Surveys, Polls, and Samples

Surveys, Polls, and Samples:

PRACTICAL PROCEDURES

By Mildred Parten, PH.D.

UNIVERSITY OF ROCHESTER

COOPER SQUARE PUBLISHERS, INC.

NEW YORK

1966

To

F. STUART CHAPIN
Pioneer in Social Survey Methods

Contents

Preface

Over twenty years of active participation in divers social surveys and polling projects have convinced me that the successful prosecution of such investigations is no simple matter, but requires the knowledge and considered application of a wealth of general principles and specific facts. From this point of view I have felt the need for a new book which would bring together in convenient form the current procedures used by population surveyors in such fields as marketing, political opinion polling, government census, radio audience measurement, socioeconomic assays, as well as in the more academic attempts of the social scientist to evaluate populations by questionnaires and related devices.

During the 1930's I began to assemble relevent information which has been continuously modified and supplemented to accord with the improvements brought by the advancing years. During this period closer contact has been noticed among various surveying groups and increasing recognition of commonly encountered problems and commonly useful techniques has become evident through the establishment of various organizations for the interchange of ideas and the formation of professional standards and practices. Naturally, in this comparatively new field there are differences of opinion with respect to the relative merits and limitations of many of the methods and techniques employed; and this situation is aggravated by the fact that practical considerations must often outweigh theoretical ones. When there are significant claims both for and against an important procedure, it has seemed worth while to indicate both sides. In general, I have sought throughout to present an organized account of problems and approaches and at the same time to supply unusually full technical details of procedure. Thus it is hoped that the forest and the trees both will remain visible and that the book may serve the dual purpose of text-book and manual.

As a textbook, it presents the historical background of population surveying, polling, and sampling in the several active fields; and then it goes on to describe the significant current practices. I have tried to avoid slighting any practically important topic. Coding and editing, topics which are generally ignored in publications of survey and polling methods, have been given careful consideration and are based on personal experience. Only quite recently have specific procedures for drawing population samples appeared in the survey literature. General principles have long been available, but persons unfamiliar with actual survey practice or unused to thinking in terms of the effect of every technique upon the findings which will eventually emerge from the survey can profit immeasurably by contemplation of the specific details. Particular emphasis has been placed upon the problem of bias, and at the risk of being unduly repetitious I have tried to warn the reader of the many circumstances in which biasing procedures are unconsciously employed.

The manual function of this book is furthered by emphasis on the specific procedures which provide the practical answers to the numerous technical problems arising at every stage of the survey operation. To be sure, surveys differ widely in various ways including plan, scope, and details; each survey possesses certain unique aspects in problem faced or approaches employed, and so each must set up its own organization, instructions, and schedule forms. Still, many of the points made will require only slight adjustment to fit the special needs of the proposed survey, whereas other points may serve merely as reminders of items to be covered. Thus an intended function of the present work is that of an overall guide for planning the survey, drafting the forms, writing the instructions, securing the information, and interpreting and reporting the results.

The surveys given primary consideration here have been those of the type conducted by questionnaires and similar techniques for gathering information about people rather than about community agencies or facilities provided for them. In other words, this work is not intended for use in nonquantitative assessments of the status, facilities, or purposes of organizations within the community. Nevertheless, it is sometimes possible to evaluate such agencies through a knowledge of their effects or influence on the people they serve; and to the extent that that is the case, most of the suggested techniques should apply.

Similarly, this book is not designed as a critique of current polling practices. Nevertheless, it should be possible to assess the work of any polling agency, whether in the field of election forecasting, product research, or public opinion by scrutiny of the procedures employed in the light of the facts of sound practice.

It is impossible to acknowledge adequately the many people who have contributed toward this book, either knowingly or unknowingly. I have drawn from the writings of numerous authors throughout and wish that I could thank each one or even mention them by name. My usual procedure was to use the reference number from the bibliography and only occasionally give personal mention of the author. Several persons whose writings were quoted rather extensively, either directly or indirectly, deserve special mention. They are: Albert B. Blankenship, Hadley Cantril, Archibald M. Crossley, A. Durost, W. Edwards Deming, R. Parker Eastwood, Albert Freiberg, George Gallup, John J. Karol, Daniel Katz, Paul Lazarsfeld, Henry C. Link, George Lundberg, Morris Hansen, Quinn McNemar, Elmo Roper, E. Dillon Smith, Frank Stanton, Frederick F. Stephan, Helen M. Walker, and Pauline Young.

I am particularly indebted to the National Opinion Research Center which permitted me to quote at length from its outstanding publication "Interviewing for NORC." Morris Hansen of the Bureau of the Census has been very coöperative about supplying me with various forms and copies of instructions. Dr. W. Edwards Deming of the Bureau of the Budget contributed through his discussions with me and by supplying important reprints from the United Nations publications. Miss Thelma Dreis of the Department of Agriculture has been exceedingly helpful whenever called upon for suggestions or material for several parts of this book. Marian Rotnem helped me collect material for an early draft of the manuscript. Dorothy McCamman wrote a paper on editing from which I drew for Chapter XIII. Wilbur Lewis wrote a short note for Chapter XVII. Dr. Sidney Merritt Newhall assisted in the writing of the chapters on sample size and evaluation of the sample as well as with numerous details in the preparation of the manuscript.

The manuscript has undergone several typings, and I am deeply grateful to the following who assisted me beyond the call of duty:

Miss Ruth S. Geyer, Mrs. Katherine Stovall Hibbs, Mrs. Helen Goldstein and Mrs. Betty Nickerson. Miss Geyer also was of immeasurable assistance in the preparation of the index.

To Miss Dorothy Thompson of Harper & Brothers fell the arduous task of editing the manuscript and seeing it through the various stages of printing. For this and for her endless patience I am indeed grateful.

I am indebted to Professor Mark A. May of the Institute of Human Relations of Yale University and to Dr. Dorothy Swaine Thomas, formerly of the Institute, for encouraging me to carry on social surveys and sampling studies during the early years of the Institute. I have drawn material from several of the studies of this period. The Social Science Research Council granted me a post-doctoral fellowship in 1931 to study the survey methods of the London Survey of Life and Labour. Work with Professor A. L. Bowley of the London School of Economics at that time undoubtedly influenced my thinking about methods of surveying. The teachings of L. L. Bernard and the counsel of Professor E. B. Wilson both, I feel, have influenced my point of view.

Dr. R. J. Reeves Kennedy of Connecticut College for Women read part of the manuscript and has given me much encouragement to complete it. Mrs. Emma Llewellyn of Sarah Lawrence College contributed numerous ideas on survey techniques while we were both on the staff at Yale.

My greatest debt is to Dr. F. Stuart Chapin who wrote one of the first textbooks on social survey methods, and as my teacher inspired my interest in surveys and set in motion the present volume. To his friendly and sustained encouragement is due the completion of this book.

MILDRED PARTEN

University of Rochester
November 30, 1949

Surveys, Polls, and Samples

CHAPTER I

Social Surveys and Polls in the United States

The American public's economic and social conditions—its income, purchases, employment status, health, housing, migration, family composition, fertility, and countless other conditions and characteristics—have become focal points for recent surveys. Furthermore, what the people think, feel, do, and plan to do about these and projected situations is of increasing interest to survey sponsors. This interest is being expressed in a great variety of attitude and opinion studies. Public opinion on social, economic, military, international, and political issues; people's preferences for various commodities, radio and movie programs, news commentators, movie stars, political candidates; the public's habits with respect to shopping, reading magazines, listening to the radio, going to the movies, driving cars, and almost every other field of human activity are being subjected to systematic investigation by social surveyors.

Of great significance also are the numerous surveys aimed at developing new survey techniques, improving upon known methods, and finding new applications for techniques already in use. Many surveyors are aware of the criticisms leveled against their findings because of the shortcomings of their techniques. Since millions of dollars are being spent yearly for surveys, surveyors cannot afford to let these criticisms go unanswered. Thus they are constantly experimenting with the ways of extracting reliable, valid, and accurate information and views whose significance cannot be doubted. They are experimenting with ways of choosing true cross-sections of the population and developing tests of adequacy and efficiency.

The information secured in surveys may consist of extremely diverse data. It may vary from easily defined or observable objective facts about the informant to relatively complex feeling tones or attitudes which the individual holds with regard to certain persons, situations, or events. It may be reported in terms of simple categorical answers to questions of fact or opinion, or it may be expressed in units on scales devised to quantify human reactions or situations.

More than a million people are interviewed annually by pollers. The public has given freely of its time and has even seemed to enjoy expressing its views. It has expected nothing in return. Most of the findings of surveys are published long after the survey interviews, but many other results never are available to the general public.

One national organization, however, recognized the potential interest of the public in what people in general think, feel, and do; hence it has been releasing syndicated newspaper reports weekly, or several times a week, ever since the middle nineteen-thirties. These releases, as well as radio programs relating to surveys and polls, have done much to acquaint the public with this phase of American social science. In 1944 a poll conducted by one of the national polling agencies revealed that over half the informants had heard of public opinion polls (363).[1] Of these, about three-fourths seemed to feel that polls were a good thing for the country. A very small minority seemed to disapprove. But whether they approved or disapproved or were neutral, most of them were ignorant about the purposes and methods of polls. Were it not for the attempts of pollers to predict the winning candidates in presidential elections and the wide publicity given to their forecasts, the public opinion poll might have received unqualified acceptance even on the part of the originally skeptical groups. Two times the nation has developed great confidence in the ability of pollers to foretell how people were going to vote, only to find that the forecasts were wrong. This confidence in the second instance was built up from the record of several hundred or more successful forecasts of city, state, or other local election results, as well as of three national presidential elections. The election pollers had such excellent records that they had begun to believe in their own infallibility. They claimed for themselves the title of "scientific pollers" to distinguish themselves from their "unscientific" predecessors. To be sure, they employed techniques which were far in advance of those used by the earlier polls. Being social scientists, they continued to experiment with techniques and to improve

[1] Bold-face numbers refer to the bibliography at the end of the book.

them. Being businessmen also, they felt justified in capitalizing on the growing body of knowledge. As scientists they knew that numerous factors such as those which will be discussed later (Chapter 12) could affect the outcome of an election, but as commercial enterprisers they were willing to make specific predictions to satisfy their public. It is unfortunate that the public was not informed as to where the science of polling ended and the personal judgment of pollers entered into the forecasts. After a careful analysis of several surveys of the reactions of the public to opinion polls—before and after the 1948 presidential election—Sheatsley (870) concluded that the public has adopted a surprisingly tolerant attitude toward the polls. People are still willing and even curious to be interviewed, and the majority also regard the polls as accurate. Selected groups such as some Congressmen and newspaper editors who were hostile to polls before 1948 were even more so after the election. Clients of polling agencies seemed to follow a middle course. A mail survey of 200 leaders in advertising, marketing and public relations revealed that about half of the respondents blamed the failure of the forecasts upon bad judgment in interpreting results rather than on faulty techniques. Almost a third felt there was a basic lack of validity in public opinion measurement techniques, but as a whole they felt that the setback was only temporary (965). Within six months after the election forecast fiasco, market research agencies as well as public opinion polls were functioning at their 1948 levels.

While some surveyors are still proceeding on the assumption that their methods are peculiar to their own fields of investigation, such as marketing research, social research, psychological measurement, election polling, or radio audience surveys, many others are coming to utilize the experience and techniques of workers in other fields. This practice proves advantageous because all have a common primary goal, that of securing information from and about the general public or a selected portion of it.

One of the first expressions of this desire for cooperative effort took the form of a conference of public opinion and survey experts which was held at Central City, Colorado, in July, 1946. It was attended by researchers from all parts of the nation as well as from abroad. Discussions were held on most of the knotty problems with which practical workers in the survey field had been faced. The conference was such a success that a second conference was called for the following year. It was held at Williamstown, Massachusetts, September 2–5, 1947. Several important organizations had their origin at this meeting. The American Association for Public Opinion Research was one of these. This new organization serves as a representative national organization in international meetings and is concerned with the development of research methods, professional standards in public opinion research, dissemination of techniques and findings, and the utilization of public opinion research in democratic policy formation.

The Office of Public Opinion Research Personnel had its origin at the Williamstown Conference. It has prepared a list of organizations known to be employing opinion researchers, their positions, salaries, and training prerequisites, anticipated future demand for workers, institutions offering training, and students now in training who will be able to qualify.

The Williamstown Conference also brought into being the International Committee for Public Opinion Research and World Peace. Its expressed purpose is to learn about, improve, and increase the amount of opinion research related to world peace; to analyze, interpret, and publicize poll data bearing on world unity; and to promote the development of an "international barometer" of opinion relevant to world understanding and world peace. The committee on research design and promotion will work on question design and publicizing results.

Interest in public opinion on an international scale was shown at Williamstown by the formation of the World Congress on Public Opinion Research. The stated purposes of this organization are: to serve as an international meeting group for individuals engaged in sample polling or in teaching; to develop scientific standards among its members; and to foster the improvement of current techniques and the development of new techniques. Members are drawn from the fields of opinion and attitude studies, publication and radio research, market research, and the social sciences.

The third International Conference on Public Opinion Research was held at Eagles Mere, Pennsylvania, on September 12–15, 1948. Two organizations sponsored this meeting—the American Association for Public Opinion Research and the World Association for Public Opinion Research (formerly the World Congress on Public Opinion Research). They set up committees on membership and standards, personnel training and exchange, and public relations. In 1949, the World Association met in Paris.

In 1947, the American Marketing Association, the Market Research Council, and the American Association of Public Opinion Research issued a proposed code of professional practices to insure honest and competent surveys. They also proposed a set of standard practices to be used in reporting survey results. One of the immediate effects of the 1948 presidential election forecast fiasco was the calling of a conference at Iowa City of specialists in the field of social science, opinion sampling, and sampling statistics. Basic problems of these fields as well as causes of the disparity between poll findings and elections were discussed.

Before turning to the practical procedures which constitute the main subject matter of the present book, the student of survey methods will be given a bird's-eye view of the survey movement as a whole, both historical and contemporary. This will include mention of research organizations as well as of some outstanding inquiries in various fields. These may suggest sources which can be tapped for current developments and for detailed methodologies, instructions, forms, and statistical background data. The principal contributions have been made by specialists in one or more of the following fields: (1) social surveys, (2) public opinion polls, (3) market surveys, and (4) radio audience research.

Social Surveys

LOCALIZED NON-GOVERNMENT SURVEYS:

European and British Forerunners. The social survey movement in the United States can best be understood in the light of its developmental history. From the earliest times governments have taken inventories of their human resources for taxing, military, and other administrative purposes. Not until the nineteenth century, however, did the social survey movement assume much importance from the point of view of social welfare and social science.[2] A first-hand in-

---

[2] Prior to this period some scattered social welfare studies were recorded. For instance, John Howard (1726–1790), an English philanthropist and prison reformer, assembled a systematic and objective body of facts about the prison conditions of his time. He not only counted the number of jails, their officers, and inmates, but also gathered detailed information on the

vestigation and analysis of social, economic, and related aspects of a community is reported in *The Description of Yarmouth*, published in 1819. In 1834 Henry Lytton Bulwer published the two-volume work, *France—Social, Literary, Political*, which contained, in addition to descriptive material, an analysis of census data and other statistical material concerning education, crime, wages, and population. Frederic LePlay, a French social reformer and economist, made studies of thousands of European workingmen's family budgets; his findings were published in six volumes in 1855 as *Les ouvriers européens* (560). From these studies he developed some theories of social organization; he also sought to use his studies as a means of revealing the need for social reform.

Charles Booth is credited with having designed and conducted the first social survey of the type that later became so prevalent in England and the United States. In 1886 he began an extensive inquiry into the economic and social conditions of the people of London to show "the numerical relation which poverty, misery, and depravity bear to the regular earnings and comparative comfort and to describe the general conditions under which each class lives" (91, Vol. I, p. 6). This survey differed from its predecessors in that it was more comprehensive; many phases of London life were covered, a greater variety and more objective and systematic methods of gathering information and defining terms were utilized, and the treatment of the data was more analytical, the discovery of causal relationships holding an important place. The facts collected by personal observations, interviews, use of secondary sources, and other techniques were defined, recorded, classified, and fitted into a statistical framework from which an integrated analysis was made.

With the assistance of social investigators, Booth interviewed several hundred school board visitors who in the course of their work had made house-to-house calls in every area of London. The information obtained during these conferences covered such items as occupation, rooms in dwelling, number of children, lodgers, etc., as well as subjective impressions. The data were checked and supple-

---

physical condition of the prisoners and the prison quarters. Supported by these facts, his testimony before the House of Commons in 1774 led to the passage of a number of measures providing for prison reform (1137, p. 5).

mented by visits to many neighborhoods, streets, and homes, and by conferences with various welfare and community leaders. From time to time Booth lived as a lodger in districts where he was not known, so that he could become more intimately acquainted with the lives and habits of the poorer classes. His classification of the London population into an ascending series of social and economic grades described by letters (from A to H), the estimated number of people belonging to each of these grades, and the graphic representation of their distribution by streets for which he used a set of colored maps, were regarded by his followers as the most striking features of his investigation (585, Vol. I, p. 2). His report, *Life and Labour of the People in London*, was published in seventeen volumes between 1892 and 1897. Following the Booth inquiry and utilizing a more precise definition of poverty, B. Seebohm Rowntree investigated the working-class conditions of York, England; his study was published in 1901.

Of the other surveys of English towns during the first forty years of the twentieth century, the studies by Bowley, a statistician and economist at the London School of Economics, were the first to apply the principles of scientific sampling in selecting the population to be surveyed. In 1912, a group of community leaders in Reading, England, asked Bowley how best to use a small sum of money they had for the purpose of investigating the economic condition of the working class in that town. He suggested the method of pure sampling in order to obtain the best results in the time and with the money and other resources available. The process of selection involved using a list of the houses in the area, usually in alphabetical order by streets, and marking for investigation one in n of the houses in this order (103, p. 475).

Bowley surveyed five different towns between 1912 and 1914, and ten years later repeated his investigations in the same communities. Thus standardized definitions and procedures for "parallel investigations in different areas at the same time and in the same area at different times" (483, p. 821) were first developed and applied by him. Surveys of other English communities by Jones (482, 484) and Ford followed plans similar to those originated by Bowley.

The New Survey of London Life and Labour, undertaken in 1928 by members of the London School of Economics and Political Science, followed in a general way the survey pattern established by Booth and modified by later discoveries in research techniques (483, pp.

823–824). The results of this survey were published in nine volumes between 1930 and 1935 (585). One volume sketched the changes in the everyday life of the people due to the development of transportation systems, wireless, the cinema, educational opportunities, social services, etc. Of particular interest are the two volumes which describe the methodology and conclusions reached in the survey of poverty and related conditions, and the two others which contain maps showing the distribution of poverty. Three volumes describe the industries of London. The ninth volume deals with the Londoners' pursuit of leisure, social organizations, drinking habits, and delinquency.

In his description of the English survey movement Jones says that from 1928 on there has been in England a more or less continuous series of surveys directed by different people and varying greatly in scope and value. Some were specially interested in the character of the region surveyed, such as a depressed area or a newly developed area. Other surveys were limited to a single aspect or one or two related aspects of social life, such as housing, unemployment, standard of living in relation to nutrition, or intelligence in relation to fertility (483, p. 821).

An interesting approach to the study of the habits, lives, and opinions of the British was undertaken in 1937 under the title of *Mass Observation*. At first, a group of 37 volunteer observers from different walks of life and living in widely scattered sections of the nation were instructed to keep detailed records of everything they thought, saw, and talked about on a given day—February 12. These reports were assembled, analyzed, and published. Much public interest was shown in this experiment and the day surveys were continued on the 12th of each month. By the end of the first year more than 1,000 volunteer observers were sending in their reports. In his description of this survey, Willcock (1093) states that at the start of the war a panel of 1500 observers was set up to observe and keep records on subjects of interest to the nation at war. Problems of evacuation from cities, rationing, spending and saving, propaganda, and numerous other war topics have been subjected to study. *War Begins at Home* (London, Faber, 1940) is one of the publications growing out of these studies. Other subjects in the fields of art, sports, cinema, religion, jazz, shopping habits, astrology, pacifism, have also been investigated in the Mass Observation surveys. Area studies consisting of detailed reports of community life by full-time observers were made of various towns. Two main areas, an industrial town in the North "Worktown" and a London borough "Metrop," were focal points for intensive surveys. In addition to volunteers, the personnel in 1942 consisted of 15 full-time trained investigators of opinion. They used standard techniques of interviewing and opinion sampling supplemented by purely observational techniques. An interesting summary of three mass-observation surveys published in 1947, *Puzzled People, Peace and the Public,* and *Exmoor,* is presented by Robinson (794). These surveys deal with popular attitude toward religion, war and peace, and community life. Other sampling surveys in England during the 1940's are described by Moser (658).

Social Surveys in the United States.   Surveys in the United States followed the trail blazed by Booth—even long after Bowley's more scientific and efficient procedures had been described and published. Like Booth's studies, the early American surveys were tremendous undertakings, covering a broad range of subjects and dealing with complete elements of the population.

The first of these systematic studies was the Pittsburgh Survey (504) undertaken by Paul U. Kellogg and his associates in 1909. The living and working conditions (including income and expenditures, crime, work accidents and factory inspection, women in industry, etc.) of the unskilled laborers in the steel mills of Pittsburgh were studied by trained social workers, sociologists, and economists. The findings of the survey were widely publicized through exhibits and the press.

In 1912 the Russell Sage Foundation, in response to many requests for advice on and cooperation in making social surveys of urban communities, established a Department of Surveys and Exhibits under the direction of Shelby M. Harrison. "The two main objectives which the department set for itself were the spreading of the survey idea and the further development of survey methods. In furthering both of these objectives advice and assistance were made available to outside organizations on their specific undertakings" (267, p. xxi). Noteworthy among the early surveys assisted by this agency was the Springfield, Illinois, Survey, which differed from the Pittsburgh inquiry in that its scope was more general; it covered such topics as public schools, care of mental cases, recreation, housing, public health, the correctional system, charities, industrial conditions, and city and county administration.

Eaton and Harrison (267) point out that after a few years the social surveys in this country tended to be more specialized, that is, to focus on one major phase of community life, such as health and sanitation, public education, housing, recreation, employment and industrial relations, child welfare, etc. The Cleveland Survey (177), which represents one of the first of these specialized surveys, covered studies on education, hospitals and health, recreation and crime. Its publications appeared between 1916 and 1922.

The number of surveys of social and economic conditions has increased by leaps and bounds since 1914. The Russell Sage Foundation Department of Surveys and Exhibits listed some 2775 surveys up to January 1, 1928; of these, 153 were general community surveys and the rest specialized in the fields of health, crime, delinquency, recreation, education, or housing (267).

In addition to the surveys which were conducted primarily for the purpose of social reform, several other types have developed in the United States. Regional surveys which stress the human use of topographical and geographical areas for the purpose of city and regional planning appeared in England around 1920. In the United States the first ones of note were the Regional Survey of New York and Its Environs (1927–1931) and the Regional Plan of New York (1929–1931).

Another group of surveys was made of small towns. *An American Town* by J. M. Williams in 1906, and *A Hoosier Village* by N. L. Sims in 1912, were pioneer efforts in this field. The Institute of Social and Religious Research, as well as sociology and economics departments in agricultural colleges and universities, have sponsored numerous rural and small community surveys. Some of these are studies in the social processes of the community, others are ecological studies in which the emphasis is on the relation between social groups and the areas in which they are located.

One of the landmarks in community surveys is the study, *Middletown*, by R. S. and H. M. Lynd published in 1929 (602). Using a variety of techniques the authors explored the life of a typical city. They studied the processes of earning a living, making a home, training the young, using leisure, engaging in religious life, and participating in community activities. This study is notable because of its extensive data and analytical summaries.

Ten years later the Lynds surveyed the same community to discover the changes that had taken place during and as a result of the boom and depression years, and to check up on whether trends observed in 1925 were continuing. *Middletown in Transition* (603), their report of the second survey, appeared in 1937. Varied research techniques were employed by the director and his five assistants who lived in homes in all sections of the city. They combed existing records of all kinds and conducted many interviews, both formal and informal. In addition to the descriptive and anecodotal material, the published report contains a wealth of statistical data interpreted by the surveyors.

Leisure: A Suburban Study, made by Lundberg, Komarovsky, and McInery (598) in Westchester County, New York, in 1932–1934, represents a cross between the specialized social survey and the social process community study.

This study covered the topic of leisure in relations to numerous aspects of community life—organizations, the family, the church, the school, the arts, adult education, and community recognition of the problems of leisure. Many techniques of social research were employed in securing the information. More than 10,000 schedules and questionnaires of various sorts were collected; data were secured through interviews, systematic direct observation, analysis of secondary data, and the participant-observer technique. All three authors lived in the area for almost two years, joined the local organizations, and attended meetings and recreational events. "More than two hundred formal interviews lasting from one to three hours were secured with ministers, school officials, and women in their homes. There were many more interviews incidental to the circulation of schedules, and a very large number through casual contact and association of living in a community. In addition to the customary analysis of secondary material such as histories, annual reports of organizations, and newspapers, we studied the mobility of the population through the analysis of telephone and other directories of fifteen villages and cities, involving a checking of more than two hundred thousand names and addresses. Among the projects of formal direct observation was the

recording of a schedule of the activities of some 6800 commuters
on trains. Constant traveling throughout the county, visits to homes,
schools, playgrounds, all major recreational resorts and all the contacts incidental to daily living complete the story of the observations
upon which this study of leisure of a people is based" (598).

Since the Bowley studies in the first decade of the twentieth century, there has been slow but increasing recognition of the necessity
for clearly defined, measurable, and comparable statistical units as
well as adequate sampling procedures. While recognized as desirable
by social surveyors, scientific sampling, especially with regard to the
selection of informants, was not usually employed in their procedures.
It is possible that the present author's own attempt constitutes one of
the first on record in this country.

In 1931 Parten drew a sample of householders from a card file of
gas meter subscribers in New Haven, Connecticut, for a study of urban
mobility. A systematic sampling similar to the method used by Bowley
was employed. Hogg of the Russell Sage Foundation, who earlier had
assisted Bowley in England (106), utilized the New Haven sample for
a study of the incidence of unemployment (446). The 2097 families in
the sample were personally interviewed and their statements about
their employment status, as well as other relevant data about family
members, were recorded on a short schedule. The sample compared
favorably with the 1930 United States census figures for New Haven.

The same sample of families (brought up to date and supplemented
to include newcomers to the city) was surveyed again in 1933. This
time the major purpose of the inquiry was to produce social statistics
on the general population which could be used in the Social Background Studies of the Institute of Human Relations (252, 716). In
addition, however, the unemployment survey questions were repeated in order to measure changes that had occurred in the labor
market since the study two years earlier. Members of various departments in the Institute of Human Relations had expressed a desire for
information on certain characteristics of the New Haven population
which were not secured in the census. Thus the facts collected in the
1933 sample survey included items on religious affiliation, education
of family members, names of family physicians, legal consultations of
family members during the year, family income, and family composition, as well as the employment-unemployment information.

In 1934 Parten and Dreis used the household address list of the New Haven city directory to obtain a representative sample of city households. The names in the sample were cleared with the Social Service Exchange, and the incidence of relief among the general population of New Haven was thus determined.[3] This is probably the first attempt to utilize the address list in a city directory as a source for sampling all the households in a community. This basis of sampling has since been adopted with considerable success in surveys throughout the country. In 1935 it was employed by Dreis in Meriden, Connecticut, and later in 1935 the Urban Study of Consumer Purchases (1010, 847) adopted it in most of the thirty-two cities surveyed. In 1941 the Employment Stabilization Institute of the University of Minnesota followed this sampling procedure for its survey of employment-unemployment and relief (287).

GOVERNMENT SURVEYS:

The Federal Government conducts the largest and greatest number of surveys of any agency in the world. It is almost impossible for anyone to keep up with current developments, not to mention its past work. Surveyors are fortunate that a summary of the statistical work up to 1946 has been made by experts in various government departments and published under the editorship of Hauser and Leonard (425). Space permits us to mention only a few of the surveys which are significant either because of the methods used or because of the statistical data yielded.

The Decennial Census of the United States. The census conducted by the Bureau of the Census, Department of Commerce, is not usually regarded as a social survey but is looked upon primarily as a headcounting of the inhabitants of this country. Actually the census is more than this. It has concerned itself from the beginning with ascertaining the incidence and cross relationships of social characteristics of the population. Thus, as early as the first census in 1790, when the number of freeholders and slaves, the size of the family, and other social facts were secured, the government may be said to have conducted a social survey. Every ten years since that

---

[3] The results were not made public but were reported to the Yale Institute of Human Relations by Mildred Parten and Thelma Dreis under the title "Comparison of the Families Receiving Relief with the General Population."

date the American population has been surveyed, not only to determine the number of representatives to be selected (in accordance
with the constitutional provision for the House of Representatives
to be chosen on the basis of population size) but also to find out facts
which leaders in this country deemed essential to shaping public
policy. Questions have been added, dropped entirely, altered, or retained unchanged, depending upon the importance of the issues involved and upon public demand for various facts. The Sixteenth Decennial Census in 1940 included, in addition to an extensive Population
Census, a Census of Housing, of Agriculture, of Business, of Manufactures, of Mines and Quarries. Furthermore, for the first time the national
population census schedule included supplementary questions answered by a 5 per cent sample of the total population enumerated.
Thus, one of the alleged distinctions between the Census and other
surveys—namely, that the census is a complete enumeration, whereas
most surveys are sample counts—has broken down.

The items obtained from the total population in 1940 ranged from
the more usual questions on sex, age, race, marital status, family
relationships, citizenship, birthplace, and occupation, to questions on
education, residence in 1935, employment status, and income. From
one in every twenty individuals enumerated, supplementary information was secured on birthplace of parents, mother tongue, usual occupation, industry, class of worker, as well as certain facts bearing
on relationship to veterans, social security, and fertility. The 1950
schedule provides for much the same type of information as was secured in 1940. As before, additional information secured from a sample
of the total provides information on income, nationality, mobility, employment, and housing.

The published material represents only a small fraction of the vast
amount available from the Bureau of the Census. Some data are in
the form of subtotals which may be obtained by paying to have the
desired figures copied. Other materials are on punch cards or on
machine runs (425, 999). The payment of tabulation costs will make
these data available and will often eliminate the necessity for an expensive field survey. A comparatively recent development in the use
of Census material is the "Matching Study." The Bureau of the Census
will compile statistics from specific census schedules of lists of con-

sumers furnished by business concerns. A given firm may provide certain information about its clients which is transcribed and placed on punch cards along with information taken from the census schedules of the same persons. Cross tabulations are then prepared to show relationships between the characteristics known to the census and those known to the enterprise. No data are given out in terms of individuals but only in frequencies or summary form. Census material serves the even more important function of checking the representativeness of sample populations being surveyed (with due allowance, of course, for changes occurring since the last census) and gives a basis for weighting stratified samples to be described later.

Aside from the valuable data obtained, the 1940 and the 1950 censuses are models of survey methodology which aspiring surveyors would do well to study. (Copies of many of the forms and instructions can be obtained upon request.) The techniques and instructions employed in the administration, field investigation, sampling, processing of schedules, and tabulation will be referred to in later chapters. At this point we wish only to call attention to two of the most carefully planned and executed large-scale surveys that have ever been undertaken. Except for the fact that the giving of census information is compulsory, the problems faced and the techniques used to secure and analyze data are much the same for the census as for any large survey.

Since 1940 national estimates of the population are prepared semiannually. Thanks to the registration for War Ration Books, post-censal estimates for local areas also were possible during the war years. The Bureau of the Census released Series P-44 No. 3, "Estimated Civilian Population of the United States by Counties: November 1, 1943." A "Map showing changes in Civilian Population of the United States, by Counties: April 1, 1940 to November 1, 1943" shows the effect of induction of millions of men and women into the armed forces and the mobility of others to production centers (1003).

Between February and July, 1944, a series of sample censuses were taken in ten Congested Production Areas (123, 1003, 1004). Estimates were made on total population and on population characteristics in these areas. Such figures were extremely valuable to various war agencies.

OTHER FEDERAL CENSUSES AND SURVEYS:

In intercensal years the federal government usually undertakes censuses in special fields. For example, after 1930 there was a census of manufactures in 1931, 1933, 1936, and 1939. During the war, the War Production Board collected a vast amount of data on manufacturing; much of this material was published in 1944–1945. A census of agriculture occurs every five years.

A "Survey of Consumer Requirements" by the Civilian Surveys Division in the Office of Civilian Requirements was conducted in November, 1943. Using the area sample of the Bureau of the Census, 5000 homes were surveyed in four geographical areas. Families were asked about shortages and the trouble people had trying to buy various items as well as how much of a hardship the shortage entailed. Results of this survey were printed and distributed within one month of the field work.

A second survey of consumer needs took place in the spring of 1944. Clothing and textile purchases by or for each member of the household between January 1 and March 18 were ascertained. The findings of the survey were used by the W.P.B. and the O.P.A. in planning and administering their programs.

The third survey, conducted in April, 1944, obtained data on the number of items consumers had bought or tried to buy during the previous week as well as the shortages they had found in various household items the previous year.

The Office of Civilian Requirements, at the request of the War Food Administration, conducted a survey of farm supplies in February 1944. A sample of 2678 interviews with farmers drawn from the area sample of the Census obtained information on farmers' attempted purchases, success in buying, and anticipated needs.

Housing Surveys. Interest in housing during the war years was shown in the more than 1000 vacancy surveys conducted between 1940 and 1946 by the federal government. Numerous efforts were made at this time to determine housing needs and solutions; several of the surveys were made in conjunction with the Labor Force Surveys mentioned below. In addition to statistics by regions, data were obtained for more than 30 metropolitan districts with samples of about 3300 households in each area. During 1946 veterans' housing was surveyed in more than 100 different localities. Information was collected about the family characteristics and income of veterans as well as facts about living accommodations and future housing plans.

One very interesting survey was made to determine what actually happens in the chain of housing shifts when new dwelling units are occupied. Enumerators secured information concerning the characteristics of the new unit and the family which moved into it. Then the enumerators secured the address just vacated by the incoming family and visited that address. Thus by tracing the shifts touched off by the construction and occupancy of a new dwelling unit, it was possible to determine how many families obtained better housing because of the new unit (124).

Current Population Statistics: Labor Force Survey. Starting as a survey of unemployment conducted by the Works Projects Administration in 1936, the Monthly Survey of the Labor Force was transferred to the Bureau of the Census in 1942. Since then it has developed as a continuing survey. In 1946 it covered 68 areas and had a full-time staff of supervisors and part-time interviewers. In addition to its surveys for estimating employment-unemployment and nonworking groups, the staff conducts numerous special surveys for various government agencies. With the readily available staff and samples, its services are solicited to conduct surveys on widely diversified subjects. Occasionally, questions are merely added to the schedule for the Monthly Report on the Labor Force; at other times, entirely separate surveys are conducted by them.

Survey of Consumer Finances. The Survey of Consumer Finances conducted for the Board of Governors of the Federal Reserve System between 1946 and 1948 covered a sample of 3000 consumer or spending units distributed in 66 sampling areas of the nation. The survey was carried out by the Survey Research Center of the University of Michigan (371). Data on saving and dissaving among the various income groups were obtained. Studies included the various types of saving as well as spending. In 1948, the median income for all spending units was about $2530 before taxes and $2380 after taxes (944). This is roughly double that of median family income shown by the 1940 federal census. For a discussion of the sample used, see pp. 274–277.

Census of Partial Employment, Unemployment, and Occupations, 1937. The National Unemployment Census had as its origin the provision of information which could serve "as a guide in the planning and administration of programs for re-employment, social security, and unemployment relief for the people of the United States" (993, Vol. IV, p. 1). This survey took the form of a voluntary registration of the unemployed; postmen distributed the registration forms. The registration was followed by a house-to-house check survey, "The Enumerative Check Census," which was conducted in sample areas throughout the country. The technique of this survey is notable because of the speed with which it was carried out and the use of postmen as enumerators. On the basis of the returns from the sample, the underregistration of certain groups of unemployed was estimated.

State and Local Censuses. A number of states regularly take a census five years after each federal decennial census. During the intercensal years of 1930–1940 particularly, a great many states and cities made complete enumerations of their populations, many of them being conducted in cooperation with the federal Work Relief Administration. Between 1940 and 1950 numerous local censuses were conducted to ascertain housing needs.

Surveys Conducted as Work Relief Projects. Of the many thousands of surveys made during the 1930's under the auspices of government relief agencies such as the Civil Works Administration (CWA), the Federal Emergency Relief Administration (FERA), and the Works Progress Administration (WPA), later known as the Works Projects Administration, it is impossible in the present summary to do more than point to a few of the larger nation-wide studies which are of interest to social surveyors. For the others the reader should refer to the *Index of Research Projects* published by the Works Progress Administration (1032).

The National Health Survey. The National Health Survey conducted by the U. S. Public Health Service was an extensive study of sickness in its social and economic setting, made through a house-to-house canvass by WPA workers. The health data covered the prevalence and incidence of acute and chronic disabling illnesses and death and the receipt of medical care from physicians, health clinics, sanitariums, and public health nursing services, in relation to such factors as income, employment status, housing conditions, age, occupation, sex, color, and amount of time lost from usual activities. The demographic information on age, sex, race, occupational distribution of the population, size, composition, income and relief status of families, and various indices of the standard of living of surveyed households was in itself of importance and of value to the surveyor. The study covered 740,000 urban and 36,000 rural families drawn from 19 states in the four main geographical regions, East, Central, South, and West. Different-sized cities were represented proportionately, the sample varying from 1 in every 2 families in small towns to 1 in 35 in larger cities. One volume of the report deals with the field organization, training methods, canvassing procedures, and administration of local supervisors (1024). It outlines in some detail the procedures used in sampling, canvassing, verifying sickness diagnosis by interviews with physicians, and coding and punching.

The Real Property Inventories. In connection with the federal housing program, the Works Progress Administration, the Central Statistical Board, and the Federal Housing Administration cooperated in inventories of real property throughout the United States. From these surveys was assembled the most detailed body of statistical information available, until the 1940 census, on the physical characteristics of housing in the United States. A great deal of information was gathered between 1934 and 1940 on all types of structures, although most of the data related to residential sections. A summary of the Real Property Inventories conducted as work projects during 1934–1936 in 203 urban areas is published in *Urban Housing* (1030). A file of the results of the various inventories is maintained by the Federal Housing Administration, Washington, D. C.

The Technique for a Real Property Survey in three volumes (1013) served as the standard procedure for making surveys of this type. The result of several outlines and revisions of the procedure, it gives detailed instructions and forms for organizing and operating a survey. It includes instructions for enumerating, editing, checking, and tabulating the physical inventory of real property in urban areas (1) for surveys of dwellings, standard and substandard, and (2) for surveys of land use. Data regarding the present use of all the land and the extent of coverage by permanent structures are also provided. A supplement issued in 1938 contains improvements and corrections (1029).

The Study of Consumer Purchases: Family Income and Expenditures. This nation-wide survey of the income and expenditures of families in the United States was undertaken in 1936 with a grant of funds from the WPA. The data were collected by the schedule method through personal interviews with families residing in different sections of the country and in communities of varying size. The Bureau of Labor Statistics of the U. S. Department of Labor conducted a survey in 32 cities, and the Bureau of Home Economics of the Department of Agriculture made a survey of some small cities and village and rural areas. Cooperating in the development of the plans were the members of the Central Statistical Board, the Consumption Research Staff of the National Resources Committee, and the WPA, as well as members of the two agencies which conducted the survey. National estimates of family income and family expenditures were derived from the urban and rural data in this survey, supplemented by other sources (1021, 1022). In all, contact was made with almost a million families. Information was collected on family income, occupations of family members, family composition, home ownership, and related questions. The details of family consumption were obtained from a smaller controlled sample. For a more detailed discussion of the procedures used, the problems confronted, and the results obtained, the reader should refer to the official reports of the survey (986, 1010) and to the article by Schoenberg and Parten (847).

Agricultural and Rural Surveys. One of the first government agencies to enter the sample social survey field and to develop systematic periodic surveys was the U. S. Department of Agriculture. The Bureau of Agricultural Economics has been especially active in this field. It has initiated or sponsored numerous rural surveys on all phases of farm life, from the crops produced to the income received and the reactions of farmers to their situation and to government programs. The experimental work on survey methodology which agricultural economists and sociologists have carried on has contributed a great deal to scientific knowledge. Especially significant are the contributions in the field of sampling techniques. In connection with the 1945 Census of Agriculture, a Master Sample of Agriculture was developed by the Bureau of Agricultural Economics and the Bureau of the Census (478, 512). It consists of approximately 70,000 small geographical areas representative of every county in the nation. Subsamples of these areas are drawn for national or regional coverage (78, p. 279). Prior to the 1940 federal census, for example, a trial sample census of agriculture was undertaken in Iowa (477, 737, 833). The findings of this experiment deserve the attention of surveyors in other fields because many of the recommendations are widely applicable. A comprehensive bibliography of sampling methods in social science prepared by Larson (540) contains a brief description of many of the surveys conducted during the 1930's.

In 1939, a Division of Program Surveys was set up in the Department of Agriculture for the purpose of securing reactions of farmers to various agricultural problems and programs. The answers were to serve as guides for administrative decisions. Under the direction of a psychologist, the Division made numerous surveys both for the Department of Agriculture and for other government agencies. Not only were efforts made to ascertain the types and incidences of various attitudes but the factors producing the attitudes and the effects of these attitudes on behavior also were probed. The extent to which people were informed about various aspects of federal programs was determined because of the relationship between attitude and knowledge or understanding of the purposes of the programs. Surveys covered attitudes toward such varied topics as the War Food Program, Victory Gardens and Home Preservation of Food, Consumer Acceptance of Dried Milk, Veterans' Readjustment to Civilian Life, and Liquid Asset Holdings, Spendings, and Savings. During World War II government agencies such as the Office of Facts and Figures utilized this survey service to keep its finger on the public pulse.

In 1946, the Division of Special Surveys replaced the Division of Program Surveys. According to the Secretary of Agriculture, the new Division was authorized to conduct special surveys and make analyses for the following purposes: (1) to obtain information on consumers' preferences for various agricultural products; (2) to obtain information on the underlying factors that influence farmers' production, marketing, or purchasing intentions and behavior; (3) at the request of the Secretary to obtain data for his use; and (4) at the request of other agencies, including agencies outside of the Department, to secure data that will help increase the effectiveness of agricultural activities or improve services to farmers.

Up to 1946 most of the attitudinal surveys employed the "open question" technique, in which the respondent answers each question in a conversational manner and the interviewer records the response almost verbatim, but check-list types of questions were used where data were readily classifiable into set answers. The surveys since 1946 tend to be more of the check-list type. In 1948–1949, the Division employed about 250 interviewers who conducted about five national surveys a year. Topics surveyed included men's and women's preferences among selected textile products for clothing, consumer and hotel preferences regarding potatoes, and pear purchases and consumer preferences regarding pears.

Surveys of Youth. During the depression period of the 1930's numerous studies of the characteristics and needs of the youth of the nation were undertaken. The Committee on Youth Problems of the U. S. Office of Education gathered information on the youth surveys conducted between 1933 and 1935. The findings were reported by Jessen. His list of more than 30 youth surveys, he points out, does not cover all of the many surveys which were undertaken during this period. While most of the inquiries centered around the topics of school, employment, and use of leisure time, a great variety of questions bearing on other topics was included in these youth surveys. Jessen remarks: "Some of the surveys report information on such matters as church and civic interests of young people, the responsibilities which they take around the home, the sources of their spending money, the guidance services which they have enjoyed, the effects which the depression has had upon them, their marital status, place of residence and mobility of residence, their health, and their attitudes toward drinking, war, work, school, and other subjects" (476, p. 273).

Harley (404) lists and describes 166 surveys—national, regional, state, and local—made in the United States from 1931 to 1937. While a great many of them were sponsored or conducted by educational agencies, a significant number were made by public agencies such as employment services, relief administrations, recreation bureaus, planning boards, and by departments of the national government; some were conducted by private agencies and individuals. Of the 149 surveys on which methodological detail is available, 138 employed questionnaires, generally alone but sometimes in combination with other techniques and sources. In over four-fifths of the surveys the questionnaire was filled out during interviews; in the remaining fifth the mail questionnaire method was used.

Notable among these surveys was a large-scale study conducted in

Pennsylvania under the direction of Updegraff. Some 23,000 youths whose names were taken from the sixth-grade school rolls for 1926 and 1928 were included in the study, and about 6000 of these were surveyed in a more intensive investigation. Data on intelligence, school achievement, social-economic background, and out-of-school experience were collected. In addition, ratings on six character traits were secured from former classmates. On the basis of these data the youths were classified according to the station in life they might eventually fill and the contributions they were capable of making to social welfare (1036).

The survey of youth in Maryland, reported by Bell in *Youth Tell Their Story*, is perhaps the best known of the youth surveys. It was conducted by the American Youth Commission of the American Council on Education. A staff of 35 interviewers working over a period of seven months gathered firsthand information and opinions from 13,528 young people between the ages of 16 and 24. The informants were selected to be representative youth of Maryland. "Every kind of neighborhood or area, every social and economic stratum, and every educational and intellectual level was proportionately represented in the final sample" (41, p. 9). The inquiry covered all phases of a young person's life—"his school, church, street gangs, neighborhood clubs, recreation centers, libraries, his job, and his home." The description of methods as well as the graphic presentation of findings in Bell's report should be of particular interest to surveyors.

Public Opinion Polls

STRAW POLLS:

Modern public opinion polls in the United States are outgrowths of early straw or trial votes conducted by newspapers for the purpose of forecasting the outcome of elections. Robinson (786, 787, 788) and Gallup and Rae (345) have described these pioneer efforts in considerable detail. As early as 1824 a straw vote was reported taken at Wilmington, Delaware, and another at Raleigh, North Carolina. The Raleigh *Star* covered political meetings in the state and attempted to learn the "sense" of the people. Other pioneer polls were conducted by the *Boston Globe* in 1883, by the *New York Herald* in 1904, and by the same paper in collaboration with other newspapers in 1908, 1912, and 1916. Many newspapers had the twofold purpose of increasing their circulation and estimating the opinion of the public.

Often the polls of this early period were conducted by persons quite innocent of the principle of scientific control. The ballot was simply printed in the newspaper, with instructions to the reader to fill it out and mail it in. People who did not have a newspaper or send in their ballot could not vote; hence an accidentally biased poll would be probable. Furthermore, people could buy many copies of the paper, fill in the ballots that favored their view, and thus intentionally distort the picture of public opinion.

There were, however, a few sponsoring newspapers that proceeded more scientifically. The Columbus *Dispatch,* for instance, secured votes by using crews of canvassers instead of printed ballots. These pollers were specially selected and trained, and they were assigned to canvass predesignated areas. Some effort was even made to sample urban, sex, and occupational groups according to size, and to run check polls in regions where the straw ballot predicted close votes.

Newspaper polls originally were devoted primarily to forecasting election outcomes. By the middle 1940's, however, newspaper polls had carried their surveying to subjects of general social, economic, or political interest as well as to readership studies. Among the better-known polls set up during this period are: the Iowa Poll (Des Moines *Register and Tribune*), the Minnesota Poll (*Minneapolis Star Journal and Tribune*), the Bulletin Poll (Philadelphia *Evening Bulletin*), the Washington *Post* Poll, and the Texas Poll. All of these polls are regional in scope.

MAGAZINE POLLS:

During the first decade of the twentieth century, national, state, and local elections provided the subject matter for numerous newspaper polls. Then magazines entered the polling field. The *Farm Journal* started a poll on the presidential election in 1912. This was followed in 1916 by the *Literary Digest,* which conducted a poll to predict the outcome of the election in which Charles Evans Hughes and President Wilson were candidates. From then until 1936 the *Digest* poll reigned supreme in the field. Because of its great success in predicting election results, it stood out in the public mind as a monument of accuracy. In 1932, for instance, this magazine predicted the total popular vote on the two presidential candidates within 1.4 per cent.

The *Digest* did not confine its polls to election campaigns but surveyed public opinion on various social issues as well. Millions of ballots were mailed out, usually to persons listed as telephone subscribers or automobile owners. As a rule, replies were received from about one-quarter of those solicited, but even so the returns tended to be in the millions. The election poll ran smoothly until 1936, by which time the *Digest's* record of infallibility had made its sponsors overconfident about their abilities in forecasting elections. In the course of the 1936 presidential campaign, some 10,000,000 ballots were mailed out and 2,376,523 were returned. The *Digest* predictions enjoyed extraordinary publicity because the returns ran counter to the estimates of a number of competing small-scale sampling polls. The election returns proved that the *Digest* forecast had been extremely inaccurate. It not only failed to predict the winning candidate but also missed forecasting the popular vote he would receive by about 20 per cent. Shortly after this fiasco, with its cost of half a million dollars, both poll and magazine passed out of existence.

One of the oldest of the current magazine polls is the "Companion Poll," sponsored by *The Woman's Home Companion*. It was set up in 1935 as a panel of reader-reporters. In 1946 about 1400 panel members were reporting periodically on the topics polled.

Opinions of farmers are reported in two magazines whose polls date back to 1938. "The Farmer Speaks," conducted by *Successful Farming*, and "The Wallace Homestead Poll," of the *Wallace's Farmer and Iowa Homestead*, both try to keep abreast of rural public opinion. Neither poll is as extensive as those conducted by the Department of Agriculture.

Both newspaper and magazine polls flourished during the 1920's. Robinson says, for instance, that approximately 85 straw polls were held during the presidential election of 1928 (787). Seventy-five of these were local in character, being confined to a city, county, or restricted trade area. Four extended to the boundaries of the home state or included that state and neighboring commonwealths. The other six, which were nation-wide in character, were sponsored respectively by the *Literary Digest*, the Hearst newspapers, the *Farm Journal*, the *Pathfinder*, the *Nation*, and *College Humor*.

As the polls began to branch out from the election issues, they were naturally first directed toward topics of special interest to voters. The war of 1914–1918 brought up the question of American participation, and Congressman Ernest Lundeen of Minnesota conducted a poll on this important point. He mailed out a ballot form to all the 54,000 voters in his district and received 8800 replies, of which 90 per cent were against participation (345). *Literary Digest* polls were designed to discover the voter's opinion with respect to prohibition, the soldiers' bonus, and the Mellon tax plan. Since the early 1930's, however, the polls have expanded to include innumerable questions on public opinion and behavior which will never be presented to the electorate. For example: "Financially, are you better or worse off than last year?" "Have you had any colds this winter?" "What do you think are the main reasons why couples do not have more children?" (See current issues of the *Public Opinion Quarterly* and the *International Journal of Opinion and Attitude Research* for recent poll topics.)

The enlistment of trained surveyors and statisticians in public opinion measurement marked the shift in emphasis from quantity of returns to quality of sample. Leaders of some of the best-known polls came from the field of marketing research where practical techniques of surveying and sampling had been developed.

FORTUNE SURVEY:

The Fortune Survey, conducted for the magazine *Fortune*, was started in 1936 by Paul T. Cherington and Elmo B. Roper, Jr. The reports are published monthly as a leading feature of the magazine. This poll enjoyed the distinction of having predicted more closely than any other poll the popular vote in the 1936, 1940, and 1944 presidential elections. The error in predicting Roosevelt's vote in the first instance was 1 per cent, and in the other two elections 0.2 of 1 per cent. This achievement was especially notable because the forecasts for various sections of the country were not nearly so accurate, the average error in 1940 being 7.8 per cent. Roper does not attempt state-by-state predictions. With such an excellent record behind him, it is not surprising that Roper began to feel that election forecasting had been reduced to a real science with most of the answers known. So, as early as September in the year of the presidential campaign of 1948, he decided that the election outcome was established and that Dewey was certain to win the election. Roper predicted that Dewey would receive 52.2 per cent of the popular vote and that Truman would get 37.1 per cent. Although some 15 per cent of the voters had not made up their minds on how they were going to vote at that date, Roper felt certain that there was no chance that a sufficient number of people would turn to Truman to elect him in November. It was after September that the factors which accelerated and increased the Truman votes operated most strongly. The drop in the price of corn in the fall, for example, caused the normally Republican farmers to vote the Democratic ticket. The drop was attributed to legislation of the 80th Republican-controlled Congress. Large-scale efforts of labor and liberal groups to bring out the Democratic vote and to defeat conservative groups in Congress got into full swing in October—*after* Roper had stopped polling. It is not surprising, therefore, that his prediction on Truman was in error by 12 percentage points and that he failed to choose the winning candidate.

Katz believes that this large error was due primarily to Roper's failure to correct for the sampling bias in his data. In the elections prior to 1948, Roper's surveys overestimated the Democratic vote of the South, since he made no corrections for the actual voting population of this section. This compensated for his underestimation of the Democratic vote in the North. Three times these figures resulted in successful predictions. But in 1948, the candidacy of Thurmond reduced Roper's estimate of the Truman popular vote and this destroyed the compensating error in the South (497).

In the fall of 1947 the *Fortune* Consumer Outlook studies were initiated. By a series of questions on how optimistic or pessimistic the informant is about his own economic future and security, and whether he is better or worse off than he was several months ago, it is possible to build up trend studies which may reveal which way the country is heading economically.

The survey is conducted by personal interviews with a sample of the population distributed according to such factors as age, sex, section of country, community, and economic level. A very small sample is drawn. In 1948, Roper and a staff of 256 interviewers employed samples of several sizes. His presidential poll was about 5000, his consumer polls covered 3500, and his surveys of management and their opinions ran to 4000 or more.

Roper has devised some extremely interesting tests to determine the effects of framing the questions and of certain kinds of arguments on opinions (318, 803, 806). Experiments on changes of opinions and reasons for the changes, alternative wordings of questions, and attitude scales to ascertain gradations of opinions were tried out in the pre-election periods of 1940 and 1944. By using a multi-step attitude scale in place of a simple for-or-against vote, Roper was able to gauge the strength of the voter's attitude as well as the possible reason for his decision (803, 806). In 1944, a week before the election, *Fortune* tried out three survey techniques on national samples of 3500 each. One survey used an attitude scale consisting of four statements about Roosevelt and the respondent was asked which one came closest to his own opinion. The second survey employed a mixed attitude scale and a secret ballot, while the other consisted only of the secret ballot. The Roosevelt scale was adopted because it was decided that the main issue of the election was Mr. Roosevelt, and that the no-opinion vote was lowest with this scale (496).

CROSSLEY POLL:

Another nationally known poll is that directed by Archibald M. Crossley of the national research organization, Crossley, Inc. This organization is primarily occupied with measuring the popularity of radio programs, but it enters the polling field during national election campaigns. The Crossley Poll was launched during the 1936 presidential campaign and again in 1940, 1944, and 1948.

In 1940, Crossley concentrated his surveys in 19 states in which a close return was anticipated. His prediction here was 1.8 per cent under the actual vote received by Roosevelt. Crossley reports that he tried a number of new departures in this poll, only some of which were successful. One was to cross-section the population of voting age rather than the intending voters; this proved to be effective in all places except in very large cities. In the latter, voter ratios would have provided a better guide for sample distribution (213). Among the other interesting departures was one designed to measure the undecided vote by a series of check questions, the use of a secret ballot (he was the first to employ this device), and the determination of the date when the decision was reached to vote one way or the other.

Crossley and Gallup were the only two pollers who made state-by-state predictions in the four presidential campaigns from 1936 through 1948. Such forecasts require relatively large samples and correct weighting of controls within each state. In 1944, for five states Crossley made an incorrect prediction, while Gallup erred in seven states. Of the thirteen that Crossley called "very close," only one elected Roosevelt by more than 3 per cent. In 1948 also, Crossley made slightly better predictions than did Gallup in his state-by-state forecasts of the Democratic party vote of the nation. The difference in their predictions of the popular vote was negligible—both giving Dewey about a 5 percentage point lead.

The way in which Crossley arrived at his predictions is noteworthy. In 1944 he used 400 sampling points and covered approximately 20,000 people in each of two surveys (mid-September and the third week in October). Only states with a margin of less than 4 per cent for either candidate were included in the October survey. Census data, ration book registration, local statistics, and market data were all utilized in the preparation of his sample. His controls took into account occupational and political factors as well as the more usual variables. This poll was the only one which estimated the probable soldiers' vote (496). In 1948, Crossley followed much the same procedure. In August he took a cross-section in 48 states; in September he confined his surveys to states where his August survey indicated a close race; and in October he restricted his inquiry to the lower economic groups whose voting intention seemed less stable than that of the upper groups. His final prediction utilized the latest interview for each economic level—therefore combining data collected from August to October (898).

Concern over the turnout problem caused Crossley to experiment with intensity of conviction and intention to go to the polls. The respondent was asked the reasons why he chose a particular candidate, how long ago he had made up his mind and how sure he was that he would not change his mind before the election. These precautions and experiments undoubtedly helped him in forecasting. In that election which was very difficult to predict, he underestimated the number of Roosevelt electors by only 78. In 1948, Crossley used a battery of "filter" or screening questions to eliminate people who were unlikely to vote. It is unfortunate that his interviews were held so far in advance of the election date, as he might have been able to predict the turnout more correctly.

GALLUP POLL: THE AMERICAN INSTITUTE OF PUBLIC OPINION:

George Gallup began experimenting with public opinion polls in 1933, and two years later he organized the American Institute of Public Opinion. A series of weekly polls was started and the results were published in newspapers throughout the country. During the 1936 presidential campaign this poll and several others gained nation-wide publicity because their findings, based on relatively small selected samples, differed so greatly from the *Literary Digest* predictions, based on one very large sample. When the actual election returns proved the polls using small samples to be more nearly correct, the American Institute of Public Opinion, also known as the Gallup Poll, assumed a prominent place in the polling field. Because of his syndicated news releases Gallup continued to hold that position in the eyes of the public. His forecasts in numerous elections between 1936 and 1948 were sufficiently good to develop great public confidence in his predictions, as well as in the results of his non-political polls. It was claimed that the findings of the pre-convention polls of 1948 played an important role in the choice of the Republican candidate. The popularity of Dewey as shown in the public opinion polls was cited in the speech seconding his nomination as evidence that he could be elected. By 1948 many people placed great stock in Gallup's prediction that Dewey was going to be elected and that Truman would get 44.5 per cent of the popular vote. It is not inconceivable that the aura of infallibility surrounding the poll forecasts was in no small measure conducive to the relatively small turnout of Republicans at the polls and to the concerted efforts of Trumanites to bring Democratic voters to the polls. Ironically, Gallup's error (as well as Crossley's) in percentage points was less in 1948 than in 1936 when he gained public confidence because he picked the winner in the election contest. In 1936, he underestimated the Democratic party vote by 6.9 percentage points and in 1948 by 5.0 points (498).

Its experience in the 1936 survey led the Institute to adopt two principles of technique which it has followed ever since. At first, both mailed ballots and personal interviews were used. The interview was employed chiefly with rural and lower income groups and the mailed ballot was used to reach the middle and upper income groups. However, when the results were analyzed, it was discovered that the mail returns came from a highly selected or non-representative group of people; hence the mailed ballot was discontinued and the direct interview adopted for all regular survey work. The other technical principle adopted was that of securing a series of successive samples throughout the course of a campaign rather than a single large cumulative one, as was the *Digest's* practice. The latter's poll contained over 2,000,000 votes, whereas the spaced polls of the Institute averaged only 25,000 to 40,000. In 1948, the cumulated interviews over a two-month period reached about 60,000. The spaced samples had the vital advantage of being able to reveal and follow shifting sentiment as the election date approached. Unfortunately, the samples in 1948 were not taken the two weeks preceding election day when shifts toward Truman might have shown up. The Social Science Research Council Committee reports that panel studies revealed that more voters said they shifted from Dewey to Truman in the last two weeks of the campaign than said they shifted in the opposite direction (898).

The staff of interviewers which the Institute maintains is selected with the aim of avoiding bias, and therefore itself represents a problem in sampling. Age, sex, political sympathy, occupation, economic status, section of the country from which he comes, and other factors are considered when the interviewer is chosen. The staff numbered about 1300 in 1948.

Not only has the Gallup Poll surveyed opinion on candidates during various local and national elections, but it also has taken the public pulse on a wide range of current social, political, and economic questions. Such questions as: "Did the atomic bombs in the recent tests do more damage or less damage than you thought they would?" (August 30, 1946) "In some families the wife manages most of the money, while in others the husband does. Who manages most of the money in your household?" (August 31, 1946) "Can you tell me what is meant by 'balancing the Federal budget?'" (September 4, 1946) It will be noted that the first of these is an opinion question, the second is an attempt to get at a fact of behavior, and third to determine how well informed the respondent is.

These "social polls" are not confined to eligible voters but include cross sections of the entire adult population. Up to 1946, the nationwide tabulations were usually based on about 3,000 cases selected according to a stratified quota sampling procedure to be described in a later chapter. During the 1944 Presidential election the Institute experimented with area sampling, and in 1946 Gallup announced a change from quota sampling to random or area sampling similar to that carried on by the Bureau of the Census (see p. 239). Actually, he did not make a major change until 1949.

Studies in the use of the secret ballot and of turnout intentions of voters also are conducted during elections. The findings of the Gallup Poll appear several times a week in more than 126 newspapers which reach an estimated ten million readers As a result, this poll is better known to the general public than any of the other polls. It is also known throughout the world, having affiliates in 1947 in Britain, Canada, Australia, France, Sweden, Norway, Finland, Denmark, .and Brazil.

In addition to election and social polls, Gallup and his associates conduct Audience Research polls. A staff of 400 interviewers, of which 200 are usually on assignment, interview from 4000 to 5000 people a week in several hundred cities scattered over the nation. They ascertain public preferences for various types of movies, books, and radio programs, including plots, titles, and stars. According to one report, changes in the title or star of a picture may increase box-office returns by two million dollars. The movie hit *Best Years of Our Lives* is one of the pictures which was pre-tested by this polling agency.

Interest in public opinion measurement is not confined to organizations affiliated with American polling agencies. In 1947 the Swiss Institute of Public Opinion was organized in Lausanne. The Netherland Foundation for Statistics has been surveying public opinion as well as market and consumer problems. The Hungarian Institute of Public Opinion Research and the Institute for Statistical Research and Public Opinion Analysis in Italy are also making contributions to the polling field. The Science Institute of Mexican Public Opinion has been conducting numerous surveys of the customs, habits, and preferences of the population. In September, 1948, the European Soicety for Public Opinion and Market Research was formed in Amsterdam.

The Princeton Office of Public Opinion Research established in 1940 at Princeton University is a nonprofit organization and operates with a foundation grant under the direction of Hadley Cantril, a professor of social psychology. This organization is interested in developing and improving the science of public opinion research. The work of the institute has centered on psychological problems of phrasing questions, influence of suggestive and emotionally tinged words, determinants of public opinion, and evaluation of sources of hidden bias.

Although not primarily concerned with election forecasting, Cantril in the 1944 election, with a sample of 2000, predicted the popular vote for President by one-half of 1 per cent (496). He used the Roosevelt attitude scale developed by *Fortune* on half of his sample and the Dewey scale on the other half. He found that the Dewey scale produced a 4.6 per cent greater Republican vote than did the Roosevelt (496, p. 476). By averaging the predictions, distributing quotas on the basis of voters in the 1940 election, counting only those planning to vote for their candidate, and adding 0.8 per cent to the Roosevelt vote for the soldier vote, Cantril arrived at his close prediction.

In 1941 the *National Opinion Research Center* (known at NORC), a non-profit, non-commercial organization for measuring public opinion, was established at the University of Denver with the aid of a grant from the Marshall Field Foundation (673). It maintains an office in New York City as well. In September, 1947, the national headquarters of the National Opinion Research Center was transferred from Denver to Chicago (4901 South Ellis Avenue). A branch office is maintained at Denver. The organization was set up "to make available to legislators, government departments, academicians, and non-profit organizations, a staff of experts in the science of public opinion measurement, and a highly trained nation-wide corps of interviewers" (673, p. 31). It is also equipped to analyze and review results made by other polling agencies, and to experiment with new methods and techniques in the polling field.

Like the Princeton Office of Public Opinion Research, the NORC did not publish its election forecast in 1944, but it made one nevertheless. Its prediction, based on a quota sample of 2000 voters out of 2600 covered, erred only 1 per cent from the true popular vote. The sample took into account 1940 electoral votes, population shifts since 1940, city size, rural voting, sex and economic groups. Also considered were registration for voting and intention to vote, together with the interviewer's judgment of whether the respondent was likely to vote.

In 1946 the interviewing staff, consisting of about 200 interviewers, located in various parts of the country, was supervised by a corps of field supervisors sent out by the central office. The main instructions and assignments, however, were sent by mail. All the surveys are conducted by interview with a small representative sample of the population. The number in the cross section usually ranges around 2500 but occasional surveys are conducted on less than half this number. The sampling procedure is known as "Quota Sampling" because interviewers are assigned a definite quota of cases to be interviewed in specified areas, sex, color, and economic groups. All of these groups are represented in the sample in the same proportion in which they are found in the population.

The NORC is continually experimenting with survey procedures. Its techniques are frequently altered to take advantage of latest developments. Outstanding among the contributions of this agency is its published book of instructions for interviewers, *Interviewing for NORC* (675). Since the quota system of respondent selection is employed, a large section of the instructions is devoted to methods of choosing sample cases and ways of avoiding biases in the selection.

In view of the limitations of the quota method, to be discussed in Chapter VII, many surveyors are abandoning this technique. Those who still use it, however, should not overlook this reference for its instructive details. The excellent discussion in this book on methods of interviewing and of recording answers deserves careful study by all surveyors. Another publication in 1946 describes how the sample is built up (674).

Government agencies have made and are making extensive use of the NORC staff and facilities. During World War II, for example, the Consumer Requirements surveys, already mentioned, as well as surveys for the Office of Price Administration, War Production Board, Office of War Information, and other Federal agencies, were conducted by the NORC. In 1949, the universities of Chicago, Cornell, Denver, Harvard, and Wisconsin, became affiliated with the NORC and contributed funds for research in which the facilities of that polling agency will be available to them.

Instructions, assignments, and payments to interviewers are accomplished by mail, but in urgent cases telegraphic communication is used. Telegraphic surveys may either mail or wire the assignments, and the interviewer is asked to complete the interviews in a short time, usually in a day or two. He then tabulates his results and wires his findings to headquarters. In this way a survey can be completed within 48 hours of the drafting of the questions. The most experienced interviewers available on short notice are used for testing schedules and questions prior to the main survey.

N. Y. CITY COLLEGE POLL:

During the Second World War the City College Civilian Defense Council of New York City organized a public information poll to ascertain by monthly house-to-house interviewing what was on people's minds in connection with our war effort. This poll used more than one hundred student volunteers as field investigators. The results, reported in the *Journal of Higher Education*, 1942, 13:279, were particularly valuable in helping officers of broadcasting stations, governmental agencies, and the military units to increase the effectiveness of their methods of disseminating information.

The School of Journalism at the University of Minnesota established a research division in 1943. During the first four years of operation approximately 100 studies were conducted on problems of polling, content analysis, reader interest, and consumer attitudes.

In the fall of 1947 an Institute of Communications Research was organized at the University of Illinois. This same year other universities were also very active in this field. The University of Denver offered a course in "Communications in Public Opinion." It included studies of the formation of public opinion and the accuracy and reliability of opinion polls. The Laboratory of Social Relations at Harvard conducted clinical and panel studies on the dynamics and measurement of opinion. In the state of Washington, a polling agency supported jointly by the University and the State College was set up. Other universities with laboratories equipped for taking polls and experimenting with methods include Syracuse, Michigan, Cornell, Iowa, Iowa State, and Swarthmore. By 1948, some thirty universities had introduced courses in polling into their curricula. Any list is necessarily incomplete since new agencies are being established by universities at an unprecedented rate.

STUDENT OPINION SURVEYS:

Since much scientific knowledge of human behavior is based on studies of college students, polls which can reveal similarities and differences between college students and the general population form a welcome advance in the polling field. The Student Opinion Surveys of America provide a promising start in this service. The project, which was begun in December, 1938, from headquarters at the University of Texas, is national in scope, with about 85 college and university newspapers cooperating in conducting the interviews and publishing the weekly reports. The interviewing is done principally by upper classmen, who receive full instructions from headquarters. Interviews are held in dormitories, lounges, libraries, or elsewhere, the informant being taken aside and asked questions concerning foreign policy, personal habits, or almost anything else. The questions are tested at headquarters before being sent out to avoid inclusion of ambiguous or biased items (39). The samples are planned and drawn by procedures similar to those used by the best commercial surveys.

A number of student polls turned their attention to the study of war psychology and problems of student morale during World War II. One such poll at Cornell was organized for the duration of the war. The procedure employed involved the systematic polling of student opinion, the testing of attitudes in groups, and intensive case studies of individual points of view.

POLLS USED BY SOCIAL AGENCIES:

Social agencies supported by contributions from the public have found that drives for funds can be made more effective if preceded by a public opinion poll to ascertain attitudes toward the agency, its operation, and the services it supports. In its publicity and special newspaper or other articles, the campaign to raise funds applies the findings of the poll, stressing those services which the public approves most, and correcting mistaken ideas regarding the agency's operations. In 1941, for instance, the Community Fund Campaign in Minneapolis employed a polling firm to conduct a public opinion survey to ascertain attitudes of a cross section of the men and women in that city toward the Community Chest. The information thus secured was utilized in conducting a drive which succeeded in achieving 97.6 per cent of its goal.

Market Surveys

No less numerous than the government studies and public opinion polls are the surveys conducted by market research groups, trade associations, and advertising groups to measure the markets for various consumer goods and determine the effectiveness of marketing programs. It is beyond the scope of this book to enumerate all the agencies equipped to conduct field surveys. A list, admittedly incomplete, of market research agencies operating in 1945 was prepared by Ernest Smith Bradford of New York City College, Bureau of Business Research. Approximately 175 agencies, some with branches in several cities, are listed in this directory, *Survey and Directory of Marketing Research Agencies in the United States* (108). *Market Research Sources* published currently by the U. S. Department of Commerce, contains an impressive list of the organizations that are carrying on hundreds of consumer studies; other lists of market surveyors are to be found in the textbooks on marketing listed at the end of this chapter. A discussion of the problems and techniques of a number of surveyors who use the questionnaire technique are described in a book edited by Blankenship, *How to Conduct Consumer and Opinion Research* (78). In the business and industrial field, it includes articles on market description, research for product development, industrial surveys, movement of branded goods to the consumer, Psychological Brand Barometers, public relations research, consumer research, development of advertising copy, copy testing, and readership surveys. In addition to these market studies, it contains articles on radio audience research, government surveys, and public opinion research.

Market surveys are focused on such problems as: testing new products, ascertaining the attitude of consumers toward products already on the market, studying the potential demand for a product in a given field, gauging the unsatisfied needs of consumers, evaluating the methods by which products are distributed, discovering new uses for products, measuring the market of competing products, studying the nature of buying habits, testing consumer reaction to a product while it is being developed and before it is put on the market on a large scale, predicting consumer behavior, analyzing consumer tastes, conditions of usage and ways of using given products.

A great many large firms have established research divisions to survey consumers' reactions to their products. For example, in 1926 the General Foods Corporation selected a panel of leading homemakers throughout the country (859), who tested recipes for jam and jelly in which a prepared pectin product made by the corporation was used. This consumer jury proved to be so valuable that in 1935 an additional and larger panel for appraising other products, packaging, and basic recipes was set up. The members of this jury, originally chosen from a radio cooking school mailing list, numbered 10,000 active testers in 1941. From 1000 to 2500 women are asked to cooperate in any given test, and on the average about 85 per cent respond to the questionnaires mailed to them. The list is classified so that groups of women with special interests, such as women who bake a great deal, may be readily selected for a given test.

The Consumer Research Staff of General Motors has sent out millions of questionnaires to car owners asking them to comment on their practical experience with their cars and to suggest needed improvements. This staff "was set up as a self-contained department in 1933." Weaver states that in the course of a year from twenty to thirty surveys are conducted. Contact is made with more than two million motorists, owners of all makes of cars, located in all sections of the country. These surveys cover topics such as features of mechanical design, styling, various aspects of advertising, sales promotion, and service. The personal interview technique as well as direct mail is employed, although direct mail is used more. Over a period of years, a panel of special correspondents or motor enthusiasts has been built up. It is "restricted to the names of people who make motoring a hobby, who take more than a passing interest in problems of engineering design, and who have the ability to project their thinking somewhat beyond what they actually see in the cars of today" (1066, pp. 150, 151). Among other large firms with research staffs are the Curtis Publishing Company, the Meredith Publishing Company, the Metropolitan Life Insurance Company, the American Institute of Food Distribution, and General Mills.

In 1939 the Advertising Research Foundation began a series of surveys in various cities to find out "how the American public reads its newspapers" (876, p. 125). In this survey, the day after the papers that are to be subjected to examination are published, interviews are held with about 450 men and women. An effort is made to control the sample with respect to occupational groups, sex, and newspaper circulation district. Those informants who say they have read the newspapers in question are asked to indicate on a fresh unmarked copy of the paper exactly what they recall having read on each page of that particular issue. Between July, 1939, and November, 1941, forty-five newspapers were studied in this manner.

The Starch Advertising Rating Service secures data on the number of people who see and read part or entire advertisements of one-half page or larger in a list of consumer magazines. In 1942, according to an article by F. M. Sheppard in the *Journal of Marketing*, the Starch Service employed forty-eight interviewers who each year question approximately 100,000 adults in primary magazine-reading families. Roughly two-thirds of the interviews with women are conducted in their homes; the other third takes place in their places of employment. The reverse policy is applied to interviews with men. Having determined which (if any) of the magazines on the Starch list the interviewee has read, the investigator makes that magazine the subject of the interview. He finds out whether the interviewee knew what was being advertised in each of the advertisements included in the inquiry.

The Magazine Audience Group, consisting of leaders in market research, have been experimenting with various methods of obtaining a true picture of how many people see and read all or part of various magazines. This group has conducted studies of ways of sampling communities and respondents within them; effect of interview fatigue on audience figures obtained for the magazine shown last in order of questioning; and techniques of interviewing which will eliminate "confusion" or the tendency to confuse two issues of the same magazine. In 1945 the group was satisfied that it had developed a technique of asking questions that made correction for confusion unnecessary (78, p. 215). Factors associated with reading and therefore with size of readership audience also have been analyzed.

The Psychological Corporation, established in 1921 by Dr. J. McKeen Cattell, is one of the leading market survey agencies in the country. Its surveys are carried on with the aid of professional psychologists who act as field supervisors and consultants. Dr. Henry C. Link started its series of Brand Barometer studies which is the oldest continuous poll of buying behavior in the United States (78, p. 76). Starting in 1932 with a study of 1578 housewives in the upper-middle income brackets, the Barometer studies have been repeated periodically ever since. Over 442,000 interviews had been made in the 68 Barometer studies completed by June, 1945. Since 1936 the sample has been increased to 10,000 and includes all socio-economic groups. From 1940 on, the studies have been made four times a year.

In 1946, 121 psychologists residing in different cities or towns supervised the work of 479 interviewers in 125 localities. All interviews are held in the home of the respondent, who is a housewife or adult female. The husband or an adult male is also asked to answer a section of the schedule questions. The respondent is asked "What brand of X (coffee, beer, etc.) did you buy last?" This is asked about such varied products as coffee, beer, water softeners, antifreeze solutions, flashlight batteries, shampoos for women, shaving creams for men, cigarettes for men and women. The purpose of such studies is to reveal whether more or fewer people are buying a given article, and to show such trends in relation to competing articles of the same type (469).

In addition to the Brand studies, the Psychological Corporation conducts surveys of public opinion on matters of business, political, and social interest. The survey of opinion conducted in October, 1946, consisted of two questionnaires covering a sample of 2500 people each. One of the questions about which data have been obtained over a period of years is "Is your family more prosperous (or better off) today than two years ago, less prosperous, or the same?" Interesting trends on the psychological counterpart of changes in wages and the cost of living can be developed from such data.

The Psychological Corporation also conducts experiments on survey techniques. In 1939, for example, studies were made on the effect of variation in the form of the question, its position in the interview, and the training of the interviewer. The following year increasing emphasis was placed on experimental exploratory studies prior to advising clients as to the nature and desirability of extensive surveys. These "test tube" studies proved useful devices for testing proposed procedures.

The Reed poll, a junior survey of views and reactions of children of school age (13–16), is conducted by the public relations office of William R. Harshe Company for the Reed Candy Company. The poll is made by means of questionnaires distributed to groups of children through Sunday school teachers, Y.M.C.A. heads, summer camp directors, etc. Ten thousand children responded to the first poll. An experimental poll was conducted at the Chicago Youth Exposition and the 4H Clubs. The children have been asked questions pertaining to subjects of particular interest to adolescents, such as movie and radio program preferences, occupational aspirations, and attitude toward school, as well as questions of more adult interest (411).

More practical procedures for conducting surveys can perhaps be found in the literature of marketing than in any other social science field. Such literature may be found in the bibliography at the end of this chapter.

RADIO AUDIENCE RESEARCH:

The measurement of the extent and character of radio audiences and the influence of various advertising techniques, while a branch of market surveying, has become so important that it deserves separate treatment. Studies of radio audiences have thrived with the aid of university research groups, private radio research agencies, and marketing groups.

Commercial radio audience measurement is directed toward two main objectives, that of furnishing the buyers of radio time with figures on the size and type of audience reached by given broadcasts, and with the determination of program preferences of the groups advertisers wish to reach.

As early as 1929 Crossley conducted surveys to discover what programs people had heard. During the same year the Association of National Advertisers and the American Association of Advertising Agencies formed the Cooperative Analysis of Broadcasting, known as the CAB. This organization functioned until 1946. It provided buyers of radio time in over eight cities with audience data. The method employed changed over the years from a day-part recall method (asking respondents what programs they had listened to during the preceding two or four hours) to the telephone interview using the coincidental method (asking the respondent what station and program he was listening to at the time of the call).

C. E. Hooper, who had been operating in the field of continuous radio audience measurements since 1934, took over many of the clients of CAB. "Hooperating" is an index of program popularity and is widely used by both buyer and seller of radio time. The telephone coincidental method has been developed largely by C. E. Hooper, Inc. The questions used are: "Were you listening to the radio just now?" "To what program were you listening please?" "Over what station is that program coming in?" "What advertiser puts on that program?" "Please tell me how many men, women, and children were listening to the radio when the telephone rang." (170, p. 62). In 1949, Hooper ratings were based on findings from telephone calls conducted by 1200 interviewers located in 36 cities throughout the country.

These five questions yield an amazingly large number of facts about the size of the available audience (persons at home and awake), hours of listening, sets in use, network program rating, urban cross-section ratings, per cent of listeners to a specific program, patterns of listening by one-, three-, and five-minute intervals, composition of the audience, long-term audience trends, and hourly, daily, weekly, monthly or yearly changes in many of the above items. *Radio Audience Measurement* by Chappell and Hooper provides a full treatment of the techniques used and the pros and cons of each (170).

Although the evidence presented on the difference between telephone and non-telephone homes does not agree with that found by other surveyors (e.g. Roslow), this book is the most comprehensive treatment of the entire subject of radio audience measurement prepared to date.

Two large networks, the Columbia Broadcasting System and the National Broadcasting Company, Inc., conducted surveys which involved interviewing about 40,000 urban and 20,363 rural residents as to radio sets in use and family availability (185). The data on when various family members may be found at home and awake are valuable to surveyors who want to limit their calls to periods when the interviewer is most likely to be at home. The research divisions of broadcasting systems are generally concerned with public response to sustaining programs and other aspects of the radio industry.

The panel method, in which a fixed sample of homes are covered over a relatively long period of time, has been used by the Columbia Broadcasting System as well as by other surveyors such as Cawl (154). In these listener panels the members keep records of stations and programs heard, of periods when no one was at home, bedtime and rising time, in addition to records of products and brands purchased.

The panel members may be solicited by mail and, in return for a gift, the prospective respondent is asked to keep a diary on specially prepared forms for recording in quarter hour periods his household's radio listening for a week. This system has come to be known as the "diary method." The fact that the panel membership changes weekly eliminates one of the disadvantages of most panels, i.e., it becomes increasingly unrepresentative as time elapses because of waning interest, migration, deaths, births, marriages, etc. On the other hand, a weekly record does not permit satisfactory studies of long-term trends and of the more complicated influences affecting radio listening.

Surveyors in the field of radio not only employ practically all the techniques known to social surveyors, but they are constantly devising new techniques. The A. C. Nielsen Company, for example, has set up the Nielsen Radio Index, a monthly report based on data secured from a graphic recording instrument, known as an "Audimeter," that is attached to radio receiving sets. This instrument was originally invented by two members of the Massachusetts Institute of Technology but has been developed commercially by the Nielsen Company. The company has about 1000 audimeters in operation. After the audimeter is installed, it makes a record of all the times at which the set is turned on and off, and the station to which it is tuned at every minute of the day or night for one month. Every month a representative visits each home in which an audimeter is installed, removes the record tape (which is about 100 feet long and three inches wide), and inserts a new one. At the same time he takes an inventory of radio-advertised commodities (found in the pantry, bathroom, etc.) to aid in determining the sales effect of radio advertising (696). The Radio-Graph Corporation also has experimented with a mechanical recorder. The type used by this agency records no station tuning of less than twenty seconds. This eliminates recording some of the dialing necessarily taking place when persons are seeking programs of interest.

In 1937 the School of Public and International Affairs at Princeton University established an office of Radio Research. This project, as well as one created later at Columbia University, was sponsored by the Rockefeller Foundation. Among the many activities of the Princeton group are the development and critical evaluation of methods of interviewing and testing in the field of radio. Other pioneer research projects are being conducted at Wayne University, Kansas State College, Ohio State University, and the University of Wisconsin, to mention only a few. *The Journal of Applied Psychology* devoted the entire issue of February, 1939, to the subject of radio studies. Reports such as *Radio Audience Measurement* (170), *The People Look at Radio* (551), and *Radio Research* (554), give some idea of the developments in this field.

The Office of Radio Research, a division of the Bureau of Applied Social Research, Columbia University, concentrates on studies of a psychological nature. For example, it has studied the influence of radio on voting behavior as compared with newspapers and magazines, who listens to small local stations, the degree of satisfaction with current radio offerings and commercial advertising, and the extent to which the acquisition of a radio changed the habit and thought patterns of a group of farm households. The Office of Radio Research has also been interested in non-listening—why people do not listen to given programs.

Just what features of given programs appeal to radio audiences has been measured by the Lazarsfeld-Stanton Program analyzer. This apparatus permits respondents to record their reactions to a program while they listen to it by pressing red (dislike) and green (like) buttons and by not pressing buttons if they are indifferent to what is being heard. A permanent record of the reactions to each program is provided by this device. Accompanying the program analyzer technique is a focused interview (in which the surveyor obtains the reasons for the listener's reaction). The usual procedure is to interview small carefully-selected groups who are called together and presented the program.

This discussion of surveys and polls is obviously far from complete. It is intended only to suggest the origin, general nature, scope, and variety of the methods employed and the various fields covered.

From 1935 to 1940 the great majority of social surveys were conducted with grants of federal funds. With each year of experience in evaluating survey techniques and appraising the outcome, the need for detailed survey plans became more and more apparent to government research project experts. They not only refused to approve poorly planned surveys but also did much to acquaint would-be surveyors with the best-known techniques. Thus the survey movement in this country may be said to have reached a new high, in terms of both numbers and quality, by the end of the 1930's. Many mistakes have been made, to be sure, and still more will be made in the future; but now it is known which techniques have been tried and found wanting, which procedures have proved useful and for what purposes, and which have as yet given contradictory or inconclusive results when tested by practical surveyors. The new techniques that are discovered must pass the ever increasingly rigid tests set up by survey experts before they will be widely accepted. Surveyors have learned that what they find out will depend largely upon how they go about finding it.

Selected References

Social Surveys and Social Research Methods

Bogardus (88), Booth (91), Bowley (100), Bowley and Bennett-Hurst (105), Bowley and Hogg (106), Box and Geoffrey (107), Brunsman (122, 123, 124), Campbell (135), Campbell and Katona (137), Carpenter (148), Cavan et al. (153), Chambers and Bell (156), Chapin (157, 158, 159, 166), Cleveland Survey (177), Colcord (181), Daniels (226), Davie (228), Dodd (247, 248), Dreis (252), Eaton and Harrison (267), Edwards (275), Elmer (285), Employment (287), Florence (317), Frankel and Stock (326), Franz (328), Fry (336), George (352), Gleuck (361, 362), Goodman (370), Goodman and Maccoby (371), Great Britain (376), Hader and Lindeman (387), Hagood (388), Harley (404), Harrison (410), Hogg (446), Horwood (453), Jessen (476), Jones (481, 482, 483), Jones and Clark (484), Kellogg (504), Kinsey et al. (517), Kiser and Whelpton (523), Kluckhon (524), Komarovsky (530), LePlay (560, 561), Lindeman (567), London (585), Lundberg (594, 597), Lundberg et al. (598), Lynd (602, 603), McKenzie (628), Moser (658), Myers (666), Myers and Webb (667), Odum and Jocher (702), Ogg (705), Palmer (715), Parten (716, 718), Phelps (739), Quinn (754), Ritchie (783), Robeson (785), Robinson (794), Rowntree (818), Sackett (828), Schmid (844), Schoenberg and Parten (847), Schuler (851), Shea (866), Smith and White (891), SSRC (899), Solenberger (900), Steiner (915, 916), Stephan (924), Stouffer and Lazarsfeld (938), Taylor (952, 953), Thomas et al. (956), U.S. (981, 986, 993, 1002, 1003, 1004, 1006, 1009, 1010, 1021, 1022, 1024, 1028, 1031), Updegraff (1036), Warner and Lunt (1058), Webb (1071), Wells (1077), Whelpton and Kiser (1081, 1082), Whitely (1086), Willcock (1093), Wirth (1113), Young (1136, 1137), Young et al. (1135).

Public Opinion Polls

Barth (33), Belden (39), Benson (50), Benson and Northcross (47), Benson et al. (49), Berelson et al. (52), Blankenship (77, 78), Blankenship et al. (80, 81), Bosse (95), Box and Geoffrey (107), Bruner and Korchin (121), Campbell (135, 136), Campbell and Katona (137), Campbell et al. (138), Cantril (142, 145), Cowell (204), Crossley (211, 213), Crum (218), Crutchfield

(219), Dodd (247, 248, 249, 250), Ferraby (302, 303), *Fortune* (319, 320, 321, 322), Gallup (338, 339, 341, 343), Gallup and Rae (345), Gallup and Robinson (346), Goldman (363), Harshe (411), Henderson (429), *International Journal of Opinion and Attitude Research* (467), Katz (493, 494, 496, 497, 498), Katz and Cantril (499), Knutson (528), Likert (564, 565), Link (574, 575, 576, 577), Link and Corby (578), *Literary Digest* (581, 582), Madge and Harrison (607, 608), Miller (645), Moser (658), *Nation* (670), National Youth Poll (678), NORC (673, 675, 677), Phillips (741), Remmers (767), Robinson (786–791), Robinson and Rhode (792), Rogers (795), Roper (801, 803, 804, 806, 808, 809, 810), Schreiner (850), Smith et al. (880), Spencer (902, 903), Springarn (904), Stagner (906, 907), Stouffer (937), *Tide* (964), Tryon (976), Turbeville and Hyde (977), Wechsler (1072), Weld (1075), Willcock (1093), Williams (1097), Wilson (1109), Wood (1118, 1119), Wulfeck (1127).

The 1948 Presidential Election Polls

Blankenship (68), Brennan (110), *Business Week* (458), Cantril (146), Chapin (163), Coutant (200), Crespi (206), Dodd (250), *Fortune* (321), *Time* (377), Guest (383), *International Journal of Opinion and Attitude Research* (467), Katz (497, 498), Likert (566), Myers (668), Peatman (729), Sheatsley (870), SSRC (898), *Tide* (965).

Consumer Surveys and Marketing Research

Advertising Research Foundation (1), Bader (20), Blankenship (76, 77, 78), Bradford (108), Brown (115–120), Burtt (128), Caples (147), Cassady (149), Cassady and Haas (150), Cherrington (171), Churchman et al. (174), Converse (191), Coutant (200, 201), Coutant and Doubman (202), Crossley (214), Deming and Simmons (242), Duffy (258), Eastman (265), Eastwood (266), Egerton (282), Engle (291), Ferber (297), Fiske and Handel (310, 311), Franzen (330, 331), Ghiselli (357), Goodman (370), Goodman and Maccoby (371), Hancock (392), Haring (401), Harshe (411), Hartwell (417, 418), Hauser and Hansen (424), Hauser and Leonard (425), Heidingsfield and Blankenship (428), Hotchkiss and Franken (454), Houser (457), Jenkins (469), Jenkins and Corbin (472), Karslake (490), Kelsey and Alexander (505), Lazarsfeld (549), Link (572, 574), Lucas (589, 590), Ludeke (591), Malcomb (610), Murphy (663), Nafziger (669), Newhall (690), Poffenberger (745), Prevette (748), Psychological Corporation (749, 750), Redmayne and Weeks (760), Reed (761), Reilly (764), Riggleman and Frisbee (780), Root and Welch (800), Roper (802), Roslaw et al.

(816), Ruch (821), Rudolph (823), Schoenberg and Parten (847), *Scholastic* (849), Sellers (859), Shaw (865), Sikes (876), Smith (882), Smith and Suchman (883), Stanton (911), Stock and Hochstim (930), Stonborough (933), U.S. (944, 986, 1010, 1021, 1022), Wagoner (1044), Watson (1060), Weaver (1069), Wheeler (1079), White (1085), Wingate (1111), Wolfe (1115).

Radio Audience Research

Beville (58), Chappell (168, 169), Chappell and Hooper (170), CBS (184, 185), Crossley (215), Curtis (223), Fiske and Lazarsfeld (312), Gaudet and Daniel (347), Gill (358), Goode (369), Gruenberg (380), Herzog (431), Hettinger (432), Hettinger and Neff (433), Hettinger et al. (434), Hill (437), Hooper (450), Karol (488, 489), Kirkpatrick (518, 519), Lazarsfeld (544, 545, 546, 547), Lazarsfeld and Field (551), Lazarsfeld and Stanton (554), Link and Corby (578), Lumley (592), Maclatchy (606), Meyrowitz and Fiske (642), Neumeyer (684), Nielson (696), Peter (735), Politz (746), Rorty (811), Sayre (837, 838), Schuler and Eubank (852), Siepmann (875), Stanton (909), U.S. (1008), Wagner and Erb (1046), *Wall Street Journal* (1054), Weld (1076), Wilder (1090), Wilson (1102), Wolfe (1114), Womer (1116).

CHAPTER II

Planning the Procedure

Designing, organizing, and conducting a survey is like establishing and running a business enterprise. Both require technical knowledge and skill, administrative ability, and specific experience or training in work similar to that being organized. In the past, to be sure, it was thought that anyone could set up a peanut stand and make a go of it, or that anyone could conduct a survey and produce reliable, meaningful results. The failure of thousands of small-scale businesses and the findings of thousands of surveys which were misleading or unwarranted in view of the procedures followed to obtain them, lend adequate testimony to the falsity of this assumption. Only by carefully planning the survey from start to finish can reliance be placed upon the results and, in many cases, will the findings ever reach the publication stage.

Before the detailed plans for a survey can be developed, a number of general questions should be answered, preferably by the person or persons to whom the surveyor will eventually have to report. The points usually needing clarification are:

1. *What question or questions are to be answered by the survey?* Before undertaking a social survey or poll or choosing the methods by which it is to be conducted, it is important *to formulate a statement of the problem* that is to be surveyed. In their enthusiasm to secure the facts, few people stop to consider just what the problem is that calls for facts, and what type of facts, if any, will solve it.

When an investigation is undertaken, the general nature of the problem has usually been determined, either by the organization sponsoring the survey or by the individual who is conducting the research. If the sponsors are asked to condense the problem into a statement or two, the formulation is of such broad scope that the director of the investigation can generally study pretty much what he pleases. It is his job to get the sponsors to define the problem so that it can be studied objectively and scientifically. Administrators in the fields of social and business relations are usually concerned with broad problems, such as whether or not the community is serving certain groups of people adequately; the reaction of the electorate to the programs of the party in power; the effect of some social measure on the social or economic situation of certain elements of the population; whether the morale of a group will enable it to bear up under certain conditions; the effect of a particular advertising campaign, etc. Before these general topics can be studied, they must be delimited to some small phase of the general problem or to some specific point or points that can be observed or studied in a stated period of time by the individual or group attacking it.

The survey designer should get the survey sponsors to agree upon what specific question or questions they wish answered by the survey. Related questions which are "interesting" but not essential to the main purpose of the the investigation should be discussed and deliberately included or excluded, according to the wishes of the sponsoring group. If included, the sponsors should be made to realize that their inclusion will involve additional expense or that they may take the place of more pertinent questions. The decisions should be recorded so that the surveyor can have them before him when he drafts the detailed plans. Should someone later propose to add still other questions to the schedule or some new tables to the proposed tabulations, the surveyor can evaluate such proposals in the light of these objectives.

The formulation of the problem should include a statement of the purpose to be served by the collection of the facts. Collecting facts for their own sake, while of probable value to someone somewhere sometime, is costly and time-consuming and usually not justified in view of the pressing need for facts about specific current problems.

The agencies or individuals who may be expected to utilize the survey findings should also be considered. By keeping the potential consumers in mind, the survey designer is more likely to select questions that will be meaningful and useful.

2. *What issues should be used for public opinion polls?* Public opinion pollers have found that the selection of issues for their polls requires intimate knowledge of current social, political, and economic events and trends. Since public interest in current affairs changes from

day to day, the poller must try to catch opinion on any particular topic while the public has an opinion. Some issues dominate public thinking over a relatively long period and so are more easily tapped than others. Opinions aroused by some temporary crisis in human affairs may soon die down when the situation is solved. For this reason telegraphic surveys are necessary if the findings are to be published while interest still exists.

In addition to the need for timeliness in the selection of issues, the topics must be of general interest. Unless most people have been touched by the problem under consideration, and unless they have developed an opinion about it, there is not much point in trying to report their opinions. Sometimes, to be sure, the poller is interested in knowing the extent to which the issue has reached the public consciousness. In such cases, the poll may provide the desired information. Generally speaking, the issues must be understood and thought about by the public if the poll is to be meaningful. Furthermore, the choice of phrases for expressing how people feel about the issue should take into account how the issue expresses itself in the mind of the man in the street. The expression of the issue must be realistic and reflect accurately all shades of opinion. All sides of the issue should be presented; otherwise critics may cause the public to lose faith in the impartiality of the polls (see 534). The work of Suchman and Guttman to be discussed later should aid greatly in a balanced presentation (942).

One of the most basic requirements in the choice of the issue is that it should be easily condensed into a brief, uninvolved statement. Issues which have not become clear-cut are of little value for polling purposes. It is better to wait until the issue can be defined before attempting to poll it. For a detailed discussion of the choice of issues see (345, pp. 93, 94, and 825).

3. *Is a survey or poll the best way to secure the desired type of information?* If the purpose of a survey is to reveal facts which, if known, would lead to a social reform, it might be more effective to select and describe a few extreme cases, for their emotional appeal may be far greater than any statistics. For example, the statement that one-third of the nation is ill-housed may not be so effective an appeal for housing reform as a picture or detailed account of the living conditions of the poorest families. Again, if the purpose of the investigation is to

find some clues as to the types of situations existing in a community, regardless of their prevalence, a cheaper technique than a survey might be used. In other words, a survey representing the total population in any group is often unnecessary when all that is wanted is a classification of the types and not frequencies of people or situations to be found in that population.

4. *How and by whom will the results be used?* This question is closely related to the preceding one. If the survey is to be made for a private concern or agency and if the findings are to be kept confidential, the only persons who need be consulted in developing the survey plan are those immediately involved. On the other hand, if the results are to be published, the wishes and suggestions of eventual consumers must be considered throughout the survey. While it is not possible to foresee all the misuses to which survey statistics may be put, many abuses can be prevented if the surveyor is aware of his public.

5. *Is it possible to secure any data by the survey method which will throw light on the problem?* Studies of change—before or after some event—are often inconclusive because of the lack of "before" information and the unreliability of memory for certain types of data.

If the problem is stated in terms of evaluative concepts, it is quite possible that the findings will not provide an answer to the questions giving rise to the survey. For example, if the problem to be solved were "Is direct relief preferable to work relief?" there could be no assurance that a survey would yield an answer, since the evaluative concept "preferable" is so largely a matter of individual opinion. When one studies "adjustment," "success," "standards," "better or worse adaptation," a subjective evaluation of the phenomena is implied. Since few persons have the same philosophy of life, few will agree that the findings of the survey actually prove or disprove these subjective problems. A glance at the literature on public opinion polls indicates that there are many "doubting Thomases" who do not believe the polls "measure" public opinion. (See especially 795, 796, 797.)

6. *Will the facts be out of date or of no interest before they can be obtained and tabulated?* Scarcely a year had elapsed after the collection of the 1940 census data before various groups were clamoring for an annual sample census because the figures on employment and other occupational data were regarded as not depicting the current situation. The labor supply in various places was changing so rapidly that

a count as of 1940 was no longer sufficient for many of the users of the statistics. As mentioned earlier, a very high percentage of the questions studied by the public opinion polls are doomed to oblivion because interest in the topics has waned by the time the returns are tabulated.[1]

7. *How much money is or can be made available for the survey?* Surveys are usually expensive undertakings, and unless the surveyor can be certain that there will be sufficient funds not only for the collection of data but for their tabulation, analysis, and presentation, he had better not start. Too many optimistic surveyors have used the limited funds allotted them for collecting the data in the expectation that more money would be forthcoming for the later stages of the survey, only to be disappointed. Even more important, however, than the likelihood of being unable to obtain additional funds is the fact that the funds which were available could have been used to complete a more limited survey. A small preliminary or "pilot" study, for example, might have been successfully carried through. In fact, some agencies which subsidize surveys have found it advisable to make a special small grant for a pilot study, and on the basis of the findings or experience with it, to decide whether or not to grant funds for a larger undertaking. At every stage of planning the survey, the amount of money available should enter into the choice of procedures and the inclusion and exclusion of items to be surveyed.[2]

8. *Will other resources be available for the study?* During periods of marked unemployment surveyors are not likely to have much difficulty in finding personnel, but when labor is scarce, the labor required by the survey may make the inquiry prohibitive in many communities. The question of the availability of trained personnel, potential cooperation of informants, and support of the study by leading citizens must also be taken into account when making plans for the survey.[3]

It is important to have an experienced full-time director for the survey rather than someone who is heading it up in addition to other work. Problems which need immediate decisions are always arising. Furthermore, constant supervision is needed to see that the survey is

---

[1] Estimates on time required for surveys are given on pp. 59–61.
[2] For cost estimates, see Chap. V.
[3] Personnel requirements are discussed in Chap. V.

progressing according to schedule. If some aspects of the survey are more time-consuming than planned or if the data coming from certain parts of the survey are not worth the effort involved in collecting them, the director should be at hand to decide whether to drop these phases of the survey or to find short cuts which will not seriously affect the survey as a whole.

9. *Is it advisable to ask an organized research agency to conduct the study?* Both private and public agencies have trained research staffs who can make the survey. If the problem is of sufficient public importance, it is possible that a few questions added to the schedule of a survey contemplated by a public agency may eliminate the need for a separate survey. Then again, any one of a number of private agencies, such as those conducting public opinion polls and market surveys, or research foundations might undertake the survey. Some commercial consumer research organizations were mentioned in Chapter I. When the research staff is already organized, a survey can get under way more rapidly and be conducted more efficiently than would be possible if it were in the hands of a relatively inexperienced group. Even though it is not feasible to hire professionals to take complete charge of the survey, it might be desirable to hire interviewers from one of the several agencies equipped to supply experienced enumerators. The Office on Public Opinion Research Personnel ought to be invaluable in this connection.

10. *Are you certain that the answer is not already known?* With the countless agencies both public and private that are engaged in social research, it is difficult for anyone to keep up with the latest findings, which may be in unpublished form as well as in published reports. For these reasons, no survey should be undertaken until the surveyors are satisfied that the required facts do not exist. Often a careful search will show that the facts desired are already on file or in published tables and require only a regrouping or retabulation to yield the data needed. Although the published data do not appear to be exactly what is wanted, an examination of the schedule forms or tabulations may reveal that the facts required can be obtained without any further field work, or with only supplementary field work.

One of the difficulties in using existing records is that the methodological procedures followed in collecting or tabulating the data often have not been carefully recorded, so the facts may have a quite different significance from what would appear on the basis of superficial examination. A further difficulty is that definitions used in classifying information may be entirely adequate for one purpose but may result in extremely misleading conclusions if used for another purpose. Still another objection is that the data usually are not up to date and therefore do not describe the current situation which has necessitated a new survey.

If the survey is made from the files of an administrative operating agency, such as cases in social agencies, records of children in public schools, lists of gas meter subscribers, etc., a cross section of current cases is difficult to obtain. Sometimes closed or inactive cases are not separated from current cases in the files, or cases presenting special problems may be in separate files, or cases awaiting filing or needing attention during the day may not be in the files. Hence, before active files are used as a source of information, it is well to look into these difficulties.

If the facts available are found not to be sufficiently conclusive or up to date for the purpose at hand, a new survey can profit by avoiding the mistakes of the earlier one or by enlarging upon phases which the original one did not emphasize.

11. *How will information be obtained?* Having clearly formulated the problem to be investigated and having decided to conduct a field survey, the surveyor has next to decide which technique or techniques he will use to obtain the desired information. To make this decision, he should be familiar with the advantages and disadvantages of various methods and techniques. If he is aware of the limitations of his procedures, he may use ingenious devices to correct the shortcomings of the method he selects, or he may employ a combination of techniques. In the following chapter the most widely used procedures are evaluated from the point of view of all phases of survey methodology.

12. *Are you sufficiently trained or experienced to conduct a survey?* The job of running a survey calls for specialized knowledge in all phases of survey procedure. It is the wise surveyor who knows when to call and whom to call upon for expert help. It is best to consult a specialist in the planning stages of the survey so that many costly errors may be avoided. As in any profession, there are capable and incapable specialists. There are those who emphasize or are familiar with one phase of the survey to the exclusion of most of the other phases. If

the survey is to be a very large or important undertaking, it may be desirable to call in a "board of experts" so that a well-rounded survey design will be drafted. Unfortunately, there is yet no way of knowing when one has the best advice obtainable, but with the development of the various university schools for training in opinion and survey methods one might turn to such agencies for advice and assistance in the selection of qualified personnel.

Designing the Survey

In order to insure that the survey will yield returns which are meaningful and are secured in the most efficient manner possible, it is essential that the entire plan of the survey be prepared before the collection of data is begun. Each stage of the survey should be planned with all the preceding and succeeding stages in mind. A single unified plan insures that a minimum number of waste motions and illogical decisions will obstruct the course of the survey. Insofar as possible, this plan should be recorded so that it can be referred to constantly. When deviations from it must be made, the effect upon the entire survey can be readily discovered and alterations can be made quickly and logically in every stage of the survey affected by a change in the plan for a single phase.

PRETESTING AND THE PILOT STUDY:

It may be argued that because it is impossible to know what the survey will discover before it is made, and because so many decisions are based upon what is discovered during the survey, the above suggestion for detailed planning cannot be followed. As a matter of fact, an efficiently conducted survey should yield little new information to its designer. This advance knowledge of the experiences to be encountered and even of the findings to be obtained should be gained through pretesting or trying out the new techniques and forms which it is planned to use, and through a small advance study during which the final design for the survey is evolved. In some instances the subject matter of and devices for the survey will have been tested by other surveying agencies, so their experience may be regarded as the pilot study; but even so, it is still desirable to check the procedures in advance of the main survey since local conditions may be different or the passage of time may have brought new problems.

Before deciding definitely upon given procedures, the surveyor should pretest every plan. He should not assume that his own reaction or that of his colleagues is "typical" of the response of the man on the street or the average housewife. The janitor, the delivery man, and the maid are usually better samples of the "average person" than are the white-collar workers associated with surveys. But even service employees like the above may not react the same as would strangers to whom the surveyor has no special entree. So, before finally adopting a technique, the surveyor should try to test it in a situation comparable to that where it will eventually be used. While the various steps may be tested individually and improved upon during the preliminary planning stage, the plans for the different operations should be combined into a unified plan and given a complete test before a large-scale survey is undertaken. This final trial, often referred to as the *Pilot Study, Test-Tube Survey,* or *Trial Survey,* is of inestimable value if properly designed and carried out.[4]

When setting up a pilot study it is important to design it in such a way that the questions for which an answer is desired are definitely settled. The results should be *definitive* and not left up in the air as they were before the pilot study was undertaken. In order to test whether one procedure is preferable to another, for example, it is necessary to give each a fair trial under comparable conditions. By divid-

---

[4] The U. S. census, for example, makes a pilot study about a year before the decennial census is to begin. In 1939 the pilot census was conducted in Indiana.

"A special census of St. Joseph and Marshall Counties, Ind., was authorized by the Secretary of Commerce to be taken as of August 14, 1939. This census, a preview of the decennial census of population, proved to be very helpful in providing a testing ground for the schedules, auxiliary forms, instructions, and procedures planned for the decennial census and indicated some necessary changes in the schedules and procedures. Two innovations of the trial census were the use of objective tests as a means of testing and selecting the enumerators after a period of census training and the employment of squad leaders as supervisors of from 10 to 20 enumerators. Both of these innovations were adopted for the Sixteenth Decennial Census.

"This trial census also provided real data for training office employees before the population schedules from the regular census were received. Preliminary editing and coding instructions, card forms, tabulations, and even table forms for the final census reports for 1940 were developed well in advance of any previous census on the basis of the substantial 'census preview.'" (*Annual Report of the Secretary of Commerce, 1940,* p. 42.)

As a result of this advance study, many of the questions raised by opponents to the census could be answered with facts.

ing the cases in the pilot study into two or more random groups of equal size, different techniques in questioning can be applied to each group. In one employment-unemployment study, for instance, there was some uncertainty as to whether the inclusion of a question on the amount of earnings received by the workers in the family would make a large number of families refuse to cooperate. Hence every other family interviewed in the pilot study was asked the question on earnings, and the refusal rate of the two groups of families was compared; the difference was found to be negligible.

The pilot survey should reveal the shortcomings of all procedures, instructions, and schedules. Even before the printed schedule is prepared and the pilot study undertaken, questionnaires for ascertaining opinions should be pretested so that glaring weaknesses in the questions or in their arrangement will be eliminated. Pretesters in opinion polls should have as their objective the discovering of how to find out what people think. To achieve this goal pretesters must be on the lookout for questions which are difficult to convey to the informant, questions which seem to mean different things to different people, questions in which the alternatives are not clear-cut or realistic, questions which give identical responses, questions which appear to be drawing dishonest or hedging answers, leading questions, or questions which have any other of the weaknesses discussed in Chapter VI. Pretesters should analyze critically each of the proposed questions and make suggestions for improving or omitting them. The early question pretests are usually not carried out so systematically or extensively as the pretests during the pilot study. By the time the pilot survey is undertaken the questions are usually in almost final form. The points to be pretested have been narrowed down to a few points which can be cleared up during this test-tube study, which also is aimed at answering cost and time as well as other administrative questions. In fact, the results of the pilot survey should determine whether or not a larger survey is desirable.

The National Opinion Research Center has most of its questionnaires tested by full-time staff members. The pilot survey type of pretest is used when the subject matter is new or complex, when new techniques are being experimented with and a cross section of interviewers' responses are desired, and when the approximate frequencies of various answers are wanted.

In setting up the pilot study, it is desirable to "practice" on groups other than those to be surveyed in the main study. If some techniques prove faulty or arouse antagonism, it is important that the effects of these procedures not be allowed to affect the main survey. Thus, if a large proportion of the population of a city is to be covered in the survey, it might be preferable to conduct the pilot study in a nearby city that has similar characteristics. Or if the city to be surveyed is large, a small number of persons who will not be included in the final sample might be the "guinea pigs."[5]

On the other hand, it is desirable that the pilot sample be as similar as possible to the final sample, for only then can the surveyor be certain that he has faced all the types of problems that are likely to arise in the more comprehensive study. If he wishes to test how the general public will react to a poll question, for example, he should not trust the experience gained from interviewing a group of college students, for the vocabulary and knowledge of the two groups is likely to be so different that the test results will be misleading. Similarly, if an entire community is to be surveyed, the selection of one section of it for the pilot study cannot be depended upon to give a representative sample of the types of problems that may arise in other sections.

While the nature and techniques of the survey and the complexity of the schedule will determine the number of cases required for the pilot study, a rough idea of the experiences of other surveyors is helpful. As mentioned below, the U. S. census covered two counties in its pilot study of 1939. In less extensive surveys in the public opinion field, surveyors have been satisfied with 100 interviews for the pilot surveys. If there is much doubt about the feasibility of various procedures, 200 interviews have been used. On the other hand, if a choice between two versions of a simple question are being tested, as few as 25 interviews may prove sufficient. If the findings of the pretest indicate that significant changes are necessary in the survey design or questions, a second or even a third pretest may be necessary before the final form is adopted.

If the survey is to be repeated periodically and if the techniques have been tested in other surveys, it may be efficient to conduct the pilot study with one of the subsamples that will be used in the main survey, with the understanding that the results of the pilot study will be incorporated in the main study if the techniques need no significant

---

[5] The techniques for drawing samples are described in Chap. VIII.

revision before being applied again. Only in rare instances is the original survey design likely to be adopted for the larger study without alteration, so it should be tried on a small scale first if no pilot study is contemplated. If the experience from this limited survey indicates that revisions of techniques, forms, or instructions are necessary, the results of this small study should not be included in the later surveys.

THE USE OF SAMPLING WHEN MAKING ESTIMATES:

When drafting plans for the inquiry the surveyor will find that he can improve his estimates of possible results and lessen the time and cost involved in various operations by employing sampling techniques whenever possible. If, for example, he needs to know how many cards of a certain type are in a large file, he can come quite close to the correct figure in an hour's time by using sampling devices.

COST ESTIMATES:

Cost and time considerations should enter into the choice of procedures and the collection of survey data at every step. While a survey can be planned on the assumption that unlimited funds will be available, the resulting plans will not be useful if the survey has to operate on a limited budget. If, however, the amount of money available is known from the start, the most efficient plans can be devised.

In drafting budget estimates, the rule-of-thumb procedure of dividing the survey into the following three parts, each of which frequently takes about one-third of the available time and funds, may be used:

1. Planning the survey and drafting schedule forms and instructions.
2. Investigating in the field, collecting data, and editing schedules.
3. Coding, tabulating, analyzing data, and writing the report.

The publication of the report is not included, since this is such a variable item. However, in some survey plans it may be necessary to give it the same importance as the other three.

When preparing the budget estimate, the surveyor should allow ample funds for nonlabor as well as labor costs. He should make a detailed statement of all the anticipated costs when the plans for all stages of the survey are ready. These detailed expenses should be totaled to arrive at the budget requirements. After every anticipated cost has been provided for, the surveyor should play safe and add 10 per cent of the total budget for contingencies—in a period of rising prices perhaps 20 per cent would not be too much. Specific costs will be discussed in Chapter V.

The above plan assumes that a detailed survey design has been carefully worked out and that all estimates are based on knowledge of the local situation—wages, rents, prices, etc. If the estimates are based on rough guesses, the surveyor will probably be wise to include every cost he can foresee and then double the estimated total. Or better yet, he had better wait for his budget until he or his associates have prepared detailed plans.

TIME ESTIMATES:

The time schedule should consist of a detailed statement of when various operations are to begin and end, so that at any time the surveyor can know what the chances are of completing the survey and whether or not a cut should be made in the total work outlined.

If the surveyor draws up his plans on the assumption that every operation will take longer than the trials or tests indicate it should, he may achieve the distinction of keeping to a time schedule in completing the survey. Few people can continue to work at the pace established during the early days at a new job. Sickness, fatigue, holidays, extremely hot or cold weather, dismissals, errors, lack of supplies, and many other factors tend to slow down the best of plans. A satisfactory time schedule takes into account as many of these contingencies as possible, but it·should also allow some time for the unforeseen.

Since surveys are usually prompted by a more or less urgent need, the sponsor of the survey seldom allows sufficient time for conducting it and making the results available. Generally speaking, the time required is much longer than the sponsors anticipate. For such large-scale surveys as the Study of Consumer Purchases, the National Health Survey, the study on the Cost of Medical Care, the Real Property Inventories, etc., several years were required from the initiation of the field work to the final publication of the findings. The final tabulations of the U. S. census are seldom published until two or more years after the enumeration. However, hand counts·as well as a sampling of the 1940 census schedules made it possible to prepare preliminary estimates long in advance of the total counts, thus overcoming this time lag. Less complex investigations can be conducted in much less time than that required by comprehensive surveys. The survey of ten congested production areas by the census was carried out with comparative speed. The work on the plans began in October, 1943. The field work started in January and preliminary counts for two of the cities were issued in March, and by July practically all of the releases were published. In a short survey conducted in New Haven, Connecticut, by staff members of the Russell Sage Foundation and the Yale Institute of Human Relations, the major portion of the field work—investigating 2097 families—was done in approximately one month, and within a few months summary tables of the findings were available. Not, however, until almost a year had elapsed was the main report published (446).

The National Opinion Research Center reports that from six weeks to three months are required from the start of a regular survey until the data are ready for final form, two to three weeks are required before the last completed schedule is received, and from one week to a month to tabulate the figures and compute percentages (675, p. 127). Telegraphic surveys conducted by this and other national polling agencies are, of course, much speedier. With an organized field and office staff always available, they can present findings within forty-eight hours from the time questions are framed. In order to make this possible, the returns are telegraphed to the central office and the staff members work in day and night shifts to complete the tabulations. The tabulations must be simple and be limited to answers to a few questions. In most surveys the subject matter is more comprehensive than in these public opinion polls and many cross tabulations are desired; hence the work of collecting, editing, coding, tabulating, and analyzing is considerably more time-consuming than it is for opinion polls. But if the survey is made periodically, it can be planned to yield quick returns even on rather complicated data. In the St. Paul study referred to on page 13, the survey procedures were so organized that tabulations for the monthly index of the labor force were available a few days after the close of the period covered by the index.

SETTING THE DATE FOR FIELD WORK:

When setting the date for the investigation, the surveyor must take several factors into consideration. First of all, the time of year is extremely important. If the survey is to extend over several months, it is desirable to begin the field work well before March. In most sections of the United States, particularly in cities, the summer months are quite undesirable for survey work. During warm weather many urban families vacation away from home, drive to nearby resorts, or seek refuge from the heat in the parks. Thus, as many as half the homes visited by the investigator may be deserted, either for the day or for several weeks or months. Generally speaking, the upper-income groups are more likely to be away during the vacation period than are the low-income groups; hence unless the study is extended into the fall of the year, the completed returns may show an underrepresentation of the upper-income groups.

If the survey is to be conducted in rural areas, however, still other stumbling blocks must be faced. Because during the winter and spring many roads are impassable, investigators calling on farmers may find the problem of transporting themselves from one farm to another more time-consuming than results warrant. However, in the winter the farmers are quite likely to have time to go over a detailed schedule with the investigator, whereas during planting or harvest season they may resent having him take up their time. When the U. S. census was first undertaken, the enumeration was made during the month of August; later this was changed to January. The decennial census is now taken in April when most people are in their homes.

Holidays such as Christmas, Thanksgiving, and Fourth of July are often unsatisfactory for surveys since people are likely to be busy or away from home. Even if the informant is home, relatives or guests may be present so the interview cannot be held in privacy. One surveyor found that if questionnaires are to be sent by mail, maximum returns can be expected if the questionnaire reaches the informant on Saturday so that he can have the week end in which to fill it out. During the summer, however, this timing is probably unsatisfactory because few people remain at home over the week end.

The various stages of survey procedure which must be provided for in time and cost estimates include:

1. **Drafting the Plans.** As mentioned earlier in this chapter, before detailed plans for the survey can be developed it is necessary to formulate a statement of the problem, to delimit its scope, to define the es-

sential concepts which will be used, and to develop a working hypothesis as to what is to be found and how it is to be measured. Once this general groundwork has been laid, the survey designer and his assistants are in a position to prepare detailed definitions, schedules, forms, and procedures for each stage of the survey. The time spent planning is usually more than justified by savings of waste motion in later stages of the investigation. The larger the survey or the newer the field of inquiry, the more work is required for drafting plans. The staff of the Census Bureau begins planning for a census several years before the actual enumeration is to start. Other large studies by government agencies have required two or more years of planning by a half dozen specialists. If the survey is of a rather limited scope and is to be conducted in a single community, a few months of planning by two or three experts may be sufficient. However, if much pretesting of terms or procedures is required, the experts must have the assistance of question testers, interviewers, and clerical and stenographic assistants. This last is essential regardless of the amount of experimentation, because planning involves the preparation of numerous forms and instructions which must be typed.

The assembling of statistical background data about the area and population and topic to be covered by the survey is an essential phase of the planning. A clerical staff under the supervision of the sampling director should assemble statistical data which can be used in determining the sampling procedures as well as in forecasting the findings that are likely to be revealed by the survey. For sources of statistics in most communities the surveyor should consult the references at the end of this chapter. Maps such as those supplied by the Census Geographer or by local civic officials are practically a must in survey work. The Sanborn maps used by the Cenus Bureau in its area sampling studies show the location and general use of individual structures. Maps can be obtained for cities having more than 25,000 population. Census and other government reports, statistics from trade journals, and published findings of surveys conducted by agencies such as those mentioned in Chapter I often contain information indispensable to the survey planner. In opinion surveys it is desirable to understand the background of the community gained from discussions with leaders of management, labor, government, social agencies, and other special groups. Such discussions may reveal the central issues to be covered by the polls as well as concrete ways in which opinions are expressed (463).

Unless the survey designer knows approximately what the study will disclose, he cannot draw up satisfactory coding instructions, table forms, or analysis procedures. If the data available from secondary sources do not provide a basis for making good estimates, the pilot study should yield the needed information. Thus the pilot study may be regarded as part of the planning procedure for the survey, and allowance for this expenditure should be made in the budget.

Of paramount importance in the survey plans is the choice of the sampling design. The ideal sampling plan should have the following characteristics: (1) It should yield an accurate, reliable picture of the total. Thus it should not be biased or too small to produce results as precise as needed to answer the question of the survey. (2) It should be possible to assess the precision of the sample, or to determine the outside limits of error which could be expected according to the laws of probability. (3) It should be as simple as possible so that chances for slip-ups will be minimized. (4) It should give the most information for the least cost. (5) Insofar as possible, the sample cases should be selected in the office by trained samplers rather than in the field by interviewers. If the sample cases are not predesignated, instructions for their selection should be so explicit that interviewers will not depart significantly from random selection. (6) It must be possible to carry out in practice the principles adopted in theory. An excellent theoretical plan is worse than none if it is impractical to follow in view of the people who are to carry it out and the conditions under which they are to do it. (7) It should be possible to draft foolproof instructions to those who draw the sample as well as to those who locate the cases and collect information from them. (8) It should represent a real saving in time and cost over complete enumeration, otherwise sampling should not be employed.

With the publication of the report on sampling methods prepared by the Committee on Measurement of Opinion, Attitudes and Consumer Wants under the sponsorship of the Social Science Research Council, the surveyor will have an up-to-date, comprehensive treatment of this subject to guide him in planning his sample.

As the complexity of the job of surveying is revealed in this book, it will become increasingly evident that it is necessary to select the initial staff of planners very carefully so that these persons may eventually assume supervisory or administrative work where a knowledge of the plan as a whole as well as of the details is essential.

2. Designing the Schedule and Framing the Questions. While drafting the schedule and the survey questions is part of the planning process, the time, skill, and effort required by this work make it stand out as a major phase of survey procedure.

In addition to the selection of the subject matter to be covered in the survey, or the issues to be polled in opinion polls, the precise wording used and the order of asking the questions must be skillfully planned so as not to prejudice or predetermine the reply. Since the opinions expressed are likely to be influenced by the form of the question, familiarity with the numerous pitfalls into which the question designers may fall is essential. In opinion and attitude surveys, the survey designer should look into scaling devices such as those developed by Guttman (see page 196) or the quality control techniques of Deming. The surveyor needs to be certain that his findings would not be significantly different or even reversed had he varied his phrasing or used different questions. Not only must the schedule or questionnaire be drafted, tested, and printed, but written instructions must be prepared for everyone who will interpret, fill in, edit, code, and analyze the items on the schedule.

3. Setting Up the Organization. The larger the survey or the greater the urgency to complete a survey quickly, the greater the task of setting up a working organization. However, even small-scale undertakings require a great deal more organization and administration than is usually provided for by the plans. Not only must sufficient and conveniently located office space be found, but arrangements must be made for obtaining the needed office equipment and supplies. Little time is allowed for this work because of the speed with which most surveys must "get going" and be completed.

In addition to providing office space and supplies, there is also the interviewing and selection of personnel, which is usually quite time-consuming. Tests must be devised for applicants. Possibly a training school for interviewers will have to be instituted so that only persons who can prove their ability in this line will be employed. In normal times when community leaders learn that the survey is about to begin, they are likely to refer many job-seekers to the survey director. Either he or his assistants may expect to devote at least a week to interviewing applicants—even for a survey which needs only a few interviewers.

Training the personnel for the various duties connected with a survey usually takes more time than the planners allow. Only if the office and field workers are carefully trained will the data secured be of any value; hence time spent on this aspect of the survey usually pays high returns.

The instructions and forms needed in the office administration include production records, payroll forms, expense forms, time sheets, checking forms, error record forms, filing instructions, inventory sheets, and the forms required for sampling, editing, coding, and tabulation. (See later chapters for a more detailed discussion of these topics.)

4. **Drawing and Testing the Sample.** Assuming that the sample of cases to be interviewed for the survey is chosen in the office rather than in the field, one of the first things to be done after the personnel have been employed is to select the sample. This involves preparing the source list, spotting or selecting the sample cases, writing sample cards, preparing the master list, and entering the name and address of the sample cases on the schedule forms which are to be used in the field. (See Chapter VIII for a detailed treatment of these steps.) Once the sample has been drawn, it should be tested by internal and external checks. For this last operation, statistical background data mentioned earlier need to be available about the population in the area of the survey.

The surveys which are designed so that the sample cases are selected by field investigators or by informants who "select themselves" must devote a considerable portion of their staff time to determining the nature of the sample thus obtained and trying to improve its representativeness. If the sample design adopted is one which calls for the proportional selection of cases from among different groups of the population, the planner has a twofold task. First, he must decide which groups of the population are likely to show significant differences with respect to the survey topic. This decision should be reached only after the surveyor is thoroughly familiar with all related studies and data which he can find. Second, he must provide estimates of the number of cases in each of the groups sampled in the total population. The statistical background data referred to above are essential for this purpose.

In any type of survey the sampling staff must keep a running inventory and analysis of the returns that are turned into the office as completed, as well as of those that present special problems and therefore may not yield completed and acceptable schedules.

5. Collecting and Processing the Data. Whatever the technique used to secure information from the sample cases, the procedure must be planned in great detail. The organization and training of the field staff, the assignment and control of schedules in the hands of interviewers, the setting up of checks to insure that the information collected is reliable and meaningful—these are but a few of the many problems to be considered.

Processing the data as soon as the interviewers turn in schedules will result in a great saving of time and will do much to insure that the interviewing is of the highest caliber. Field workers who do inferior work can be quickly detected and taken out of the field before scheduling has advanced too far.

The processing should include editing for completeness, consistency, and reliability. If the data are to be transcribed to a form more suitable for office manipulation, this, too, is part of the processing procedure. If, after editing is completed, the data are classified or coded and made ready for the tabulation stage while the field staff is still collecting them, the number of usable returns will be much higher than if the coding is carried on after completion of the field work. Return visits to an informant may clear up cases which might have to be discarded were such visits impossible.

As mentioned above, throughout the collection period careful checks on the samples should be made and every effort exerted to secure returns from all cases in the sample.

6. Tabulating the Returns. Whether hand or machine tabulation is employed, the table forms which will provide answers to the questions giving rise to the survey should be prepared before the final plans for the survey are adopted. The sorts or counts which will constitute each table and the order in which the tables are to be built up are an important part of the tabulation plans. If hand tabulation is to be efficient, the data should be placed on small cards to facilitate sorting and counting. If machine tabulation is employed, the punch cards, punching and verifying instructions, and instructions to machine operators should be ready well in advance of the time when tabulation is to begin. Tabulation includes such various operations as making sorts and counts; entering the counts on a table form; computing totals, averages, percentages, and other statistical measures; entering these computations on the tables, and typing the completed tables. Each of these operations must be checked; if an error is found all the records affected by it must be changed. The editing of table titles and the preparation of summary and text tables from the raw data or detailed tables also must be provided for in the tabulation plans.

7. **Analyzing Figures and Writing the Report.** A few of the staff members who have followed the survey from the beginning should be entrusted with the task of writing up the procedures and interpreting the findings for the user of the statistics. Only persons who are thoroughly familiar with the plans and the reasons for adopting one procedure rather than another and who know what deviations from the plans occurred are really capable of writing the report of survey findings. The writer should know the limitations as well as the possibilities in the figures obtained.

If detailed records of procedures are prepared while the survey is in progress, the writer's task is simplified. By incorporating these methodological notes, he may have a good start on the report before the final tabulations are ready. Statistical assistance for checking figures, grouping into classes, and making computations to determine the significance of differences, etc., should be available at this stage of the survey. Plenty of stenographic help is, of course, a prime essential.

Expert draftsmen who can prepare charts and other graphic material to be included in the report should also be available, if such material is to be prepared by the survey organization rather than by an outside agency.

8. **Publishing the Findings.** Budget estimates should include the cost of publishing the report if publication is contemplated. This should include the actual printing cost as well as the cost of copies for free distribution.

9. **Terminating the Survey and Disposing of the Data.** Plans for dismissing the staff, vacating the premises, disposing of the supplies, and insuring that the data are placed where they will be safe and ac-

cessible to qualified research groups should be made before the survey is actually terminated.

After looking over the above program for detailed planning, the reader may wonder whether survey procedures really need to be so complicated. When one enthusiastic survey sponsor was shown the several feet of shelf space needed to hold the forms and instructions for a state-wide survey of family income, he threw up his hands in despair, saying, "If it takes so many instructions to make a survey, I couldn't be bothered making one!" It is very probable that he was too impatient, not to mention unqualified, to undertake the survey.

In order for the findings which result from the expenditure of much time and effort to be all that they are supposed to be, the survey architect needs to prepare very detailed plans and to follow them as meticulously as possible throughout the investigation. Before the plans are finally adopted, the surveyor should review the standards outlined by Dodd (248) to see whether his survey will be able to meet the requirements of good survey procedure. While these standards as yet are not official, it is only a matter of time before these or similar ones will be required for the results to be acceptable. The United Nations bulletin *The Preparation of Sampling Reports* is a step in this direction (980).

The plans presented so sketchily in this chapter are discussed in greater detail in the succeeding chapters of this book.

Selected References

Bibliographical Sources

Brunsman (124), Buros (126, 127), Colcord (181), Conover (188, 189), Culver (222), Day (232), Deri et al. (245), Droba (256), Dunham (259), Eaton and Harrison (267), Good (365, 367), Good et al. (368), Harrison (410), Hauser and Leonard (425), Hildreth (435), Hopkins (451), *Index* (465), Kaplan (487), Kelsey and Alexander (505), Kirsch (521), Larson (540), McNemar (630, 631), Moser (658), Mudge (659), Quinn (753), Schettler (841), Schmeckebier (843), SSRC (896, 897, 898), Stephan (924), U.S. (990, 1005, 1016, 1025).
Also see current issues of the various journals in Sociology, Psychology, Economics, Marketing, Public Opinion, Statistics, Education and Re-

search as well as current periodical indexes such as *Readers Guide*, *International Index*, *Education Index*, *Psychological Abstracts*, etc.

Social Background Data

Brunsman (124, 125), Colcord (181), Davie (228), Deming and Hansen (241), Dreis (252), Dunn (264), Eberle (268), Eckler (270), Eckler and Staudt (272), Edwards (275, 276), Green (378), Hagood and Bernert (390), Hauser (421), Hauser and Leonard (425), Hyman (463), Kaplan (487), Mangus (613), Newcomb (689), Parten (716, 717), Parten and Reeves (721), Quinn (752, 753, 754), Schmid (845), Shryock and Lawrence (871), U.S. (986, 992, 1002, 1003, 1004, 1005, 1006, 1010, 1021, 1022, 1025), Watson (1060).

CHAPTER I I I

Methods of Securing
Information

A great variety of techniques are being employed to secure information from and about the population. Once people are located and contact is established by the surveyor, practically all the methods of social and psychological research may be utilized to reveal their situations, characteristics, or views. Although we shall describe separately each of the techniques most widely used in surveys, it is not unusual to find combinations of them employed effectively in many investigations. As a matter of fact, it is often expedient to overcome the limitations of a given technique by using several methods, as will be seen in the detailed procedures discussed in later chapters. The following methods refer to ways of obtaining information directly from the persons surveyed, sometimes called the collection of "primary data"; they do not include the use of secondary sources which is discussed elsewhere (Chapter I). The methods for securing information are: (1) Personal Interview (which, unless otherwise specified, will refer to face-to-face contacts); (2) Observational Methods and Recording Devices; (3) Telephone Interview; (4) Mail Questionnaire or Ballot; (5) Radio Appeal; (6) Panel Technique. The following information on the practical applications and limitations of each of these methods should enable the surveyor to choose the one most suited to the problem confronting him. He should bear in mind, however, that any method can yield misleading or incorrect results in the absence of careful planning and attention to details. Furthermore, in evaluating the various methods, he should realize that the cheapness or quickness of returns from 10 or even 50 per cent of the most cooperative or accessible informants does not guarantee that the method is any cheaper or will yield speedier returns from a representative or an unbiased sample of informants.

The Personal Interview

The method of direct investigation in which skilled interviewers call upon and solicit information from selected individuals is known as the personal interview method. The investigators must be carefully chosen and trained in techniques of selecting informants, methods of securing cooperation from persons covered by the survey, and procedures for recording the information secured.

The choice of the people to be interviewed may be made either in the survey office under the supervision of a sampling expert or in the field by interviewers who have been instructed as to the type of informants wanted. Several of the large-scale public opinion polls leave the final choice of specific informants up to the interviewers who are specially instructed on this point. Some large government surveys have employed the other technique—predesignating the addresses at which the interviewer is to call—with considerable success. If any adult who comes to the door can supply the information desired, the predesignated address sample can be covered more rapidly than if a specific member of the family, such as the chief breadwinner, has to be seen. When the field worker's assignment designates specific names, the time required to locate each person, if necessary trace him to a new address, and find him at home and available for an interview is usually much greater than when any occupant of the dwelling or any adult member of the family can give the information.

Although the informant is usually more accessible and has more time for an interview at home, informants in some surveys are interviewed wherever they can be reached—places of work, social agencies, stores, public gatherings, the street, or any other place where the type of people included in the survey can be found. The home interview, at least for the initial contact, is recommended in studies of the general population.

The personal interview method should include the checking of a sample of each interviewer's work by other investigators. This process, often referred to as "check interviewing," guarantees that the data turned into the office have been collected and recorded in accordance with instructions. If certain returns do not come up to specifications or if the accuracy of the information is questioned, the check interviewer can, by revisiting the informant, secure the correct information before the data are prepared for tabulation.

The length of time usually consumed by the personal interview varies from survey to survey. Some people have cooperated in surveys which took many hours of their time. The more usual practice, however, is for an interview to last from a few minutes to about half an hour. The type of information to be elicited as well as the type of people surveyed enters into the consideration of time.

One of the most striking features of the personal interview method is the high percentage of acceptable returns obtained, especially in a well-organized and carefully planned undertaking. In studies of the general public, for example, almost any survey can depend on cooperation from about 80 per cent of the cases solicited; with special procedures, well over 95 per cent should yield complete and acceptable information.

USING A SCHEDULE:

The form that the interview takes will, of course, depend upon the type of information to be ascertained. In the usual procedure the interviewer uses a schedule form containing definite items about which information is to be secured. After brief introductory remarks he proceeds to ask for the information designated on the schedule, recording the informant's responses in accordance with instructions. The data to be secured may cover a variety of topics. They may be census-type factual questions, such as age, sex, family composition, country of birth, etc.; they may be questions of opinion or feeling about an existing situation or current social issue; or they may be questions as to usual habits, behavior, or preferences. Whether the purpose of the survey is to count the number of persons having given characteristics or living under various conditions, the number holding certain points of view, or the number behaving in specified ways, the construction of the schedule and the framing of the questions require technical skill, knowledge, and experience. Some procedures for designing the schedule are given in Chapter VI, but these by no means cover the subject. The wealth of literature in the field of attitude or opinion measurement, for example, indicates how difficult it is to devise questions that measure what the surveyor hopes to measure.

FREE STORY TECHNIQUE:

One procedure that is popular among some surveyors is the free story technique. The interviewer encourages the informant to talk about the subject matter of the survey and from his remarks obtains a general impression of his attitude or situation. This procedure usually results in a mass of notes which contain chance impressions, usually biased by the investigator's own opinions and seldom capable of being expressed in quantitative form. When reactions to various items are omitted, it is impossible to know whether this is due to the failure of the investigator to ask about the question or to record the informant's remarks, or the failure of the interviewee to mention the item either because he did not regard it as important or because he forgot it. In fact, these general impressions are usually quite unreliable; a second interviewer is likely to obtain and record an entirely different response from the same informant.

FOCUSED INTERVIEW:

A modified "free story" technique known as the "focused interview" has more or less replaced the completely unguided type of interview. In order that the interviewer may obtain the same type of facts about each informant, he may carry a reminder or list of questions on which he is to secure the informant's reaction. He may have a few standard questions that are supposed to make the interviewee talk, and rate or classify the latter's attitude when the interview is over. In some surveys it has been found feasible to have the informant classify his own attitude on a rating scale. The focused interview is usually more time-consuming than when a set schedule is used. One of the advantages of the long interview is that it enables the interviewer to become better acquainted with his informant and thus to secure a closer understanding of the latter's real attitude. Unless the interview results in a uniform objective classification of the respondent's remarks, however, this general conversation is not susceptible to statistical treatment. It may serve as illustrative material or contain leads as to why the respondents react as they do. Therefore it is often advisable, at least in the early stages of the survey, to record verbatim comments of the interviewee or to obtain the field agent's impression. If a survey topic is more or less new to the surveyor it is especially desirable to seek a certain amount of free response. Open-end questions in which the respondent is asked for his opinion without being given any suggestions as to possible reactions are usually employed in the focused interview. These questions are particularly helpful in the exploratory phase of opinion polling because they may reveal what form the issue is assuming in the mind of the public and what words or phrases are commonly used to express the issue.

UNAIDED RECALL:

Marketing and advertising research groups employ an interview procedure which they call unaided recall. Here the informant is asked to report on what he remembers about a given situation. In radio listening surveys, for example, the listener may be asked, "What radio programs did you listen to last night?" The weakness of this technique lies in its dependence upon memory. Since ability to recall depends upon such factors as recency, strength of association, length of association, and other factors discussed on pp. 179–181, the programs which will be recalled will probably be those that have been running for a long time, those well advertised, and those immediately preceding the interview period.

In one experiment "memory loss" of the unaided recall interview was measured by checking the informant's report against an automatic record of the actual operation of his radio set during the period. It was found that the average person was able to report correctly the names of only 31 per cent of the programs to which he had had his radio tuned in on the preceding day.

In magazine advertising research, the unaided recall test may take the following form: "Have you read this week's issue of the Blank magazine?" An answer of "Yes" is followed by: "What advertisements in it do you remember having seen?" Freiberg claims that the results from this type of questioning are too general to be of much use to advertisers (78, p. 124).

AIDED RECALL, RECOGNITION, AND IDENTIFICATION:

The aided recall technique is widely used in market and radio research. In radio surveys it consists of showing the informant a printed list of the programs that were on the air during the period his radio was tuned in. Usually two printed lists are employed—one a list of broadcast periods by fifteen-minute intervals, and the other a complete list of the programs of each station in the area (488). The programs also are identified by talent, broadcast time, and (for commercial programs) sponsor and product. After the informant indicates on list 1 the periods his radio was turned on, he is asked to check on list 2 the programs to which he listened. Comparison of the two lists reveals that the recall technique results in an underestimation of the listening period while the recognition technique results in an overestimation. Respondents tend to check full programs even though they heard only part.

One advantage of the aided recall method is that it stimulates cooperation from informants. Checking against an automatic record of the operation of the radio set, surveyors found that persons with recognition sheets remembered 59 per cent of their listening experience as compared with 31 per cent recalled without aid (488).

An illustration of aided recall as used in copy testing is found in the following type of question: "Which of the following brands of coffee have you seen or heard advertised lately?" The informant is then shown a list of brands. Results from this type of question throw light on brand dominance. When repeated periodically the comparative standing of given brands as well as improvement or loss in rank is shown.

"What claims made by the advertising impressed you?" or "What did this advertising say?" (78, p. 124) may also be asked. Results from such questions reveal impressions made by the advertising. As Freiberg points out, however, factors other than advertising, such as experience with the product, may also influence responses.

The triple associates tests developed by Link (78, p. 126) attempt to measure the strength of the advertising theme associated with a certain brand. The following is a typical example of such a test: "What coffee company advertises 'Good to the last drop!'?" This type of test is used when a central advertising theme has been linked with a particular brand or company.

In magazine and newspaper advertising research, the recognition method is widely used. It consists in going over a magazine or newspaper with someone who has read it and asking him what he has seen. In addition, he may be asked whether he has read it, whether he has read all of it, or whether he has read most of it. He may be asked whether he definitely remembers seeing it or is uncertain. Sometimes the brand name or other identifying material is blocked out and the respondent is asked "What product, brand, or company is advertised?" This is called the "identification" test.

This technique has been shown to have high reliability, i.e., it yields consistent results upon repetition. On the other hand, the *meaning* of the results obtained from these questions is not always clear-cut. It is a well-known fact, for example, that informants "identify" material which has not yet appeared. The "controlled recognition" test described on page 491 has been developed to adjust for this source of error.

The controlled opinion test consists in presenting the informant with two or more advertisements or products and securing his preference. Most of such tests are administered to consumer panels such as those described later in this chapter. They are particularly useful for testing out products or advertising slogans before they are adopted on a large scale.

Numerous variations or elaborations of the above techniques are to be found in the literature of consumer research. The surveyor should refer to the more detailed treatment of these methods if he considers using them.

THE USE OF HOME AND NEIGHBORHOOD SCORING DEVICES: One of the advantages of the personal interview method is that the interviewer can collect data on the informant's cultural and social environment which can be utilized in interpreting his attitude, behavior, and other personal characteristics. A number of sociometric scales for the measurement of environment have been developed and standardized. Chapin describes several types of these scales and suggests various uses for them (166, Chapter VI). These scales could be used to advantage in surveys where interviewers now rely on subjective impressions of social environment which often prove quite unreliable.

Chapin's Social Status Scale (158) is one of the most objective and carefully tested scales. As revised in 1936 it consists of an inventory and scoring of all the living-room equipment in the home. This provides a good measure of social status in terms of social-economic data. Chapin reports that different raters make nearly identical independent ratings of a given home; this is also true of the same observer rating at different times. Furthermore, the ratings based on the social status scale agree closely with other measures of this factor.

The scale for the Measurement of Urban Home Environment (866) is designed to measure the factors in the home that influence the behavior and development of the child. Other well-known scales are the Chapman-Sims Socio Economic Scale (167), A Scale for Grading Neighborhood Conditions (1099), and A Scale for Grading Social Conditions (175). (For others, see page 103.)

SCALES FOR MEASURING INDIVIDUAL BEHAVIOR AND PERSONALITY:

The informant's social behavior, personality traits, intelligence, information, morale, attitudes, and opinions can also be measured during the personal interview. A great number and variety of such scales are found in the different fields of social and psychological research. Some may be administered orally, but others require the informant to take a written test. Some are brief and expressed in terms intelligible to the man on the street, whereas others are long and complicated and of value only in the classroom. The selection of tests suitable for use in surveys requires an intimate knowledge of the composition of the population and of the conditions under which the tests will have to be given. Except for the scales developed in modern public opinion polls and in marketing research, very few are designed for the people and conditions encountered in surveys. Thus surveyors frequently find it necessary to devise their own scales or to adapt others to fit the survey situation. (A more detailed treatment of these scales and the technique of scale construction appears in Chapter VI.)

GROUP INTERVIEW:

A variation in interview technique is to present the schedule to a group of people assembled in one place. For example, to measure the response to special features on a radio program, people were invited to parties at which transcriptions of radio programs were played. They were asked to record their reactions on questionnaire forms. Movies have also been presented in this way to measure audience reactions. Sometimes push buttons are used, different colored lights being employed to indicate different responses from a strong liking to a definite dislike. To secure any adequate cross-sections of public opinion or re-actions, the audience must obviously be carefully selected to be repre-sentative of the public about which generalizations are to be made. Since it is known, for example, that preferences for large or small net-work radio stations vary for different income levels (642), the experi-mental audiences must be chosen to represent proportionally the groups for which a radio program is intended.

SECRET BALLOT TECHNIQUE:

Because of the reluctance of some informants to state their opinions to a "total stranger," certain polling agencies have experimented with asking the informant to record his vote on a ballot handed to him by the interviewer; the ballot is then dropped into a container carried by the investigator. Benson (50) reports that this procedure definitely re-duces the number of cases in which "no opinion" is reported. However, he recommends that a combination of the secret ballot and the oral vote is probably most desirable. People who wish to use the secret ballot are asked to do so, but ballots are not given to those who have no reluctance to expressing their views.

EVALUATION OF THE PERSONAL INTERVIEW METHOD:

Before the survey designer selects the method of approach for col-lecting data, he should weigh the advantages and disadvantages of each method and see how or whether it is suited to the problem that is to be surveyed.

The *advantages of the personal interview* are:

1. The personal interview usually yields a high percentage of re-turns, for most people are willing to cooperate.
2. It can be made to yield an almost perfect sample of the general population because practically everyone can be reached by and can respond to this approach.
3. The information secured is likely to be more correct than that se-cured by other techniques since the interviewer can clear up seemingly inaccurate answers by explaining the questions to the informant. If the latter deliberately falsifies replies, the interviewer

may be trained to spot such cases and use special devices to get the truth.

4. The interviewer can collect supplementary information about the informant's personal characteristics and environment which is valuable in interpreting results and evaluating the representatives of the persons surveyed.

5. Scoring and test devices can be used, the interviewer acting as experimenter.

6. Visual material to which·the informant is to react can be presented.

7. Return visits to complete items on the schedule or to correct mistakes can usually be made without annoying the informant. Thus greater numbers of usable returns are assured than when other methods are employed.

8. The interviewer may catch the informant off guard and thus secure more spontaneous reactions than would be the case if a written form were mailed out for the informant to mull over.

9. The interviewer can usually control which person or persons answer the questions, whereas in mail surveys several members of the household may confer before the questions are answered. Group discussions can be held with the personal interview method if desired.

10. The personal interview may take long enough to allow the informant to become oriented to the topic under investigation. Thus recall of relevant material is facilitated.

11. Questions about which the informant is likely to be sensitive can be carefully sandwiched in by the interviewer. By observing the informant's reactions, the investigator can change the subject if necessary or explain the survey problem further if it appears that the interviewee is about to rebel. In other words, a delicate situation can usually be handled more effectively by a personal interview than by other survey techniques.

12. More of the informant's time can be taken for the survey than would be the case if the interviewer were not present to elicit and record the information.

13. The language of the survey can be adapted to the ability or educational level of the person interviewed. Therefore it is comparatively easy to avoid misinterpretations or misleading questions.

Some *limitations of the personal interview* follow:

1. The transportation costs and the time required to cover addresses in a large area may make the personal interview method unfeasible.
2. The human equation may distort the returns. If an interviewer has a certain economic bias, for example, he may unconsciously ask the questions so as to secure confirmation of his views. In opinion studies especially, such biases may operate. To prevent such coloring of questions, most opinion surveyors instruct their interviewers to ask the question *exactly* as printed on the schedule.
3. Unless the interviewers are properly trained and supervised, the data recorded may be inaccurate and incomplete. A few poor enumerators may make a much higher percentage of returns unusable than if the informants filled out and mailed the interview form to survey headquarters.
4. The organization required for selecting, training, and supervising a field staff is more complex than that needed for surveys conducted by other methods.
5. It is usually claimed that costs per interview are higher when field investigators are employed than when telephone or mail surveys are used. This may not be true if the area to be covered is not too great. If the general public in a community is to be surveyed, the costs of securing a *representative* sample by telephone or mail inquiries will probably equal or exceed the cost by the personal interview method, since in the end personal follow-up will be necessary to round out the sample.
6. The personal interview usually takes more time than the telephone interview providing the persons who can be reached by telephone are a representative sample of the type of population to be covered by the survey. However, for a sample of the general public a telephone inquiry is not a substitute for a personal interview. The lowest income groups often do not have telephones.
7. If the interview is conducted in the home during the day, the majority of the informants will be housewives. If a response is to be obtained from a male member of the household, most of the field work will have to be done in the evening or on week ends. Since only an hour or two can be used for evening interviewing,

the personal interview method requires a large staff for studies requiring contacts with the working population.

Observational Methods and Recording Devices

Observational studies fall into two general categories, the uncontrolled and the controlled. In uncontrolled observations, the conditions under which the observation is made and the type of material noted and recorded are left to the observer and to factors which may happen to influence him.

Many of the early surveys utilized uncontrolled observational methods to arrive at their findings. Some surveyors felt that their observations would be more meaningful if they shared the lives of the people they were studying and tried to identify themselves with them. This procedure, designated the *participant observer technique* by Lindeman (567), found its greatest popularity in the social survey field. Studies by Booth (91), the Lynds (602, 603), Lundberg and others (598)—to mention a few—utilized it as one of the instruments by means of which their data were collected. Much interesting descriptive material has been secured in this manner, but the discrepancies in observations made by different observers and those made by the same observer at different periods could seldom be reconciled without recourse to more objective procedures. While many valuable leads for further research may be unearthed by uncontrolled observational reports, the unreliability and subjectivity of the observations make such data of little scientific value.

Controlled observation according to Lundberg (597) consists in (1) a careful definition of the units to be observed and the information to be recorded; (2) the selection of pertinent data for observation; (3) the standardization of the conditions of observation—time, place, persons, etc.; (4) whenever possible, the use of mechanical devices, tests, and other aids to accuracy.[1] An excellent treatment of the technique of controlled studies is described by Chapin in *Experimental Designs in Sociological Research* (166).

In social surveys it is difficult to set up experimentally controlled conditions in the places where people are to be observed. When observational techniques are used, the investigator must be trained to

---

[1] For a more detailed discussion see Lundberg (597).

observe, classify, and record objectively. He must also be able to recognize significant deviations in the phenomenon observed.

The assistance of all types of people in observing and reporting on the behavior of others has been enlisted in the cause of research. One novel example was a large taxicab concern which cooperated in a study of radio listening habits. Half of its drivers were instructed to have the radio turned off when passengers entered the cab, and the other half were told to have their radios turned on. The drivers were asked to note the reactions of the passengers—whether they requested that the radio be turned on or off or changed to another station. To be sure, persons who ride in cabs constitute a highly selected portion of the general population; hence the results of such a study cannot be regarded as of wide applicability until so demonstrated. The proper sampling of periods during the day or evening should also be controlled. In this study, for example, it was found that evening passengers had quite different radio preferences from people who rode during the business rush hours.

A combination of controlled and uncontrolled observation was utilized in the Mass Observation study in Britain (608) described in Chapter I. The technique of controlled observation in the social field has seen its greatest development in the studies of the behavior of young children. The use of repeated short samplings of behavior (718, 956); the utilization of devices such as stop watches, one-way screens, and reruns of movies depicting social situations for establishing observer reliability (16); and the breaking up of behavior concepts into very detailed observable elements constitute some of the advances made in observational studies. While most of these studies are too specialized for survey purposes, some of their methods, schedules, and attention to detail may suggest techniques that might be applied in controlled observation in social surveys.

AUTOMATIC RECORDING DEVICES—AIDS TO CONTROLLED OBSERVATIONS:

The use of an electric-eye ticker which counts the number of autos passing a given spot became popular during the 1930's. The counting apparatus attached to gates at fairs to keep a current record of attendance received great publicity at the New York World's Fair. Business concerns contemplating location of stores in various downtown sections of large cities have employed investigators to make a count of the number of potential customers passing given locations in the course of the day. To facilitate the counting, the observer holds a "ticker" device in his hand and presses the key to make the count as each person passes him.

Interesting experiments with a mechanical recording device attached to radios in homes that makes it possible for individuals to press a button and indicate at headquarters that their radio is in use, and to press another button to indicate a vote of yes or no on questions presented over the radio, have been conducted by radio research organizations. The sponsors even visualized its use for voting purposes. The audimeter developed by the A. C. Nielsen Company has already been discussed (p. 43).

The recorder indicates when the set was turned on, how long it was in operation, and which stations were tuned in. Among the advantages claimed for these automatic radio recording devices are: (1) that they do not depend upon memory as do the recall techniques; (2) interviewers do not influence the results except in so far as they are successful or unsuccessful in securing cooperation of the radio owner to install the recorder; (3) data can be obtained for the entire 24-hour period, whereas telephone and personal calls are limited to certain periods; (4) they do not take much of the informant's time; (5) it is possible to get comparable data over a long period of time; (6) the data are not biased by the report of any one family member (488, p. 96). These devices yield information on minute-by-minute flow as well as on turnover of audience during a program period (78, p. 186). The main objections which have been leveled at these automatic recorders are: (1) that the devices are expensive to install and operate so that their use is restricted to a relatively small panel of homes; (2) all the limitations of panels apply here; (3) the problem of obtaining permission to install the recorder may result in a biased sample of panel members; (4) information on social characteristics of panel households must be obtained by other research methods such as the personal interview or mail ballot and therefore will be subject to the limitations of such methods; (5) the devices measure only sets in use and not necessarily stations or programs heard by some member of the household. In regard to this last mentioned item, there seems to be disagreement among researchers in this field as to the relation between listening and sets in use. Definitive evidence ought to be forthcoming soon.[2]

The Telephone Interview

Surveys conducted by telephone interviews have found wide popularity in recent years, especially in radio audience research. In addition to a number of nation-wide surveys, numerous local surveys have been conducted over the telephone. These surveys of radio listeners employ a variety of techniques.

THE COINCIDENTAL METHOD:

The person answering the telephone is asked whether or not his radio is turned on and, if so, the name of the program or station to which he is listening. Other questions on the product being advertised on the program are also frequently asked. The chief advantage of this method is that it does not depend on the memory of the informant, but asks about his radio listening at the time of the phone call.

The disadvanages are (1) since only a short period can be covered with each interview, many calls are required to yield data for a whole day, and (2) programs late in the evening or early in the morning cannot be covered because of the undesirability of telephoning at these times.

THE RECALL TECHNIQUE:

The informant is asked to report on the programs he has heard in a certain period preceding the phone call. The length of time covered varies from survey to survey—from a few minutes to four hours or more. The lapse of time between the program and the call also varies from about fifteen minutes (immediate recall) to a day.

Two types of recall are employed—the aided recall and the unaided. In the former, the informant is told the names of the programs that were on the air and asked to identify those to which his radio was tuned. This technique is more widely used in personal interview surveys than in telephone surveys.

In the unaided recall technique no attempt is made to assist the informant in recalling the data asked for. It is most effective when

---

[2] For a detailed discussion of automatic recorders, please consult references **78**, **696**, **908**, and **114**.

the period between exposure and report is short because memory loss is not so great. Although the interview must be brief the informant must be given ample time to orient his thinking. Even so, it is practically impossible to avoid bias in recall since programs immediately preceding the call tend to be reported more frequently (488).

Not only have radio research services found the telephone ·a useful device for interviewing, but other surveys wishing to save transportation time and cost have also adopted this technique. In one city a social agency telephoned housewives to obtain data on wages, hours, and training of colored maids in private homes. The method by which the maid was secured, i.e., a public or private employment agency, former employee of the housewife, maid of the housewife's friend, etc., was also obtained. Maids were then interviewed in employment agencies, church groups, settlement houses, or wherever it was possible to see them. The telephone survey provided an estimate of the incidence of maids who secured employment by various methods, and these figures gave the weights used when tabulating the schedules obtained from the maids who had been interviewed on a more or less opportunistic basis, i.e., without regard for their proportional representation in the total population of maids.

In another survey which was setting up a monthly index of employment and unemployment, it was planned to reach by telephone as many people as possible in a random sample of the city population, and to visit personally only those households that did not have telephones. The first contact with each household was made by personal interview, at which time those with telephones were asked to cooperate by giving the information over the telephone for the future monthly indices of employment.

With the tremendous saving in transportation time and costs, the telephone may appear to be a solution for surveys that have to be conducted quickly and cheaply. One or two interviewers can investigate a large portion of the population of a community in a short time because several hundred calls can be completed per day.

The chief objection to the telephone interview technique concerns the representativeness of the sample as a picture of the total population. People who have telephones do not constitute a true cross-section of a community's inhabitants. More telephone subscribers are in the higher-income or upper socio-economic groups than is true of the population as a whole. Since economic status is so closely correlated with almost every social characteristic surveyed, the restriction of a sample to telephone subscribers seriously limits the general applicability of the findings. If, however, an investigation is to be focused on the characteristics of the middle-class and well-to-do members of a city, it is quite likely that the vast majority can be reached by telephone.

In one large city in which the relationship between home tenure and telephone subscription was studied, it was found that 37 per cent of the renters as compared with 73 per cent of the home owners were telephone subscribers. As is well known, stability of residence is much greater among people who own their homes than among renting families, so a sample of telephone subscribers would be biased in favor of the stable groups in the population.

In addition to the problem of securing a representative sample of the total population, certain other limitations of the telephone interview should be recognized. The interview must be quite short, so only a few brief items can usually be investigated. Most of the radio surveys limit their interviews to about two minutes. In this short time only a few definite facts can be secured. Studies in which the attitude of the informant is to be ascertained on the basis of his reaction to numerous questions should not be conducted by means of the telephone interview. Furthermore, the interviewer must "sell" the survey idea to the informant without being able to see his reactions and thus judge which approach would be most effective. This is not a serious limitation, however, if the questions are carefully prepared and tried out in advance of the main survey. The refusal rate among telephone subscribers seldom amounts to more than 2 or 3 per cent of the total. The loss in sample size comes more from unanswered calls or busy signals than from refusals.

Closely associated with the brevity of the telephone interview is the undesirability of asking many questions about the informant or his replies. In the personal interview the investigator can observe a number of characteristics which bear upon the qualifications, classification, and reactions of the interviewee, but over the phone he must accept the answers without evaluating them or sizing up the informant's qualifications. If the respondent is.annoyed by the call he may deliberately give misinformation, and the interviewer cannot question it.

As a rule the housewife answers the telephone, so surveys using this technique are likely to be most successful if directed to the woman of the house. However, surveyors of such groups as automobile owners, businessmen, magazine subscribers, store owners, etc., have found the telephone interview satisfactory.

One of the problems of rural, or party-line, telephone surveys is that of securing private interviews. The informant knows that the conversation may be heard by other people on the line so he may respond accordingly. The interviewer is also at a disadvantage, since the informant may know what questions are coming and how others have answered them.

Many of the procedures employed in personal interview surveys are also applicable to surveys conducted by telephone. The selection of good telephone interviewers, for example, is extremely important for keeping down the refusal rate. Numerous devices may be used to determine whether or not a given applicant possesses a satisfactory "telephone" voice and manner. Personnel managers in such places as the Telephone Company, radio research agencies employing the telephone technique, and telephone order departments in large mercantile establishments often have excellent suggestions as to ways of choosing interviewers who will appeal to the public. One radio survey director who employed a great many interviewers always asked the applicants to call one member of the survey staff and read the script which was to be used in the survey. Several extension lines were on the same hook-up so a number of other members of the staff listened in on the conversation and rated the applicant. If this "test" was passed, the applicant was given a list of numbers to call, among which were phones of members of the staff who usually pretended to be difficult cases. The ability of the interviewer to think quickly and win over the reluctant informant was rated. In addition, the records made by the interviewer were examined as to legibility and conformity with instructions. Even after the interviewer was hired, "check" calls were employed periodically so that the original high standard of work of the interviewers was maintained. The interviewers were told that with each day's assignment of numbers some check calls could be expected. Daily records were maintained on the number of completed calls, "no answers," "busy," "disconnected," "wrong numbers," "non-resident or business phones," and "refusals." Thus, it was possible to detect abnormally high refusal rates before much damage had been done to the sample.

The difference between the number of telephone numbers assigned and the number yielding completed schedules will depend chiefly upon whether or not recalls are made on "no answers" and "busy signals." In one investigation covering about 150,000 telephones, only about two-thirds of the calls made were answered and the completed information obtained. Since only about one and one half per cent refused, the bulk of the incomplete calls were attributable to those who did not answer or were busy. The interviewers were instructed to wait for half a minute, if no one answered the phone, before hanging up. In certain sections of the city (those having a given exchange) the interviewer waited for five rings before hanging up. It was assumed that in large homes it might take longer to get to the phone. The effect on the sample of the omissions of "no answer" calls may be to distort it markedly. In the radio survey under discussion, it was assumed that people who do not answer their phones are not at home or are not awake, and therefore do not have their radios tuned in. Thus, they were not to be included in the "available" radio audience which was being surveyed. Before making such an assumption, however, careful tests should be made to determine how many people who do not answer their phones are actually at home. How frequently, for example, does the person at home refrain from answering the telephone ring, if he or she is listening to a favorite radio program? If there were a significant proportion of such cases, a survey of radio listeners should make some provision for contacting such persons in order not to bias the sample. In one-room apartments or small homes it may be more difficult to avoid answering the ringing phone than would be true in a large home. Thus economic biases may enter. People who spend a great deal of time in their gardens or yards, in the basement, in the garage, etc., may not answer the phone, and may be quite a selected group from many points of view.

If the survey is not directed toward an "available" radio audience, but rather aims to be a cross-section of all telephone users, the omission of the "no answers" is even more serious. As in the case of "not-at-homes" when the interviewer rings the doorbell, people who are not at home to answer the telephone are likely to be a highly selected sample.

The effect of omitting the "busy signals" may also be quite serious. In the first place, there may be an economic bias due to the fact that party lines are more popular among certain economic groups than others. The chance of getting a busy signal is probably greater when several parties share the same telephone line. There may also be a family composition bias if "busy signals" are not called back. The more members there are in a family the greater is the chance that someone is telephoning at any given time. To be sure, the "telephone habit," sufficient leisure time to carry on a long telephone conversation, participation in many social groups, etc., also may affect the number and length of calls made and thus the chance of a "busy signal" being given. The relationship between such characteristics and the subject matter of the survey should be carefully considered when planning the procedure for controlling the sample. Generally speaking, it is wise to re-call a sample of the "busy" cases until all in this subsample have been reached, and then to compare the information received from this group with that obtained from persons replying on the first call to see what effect the omission of such cases would have on the findings of the survey.

If good interviewers are employed, the number of refusals (providing the schedule is short and has been pretested) will be low. Early in the survey an analysis of refusals by time of day called may cut down the number even more. Calls too early in the morning or late at night may result in a disproportionately large number of refusals and so should be avoided. It is possible to tabulate the refusals by other characteristics such as telephone exchange, district (census enumeration district or ward), home tenure, and number of families in dwelling (often obtained from the address list of the city directory). These tabulations should be compared with similar tabulations of a random sample of cooperative informants to discover biases. If it is found, for example, that three-fourths of the refusals are home owners and that one-fourth of the cooperative informants own their homes, the surveyor may be quite sure that other biases also exist. A tabulation of replies secured from home owners and from tenants among the cooperative cases will probably show significant differences in the phenomenon surveyed. So a large refusal rate concentrated among home owners should either be reduced by personal visits to "recapture" the uncooperative cases, or should be adjusted by means of weights or other procedures described on pages 400–402.

Since it is easier to interview large numbers of people by telephone than by field visits, most telephone surveys deal with very large samples. In doing so, however, they multiply the task of maintaining an accurate control of the sample in the office. The importance of installing and using a good file system and of setting up automatic checks of the number of schedules to be accounted for during each operation in the office cannot be overemphasized. If schedules belonging to a sample are misfiled, destroyed, not counted, counted more than once, never assigned to interviewers, etc., the sample tabulated may prove to be totally different from that selected as a cross-section of the population surveyed.

A summary of the merits of the telephone interview method follows:

1. The telephone interview is the quickest of the survey techniques. Interviewers can complete about thirty calls per hour if the calls are brief. It is especially adapted to surveys of radio programs where a great many interviews must be made during a given program.
2. The refusal rate is usually low among people who are reached by phone.
3. The coincidental method can be used, thus eliminating the memory factor.
4. It is easy to train and supervise interviewers since they can work in one room directly beside the supervisor.
5. The approach and questions are easy to standardize from one interviewer to another.
6. The cost per completed interview is low for the sample covered.
7. The geographic distribution of the sample can be easily controlled. An address listing of numbers is usually available and can be used for drawing the sample.
8. For studies of middle- and high-income groups the telephone interview may be satisfactory because most of them have phones.
9. Interviews may be scattered over a wide area within a city without adding to the cost.

10. As compared with a mail questionnaire, the telephone survey is preferable because it usually costs less per return. Returns are higher on first solicitation, and they can be more effectively controlled from the point of neighborhood distribution.

The *disadvantages* of this method may be summarized as follows:

1. As a sample of the general population, telephone subscribers are not representative. So unless the telephone interview is supplemented by a method that covers nonsubscribers, it should not be used. Less than half of all homes in towns over 2500 have telephones.
2. Detailed data cannot be gathered by this method because the informants soon become annoyed or impatient. If the schedule is too lengthy, the informant may either hang up or give unreliable answers.
3. When observation of the situation is an important element, the telephone interview is not useful. If the interviewer is supposed to evaluate the answers as to trustworthiness, he has very little to go on in a short telephone conversation.
4. Information about the respondent must be limited to one or two facts. Such items as age, nationality, income, etc., are difficult to secure by telephone.
5. Attitude scales must be used with caution. Also opinions are less likely to be given freely since the informant cannot be certain of the credentials of the person calling.
6. Since rural telephone ownership is low, the telephone interview is not useful in such areas. Also, because rural rates are higher than urban, the cost of telephone inquiries is greater than in cities.
7. The brevity of the introduction and questions does not give the informant much time to orient himself to the subject matter of the survey. Reactions requiring careful thought—such as criticisms of various products, suggestions as to new uses of products, appeals, etc.—should not be obtained by this technique.
8. The telephone situation neither encourages the respondent to amplify his replies nor gives the interviewer much time to jot down the comments. A face-to-face interview is more conducive to a considered response.

9. The task of checking the no-answers, wrong numbers, busy signals, etc., is time-consuming but must be done if the sample is to be representative of telephone subscribers.
10. It is difficult to secure privacy on party lines.
11. The time may come when the telephone technique will be used by so many groups that informants will develop an antagonism to all telephone inquiries.
12. The surveyor must be careful not to antagonize informants by phoning too early or too late in the day. One well-known survey agency makes it a policy never to call before 8:30 A.M. or after 10:30 P.M.
13. Misinformation is hard to detect and check in short inquiries.

Mail Questionnaire or Ballot

While the mail questionnaire is the most widely used of survey techniques, it is also the most criticized. Although a great deal of the criticism is justified, a fair portion is directed at features that are not inherent in the mail questionnaire technique per se.

In its simplest form, the mail questionnaire consists of a schedule of questions sent by mail to persons on a list or in a survey sample. The form is supposed to be filled in by the recipient and mailed back to the sender. This procedure may vary, depending on the manner in which the form or question list is placed in the hands of the potential informant. Instead of being mailed out by the surveying organization, it may be:

1. Published in newspapers, magazines, etc., and returned by mail.
2. Attached to consumers' goods, such as cereals, as coupons or ballots to be mailed in.
3. Given over the radio, informants being asked to mail in their answers.
4. Delivered to members of a group and collected by designated persons or officials of the group.
5. Telephoned to the informant and mailed by him to survey headquarters.

For purposes of simplicity in presentation, the discussion of the questionnaire technique will assume that the question list is sent to and returned by the respondent by mail.

The *advantages* of the mail questionnaire may be summed up as follows:

1. If mailed questionnaires are used, it is possible to cover a wider geographical area and to reach a much larger population with given funds than could be accomplished by personal interviews with each informant. This lower cost applies primarily if personal follow-ups are not made.

2. Mailing costs are relatively low compared with the transportation and time costs for a field staff.

3. The expensive and time-consuming task of training a staff of investigators is eliminated. This assumes, of course, that a large staff will not be needed to collect the schedule data from the people who do not answer the questionnaire.

4. The informant may answer questions more frankly by mail since anonymity is assured. On the other hand, some respondents may hesitate to put their ideas in writing for fear that their schedules may be identified even though unsigned. Actually, it is questionable whether anonymity is either an advantage or a disadvantage.

5. The questionnaire may reach groups who are more or less protected from solicitors and investigators. In high-rent apartment houses or private homes where servants protect the occupants from solicitors and other doorbell ringers, for example, it is often difficult for investigators to gain admittance. Of course, the mere fact that the mail is received does not guarantee that it will not be filed in the wastebasket by a secretary or even by the addressee as soon as he glances at the heading.

6. Personal antagonism to investigators which may lead to a refusal to give the desired information is avoided.

7. If time is not an important consideration and if the sample extends over a wide area, the cost of securing practically complete returns is probably lower than in the personal interview method.

8. The questions are standardized, whereas in the personal interview the investigator may alter them or suggest answers.

9. The questionnaire can be answered at the convenience of the respondent. This gives him time to deliberate on each point, and if necessary to look up information needed to fill in the items. However, he may consult other members of his household, so his

reply may be more representative of the family's point of view than of his own.

10. It is claimed that the mail questionnaire brings many more returns from the *man* of the house than does the telephone or personal interview method.

11. Where the persons to be reached are located in widely scattered areas of cities and are a mobile element of the population, it may be easier to locate them by mail (registered or special delivery) than by other methods.

Most of the advantages of the mailed schedule over the personal interview are offset by the following serious *drawbacks*:

1. The people who return questionnaires are not representative of the groups to whom the schedules are sent. This limitation is sufficiently great to outweigh almost all the advantages listed above. Some of the many types of biases that have been found in mail questionnaire surveys are discussed in Chapters XI and XII. Suffice it to say at this point that unless every effort is exerted to adjust for nonresponse or to obtain practically complete returns from everyone solicited by mail, the technique should not be used.

2. The returns from mailed questionnaires sent to the general public are usually very low, often ranging from about 10 to 20 per cent. The percentage of returns varies greatly, however, with different schedules and informants. One survey of M.D.'s in New York State received about 50 per cent returns without follow-ups. By continued effort the returns may be increased considerably over the first responses. The techniques for increasing mail returns are dealt with in Chapter XI.

3. Since the informant fills in the data on the questionnaire without the assistance of an investigator, he may misinterpret questions, omit essential items, or send in material which cannot be put in form for tabulation, thus making it necessary to discard many of the questionnaires.

4. The questions used must be simple and practically self-explanatory, since no training can be given the informant on their meaning and on how to fill out the schedule.

5. In most studies the questionnaire must be relatively brief if high returns are to be obtained.

6. If the sample is to be unbiased, it is necessary to supplement the mailed returns with information obtained by ꞌpersonal interviews with the nonrespondents.

7. Checks on the honesty and reliability of returns are difficult to devise when the personal interviewer does not see and size up the informant.

8. It is practically impossible to return unsatisfactory or incomplete schedules to the informant for correction.

9. Because most people would rather talk than write, questionnaires must be made very interesting to induce responses.

10. An up-to-date address list of potential survey informants is difficult to find.

11. Mail returns from the last third of the respondents come in slowly; hence the mail survey must be spread over a relatively long period, if a high percentage of returns is to be secured.

12. Many questions which might antagonize the respondent cannot be included on the mail questionnaires but can be asked in personal interviews when the informant gradually can be led around to the subject.

QUESTIONNAIRES DISTRIBUTED AND RETURNED BY
MEMBERS OF GROUPS:

Instead of mailing the questionnaires to informants, better results may be obtained by using messengers or interested individuals to deliver them and be responsible for their return. For example, school children have been used with marked success for delivering questionnaires to their parents. In such cases it is essential, of course, that generalizations be made only about the group from which the sample is drawn, i.e., parents of school children and not all adults in the community.

Radio Appeal
Several developments in the radio survey field appeared in the 1940's. In the course of ascertaining the number of persons listening to given radio programs, techniques were devised to increase the size

of the listening audience and to encourage listeners to learn something about the product advertised on the program.

One device is to give a prize to listeners. Each day during the program a few telephone calls are made to a small sample of names chosen at random from the telephone directory. If the person called is listening to the program and can answer a simple question about the product advertised that day a money gift is sent to him. If no one passes the requirement that day, the prize the following day is increased. The amount is cumulated until someone is listening when called and is familiar with the product. Persons who answer the phone but are not listening to the program receive a small consolation prize; this tends to leave a feeling of good will toward telephone sample surveys.

A number of variations in this prize technique are in use. One program which advertises the same product every day asks the telephone respondent to give the "key word" of the day; another asks for the "lucky number"; another asks him to "identify the song which the announcer has just sung."

Although these studies are not primarily surveys, they provide a wealth of data on telephone respondents and on the listening habits of the population in the telephone directory. As we shall point out in later chapters, the lowest income groups are greatly underrepresented there. In order to overcome this limitation some radio programs ask the person whose name is mentioned on the program to telephone to the radio station within half an hour and receive a prize. Thus listeners who do not have a phone at home can phone from a pay station or a neighbor's home.

Panel Techniques

The panel technique is of more recent origin than most of the methods described above. It consists in making more than one contact with the groups being surveyed. A consumer jury, for example, may consist of several thousand women distributed geographically, who are asked periodically to report their reactions to new products which are to be placed on the market or to advertisements which have appeared in particular magazines. Sometimes they are asked to keep diary records. Usually the women volunteer their services in return for prizes or points which can be turned in for desirable commodities. These prizes may be offered to the housewife or to the children in the house who see to it that their mothers keep up their panel records. The approach may be made by any one or more of the techniques already described in this chapter. This technique is adapted to studies in which changes in social situations or trends in opinion are to be measured, or in which periodical indices of certain aspects of community life are desired.

The panel technique offers several advantages:

1. When small samples of the population are surveyed by single contacts and differences in the results are noted from one period to another, the sampler cannot know whether these differences are due to differences in the sample populations or to true shifts in the phenomena measured. If, however, the sample surveyed during each period includes the same persons or groups, the variations in the findings may be attributed with greater certainty to a real change in the phenomena studied. Thus for trend studies, data secured from relatively few persons can be as reliable as the results secured from a larger number of people who are contacted only once.

2. Data gathered from the same persons over a period of time can be cumulated and a detailed picture of the factors underlying shifts in opinion or situation can be secured for everyone in the panel. An analysis of the charted profiles of the individuals in a panel may give the surveyor an insight into causal relationships which he might not secure from single contacts with more people.

3. Closely allied with the above is the fact that the information collected about each informant tends to be more voluminous than can be obtained in single contacts. Many such items change either very little or not at all with the passage of time, so that a comprehensive case history of each panel member can be built up. These data can be cross tabulated with the more limited material secured in a single interview for a better understanding of the phenomena being studied.

4. If the group constituting the panel is cooperative, it may be possible to set up experimental situations which expose all the members to a certain influence and thus enable the effectiveness of this influence to be measured. For example, if the effectiveness of a

propaganda or promotional campaign is to be measured, it might be possible to leave literature at the home of each panel member with the request that he read it. Then, at the next interview with the group, the influence, if any, of this literature can be tested. If panel members are asked to listen to certain radio programs or to attend certain movies, or to expose themselves to the same environmental influences, valuable data may be obtained by agencies that are considering certain programs for promoting a specific idea, product, or behavior pattern.

5. It has been claimed that members of a panel learn to express themselves in the course of several interviews so that valuable comments and elaboration of points made by them can be secured. Whereas some informants may stop with a "yes" or "no" on the first interview, the survey may start them thinking about the survey topic so that a second or third contact will find them full of ideas. Part of this increase in volubility may result from a feeling of familiarity either toward the interviewer or toward the survey as a whole. On first contact some informants may be suspicious of the investigator and therefore give only enough information to satisfy him so he will leave. Critics of public opinion polls have questioned the accuracy of information obtained during a single contact. They point out that the information given to a stranger in a brief interview is not likely to be indicative of what the informant really believes. Actually, experiments in which panel groups have been compared with non-panel groups do not seem to bear out this criticism.

The problems raised by the panel procedure are often sufficient to offset the advantages. Among these limitations are the following:

1. Probably the most important problem is the loss of panel members. People move, become ill, or die, or are subjected to other influences which make it necessary for them to drop out of the group. Thus what was originally a representative sample of the population may soon become unrepresentative. Losses from so-called natural causes, however, are not so great as those due to lack of interest or a change in attitude toward the panel idea. Many people agree to cooperate in what seems to be a novel undertaking, but after the first interview or two the amount of time or work involved becomes more apparent and their interest dies down; the result is an almost in-

evitable dropping off of membership. Lazarsfeld points out that in his experience the largest losses occur between the first and second interviews. At the second interview a number of people simply refuse to continue. There is always a floating group of 6 or 7 per cent who cannot be reached for an interview because they are out of town or are ill. In addition, a small percentage move away permanently or die. In a series of panel interviews Lazarsfeld noted that the average loss for all reasons was about 13 per cent. This is somewhat less than the losses experienced by the group of "reader editors" of *The Woman's Home Companion.* Contact with this panel is by mail questionnaires. After about six years of surveys, approximately 80 per cent of the 2000 questionnaires mailed out periodically were returned. This is not the outside limit of losses, because women who failed to return three consecutive questionnaires without explanation were dropped from the panel. In the earlier years of the survey the mortality fluctuated around 25 per cent.

The number of drop-outs can be reduced by various devices for holding the interest of panel members. *The Woman's Home Companion,* for example, issues a small monthly magazine to panel members, and occasionally one of the members is selected to spend a short time in New York at the magazine's expense. In St. Paul, where a panel of some 400 householders were interviewed each month to secure employment data, cooperating members received a "certificate of appreciation" that contained the individual's name. This was accompanied by a short note thanking him for his participation in the project, signed by a prominent member of the university sponsoring the study. Early experience with this device indicated that it was apparently successful in preventing losses in membership. The St. Paul panel differed from the panels reported by Lazarsfeld and others in that it was a panel of *addresses* or *dwelling units* rather than of *individuals.* Thus persons or families who moved out of the dwelling unit were automatically dropped from the panel and the new occupant became a member. This type of panel has the advantage of changing with the changing character of the city population so that at any given time it is representative of the total population of the community—assuming that provision is made for including periodically a sample of newly constructed dwelling units. People who migrate to the city from other communities and move into an address in the panel sample become members of the panel. Similarly, population changes arising from the migration of families away from the city or from homes that are broken up by divorce or the death of the head of the family are reflected in the changing character of the panel. Of course, the most detailed and the greatest number of records will be available for the most stationary elements of the population. The mobile groups belong to the panel a much shorter time than the others. However, in order to retain representativeness this loss of background data is inevitable. As a matter of fact, panels composed of the same persons for many years will gradually become panels of old people and eventually all the members will die. Even in panels that last only for a year or so, the people who continue to cooperate with the survey may be a biased element of the original group unless a definite effort is made to keep them from dropping out.

2. According to Lazarsfeld, members of a panel develop a "critical set"; as they do this, they cease to be representative of the general public. The panel has an educational effect; it tends to dramatize and increase one's interest in otherwise unobserved elements and to heighten one's awareness of the things and people about him. Hence, the mere fact of participation in a panel may change a person's attitudes and opinions. The effect of panel membership probably does not show up for some time. A unique experiment to measure the effect of belonging to a panel on the opinion of members was conducted by Lazarsfeld. He set up four evenly matched groups of 600 people each. One of them was designated as the panel while the other three were control groups. After the initial interview, panel members were re-interviewed six more times while each control group was re-interviewed only once and at different times. Thus if the panel members had been influenced by the interviews the discrepancy between the panel and the control groups would have become more and more pronounced as more interviews were held. The findings did not show up this influence. Except for the tendency for the don't-knows to disappear faster in the panel than in the control group, the differences between the panel and the controls were negligible for the great majority of questions (547).

3. Once members of a panel have stated an attitude or opinion ex-

plicitly, they tend to try to be consistent and to "stick" to it, according to Lazarsfeld. Thus panel members may be less likely to change than the general public. However, the studies that have been made on cumulative change and on whether or not individuals will admit changes suggest that enough people do admit shifts to make it valuable for the investigator to locate such groups and to investigate further the reasons for the change.

One panel design which has proved to be very valuable is that used by the Government Information Service of the Bureau of the Budget. Its "Correspondence Panels" were set up in 1942 (676, p. 82). These panels provide qualitative information which is used in conjunction with the more quantitative opinion polls. The panels include six occupational groups—editors, labor spokesmen, housewives, social workers, clergymen, and small businessmen. Two members from each of these groups in each of 68 sample areas constitute the panel. These representatives serve as informants—reporting on the opinions of people with whom they associate. These informants are supposed to be fairly articulate and relatively unbiased. The survey employs open-end questions and the informant is encouraged to discuss each topic fully. These correspondence panels provide a broader picture of the elements associated with public opinion than is usually obtained in shorter and more quantitative polls. The returns from the panels reveal the presence of various emotional tones in opinions; they disclose the level of information and misinformation about various topics; they bring to light the doubts, qualifications, and contradictions in opinions; and they suggest reasons for favorable and unfavorable attitudes. The stereotypes and phrases used by the various groups also are revealed by the panels. For example, small businessmen think of the worker as a shiftless type, unconcerned about his future, while labor spokesmen report that workers are greatly concerned about their future. Shifts and trends in attitudes and opinions also can be charted by these studies.

Findings of correspondence panels tend to corroborate those of various public opinion polling organizations. When significant differences have been found they seem to be due to the fact that panels permit greater qualification of opinion than the straight yes-no type of question (676, p. 84).

When designing a panel, the surveyor should keep in mind the fact that certain types have a greater mortality than others. A panel of individuals is likely to suffer the heaviest losses. A panel of families is easier to maintain because there is less chance that something will happen to all the adult members of a household than that circumstances will prevent any given person from participating in the panel. A panel of dwelling units is even more stable—the building itself usually remains even though the inhabitants migrate. Which type of panel will be best for a particular survey is, however, a matter which cannot be determined on this basis alone; it must be decided with the survey as a whole in mind.

Final decision on the choice of techniques to be employed in the survey should be made after the detailed procedures and technical problems presented in the following chapters have been thoroughly evaluated.

Selected References

Research Methods
Alexander (4), Dartmouth (227), Deri et al. (245), Desing (246), Dodd (247, 248), Good (365), Horwood (453), Kelley (502), Kirsch (521), Meredith Pub. Co. (638), Monroe and Englehart (652), Murphy and Newcomb (662), Rice (774), Ritchie (783), Smith (891), Spahr and Swenson (901), U.N. (979, 980), Webb (1071), White (1085), Whitney (1088, 1089).

Social Survey Methods
Bernard (56), Bogardus (88), Chambers and Bell (156), Chapin (157, 166), Colcord (181), Elmer (285, 286), Fry (336), Lindeman (567), Lundberg (597), Odum and Jocher (702), Smith and White (891), Young (1137).

Scales for Measuring Social Phenomena (See also books and references on Attitude Measurement)
Bogardus (87, 89), Chapin (158, 159, 161, 166), Chapman and Sims (167), Clark (175), Colcord (181), Guttman (386), Rundquist and Sletto (826), Sewell (860, 861), Shea (866), Thomas-Baines (957), Williams (1099, 1100).

Opinion Poll Techniques
Benson (46, 50), Benson et al. (49), Blankenship (77, 78), Bogardus (86), Campbell (133), Cantril (142), Coutant

(200), Crossley (213), Droba (255), Gallup (343), Hyman (462), Lazarsfeld and Fiske (552), Lockley and Watson (584), Max (619), NORC (674, 675, 676, 677), Robinson (788, 789), Roper (801, 806, 810), Ruch (819, 820, 821), *Scholastic* (848), Stagner (905).

Public Opinion, Election Forecasting, Voting, and Attitude Measurement

Albig (2), Bean (37), Blankenship (77, 78), Cantril (142), Childs (172, 173), Crum (218), Gallup (343), Gallup and Rae (345), Key (509), Likert (563), Lydgate (601), Maclatchy (606), Madge (607), Madge and Harrison (608), Max (619), Menefee (637), Merton et al. (640), Murphy and Likert (661), NORC (676, 677), Rice (770), Robinson (786, 793, 794), Rogers (795), Roskelley (814), Smith et al. (880), Thurstone and Chave (963).

General Discussion, Criticism, and Significance of Polls

Albig (2), Allport (5, 6), Berelson et al. (52), Bernays (57), Blanar (67), Blankenship (69, 75, 79), Blankenship and Manheimer (81), Blankenship et al. (80), Bower (96, 97, 98), Bruner and Korchin (121), Cahalan (130), Campbell (136), Cantril (140, 143, 146), Chapin (163), Cook and Welch (192), Cowell (204), Crespi (206, 209), Dodd (248), Fink and Lutz (305), Gallup (343, 344), Gallup and Rae (345), Goldman (363), Gosnell (372), Gosnell and deGrazia (373), Guest (383), Harper (406), Hart (412), Hartwell (417), Hearings (427), Katz (493, 496, 497, 498), Katz and Cantril (499), Kornhauser (534, 535), Lee (556, 557), Link and Freiberg (579), Link et al. (580), Lurie (599, 600), .Martin (617), McGuire (627), Myers (668), Payne (725), Pierce (743), Ranney (759), Riesman and Glazer (778), Robinson (790, 791), Rogers (795, 796), Sheatsley (870), SSRC (898), Spingarn (904), Stagner (906, 907), Studenski (941), *Tide* (965), Updegraff (1037), Wallace and McCamy (1055), Warner (1057), Wechsler (1072, 1073), Woodward (1120).

Market Research Methods

Advertising Research Foundation (1), American Marketing Assn. (8, 9), Blankenship (77, 78), Brown (115, 116, 120), Cantril (142), Caples (147), Chappell and Hooper (170), Cherington (171), Churchman et al. (174), Converse (191), Duffy (258), Eastwood (266), Eckler and Staudt (272), Egerton (282), Hauser and Leonard (425), Heidingsfield and Blankenship (428), Hotchkiss and Franken (454), Houser (457), Kelsey and Alexander (505), Killough (511), Lazarsfeld and Field (551), Lazarsfeld and Stanton (554), Link (572), Lucas (589, 590), Ludeke (591), Lumley (592), Phelps (738), Poffenberger (745), Psychological Corp. (750), Redmayne and Weeks (760), Reed (761), Reilly (764), Stephan (918), Stock and Hochstim (930), White (1085).

Panel Techniques

Box and Geoffrey (107), Cawl (154), Churchman et al. (174), Employment Stabilization Inst. (287), Fleiss (315), Gaudet and Daniel (347), Lazarsfeld and Fiske (552), Moser (658), Root and Welch (800), Ruch (819), Sellers (859), Sikes (876), Stonborough (933), Weaver (1066), Yoder et al. (1133).

CHAPTER IV

The Role of Sampling

The process of sampling, or the selection of part of a population from which the characteristics of the whole are inferred, has long been accepted as a legitimate and expeditious method of research procedure. Until the twentieth century, however, the use of carefully designed sampling procedures was more prevalent in the physical sciences, especially in applied fields, than in the social sciences.

In a comprehensive discussion of the history of modern sampling procedures Stephan (924) pointed out that sampling has generally preceded the establishment of regular censuses. In 1754, for example, estimates of population in England were based on number of dwellings taxed and not taxed, multiplied by a more or less arbitrary figure of 6 persons per dwelling (364, pp. 279–280). In 1800, the population of Great Britain was estimated from sample data on the average number of persons per house and on the number of births (924). Estimates of the population of France in 1765 and 1778 were based on enumeration of populations in certain districts as well as on births, deaths, and marriages reported in the entire country (924, p. 14). Laplace also used vital statistics in thirty sections of France in preparing his estimates of the total population of that nation from 1799 to 1802. Stephan points out that Laplace made a remarkable step forward in attempting to measure the precision of his estimate. The odds, the estimator claimed, were 1161 to 1 that it was not in error by more than 500,000, or 12 per cent of the total population (924, p. 15).

The recorded instances of the deliberate use of sampling plans in the fields of social investigation prior to 1900 are relatively few in number. In 1891 a survey of income and wealth was conducted in

106

Norway on a sample basis. Instead of canvassing the entire country, representative towns and parishes in the rural districts were selected. Within each one only persons of certain ages (17, 22, 27, etc.) and with certain initial letters in their names were enumerated (921). Another early instance of sampling in Norway may be cited. A. N. Kiaer and E. Hanssen applied sampling in a survey conducted for a parliamentary labor survey to determine the relationships between age, income, invalidism, and occupation. In each community a number of streets were selected which were as representative as possible of the various classes of the population. A number of houses chosen at random were then visited and the adults scheduled. In the capital every tenth house in populous streets were included in the sample, and in each village three or four houses were enumerated. Kiaer labeled his method *"representative"* sampling (510). Snedecor (893, p. 848) remarks that "the essence of Kiaer's representative sampling was large numbers of small units distributed with some uniformity over the region of inquiry." Another early use of sampling methods was made in Denmark in connection with the harvest in 1901.

It was A. L. Bowley of London, however, who first designed a plan for securing a random sample of households which has met the more rigid tests of scientific requirements. As early as 1906, in his presidential address to the Royal Statistical Society, Bowley stated that the method of sampling, which had been well known and accredited for twenty years, had been sadly neglected. Accordingly, he proceeded to develop this field. His surveys from 1912 on have already been described in Chapter I. He did not limit sampling to field investigations, however, but applied it also in studies of secondary data. In 1915 he drew a sample of 1 in 50 schedules in the census office for the purpose of developing a classification.

By 1925 the interest in sampling had grown sufficiently for this procedure to command a place on the program of the International Institute of Statistics held in Rome. Bowley (102) and Jenson (473) were the chief contributors. Snedecor remarked in 1939: "Bowley's monumental investigation of the mathematical theory of representative sampling has since been improved in only minor details. With two notable exceptions it may be said that most of our present knowledge of the sampling of social facts is set out in the pages of the 1926 volume of the Journal of the International Institute" (893, p. 849).

Other applications of sampling methods appear in the literature. When a large part of the tabulations of the Japanese census were destroyed by the Tokyo earthquake in 1923, a new tabulation was prepared from a sample of the household schedules. One in every 1000 (numbers 500, 1500, etc.) of the 11 million schedules were included in the sample. The tabulations relating to age, sex, size of household, etc., were published in 1924.

Hilton utilized a sampling plan in the study of the circumstances of the unemployed in England in 1926 and in 1930. He summarized the procedure used in the latter study as follows: "The sample was selected from the files at the Claims and Record Office, Kew, of unemployment books for the year 1929–30. . . . The sample was selected by measuring off, while in the racks, each block of 100 books, and extracting the last book in each measured block. . . . The number of books selected in this manner approximated closely to 1 per cent of the total known to be in the racks. The new sample was, therefore, selected in a different manner from that of April, 1926. The latter was taken from the ledger accounts direct and the change was made for economy in time and labor. . . . The sample was reduced to a total of 120,000, including 86,740 books for males and 33,260 for females. These figures represent 1 per cent of the estimated insured population on July, 1930. . . ." (Quoted by Larson, 540, pp. 69–70.)

In the United States, agricultural economists have given considerable attention to the problem of practical procedures for the selection of samples. Under the direction of John Black they prepared a report to the Social Science Research Council in 1928, which included a detailed treatment of methods of sampling agricultural data (896). Since the 1930's, an increasing number of people have become "sampling conscious" and have either devised new techniques for drawing or testing samples or attempted to bring together the wealth of material in this field, both practical and theoretical.[1] With the adoption of sampling for a large part of the 1940 census, concerted efforts have been made both for wider adoption of sampling methods and for the improvement of techniques. In 1946, the Social Science Research Coun-

---

[1] Specific examples of surveys and polls that employ sampling in various fields were presented in Chap. I. For further discussion of these surveys as well as of sampling procedures in general, consult the Topic References at the end of the present chapter.

cil again tackled sampling methods; this time as part of a larger study of the entire field of social surveying. The reports of the Committee on Sampling Methods as well as the reports of the United Nations subcommission on statistical sampling will do much to bring order and standards to this very controversial field. (See 898, 979, 980.)

ADVANTAGES OF SAMPLING:

Most of the reasons for using sampling procedures rather than making complete enumerations of the population in a survey are well known and generally accepted. Occasionally, however, the survey designer meets a skeptic and thus needs to have the arguments at his fingertips. The following summary may be helpful:

1. If small samples are employed, an estimate of the characteristics of the total can be secured in a much shorter time than would be possible otherwise. This time-saving advantage is especially important in studies of our modern dynamic society. Conditions change so rapidly that unless short-cut methods are devised for measuring social situations, the measurement is out of date before the survey or poll is completed. The saving in time applies not only to the actual collection of data but also to their processing and tabulation. Thus at almost every step of the survey the amount of work to be done is decreased by the reduction in the number of cases in the survey.

2. If properly designed, sampling should make the survey much less expensive than complete enumeration. Fewer people need to be interviewed and a smaller staff is needed to collect, process, and tabulate the data. The space and equipment required are correspondingly reduced. Thus both labor and nonlabor costs are lower than they are in a complete canvass.

3. Granted that the same amount of money is allotted for sampling as for a complete count, the money saved by the sampling procedure can be used to learn more details about the cases studied, to extend the scope of the survey to groups other than those originally included, or to prepare more analyses and tabulations than were planned at first. The findings of most surveys would assume added significance if comparisons could be made with other groups, times, or places.

The surveyor may argue that he wants large numbers of returns in order to impress those who will pay for the survey. This is a foolish waste of funds. It would be far better to distribute an equal number of cases over a much larger area or repeat the same survey several times in the same area and thus secure enough cases to "impress" those who haven't much faith in small samples. The consistency of returns for different areas or for different periods of time is usually impressive. Furthermore, the surveyor should be able to convince his sponsors that large numbers are no guarantee of correct results by citing the fiasco of the Literary Digest Poll with its millions of ballots.

4. From the administrative point of view, it is often impossible to conduct a complete canvass. The hiring of a large staff, the task of training and supervising them, and the space required to handle and file the schedules from a canvass of the total population may necessitate the development of a sampling plan if the survey is to be made at all.

5. When small samples are used, it is possible to give more attention to each return received and to make certain that the schedule data are as accurate as possible. Thus the tabulations and analyses prepared from the data may be more trustworthy than if the raw data were less carefully collected.

The above arguments assume that the sample represents a relatively small proportion of the total population. Samples that are almost as large as the total do not justify either the effort involved in designing and controlling them or the returns received. In the sample surveys of congested areas conducted by the Census Bureau, formulas were developed whereby it was possible to determine when a complete count would be as cheap or cheaper than a sampling survey (1004, p. 11). In these studies a complete count was taken when the population was about 100,000 or less. The considerations that prompted this decision would not be likely to apply to other surveys and problems, but is cited here as illustrative only.

From one point of view, sampling is always employed in investigations, for it is clearly impossible to study all the manifestations of phenomena for all times and places. Thus, even the census is a sample of the country's population at a given point of time. No sooner is it taken than it is a sample of the past. It "describes a population that is subject to the variations of chance, because it is only one of the many possible populations that might have resulted from the same underlying system of social and economic causes" (243, p. 45). From the practical point of view, however, surveyors can and do differentiate between a sample count and a total enumeration.

DISADVANTAGES OF SAMPLING:

Sampling is not without its limitations. The following disadvantages may be pointed out:

1. The sampling procedure must be correctly designed and followed; otherwise the results obtained may be incorrect or misleading. Of course, complete canvasses must also be done carefully; but additional sources of error arise in sampling when improper sampling procedures are employed.   .

2. When the characteristic to be measured or tabulated occurs only rarely in the population, a very large sample is required in order to yield enough cases to give statistically reliable information about it. For example, if one were interested in surveying people over 90 years of age in a community, the number of such cases in a sample of, say, 5000 persons in the general population would be so low that no reliable estimates or tabulations could be made. If detailed breakdowns or many subclasses are to be shown, small samples of infrequent characteristics are not adequate. Fluctuations within the groups may be so great as to make accurate prediction from the sample impossible. On the other hand, if only totals for the main population groupings are desired, relatively small samples will suffice.

3. The number of breakdowns and subclassifications for which detailed tabulations will prove useful is lower for samples than for complete counts because of the smaller number of sample cases. So if information is needed for very fine groupings of the population, it may be necessary to take a complete count so that there will be enough cases for the analysis. Of course, even complete counts may not yield enough cases to warrant some of the detailed analyses desired, but a sample will reach this point sooner than will a census (243).

4. Most sampling requires the services of experts, if only for consultation purposes. At present there is a shortage of well-qualified sampling experts. To be sure, there are many statisticians. But sampling of human populations requires considerable experience with social data and a knowledge of the various interrelationships. The surveyor thus runs the risk of getting poor advice when he hires technical assistance. With the establishment of survey personnel services and standards, this risk will gradually be reduced.

5. Each type of sampling has its limitations. These will be discussed in Chapter VII.

6. Complicated sampling plans may prove in the long run to require more labor than a complete count. This is particularly true if the sample is a large proportion of the total, and if complicated weighting procedures are used. The chances of errors occurring are multiplied with each additional complication in the survey. The more chances for error, the more checks must be set up and the more operations must be repeated when errors are found.

In the measurement of human populations, much of the sampling has been on an intuitive level and the principles of sampling laid down by statistical experts are often violated. Furthermore, much of the sampling that has followed a consciously conceived "design" has given an erroneous picture of the population sampled. The reasons for the inadequacies of a great deal of the sampling in the social sciences will become apparent as the complex nature of sampling procedures is shown.

The subject of sampling is dealt with in the present book primarily from the point of view of practical procedures and the problems that arise in the selection of unbiased or representative samples of the population. It is often assumed that little attention need be paid to the method of selection because formulas for correcting the sample will take care of such problems after the analysis of results is begun. This view is erroneous because correction for bias cannot be made unless the nature of the bias is known, and this can be ascertained only by the systematic drawing and checking of the sample. Corrections to reduce errors from chance fluctuation usually have only a slight effect upon the results. Moreover, such corrections are often not justified because of the unrepresentative character of the original sample.

Only a few elementary formulas which may be applied when planning the size of the sample and interpreting the significance of differences observed in the results will be presented. Adequate treatment of the theory of probability and of the mathematical derivation and practical application of probability formulas may be found in the extensive literature on statistics.

THE SAMPLING PLAN:

The surveyor is confronted with sampling problems at every stage of the investigation, from the minute he decides to make a survey until the report of findings has been completed. Who shall be studied? When shall the study be conducted? How shall the sample be selected? What size sample is necessary? What shall be done about refusals, families who cannot be reached, substitutions for the cases drawn in the sample, inaccurate and incomplete returns? To what groups are the findings applicable? These questions and countless others are essentially sampling considerations and should be decided in the light of a well-organized, consistent sampling plan. Each decision must be made not only in terms of the immediate situation but in terms of its effect upon the representative character of the findings. Thus sampling procedures do not begin and end with the choice of the sample; instead, they must be employed throughout the course of the investigation. Conversely, until the plans for the study as a whole are clearly outlined, no final decisions as to sampling techniques should be made. Since human beings are not so tractable as black and white balls drawn from an urn (as in the textbook illustrations of sampling principles), and since usually little is known about the characteristics of the human population, especially with respect to the characteristics to be surveyed, the sampling procedure should be directed more toward finding and using practical devices to avoid distorted samples than toward using refined mathematical formulas to measure chance fluctuations in sampling. To be sure, the extent to which the sample can be relied upon to give a true picture of the universe should be measurable. Furthermore, it is efficient to determine mathematically the smallest size sample needed to give a satisfactory measure of the total. But if the choice must be made between employing a logical, nonmathematical approach which might do no more than guarantee that the sample is unbiased, and using a theoretically efficient sampling design which in practice might permit the introduction of biased errors, the author believes the former is preferable. It is better to have too large a sample of the right things than just the right size of the wrong.

Mention has already been made of the characteristics of an ideal sampling plan (Chapter II). Some of the points deserve further emphasis:

1. The sample should yield an unbiased picture of the population of which it purports to be a sample. Whether its purpose is to give an estimate of the frequency of given cases in the population or universe or to reveal the existence of certain interrelationships in the total, the sample should constitute a true cross-sectional picture of the whole.

2. The sampling method chosen should be the most efficient way of securing the desired information with the funds available. Thus the type of sampling should be suited to the survey design as a whole. The sample should be relatively easy to plan, to select, to collect information from, to test, and to interpret.

3. The sample should be so defined that there is no question as to which groups are included or excluded, or as to what group it represents.

4. The sample should be large enough to give statistically reliable results for the characteristics which are to be measured by the survey. It should not be so large, however, as to involve collecting and handling data which are not needed for reliability or for the interpretation of findings.

5. "A sampling method is said to be satisfactory for the questions under consideration if it can be depended upon to yield samples (less than 100 per cent) that lead to the same action as would have been taken on the basis of a complete count" (243, p. 48).

6. When possible, the sampling plan should be designed so that the sample cases will be selected in the office rather than by interviewers in the field. The task of teaching interviewers how to avoid the many sources of bias in selecting cases, the many controls required for checking on their sampling techniques, and the stupendous task of analyzing and interpreting their samples more than offset any advantage to be gained by shifting the responsibility for case selection from the sampler to the field workers.

A number of regular survey agencies which employ trained interviewers have been able to develop fairly satisfactory sample designs in which the final selection of informants is done by the interviewers. Very elaborate instructions and close supervision and analysis of returns are necessary for such samples to be acceptable. Among the more successful agencies, instructions are becoming so specific that the interviewer is given very little leeway in his selection. Surveys which are one-time propositions can hardly hope to develop adequately trained interviewers or to prepare foolproof instructions which would make interviewer selection of respondents as good as office selection.

Even less justification can be found for using self-selected samples, as in voluntary straw votes or radio appeals answered by mailing coupons or labels from packages to the sponsor of the program. Of course such poor samples may be good publicity stunts even though they are not representative of the general public.

7. When the type of sampling is being decided on, the difficulty of locating persons who fit several qualifications must be borne in mind. For example, it is relatively easy to find people in a given age group, say from 20 to 40 years; but when the sampling plan calls for individuals in specified age, sex, occupational, and income groups, the difficulty is increased. The more characteristics by which a sample is controlled, the more time-consuming and expensive is the task of finding people who meet the specifications. Thus, when the selective procedure is being planned, the number of controls used should be kept to as few as is feasible.

8. It is advisable to set up the sampling plan so as to avoid biases which may result from careless or illogical procedures. For example, no plan for sampling human beings is satisfactory unless it includes techniques for handling the nonresponses, the refusals, the not-at-homes, and other problem groups. The many ways in which biases may arise during the selection and collection of samples are discussed in Chapter XII.

The surveyor should learn to think in terms of the effect of every decision upon the type of sample. No formal rules can replace the application of logic to the problems encountered. Ideally this logic should be accompanied by experience in the field of sampling and a knowledge of all relevant aspects of the phenomena to be sampled. If he approaches his problem with a determination to understand the phenomena he is to sample before he decides on which techniques to adopt, he can avoid many mistakes in sampling.

The sampling plan should cover all phases of the survey. The various steps to be considered are listed below and are discussed in detail in later chapters.

PRELIMINARY PLANNING OF THE ENTIRE SAMPLING DESIGN:

1. *Define the universe.*[2] The decision must be made early in the survey regarding the population or group to which the findings are to apply. The definition should include the place, time, and relevant characteristics of the group to be sampled.

Although the findings of the sample inquiry may prove to be applicable to groups, times, and places other than those covered in the survey, the surveyor can be certain of applicability only to the universe from which the sample has been drawn. Thus before deciding how to choose the sample cases, he must know what population is to be sampled. First, he usually has to define the geographical boundary. Is the survey to cover the people residing within the city boundaries, or should it include the population of the suburbs, of the county, of the state, of the nation and its possessions, or of other geographical areas? It is often difficult to limit the scope of the survey at this state, but unless the geographical limits are definitely set, the sample cannot be selected efficiently or correctly.

Whenever possible, it is desirable to survey an area for which population counts are available. Thus, instead of surveying territory served by a public utility such as an electric light company, it is better to confine the survey to the population residing within the city limits. Public utilities frequently serve sections of the suburbs that happen to be well settled or that have requested service from the city public utility. When comparisons of the sample and the census counts are to be made, no statistical background data are available for these sections of the suburbs.

If the survey is limited to the resident population in a given area, how is residence defined? Many individuals consider a city their legal residence but actually spend little or no time there. Members of the

---

[2] The term Universe of discourse is used in statistics to cover the total population from which any sample is drawn or which it is supposed to represent.

armed forces, the "Bar Harbor" set, hobos, traveling salesmen, circus performers, and countless others who are away from home most of the time must be given special thought by the survey analyst if they are to be included.

In addition to geographical boundaries, the population to be sampled must also be defined as to period of time. Is the sample to apply to the situation as of a given day, week, month, or year? The longer the period, of course, the more difficult it is to select a representative sample, because populations are constantly changing. Whatever the period chosen, the surveyor will be able only to approximate an ideal sample of it. Surveys take time; before they are completed the situation which was being measured will have altered. Many people who should have been included in the sample will have moved away or died, thus changing the composition of the sample.

The population to be sampled should be further described in terms of social groups included. What age, sex, color, occupational socio-economic groups belong in it? If the survey covers heads of families, how is the head defined? What is a family? Does it include persons living alone, remnants of larger families, families within families, partnership households, dormitories, clubs, etc.? If the population is that of voters, are only those who voted in the last election included, or does it also include persons coming of voting age, registered voters, or others? Are people who live in institutions as caretakers, employees, or inmates to be surveyed? Is the population one of all persons, adults, family heads, or householders, or does it cover families of cases, events, behavior, opinions, or other phenomena? Just because human beings happen to be the form through which the many social phenomena are expressed, this does not mean that a universe of people is necessarily equivalent to a universe of other social factors. Until the answers to these questions are determined, the universe to be sampled cannot be clear to the surveyor.

2. *Selection of the sampling unit and the unit of tabulation.* The choice of the sampling unit and of the unit to be used in tabulations— i.e., geographical, social group, family or dwelling, individuals, events, behavior segment, or trait—should be made before the sampling procedure is developed. The preparation of the forms for tables at this stage often reveals the need for an early choice of the unit to be used in them and the one which should be used as the sampling unit.

Unfortunately the concept of the sampling unit has received little attention in the social sciences. This is due, among other things, to the complexity of the problem. Just what is it that is being sampled in each study? To answer this question it is necessary to examine the list of sources from which the sample is taken. Surveyors have fallen into the error of thinking that as long as they are dealing with human populations, the individual persons are the sampling units. Actually, however, relatively few studies have used people as sampling units. To be sure, tabulations are often presented in terms of individuals, but this does not mean that the units sampled were necessarily individuals. The most commonly used sampling units may be grouped in the following classes: (a) Geographic or political administrative units; (b) social groups—agencies or institutions; (c) families, households, dwelling units, farms; (d) individuals; (e) events, behavior, opinions, or traits of individuals.

a. An examination of the samples employed in many studies reveals that they have been drawn from a list of geographical areas such as states, counties, small rural areas, cities, wards, tracts, postal routes, census enumeration districts, city blocks, block segments, etc. Usually every individual residing in the areas or included in the groups selected from the list is interviewed. The number of persons included is generally large, but the sample is not necessarily very reliable because it is a sample of *areas* or of clusters of elements rather than of individual persons. Often only eight or ten areas are actually included in the sample; hence the number of sample cases is exceedingly small. These area samples are most applicable to studies in which tabulations are made in terms of areas rather than of individuals. For example, if city blocks were sampled in a survey, tabulations showing the number of *blocks* having specified characteristics (e.g., Negro-occupied dwellings) could be made from the sample without difficulty. But tabulations of the number of Negro-occupied dwellings in the city should not be derived from such a sampling unless special procedures are used.

If, as is often the case, the surveyor desires to estimate the characteristics of the various elements such as dwellings, persons, families, farms, etc., from the sample, he runs into difficulties. The sample cannot be treated as if these elements were the sampling units employed in the selection of the sample. The "clusters of ele-

ments" which constitute the sampling units do not have the same
sampling errors as do elements drawn separately. As Hansen and
Hurwitz point out, "When clusters of elements are the sampling
units, the correlation between the elements within clusters will influence the sampling error. . . . Usually, this correlation is positive, so the sampling of clusters tends to be less efficient than the
sampling of individuals" (396).

b. It is not uncommon to find samples drawn from lists of churches,
clubs, schools, social agencies, etc. Only those agencies included in
the sample are surveyed. The resulting sample is thus one of organizations and it may be no larger than the number of different
agencies involved. Here, as in geographical samples, there is a
cluster of elements. Although each agency may be requested to survey its entire membership and the number of persons giving information may consequently be large, the sampling unit is still the
agency. To be sure, each agency may be considered as a separate
universe and a random sample of individuals may be selected to
portray the situation therein. In this case, the individual is the sampling unit for the agency. The generalizations to be made from such
a sample will pertain to the agency that was sampled and not to individuals in *all the agencies.*

c. The most practical sampling unit for surveys of a community is
the family. If the surveyor is satisfied with a definition which makes
"family" synonymous with the occupants of dwelling units, a source
list is likely to be available. Since it is difficult to find a completely
up-to-date list of families, a more satisfactory way of securing a
"family sample" is to sample addresses or dwelling units. The dwelling unit is a more stable phenomenon than the family, it is easier to
keep track of, and all that needs to be known to make it up-to-date
is the number of dwelling units torn down or condemned and the
new ones being built. Such lists as addresses taken from the city
directory, telephone subscribers, gas meter subscribers, home owners, relief applicants, car owners, etc., tend to provide better samples of families than of individuals. When used as a source list for
family sampling units, however, the list should be corrected for
multiple listings of families (see Chapter VIII).

A great many *tabulations* from data obtained in social surveys are
expressed in terms of families or of family heads. As a rule, the

characteristics in which surveyors are interested tend to be associated with family characteristics because most people are brought up in and are allied with family groups. Thus selection of the family as a sampling unit as well as a tabulating unit is usually satisfactory. The computation of the sampling error is a straightforward procedure depending on the number of different families included in the sample.

For a sample of individuals, the family unit is generally fairly good. The clusters of elements (persons) in the family is not large except for households that have many lodgers. If precautions are taken to avoid including too many individuals from any one of these large clusters, samples in which dwellings or families are used as units give good estimates of the individual population without much distortion.

d. Samples in which persons are the sampling units are ideal for studies in which tabulations are to be made in terms of the number of individuals possessing specified characteristics or holding certain opinions. The greatest difficulties about using persons as sampling units are the lack of source lists from which to sample and the inadequacy of such lists as are in existence. After a sample of individuals is drawn, it may be extremely difficult to locate and schedule them. Whereas dwelling units remain more or less fixed over a period of months and thus make it possible to sample families residing in them, there is no such source for sampling individuals. Consequently surveys which are interested in generalizing for individuals .are usually forced to use the family or dwelling as the sampling unit. As mentioned above, special attention must be given to selecting a good sample of persons who live in rooming houses, clubs, dormitories, or other similar places. A chance selection of one or two large rooming houses in a very poor section of the city might load the sample of individuals with an unrepresentative sample of lodgers.

If the list employed is that of members of organizations, employees of concerns, social security registrants, or some other definitely defined group, the individual is the sampling unit. It should be kept in mind that such lists may include more than one member of a family. Thus, before making tabulations in terms of family heads, it is necessary to take into account the fact that large families have a greater representation among a sample of individuals than do small families.

e. Sometimes the surveyor desires to know the number of times specified events have occurred, or the number of instances of a certain type of behavior, regardless of the number of persons involved. Sampling units composed of records of events may yield quite different results from sampling units representing individuals. For instance, a sample of the names of mothers taken from birth records would not be the same as a sample drawn from a list obtained by means of a house-to-house canvass of the community in question. The sampling unit in the first case would be a birth record; in the second, a household. Thus it follows that a representative sample of births would be quite different from a representative sample of mothers. Since some women have several children, lists of births will contain their names several times. These mothers would have a greater chance of being included in a sample drawn from birth records than would those who have had only one child. Conversely, if a sample of children were drawn from a list of the names of mothers, the sample would overrepresent the children from one-child families.

Surveys based upon intensive studies of one or a few people, or "case" studies, usually employ *segments of behavior* of the individual as their sampling unit. The time sampling studies of the behavior of preschool children in which a number of one-minute samples of social behavior were observed and recorded by the author (718) as well as similar studies by Thomas and others (956) show how carefully drawn samples may yield measures of individual behavior. The generalizations should not legitimately go beyond the description of the person studied or of the behavior traits. To generalize for a community of persons, the sampling unit should be composed of individuals.

3. *Locate and select the source list.* Although the universe and sampling unit are usually decided upon with a source list in mind, the selection of the list from which to sample may be regarded as the next step in planning the survey sample.

4. *Decide on the type or types of sampling to be used,* i.e., whether to use random, stratified, purposive, or other techniques (Chapter VII).

5. *Decide on the size of the sample or the sampling ratio.* To make an intelligent decision, it is necessary to have a thorough grasp of the survey problem as a whole—the precision wanted in the results, the tabulations planned, the characteristics of the population, the type of sampling to be employed, funds and personnel available, and many other considerations (Chapter IX).

6. *Plan the sampling procedure as a whole and write sampling instructions.*

7. *Prepare the source list for sampling and draw the sample.*

8. *Check the selection.*

9. *Transcribe identifying information to sample cards,* e.g., name, address, sample number, district, etc.

10. *Prepare sampling tables to test the sample before the field investigation.* Number of cases, geographic distribution, telephone possession, etc., of the sample cases should be compared with total counts from other sources such as the census.

11. *Control the sampling during the collection period* (Chapters X and XI). This involves instructing the field workers how to meet various problems encountered during the collection of data; checking on selective factors operating to distort the sample; and setting up procedures for overcoming biases in the returns. If the sample is selected by interviewers, close supervision and numerous checks on the randomness of selections is necessary.

12. *Office control of the sample.* Set up controls in the office so that no sample cases are lost during the editing, coding, or tabulation stages of the survey. If the surveys employ mail questionnaires and telephone interviews, specific precautions must be taken to avoid biases in the returns.

13. *Test the sample* (Chapter XVI). Check the sample finally obtained against the universe for certain known characteristics in order to reveal deficiencies in the sample which may have been overlooked in early stages of the survey.

14. *Adjust or correct the sample if necessary* (Chapter XV).

15. *Interpret the data obtained in the survey in the light of the reliability of the sample* (Chapter XVI).

16. *Publish sampling methods* (Chapter XVII). The surveyor owes a detailed account of his sampling method to his reader. Only by such means can the significance of his findings be evaluated.

Selected References

Some Sample Surveys

Bowley (99, 100, 103), Bowley and Bennett-Hurst (105), Bowley and Hogg (106), Box and Geoffrey (107), Callandar and Sarle (132), Employment Inst. (287), Goodman (370), Goodman and Maccoby (371), Hansen et al. (398, 400), Hauser (422), Hilton (439), Hogg (446), Jessen (476, 478, 479), Jones (481, 482), Jones and Clark (484), Katz (497, 498), Katz and Cantril (499), King (512), Kiser and Whelpton (523), Larson (540), Lazarsfeld (545), Likert (565), Link (575, 576), London (585), Maclatchy (606), Madge and Harrison (608), Mangus (612), Moser (658), NORC (674, 675, 676, 677), Robinson (794), Roper (808), Ruch (821), Schoenberg and Parten (847), Stephan (918, 924), Stephan et al. (927), Stock and Hochstim (930), U.S. (993, 1004, 1006, 1010, 1021, 1022, 1024), Whelpton and Kiser (1080, 1081, 1082), Winslow (1112).

CHAPTER V

Organization and Personnel
of the Survey

The first step in setting up a survey is to develop detailed plans such as were discussed in Chapter II. The importance of having these plans completed before the collection of data is begun cannot be stressed too strongly. If the plans are developed while the survey is in progress there is great likelihood of considerable waste motion because of inconsistent instructions or plans, changes in instructions, delay while waiting for schedule forms, and other conditions that interfere with the smooth flow of work. The data collected under such conditions are often inaccurate and not worth tabulating. If later an effort is made to correct the errors made during the early stages, the time and cost required if correction is possible are greater than would have been the case if the field work had been postponed until the plans were completed.

Survey directors are often surprised at the rapidity with which returns come in during the first few days of a survey. If the staff is unprepared and falls behind in handling these schedules, it is difficult for them to catch up, and it will be almost impossible to detect and correct mistakes or erroneous procedures. Most survey directors find themselves unable to cope personally with the innumerable problems that confront them during the first few days or weeks of investigation. Thus, a number of major decisions affecting the ultimate success or failure of the survey may be left to members of the staff who are neither trained nor hired to direct it. Some of the procedures need not be planned in as great detail for small- as for large-scale surveys because the director is likely to be available to decide on problems as they arise. Even in small studies, however, he often has little time for technical planning because he must devote a large portion of his time to organization and public relations.

Although we have chosen to concentrate upon the more general problems of the organization and administration of surveys in this chapter, the detailed problems that arise during the execution of the various operations will be discussed throughout the book.

The problems of survey organization and administration are like those encountered in most business undertakings. Standard treatises on business organization, office supervision, and administration contain many helpful suggestions to the surveyor, especially to one who is to direct a large-scale study. Among the pertinent topics discussed in such books are the factors to consider in laying plans, the setting up of the organization, the control of quality and quantity in the work produced, and problems of personnel.

There is one difference between business organizations and surveys which must be kept in mind, however. Most surveys are temporary undertakings and are known to be so by the staff members, whereas business enterprises are more permanent. The task of hiring and training qualified personnel and maintaining high standards as to quality and quantity of production during the relatively short period of the survey is much more difficult than is the case when permanent tenure or a future with the organization can be guaranteed. During periods of unemployment, when many white-collar workers are seeking jobs, the temporary employment offered by the survey is readily accepted. But when the labor supply is low, special inducements must be offered to secure capable temporary workers.

During the final stages of the investigation, when the staff members anticipate losing their jobs, some of the better qualified will leave to accept new positions. Others may not exert their best efforts because they are job hunting; still others may be influenced by the knowledge that the higher their production rate the sooner the study will be completed. This may be counteracted early in the survey by promising to retain the most efficient field workers for later phases of the work. The director may know of another survey which is just being launched and which can take over many of the workers released when his own survey is completed.

SUGGESTIONS TO ADMINISTRATORS:

The size of the survey, the techniques used in collecting data, and the amount of tabulation and analysis to be done will determine to a large extent the complexity of the organization required. Some general principles of organizatfon and administration, however, are applicable in some degree to every survey. While many of them seem self-evident, they are frequently violated, thus causing confusion and inefficiency, not to mention poor quality of the data. The following general practices which the survey director should observe and enforce may have an important bearing on the success of his project:

1. *Whenever possible, put instructions in writing.* This insures against making hasty and inconsistent judgments. Frequently when a survey director or supervisor is faced with what seems to be a unique case, calling for a special decision, he gives an offhand ruling which he would not make if he considered it in the light of the procedure as a whole. Another advantage is that the written statement precludes errors arising from forgotten instructions. It serves as a reminder as well as a handy reference guide on how to proceed. People sometimes claim to understand an oral instruction because they do not want to appear stupid. A person who receives a written statement has more chance to think it over and make sure of the meaning. A collection of these written instructions should serve as a guide for training new employees, thus simplifying this task. Even more important is the fact that recorded instructions tend to insure that the procedures are uniformly carried out. Thus the quality of work is likely to be more dependable If questions arise as to lines of authority and responsibility for the performance of certain operations, the written instructions help to answer them. In small-scale surveys they may serve as a manual for other surveyors who will repeat the survey in a different locality or later in the same place. In both large and small surveys written instructions simplify the task of writing up the methodological aspects of the study as well as of interpreting the data.

2. *Guard against too much division of authority and overlapping of responsibility.* The lines of authority should be clear, and definite responsibility should be assigned for the performance of each operation. Everyone should know (a) .to whom he is responsible, (b) for what operation he is responsible, (c) whom he should consult if his instructions do not appear to cover a specific situation, and (d) what types of cases should be turned over to persons specializing in "problem cases."

If responsibility can be fixed and if the work is checked, it should be possible to discover which people are doing incorrect or inefficient work. Possibly further training or discipline may be necessary. Friction among workers is lessened if each one has definite duties for which he is responsible.

3. *Delegate some authority but also keep in touch with the details of operation.* The survey director is in the position of an executive of a business undertaking. His job consists principally of planning, organizing and controlling the work of his staff. If he gives too much time to details he may lose sight of the broader aspects of his job. On the other hand, he must be sufficiently close to actual operating conditions to make decisions that meet the practical needs of the situation. If a particularly knotty problem arises, the director would be wise to probe into the causes of the situation by inspecting the processes immediately involved. If necessary, he should examine a set of schedules to learn exactly what the problem is. After a decision to proceed a certain way has been reached, the director should try out a few cases to see whether it is practicable. Although the supervisors of the various operations in a large-scale survey should be in a position to recommend the best procedures in problem situations, it is better for the director to see for himself before accepting many of the recommendations.

Just as the director should keep in touch with details, the supervisors should be posted on the broader phases of the survey. Too many directors like to keep the facts about the project as a whole to themselves. In so doing they run the double risk of not having one or more trained persons who could take over in an emergency and of having conflicting procedures develop within the survey because of poorly informed supervisors.

4. *Keep account of the time and cost of the survey.* Actual performance should be compared with the plans; if the survey is running behind or ahead of the schedule or the budget, the plans should be adjusted. For example, if the survey director finds that his collection costs are greater than he anticipated, he may have to reduce the number of tabulations or the amount of analysis. The condition of the budget should not come as a surprise to him, when it is too late to limit the project in a satisfactory way.

5. *Set up a routine check of the quality of every operation.* It should be clearly understood that all work will be checked and that incorrect work will have to be corrected. Standards as to what consti-

tutes an "allowable" amount of error should be established and enforced. Since the whole purpose of a survey is to supply accurate facts about a given situation, incorrect data are worse than useless. If errors are caught and corrected from the beginning, the amount of correction necessary in the later stages is manageable. But if errors are permitted to persist until the final tabulations are prepared, the cost of tracing and correcting each step in processing the schedules is often prohibitive. It is cheaper to spend time and effort on having the material correct in the first place than in trying to make corrections later. As far as possible, use checks that will become more or less automatic. For example, the total of a given count should be the same as the total that appears in a certain place.

6. *After errors have been detected, see that someone is responsible for making corrections at every point affected.* Too often a staff worker corrects a mistake where he happens to catch it without going back to other tabulations or data in which the same error may have been made. The result is that when analysis is begun, figures which should agree do not.

7. *Require production reports periodically on the quantity and type of operations performed.* Frequent comparisons should be made between the amount of work planned and the amount accomplished by various individuals and by different sections of the survey. By studying these reports the director should be able to spot or foresee bottlenecks which may hinder the smooth flow of operations.

8. *Avoid labor turnover.* Since the cost of training workers in the techniques and procedures of the survey is relatively high, a stable force is desirable. Adequate wages and pleasant working conditions are helpful. Transferring employees from one phase of the work to another as the survey progresses reduces turnover expense by avoiding the need for training new workers. Many mistakes in interpreting or analyzing results have been made by people hired for analysis who were not familiar with the procedures through which the data passed prior to that stage.

9. *When possible, divide each job into several definite operations* which can be done by one worker and checked by another within a specified time. The operation as a whole should also be reviewed by someone assigned to this task.

10. *Avoid too many transcriptions of the data.* The more times the

data are transcribed from one form to another, the greater the probability of mistakes in copying or verifying the transcriptions. Since the
arrangement of material for field interviews may not be satisfactory
from the point of view of work in the office, transcription may occasionally be desirable. In general, however, this should be limited.

11. *Ask the worker who does each operation to initial the record of
it.* This makes it possible to determine who makes an error or whose
record needs further clarification. It is important to discover and correct wrong or misunderstood procedures when workers are being
trained rather than later on when many errors have been made.

12. *Do not keep inefficient workers.* An employee who is incapable
of doing accurate and efficient work should be discharged. It may be
cheaper to train a new employee than to permit an inefficient one to
affect the morale of the more industrious and efficient workers. Furthermore, too many other employees may have to spend time correcting
the errors made by a careless worker.

SECURING COOPERATION FOR THE SURVEY:

One of the first steps in conducting a survey is to develop favorable
local interest in it. In small communities particularly, the backing of
community leaders is essential. If the town is divided into opposing
factions, both groups must be approached. For surveys of selected
groups such as doctors, lawyers, teachers, etc., the surveyor runs into
the danger of getting the cooperation of leaders who speak for only
one element in the profession. For example, if one group belongs to a
certain trade or professional organization while another does not, the
leaders of both the members and nonmembers must be consulted before the survey gets under way. Familiarity with the community or
with the group to be surveyed is necessary if oversight of influential
persons is to be avoided. If the aid of a committee of leading citizens
can be secured for the proposed survey, the project should get off to a
good start. Surveys undertaken to secure factual data for social planning and amelioration may find such committees extremely helpful
later on in carrying out the recommendations made in the report.

Whether or not the public as a whole should be informed in advance depends upon the nature of the investigation. Some schedules
should never be published, as, for example, those which may tempt
people to respond with false information and those which contain ex-

tremely personal questions. It is preferable to catch informants off guard so that their answers will be spontaneous, for such responses offer little opportunity for deliberate misinformation. Advance knowledge may make informants flatly refuse to answer personal questions; but if they are ignorant of the nature of the questions the interviewer can sometimes secure the desired information so skillfully that the respondent is unaware of having given it.

The Bureau of the Census begins its publicity campaign many months before the actual date of the field enumeration so that the public will be prepared for the enumerators. The publicity is increased as the date approaches. An interesting account of the program for the census of 1940 is given in the report of the Secretary of Commerce:

A Division of Public Relations was organized in August, 1939, under specific authority of Congress to plan and execute an educational campaign for enlisting Nation-wide cooperation in the decennial census.

Operating through various media of public expression—newspapers and periodicals, radio, motion pictures, local committee organizations, public officials, and the Bureau's field force—an intensive campaign was conducted in advance of and during the enumeration. More than 2000 cooperating local committees sponsored by chambers of commerce and State, county, and municipal officials assisted this program in their localities.

School officials, church leaders, civic groups, and fraternal organizations throughout the country also gave their assistance toward insuring the completeness of the census. Valuable contributions in services were received from county farm agents, home demonstration agents, and other leaders in the rural sections of the country. Other agencies of the Federal Government also cooperated in passing the word along through their local offices everywhere. The 40,000 postmasters throughout the Nation gave space on lobby bulletin boards to posters and other expressions of census information.

Editors of more than 10,000 daily and weekly newspapers and of more than 1600 general magazines, business and professional periodicals, agricultural publications, and organs of trade associations and commercial organizations also cooperated in giving space to explanatory articles about the census as well as editorials urging the fullest cooperation on the part of their readers.

The Office of Education contributed much to the success of the radio program as did, of course, the various radio broadcasting chains, commercial program sponsors, and hundreds of individual radio stations. Similarly, the cooperation given by national news-reel companies and by several thousand individual motion picture theatre operators is to be credited as a contribution of major importance.

Other agencies and groups, too numerous to mention in detail in consideration of space limitations, contributed also—as, for instance, news services and press associations, Washington newspaper representatives, free-lance writers, volunteer speakers, library officials, heads of individual business organizations, and so on. The Bureau also had the benefit of consultative service by technical experts on the various media of publicity (1001, pp. 40–41).

Some surveyors claim that too much advance publicity may be harmful to a survey, especially if an opposition group induces its members to refuse to cooperate. An outstanding example of opposition of this sort occurred in connection with the 1940 census, when a Senator objected to the questions on income as an invasion of the right of privacy in personal affairs. It was claimed that census takers, although sworn to hold confidential the information given them, could not help but pass on the most "interesting" bits they obtained. One precaution against this was the assignment of enumerators to districts other than those in which they lived. A second measure met such objections even more effectively; each enumerator was supplied with special blanks and with envelopes addressed to Washington, D. C. An informant who refused to answer these questions was given one of these blanks and an envelope to be filled in and mailed direct to the Bureau of the Census. This created extra work for the Washington staff because these returns had to be matched with the enumerators' schedules and entered on the proper line. Fifteen million of these special slips were printed, but when the final tabulations were made, it was found that fewer than 200,000 had been used. Enumerators reported that a few people who had never questioned the right of census takers to ask about personal matters were uncooperative as a result of the advance publicity; many others proved to be especially cooperative because the questions were much less personal than they had anticipated.

Throughout the survey the maintenance of good public relations is essential. Periodic news releases on the excellent cooperation received from the community, a word from leading citizens or civic groups on the need for cooperation, and a general statement regarding the type of data desired will do much to solve the interviewer's problems. If local opposition develops, there are usually ways of reaching and changing the attitude of the leaders and their followers. Several WPA projects met with an unfavorable response in strongly anti-New Deal communities. Surveys of wages and living conditions of workers may be objected to in towns dominated by employer groups. Unless the co-operation of the leading opposition groups is secured early, the most carefully planned survey may fail. If the antagonism is too great and there is no immediate prospect of overcoming it, it may be desirable to survey another community or wait until later when the opposition may have subsided.

Schedule Forms and Instructions

The number of forms and instructions needed for a survey depends primarily upon the size of the field and office staffs. But even in a survey that has only one or two investigators a record should be kept of interpretations and procedures so that the data on any two schedules will be comparable and the schedules themselves will be comparable from one period of the survey to another. The written instructions are also valuable when the written report of the survey is prepared, because the passage of time makes it difficult to recall the details of the procedures adopted during the collection period. A schedule containing a list of questions or a group of items is not enough; the definitions of these items and the interpretations to be given the various answers must also be standardized. (See items to be included in instructions to enumerators in Chapter X.)

In large-scale studies the necessity for written instructions to be in possession of the staff members soon becomes apparent. Every form that is prepared must be accompanied by instructions for filling it out. If the schedule is extremely short, these instructions can be included on the form. When the schedule forms and instructions issued in the course of several recent nation-wide surveys were assembled at the completion of the surveys, they constituted several volumes of mimeographed and printed material. The book of instructions to enumerators issued in 1940 by the Bureau of the Census contained 173 pages. Detailed instructions were prepared for every item and subitem on the schedule. Furthermore, the following processes involved in taking the census were outlined and were accompanied by detailed instructions.

1. The design of the schedules and the writing of the instructions which accompany them (performed by the Population Division

with the approval of the other divisions affected, that is, the divisions of Geography, Field, and Tabulation).

2. The actual enumeration (performed by the Field Division with technical questions being referred to the Population Division).

3. Processing of the schedules necessary prior to the tabulation of data for individuals and for dwelling units. (This is performed by the Population Division and the individual steps are outlined below.)

4. The punching of cards and the mechanical tabulation of data for individuals and dwelling units (performed by the Tabulation Division according to specifications furnished by the Population Division).

5. The transcription of data from the schedules in order to prepare for tabulation of information for households, families, women in the fertility sample, and other special studies. (This is performed by the Population Division.)

6. The punching of cards and the tabulation of data for households, families, etc. (performed by the tabulating division according to specifications furnished by the Population Division).

7. The assembling of the tabulated data into table form in order that it may be published.

8. The analysis and interpretation of the data which accompanies the published results.

9. The publication of the results of the censuses.

An example of the many operations involved in a single process is afforded by the instructions prepared for Process 3 above, the processing of schedules or the preparation of data for tabulation. Each operation was done by different groups of clerks, but in almost every case one clerk carried out all the steps in one operation. Process 3 was composed of the following 12 operations:

Operation 1. Receipt and Examination by Field Division.
Operation 2. Receipt and Examination by the Population Division.
Operation 3. Matching.
Operation 4. Verification of Matching and Hand Count of Population and Housing.
Operation 5. Verification of the Hand Count; Transcription and Verification of the Preliminary Sample Data.
Operation 6. Separation of Population Schedules, Housing Schedules, and Other Materials.
Operation 7. General Population Coding.
Operation 8. Verification of General Population Coding.
Operation 9. Coding of Occupation, Industry, and Class of Worker.
Operation 10. Verification of Coding of Occupation, Industry, and Class of Worker.

Operation 11. General Housing Coding.
Operation 12. Verification of Coding of Housing Census.

Each of these operations was divided into steps for which detailed instructions were prepared. Operation 5, for example, was described in 42 paragraphs, and Operation 3 in 80 paragraphs.

The Low Income Housing Area Survey (1019) plans contained 207 pages of instructions on the various procedures, such as enumerating, editing, coding, tabulating, etc. The Real Property Inventory Technique (1013) required three volumes of instructions.

The number of forms and instructions needed for a survey, aside from those required for purely administrative purposes, such as time sheets, filing instructions, etc., is surprising to people unfamiliar with survey methods. The following are commonly required for large surveys:

1. Sampling instructions—general plans.
2. Sampling instructions for drawing sample.
3. Sampling instructions for field control of the sample.
4. Schedule forms.
5. Instructions to interviewers.
6. Instructions to check interviewers.
7. Instructions to editors.
8. Instructions to check editors.
9. Transcription card or code card.
10. Instructions for transcribing data from schedule.
11. Instructions to coders.
12. Instructions to code verifiers.
13. Punch cards.
14. Instructions to punch card operators and punch verifiers.
15. Instructions to machine operators as to machine runs desired.
16. Instructions for sorting, counting, and tabulating data.
17. Instructions for verifying and editing machine runs.
18. Instructions to control section and forms for administrative purposes.

This last-mentioned set usually includes assignment sheets, production record forms, daily, weekly, or monthly progress tabulation forms, time sheets, error record forms, filing instructions, inventory sheets, routing slips, receipt slips, payroll forms, expense account sheets, and numerous others depending on the survey method and size.

The file of instructions and forms should be kept in a loose-leaf notebook that is indexed. All instructions should be dated, and the file should be kept up to date. When revisions are made, the phrase "superseded by instruction of —— date" should be stamped on the earlier instructions.

In some cases instructions may become too cumbersome, so that it is impossible for the survey staff members to familiarize themselves with the essential points. Hence a condensed set of instructions may be desirable for daily use, the detailed set being available for reference on specific problems. No time and effort should be spent on drafting instructions and forms for their own sake; this is particularly true of intra-office forms, which sometimes become so numerous and time-consuming that the staff cannot fill them out.

The Survey Personnel

THE LABOR MARKET:

Before undertaking any large-scale survey, it is advisable to find out whether sufficient workers with the necessary qualifications are available for temporary employment. In case a survey already in operation may have engaged all the qualified workers in the community, it may be necessary to delay the new project until this labor force is available unless the budget permits workers to be brought in from nearby localities. In some cases it may be preferable to select another community where labor conditions are more favorable.

Although occasional surveys are projected in the hope that the labor cost will be met largely by unpaid volunteer work on the part of interested people or cooperating agencies, dependence on this is usually unwise for several reasons. Interest lags, certain jobs require specialized workers not found among volunteers, and, most important of all, high standards of work cannot be maintained because the threat of dismissal cannot be used as a disciplinary measure.

EMPLOYING THE PERSONNEL:

While the sources which can supply qualified workers vary with the community and the condition of the labor market, the following usually should be investigated: public and private employment agencies; the employment bureaus connected with universities, business or vocational colleges, and high schools; college women's clubs (their members often want temporary or part-time work); and graduate students or their wives as well as wives of professors, who are frequently interested in survey work. If the survey is conducted during the vacation period, teachers or college students or even high school pupils who meet the requirements and are seeking temporary work are often available. Help may be obtained from the list of survey personnel compiled by the Committee on Opinion and Attitude Research Personnel and the lists of qualified interviewers prepared by the Institute of Market Research (19). The *International Directory of Opinion and Attitude Research* (757) should be consulted also for experienced assistance.

Before being hired, however, each applicant should be tested. Standard tests of clerical workers (751), and of other office workers ought to prove helpful. The limited time and financial resources of most surveys make the employment of even one inefficient worker a retarding influence. Too often the sponsors think that anyone can do work on a survey and before the director realizes it, he finds that his staff has been chosen by the sponsors without regard for qualifications.

Interviewers' tests such as those developed by government survey agencies might be used in conjunction with ratings like those described by Rugg (142, p. 88). Alderson has developed a quiz to accompany interviewers' instructions (78, p. 20) which might be adapted for other surveys.

Since it is seldom possible to secure trained interviewers for temporary positions, training and testing may be combined. One survey held a one-week evening training school for candidates for interviewers' positions. Office instructions and practical experience in the field (a suburb of the city to be surveyed) were alternated during the training period. Some candidates dropped out after a few days; of those who remained, about one-third were hired. The cost of running the school consisted principally of the salary of the director and the assistants who conferred with the candidates and edited their schedules. Some of the candidates had full-time jobs but were willing to leave them for a relatively good salary with a one-year guarantee of employment in a type of work which appealed to them.

One survey director who hires interviewers by mail sends out sample assignments with instructions to aspiring interviewers and only those who do creditable work are hired. He claims that many people who think they might like to become interviewers find out that this type of work does not appeal to them. Thus, the survey agency as well as the candidate are saved a lot of trouble by this preliminary test (409).

THE SURVEY STAFF:

The personnel usually required for a survey may be classified as follows: (1) the director and other supervisory personnel, including analysts; (2) interviewers; (3) nonsupervisory office workers; and (4) service employees.

The Director; the Supervisory Staff. Before field work is begun, a small technical staff should be employed to draw up the plans for the survey. As a rule, only people who have actually conducted surveys realize the need for technical assistance in planning. The number of persons required depends on the size of the survey and the time available for preliminary work. Large-scale surveys customarily have, in addition to the director, an assistant director of the project as a whole, and a director for each of the major divisions—sampling, collection of data, editing and coding, and tabulation. A nation-wide survey may require area managers and district and city supervisors in addition to the headquarters staff.

Unless well-developed techniques are available from earlier surveys, a pilot study should be undertaken to test the schedule as well as the reactions of the public and interviewers toward it. To do so, a skeleton staff of interviewers and office personnel is needed practically from the start. Some nation-wide surveys have required more than a year and a staff of several people for this preliminary work. The administrative procedure, sampling instructions and forms, interviewers' instructions, office control forms, schedules and forms for the data, and coding, editing, and tabulating procedures must all be prepared in advance. After the survey is under way, little time is available for preparing and having forms printed and for writing the instructions to accompany them; hence as much as possible should be done before the full staff is employed.

Once the field work has begun, the supervision of the staff should concern itself with both the quality and quantity of data collected and processed. In nation-wide surveys this may involve considerable correspondence with the field staff, occasional visits to the various local headquarters, and evaluation of the field work. Routing the schedules through the processes necessary before the finished tables appear is the work of the director, his assistant, or the control division of the survey. They must see that the work flows smoothly from one process to the next. Routing becomes complicated, for example, when incomplete schedules must be returned to the field staff after they have gone through several operations. Moreover, special technical problems inevitably arise in preparing the schedule data for tabulation. Constant care is necessary if all the divisions are to function with equal effectiveness, for schedules may pile up in one division while another is without work. Staff conferences in which the heads of the various divisions discuss their problems and formulate a production program which will be compared with performance at the next meeting may disclose the weak links in this chain.

After the field work has been completed and the report on the method has been prepared, the headquarters staff should prepare the report on the findings. Too often the analysts and report writers are not hired until the analysis stage; the result is that either they have to spend months familiarizing themselves with the data or else they interpret the data inadequately or even incorrectly.

Weekly progress reports from each division head will help the director to determine whether the survey is keeping to its schedule and whether short cuts or curtailment of certain plans is needed if it is to be completed on time.

Interviewers. When selecting his staff of interviewers, the survey director should keep in mind the classes of people to be interviewed, the type of information to be secured, and the qualifications required of a good interviewer.[1]

Market and public opinion surveyors have presented lists of characteristics which the "ideal" interviewer should possess. These and other suggestions which the writer has found to be important may be condensed into the following list:

1. Ability to talk easily with all types of people. Extrovert individuals.
2. Ability to size up people and situations quickly and correctly.
3. Keen powers of observation and regard for details.
4. Persistence and thoroughness. He should not give in to the temptation to secure an incomplete schedule if difficulties are encountered.
5. A sympathetic as well as an enthusiastic interest in human beings.

[1] See p. 88 for the selection of telephone interviewers.

6. Conscientiousness, honesty, and reliability.
7. Quick wit and resourcefulness. He should not appear to be too intelligent, however, or the informant may distrust him.
8. A good memory or ability to take shorthand. This is particularly useful for verbatim recording.
9. A legible handwriting—if many entries require written comments.
10. Interest in research and ideas. An inquiring mind.
11. An appearance and manner which inspires confidence.
12. Ability to grasp and follow instructions precisely.
13. Ability to summarize and record objectively and accurately the information obtained.
14. In so far as possible, freedom from bias in observation and in eliciting and recording of facts and opinions.
15. Plenty of physical energy. Good health.
16. Freedom to travel if necessary.
17. Freedom and willingness to work evenings, Saturday afternoons, Sundays and holidays.
18. Possession of a car (often desirable).
19. A high school education or more—in most cases. Whenever possible the education of the interviewer should be superior to or at least equal to that of the informant. It has been suggested that interviewers should be drawn from the same social or economic groups as the informants in order to develop closer rapport and avoid tension. The present author does not agree completely. A wider background on the part of the interviewer does not preclude a sympathetic insight or understanding of the informant's situation. Furthermore, the public is accustomed to giving its confidences to superiors such as the priest, the social worker, the doctor and psychiatrist and numerous others in positions of authority in the community. Thus for some types of questions at least, such as those dealing with intimate family situations, a person with prestige might be more successful than a member of the same economic group as the informant. On the other hand, as is pointed out later, in surveys of opinions in economic fields, of racial and religious prejudices, and possibly in other fields not yet explored for interviewer effect, it may be possible to avoid biased responses by using interviewers of the same economic or racial groups as the informants. Another solution is to select interviewers

biased in opposite directions so that their effect will be counter-balancing.

Whether to employ men or women for interviewers will depend primarily upon the type of survey and the nature of the questions to be asked. In some surveys—public opinion polls, for example—both men and women have proved satisfactory, but in others there has been a definite preference for one or the other. Women are sometimes preferred for interviewing housewives, but for interviewing garage mechanics about the mechanical features of cars men may be better. According to Brown (115), women are usually employed for consumer calls and men for dealer calls, but other market surveyors claim that a woman can sometimes secure information from a man who would flatly refuse to talk with another man (8). Night interviewing in the poorer districts of a city can be done best by men.

Brown (115) suggests that 25 to 40 years is a desirable age range for interviewers. He says that investigators who are too young often lack tact and the ability to approach people, while those who are too old are often not willing to follow instructions carefully, or not aggressive enough to obtain an interview.

The class of people to be interviewed is another factor that influences the selection of interviewers. Residents of the high-rent sections of a city will be likely to refuse to talk with interviewers who appear to have a narrow background and little education. On the other hand, in sections inhabited by the foreign-born laboring classes, the interviewer's ability to speak a foreign language may be more important than his education or background. "Junior Leaguers" might obtain good interviews in the Gold Coast area of a city but they might not get cooperation in the slum sections (8).

When interviewers are being selected for public opinion polls, the surveyor must exert every effort to avoid hiring those who would bias the returns. If the respondents are to be selected by the interviewers, various economic groups should be represented among the interviewers. Katz found, for example, that middle-class or white-collar workers did not find the same public sentiment on labor and war issues as did working-class interviewers in a low income area. More liberal and radical opinions on labor issues were found by the working-class interviewers while more conservative attitudes were reported by the middle-class interviewers. Katz suggests that these differences may arise from the tendency of respondents to give answers they think their questioners expect, or from deliberate deceit, or from noncooperation in labor districts where people are suspicious of company spies, or lastly, from biased selection of respondents by white-collar interviewers (495).

When respondents are preselected in the office, there is still a danger that interviewers may reflect their own biases in asking questions or in obtaining and recording responses. In a survey of anti-Semitism, for example, one surveyor found that respondents, particularly those in lower economic and educational groups, tended to withhold anti-Semitic views from interviewers of Jewish appearance or name (792). In another study, two comparable samples of Negroes were interviewed—one entirely by whites and the other by Negroes. Answers to political questions did not differ, but those on the Germans (white race) and Japs (yellow race) differed slightly for the two groups of interviewers. Apparently the Negroes tended to hide their views that the white group was a greater threat than the yellow (1098).

The best way to select good interviewers is to give them a trial and choose them on the basis of performance. Few commercial survey concerns employ interviewers until they have been given a field trial and have proved their ability to secure the desired information and record it satisfactorily.

The number of interviewers needed for a personal interview survey depends essentially on how many interviews can be conducted per day or hour. This in turn depends upon many factors, among which are the following:

1. The geographical distribution of the informants is perhaps most important. If interviewers must spend a half hour or an hour traveling to the interview, they will be able to hold fewer interviews than if the addresses are concentrated in a relatively small area. Moreover, if no one is at home, almost as much time is spent as if an interview had been secured.

By careful charting, the assignment clerk can greatly reduce the time lost from this factor. It may be most efficient to assign scattered not-at-home revisits to an interviewer with a car. In cities with adequate transportation facilities it is often advisable to pay the interviewers' carfare from one address to the next, as well as from the office to the district in which the addresses are located. The *distance* between calls

may be less important than the *time* required with available transportation facilities to reach given addresses. For example, although
New York City extends over a large area, the bulk of the population
can be reached by the subway system in a relatively short time. In
most cities, a widely scattered list of addresses should be assigned to
investigators who have their own cars.

2. Can any adult member of the household be questioned? If the interviewer can secure the information from any adult who happens to
be at home, he can conduct more interviews per day than if he has to
see a particular member of the family.

3. The type of information desired is important in determining the
number of interviewers. For example, information sought from women
in the home is relatively easy to secure, since the chances of finding
a housewife at home are good. On the other hand, collection of information from business people who cannot be interviewed in their
offices or from roomers who are seldom home requires more callers in
a given area because only a couple of hours in the evening or on weekends are likely to be productive.

4. Does the interviewer have to complete all his assignments before
he is given another list, or can he pick the easy and most accessible
cases? In the early stages of a survey an investigator may not bother
with cases that require return visits, night calls, special persuasive
techniques, or too much travel time. Consequently he can complete
many more schedules than he can when a good sample is secured.

5. Can the interviewer select the informants? If so, he may choose
the most accessible so that he can complete more interviews. If a
good sample is to be obtained, controls or quotas are set which limit
the interviewer's tendency to select easy cases. For example, one
agency now requires the selection of informants by rent groups distributed over the entire area of assignment. Naturally this will take
much longer than would interviews concentrated in one district. If
quotas are assigned which require the interviewer to find people of
given economic, age, sex, and occupational groups, the task of locating
potential informants with the desired characteristics becomes extremely
time-consuming when the last few cases are needed to fill the quota.

6. How long is the schedule? If it requires four or five hours of the
informant's time, as did the schedule of family expenditures secured
by the Study of Consumer Purchases (1010), the interviewer has

difficulty in completing even one schedule per day on the average. The sheer mechanics of filling in and examining long schedules takes a great deal of time. Before handing in a schedule, the interviewer must examine it to see that the entries are properly made, all questionable items are explained in notes, and the schedule itself looks as if it would be acceptable to the editor. He has to spend time traveling to and from the office and the assignment area and from one address to another within that area, waiting for someone to answer the door, interviewing, writing up the interview, examining the schedules before turning them in, reviewing assignments at the office, securing supplies, consulting with the editors, and receiving further training, instructions, and schedules. Thus the interview itself may occupy only a fraction of the total time required for the interviewer's task.

The following figures on numbers of interviews are presented merely to give the surveyor a basis for estimating what he may expect with a city directory type of survey and a survey based on telephone interviews.

In 1940, the author participated in a trial study of the length of time required to ring every doorbell in a middle-class residential area in a midwestern city and secure answers to about ten census-type questions. The purpose of this canvass was to locate people of specified age, sex, marital, religious, and educational status. If the doorbell was not answered, an attempt was made to secure some of the information from neighbors, but no return calls were made. When a complete schedule was obtained from each informant, between 20 and 25 addresses could be visited per hour. About two hours of an eight-hour day were needed for examining the schedules before turning them in. Several city directory canvassers have corroborated the writer's experience. They report covering about 175 or 200 households per day. In heavily populated areas canvassers have secured data on 350 households a day, but this speed cannot be maintained in all sections of the city. These quick canvasses cannot be considered satisfactory for most purposes because return calls are usually necessary and thus the average rate would be considerably less than 20 per hour. As a matter of fact, the percentage of no-information schedules was much lower than is usual when one mailing of mail questionnaires is used. In the canvass described above it was possible to determine whether or not the person not seen was the type in which the survey was interested, for in all but about 5 percent of the cases the neighbors could give sufficient information on this point. Thus for this particular survey only a small number of return calls would have been necessary. These figures represent a more or less maximum rate for skimming the population and reaching the most accessible cases.

The U. S. census schedule included many more items than the foregoing survey and hence required more time. According to one report the average time was about eight minutes per interview. Except for call-backs the amount of travel time necessary for the census canvass is negligible compared with that required in most surveys.

Consumer market surveys have made estimates on the basis of their experiences. Louis Bader describes a study of the effectiveness of house-to-house canvassing in three suburban towns (20). Of the 581 persons interviewed, 381 took no more than five minutes to answer the 20 questions; 145 took no more than ten; 33 took from ten to fifteen minutes; and only 22 took over fifteen. He concluded that at least seven interviews could be held per hour, or 35 a day, even though the questionnaire was lengthy. This allows for practically no time getting from one address to the next.

Market surveyors have sometimes required about 20 consumer interviews a day from their investigators. If no restriction is placed on the sample of informants selected by interviewers it is not unusual for them to average about 24 a day. This rate is close to that found in public polls when interviewers select informants of the types specified in the assignment quota. The National Opinion Research Center advises its interviewers that two or three interviews per hour are usually obtained but when long distances are to be covered or when the interviewer is searching for the last two or three respondents needed to fill the quota it is difficult to average two. Three schedules per hour could be completed also by the enumerators in a rather detailed Real Property Inventory (1013). The survey and schedules were similar to those used in the U. S. Census of housing in 1940. A lower quota consisting of 1.25 schedules per hour was set in a substandard dwelling survey (1019) which entailed calling at addresses separated by some distance within the poorer areas of a city.

In a random sample survey consisting of every twentieth address in New Haven, Connecticut, interviewers averaged 7 completed schedules per day, thus closely approximating the quota set in the above substandard dwelling survey. The one-page schedule contained some twenty questions about each family member, in addition to an equal number about the household as a whole. This average of about one an hour is close to what can be expected if the sample extends over a city and the interviewer has no car, the interviewer must see an adult at a specified address, the schedule takes no longer on the average than 20 minutes to complete, the interviewer is given no new assignments until he has made several calls on individuals recorded as not at home, and only completed and acceptable schedules are counted (no credit being given for unproductive calls, incomplete schedules, or refusals).

If cars had been used, this average might have reached about 10 or even 12 schedules per day. The saving in travel time occurs not only on the original call but on every return call. While an average of one hour per schedule is low during the first few days of a survey when the most accessible people are located and interviewed, the rate usually drops rapidly as the survey proceeds, thus lowering the average.

An average of about 30 telephone interviews can be held per hour when only a few questions are asked and no return calls are made on originally busy signals, wrong numbers, and no answers. If call-backs are made in the latter cases, however, this rate is greatly reduced, probably by 75 per cent.

The Non-Supervisory Office Force. The non-supervisory office force should consist of (1) an assignment editor who gives the interviewers their assignments; (2) intake editors who examine the schedules turned in; (3) schedule editors and check editors; (4) clerks who code data and check the codes; (5) statistical clerks who sort, count, and tabulate the returns (if tabulation is done by hand; if it is done by machines in the survey office, card punchers, punch verifiers, and other machine operators will be needed); (6) statistical clerks who prepare the tables, calculations, graphs, charts, etc.; and (7) typists and stenographers. For every interviewer it would not be too much to have one office employee to check, process, and tabulate the data.

In large surveys as the field work lessens, it is usually advisable to transfer the few interviewers who have ability or experience in writing reports to work on tabulations and analyses. Their background of field work often enables them to make significant contributions to the analysis.

It is advisable for every survey to hire some typist-clerks because so many of the processes in a survey require typing. People whose training includes the use of calculating machines, draftsmanship, bookkeeping or accounting, filing, etc., are equally valuable. Tests on the various abilities required of survey personnel are available, but for most purposes a simple performance test is satisfactory.

The length of time required to check, edit, code, and tabulate the data from schedules varies greatly with the amount of information handled and the quality of work done by the field staff and expected of the office force.[2]

Clerks in the Real Property Inventories were expected to check 15 schedules per hour; editing was to proceed at the rate of 20 per hour, coding at 15 per hour, and hand tabulation at 4 per hour. Because editing was more complicated in the Substandard Dwelling survey, 8 schedules per hour was the average.

The abilities which make for a good interviewer are sometimes far different from those needed in a good office worker, and vice versa. Frequently survey directors are tempted to use the same staff for both functions, the employees spending one week in the field and the next week in the office. This appears feasible but is likely to be inefficient because of the difficulty of finding interviewers who are also qualified for routine office work. Furthermore, there is not the same opportunity to check the interviewers' work as there is when the editing is handled by a separate staff. Finally, the salary scale for clerical workers is usually much lower than that for interviewers, which makes using the field staff for office work relatively expensive.

Service Employees.   In addition to the staff who collect and process the schedules, it is often necessary to employ a supply clerk, a bookkeeper, a time clerk, a messenger boy, and a janitor, among others. Many survey plans fail to include these purely service or payroll employees.

Examples of Personnel Requirements.   The wide range of personnel required in a field survey may be gauged from the following list adapted from the one prepared by the U. S. Housing Authority for its "Plan for the Study of Housing of Low Income Families" (1019). This list was based on the assumption that the plans and instructions

---

[2] For a report on the time required to sort and count data coded on 3 × 5 cards, see pp. 463–464.

for the project had already been formulated by the headquarters staff in Washington and that the completed tables would be sent there for analysis and publication.

City director of the survey.
Regional supervisor in cities of 150,000 population or more. They are under the city director.
Office manager. He is responsible for the checkers, coders, and tabulators in the office.
Enumeration supervisor. He is in charge of enumeration and spot checking.
Squad leaders, usually one per 15,000 population. They have direct charge of all the enumerators in their squads and must master and be able to explain every detail of the survey.
Draftsman. He draws maps of the city and keeps a geographical check on the progress of the survey.
Enumerators. After enumeration is completed, the best-qualified interviewers are retained for coding and tabulation.
Spot checkers, sometimes called "check interviewers." Their duty is to reinterview a sample of the families already seen. They may be selected from the best-qualified enumerators, but they must never check their own interviews.
Clerks. They check, code, and file the forms as they are completed, prepare tabulations while the data are being collected, and later work on the final tabulations.
Stenographers, one for the city director and one for each regional supervisor.

If machine tabulation is to be used, machine tabulation supervisors, machine punch operators and verifiers, and tabulating machine operators will be required in addition to the above personnel.

The field organization for the 1940 census also illustrates the complexity of the problem (1001, p. 39).

To administer the census field activities, the United States, including its territories and possessions, was divided into three regions. Each region was administered by an Assistant to the Chief of the Field Division with headquarters in Washington. The three regions were divided into 105 areas, each area in charge of an area manager who had been trained in Washington.

The areas in turn were divided into districts, each district in charge of a supervisor. There were 532 of these districts in the United States. Each supervisor's district was divided into enumeration districts—the smallest field unit for census administration and the territory normally canvassed by one enumerator. This field organization, whereby the United States was divided into regions, areas, and districts, was an innovation of the 1940 census and provided a better control and quicker action on field problems than was possible under the field organization of previous censuses. Squad leaders were appointed in cities of 50,000 or more population in the ratio of about 1 to every 20 enumerators. At the peak of field activity there were 2464 squad leaders and 101,916 enumerators employed on the enumeration of the censuses of population, housing, and agriculture.

The following staff might be adequate to collect and tabulate data on census-type questions on employment and family composition for a random sample of 1000 households in a large city, for in such a small-scale survey several employees should be able to do more than one kind of work. This list is based on the assumption that the plans, instructions, and forms have been prepared and that office space and maintenance service are supplied, and that the survey is to be conducted and the tabulations prepared within one month. If a detailed analysis and written report were called for, this would require several of the workers for at least another month.

1 director
1 assistant director
7 interviewers (with cars)
1 check interviewer
1 rooming house and hotel interviewer
1 intake and assignment editor
2 editor-coders
2 check editor—code checkers
1 sampling assistant
1 statistical clerk
2 typists or stenographers

TRAINING THE PERSONNEL:[3]

In order to have his organization running smoothly as quickly as possible, the survey director should see that the employees are started correctly. Definite information on what is expected of them and on

[3] A detailed discussion of the instructions to interviewers, editors, and coders is presented in later chapters.

the general policy with respect to the work routine—hours of work, overtime, absences, method of payment, lunch period, vacations, holidays, tardiness, phone calls on office time, chatting in the office, etc.—will do a great deal toward this end.

The importance of written instructions has already been pointed out (page 126). These instructions should also include a statement regarding what production records are required and how and when they are to be filled out. Every worker should have access to the manual of instructions on survey procedures as a whole and he should be given a copy of the instructions concerning his own work. The importance of knowing these instructions should be emphasized. Periodic tests will do much to insure uniformity in interpretation and to avoid errors arising from lack of familiarity with instructions and their revisions.

The confidential nature of the data secured should also be stressed. If the good will of those who cooperate with the survey is to be maintained, respect for the confidential nature of the data given the survey must be guaranteed. When employees leave their jobs they must be required to turn in all the material they have received from the survey. Occasionally confidential material has fallen into the hands of newspaper reporters and been published.

Cost Estimates

Basic to the efficient conduct of a survey is the detailed budgeting of funds to cover expenses for labor and nonlabor items. Unfortunately, it is impossible to set up close estimates which can be used as "standards" for future surveys. The cost of the survey varies with the thoroughness with which plans are developed and executed, with current wage rates, with the techniques used in collecting data, with the type and amount of information collected, and with the editing, tabulation, analysis, and publication plans, as well as with nonlabor expenses. However, lists of expense items frequently encountered in surveys and some examples of costs drawn from the literature which are presented below should give the survey director some basis, admittedly inadequate, for preparing cost estimates. In many surveys certain overhead expenses and supervisory services are paid by the sponsor or by groups who expect to utilize the findings. In such cases the survey director and the contributor should have a definite understanding on what is to be covered—the length of time borrowed material will be available, the amount of supplies, the minimum number of hours of work that will be contributed, etc. Carelessness here may result in unanticipated expenses.

NONLABOR COSTS:

Nonlabor costs include the cost of office space, equipment, and supplies. One of the major items of expenditure when office space is not contributed is rent. The office should be centrally located and should provide good working conditions—adequate light and ventilation, cloakroom and sanitary facilities, and quiet. The size and arrangement of the space are also important. The office should be large enough to accommodate both the field and the office forces because the interviewers are in the office frequently. A private office should be available for staff conferences and interviews with the public, and there should be some space that will offer privacy, and hence better thinking, when instructions and reports are being written.

In addition to rent, the budget must include funds for heat and for electricity for both light and machinery. Buying or renting furniture and equipment is another drain on the budget. Desks, tables, chairs, filing cabinets, and certain machines and appliances must be provided. Even relatively small surveys require several typewriters and occasionally a dictaphone. Larger surveys need such equipment as mimeographing machines for duplicating instructions and forms. One or two calculating machines and a listing machine are usually essential. If tabulations· are to be done by machine in the survey· office, several tabulating machines must be rented. Surveys require a wide assortment of office supplies—correspondence paper and envelopes, typewriter, carbon, and scratch paper; ruled and graph paper; plain and colored pencils; erasers, ink, glue, and notebooks; manila folders and folders in which schedules can be carried; paper clips, stapling machines, and rubber stamps; rulers and scissors; white and colored index cards; a bulletin board, maps, and drafting instruments. The cost of postage stamps must be provided for in surveys that are conducted by mail. Telephone surveys may involve special charges for the use of commercial telephones or for obtaining an alphabetical list of the names and addresses of subscribers. Charges for city directories or other similar sources used in sampling should also be included in the budget. The cost of printing the schedules for the survey should be provided for. Other special costs may include tabulations or graphs or charts prepared by commercial agencies. The cost of printing and distributing the final report of the survey may also have to be included in the budget.

Labor costs include the salaries of the entire personnel, as well as traveling expenses. The office staff must be organized long in advance of the field staff and its work continues after that of the field force is completed. The number and kind of workers required depend on the size and type of survey and the speed with which the report must be completed. Since salaries for white-collar workers vary in different sections of the country, and within some communities at different seasons of the year, the survey director should familiarize himself with current salary and employment conditions in the community before setting up his cost estimates.

Because of these salary-scale variations the number of man-hours of work have proved the most useful basis for estimating, particularly in the case of nonsupervisory workers. It is hoped that, as interest in scientific social surveys develops, more information on the length of time required for the various operations in a survey will be accumulated and made available.

If the city has good public transportation facilities it may be cheaper to require the interviewer to use such facilities rather than his own car. This has to be worked out for each community.

Traveling expenses are a large item in field surveys. The personal investigator must be paid for his transportation; if he uses his own car, he should receive a mileage payment. If he uses a bus or street car, it is customary to reimburse him for all fares except to his first interview and from his last at night. Also, rural interviewing or surveying in a community at some distance from the residence of the interviewer may require payment for overnight expenses such as hotel rooms, meals, telephone calls, or postage. In regional or national surveys, railroad fares or per diem payments to supervisory staff members who have to travel extensively may be a considerable item. Conference expenses may come under this category.

Before any decision is made on the payment of interviewers, the relative merits of a per schedule, per hour, or per diem basis should be carefully considered. The Bureau of the Census has found payment per schedule the most satisfactory because enumerators have to make their calls when there is a chance of finding people at home. This means many evening calls in the apartment house districts in larger cities where so many people work during the day. Thus an enumerator who makes a conscientious effort to find families at home will have very irregular hours of work and it will be difficult to pay him on an hourly basis. Payment per schedule has the disadvantage of stimulating hasty or inaccurate work, or the making of false returns; it tends to penalize the more careful, conscientious workers. But any adequately planned large-scale survey should have a system of checking that will locate the people who are faking or carelessly filling in the schedules.

While the survey director should not increase the cost of the survey by paying higher salaries than necessary, he must bear in mind that there is small economy in hiring low-grade workers for little money and in having the high labor turnover that usually results when the survey offers only slight financial inducements to remain with it. The cost of errors and of training new workers soon offsets the money saved from low salaries.

No satisfactory salary scale has been set up for interviewers because the labor market as well as work standards are so variable. One scale which has been adopted in several surveys calls for the field interviewers to receive about double the salary paid to typists. In surveys requiring special technical knowledge the rates should be somewhat higher than those in the interviewers' regular field of work.

SOME EXAMPLES OF SURVEY COSTS:

The cost estimates that are available are usually not comparable because some of them include only the enumerators' salaries, and others are expressed in terms of the cost per schedule. In the latter, the total expense of the survey—from the preliminary planning to the publication of the report—is divided by the number of completed schedules obtained.

In 1940, the Bureau of the Census paid its enumerators four cents per individual interviewed for the population information. In addition, it paid eight cents for the housing schedule, two cents for the infant card, and six cents for the housing vacancy schedule. At certain addresses the enumerator filled out more than one of these forms, thus increasing his earnings above the average of twelve cents per family (of three persons) for the population schedule. The rate of pay per schedule was also adjusted to take into account the density of population, or the distance between addresses. For the farm schedule, for example, enumerators received twenty-five cents. In 1940, the year of the census, $26,900,000 was appropriated for the expenses of the census and an additional $17,850,000 was appropriated for the fiscal year ending June 30, 1941. Census reports were received for more than 131 million individuals, 6 million farms, 3 million places of business, 180,-000 factories, and 30,000 mines and oil wells. The expenditures during the first two years of this census covered planning and enumeration primarily.

In 1947 several city directories in New England towns were paying interviewers 2 to 4 cents per household. It was not always necessary for the interviewer to contact the householder because the information obtained from neighbors often proved adequate for filling out the card. High school boys who were making the canvass reported that they could do as many as 360 households a day but that they actually averaged about 200. Approximately two hours a day were used for checking entries on the cards. Although 2 cents proved sufficient for the initial skimming of the population, the total cost per household amounted to 4 cents according to one directory owner. The call-backs made it necessary to double the original cost estimate.

In a much smaller survey (446) of a random sample of 2097 families in New Haven, Connecticut, in May to June, 1931, in which the questions covered both sides of a one-page schedule, it cost an average of about 50 cents per schedule for collection and first edit. This did not include the rent for office space and equipment or the salary of the director, the supervisor, and two assistants. It did, however, include the salaries of field workers and typists and the costs of printed schedule forms, paper, pencils, and other supplies, as well as carfare and automobile transportation. The cost of editing and machine tabulating the data for about 3000 gainful workers in this sample amounted to about $685.00, distributed as follows:

Punching and verifying operators	25.6%
Rent of key punches and vertical files	5.0
Sorting and counting operators	15.0
Rent of counter-sorter	21.1
Clerical work	23.5
Preparation of tables	6.7
Hollerith cards	2.1
Paper	1.0
	100.0%

The budget of one survey which required extremely skilled enumerators and several hours per schedule allowed $25 for collecting and editing each completed schedule.

In 1945 the National Opinion Research Center reported that its interviewers averaged between $30 and $40 per month for about 50 hours work—or between 75 and 80 cents an hour. In 1948 several national polling agencies paid interviewers who worked part time at an hourly rate of 85 cents. Snead (892) stated that some market research organizations paid from $5 to $7 a day in 1941. Others paid by the number of interviews in the assignment. Such agencies have paid from 10 cents to five dollars for consumer interviews (115).

Hancock (392) studied the following methods of surveying attitudes toward retail stores:

1. A questionnaire was mailed out, together with a letter explaining the purpose of the study and giving instructions on how to fill in the form.
2. The mailed questionnaire was accompanied by twenty-five cents to reimburse the informant for filling out the questionnaire.
3. The mailed questionnaire was accompanied by a promise that twenty-five cents would be paid on receipt of the completed schedule.
4. Two investigators personally interviewed informants and recorded their answers.

He secured about 1500 usable returns—or 375 from each method—at a cost of $1315 (excluding the salary of the two interviewers). This cost was divided as follows:

Transportation of two interviewers (from one community to another and within each community) . . . .$	288.33
Twenty-five cent pieces used as inducements	253.00
Rental of cars	148.25
Clerical help	286.47
Stamps and supplies	339.31
	$1315.36

Hancock estimates the cost per usable schedule obtained by each method (excluding clerical labor and the interviewers' salary) as $1.22, $0.79, $1.06, and $0.74 respectively. No study was made of the cost had follow-up letters and other devices been employed to secure an unbiased sample with each method. Undoubtedly the cost of each of the mail techniques at least would have been considerably higher because the number of usable returns was so low in comparison with the return from the personal interviews. The returns in percentage were as follows: 9.56, 47.2, 17.6, and 85.5 respectively.[4]

Filing and Storing Data

The filing and control system used in a survey should be so planned that there will be practically no danger of losing the data once it is collected. Fireproof files for the original schedules safeguards them against one type of loss. In large-scale surveys it may be wise to carry fire and burglary insurance. Although such insurance could not restore the lost data, it might partially offset the cost of repeating the survey. Material sent through the mails should be insured or registered, and whenever possible duplicates should be prepared and filed in the office.

Insistence that all schedules be in the files at the close of each day will do much toward preventing the loss or misplacement of schedules. Whenever individual or blocks of schedules are in temporary use, a signed receipt for them should be placed in the files.

The disposal and storage of the material when the survey terminates also deserves consideration. Since the original schedules are often required for additional tabulations or for checking purposes, they should be readily available until this period of usefulness is over. If the agency sponsoring the survey has no filing or storage space available, it may be possible to file these records in the city hall, public library, university library, university social research division, or some similar place. If anonymity has been assured informants, the survey director must make sure that when the survey terminates the individual schedules cannot be identified except by responsible persons who will respect the guarantee to the informants. One procedure is to block out the respondent's name and address before storing the schedules. It may be desirable to prepare a code list by which the individual schedules

---

[4] Hancock expresses doubt as to the advisability of using the interview technique in other surveys of this topic because the results differed so much from those obtained by the three mail techniques. A more likely explanation of the discrepancy in findings is that the sample of respondents to the mail surveys were much less representative of the total population surveyed than were the interviewed respondents, and their reactions were correspondingly different or less representative.

might be identified again for use in other scientific studies; the list could be kept by some responsible agent.

Selected References

Personnel Supervision and Administration

American Marketing Assn. (8), Bader (18, 19, 20), Bennett (45), Bevis (60), Blankenship (77, 78), Blankenship et al. (82), Borg (94), Brown (115), Cantril (142), Cooper (193), Copeland (194), Cornell (199), Crespi (207, 208), Davis (230), Deming (239), Deming and Geoffrey (240), Deming et al. (244), Eckler (271), Elinsen and Cisin (283), Guest (382), Hancock (392), Harris and Connelly (409), Huey (460), Katz (495), Maccoby and Holt (605), Manheimer and Hyman (614), McPeak (633), Neuner and Haynes (685), Niles (698), Psychological Corp. (751), Radvanyi (757), Richards and Rubin (776), Robinson (792), Snead (892), Thomson (959), U.S. (1001, 1013, 1019), Whitney (1088).

See books on social surveys, market research, and research methods.

CHAPTER VI

Construction of the Schedule
or Questionnaire[1]

After looking at the lengthy, comprehensive questionnaire sent out under the Selective Service Act, a young farmer scrawled across the first page, "I am ready when you want me," and returned it. How many questionnaires other than those backed by the law have been disregarded because they "looked too complicated or too long" will never be known. But this much surveyors do know—careful planning of the physical design of the schedule and careful selection and phrasing of the questions will affect not only the number of returns but also the meaning and the accuracy of the findings.

Several considerations should be borne in mind when the schedule or questionnaire is being designed. The most important are:

1. Who will make the entries on the schedule? If a highly trained investigator will ask the questions and enter the replies, the form should be different from one drawn up for the informant to fill out, for the interviewer can be instructed regarding details which will insure uniform definitions, entries, and interpretations.[2] Hence the exact wording of the questions is secondary to their "underlying meaning." In large-scale surveys, however, interviewers are frequently no better pre-

---

[1] The terms "questionnaire" and "schedule" are used synonymously in this book because this seems to be the current practice among research workers. A technical distinction is sometimes made, however. The term "questionnaire" applies to forms distributed through the mails or given to informants to be filled out without the assistance or supervision of the interviewer; a "schedule" is the form carried and filled out by the investigator or filled out in his presence.

[2] Sometimes in ascertaining public opinion no latitude is given interviewers; the exact wording on the schedule is repeated to insure comparability of responses.

pared than the informants. Schedules to be used by such relatively untrained enumerators should be drafted very carefully.

The terminology and questions should be adapted to the type of people who will give the information. For example, a questionnaire addressed to specialists familiar with the subject matter of the survey can be much more technical than one directed to a cross-section of the population. Public opinion surveyors have come to realize that the vocabulary and interests of the "man in the street" are quite unlike those of the survey designers. In designing schedules that are to be filled out by farmers, housewives, employers, or any other group, the level of education, the biases, and the interests or other characteristics which affect the ability and desire to fill in the form truthfully and correctly should be taken into consideration.

2. Does the physical appearance of the schedule affect the coopera-tion the survey receives? In surveys by mail, there is no doubt that an attractive looking questionnaire is a selling point for cooperation. Con-versely, an unattractive one may cause the recipient to put it aside or throw it in the wastebasket.

Attractiveness of the record blank is not an essential feature if the interviewer enters the data. The fact that the form looks "short," how-ever, often contributes to securing the individual's consent to be inter-viewed. Informants will tolerate a short interruption if only to get rid of the interviewer, but they may flatly refuse to answer a long list of questions.

3. How are the questions to be worded? If the respondent sees or hears each question exactly as it appears on the schedule, the choice of words is much more important than if the questions serve only as reminders to the interviewer. If the investigator is permitted to adapt the question to the respondent's educational level or other character-istics, it is more essential that he grasp the spirit of the question than its precise wording. One common procedure in field investigations is for the interviewer to read the questions as they are given on the schedule and to explain in his own words those that are not clear to the respondent. In public opinion surveys, however, explanations usu-ally are not permissible. The interviewer repeats the original question instead of varying the phraseology.

4. Is the sequence of questions on the schedule to be followed ex-actly? For investigating attitudes in particular, it may be important for

certain questions to follow certain others so that the proper "set" will be developed. In this case, special attention must be given to the sequence of the items.

5. How many questions are to appear on the form? If there are only a few, their arrangement on the schedule will not require the detailed planning necessary when a great amount of material must be condensed in a very limited space.

6. Is the purpose of the questions to ascertain facts, test the knowledge of the informant, or discover his beliefs, opinions, or attitudes? If attitudes are desired, for example, care must be taken to see that the questions do not bring out only points of fact. Two persons who may agree on the facts may have entirely different attitudes about them. Various problems of attitude measurement must be considered when questions to reveal people's attitudes or opinions are being framed. This is discussed later in this chapter.

7. Is the schedule to be used in future or periodic surveys? If so, the questions should be designed with a view to the uniformity and comparability of results.

8. What manipulation and processing by the office staff will the schedules receive after the field collection is completed? When designing the form and wording the questions, the surveyor should keep in mind the study as a whole. He should consider such questions as the following: Are the schedules to be precoded (code symbols printed on the form) or is coding to be a separate operation? Will a transcription sheet or code card be used or will the codes be placed on the original schedule? Will the tabulation be made directly from the schedules or will the data be put on code or punch cards which will be sorted and counted?

The Physical Form of the Schedule

SIZE:

Although the size of the schedule depends to some extent upon the scope of the survey and the number of items to be included, the designers of the schedule can take advantage of certain devices to bring it to the desired size. The fundamental question therefore is, "What size schedule is preferable?" This can best be answered by considering the advantages and disadvantages of various sizes. If the schedules are small they can be carried in a purse or coat pocket and brought out only after the doorbell has been answered. If the questions can be put on a 4 x 6 or 3 x 5 card, the sorting, counting, filing, checking, etc., in the office is facilitated. Moreover, it is easy for the interviewer to write on small cards while holding them in his hand.

Standard letter-size schedules 8½ x 11 inches have been widely used, however, and have not been found too objectionable by field workers, especially if they can be folded while being carried. Some investigators object to carrying a large folder because they may be mistaken for magazine salesmen. From the interviewer's point of view, the schedule should not be too cumbersome. One disadvantage is that this size is too large to be sorted and tabulated easily if this is done by hand; but if the data are to be transcribed to a code or punch card, size is no consideration. Furthermore, this size fits standard file cabinets.

Whatever size is adopted, it is best to use only one side of the schedule form, the reverse being left blank for special notations by the interviewer. If both sides are to be filled out, this makes such processes as filing and sorting the schedules difficult.

The Bureau of the Census uses a sheet 16 x 23 inches which allows data for 40 individuals to be recorded on each side. This size has a number of limitations. It is extremely difficult for the enumerator to fill it in unless he can sit at a table or desk. The handling and filing of such large schedules in the office is also difficult. The Bureau has had to design special bindings for these sheets.

Short questionnaires sent through the mail can be printed on post cards. A double post card, of which the questionnaire half is to be torn off and returned, has been used extensively in market surveys. Return post cards, sealed in envelopes and sent first class, are also used. Experimental findings do not seem to favor either method over the other.

Mail questionnaires should be large enough to provide adequate space for comments if such supplementary material is desired. There is apparently a definite relation between the amount of space and the amount of comment. A camera company at the Chicago World's Fair distributed a questionnaire regarding photographic interests. At the end of the blank there was a relatively large or a relatively small space in which the respondent was asked to add any comments he felt were important. Returns were received from more than 20,000 people; 8 per cent of the forms with less space and 13 per cent of those with more space contained comments (8, p. 88).

Charts, diagrams, and pictorial material have been introduced in mail questionnaires to create interest on the part of the recipient, but such material usually requires considerable space. In order to avoid too large a schedule, a booklet may be used. Much of the customer research done by a large automobile concern is conducted by means of a 5 x 8 inch booklet. A booklet may bring in more returns than a large schedule chart, but processing the data from booklets is awkward and time-consuming. For efficient processing it is almost essential that the information be transcribed to a form better adapted to office procedures.

QUALITY AND COLOR OF PAPER:

The quality of paper for the schedule depends primarily on how the schedule is to be duplicated, but several other factors are also worth considering. The schedule is handled a great deal after it reaches the office; therefore the paper should be durable. If feasible, card schedules should be stiff enough to facilitate filing. If sorting and counting are to be done by hand, a strong flexible card with a smooth surface is desirable. Since entries should be made in ink whenever possible, the paper should take ink without blotting, unless investigators and office staff are supplied with pens which do not blot on any surface.

The less conspicuous the schedule, the less likely interviewers are to encounter people who object to giving information. Hence ordinary white and light-colored schedules are preferable from the collection point of view. Furthermore, printing and writing show up better against a light background. If several types of schedules are to be used, different colored forms will prevent their being confused in either the field or the office. The colors should be light tints (high in lightness and low in saturation) to favor legibility.

When planning mail questionnaires, it may be desirable to use a color which will attract the recipient's attention. However, before a color is selected, pretests to determine its effectiveness may well be made. In certain marketing studies yellow paper was found to have the highest percentage of returns and pink followed closely, but dark colors were not effective. When several questionnaires are sent out in sequence, alternation of lighter colors apparently elicits more returns than a single color (266, p. 290).

THE ARRANGEMENT OF ITEMS ON THE SCHEDULE:

It is important to avoid a complicated or cluttered-looking schedule. The interviewer or the respondent to a mail questionnaire should be able to tell at a glance whether or not all questions are answered. He can do so if spacing, indentation, underlining, vertical lines, numbering, and variations in type are used appropriately in setting up the schedule. Questions which belong together should be easily distinguished. When a question is dependent upon the answer to the preceding one it should be given a subordinate place. By paying attention to the appearance of the schedule the surveyor will avoid many errors and will insure a greater percentage of usable returns than would be obtained from a poorly arranged questionnaire.

THE NUMBER OF SCHEDULES AND THE METHOD OF
REPRODUCTION:

The decision as to the number of schedules to be printed should take into account the fact that, in field studies, about one-third of the forms are usually wasted or consumed for purposes other than scheduling. Schedules are used for training investigators during the early stages of the survey; interviewers may have to copy some of the less legible schedules before handing them in; the wrong individuals may have been interviewed; some cases may require two schedules; requests for samples of the form will be received from research organizations and others interested in the survey; and some schedules will be lost. Therefore it is cheaper in the long run to have many more printed than will be required for the actual enumerations.

The method of reproduction depends chiefly on the number of schedules desired. "As one proceeds from a few dozen copies to many thousands of copies, typing, mimeographing, multigraphing, reproprinting, and printing become successively available as economic methods of reproducing the questionnaire" (266, p. 290).

The Three Kinds of Schedule Items

The information included on the schedule may be classified under three headings: (1) *Identifying information*. This insures that the schedule will not be mislaid, lost, or duplicated; that the information on it pertains to the particular sample case; and that the interviewer and informant can be identified. (2) *Social background or census-type factual data.* This information about the respondent provides the variables by which the survey data are to be classified and also the bases for evaluating the sample. (3) *Questions on the subject of the survey.* These questions may be directed toward obtaining more or less objective facts or toward revealing attitudes and opinions on matters of current interest.

SCHEDULE ITEMS FOR IDENTIFYING INFORMATION:

At almost every stage in the survey from the selection of the sample to the analysis of the results, questions of omission, duplication, and accuracy make it imperative to locate certain schedules, to check the entries made by the interviewer or the information given by the respondent, or to check the processing of the schedule in the office. Although the amount of identifying data required varies from survey to survey, the following are frequently useful, especially in surveys conducted through personal interviews.

1. Schedule, Case, or Sample Number. This number is usually placed in the upper right corner of the card or schedule so that it can be easily located. In sample surveys, the person drawing the sample should assign this number to each case in straight numerical order. It may be desirable later to code the schedule with another number to indicate certain characteristics of the case, but considerable confusion and duplication will be prevented if the original serial numbering of schedules remains unaltered throughout the course of the survey.

2. Cross-Reference Schedule Number. If more than one type of schedule is to be secured from certain cases or if completed schedules are to be given numbers different from the original serial numbers, the schedule should contain space for a cross-reference number. This number may not be filled in until the field work and editing are completed, but it becomes important for locating individual cases or blocks of schedules which require special attention whenever a second system of numbering is adopted.

3. Name of Survey. Except when it is desirable to conceal the purpose of the survey,[3] the title of the survey should be stamped or printed on the schedule form. Many informants glance at the form

---

[3] In some market surveys even the interviewer is not told the name of the brand whose popularity is being investigated or the name of the concern sponsoring the survey. It is felt that answers will be secured more impartially if this anonymity is maintained.

while the interviewer is filling it out; some ask to see it before they agree to be interviewed. Hence in selecting the name of the survey, the importance of the wording of the title in determining cooperation should be kept in mind. If a survey organization is to conduct several studies simultaneously or over a short period of time, the survey designer should see that the title is sufficiently differentiating to avoid confusion with the other surveys.

4. Title of Schedules. If more than one type of schedule is to be employed during the survey, it is important that each be given a title in addition to a form number. This prevents confusion in both field and office work.

5. Name of Agency Sponsoring Survey. It is usually desirable for the name of the sponsoring agency to appear on the schedule. If the agency is well regarded in the community, its name on the schedule serves as a guarantee to informants that the data will not be misused, that it is a legitimate cause, and that the informant's confidence will be respected. Although most people do not question the purpose of a survey, the few who do may cease to be suspicious if they see that a reliable agency is sponsoring it. If a significant portion of the community to be surveyed feels antagonistic toward the agency, it may be advisable to omit its name from the schedule. Many of the middle-class and poorer residents in one college community, for example, felt that the privately endowed college in their midst was not carrying its burden of the taxes; consequently the mere mention of its name was sufficient to create a feeling of resentment toward it and all its undertakings. In most cases, however, universities or educational institutions rate very high in their communities and sponsorship of surveys by them produces excellent cooperation.

6. Name of Individual or Family Interviewed. In field studies in which the sample is drawn from a city directory, the name of the occupant at the address to be visited is transcribed from the directory to the schedule by the sampling clerk. If the sample consists of dwelling units and the interviewer finds that the name in the directory is incorrect, he may be asked to cross out the original name and to insert that of the new occupants. Having the exact name of the family or individual appear on the schedule facilitates the work of the check interviewer, for he must know whom to ask for when he calls. When apartments in multiple-family dwellings are not numbered, often the only clue to whether an apartment belongs in the sample is the name of the occupant listed in the city directory. The inclusion of names serves an even more important purpose, for it makes possible the collection of information about the individual from other records, both public and private.

In a great many surveys, particularly public opinion polls and those using mailed questionnaires, the fact that the informant is asked his name may make him more cautious than he would be if his replies were to remain anonymous. In an address sample, the length of time the informant has resided at that address may be substituted for his name and only those families that have moved in since the enumeration for the city directory need be asked for their names. Interviewers can ask for an interviewee's name near the end of their call after they have gained his confidence. If many people are reluctant to supply this information, the investigators may keep a separate record book for these names and schedule numbers, telling these informants that their names will not appear on the schedule but will be used only as proof that the interview took place. Some informants are greatly impressed by the care and checks necessary to assure accuracy.

The name problem is not so easily solved in the case of mailed questionnaires. Usually surveyors use some device such as a code number which enables them to identify the schedule received from each respondent. Evidence suggests that for most survey topics asking for the informants' signature does not affect returns greatly.

7. **Sex of Informant or of Family Members.** This item can be secured without asking questions if recorded for the informant only.

8. **Relationship of Informant to Family Head.** The member of the family interviewed may have a bearing on the type or amount of information secured. Schedule editors may find, for example, that the person interviewed could not be expected to know the facts called for on the schedule and that another interview with some other member of the family is necessary. Knowledge of the identity of the informant is particularly useful to check interviewers, for they need to know who was seen during the first interview. If the person first interviewed refuses to cooperate, it may be desirable for the second investigator to interview a different member of the family.

9. **Address of Sample Case.** The exact address of the respondent should be recorded if check interviewing is to be done efficiently. The

record of the location of the dwelling unit within the building should include the apartment number, or such terms as rear, front, side, alley, upper, or lower.

When a dwelling unit sample is not used, it is difficult to devise means of identifying informants for check interviewing. One public opinion poll does not record the name and address of the informant but notes only the street on which he lives. Although check interviews with the original informants are thus impossible, comparisons of findings with those secured for other people in the same neighborhood will give some indication of the reliability of the work done by a given interviewer.

In national surveys the name of the place and the state should be on each schedule. Sometimes also the size-group of the community is recorded by the interviewer or stamped on the schedule by the local office staff. In rural surveys the township or county as well as the classification rural-farm, rural-nonfarm should be designated.[4]

10. District in Which Address Is Located. The number of the census enumeration district, ward, block, or some other geographic unit should appear on the schedule. This district number is utilized throughout the survey. Classification of addresses by districts enables the assignment clerk to assign interviewers efficiently. Refusals should be checked constantly by districts so that economic or other biases can be detected. If the city surveyed is a Census Tract or Block city, published data are available on the population characteristics of enumeration districts or blocks, and the representativeness of the sample may be thus checked (see page 66). If block sampling is used, the block or block section should be prominently placed on the schedule.

11. Place of Interview. When the interview takes place on a street corner, in a place of business, in a department store, in front of a theater, in a park, etc., a record of the type of place should appear on the schedule as a check on the representativeness of the informants enumerated and of the conditions which could influence the responses. Although samples selected in this manner are of doubtful scientific

---

[4] Rural farm refers to all persons who live on farms regardless of their own particular occupation. A farm by census definition consists of three or more acres or an area which produces at least $250 worth of produce annually. Rural-nonfarm residents are those living within the limits of a town of less than 2500 population and who do not live on farms.

value, the more information obtained about the process of selection, the better the evaluation of the sample.

12. Telephone Possession and Numbers. Opinion surveyors have found that telephone possession is associated with other economic factors so they ask, "Do you have a telephone in your home?" (Not a pay phone.) If the answer is yes, "Is it listed either in your name or in your family's name?" In telephone interviews the informant's telephone number should appear on the schedule. This number is also useful for panel surveys when the informant is interviewed periodically. Surveys of the general population have shown that about one-third or more of the informants have no telephone. If the telephone numbers of the others are secured, staff members may save time in making appointments to interview specific members of the family and in checking one or two items to test the accuracy of the initial investigator.

13. Interviewer's Name or Initials. The inclusion of the interviewer's name or initials on the schedule simplifies the task of locating him in case questions arise concerning his schedule entries. Furthermore, if any interviewer's work is found to be unsatisfactory, all the schedules bearing his name can be easily identified and check interviews held. To avoid confusion in large-scale studies the entire name should be entered rather than the initials.

14. Date and Time of Interview. When the date and time the interview started appear on the schedule, such information serves as a measure of production and also aids check interviewers to choose a time for their calls. The date and time of interview are also significant from the methodological point of view because they throw light on the problem of finding different individuals at home.

The date of the interview is especially important if the survey extends over a long period. In such cases, a tabulation by date of interview is usually made to determine whether any significant trend has occurred during the survey.

If several calls at an address may be required before the desired informant is seen, space should be left on the schedule for recording the date and hour of each call. A circle may be drawn around the date and hour of the call that was successful.

15. Monthly Rent of Rented Dwellings or Rental Value of Owned Home. The monthly rent or rent estimation of each dwelling unit in the sample is exceedingly useful in connection with interviewer assignments and for detecting economic biases in the samples. When housing is in adequate supply rent tends to be a function of income and thus it provides an indirect measure of the economic status of each case in the sample. Interviewers should estimate the rent if an informant refuses to give this information. Field agents who know the actual scale of rents in a given neighborhood can usually estimate the rent of a given dwelling very closely. An analysis of refusals or of people not interviewed, in terms of rent, often reveals significant sampling biases which must be overcome or adjusted in the tabulation.[5]

16. **Cooperation of the Informant.** It is usually helpful for check interviewers to have some idea of the cooperation to be expected on their assignments. The first interviewer's rating of informants' attitudes serves this purpose. If the difficult cases are assigned to the most skillful check interviewers, refusals may be avoided. A city editor of a metropolitan newspaper remarked that he always sent a woman reporter to get stories from men who were allergic to reporters and conversely sent men reporters to secure information from women. Even telephone calls of complaint were handled on a sex basis. In panel studies it is especially important to flag potential problem cases. In one such study the word "special" in the space for cooperation indicated that further information would be found in the special problem file. The schedules in this file included such information as the name of the most cooperative member of the family, the methods of approach which had been found most effective, the situations which had caused difficulties, and particular "peeves" and "likes" of the informant. Interviewers were instructed to look up the material in this file before calling on these people.

17. **Notes as to the Confidential Treatment of Returns.** Although this is not identifying information, a statement to the effect that the information received will not be disclosed in any form which will identify the individual is usually placed near the identifying items. Such statements as the following have proved satisfactory: "Information given will be used for statistical purpose only. The confidence of the informant will be respected."

If the informant sees such a statement on the schedule, it will do much to set his mind at ease about giving information regarding his personal life or opinions on which he does not wish to be quoted.

[5] See pp. 372, 413–417, 483–484 for further discussion of this point.

SCHEDULE ITEMS FOR SOCIAL BACKGROUND OR CENSUS-
TYPE FACTUAL DATA:

Regardless of the type or purpose of the survey, a few basic facts about the informant must be secured. These data are essential to the evaluation of the sample and the interpretation of the results. If this information is comparable to the census or other standard and recent data for the population in the area covered by the survey, the extent to which the sample is a cross-section of the total population can be determined. For this reason it is important to use definitions and groupings which are comparable to those used in the census or other complete canvasses. In some communities, statistical background data are available from school records, from the records of social agencies, or from "stock-taking inventories" of the population. If these "inventories" cover an up-to-date and tested cross-section of the population, the information from them may be more useful than a census of an earlier date.[6]

Among the data that are available and have proved to be highly correlated with most social phenomena are the following:[7]

1. **Age (Last Birthday) of Head of Family and Family Members.** For some purposes the date of birth may be preferable to age, but if the age is needed for tabulation purposes, the original entry should include the age. If age groups are used for classifying informants, they should be carefully selected in advance; such overlapping categories as 10–15 and 15–20 should be avoided because an individual 15 years of age can be classified in either one. Moreover, the age groups selected should be comparable to the census or other statistics for the entire population.

2. **Country of Birth of Family Head.** This item was formerly extremely important in surveys in this country, but owing to the small amount of immigration since World War I, the number of foreign-born is not large enough in most communities to warrant space for this entry on the schedule. In some surveys, however, information regarding the national background of parents and grandparents may be of

---

[6] In addition to the federal, state, and local censuses, such national surveys as those discussed in Chapter I have collected considerable information on many communities.

[7] The chapter on coding suggests definitions and subcategories to be used in defining and recording this type of information.

considerable significance. For example, attitudes and opinions regarding the international situation, economic philosophies, our participation in World War II and our post-war activities are probably strongly influenced by this factor. The recent rapid changes in the status and national affiliations of many European countries have made it difficult to secure accurate and consistent information on questions relating to nationality. Some surveyors have found the language spoken in the home a better indicator of national ties.

3. **Marital Status.** For most purposes it is sufficient to use the categories: Married, Single, Other (widowed, divorced, separated, etc.)

4. **Education.** There are times when education is a better measure of socio-economic status than is rent or income. During periods of housing shortages and instability in economic conditions, many families are found in rental or in income groups which are not "normal" for them. Their tastes and opinions may be undergoing rapid changes also, or they still may be unlike those held by groups who have been in those classes longer. "Highest school grade completed" may be printed on the questionnaire. Night school courses, business college courses, correspondence schools are not regarded as formal schooling. One polling agency has found it advisable to precede the education question with "Do you remember the name of the last school you went to?" Then "What was the last grade (or year) you completed in that school?" This first question avoids the tendency of the informant to exaggerate his educational attainment. It is not printed on the schedule but is included in the instructions to interviewers.

5. **Religion.** Religion is seldom included among the items of basic information. One reason is that some surveyors fear that people resent being questioned on this topic. The New Haven Survey described earlier included this item and did not encounter the expected resentment. The limited uses made of information on religion may be a better reason for omitting this item. If religion is regarded as a significant variable, questions may consist of two parts: (a) "How often do you go to church or religious services (number of times per week ..... month ..... year ..... 5 years ......) and (b) What denomination do you consider yourself?" (**675**, p. 119.) The Census of Religious Bodies contains membership information which may be used in conjunction with the survey data on this topic. Recent figures

from national polls and surveys would perhaps be better, however, because the census is out of date. The information collected by air raid wardens during the household inventory in the spring of 1942 included a question on the religion of each family member.

Intensity of religious feeling probably has a more important bearing on other social phenomena than does denominational affiliation; hence detailed figures on specific sects are of comparatively little value in interpreting survey results. On the other hand, broad categories such as Protestant, Catholic, etc., often correlate highly with other social phenomena.

6. **Political Preference.** This item is widely used in polls for election forecasting as well as for interpreting reactions to government policies. Sometimes the name of the candidate for whom the respondent voted in the last presidential election is obtained. Sometimes the name of the candidate *favored* is secured so that those who did not vote or who were too young to vote can also be classified. The name of the party preferred is also of use for some polls.

7. **Union Membership.** Since so many polls are taken on subjects related to labor and unions, a space for union affiliation is often provided. The question takes the following form: "Are you (is the family's breadwinner) a member of any union?" If yes, "Is that CIO, AF of L, Independent, or don't know?"

8. **Veteran.** In view of the large number of persons who served in the armed forces and in attempts to organize them into a political force, opinion surveyors frequently ascertain whether or not their informants are veterans. The question sometimes used is, "Did you serve in any of the United States armed forces during World War II?" If yes, "What was your branch of the service? Army, Navy, Marine, Coast Guard?" "Did you serve overseas?" (See 675.)

9. **Home Tenure.** This information tells whether the family owns or rents its home. Except in periods of housing shortages when families are forced to buy homes to secure housing, the group who own homes tend to differ from renter groups in many social characteristics.

10. **Monthly Rent of Rented Homes or Rental Value of Owned Homes.** This item may be placed with the identifying information (Item 15). The 1940 and 1950 Census of Housing secured the estimated monthly rental value of owner occupied homes as well as their actual value.

11. **Color or Race of the Individual.** This item is unnecessary in schedules which are confined to only one racial group. In some national polls the interviewer is told not to ask the color question but to report white or colored (Negro) from appearances. In surveys of family situations it is customary to secure the race of the head of the family only, but if this is likely to be a significant factor in a given survey, the race or color of other family members may be secured.

12. **Family Size and Composition.** Although the definition of "family" and "household" has long been a stumbling block to statisticians, few surveyors feel that they can omit information on family size and composition.[8] Complex human relationships—marriage, blood, economic, or social—are usually difficult to classify in categories that are meaningful for survey purposes. Therefore, although information regarding each member of the family is recorded on the schedule, only the number of persons per family—adults and children—is tabulated as a rule.

13. **Occupation of the Head of the Family or of the Respondent.** Since so many social phenomena are correlated directly or indirectly with the type of occupation in which the chief earner of the family engages, this item is practically always obtained in surveys. Often the occupation of all the gainful workers in the family is also secured. Whether to ask for "present occupation" or "usual occupation" or the occupation for which the individual is trained, if it differs from the present one, should be decided before enumeration begins. In order that the occupational data be reliable, it is necessary to use objective and adequate definitions. Classifications and definitions such as those developed for the last Federal Census or for current surveys of employment should be used. (For further discussion of these classes see pages 455–457.)

Information on the industry in which the individual is employed is sometimes collected along with the occupational data. Although this fact may be very pertinent in national surveys, the name of the firm employing the worker may be more useful in local surveys. Knowledge of pay rates and employment policies of the larger concerns in the survey community will provide a check on the reliability of information secured through home interviews.

---

[8] See pp. 452–453 for classifications sometimes used.

14. Employment. An item on the employment or unemployment of the main earner, or of the informant or of all adults in the family, is sometimes included on survey schedules. The United States government provides current total counts on the numbers of unemployed; consequently some comparative data are available. For the classifications used see pages 455–457.

15. Family Income. Information is sometimes requested on the income group in which the family's income during the past year would place it. This gives a rough economic grouping which is useful during the analysis of data. Public opinion surveyors frequently find this factor the most significant of any control used. Instead of a gross estimate of family income, the wages and salaries received by each member of the family during a specified period may be ascertained. The earnings of individuals may be totaled to arrive at family income. Income from sources other than wages, such as interest and dividends, rent received, pensions, professional fees, bonuses, etc., must also be ascertained if the income estimate is to be reliable—particularly in the middle and highest brackets. Very exact figures on income are particularly difficult to obtain for certain groups of people such as farmers, retail merchants, and others who live on profits and withdrawals from the business rather than salaries, and for janitors, ministers, and servants who receive the use of a home or room as part of their compensation. Census instructions for the ascertainment of income from these "problem cases" are perhaps the best available and should be consulted if close estimates are wanted.

16. Car Ownership. This item may be used as a check on the sample by comparing the information with that obtained through motor vehicle registrations. The question may take the following form: "Do you happen to have a car in your family?" Trucks, motorcycles, or cars used primarily for business do not count (675, page 119).

17. Socio-Economic Status. Several objective rating scales for measuring the family's socio-economic status have been devised. Chapman and Sims (167) developed one of the first such scales. Chapin (158) was also a pioneer in this field. His scales have been refined and simplified so that high reliability of ratings is obtained with a relatively simple procedure. Other scales of value to surveyors are those by Shea (866) and Sewell (860, 861). Remmers (767) describes the Kerr-Remmers scale, which is relatively easy to apply. The Committee on

Hygiene of Housing of the American Public Health Association has developed "an appraisal method for measuring the quality of housing." It takes into account physical equipment and facilities, structural condition of the dwelling unit, room crowding, area crowding, environment of structure, community facilities, hazards, nuisances, etc. Lundberg (597) presents an excellent summary of the existing scales and of the technique of constructing such scales. Young's discussion of sociometric scales (1137) is also valuable.

The economic levels used in public opinion polls may be regarded as a socio-economic grouping. The NORC uses the following classes: wealthy, upper middle class, middle class, and poor. According to the NORC instructions, the interviewer sizes up the family situation using certain specified criteria and then classifies the respondent.

Economic level of farmers is not so easily estimated as that of city dwellers. Interviewers for the NORC are instructed to judge the farmer's economic level by comparing his situation with that of other farmers in the same locality. Such factors as the size and condition of his home, the number and condition of repair of the farm buildings, the acreage, productivity, and stock are to be considered.

Nonfarm residents are rated by taking into account their situation as compared to the entire rural area, rather than by comparing them to their immediate neighbors who might be equally poor or well off. Thus the "average" standard of living among nonfarm residents is judged by the level in the entire rural area, not just by the locality in which the nonfarm groups reside.

QUESTIONS ON THE SUBJECT MATTER OF THE SURVEY:

In addition to the identifying data and the census-type items, the schedule, of course, contains questions which it is hoped will throw light on the problems with which the survey is concerned. Questions on the survey topic may be broached in any of several different ways. The informant may be asked a direct question on the facts as he understands or remembers them. The census-type questions already discussed generally are obtained in this manner. The respondent's overt behavior, such as what products he buys, what radio programs he listens to, what customs he follows in his home life, is also rather easily secured by straightforward questions. The opinions which he holds, however, are not so readily ascertained. Whether opinions are sought about some existent situation or about some hypothetical or future likelihood, there are many pitfalls into which the unwary question designer is likely to fall. Techniques and limitations of various opinion-type questions are discussed in greater detail later in this chapter. In addition to the more or less direct approaches described therein, three others deserve mention. First, there is the so-called "information question." With the realization that the public as a whole is relatively uninformed about social problems, programs, or leaders, surveyors are finding it necessary to ascertain the extent of the informant's knowledge about the survey topic before getting his opinion. When knowledge about the topic is definitely correlated with the opinions held, these information questions are particularly important. Too often respondents are tempted to answer "yes" or "no," or "satisfactory" or "approve" without really knowing what the question is to which they have replied.

Questions about complicated issues are preceded by a question designed to separate the informed respondents from the uninformed. Then opinions may be elicited only from those who are in a position to hold them. Questions such as: "Have you heard about . . . . .? Did you read . . . . .? Have you ever used . . . . . product? Do you happen to know what is meant by . . . . .?" may be used for this purpose. These questions may serve not only as filter questions but for analysis purposes when opinions are obtained from all respondents regardless of their familiarity with the subject. Comparison of the reactions of the uninformed with those of the informed may reveal the effect of knowledge upon opinion.

A second approach is that of "seeking advice." This is particularly valuable for opening the interview. The informant is usually flattered by the fact that his advice is considered important and good rapport with the interviewer generally results. It is easy to make the transition from the general case to the specific case of the informant. This approach was used effectively in a study of factors associated with family size. Housewives were asked what they would do in a hypothetical situation such as: "John and Mary have been married ten years, during which time Mary has held a job. Now she wants to give up her job and start having a family. John's job as a salesman is not very certain, so he doesn't think they should risk not being able to support a child. Shall Mary quit her job and have a baby or should she wait until her husband's job is secure? Why?" By the time respondents had given advice to several such controversial cases, the interviewer had no difficulty taking up the informant's own situation.

Another approach which opinion pollers use is the "explanatory question." In questions of this type the informant is given a sufficient background of information about the survey topic to enable him to make a sensible judgment. If opinions are wanted about a situation, issue, or law, it may be advisable to inform the respondent about the situation before getting his reaction. For example, one poll used the following question: "At the present time American citizens cannot vote until they become 21 years of age. Would you favor changing the law to allow persons 18, 19, and 20 years to vote?" (AIOP, 1947). Another of this type was: "Mr. Byrnes was Secretary of State for about a year. In dealing with foreign nations do you think that he did an excellent, good, fair, or poor job?" (AIOP, 1947). There is a danger in giving information of this last type because many respondents will give an opinion before they have had time to think over all the aspects of the situation and not just the one or two facts presented by the interviewer. Unless informants are asked to give reasons why they said "Good," in the above example, for instance, the poller cannot be certain that they know anything about what Mr. Byrnes did. The "briefing" of respondents is a double task because the surveyor must not only design the opinion question, but he must frame the explanation which precedes it so that it will be a fair presentation of the issue. If people with opposite opinions cooperate in the drafting of the preliminary statement, there is a greater chance that the resulting explanation will be unbiased.

Questions should be selected and worded only after considerable deliberation and testing by experienced "question testers." As pointed out above, the questions designed to elicit definite facts do not create as many problems as do those directed toward the polling of opinions of the measurement of attitudes toward past events, current situations, personalities, or proposed actions. A glance at the vast literature on attitude measurements should show any aspiring attitude tester that his is not an easy job. Space does not permit more than a condensed discussion of the problems incidental to the selection and framing of questions for both attitude and opinion polls.

CHOICE OF QUESTIONS:

When deciding what type of questions to include, by seeking the advice of experienced surveyors in such varied fields as marketing research, public opinion polling, radio audience research, and other economic and social research the surveyor may be prevented from falling into certain known pitfalls. The following suggestions are taken from the literature in this field as well as from the author's own experience.

1. Include only questions which have a direct bearing on the problem itself or on the evaluation of the methodology used in the survey. As a rule, questions which elicit answers that are merely "interesting" or of value to some unknown consumer of statistics do not justify the time and cost involved.

2. Do not include questions if their answers can be secured more accurately and effectively from other sources, unless they are desired as a check on the sample or are to be used in tabulations of new facts collected in the survey. Evaluate each question on the basis of whether the proposed survey will be the best source for such information.

3. Keep the tabulation plans in mind when you are selecting the questions. How will the data on a given item be grouped in the tables? If the survey planner considers this in relation to every item on the schedule, he will find that some questions may be dropped, others should be revised, or new ones should be drawn up.

4. When possible secure comparable data. In drawing up the schedule, keep in mind other studies or surveys on comparable material, and as far as practicable use identical questions, terms, definitions, and quantitative units of measurement. This insures that the results of this survey will be more meaningful because they can be compared with the findings of other similar or related studies. The lack of uniformity in selecting units and the failure to utilize existing qualitative and quantitative indices make much survey material less valuable than it would be if this comparison could be made.[9] For example, when the Gluecks (362) repeated their study of criminal careers, they found that it would have been better had more items been made com-

---

[9] It is sometimes possible to compare different materials by making due allowances for differences in definition or classification. If many sources confirm the findings of a survey, some faith may be placed in the substantiating evidence secured.

parable with items in their earlier studies. Unfortunately, however, when they planned their first survey they did not anticipate that they would repeat it several years later.

5. Be careful how you ask personal questions or those which may embarrass the respondent. Statisticians have warned surveyors not to ask questions that apparently pry into the informant's personal life. The reaction of a resentful informant is likely to be, "That's no one's business but my own." Such questions may be seized upon by pressure groups and respondents may be encouraged in their belief that certain facts should not be disclosed regardless of the purpose of the survey.

On the other hand, however, there is ample evidence that people really like to tell an objective interviewer about their personal and even intimate affairs—or at least do not object to telling him. Many people who objected to giving census enumerators information about their income willingly gave these figures to income tax collectors; furthermore, they did not complain even when the returns were published. The evidence in the survey field indicates more and more that surveyors need not be overly concerned about topics which are "too personal." They must, however, be careful how the questions are presented, by whom, and under what conditions. If a certain question may be embarrassing or antagonizing, it should be put in between innocuous questions. Very personal information often may be secured by leading up to the desired question through a series of impersonal preliminary questions which may or may not appear on the schedule. These can take the form of asking the advice or opinion of the informant. Often he will volunteer remarks on how that advice applies to his own case. If he does not, a series of questions focused on the desired information will usually prove successful. An expedient which sometimes may prove effective is to arrange for two interviews. In the first, the informant may be made to feel sufficiently well acquainted with the interviewer to give the "personal" information in the second. Relatively few people require such treatment, and many there are who would rather tell a "stranger" than a "friend."

6. Ask only those factual questions the answers to which most of the informants can reasonably be expected to know.[10] When choosing

----

[10] This rule does not apply if the determination of the *extent of knowledge* is the purpose of the inquiry. If, as in certain marketing studies, the survey

questions, the surveyor should bear in mind the type of people who will act as informants and the chances of their having had access to such information and reason to remember it.

The time factor is also important. Schedule questions may be designed to deal with the situation at the time of the interview or over a long period of time. Facts pertaining to the current situation are relatively easy to collect and they are likely to be comparatively reliable. The fallibility of memory increases as the lapse of time increases. For example, the housewife has difficulty recalling the dates of her husband's various jobs, particularly those held years ago. But she usually knows whether or not he is working at the present time.

Sometimes only one member of the family has the information desired. During the post-1929 depression, one unemployment survey investigator discovered a family where the husband had been out of work for three months but had not told his wife. He left home each morning at the usual time and spent the day searching for work, and he drew out money from the savings bank on pay day. Thus his wife had no way of knowing the real situation. To be sure, this was an unusual case. Most women are familiar with their husbands' employment status.

What people remember and are able to report depends upon the impression made by the experience itself and the conditions under which it is recalled in the present. The principal factors in remembering are:

a. *Recency.* Other things being equal, the more recent the event the more readily and accurately it is recalled. Chappell found that recall of a radio program was inversely related to the length of the time interval between hearing the program and the subsequent recall test (169, p. 114).

b. *Primacy.* Associations that are formed first have an advantage over those formed later on. This principle partly accounts for the ease of recalling the first items on a learned list. Primacy may well play a part in determining which trade names a housewife remembers while

---

sponsor wants to know how many housewives notice and remember the brand names of the products they purchase, it may be desirable to ask questions which many informants cannot answer. The characteristics associated with knowing or not knowing may be what the survey is attempting to discover.

marketing or which ones she gives in response to an interviewer's questions.

c. *Frequency.* The more frequent an experience, the more chance of its being remembered, if there is an appropriate stimulus. The recall of radio programs, for instance, increases markedly after months and years of repeated presentation (169, p. 109).

d. *Duration.* The longer the time, especially distributed time, during which a person is exposed to an experience, the more likely he is to remember it. Thus his ability to recall a radio program which he has heard previously is affected significantly by the length of time it lasted (169, p. 110).

e. *Vividness.* The strength of the impression is an important factor. Personal experiences are generally more vivid than the experiences of others which we can learn about only secondhand.

f. *Interest.* Interesting experiences are more easily remembered. Interest overlaps vividness. Chappell observed that the ability to recollect radio programs varies widely with the type of program, whether variety, concert music, drama, news, etc. The recall of a program is strongly affected by the same inherent elements which determine the size of the audience it attracts (169, pp. 111–112).

g. *Meaningfulness.* It is easier to recall what is comprehensible than what is meaningless. Newspaper reports on battle positions, for example, are less likely to be noticed or recalled by persons who have traveled little or are unable to visualize the setting.

h. *Setting.* An appropriate environmental setting is a great aid to remembering. Such a setting supplies stimuli which are likely to elicit the desired response or memory. The housewife is more likely to remember her marketing list in a grocery store than in a movie show.

i. *Set.* The set or readiness to remember a particular experience is not well understood. Often the desired information seems "on the tip of the tongue" but cannot be given until the informant relaxes or thinks of something else. Apparently a temporary interference or block by conflicting responses must be resolved before the experience or fact can be recalled. Sympathetic encouragement at this point may make all the difference between securing and not securing the information.

j. *Mode.* Ability to remember varies greatly with the mode of remembering called for by the situation. It is a well-known fact, for instance, that the *recognition* of what is present is far easier than the *recall* without any clues of a past experience. It is much easier to recognize or pick out the name of an acquaintance from among a group of names than to recall his name without any clues. Though recognition is the more sensitive faculty, both modes are constantly required in surveys.

In connection with surveys of the use of radios, Stanton (908) has found that questions that depend upon the listener's memory are unsatisfactory for determining the actual periods when the radio was in operation or the programs were heard. One radio surveyor found a decrease of from 27 to 90 per cent in the proportion of persons who listened to a program and the proportion who could name the program the next morning (908, p. 24). It would be naïve indeed to assume that the fallibility of memory must be the sole cause of such a phenomenon.

7. Avoid questions that are likely to yield inaccurate responses unless you take adequate precautions to guard against misinformation. People frequently resort to a form of wishful thinking in answering questions on such matters as the amount of education they have had, the newspapers they read, the jobs they have held, or the stores they patronize. In surveys, particularly, the replies concerning personal achievements may be inaccurate because many people seem unable to resist the temptation of creating a favorable impression by overstatement.

8. Do not ask questions which will necessitate too much extra work on the part of the informant. Thus questions requiring research or mathematical calculation should not be used. Few people will go to the trouble of giving correct answers to such questions unless they are required to by law, as in the income tax questionnaire.

9. As a rule, use no opinion questions unless, of course, it is opinions themselves with which your survey is concerned. The effective use of questions involving motives, attitudes, or opinions demands especially careful study of techniques and pitfalls. An opinion question may occasionally be justified when it is a means of subtle flattery or of lessening frustration in an inhibited informant.

FORMS OF OPINION QUESTIONS:

The task of drafting questions which can be relied upon to reveal what the respondent thinks about a given issue, person, commodity, or situation is no easy matter. It is as difficult as the selection of representative samples of the population and it may distort the results even more than would a poor sample. Surveyors and pollers have recognized the importance of this phase of their work and are constantly experimenting with different types of questions and with different phrasings in their search for unbiased questions. At the present time there seem to be no generally accepted types of questions and phrasing which are universally recommended for all surveys. Gallup finds that as many as five different approaches can be used effectively to gauge opinions about a single issue (342). Suchman and Guttman report a method by which they can divide respondents pro and con on an issue despite differences in question wording (942). No one form will probably ever meet the needs of all who try to gauge opinion in all of its various manifestations. Some surveyors prefer types of questions which will get at the intensity of the feeling which the respondent holds toward the question at issue, other surveyors lean toward questions which enable the informant to talk freely about the survey topic, while others prefer questions which ask the respondent to make a definite choice between two or more alternatives. The type of question used will depend upon such factors as the amount of exploratory work needed to reveal the breadth and intensity of the opinion; the extent to which the opinion has been crystallized or is in a vague, unformed state; the amount of popular knowledge about the subject matter of the survey and the likelihood that the public is in a position to hold an opinion about it, and the complexity of the topic or the many qualifications accompanying each opinion. The surveyor will need to consider these points and the limitations of various forms of questions when he selects from the more commonly used types of opinion questions.

1. **Open-End Questions.** During the exploratory phases of a survey it is usually necessary to employ questions which give the respondent free latitude in his responses. Only by finding out what aspects of an issue have made an impression on people and what words the public uses to express its reactions can intelligent planning of categorized questions proceed. In large-scale studies open-end questions yield such a variety of responses that the task of classification and analysis is both time-consuming and difficult to handle statistically. For these reasons the open-end questions are more suitable for small surveys or pilot studies. However, the Division of Program Surveys of the

United States Department of Agriculture has used such questions widely as has the Research Center of the University of Michigan whose director came from the aforementioned government agency. Techniques for analyzing narrative material systematically are gradually being developed so that the data can be more objectively handled. Following are examples of open-end questions:

In general, what do you think is usually the main cause of wars? (NORC, November 24, 1946)
What do you think about a city sales tax?
What were two or three things, if any, the Roosevelt administration did that you really liked? What were two or three things, if any, the Roosevelt administration did that you didn't like so well? (*Fortune,* March, 1947)
What is the principal reason for your dislike of . . . . . ?

A series of open-end questions centering around the survey topic are sometimes referred to as a "focused interview" or a "'depth interview" (see page 74). Such focused interviews may take an hour or more. The interviewer attempts to give a verbatim account of the respondent's replies. Concrete and factual questions on how the situation being discussed applies to the respondent are usually interspersed between the open questions. As in the "advice seeking questions," good rapport between the interviewer and informant is readily established by the conversational nature of open interviewing.

2. **Free Story and Case Method.**   (See page 74.) Instead of using specific questions interviewers can ascertain opinions or attitudes from extended conversations with the informant. Sometimes case histories also contain expressions of opinion. The case method most applicable to survey procedures is probably the controlled oral interview. Some surveys employ interviewers who have psychiatric and social work training. After an extended interview with the informant, the investigator writes up a summary in which he calls attention to various statements or behavior which seem to indicate attitudes. If he follows an outline and can classify each informant's reaction to all the questions on every topic in the outline, the data may be of value in statistical analyses. In the absence of some such systematic procedure, however, case material thus obtained is unlikely to be adaptable to quantitative analysis.

3. Coincidental, Recall, and Recognition Questions. We have already discussed in Chapter II other types of questions used in market and radio research such as coincidental questions, aided and unaided recall tests, and recognition and identification methods. While these market survey questions may be classified under the various types described in the present chapter, the phrasing used in these methods of questioning should not be overlooked when the surveyor is searching for suitable question forms.

4. Dichotomous Questions. Usually poll questions present opposite alternatives designed to elicit a response of yes or no, agree or disagree, true or false, right or wrong, approve or disapprove, good or bad, fair or unfair, etc. The following are typical dichotomous questions:

Do you approve or disapprove of spanking children?[11]
    Approve   Disapprove   No opinion
If hard times come again, would you rather have the Republicans or
    Democrats in office?[12]
    Democrats   Republicans   Neither   No opinion
Do you have a favorite brand of toothpaste?
    Yes   No
Do you happen to have any idea about what is meant by collective
    bargaining?
    Yes   No

The first three of these questions ask for an opinion, the fourth is directed toward determining the informant's knowledge.

Although these questions are designated as "dichotomous" they usually should and do allow for a third response, such as, "don't know," "no opinion," or "neither." Surveyors have found that if the non-committal third alternative is not openly mentioned by the interrogator, relatively few people will fail to make a choice between the two presented. But if the question explicitly contains the third alternative, more such responses will be obtained. In a sense, then, the dichotomous question more or less forces some people to take a definite stand when actually they would not do so otherwise.

Questions by mail may be so framed that the respondent puts a

---

[11] Asked of a national cross-section of parents by the American Institute of Public Opinion, March 8, 1947.
[12] April 9, 1947, AIPO.

plus, a minus, or a check in the appropriate column or box, crosses out one or the other of the terms, or circles or underlines the word which represents his reaction.

The chief advantage of the dichotomous question is its simplicity both from the point of view of interviewing and of statistical manipulation. It takes relatively little time to ask, and gives a clear-cut answer which can be easily recorded and tabulated. It is particularly adapted to polling of election issues because that is the form employed in the official ballot. If the survey is to be used for predicting the outcome of the election, the exact wording employed in the official ballot is advisable but it should be supplemented by methods used to measure intensity of feeling and to predict the voter turnout. The dichotomous question, which is more familiar to the general public than the multiple-choice question discussed later, is useful when opinion is so crystallized that the issue can be reduced to a specific proposal.

One of the limitations of the yes-no question arises from the fact that a slight misunderstanding of the meaning of the question may result in a complete reversal from a positive to a negative opinion, or vice versa. When the scales allow for a greater number of possible reactions, such misunderstandings and reversals are less likely to occur. It is quite possible that these misunderstandings are as likely to tend in one direction as the other, and that consequently the final percentages of the affirmative and negative answers will not be affected. This limitation is not serious if no individual scores are to be prepared.

Unless people easily choose one or the other of the alternatives mentioned, the alternatives are not properly chosen or the dichotomous question is not suitable. If the opinion is not expressed readily in an unqualified affirmative or negative it may be because opinions on the topic in question are actually held along a series of graduated steps rather than as discrete reactions. Some type of scale question would be better suited for eliciting such opinions. If there is reason to believe that an intermediate position or middle ground is just as tenable as the extremes, it is better to employ a three-alternative question rather than a dichotomous question. The arbitrary "forcing" of opinion into one of two categories will not reflect the true situation.

The alternatives presented may need rephrasing if too many respondents remark that "neither" or "both" alternatives could express their opinions. Then again, if many respondents feel that they must qualify .their replies to make them correct, the surveyor can be sure that the question needs revision.

5. Check-Lists. In a sense, check-lists are multiple choice questions but we shall discuss them separately. They are perhaps the most common of the multiple choice questions. They usually consist of a statement of the problem or question followed by a list of from three to to fifteen possible answers from which the respondent is asked to check his choice of a reply. Examples of the check-list type of question follow:

If prices do go up in the next six months, whose fault do you think this will be? (AIPO, August 12, 1946)
Congress
The people, everybody
Big business
Government officials
Laxness of O.P.A.
Truman administration
Labor unions, strikers
Others
No one, rises are to be expected
Don't know

Here is a list of some things the government in Washington might try to do in the next year. Which two things on the list would you pick as the most important to make an immediate start on? (*Fortune*, December, 1946—asked of a cross-section of World War II veterans)
Make better housing available
Prevent inflation
Arrange for international control of atomic bomb
Regulate labor unions more strictly
Pay a cash bonus to veterans
Make more jobs available
Reduce taxes
Tell more people abroad about our way of life
Regulate business more strictly
Others (volunteered)
None of the above
Don't know

Which brand of cigarettes do you like best?
Brand A   Brand B   Brand C   Brand D   Other   No preference

Which of the following magazines did you glance at or read last month?

Magazine A   Magazine B   Magazine C   Magazine D   None of them

As a rule these lists are made up only after some preliminary surveying has been done to determine what types of replies may be expected. Only by pretests can the surveyor be sure that most of his answers will not fall in the "other" category which is usually provided with a limited list. The advantage of the check-list is that it serves as a reminder for respondents who might otherwise fail to give a certain reply only because they had not happened to think of it at the moment. On the other hand, the check-list might suggest answers which the respondent checks for some extraneous reasons such as that it is first or last on a list or because he thinks it is the "proper" response to make. It is a well-known fact that the number of responses within a given category is higher with a check-list than when no suggestions are made to the informant. If the check-list is presented orally, it should be short with preferably fewer than five items for the listener to grasp. If the list is long or if each item is complicated it is better to print the list on a card which the interviewer can hand to the respondent for him to read. There is still some danger that the informant will not bother to read the list but will pick out an answer at random. But this is a problem which can be handled by adequate interviewer's instructions. In addition to the number of items, the order or arrangement of the list has an important effect upon replies. This problem is discussed on page 211.

The check-list type of question seems to be popular in mail questionnaire surveys where the respondent may be asked to indicate his choice in any one of several ways: He may be asked to place a check mark ($\sqrt{}$) or cross ($\times$) in an answer box. He may be told to cross out answers which do not apply. This technique is sometimes used in the measurement of attitudes. The informant is given a list of words representing political-social or other programs, or stereotyped ideas centering around the subject on which his attitude is to be measured. He is to cross out the words which he finds disagreeable, distasteful, annoying, or agonizing. This type of device apparently elicits a more or less natural response, and it offers little chance of misunderstanding.

Both the number and the type of items crossed out are taken into account in scoring (905, p. 89).

6. **Ranking of Items.** The Ranking or Order-of-Merit Method is also used in attitude measurement. In this type of device the informant is asked to arrange a list of statements, words, phrases, pictures, or other forms in the order of his preference. The following is an example of this type of question:

How important to you are the following features in a good glove?
Place (1) beside the most important, (2) next in importance, etc.
(   ) Its color
(   ) Its fit
(   ) Its style
(   ) Its quality

One limitation of this technique is the fact that in arriving at an individual attitude score no assumptions are made with regard to the size of the intervals between the steps. For instance, the difference between the statement ranked (1) and the statement ranked (2) may be much greater or much less than the difference between the statements ranked (3) and (4). Another limitation is the relatively small number of items which it is feasible to include. If the list is long, the informant tends to become increasingly careless as he nears the end of it. The first rank may seem relatively easy because he is likely to have an extreme attitude concerning items which he classifies as first or high. By the time he reaches the fifteenth or twentieth rank, however, he is likely to be working haphazardly and merely for the sake of completing his task. Although it has been suggested that as few as three choices give the best results, the optimum number probably varies with the subject matter.

An important variation in the ranking technique when applied to oral interviews has been used in market investigations. The items to be ranked are placed on 3 x 5 cards, one item to each card. The cards are shuffled after each interview and handed to the informant, and he arranges them in the order of his preference. This procedure avoids the disadvantage of disproportionate attention being given to the items at the head of the list and of the last items on a long list being skimmed through hastily. Finally, the actual manipulation of the cards seems more likely to indicate the respondent's true preferences. Special care is required, when selecting and wording statements to be ranked, to insure that the attitude to be measured is adequately covered.

The scoring of ranking tests is less difficult and may be done in various ways. As Lundberg has pointed out, the usual procedure is to score "according to the degree to which the responses agree with a predetermined assignment of attitude-value for each item. The responses may also be scored according to the degree to which they deviate in a significant manner from chance expectancy" (597, p. 226).

7. **Multiple Choice Questions.** Multiple choice questions, sometimes known as "cafeteria questions," are so framed that the informant must choose which of several possible answers represents his opinion or comes closest to it. Such questions are particularly useful when the issue is not clear-cut and cannot be represented accurately by a dichotomous question. With multiple choices all degrees of opinion can be given an opportunity for expression. The difficulty lies in framing questions which represent the whole range of opinion on the issue in question. It is important that the list of the alternatives or categories must be complete enough to cover the possible answers or the issue. If the list is incomplete there is grave danger that the respondent will think that one of the specified alternatives takes care of his response and he will read into it something which belongs in an entirely different category. It is difficult to phrase statements which are mutually exclusive so that the respondent will not be undecided between two equally desirable choices. Aside from the problem of drafting the questions, long or complicated lists of choices are confusing and irritating to informants. Just as it is difficult for the restaurant patron to remember the various items on a menu when the waitress reels off the list, so it is very hard for the average respondent to keep in mind all of the different alternatives.[13] Even when the alternatives are understood and remembered, the multiple choice questions might still give misleading results because of man's well-known tendency to choose the middle course and thus to give too much weight to the intermediate categories in the scale.

Multiple choice questions may take any of several different forms. The most popular are the rating or intensity scales which use three, four, or five points, and the check-lists which also may take various forms.

---

[13] The card questions described above help to overcome this difficulty.

RATING OR INTENSITY SCALES:

In these scales the informant is asked to choose among various *degrees* of opinion on a given question. The number of degrees presented is largely a matter of judgment and depends on such general considerations as the purpose of the survey and the nature of the issue (807, p. 479). It may vary from three to the maximum number the tester believes the informant capable of differentiating. Generally speaking, no more than five steps are used by surveys employing the interview method. The rating scale attempts to get a quantitative expression of responses that are supposedly at various steps on an attitude continuum.

Three-Point Rating Scales. The following is a typical example of the presentation of items on a three-point rating scale: "How important do you think it would be for all nations to get together and set up a special organization to increase world trade—very important, only fairly important, or not important at all?" (NORC, March 9, 1947.)

Other words or phrases commonly used in three-point scales are:

Higher	Same	Lower
Harder	About the same	Not so hard
Greater	Equal	Less
Yes	Depends	No
Above average	Average	Below average
Most	Many	Few
Exceptionally good	Average	Very poor
Definitely agree	Middle position	Definitely disagree
More than most people	Like most people	Less than most people

The particular words employed to express the degree of feeling depend upon the phrasing of the question or issue as well as on the judgment of the persons devising the scale. A common practice is to place the neutral, undivided, and "no opinion" reactions in the center of the scale and the most extreme reactions at the ends.

As has already been pointed out, the middle-ground position should be used with caution. If an issue is not well defined or if people have not been thinking about the subject, many people will choose the "about right" alternative if it is suggested. If they do so to avoid the issue, it might be better to exclude the middle position and use only a dichotomous question.

The informant may be asked to classify his reaction to a series of graded statements like the following (*Fortune*, September, 1947, p. 10):

Opinions differ as to how certain racial and religious groups are treated in this country. Which of these ideas comes closest to expressing your opinion of what the real situation is?

Racial and religious groups in this country are, on the whole, as well treated as they should be. ....

While certain racial and religious groups in this country are sometimes not treated as well as they should be, we are now improving the situation as fast as is practical. ....

Certain racial and religious groups in this country are treated very badly, and some strong measures should be taken to improve the situation. ....

Express no opinion. ....

Four-Point Rating Scales. This scale is constructed like the three-point scale, with provision for a choice between four degrees of opinion instead of three. A few of the many terms used for such scales are:

Many .... Some .... Very few .... None
Excellent idea ... Good idea .... Fair idea .... Poor idea
Highest .... Next to the highest ... Next to the lowest .... Lowest

The following example illustrates the use of the statement indicator in a four-point scale:[14]

Which of these four statements comes closest to expressing your own opinion of Mr. X?
1. In times like these it is essential to have a man like Mr. X for President.
2. There may be some reasons against having X for President for another four years, but on the whole it is the best thing to do.
3. While X has done some good things, the country would be better off under Mr. Y for the next four years.
4. The reelection of Mr. X for another four years would be a very bad thing for the country.

Don't know.

Just before the 1940 presidential election, a comparison was made between the direct "For whom do you expect to vote in November—

---

[14] Adapted from the Fortune Poll preceding the 1940 Presidential election. It used the above statement with the words Roosevelt and Willkie in place of Mr. X and Y in the above example. Reported in *Public Opinion Quarterly,* March, 1941, page 89.

Roosevelt or Willkie?" and the above four-point attitude scale. The percentage of the Roosevelt vote on four such surveys was about three percentage points higher in response to the four-part statement indicator than by the direct question.

Five-Point Rating Scales. Five-point rating scales have been widely used in attitude measurement.[15] Listed below are some of the words or phrases indicative of degrees of opinion or feeling that have been used in various surveys. This list is, of course, only suggestive of the many five-point scale responses that might be selected. The choice in a specific instance naturally depends on the statement or issue involved.

Strongly approve	Approve	Deadlocked; undecided	Disapprove	Strongly disapprove
Certainly right	Probably right	Doubtful	Probably wrong	Certainly wrong
Much greater	Somewhat greater	Equal	Somewhat less	Not at all
Very high	A little above average	Average	A little below average	Very low
Practically all	Many	About half	A few	Practically none
Like very much	Like somewhat	Neutral	Dislike somewhat	Dislike very much
Everyone	The majority	Quite a few	A few	None
Strongly urge	Approve	Neutral	Slightly disapprove	Strongly disapprove
Favor in all respects	Favor in most respects	Neutral	Favor in a few respects	Do not favor at all
Absolutely true	Probably or partly true	In doubt; divided; open question	Probably or partly false	Absolutely false

The informant may be asked to rate his attitudes in numerical terms, from 1 to 5, instead of words. The number 5 is used for the strongest reaction. When both positive and negative reactions are to be expressed, the scale numbers may be arranged as follows:

$$+2 \qquad +1 \qquad 0 \qquad -1 \qquad -2$$

----

[15] Day (232, p. 410) found in the literature he examined that slightly more than three-fourths of the attitude scales were of the five-point type. Ghiselli (355) found people more willing to respond to a four-step scale.

Graphic Rating Scales. Strength of opinion may also be indicated on a line, only the significance of the two ends and the middle being designated. To the informant this line represents a continuum; he or the rater marks the point on the line at which his reaction seems to fall. For example:

Definitely approve	On the fence	Definitely disapprove
+10	0	−10

The graphic rating system is not especially adapted to surveys of the general public unless rating is done by the interviewer.

Attitude Scale Construction

The literature on the definition and measurement of attitudes is extensive and embodies many different points of view. Among the controversial subjects in this field are such questions as: What is an attitude? Are attitudes general or specific, or both? How do attitudes and opinions differ? Can attitudes be measured? What do opinion tests test? What is the relation between opinion and behavior? Space limitations do not permit extended discussion of these points; but the surveyor who is planning a study on attitude measurement would do well to acquaint himself with the literature.

Many psychologists agree that an attitude is the preparation and tendency to act, either overt, inner, or psychic (2, p. 173). It is more general than opinion, which is merely an overt expression on a controversial point. Social surveyors, particularly those in the fields of marketing research and political opinion, have tried to measure attitudes or tendencies to act in order to predict how people will act when confronted with a specific situation, as in purchasing a commodity or voting in an election, or in responding to a question on opinion. Although opinions usually are verbal expressions, they may be revealed by gestures, facial expressions or other symbols.

The data obtained in public opinion and attitude surveys may be used in either of two ways: (1) to discover the number or percentage of the people who respond in a particular way to a single statement, phrase, or other attitude indicator; or (2) to measure the strength of the attitude of each individual by a series of questions the answers to which are combined into a single score for each person. Then the number or percentage of people holding attitudes of varying intensity may be ascertained. The great majority of opinion surveys are still of the first type. Usually a single question is devoted to a single topic on a schedule concerned with various topics, and the number of people making each type of response is counted. There is no attempt to discover the complex factors which might enable the surveyor to predict individual reactions, and consequently no individual scores are kept. Without extensive pretesting, the surveyor cannot be sure that his counts would not have come out very differently had he worded the question a little differently or placed it in another context. For this reason surveyors are searching for techniques which will measure more basic response tendencies—measures which will hold true regardless of the specific opinion questions utilized in the survey. Thus it is that surveyors are turning more and more toward the measurement of attitudes.

Attitude scales are employed in the measurement of the attitudes of individuals or groups of individuals. The construction and interpretation of these scales require expert attention. The choice of questions indicative of certain attitudes, the framing of these questions, the weights to be used for the responses in arriving at a single useful score, the standardization of the scale, the development of tests of reliability and validity, and numerous other technical problems must be considered. The ideal attitude scale is not only reliable and valid but also takes little time to administer, does not involve paper and pencil work on the informant's part, and can be given without rigid control of the test situation. This ideal has never been approximated in survey practice, but some useful technical and statistical procedures have been worked out for the development of attitude scales.

An effective attitude scale consists of a limited series of varied statements of opinion about some given subject, presented in the form of a questionnaire, and evoking responses indicative of the individual's attitude toward the given subject. The development of an attitude scale involves several essential phases. (1) The first phase is the collection of numerous diverse statements of opinion, known as items, about the subject in question. This collection is generally the result of searching in likely places and asking various people for their opinions. (2) The second phase is the reduction of the collection of statements by editing to those which are generally suitable with respect to form and scope. Edwards and Kilpatrick gave six rules for the elimination of unsuitable material (280). Careful attention to these initial phases is obviously worth while, because in the absence of suitable material it is of no avail to proceed further. Suitable material will consist of 100 or so clear-cut statements covering the range from extreme approval to extreme disapproval of the attitude subject. (3) The next phase is the selection from among these likely items, by some test technique, of about fifteen or twenty which are sufficiently discriminating to actually use. Discriminating items are those which help to discriminate or differentiate between persons who approve and persons who disapprove or who hold opposite viewpoints on a subject. The more highly discriminating an item is the more it helps in separating persons according to how much they approve or disapprove. This selection of the most discriminating items for the scale is a vital phase of attitude scale development, because the effectiveness of the finished scale in discriminating or measuring the attitude depends inevitably on its component items. Selection of discriminating items is based on the principle of correlation with some criterion of the attitude—the better the responses to the item agree with the criterion, the better the item. The principle is applied differently in several techniques of item selection which have been found useful in practice (536). (4) Another phase of attitude scale development is the combination of the chosen discriminating items into the completed questionnaire for diagnosing the attitude. This is largely a matter of efficient arrangement of the material and format. (5) The method of scoring performance on the attitude scale is likely to develop in conjunction with all the later phases. The most important function of the scoring is to so weight the various possible responses to the items as to make the most of the test material. (6) A desirable final phase is to try out the completed questionnaire for the purpose of evaluating its overall reliability and validity. Try-outs sometimes show that minor changes in arrangement, content or scoring will yield needed improvement.

The best-known current techniques for use in attitude scale development are those of Thurstone (963), Likert (563), and Guttman (385). While all of these have techniques in common, such as requiring some relevant collection of items to work with, all of them are different in other essentials. The special feature of each may be briefly characterized at this point. The unique feature of Thurstone's technique is the sorting of the opinion items into a number, say 9, of equi-spaced categories lying along the continuum which ranges from extreme unfavorable to favorable. (A continuum is merely a continuous series of quantitative variation in one dimension, e.g., all neutral grays no matter how light or dark lie along the continuum from absolute black to white. Similarly, all intensities of opinion toward war under given conditions lie along an opinion continuum ranging from strongly against to strongly in favor of war.) The median location of any item along the continuum determines its scale value. The interquartile range (a common statistical measure of variability) of the scatter of any item along the continuum determines its ambiguity. About twenty items to be used in the scale are chosen partly on the basis of their scale positions and partly on the basis of their lack of ambiguity. The aim is to secure for the scale, items which are approximately equi-spaced along the continuum and which are least ambiguous. The score of any person on the completed attitude scale is the median scale value of the various items which he endorses (963).

Whereas the feature of Thurstone's technique is the sorting procedure, the feature of Likert's technique is the scoring procedure. For the development of his scale numerous people are asked to indicate the intensity of their agreement or disagreement with respect to each item by reference to five categories ranging from strong disagreement through neutral to strong agreement. These categories are assigned the respective weights 0, 1, 2, 3, 4, and then each person is given a score consisting of the sum of his item weights. For instance, if the weights corresponding to a particular person's response categories for five items are 4, 2, 2, 3, 1, his score covering those items is 12. This is all preliminary, however, to the selection of the discriminating items which proceeds by a common method. On the basis of the trial scores obtained as above, the trial subjects are divided into two groups, a low group and a high group. Then about twenty of the more discriminating items, viz., items which were rated higher by the high group but lower by the low group, are chosen for inclusion in the attitude scale. Any person's score on the completed scale is based on the sum of the weights of his responses to all the items in the scale (563).

Guttman's procedure of scale analysis is essentially a test to see to what extent any given set of opinion items are scalable in the particular technical sense of lying along a continuum rather than falling off to one side or another. In the ideal case where the items form a perfect, uni-dimensional scale, it would be possible to predict or reproduce exactly from a person's rank score based on all the items, his separate responses to the individual items. Approach to a perfect scale is a matter of degree, and closeness of approach is evaluated numerically by calculating what is called the coefficient of reproducibility (279). This coefficient comes out 100 per cent for perfect reproducibility, but coefficients of 85 per cent or more are said to suffice in practice. Needless to say, more than one set of questions may have to be tested before an acceptable set is secured. More than one way of making the test has been proposed (385, 386). A careful critique, presenting the advantages and limitations of Guttman's technique (Cornell version) recently has become available (536). At present the greatest usefulness of scale analysis lies in the checking for uni-dimensionality of seemingly suitable items which have already been chosen by other procedures.

A noteworthy aspect of Guttman's technique is the different approach which it suggests to the traditional problem of item bias. The seriousness and complexity, in social survey design, of the problem of avoiding by pretesting and careful selection all words, phrases and arrangements of materials which might invalidate results, has been evident throughout this chapter. According to Guttman, if any series of questions is subjected to scale analysis, found to be scalable, and is then rescored for intensity; an appropriate plot of the data will correctly separate the favorably from the unfavorably disposed members of the group. The point is made that the group will divide into the same proportions regardless of the wording, loading or other bias of the questions which happen to comprise the scale. Superficially this may seem to be the answer to the surveyor's prayer for a way of circumventing the whole difficult problem of pre-testing and study to eliminate biased items; but unfortunately for the present it is altogether too difficult and time-consuming for routine application. Moreover the social survey is likely to require data on a number of different matters of opinion, and so would have to construct and administer a number of different attitude scales. However, there is unusual activity in this field and forthcoming publications may provide a practicable solution to the problem of item bias.

The most promising recent development in attitude scale construction is the technique of Edwards and Kilpatrick which combines essential advantages of the techniques of Thurstone, Likert and Guttman, and also possesses advantages of its own not present in the others taken separately. This technique is best reviewed by reference to the author's own account of their investigation (280). It is beyond the scope of this book to go into the specific details of applying the various techniques of attitude scale construction, but complete descriptions are given in the literature.

Work in progress is aimed at simplifying the technical procedures of attitude scale construction, but at present these are still so laborious that they are largely unsuitable for general social survey application. Only when a particular attitude scale has already been developed which happens to apply to the surveyor's problem, is it likely that advantage can be taken of this important device. The main trouble is that there are so many attitudes and so few developed scales that the probability of finding what is needed, ready-made, is small indeed. On the other hand, prospect of repeated use in successive panel or other tests, will sometimes justify the development and standardization of a new scale for some single situation. Even then the developmental work may best be left in the hands of specialists who know the surveyor's needs.

BEHAVIOR STATEMENT TESTS:

Instead of asking the informant for a generalized opinion about a series of generalized statements, a behavior statement test requires him to indicate how he would react to a series of specific situations. The results obtained with this technique may be very different. For example, Pace (712, p. 376) compared stated behavior with stated opinions in a study of liberalism-conservatism among students at the University of Minnesota. In one test they were asked to underline the phrases in a series of thirty questions which most nearly expressed their opinion. The following question was included in this particular test: "People should not patronize stores that are being picketed by labor unions." In the behavior statement test the wording was: "If a picket was parading with a sign 'This store is unfair to union labor, in front of the store at which you usually bought your groceries, what would you do?" The total scores on these two types of tests were very similar; either test would serve if a general index of liberalism-conservatism were desired. However, there were striking differences in the individual responses to the two types of tests. Pace concludes: "It seems important for the experimenter to ask himself what he wants to measure and how he wants to use the results. . . . Does he want to know how many people are favorable toward the general idea of labor union picketing? Or does he want to know how many would . . . withhold patronage from a store that is being picketed?" The example cited on pages 191–192, in which reactions to attitude questions were compared with replies to a direct question on voting intention (behavior test) confirms Pace's results. The evidence suggests that for opinion polls whose purpose is to determine the percentage of the people with specified opinions or reactions, attitude questions and behavior statements will yield similar results.

THE WORDING OF QUESTIONS:

The amount of attention that must be given to the wording of questions on the schedule depends on whether facts or opinions are sought, on whether or not an interviewer is to fill in the form, and on the amount of leeway he is given for interpreting the questions to the informants.

If the interviewer is to read the questions exactly as they are printed or if the informant is to reply to the questions without the investigator's assistance, great care is required in formulating the questions so that reliable and meaningful returns will be assured. While certain precautions in the phrasing of questions are necessary when factual information is to be secured, even greater care must be exercised when opinions are to be obtained. Investigators in the fields of public opinion and marketing have shown how only one seemingly innocuous word may influence the response of the interviewee. Among the many subjects which have been studied by survey experts are words which are likely to color responses, the conditions under which responses are most affected by word connotations, and question forms which are most effective for revealing true opinions. Aside from the specific suggestions discussed below for wording questions so as not to bias the responses, characteristics or conditions favorable to respondent suggestibility deserve mention. Respondents with limited vocabularies are likely to be suggestive. If questions are unintelligible to the respondent, he may choose one of the alternative responses without having any idea as to what his response means. Even if he is unfamiliar with all of the key words in the question he can still reply in meaningful terms (from the point of view of the surveyor) if he says Yes, No, Average, the Same, etc. In the 1947 New York State election, for example, voters were asked to vote on three issues about public housing. It is doubtful whether many voters knew what they were voting on. They knew that they wanted more housing so they voted for the bill. To be sure, many had been told by their party leaders that they should vote Yes, or No, but had they not been told so and had the interviewer read the complicated bill to them, they probably would have voted Yes, just because they heard the word "housing" and they knew they favored it.

If the informant knows very little about the survey topic he is more likely to be influenced by the specific words or phrases used than would be the case if he were thoroughly familiar with the topic. He will grasp at such clues as familiar words or phrases and will react to them rather than to the question as a whole.

If opinions are not strong the respondent is more likely to be influenced by wording construction than when he feels intensely about an issue. To be sure, those with strong feelings are usually very much interested in the subject and will listen to the entire question. They also have a definite reaction and look for the words or phrases that correctly express how they feel. They are on the alert for slight differences in the expression of the point which they wish to have emphasized. Neutral persons, on the other hand, may not feel emotional about the question either because they lack information or cannot see how it will affect them or their interests. Relatively few people have so much information on both sides of an issue that they think the answer is a toss-up. The great mass of disinterested and neutral responses result from lack of knowledge which in turn is commonly associated with lack of interest in the subject. To be accommodating, many will lend a half-ear to the interviewer's question and if any words or phrases are uttered which do carry interest, the response is likely to depend on such words instead of the question as a whole.

SUGGESTIONS FOR WORDING QUESTIONS:

1. *Use simple words which are familiar to all potential informants.* Surveyors should keep in mind the fact that the average adult in the United States in 1940 did not go beyond the eighth grade, and that half of all adults had had less than a grammar school education. Thus

it is not surprising that relatively few people understand such words as conscript, indirect taxes, collective bargaining, filibuster, portal-to-portal pay, and tariff. Less than half of the people interviewed in public opinion polls early in 1947 knew what the last three of the above words meant. Words like commercial, radical, liberal, conservative, also are widely misunderstood. A glance at questions commonly used in modern polls shows that pollers are still overestimating the breadth of the average vocabulary.

One practical procedure for the question designer is to think in terms of some sixth to eighth grade child of his acquaintance before deciding whether to employ a given word. The designer might well ask himself, "Would this child know what I am talking about?" When in doubt the question may be tried out on a few persons with such a limited education. Thorndike prepared a list of the 20,000 words most frequently found in general reading for children and young people (960). These words are rated in terms of frequency of occurrence; consequently their level of general familiarity can be gauged. It has been recommended that only the first 5000 of these words be employed in surveys of the general public.

The Flesch Reading-Difficulty Formula (Ph.D. thesis by Rudolph Flesch, Columbia University) may find considerable application in question framing by public opinion surveyors. The formula affords an objective evaluation of the readability of reading material by taking into account the sentence length, number of difficult words, and the number of personal references. Difficult words are scored in terms of number of prefixes and suffixes built onto the word-root. Personal pronouns, together with words like mama, papa, aunt, etc., indicate personal references (316). This formula has been adjusted to make material scaled to the sixth grade level of moderate difficulty for the average fifteen-year-old (676, p. 100). Terris (955) reports a study of the difficulty of questions employed by three nation-wide surveys. She found that slightly more than 90 per cent of the questions were too difficult for 12 per cent of the population. In addition to references (316, 676), and (960), the following publications should be of help in the selection of simple words: Chall, Jeanne S. and Edgar Dale, "A formula for predicting readability," *Educational Research Bulletin,* Ohio State University, 1948, 27:11–20; Farr, J. N., and J. J. Jenkins, "Tables for use with the Flesch Readability Formulas," *Journal of Ap-*

plied Psychology, 1949, 33:275–278; Flesch, Rudolph, "A new readability yardstick," *Journal of Applied Psychology,* 1948, 32:221–233.

As a rule, it is best to aim at comprehension by the least intelligent and educated of the group to be surveyed (155, p. 389). The questions should not be aimed at people with average intelligence because the imperfect answers given by the ignorant will destroy the completeness of the results. Another approach would be to prepare several phrasings of the same question of varying difficulty so that the interviewer could choose the one adapted to the educational level of his informant. It is perfectly possible, however, to use simple words without making the questions appear too elementary for those of higher mental or educational level. Here is where the art of question framing comes in.

Pollers who are aware of the extremely limited vocabulary of the general public have come to make wide use of the "information question" mentioned earlier. Before the informant is asked for his views on the survey topic, his knowledge on the subject is ascertained. For example, phrasing such as the following is often used: "Do you happen to know what . . . . . is?" "What is it?" "Will you tell me what is meant by the word . . . . . ?" or "What does the word . . . . . mean to you?" When the question was raised, "Can you tell me what the term 'filibuster' in Congress means to you?" (AIPO, April, 1947) only 48 per cent knew what it meant. So only these people were asked about proposals to change the system.

Words commonly used to denote certain items may vary in different parts of the country. Thus, "soft drink," "tonic," "soda pop" may mean the same thing depending on whether one is in the west, New England, or Missouri. "Harvester" may be familiar to farmers and "subway" and "elevated" to city dwellers.

2. *Make the questions as concise as possible.* A question that contains long dependent or conditional clauses may confuse the informant, even though he understands the words. In trying to comprehend the question as a whole he may overlook or forget a clause; hence his answer may be wrong.

It is not necessary to phrase items in question form if the interviewer is to fill in the schedule because he can supply the needed wording in the interview. In measuring opinions or attitudes, however, it may be important to have the complete question printed on the schedule.

Concise wording and clear arrangement of columns and column headings make it possible to condense a wide range of information in a very short schedule. The advantages of using only one side of the schedule for the actual questions have already been discussed (page 160).

3. *Formulate the questions to yield exactly the information desired,* in terms that lend themselves to tabulation and statistical treatment. Make them self-explanatory as far as possible. For example, an item calling for "birthplace" may be answered in terms of home address, or city, county, state, or country. If the country of birth is entered on some schedules and only the city on others, the schedules cannot be tabulated on either basis. Even when the country of birth is specified, there may be confusion as to what name to enter because the names of so many countries were changed after the World Wars. The name of the city is likewise not entirely satisfactory, for there may be more than one city of the same name in the world. The more specific the question, the greater the assurance that the answer will be satisfactory for tabulation purposes. Before the final wording is adopted, the surveyor should see how the answers can be coded and whether they are suitable for the tabulation forms he plans to use.

The question beginning "How long ago . . . . . ?" is not so satisfactory as "How many days (weeks, months, years) ago . . . . . ?" Similarly, the question, "How often do you buy X?" is not so manageable as "How many times a year is X bought?" or better still, "How many times did you buy X last year . . . . . ? The year before last . . . . . ?" To make it more specific, the question can be worded, "When did you last buy X . . . . . ? less than 1 week ago . . . . . from 1 week to less than 1 month ago . . . . . from 1 month to less than 1 year ago . . . . . 1 year or over a year ago . . . . . ."

If the questions call for an answer in terms of units, these units must be clearly defined. In the case of money, for instance, is the entry to be in terms of dollars or cents, or both? When costs are involved, is it the retail, wholesale, market, or some other cost which is wanted? With questions involving computations, it is generally desirable to ask the informant only for detailed figures and to have someone in the office compute the percentages or averages or other figures desired. Dependence on the informant for these computations introduces another source of error into the data.

If questions are not sufficiently explicit, they will not yield comparable results. For example, "What kind of radio do you own?" might refer to whether it is a table or cabinet model, whether it is an earphone set, a television set, whether it has FM or any other of a number of characteristics, or which particular trade name it carries. It is necessary to make questions specific enough so that the one desired interpretation will be made.

Surveyors for the Monthly Report of the Labor Force found that the question "Was this person at work on a private or government job last week?" was not interpreted by many people to include part-time workers. After some experimentation the question was changed to "What was the person's major activity during the census week?" For all persons whose major activity was something other than working, the interviewer asked whether such persons "did any work for pay or profit during the census week." The new phrasing increased the estimate of the national count of employed males by 900,000 and of employed females by 1,600,000. Most of the additional male workers were students, and the additional females were housewives. Almost half of these additional workers had worked 35 hours or more during the census week (30).

4. *Avoid "double-barreled" or multiple-meaning questions.* Unless each question covers only one point, there will be confusion as to which one the answer applies to. Such items should be formulated as two or more questions so that separate answers can be secured.

5. *Avoid ambiguous questions.* If the question does not direct the response so that it will answer the question the surveyor had in mind it is unsatisfactory. The best means to this end is to pretest the questions and thus detect the ambiguities. Persons who draft questions seldom are aware of ambiguous phrases. A question which means different things to different people is ambiguous. If respondents with opposite points of view use almost the same words in their replies, the point of the question has not been made clear. Ambiguity may arise if the vocabulary is beyond the comprehension of the respondent, if the phrasing is too complex, if the phrasing is in such general terms that informants may start with entirely different assumptions, or if words with double meanings are used. One study is reported in which informants were asked if they took many colored pictures. The replies were satisfactory until the survey was conducted among Negroes. Neg-

ative phrasings are particularly confusing. For example, a "yes" reply to the question, "Don't you think . . . . . is true?" might mean "Yes, I do not think . . . . . is true" or it might mean, "I think . . . . . is true."

Perhaps one of the greatest faults of the amateur question designer is his use of too many conditional or limiting phrases and clauses. These phrases make it difficult for the informant to grasp the main point of the question. The length alone makes it practically impossible to carry the question as a whole in mind. It is little wonder then that the respondent escapes with "I don't know" or "I haven't decided" when he really means "I don't know what you are talking about."

6. *Avoid leading questions,* i.e., questions worded in such a way as to suggest the answers. In a sense, all questions which produce biased answers may be regarded as leading questions. In addition to the numerous biasing questions specifically mentioned in this section on question wording, a few other leading questions deserve mention. There is, for example, the question that does not permit of exceptions. "Do you always read the X newspaper?" Many people will answer "Yes" even though they may not read the paper named when they are on vacations, ill, or too busy. Another phrasing that usually elicits a favorable response is "Did you see this advertisement?" Tests show that 73 per cent of the people interviewed answer "Yes" regardless of whether they saw the advertisement; other tests indicate that less than 20 per cent have actually seen the advertisement (115). Methods for correcting these responses to get the true number of recalls will be discussed on page 491. Questions in market surveys that tell the informant for which brand the study is being made (the brand name may be repeated frequently in the schedule) influence the responses. Respondents tend to give answers favoring that brand. The surveyor must be on guard also to avoid questions which are likely to produce what has come to be known as the "halo effect." In market surveys this shows itself in the tendency of informants to rate their favorite brands high in most characteristics.

7. *Decide as to your use of prestige names.* Answers to questions in which prominent personalities are injected will be conditioned by the informant's personal feeling toward the individual mentioned. Rugg and Cantril (825), who have investigated this factor in opinion polls, advise against an indiscriminate ban of important names. They suggest that the surveyor use a split ballot to determine whether a specific is-

sue can be presented more fairly and realistically with or without a prominent supporter's name. They point out that the public often responds to issues *plus* prestige names and that the two cannot always be divorced.

If opinions are not solidly structured or if the names carry a great deal of weight, the influence of prestige names on responses may be very great. In a question about whether or not the War and Navy Departments should be combined and run as one department, two different forms were used. In one, which read "General Eisenhower says the Army and Navy should be combined . . . . ." 49 per cent of the respondents approved of one department, but when his name was not used only 29 per cent favored the idea (676, p. 73). In another survey reported by the Psychological Corporation, the injection of the phrase "President Roosevelt's idea" in the question "Do you approve of President Roosevelt's idea of having Thanksgiving a week earlier this year?" resulted in 5 per cent more favorable responses than when his name was not used (70).

8. *Avoid "danger words," catchwords, stereotypes, or words with emotional connotations.* This discussion will be based on some of the many studies that have been made in this field.

a. Among the words reported by Blankenship to arouse the emotions and prejudices of the respondent are the following: Reds, Communism, radicalism, Fascism, capitalistic, sane, guarantee, rich, alien, economic royalist, Tory. Most of these words are biased only in certain contexts. Similarly, the words "involve," "forced," and "government spending" have all been found to affect responses when used in certain ways. "Trusted," "politics," "big business," and "labor union" have been found to carry derogatory connotations and affect replies (676, p. 73).

b. Names of political parties and political figures may color the response. Examples have been cited above.

c. A suggestive word is one that so qualifies a statement that the response will differ when the word is omitted. For example, tests proved the word "reasonable" to be in this class. The question "Are you willing to have a *reasonable* increase in prices with the hope that it will bring back prosperity?" resulted in 11 per cent more affirmative votes than when the word "reasonable" was omitted.

d. Words whose meaning is vague are danger words because they elicit meaningless or noncomparable responses. The word "why" is an example. People often give a great variety of responses to such a question as, "Why do you buy X's brand of coffee?" and most of them are unclassifiable. The words "mediums" and "kinds" were also found to have multiple meanings in market surveys. In the question, "Is the electric utility in your community privately or publicly owned?" many respondents understood the term "publicly" to mean ownership of shares by the public (791).

e. Name-calling and extremist phrases are to be used with caution. A questionnaire study of 218 University of Washington students indicates that stereotyped phrases or catchwords have a decided influence on the acceptance or rejection of ideas in the controversial fields of politics and labor. Extremist phrases, either reactionary or radical, were less effective than the milder conservative or liberal expressions. References to the Constitution, the flag, and the open shop were popular, but the term "Fascist" and certain of the older communistic phrases were usually rejected (636, p. 614).

9. *Decide whether to include indirect questions.* Chapin suggests the occasional use of "slant-side questions" and cites a study in which homeless men were interviewed. When they were asked "Are you married" most of them replied in the negative, but when the question was changed to "Where is your wife?" a much higher percentage proved to be married (157, p. 172). When there is danger of reflecting on the attainments or cultural background of respondents, the surveyor might get at the true situation through indirect rather than direct questions. For example, in a readership survey instead of asking the respondent "Have you read *Gone with the Wind?*" the interviewer asked "Do you intend to read *Gone with the Wind?*" Those who had already read it had no hesitation to say so, while those who felt that they should have read it were not embarrassed by the question (77, p. 64).

10. *Be cautious in the use of phrases which may reflect upon the prestige of the informant.* For example, most people like to feel that they are reasonable, intelligent, generous, understanding, and respected members of their community. They tend to answer questions in terms of what they "ought" to think or feel about a situation. For instance, the question "Do you favor the good neighbor policy?" brought out a great many favorable replies which subsequent questioning indicated were untrue.

11. *Decide on whether to personalize some of the questions.* Such questions require the respondent to state whether or not he would follow a specified course of action if the decision were up to him. They have been found valuable in some cases. They elicit a different response than do general or impersonal questions. For instance, "Would you vote to . . . . ." or "If you had to pay . . . . ." may make an informant more conservative in his reaction. The personalized question is sometimes referred to as subjective phrasing. Blankenship experimented with such phrasing as "Do you consider it desirable to balance the budget?" and "Is it desirable to balance the budget?" A slightly greater number of persons favored the proposition when the second or objective phrasing was used. Burtt and Gaskill (129) and Muscio (664) studied the suggestibility of the personal versus the impersonal form. They also tested the use of the definite versus the indefinite article. In other words, these experimenters wanted to test the extent to which the wording of the question influenced their subject's responses, in some cases erroneously. A group of subjects was shown a film and subsequently questioned concerning the details they observed. The forms of the questions were: Did you see . . . . . ? Didn't you see . . . . . ? Did you see the . . . . . ? Didn't you see the . . . . . ? Was there a . . . . . ? Wasn't there a . . . . . ? The findings of these studies cannot be easily summarized, nor can their applicability to phrasing questions in opinion polls be recommended without qualifications. However, the fact that such small differences in wording do influence responses is worthy of note.

12. *Allow for all possible responses.* Phrase the questions to provide for such indefinite answers as "Don't know," "No choice," "Doubtful," "Other (Specify)." If the informant refuses to answer, this reaction should be recorded by the interviewer. However, no special refusal column should be provided on the schedule, because some interviewers may use it instead of exercising their ingenuity to secure the information. In opinion surveys the questions should include all the important alternatives which a given issue may present (345, p. 10).

If the respondent is to underline or check his answer, provision should be made for all possible replies. Generally the most usual responses are listed, and there is additional space for "Other—specify." The danger of using a check-list that does not include all the significant responses was brought out by Young (1138) in a report of a study of the sources of community funds. Although endowments are one of the chief sources, they were not reported because they were not included in the check-list and there was no space for "Other."

A second danger of supplying a series of answers to be checked is the fact that this suggests the replies. Relevant data may be excluded, or the answers listed may be given undue weight merely because they are included. This difficulty can be avoided by using a pilot survey in which "free answers" are received and, on the basis of this information, choosing the specific items to be included on the list.

If the questions are read and the check lists are long, the lists should be put on a card so that the respondent can see them. Most people cannot remember a long list of alternatives (345, p. 101).

13. *Make the alternatives in multiple choice questions realistic.* They should conform more or less to the way people really think and feel about the problem and the issues involved.

If alternatives are phrased in terms of concrete situations, the question will be more meaningful and will give different results than if general phrases are used. Tamulonis cites the following question as an example: "If a young single woman is doing exactly the same kind of work which she is doing as well as a married man with children, do you think she should receive exactly the same rate of pay?" Sixty-six per cent answered "Yes" to this specific question. When the more general phrasing was used "Do you think women should or should not receive the same rate of pay as men for the same work?" Seventy-seven per cent approved of equal pay for equal work (676, p. 74).

Before the armed forces were to be demobilized after World War II, the War Department secured the soldier's viewpoint on priority for discharge. Questions took the form of a series of situations about which a judgment was wanted. "John Smith, age 38, father of two children, has not been overseas, while Jack Jones, single, has served in Germany for two years. Who should be discharged first—John Smith or Jack Jones?" Answers to a series of such questions provided the basis for the discharge system adopted, which by and large was regarded as fair by the majority of soldiers.

When framing alternatives the question designer should bear in mind that people answer questions in terms of the *relative* value of the choices presented in the question and *not* in terms of absolute preferences. The more desirable of two given alternatives might seem much less desirable than a third alternative, if it were presented. Thus before various alternatives are adopted, the question designer should try to ascertain what alternatives are most likely to confront the public.

The arrangement of the alternatives is important. When a choice is to be made of different alternatives in public opinion polls, for instance, it has been suggested that this choice appear as early in the question as possible (345, p. 101). There should be the same number of alternatives for each side of the question, so that an informant who is asked to choose the one most nearly resembling his own point of view will have an equal choice of pro and con statements. It might be helpful to consider the presentation of an issue to the informant similar to the presentation of a case to a jury; the wording must be balanced to avoid biasing the results.

Avoid combining issues and partisan arguments. According to Tamulonis (676, p. 74), if an argument for or against an issue is presented with a statement of the issue, the respondent will tend to reply in the direction toward which the argument points unless his opinions are strongly held. When the respondent is to identify the statement which most nearly represents his point of view, the alternatives that appear on the schedule must be mutually exclusive.

Whether to mention both alternatives in a dichotomous question, or to mention only one and let the informant infer the other, depends upon the extent to which opinion on the issue has crystallized. If it is structuralized the presentation of one or both alternatives apparently makes no difference, for approximately the same results are secured (806). But if opinion is not yet set, the alternative that is presented receives more favorable consideration than the one that is implied. Rugg and Cantril (825) give the following example of expressed versus implied alternatives:

Implied form: "Do you think workers should have the right to elect a representative on the board of directors of the company they work for?" *Answers*: Yes 61%. No 23%. No opinion 16%.

Explicit form: "Do you think workers should have the right to elect a representative on the board of directors of the company they work for, or should all the directors be elected by the owners of the company?" *Answers*: The workers should have right 53%. By owners 31%. No opinion 16%.

The explicit statement raised the vote from 23 to 31 per cent for the owners.

In any list of alternatives the response of the informant is limited to the items in the list. If two or three alternatives in the list were changed, the respondent would be making his choices from a different set, and the result might be quite different from his choices with the original set. In a list of alternatives, those placed last in the list generally are chosen more frequently than those in other positions. Items in the final position tend to be favored by the recency of their perception.

The alternative placed first may affect the response. For example, the question, "Do you think the United States will go into the war in Europe or do you think we will stay out of the war?" brought a different response when worded, "Do you think the United States will stay out of the war in Europe or do you think we will go into the war?" According to Rugg and Cantril: "There is evidence to show that when one of these alternatives is mentioned second it receives a few more votes than when it comes first. . . . It appears that there is a tendency for the respondent to select the last, more easily remembered alternative when the question is a fairly complicated one" (**825**, p. 480). If opinion has not been structuralized on a given issue, it may be advisable to use a split ballot technique, placing a given alternative first on one form and second on the other. This eliminates the effect of the order.

The number of alternatives suggested will affect the answers. The more alternatives, the more the answers tend to avoid the extremes and favor the moderate or qualified positions.

14. *When a long check-list is used, either use card questions (p. 188) or see that the items are rotated on different runs of the schedules.* In answer to the question "Which magazines do you usually read? Magazine A . . . . . Magazine B . . . . . Magazine C . . . . . Magazine D . . . . . Magazine E . . . . . Magazine F . . . . . people check many more magazines with such a list than they would if the question did not present the list. Furthermore, magazines not included will not be mentioned, and those at the lead of the list will be checked more frequently than those at the end.[16]

---

[16] With complicated alternative propositions, it will be recalled, the informant tends to select the last mentioned alternative.

15. *Keep to a minimum the amount of writing required on the schedule.* Most handwriting is so poor that there is danger of misinterpretation and hence of errors. When feasible, use symbols for the replies. The symbols should be explained either at the bottom of the page or on the reverse side of the schedule. It is not advisable to rely on the investigator's memory. One device which helps avoid this source of error is the use of abbreviations that are easily associated with the items they represent. Usually the first letter or two of a word serves as a satisfactory symbol unless, of course, two entries have the same first letters and hence may cause confusion.

If the possible responses can be foreseen or discovered by pretesting, the questions can be formulated so that the respondent or interviewer does one of the following:

    a. Writes Yes or No.
    b. Writes a number.
    c. Puts a cross ($\times$) after the correct answer or in an answer box.
    d. Underlines the correct answer.
    e. Crosses out all answers which do not apply.
    f. Puts in a symbol.
    g. Circles the correct answer.[17]

16. *Plan to include a few questions that will serve as checks on the accuracy and consistency of the questions as a whole.* Two questions that bring out the same fact but that are worded differently and placed in different sections of the schedule serve to check the "Internal consistency" of the replies.

17. *Avoid questions that call out responses toward socially accepted norms or values.* Such questions often fail to indicate a person's real opinion unless they are followed by others which make the issues concrete or place them on a behavioral level (825). Rugg and Cantril observe that questions that bluntly state a deviation from an established norm or value are less likely to be answered favorably than those which express the same deviation but state it more by implication. People are reluctant to favor a statement of a policy which suggests that a law must be changed to carry it out (825). Individuals who might otherwise favor a certain policy will oppose it if the way it is stated indicates the need for a change in existing laws.

18. *Avoid apparently unreasonable questions by using a brief ex-*

---

[17] See pp. 182–200 for various ways of framing opinion or attitude questions.

planation justifying the question. This might prevent "Don't knows" or untruthful answers. Encourage respondents to answer by the use of such phrases as "Of course no one can tell for sure as yet," "Taking everything into consideration ....." or "Nobody knows for certain, but what is your best guess about ....."

19. *Plan to compare the responses to many single questions with responses to other questions which put the same issue in different contexts.* This is essential because any opinion datum is meaningful only in a large personal and social context (825, p. 494).

SEQUENCE OF QUESTIONS:

Just as it is necessary to pretest the wording of the questions, so it is essential to test the order in which questions are to be asked. The pretest is particularly important in opinion surveys, but even in factual surveys many refusals and misunderstandings can be eliminated by proper arrangment of the questions. The following suggestions on question order are not exhaustive, but should be supplemented by discussions of this problem in such books as *Consumer and Opinion Research* (77) and *Gauging Public Opinion* (142).

Questions should be arranged logically if confusion and misunderstanding are to be avoided. When the data are to be secured by the interview method, the questions should be grouped so that the conversation will lead logically from one question to the next. Transitions in subject matter are not easy to convey to the listener. If the interview seems to skip around a great deal, many more "don't knows" or "undecided" answers will be received.

It is possible to determine the direction of the response by question arrangement. For example, in one study of the attitudes of people toward advertising, it was possible to get the respondents to think in terms of advertising toward which they approved without actually mentioning advertising. They were asked about dresses. Then when the question on advertising was asked they thought of dress advertising and responded more favorably to the idea of advertising than when the dress question was omitted. The question or questions preceding a given question may produce a certain "set" in the informant and cause him to reply very differently from the way he might if the preceding questions were different. Since it is difficult for the respondent to grasp a change in subject matter unless warned by the interviewer that a shift is going to take place, any given question will be likely to be interpreted and reacted to in the light of earlier questions. Many people do not listen carefully. They try to get the "gist" of a question and then give a reaction without even waiting for the question to be completed. Thus their response is very likely to be influenced by the frame of reference already developed.

When two or more related questions are used, the answer to the later questions are likely to be influenced by the answers already given. People try to be consistent in their replies, so if they have taken a stand at the beginning of the interview they may be tempted to carry out their point of view throughout the interview. An interesting experiment is reported by Link in this connection. The two questions which follow were asked in a national survey: 1. "Do you believe that workers and unions have the right to strike when wages and working conditions don't suit them?" 2. "Do you believe that business men have the right to shut down their factories and stores when labor conditions and profits don't suit them?" When question 1 was asked first, 65.9 per cent of the respondents said that the workers had the right to strike, but when question 2 was asked first 61.6 per cent held this view. The per cent who replied that businessmen had the right to close down their shops was also greater when question 1 preceded question 2. When question 1 came first, 52.3 per cent approved of the right to close the establishment, but when question 2 was presented first 46.7 believed in the employer's right.

If general and specific questions are used, the general ones should precede the specific ones. Otherwise the respondent is likely to answer the general ones in terms of the earlier specific ones. For example, if the general question "What improvements do you think can be made in kitchens?" is preceded by the specific question "Is there enough work space in your kitchen?" this will get the informant to thinking about the space question of kitchens and his suggested improvements are more likely to be along this line than if the order of questioning were reversed.

The opening question should have human interest appeal. If interest is aroused at the start the respondent is less likely to refuse to cooperate. Questions on fashions, movies, family customs, cost of living, psychological differences between sexes, and topics of the day are usually good openers.

The opening questions should be easily answered. It is advisable to use short questions which can be answered with a simple yes or no. If the respondent is asked to express the answer in his own words he usually finds difficulty at first. Pollers have found a greater proportion of don't know answers to the first than to later questions, so it is a good idea to keep the first question very simple. If it frightens the respondent or makes him feel apologetic or ignorant, he may refuse to be polled on the ground that he doesn't "know anything about that stuff." A few simple questions at the beginning will give the respondent confidence in himself which is invaluable for carrying the interview through later, more complicated questioning. Advice-seeking questions (p. 175) are good for bolstering the ego of respondents.

The opener should not give the impression that the interviewer has an ax to grind or that he is selling or advertising something. If the first few questions make the informant suspicious, he may either give biased replies throughout or he may refuse to go on with the interview.

Questions which might embarrass the informant should be placed toward the middle or end of the questionnaire. Those on economic status, those that reflect on the knowledge or ability of the interviewee, those of an intimate personal nature are best given after rapport has been established with the investigator. When asked "Do you know what 'reciprocal trade' means?" one college professor complained, "Say what is this, an intelligence test?" If this question had been asked after rapport had been established the professor probably would not have resented it.

Questions to which the informant may be sensitive should not be placed at the very end because this may leave him with misgivings and make it difficult to check-interview him later. In long questionnaires, questions with an emotional tinge may be interspersed between items which elicit more neutral reactions. In general, the questions should be arranged in the best sequence possible from the point of view of the interviewer and the arrangement preferred for analysis. If the arrangement differs too widely for these two purposes, the schedule should be arranged to suit the interviewer's requirements. The data can then be transcribed to another form better adapted to tabulation and analysis. Whenever possible, however, the need for transcription should be avoided by careful planning of the schedule.

In designing mail questionnaires, the arrangement of questions in order of interest is particularly important. Lacking the personality of an interviewer to "sell" the respondent on the survey, the mail questionnaire must be its own salesman. Since there is serious danger that the mail informant will lose interest as he proceeds to fill in the form, important questions should be placed near the beginning. Thus the respondent will not only be more likely to fill it out, but he will probably give it more attention. Eastwood (266, p. 289) suggests that if a choice must be made between importance and interest, importance should be sacrificed because without interest there is little chance of the questions being answered at all.

Opinion questions placed on mail questionnaires should be tested for best placement. Somewhat the same principles that are important in interviews need to be considered for mail surveys. It is particularly important to group questions under headings which emphasize the principle topics upon which information is being sought. Grouping makes the page appear interesting as well as easy to fill out, and it helps the respondent to catch shifts in subject matter.

The following suggestions on the physical arrangement of items give some idea of the variety of devices which can be used to facilitate filling out the schedule correctly and efficiently:

1. Number each item consecutively. Never repeat a number on the schedule. This facilitates reference to items when the instructions and definitions are prepared. It is also important to have each item clearly distinguished for tabulation purposes.

2. When material is to be written in, allow enough space for clear and legible entries, e.g., names of organizations, type of work, etc. Completeness of response is frequently related to the amount of space provided. Avoid crowding the items unduly, for this leads to confusion and errors.

3. Set off questions by dotted lines, solid lines, bold face type, or spacing.

4. Vary the type within a question to emphasize the most important words or phrases.

5. Arrange the items in columns or rows so that items not filled in can be seen at a glance.

6. Allow space on the back of the form for notes, coding, checking, etc.

7. Place answer boxes, circles, X's, numbers in parentheses or brackets after questions so that all the interviewer or respondent has to do is encircle or check the correct answers. If the questionnaire has been pretested, relatively few answers should fall in the "other-specify" category which is provided for rare and unforeseen answers.

8. If the respondent is to be asked to choose between several long or involved alternatives presented by an interviewer, it is a good idea to put the various answers on a card which can be handed to the informant to look over. The interviewer reads aloud only the question proper. Not only do these card questions make it possible to present more complicated issues than might be possible if the respondent had to depend on verbal presentation, but the questionnaire carried by the interviewer is correspondingly simplified. Whatever devices used, the schedule should appear to be neat and easy to fill out. This is particularly necessary in a mail questionnaire where a complicated looking form may so discourage the prospective respondent that he will not even attempt to fill it out.

Selected References

Phrasing of Questions
Bancroft and Welch (30), Bennett (43), Benson (46), Blankenship (69, 70, 71, 73, 74, 76, 77, 78), Brown (115), Burtt and Gaskill (129), Campbell (133, 134), Cantril (139, 142, 143, 144), Chapin (157), Chappell (169), Crutchfield and Gordon (220), Eastwood (266), England (290), Erdos (292), Flesch (316), *Fortune* (318), Franken (327), Franzen (330), Gallup (340, 342), Gallup and Rae (345), Ghiselli (355, 357), Gosnell and de Grazia (374), Harper (406), Hettinger et al. (434), *International Journal of Opinion and Attitude Research* (467), Jenkins (470), Karol (488, 489), Katz (491), King (515), Kornhauser (534, 535), Kulp (537), Lazarsfeld (542), Lee (558), Likert (565), Link (576), Link et al. (580), Lurie (600), Marsh (616), Mathews (618), Max (619), Menefee (635, 636), Muscio (664), NORC (675, 676), Newhall (690), Osgood and Stagner (708), Osgood et al. (709), Pace (711, 712), Payne (725), Perry (734), Psychological Corp. (750), Rogers (797), Romine (799), Roper (803, 806, 810), Roslow and Blankenship (815), Roslow et al. (816), Ruch (819), Rugg (824), Rugg and Cantril (825), Rushmore (827), Sheatsley (868, 869), Sletto (878), Stagner (905), Stanton (908), Studenski (941),

Suchman and Guttman (942), Terris (955), Thorndike (960), Vicary (1041), Welch (1074), Young (1138).

Attitude Measurement and Scales

Albig (2), Bain (23, 24), Ballin and Farnsworth (28), Bernard (54), Beyle (62), Bogardus (87, 89), Campbell (136), Cantril (144), Chapin (166), Churchman et al. (174), Conrad (190), Crespi (209), Day (232), Day and Quackenbush (233), Deri et al. (245), Droba (253), Dunham (259), Dunlap and Knoll (261), Edwards and Kenney (278), Edwards and Kilpatrick (279, 280), Farnsworth (295, 296), Ferguson (298, 299), Fromme (335), Gilliland and Katzoff (359), Guilford (384), Guttman (385, 386), Hildreth (435), Hinckley (440), Horst (452), *International Journal of Opinion and Attitude Research* (467), Jaffee (468), Kirkpatrick (518, 520), Knower (525, 526, 527), Kornhauser (533), Kriedt and Clark (536), Kulp (537, 538), Likert (563), Lorge (586, 587), McNemar (631), Mitchell (648), Murphy and Likert (661), Noll (699), Pace (711, 712), Pemberton (732), Remmers (765), Remmers and Silance (766), Riker (781), Rosander (812), Roskelley (814), Rundquist and Sletto (826), Sayre (838), Schettler (841), Seashore and Hevner (857), Smith (886, 887), Strang (940), Suchman and Guttman (942), Symonds (948, 949), Thurstone (962), Thurstone and Chave (963), Vetter (1040), Whisler (1083), Wrightstone (1126).

CHAPTER VII

Types of Sampling

Although a uniform terminology has not yet been adopted by statisticians to describe the types of sampling in general use, the principles underlying the various techniques are quite widely recognized. Confusion has arisen because in practice combinations of the various principles are often employed, and it is difficult to label any given sample with a single correct designation. Furthermore, these principles relate to the manner of drawing samples. In studies of human populations the sample of cases selected for study in actual practice is seldom exactly the same as the one from which data are obtained and tabulated. Thus one type of sample, selected in conformity with the principles of one sampling technique, may prove to be another type if the procedures followed during the collection of data are not in accord with the essential characteristics of the original sampling design.[1] In the following discussion, the advantages and disadvantages of each type for social surveys are briefly summarized from the point of view of both selection and collection. The differentiated types of sampling are random, stratified, purposive, double or mixed, and unsystematic. Combinations of one or more of these are often found most expedient for social surveys. Illustrations of these combinations are quota sampling, area sampling, and regular-interval city-directory sampling. The term "probability sampling" is employed when the sample is chosen in accordance with probability theory and its sampling error can be computed.

Random Sampling

Random sampling is the term applied when the method of selection assures each individual or element in the universe an equal chance of being chosen. The selection is regarded as being made by "chance."

---

[1] Detailed procedures for selecting and collecting the various types of samples are presented in later chapters.

Many surveyors have assumed that they could achieve chance selection through unpremeditated and unsystematic procedures which follow no law of choice. Unfortunately this is not the case. Unless every precaution is taken to avoid biasing the elements and a conscious effort is made to insure the operation of chance factors, the resulting sample is not likely to be a random sample. Before a random sampling technique can be properly designed, knowledge of the interrelationships of social data and of the characteristics of the group to be sampled is essential. Lacking this knowledge, many sample designers unwittingly introduce nonrandom selection into their sampling procedures. The requisite of random selection, that every unit in the population or universe has the same chance of being selected as every other unit, is not easy to achieve in sampling human populations, for there are usually conditions or situations which favor certain units over others. It is impossible to enumerate all the ways in which these selective factors may operate; some suggestions appear in Chapters VIII and XII.

Random sampling has sometimes been referred to as "representative" or "proportional" sampling. If the sample is chosen at random and if the number of cases in it is sufficiently large, it will represent all the groups in the universe in approximately correct proportions. Thus a large enough random sample, properly drawn, is both a representative and a proportional sample. If the sample is not large enough, there is the chance that it may be an extreme deviate and therefore nonrepresentative. Fortunately the laws of chance assure that such "bad samples" are infrequent and are not likely to turn up often enough to disturb our calculations. In fact, this chance of turning up can be mathematically computed, and we can decide whether or not to accept the probability.

Whether or not random sampling is used as the primary sampling procedure, an attempt usually is made to use it in the final selection of cases. Within strata, for example, the choice of cases to constitute the sample for each subgroup of the population should be a chance selection. If it is not, elements of bias are likely to enter and the sample will be unrepresentative.

PRINCIPLES:

To insure each unit an equal chance of inclusion, the following principles must be observed:

1. The population to be sampled and the units composing it must be clearly defined so that there will be no question as to what the sample represents.

2. A universe composed of many small units is preferable to one composed of fewer but larger units.

3. The units should be of approximately equal size. The importance of this prerequisite is easily understood when we consider drawing capsules blindfold from a goldfish bowl; the fingers are much more likely to grasp the large than the very small capsules. The application of this principle to other units of selection is not so readily recognized. To be of the same size, no unit should cover a larger area than any other if the selection is to be made on the basis of area. Violations of this rule are frequent. For example, if a random selection of 100 counties in this country were desired in order to determine how many counties had consolidated schools, the sample would not be random if the well-known "grid" procedure was used. This would consist in dividing the map of the United States into equal-sized squares, say 10,000, and selecting the counties in which squares 4, 104, 204, 304, or any other numbers secured in a chance drawing, are located. Large counties will have a much greater chance of containing a square or even several squares than the smallest counties. A sample like this that is biased in favor of large geographic areas would probably also be biased in respect to degree of urbanization or date of settlement or other factors too numerous to mention, but which in turn might be related to school provisions which constitute the subject of the survey. Similarly, the selection of city wards, city blocks, farms, etc., based on an area principle of selection for sampling populations, also violates the requirement of equal-sized units.[2]

If a card file is to be sampled by selecting cards on the basis of a measured number of inches, the cards should be of uniform thickness for otherwise the thicker cards will have disproportionately greater chance of being drawn.

4. If any unit appears more than once in the population to be sampled, all the other units should appear the same number of times. This principle, a variation of the preceding one, is frequently violated

---

[2] This requirement is not violated when the subject of inquiry happens to be the number of square miles or acres of crops (not by counties) or other characteristics expressed in terms of area, and the units to be sampled are divided into equal-sized areas.

in sampling social data. It is not unusual to find that certain cases are duplicated in the source list from which random samples are to be selected. To assure each case an equal chance of being drawn, the duplicate listings should be removed, or duplicates should be inserted for the cases that are listed only once. Special safeguards are required for making a random selection of names from files of cards in which some persons have several cards and others have only one (see pages 268–269). For instance, if a sample of parents whose children go to a given school were wanted, the parents of large families would be over-represented if parents of every hundredth child in the school were chosen for the sample. Parents with six children would have six times the chance of being drawn as would parents with one child in the school.

5. All the units should be independent of each other so that if one is drawn it will in no way affect the choice of another. For example, if a sample of the heads of families in a given community were chosen by taking every hundredth dwelling unit in the city, the sample would be quite unrepresentative of family heads if, in addition to this procedure, all married children belonging to the hundredth households but living elsewhere in the city were also re-garded as part of the sample. The selection of these other married couples would not be independent of the first group. In fact, these younger heads would have two chances to be chosen—either as one in one hundred, or as married children of the one-in-one-hundred house-holders.

6. The same unit should be used in sampling and in tabulation and analysis. A sample of individuals is preferable to a sample of families for generalizations about individuals. Similarly, a sample of dwelling units is preferable to one composed of city blocks or wards when the tabulations are to be made in terms of households.

7. The chance of selecting a certain unit in the total population must be uniform from one sample to another. In truly random selec-tion, the item selected should be returned to the universe so that in another sample it might theoretically be chosen again. In most social surveys, subsequent samples are usually drawn from universes which exclude the orginal sample. This is like drawing balls from an urn and not replacing them before drawing again. Thus if one happened to draw out most of the black balls in a million to one chance, sub-

sequent samples drawn from that urn would necessarily be deficient in black balls.

8. The universe must be present or catalogued so that every unit in it is listed or can be given an identifying symbol to be used during the drawing of the sample. This is one of the objections raised against random sampling of human populations. The catalogue or listing is often difficult to obtain, or time-consuming and expensive to assemble. However, by first classifying the population into groups, it becomes unnecessary to list every case in the universe. If the total number of cases in each of the various groups is known, it is possible to decide by lot which group the sample case falls in and then list or number only the cases in this group in order to identify the particular case belonging in the sample. (See page 275 for an example of this technique.)

9. The method of selecting the sample should be completely independent of the characteristics to be examined. For example, it has sometimes been assumed that selecting from a list of all the names that begin with one of the first 13 letters of the alphabet is equivalent to choosing names by "chance," because the initial letter of the name seems entirely unrelated to any characteristics to be surveyed. This assumption is usually false. Names are associated with nationality and this in turn is related either directly or indirectly to numerous economic and social characteristics.

10. All the units in the population should be available at the time the sample is drawn. This is possible, of course, only if a complete list or catalogue of the population is accessible to the sampler. If one were sampling a card file all cases should be in the file and all file drawers present when the sample is drawn.

11. In order for the sample to remain random throughout the survey, every unit drawn must be accessible to the surveyor for the collection of information. In a sample of the general population it is necessary to reach all groups drawn in the sample—people living in trailers, houseboats, institutions, as well as residents of exclusive homes or apartments. Insofar as any of these groups is not accessible to the surveyor, the sample loses its randomness. Surveys conducted by telephone cannot be random samples of the public because the more than fifty per cent who live in homes without telephones are not accessible.

12. Once selected, no unit drawn at random can be discarded without risk of introducing bias or changing the universe of which the sample is representative. Thus omission of schedules for people who are not at home when the interviewer calls or who refuse the information results in a departure from randomness.

13. No selective factor should be present in the tabulations made from the sample. In mail surveys it is not uncommon for tabulations to be based upon returns from 15 or 20 per cent of the number who received questionnaires. Analyses of characteristics of respondents and nonrespondents have shown the nonrandom nature of such returns.

Tabulations made from the first few hundred schedules that happen to be ready for the tabulation process are unlikely to be random selections. Cases presenting special problems either in field work or in editing and coding do not show up in sufficient numbers in such tabulations.

PROCEDURES:

The following procedures are commonly used to select random samples of human populations: (1) drawing by lot numbered slips of paper from a container, capsules from a goldfish bowl, or balls from an urn; (2) using tables of random sample numbers; (3) using a roulette wheel; (4) selecting units at regular intervals from a list or card file or map; (5) selecting line numbers or fixed positions; (6) using a grill or screen. These procedures are discussed fully in Chapter VIII.

ADVANTAGES:

The advantages of random sampling may be summed up as follows: 1. No advance knowledge of the characteristics of the universe or of their distribution within it is necessary in random sampling. The surveyor does not need to depend on "hunches" regarding the relationship between the various characteristics and the phenomena to be studied by the survey. Neither does he need to know the relative frequencies of the various strata in the universe in order to devise the correct weighting procedures when applying the results from the sample to the total universe. Thus random samples are free from biases which may be introduced by the use of incorrect weights.

2. The analyst can easily assess the accuracy of his estimates because sampling errors follow the laws of chance. The theory of random sampling is further developed than that of any other type of sampling. This theory enables the surveyor to provide the most statistically reliable information for the least cost.

3. The units in a random sample are likely to reveal the variability of the population better than the same number of cases chosen deliberately. The random sample tends to represent the universe in all of its variable aspects.

4. As the random sample is enlarged, it becomes increasingly representative of the universe, and the extent to which it can be relied upon to give a true cross-section can be determined in accordance with the laws of probability. If the random sample contains a small number of cases, it may deviate considerably from the universe, but by and large, most of the samples will tend to resemble the universe from which they are drawn. Further discussion of this point is given in Chapter IX.

DISADVANTAGES:

Random sampling has the following disadvantages:

1. The need for a completely catalogued universe from which to draw the sample has often prevented the use of the random sampling method. Surveyors seldom can find an up-to-date list of all the units in the population to be sampled. However, they should not give up too easily, because such sources as city directories (see page 255) are satisfactory for the purposes.

2. The task of numbering every unit before the sample is chosen is time-consuming and expensive. This limitation is not insurmountable, however, because it is not always necessary to number each unit. Regular-interval sampling (see page 266), for example, if applied to a list that is not classified in any way, will yield a random sample without every item being numbered. Furthermore, if the number of cases in the groups comprising the total is known, it is possible to devise a numbering scheme whereby only the groups in which the randomly drawn numbers happen to fall need to be identified in detail.

3. The possibility of obtaining a poor or misleading sample is always present when random selection is used. As Stephan says: "It provides but little aid and comfort to the victim of a poor draw in ran-

dom sampling to assure him that in the long run the random method of selection will give him errors in one direction just as often as it will in another" (921, p. 349).

4. The size of the sample required to secure equal statistical reliability is usually larger with random than with stratified sampling.

5. From the point of view of field surveys, it has been claimed that cases selected by random sampling tend to be too widely dispersed geographically, and that the time and cost of going from one address to another are too large. This disadvantage may be offset by considerations discussed on page 279.

Stratified Sampling

Stratified sampling is frequently recommended as the most efficient procedure for insuring representativeness. It consists in first classifying the universe into two or more strata or classes and then drawing a sample from each stratum. The following is a simple illustration of stratified sampling: if a sample of men and women telephone subscribers is desired, the sampler first prepares two lists, one containing the names of the men subscribers and the other the names of the women subscribers. To secure a 10 per cent stratified sample, he draws a sample of one in ten from each list. This sample resembles a 10 per cent *random* sample which could have been drawn without separating the men and women subscribers, i.e., without stratifying. However, if the sample contained relatively few cases, the sampler could not be certain that the sexes would be represented in the same proportion as they occur in the universe. With small numbers of cases, occasional samples might deviate considerably from the universe. Thus, stratification by sex guarantees proportional representation for each sex and eliminates the possibility of drawing a poor random sample.

The final selection of cases within each stratum should be made at random. However, unless this is done in accordance with a carefully designed plan and under the direction of a sampling supervisor, a random selection within strata is seldom achieved.

TYPES OF STRATIFIED SAMPLING:

There are several types of stratified sampling. The number of cases selected within each stratum may be proportional or disproportional; it may be the same from stratum to stratum or vary from one stratum to another, depending upon the sampling plan. Furthermore, if each stratum is not represented in the sample in the same proportions as in the universe from which the sample is drawn, the findings for the strata may be weighted or multiplied in such a way as to give a picture of the universe; they may be left unweighted if only comparisons between comparable subgroups are contemplated.

Proportional Stratified Sampling. In proportional sampling the cases are drawn from each stratum in the same proportion as they occur in the universe. If the strata have different totals, proportionality for each stratum is achieved by drawing a constant proportion of cases from each one. For example, to secure a 10 per cent sample of the voting population, stratified by wards within a given city, the wards should first be listed and then one in ten of the voters within each ward should be selected. If 30 per cent of the population resided in Ward X and 15 per cent in Ward Y, drawing every tenth case in these two wards would make the sample contain twice as many cases from Ward X as from Ward Y. A proportional stratified sample should closely resemble a random sample. The only difference is that proportional sampling enables the sampler to be sure that he is obtaining the right proportion from each stratum. If he drew a purely random sample which was quite small, it might by chance contain more than the correct proportion for one district and less for another; it might even fail to include any cases from some districts with small populations.

If selection at regular intervals, e.g., every tenth case from a list is employed, the basis on which the list is made determines whether or not the resulting sample is a proportional stratified or a random sample. For example, if every third name is selected in regular sequence from an alphabetical list, the resulting sample should contain approximately one-third of the names beginning with each letter of the alphabet. Hence it would be a *proportional stratified alphabetical sample*. If the alphabetical arrangement was entirely unrelated to the problem being surveyed, either directly or indirectly, the sample might be considered a random sample. Also, if the list was not classified in any way and the arrangement of names appeared completely unrelated to any known characteristic, sampling at regular intervals would yield a random sample. For further discussion of the effect of the arrangement of the list from which the sample is drawn, see pages 267–268.

The chief advantage of stratified proportional sampling is that it insures proper representation of the attributes or variables which the investigator considers most important for the subject of the survey. If he uses poor judgment or has inadequate information upon which to base the stratification, the sample will be no better (or worse) than one secured by random selection. Thus the surveyor has nothing to lose and much to gain by stratifying the universe before drawing the sample.

The more strata there are, the more complicated becomes the problem of securing proportional representation for each one. In fact, the problem is often so difficult that the selection of cases within the substrata is rarely made on a random basis if left up to interviewers.

Disproportional Stratified Sampling. In disproportional stratified sampling, usually an equal number of cases is secured from each stratum, regardless of how the stratum is represented in the universe. The number of cases drawn from each one is restricted to the number predesignated in the plans.

This form of sampling is sometimes called controlled sampling because the number of cases to be selected in the various strata is limited. A controlled sample of this type was employed in the Urban Study of Consumer Purchases conducted by the U. S. Department of Labor (1010, 847) because the cost of collecting and analyzing detailed data on family expenditures was so great that the number of schedules to be secured had to be set as low as possible. Only five schedules were obtained from families in each income, occupational, and family composition group, regardless of the frequency of the cases within each group in the general population.

One advantage of this method of sampling is the fact that all the strata are equally reliable from the point of view of the size of sample. Hence when an equal number of cases is taken from each stratum, comparisons of the different strata are facilitated. An even more important advantage, however, is the economy. The controlled sample prevents the investigators from securing an unnecessarily large number of schedules from the most prevalent groups in the population. In the Study of Consumer Purchases mentioned above, for example, families of wage earners comprised about 60 per cent of all the urban families whereas families of professional men constituted only between 5 and 10 per cent. To secure schedules from a sufficiently large number of people in the latter group for the detailed analysis proposed, it would have been necessary to obtain a very large random sample—one that contained far more wage earners than were needed for the analysis of occupational differences in expenditures.

The practical difficulty of locating an equal number of individuals who have the desired qualifications when the sample is controlled by several variables is usually great. If the 'specifications require that people possess three or more definite characteristics in common, few will be eligible in most communities. Thus, before the controlled sample can be surveyed, it may be necessary, as in the Study of Consumer Purchases, to conduct a preliminary random survey of the community to locate eligible cases. If some time elapses between the preliminary survey and the interview for the controlled survey, such problems as the tracing of mobile groups, the arrival of new eligible cases in the community, and the choice of correct weights arise. The goal of equal numbers of cases is seldom achieved in field work surveys. In the end, the sampler is likely to find that his sample has the combined disadvantages of unequal numbers of cases, smallness, and nonrepresentativeness.

Unequal Number of Cases from the Various Strata. The number of cases desired in the sample can be selected purely for analytical or tabulation purposes and regardless of their frequency in the universe. For example, instead of selecting 1000 families with incomes of $2000 and over, the surveyor might find it expedient to study twice as many in this group as in the lower-income class. Not only would the number from each income class be disproportional to the number in the universe, but the two strata would contain unequal numbers of cases. Thus the advantage of comparability from the point of view of size of sample would be lost. But this type of sampling might be desirable if the survey were directed primarily toward ascertaining the characteristics of the upper-income group, and if the more detailed tabulations were to be based on the groups with an income of $2000 or more.

The proportion of cases to be drawn from each stratum may also be varied according to the homogeneity or heterogeneity of the population in the stratum. To make an accurate estimate of the properties of a stratum composed of a mixed population requires a larger sample than is needed if the stratum is internally homogeneous. In a study of food habits, for instance, the sample required for a city whose popu-

lation is 95 per cent American-born would not be the same size as that
required for a city containing 50 per cent native-born and 10 per cent
each of five foreign-born groups. To secure equally reliable results
for each nationality group, it would be necessary to sample the second
city more heavily than the first.

Another example from the field of election forecasting may serve
further to clarify the point. Stratification by states is necessary for
presidential elections because the electoral college system makes the
candidate's state pluralities rather than his national plurality the determining vote. Certain states are usually recognized as "sure states";
hence relatively small samples will give a satisfactory forecast for
them. "Doubtful states," on the other hand, require relatively large
numbers of cases to get a precise measure of the direction of the vote.
If the forecaster makes a correct judgment in his classification of states
by certainty, he can distribute his limited sample efficiently by con-
centrating it in the states where he most needs precision in his figures.
This procedure was followed effectively by Crossley in the 1940 presidential campaign (**213**, p. 83). If the sampler's guess about the characteristics of the strata is incorrect, the results may be disastrous unless
last minute adjustments in the sample can be made and the controls
junked.

Stratified Weighted Sampling (Adjusting for Disproportionality).
It is possible, by multiplication or weighting of the averages and other
statistics from each stratum, to produce a result which closely resembles a random sample or cross-section of the universe being studied. In the Urban Study of Consumer Purchases, cited above, an estimate of the expenditures of the income groups as a whole was secured
by multiplying the average expenditures of each income group by the
frequency of that group in the general population. (The frequency of
the various income, occupational, and family composition groups was
ascertained previously by means of a random sampling (**847**). Thus
weights were used to adjust the proportions of the sample so that it
would represent the universe.

The problems arising in connection with the determination and application of weights are discussed on pp. 235–483. Suffice it to say here
that these problems often either are overlooked or underestimated
when sampling plans are being developed.

THE NUMBER OF FACTORS FOR STRATIFICATION:

Although theoretically the number of controls used for stratification is more or less unlimited, the number of those which are practicable is very limited. In the first place, many characteristics frequently used in controls are intercorrelated so the addition of new factors for stratification does not reduce the variability materially. Thus if an income control is used, a control by rent level or even by education is not likely to add a great deal to the homogeneity of the groups. In the second place, the addition of controls complicates the survey work at all stages from the planning of the sample to the collection and handling of schedules and the preparation of tables. With increased complications come greater chances of error, loss of time in carrying out the program, and added costs to cover the attendant problems. The more controls used, the greater the task of finding people who meet the specifications of the various subgroups or cells. After the schedules are in the office, the problems do not cease. The difficulty of deciding upon the weights for each substratum as well as the complications arising during tabulation cannot be stressed too strongly. Surveyors who have faced the practical and technical problems of surveys in which several controls have been imposed are not likely to recommend a sampling plan which includes more than two significant controls and division into more than three classes of substrata within each stratum.

If the sample is being used more or less continuously for surveys, the sampling plan can be more complicated than that used in an unrepeated survey. The National Opinion Research Center which is making surveys periodically has employed more controls than that recommended above and has been rather successful. Its social cross-section of the civilian adult population is controlled by geographic distribution (regional and rural-urban), and by sex, color, and standard-of-living level. Age groups under and over 40 years of age are also used in the assignment quotas (674).

THE CHOICE OF VARIABLES FOR STRATIFICATION:

The following considerations should enter into the selection of controls for stratification:

1. **The Kind of Information Available.** It is important that the information about the strata be up to date, accurate, complete, appli-

cable to the population, and available to the surveyor. Shortly after a federal or state census has been made, it is relatively easy to use stratification in sampling because the counts meet these requirements. When the latest census is several years old, or when great upheavals have occurred in the population owing to war, heavy migration, or other factors, the surveyor who employs stratification runs the risk of being quite wrong in his estimates of the size of the strata he employs. If he attempts to combine figures for the different strata, he may build up an entirely erroneous figure for the total. The National Opinion Research Center has recognized this problem and is constantly looking for population trends that may affect its sample. Much of the information it is forced to use is incomplete, or at best a rough estimate on the part of some government agency. In May, 1946, for example, their results showed that 15.2 per cent of the adults 21 years or over had attended college. The 1940 census figure for this group was 10.4 per cent. Whether the observed difference between the two figures could be regarded as correctly indicating the advancing educational level of the population, or whether it should have been looked upon with alarm by the sampler cannot ever be known with certainty, and can be checked approximately only after the 1950 census figures are available. Fortunately, educational level is not used as one of the controls of the NORC sample, so the sampler does not have to decide what weights to give the various educational groups.

Many characteristics of the population cannot be used as controls because no satisfactory statistics about them are available. Religion, for example, cannot be used as a control in surveys of the general population for this reason. Although income or economic level is frequently used as a control, the incidence of various income groups just a few years after a census has been more a matter of conjecture than of knowledge. Thanks to the current sampling surveys of the census bureau, however, population trends are being charted with greater and greater accuracy and the time is not too distant when the surveyor will have at hand current information which will enable him to use income and other controls without too much risk.

2. The Variable in Relation to the Survey. The surveyor should have reason to believe that the factors he uses for stratification are significantly related to the topic under investigation. Critics of public opinion surveys have claimed that controls are too often selected

blindly by adopting the customary controls of region, income, and sex. More attention to the factors most closely associated with the survey topic might yield better samples and more meaningful information. In a study of racial prejudice, for example, political boundaries, while having the advantage of statistical background data, may not be so important a control as the percentage of Negroes in the area. Gallup found in measuring opinion toward foreign countries that racial derivation was an important control but that this factor did not show up significantly in other issues (345, p. 78).

3. **Size of the Strata in the Total Sample.** Unless the stratum under consideration is large enough so that the sampler and field force will have no great difficulty locating candidates for it, it should not be used. An exception to this rule is found when the characteristics of the proposed stratum constitute the subject of inquiry.

4. **Internal Homogeneity of the Strata.** When selecting the factors for stratification, the surveyor should try to choose those that are homogeneous with respect to characteristics that are closely related to the subject of the inquiry. Insofar as the items within a stratum are like each other and different from items in other strata, the stratification is successful. If the items were identical in a given cell, only one case would be necessary to reveal the characteristics of that cell. Such similarity is practically nonexistent in the world of human beings, so the most that can be hoped for is the reduction of variability within cells so that the characteristics can be shown with relatively few cases.

ADVANTAGES AND DISADVANTAGES OF STRATIFIED
SAMPLING:

In summarizing the pros and cons of stratified sampling in general, it should be pointed out that the type of stratification used, as well as the topic and plan of the survey as a whole, determine the feasibility of stratification for any particular purpose.

Stratified sampling has the following advantages:

1. Since the population is first stratified and a sample is then drawn from each stratum, the surveyor can be certain that none of the essential groups will be excluded from the sample. Greater representativeness of the sample is thus assured, and the occasional mishaps that occur in random sampling are avoided.

2. With more homogeneous populations, greater precision can be

achieved with fewer cases. This usually means a saving in the time and cost of collecting and processing data.

3. When an interviewer is told to choose representative sample cases, the samples he chooses may be more representative if his quota is allocated by strata than if he is told to use his own judgment. When the interviewer's selections are restricted to groups with a small range of variation, his choices are less likely to be completely unrepresentative than would be the case were he given free reign in his selections. With all the research that has been done on bias in interviewer's selections, few surveyors now permit their field workers to choose the sample without numerous restrictions.

4. Samples that are self-selected, such as the returns from mail questionnaires, are likely to be less biased if stratification is used. To cite Stephan: "By providing that a fixed proportion of the sample shall come from each geographic area or income class, stratification automatically brings about the replacement of persons lost to the sample by persons of the same stratum, thus partly correcting the bias that would result if there were no replacement of losses. The numbers of questionnaires mailed to persons in strata with low rates of return can be increased to compensate for the lower rates so that the number of usable returns received from each stratum will be proportional to the size of the stratum. It may also be possible to introduce into the stratification scheme a classification that will separate effectively the kind of people for whom the loss rates are high from those for whom they are low, thereby controlling the major part of the bias due to losses" (923, p. 41).

5. As compared with random samples, stratified samples can be more concentrated geographically, thereby reducing the interviewer's time and expenses in going from one address to another.

Certain disadvantages, however, are inherent in stratified sampling:

1. In order to choose significant controls for stratification, the investigator needs to know a great deal about the subject of the survey and its relationships to other factors. For example, in public opinion polls income is used as the control. But if the issue on which the voters are divided is not associated with income class, a sample stratified on this basis that omitted the controlling influence by which the voters are divided might give absolutely unreliable results in the absence of randomness within the strata. In the last few

national elections particularly, voting has followed economic class lines so the income stratification has worked quite well. Furthermore, there are few social, psychological, or economic characteristics which do not show differentials by income class; hence income is a wise choice for a control. The surveyor must be on the lookout for any other factor not correlated with income that becomes a more powerful control.

2. Disproportionate stratification requires the weighting of results, stratum by stratum. The relative frequency of each stratum in the universe must be known or estimated in order to determine the weights by which averages, distributions, or totals for each group are to be multiplied to produce the cross-sectional picture of the whole. Ascertaining the correct frequency of each stratum and substratum is often impossible because of the absence of up-to-date statistics. The problem of weighting was solved in the Urban Study of Consumer Purchases by conducting a random sample investigation in which a short schedule was used simultaneously with the controlled stratified sample. Thus the frequency of each income, occupational, and family composition group was ascertained from the random sample (847).

3. It is difficult to locate cases that fit the specifications. Unless the cases can be selected from a random sample or from a total universe in which each case has been catalogued and described, the field work involved in locating the types desired in the sample consumes a great deal of time. In the Study of Consumer Purchases a random sample of families was visited; this served as a guide to selecting the controlled sample. If this random sample had not been drawn, it is doubtful whether the stratified controlled sample would have been possible.

4. If disproportionate stratification is employed, special problems arise in connection with weighting. Among these problems are the effect of combining data for different strata without first weighting them, the administrative problem of keeping weighted and unweighted figures separate and properly labeled, and the problem of changes in weights or of cell shifts that are required when new information or sources of information come to the surveyor's attention. If there are many controls and only a few cases are to be secured in each stratum, and if the choice of strata has been poor,

occasional cases in the sample may show great heterogeneity with respect to the subject of the survey. Whether to discard "freak cases" which may greatly distort the total picture if given large weights, or to "smooth" such returns, is often a serious problem. Instead of struggling with the problems of disproportionate stratification, Stephan suggests that it may be more advisable in some cases "to take a uniform proportion from each stratum for the total sample and then supplement it by a separate sample drawn disproportionately in such a way as to make the two samples, when combined, the equivalent of a disproportionate sample appropriate to the need for inter-strata comparisons and special estimates" (923, p. 43). If the surveyor has to locate the cases in each strata and estimate and apply weights, he will do well to consider the advisability of drawing a random sample instead of a disproportionate stratified sample, or at least of limiting his controls to one or two strata which are easily defined and for which weights can be obtained and applied.

Purposive Sampling

In a sense all systematic sampling may be said to be purposive, but the term "purposive selection" has taken on a more limited meaning. According to Jensen: "Purposive selection denotes the method of selecting a number of groups of units in such a way that the selected groups together yield as nearly as possible the same averages or proportions as the totality with respect to those characteristics which are already a matter of statistical knowledge" (473, p. 359).

Neyman (694) describes the work of Gini and Galvani, two Italian statisticians who in 1926 were confronted with the problem of taking a sample of 29 districts which would be representative of Italy as a whole. In order to use purposive selection, they divided Italy into 214 administrative districts called *circondari*. These districts were large, some having populations of over one million. Numerous statistics were available from a census, and averages on many items were computed for each district. Then 29 districts were selected for the sample, using primary and secondary controls. The sample districts were chosen so that the averages calculated from the sample were practically identical with those for the whole population with respect to the primary controls, and the agreement was also pretty close for the characteristics of secondary importance. Then a comparison was made between the sample and the total population in other respects. It was found that all characteristics other than those used in the controls were in extreme disagreement with those of the general population.

Snedecor reports a similar experience with purposive selection. He and a colleague tried to select townships in Iowa which had the same averages as the entire state for a number of characteristics. With the use of assessor's data they found such areas. But when they examined the statistics for the years preceding and following the assessor's data, they found that the means drifted away from the state values. Snedecor concluded that the townships chosen could serve in purposive sampling only in the particular year in which the computations were made (893).

In a sense, the so-called "barometer" states or districts that are chosen because the votes for each candidate in any given election or even in several elections have coincided with the percentages of votes obtained by these candidates in the nation may be regarded as purposively selected. Experience has shown that it is dangerous to assume that because this similarity to the national vote has occurred, it necessarily will occur again.

There are several ways of proceeding to make the sample look like the universe: (1) to see that the combined averages of the units are the same as the averages in the universe for known characteristics believed to be relevant to the phenomenon being investigated, as in the first two foregoing examples; (2) to select the sample so that it will resemble the universe from the point of view of its frequency distribution; (3) to select it so that it will contain the same proportion of cases at the upper and lower ends of the distribution (deciles, quartiles, etc.); or (4) to select it so that the variability is the same.

Statisticians as a class have little to say in favor of purposive sampling. Snedecor summarizes their position when he writes: "One advantage claimed for purposive sampling was that it is sometimes possible to carry it through where randomization is not feasible. Another was that the enumeration, assumed to be in selected districts, may be cheaper. The disadvantages are that (i) a considerable knowledge of the population must be available in advance of the sample, (ii) the controls are often not effective, and (iii) the estimate of sampling error rests upon hypotheses which are seldom if ever met in practice" (893, p. 850). Neyman characterizes this method of sampling as "hopeless" (694, p. 90).

While it is unwise to use purposive selection without being aware of its limitations, there are sampling problems which can best be solved by resorting to some kind of matching of districts. For example, it has been possible to build up fairly good national figures for various economic characteristics by taking "typical" industrial counties, manufacturing areas, wheat farming districts, etc. Even though the matching of the smaller districts with the larger areas they are supposed to represent is only approximate, these so-called "typical" or representative areas have provided statistics which are close enough to the total to be acceptable.

Double or Mixed Sampling

When two or more of the types of sampling discussed above are employed in an investigation, double or mixed sampling results. This often makes it possible to utilize some of the advantages and avoid the disadvantages of particular sampling methods. The different principles may be applied at various levels of selection, though this is not essential.

The Study of Consumer Purchases (847, 1010) employed purposive selection in choosing 51 cities. A cross-section of the population in 32 cities surveyed by the Bureau of Labor Statistics was then selected by regular-interval sampling of addresses.[3] A few basic facts regarding color, nativity, and size of family in this cross-section (consisting of about 500,000 families) were secured. For certain groups (such as native-born white families of two or more persons in certain cities), details on family income, occupation, and family composition were obtained, in addition to the preceding facts, during the initial interview. This income sample comprised about 300,000 cases of the larger cross-section. At this point disproportionate stratification was employed. From the 300,000 cases, roughly 25,000 were chosen to be interviewed again concerning their expenditures. This final sample was limited to a given number of cases in each unit, the unit being described in terms of income, occupation, and family composition. Thus

---

[3] This was designated in the plans and reports as a "random sample," but strictly speaking it is a stratified random sample.

the random sample was used to locate cases with the desired characteristics for the controlled stratified sample, and it also provided the weights employed when the stratified sample was inflated to represent the total population.

Combinations of proportional and disproportional stratified sampling are often useful when certain strata are to be analyzed in greater detail than others. Purposive selection of communities in nation-wide studies is often necessary because of administrative considerations. Within communities, however, stratified or random selection is usually most effective; therefore mixed sampling is adopted.

AREA SAMPLING:

Noteworthy among the examples of mixed sampling is that known as "area sampling." The sampling techniques employed by the Bureau of the Census in its sample surveys of congested areas in 1943 and 1944 really started a new era in sampling procedure. The technique employed is known as "area sampling" and provides a stratified, regular-interval sample. (See pp. 274–277 for a description of the area sample employed in the Surveys of Consumer Finances.) The chief purpose of these government surveys was to determine various population characteristics, including total population within 3 per cent, in ten particular areas of the nation.

A brief description of the sample design will suffice here because it has been described in detail in *A Chapter in Population Sampling* (1004). Direct reference to this publication is recommended, however, for information regarding the theory and formulas for the determination of sample sizes. To determine the total population, it was necessary to record from the block statistics of the 1940 Census the number of blocks within the limits of each of the cities. If the average number of people per block could be determined, then it remained only to multiply these two items together to secure the estimate of total population.

The surveyors determined the number of persons per block by first discovering the average number of dwelling places per block and then by getting the average number of occupants per dwelling. To obtain the average number of dwelling places per block it was decided to make a list of dwelling places in only a sample of blocks. Canvassers inspected every dwelling in the selected blocks and listed the number of occupants. Then a sample of dwelling places was drawn from this listing for revisitation to determine the population per dwelling place. In other words, this sampling was in two stages—first the sample of blocks, and then the subsample of dwelling places.

Before the sample blocks were chosen, all the blocks in the given city were classified by census tracts and by the number of occupied dwellings in 1940. Thus some geographic control as well as size stratification was employed. The class intervals for number of dwelling units were: 1 and 2, 3 and 4, 5–9, 10–14, etc., by fives to 99, 100–109, 110–119, and continuing thereafter by tens. The sampling ratio, which varied in the different cities, was calculated by the formula given in the aforementioned publication. In Los Angeles, for example, one block in seven was included in the sample. Blocks which contained no dwelling units in 1940 were listed and canvassed completely rather than by sample.

The one-in-seven blocks also were canvassed completely by enumerators who compiled a list of the number of dwelling places by inspection without asking questions. From this list, one in every eleven dwelling places was marked off at regular intervals to constitute the final sample of dwelling units which were enumerated to determine the number and other characteristics of the inhabitants.

In addition to the information secured from these blocks within the city limits, information was desired from the suburbs and areas surrounding the city proper. Where block statistics were not available for such territory, a complete listing of the dwelling places was made and on such listing every nth place was marked for inclusion in the sample of dwelling places. In the area outside of Los Angeles and its surrounding block-cities, for example, every seventy-seventh dwelling place was drawn for the sample.

Careful instructions were prepared for listing, for enumerating on the dwelling unit schedule, and for sampling procedure to be used by supervisors. Listing instructions covered items on order of listing, vacant dwelling places, types of dwelling places, dwellings under construction, rear dwellings, and alley dwellings. Interviewers were not permitted to substitute another dwelling place for the one assigned. They were given specific instructions on what to do if unable to locate the dwelling place, if it turned out to be an institution, if householders were not at home at the time, or if the unit were vacant. Supervisors'

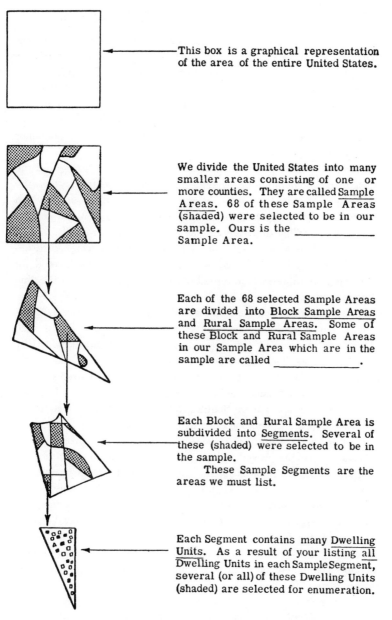

This box is a graphical representation of the area of the entire United States.

We divide the United States into many smaller areas consisting of one or more counties. They are called Sample Areas. 68 of these Sample Areas (shaded) were selected to be in our sample. Ours is the _____ Sample Area.

Each of the 68 selected Sample Areas are divided into Block Sample Areas and Rural Sample Areas. Some of these Block and Rural Sample Areas in our Sample Area which are in the sample are called _____.

Each Block and Rural Sample Area is subdivided into Segments. Several of these (shaded) were selected to be in the sample.
These Sample Segments are the areas we must list.

Each Segment contains many Dwelling Units. As a result of your listing all Dwelling Units in each Sample Segment, several (or all) of these Dwelling Units (shaded) are selected for enumeration.

FIGURE 1. Area Sampling System of the Current Population Surveys. (From U. S. Bureau of the Census, *How to List*, P-1450b.)

instructions covered the steps in the selection of the sample dwelling places, the summary of the sampling operation, supplementary lists made up from unlisted dwelling units, sampling within institutions, and sampling for areas with block sampling. The instructions included, further, the handling of refusals, call-backs, erroneous addresses, moved and demolished dwellings. The problems of listing and types of errors arising in the field are clearly stated in the article by Manheimer and Hyman (614).

Because of the lapse of several weeks between the listing and the subsequent enumeration of dwelling places and units, and because the enumerator and the lister were different people, problems arose which had to be taken care of in the sample inflation. Among these may be mentioned dwelling units not enumerated because of refusals, no one home, out of town, etc., supposedly habitable but unoccupied dwellings, those moved or destroyed since the listing, those which could not be located, and those which turned out not to be dwellings at the time of enumeration.

Special treatment of quasi-households such as trailer camps, institutions, hotels, and lodging houses was necessary. The list of such places was supplied by the census geographer and supplemented by local authorities. The enumeration of people within these places was carried on as a separate process. The files of institutions were sampled by taking every nth name; the same was true of trailer camps. In hotels and lodging houses of more than 24 roomers, every room or suite was listed separately and sampled at regular intervals.

In spite of the variety of special problems and the speed of these surveys, the results proved to be highly reliable and satisfactory. The expense of the listing was regarded as one of the main drawbacks, however, and subsequent sampling procedures of the census have more or less eliminated this step. Sanborn maps which show the number of dwelling units as well as other structures in every block began to be used by the Census about 1945. With the aid of such maps it is possible to divide cities into small block segments which may be enumerated completely or from which individual sample cases may be drawn.

Unsystematic Sampling

The terms unsystematic, careless, and opportunistic may be applied synonymously to sampling which follows no logical plan, as when the samples are selected accidentally or are self-selected. If one were to examine the sampling procedures in the majority of the surveys conducted to date, one would find this type of sampling quite prevalent. In fact, many studies include no statement concerning the sampling procedure; if there is one, it may be couched in such vague terms as to make it impossible to gauge the nature of the actual sample. Just what the sample is or whom it represents, even the investigator seldom knows. One might think that unsystematic sampling would result in random samples, but it is more likely to yield biased samples.

Accidental sampling results when the universe is not clearly defined. Many surveyors fail to decide what universe they are sampling, and consequently they have no way of knowing whether they are exposing all of it to the sampling process. In some cases the sampling unit is not defined. Then the surveyor does not know whether he is sampling individuals, families, households, occupied dwelling units, blocks, block segments, residents of a city, transients, or such population characteristics as unemployment, sickness, social attitudes, etc.

Accidental sampling also results when the source or list from which the sample is chosen does not represent the universe for which generalizations are to be made. People whose names appear on lists usually differ from those whose names are seldom included. Lists generally contain the names of people who are specifically interested or involved in the activities in connection with which their names are recorded. Members of organizations, purchasers of certain commodities or services, registered voters, users of public utilities, clients of social agencies, graduates of schools, students in school or college, property owners—all these represent selected elements of the population. Sampling from such lists to secure a cross-section of the general population is opportunistic, and is likely to be biased unless supplemented by other sources for the unlisted population.

Self-selected samples, those in which informants include themselves by being cooperative or exclude themselves by being uncooperative or inaccessible, may be classed as accidental samples. Even though the original sample is meticulously selected to conform to correct sampling principles, the final result is likely to represent a self-selected group, unless the sample as drawn reaches the collection and tabulation stages of the survey.

Although it is generally assumed that the persons or groups who do not cooperate with the survey are like those who respond, it is fairly safe to assume that the opposite will be true. All the tests of non-respondents and noninterviewable people or groups indicate that they are highly selected. The most accessible, cooperative, and able inform-ants are known to differ from the "difficult" cases. Homes in which someone is in during the day are more likely to contain larger families than those whose inhabitants are away during the day; people who own their own homes are more easily located than the more mobile groups; families in which the housewife is a wage-earner are not so apt to have other members at home during the day; families passing through such a crisis as sickness, accident, birth, death, etc., are likely not to have the time or the inclination to give information; and persons who are prejudiced against the agency conducting the study may yield a high refusal rate. These and many other differentials lead one to be very suspicious of the sample secured with little or no effort to avoid refusals. The studies which give the interviewer leeway to select a "random" sample of people for interview also are open to suspicion because field workers often cannot resist the temptation to question only the easily accessible groups. For a more detailed discussion of these points see Chapters XI and XII.

Selected References

Sampling Methods, Types, and Problems
American Marketing Assn. (9), Bartlett (34), Blankenship (77, 78), Borden (92), Bowley (99–104), Brandt (109), Breyer (111), Brown (114, 116, 118, 119), Brunsman (123), Callandar and Sarle (132), Cantril (142), Cassady (149), Chappell (168), Churchman et al. (174), Cochran (178, 179), Colley (183), Corby (195), Cornell (198, 199), Cover (203), Crossley (212, 213, 214), Curtis Pub. Co. (224), Deming (235, 236), Deming and Hansen (241), Deming and Simmons (242), Deming and Stephen (243), Dodge and Romig (251), Dunlap (260), Eastwood (266), Elmer (284), Ferber (297), Frankel and Stock (326), Goodman and Maccoby (371), Hagood (388), Hagood and Bernert (390), Hansen (394), Hansen and Hauser (395), Hansen and Hurwitz (396, 397, 398, 399), Hansen et al. (400), Haring (402), Hauser (422, 423), Hauser and Hansen (424), Hilton (439), Hitt (442), Hochstim and Smith (444), Hogg (446), Holmes (447, 448), Houseman (455, 456), Jensen (473, 474, 475), Jessen (477, 478, 479), Kameda (486), Katz (496, 497, 498), Kelley (503), Ken-dall and Smith (507, 508), Kiaer (510), King (512, 516), King

and McCarthy (513), King and Simpson (514), Larson (540), Levinson (562), Lindquist (568, 569, 570), Link (573), *Literary Digest* (582), Lloyd (583), Lundberg (597), Madow (609), Mangus (612), Manheimer and Hyman (614), Mann (615), McCormick (621, 623, 624), McNemar (629, 630, 632), Mills (646), Moser (658), NORC (674, 676), Neiswanger (681), Neyman (693, 694, 695), Parten (718), Patte (724), Pearson (727), Peatman (728), Pechanec and Stewart (730), Pettet (737), Pietra (744), Sarle (831, 832, 833, 835), Schoenberg and Parten (847), Schultz (853), Schutz (854), Sibley (874), Smith (882), Smith and Duncan (888), Snedecor (894), Snedecor and King (895), SSRC (898), Stanton (911),. Starch (914), Stephan (918–924), Stephan and Deming (925), Stephan and McCarthy (926), Stephan et al. (927), Stock and Frankel (929), Stouffer (935, 936), Tepping et al. (954), Tippett (966), U.N. (979, 980), U.S. (981, 983, 1003, 1004), Vernon (1039), Vickery (1043), Wald (1047), Walker (1049), Walker et al. (1051), Watson (1062), Weaver (1068), Webb et al. (1070), White (1084), Wilks (1091, 1092), Winslow (1112), Wood (1117), Woofter (1123), Yates (1131, 1132), Yoder et al. (1133), Yule (1139, 1140), Zeisel (1141).
See also books on Statistical Methods.

CHAPTER VIII

Procedures for Drawing Samples

The procedure for selecting the particular cases for the sample should not be decided upon without first taking into account the design of the entire survey. The population to which the generalizations are to apply, the period to be covered, the detailed plans for collecting and tabulating data, the type of sampling to be employed, and the availability and condition of a catalogue of the universe should all be considered. Since the combination of circumstances encountered when survey plans are being made will vary from survey to survey, it is impossible to set up detailed sampling procedures which will be generally applicable. Hence the rules and procedures presented in this chapter should be regarded as suggestions that should be modified to fit particular conditions.

After deciding what population is to be described by the survey and what sampling and tabulation units are to be used, the surveyor should try to locate an up-to-date list of the population to be sampled. Unless such a list is available to the sampler, the cases for the sample will have to be drawn by the field workers who as a rule are not so well versed in sampling theory or technique as the sampling specialists employed to supervise the drawing of the sample in the office.[1]

If no published lists are available, or if the available lists are out of date or lack the information needed to select a sample, the investigator will do well to compile his own directory. If the survey is directed toward selected groups of the population, it may be more efficient to canvass the entire community and thus locate every case of the type required. For example, a survey may be directed toward everyone in

---

[1] Other disadvantages of having the field force select the sample cases were discussed in Chapter IV.

the city who has graduated from college, regardless of the year of graduation or the college. The U. S. census will give the surveyor a rough idea of the number of college graduates in the city, but he cannot obtain a complete list except by a house-to-house canvass. If the number of graduates is so few that a 25 per cent sample of the population will not produce enough cases, it may be more efficient for him to make a complete enumeration of the population and to include a few census-type questions, among them the grade completed in school. He can then segregate the college graduates and survey them for the detailed information desired. Compiling a directory, whether by complete canvass or by systematic sampling, may cost less in the long run than a sample culled from several sources which still lacks the type of people whose names do not get on lists. In compiling the directory, however, the surveyor should see that good survey procedure is followed, and he should guard against the omission of addresses as well as of the names of people who are out when the enumerator calls.

Source Lists

Although the lists available for sampling purposes in any community vary from one place to another and from time to time within one community, there are a few sources that are commonly used in surveys and polls. These sources may suggest others which the surveyor may use when designing the sample.

1. CENSUSES:

For a catalogue of the general population, recent state or city censuses may prove ideal sources. During the various work projects inaugurated by the federal government, many city and state governments enumerated their population. The U. S. Decennial Census cannot be used for such purposes, but most state and local censuses are available to reputable agencies or groups who wish to conduct surveys in the interest of science or public welfare.[2] Before deciding to use a local census for sampling purposes, the surveyor should first ascertain how carefully the field work was done and what limitations, if any, the census imposes on him.

If the censuses are to be used as a sample of individuals and the surveyor is permitted to transcribe the names of specific individuals

---

[2] See pp. 14–15 for the "Matching" service offered by the U. S. Census.

for his sample, the chief question in his mind will concern the recency and completeness of the census. For most surveys, if the census dates back even one year, too many changes will have taken place to make it practicable to draw a sample of people from this source. This is especially true in periods of great mobility of the population, when it is not unusual to find as many as one-third of the families moving to new homes during a given year.

Although it may not be possible or desirable to use the names of individuals in the local census sheets, a sample of addresses may be drawn from them. If a sample of dwelling units is desired, the census enumeration may prove satisfactory even if it is several years old. The census list of addresses can be supplemented with the addresses of newly constructed or remodeled dwellings obtained from building permits. A list of demolitions does not need to be obtained because the dwelling units no longer in existence will be eliminated automatically when the investigator calls at the addresses assigned him.

When evaluating the census enumerations of addresses, the surveyor should watch for multiple listings. The addresses of lodging houses are likely to appear more than once on the census list. For example, if only the head of the household and his wife were at home when the census enumerator called, and they told him to come back later for information for their three lodgers, he would have to repeat the address later when he entered the data for each of the lodgers unless he left a blank space for them on the form. This particular address might be entered two or more times on the sheet and thus have a greater chance of being included in a sample than would an address entered only once, because all the information for all the inhabitants was obtained on the first interview.

Another point to be kept in mind when evaluating the local census as a source for sampling is whether or not the survey is interested only in residents of the community as defined by the census. It is conceivable that the survey will need to include temporary residents and not just those who regard the community as their usual abode. Supplementing the census with special canvasses of rooming houses, hotels, and other places in which transients are likely to be found may provide a satisfactory inventory of the population from which to draw a sample of current inhabitants.

The federal census will supply statistics by blocks for large cities and metropolitan areas. If some type of area sampling is used, the surveyor will find the maps as well as the block statistics invaluable.

2. TELEPHONE DIRECTORY:

Although the telephone directory is one of the most popular sources for sampling, it should be used only if the surveyor has all its limitations in mind when he designs the sample. In the first place, telephone subscribers are not a cross-section of the population of any community, for the lowest economic groups are often almost entirely omitted. If the surveyor is interested in only the middle- and upper-income groups, the limitation may present no serious objection to using this source. But the extent to which the middle-income groups are telephone subscribers may vary from city to city and in different periods of the business cycle. During a depression the proportion of subscribers is apt to be rather low; during more prosperous periods it is likely to be much higher. In view of the many types of services offered by telephone companies, not all of the subscribers are equally likely to be listed in the directory. A large apartment house, for example, may have its own switchboard; thus only the building is listed in the directory. The telephone in a lodging house may be listed under the proprietor's name; roomers are quite unlikely to have their own phones. In recent years the "unlisted" number has become popular, and it is possible that subscribers with unlisted numbers constitute a highly selected group.

Another point to be taken into account when drawing a sample from the telephone directory is that for households that contain several adults, more than one name may be listed for a single number; some companies make only a slight extra charge for the second listing. In most if not all communities the telephone company has a list of subscribers compiled by street addresses, either alphabetically or numerically. The surveyor is likely to have to pay for the use of this list, but if he is sampling households this list may enable him to eliminate multiple listings. Still another difficulty is that telephones listed for places of business which do not contain dwelling units often cannot be differentiated from the phones listed for private households. Thus it is important, when surveying names or addresses secured through the telephone directory, to ascertain whether the listing in question is residential. In addition to nonresidential listings, the telephone directory may list subscribers who reside outside the corporate limits of the community but are within the company's service district. Therefore, when drawing a sample for a given city, cases outside the city boundaries should not be included in the sample of the city. It is easier to draw the sample, classify the addresses by wards, and discard the cases outside the city than to eliminate suburban addresses (if they are listed with the others) before the sample is drawn.

3. LISTS OF SUBSCRIBERS TO OTHER PUBLIC UTILITIES:

The surveyor encounters some of the above difficulties when he samples other public utility sources such as files of subscribers to gas or electric services. A complete, up-to-date list is usually difficult to obtain. The arrangement of the lists, although perfectly adequate for the purposes of the utility companies, may not meet his requirements. The active accounts may be kept out of the file during the work day, thus making it difficult for the surveyor to have access to the complete list long enough to draw his sample. Often the files are in congested quarters so that he is likely to be in the way while he draws his sample. The suburban customers are usually listed with the urban subscribers. The service may be listed under the name of the original subscriber who has long since died or moved away; as long as the bill is paid, the company is not likely to question who pays it. It may be listed under the name of another member of the family if the real subscriber's credit rating is not good. Large apartment buildings or offices may have special arrangements, such as master meters or private meter systems under which the consumer deals entirely with the landlord instead of the utility company and therefore is not listed in the latter's files.

4. LISTS OF MEMBERS OF ORGANIZATIONS, GRADUATES OF SCHOOLS AND COLLEGES:

An organization that wishes to survey the characteristics or attitudes of its members usually has relatively little difficulty in finding a source, for a membership list is generally available. The question of what constitutes membership—dues paid up to date, dues paid the previous year, attendance at meetings, etc.—should, of course, be decided before the survey is begun. Few membership lists, however, are up to date, for several of the members in good standing will have married, moved, died, or in some way changed their status or interests since the list was compiled. Lists of school and college graduates are also not very satisfactory. The data usually relate to the individual's name, address, etc., at the time of graduation; and since some of the greatest changes in a person's life—economic, social, and residential—usually follow graduation, such a list is likely soon to become unusable for survey purposes if the plans call for personal interviews. Moreover, from the point of view of evaluating the curriculum, it may be desirable to survey students who did not graduate—those who left school either temporarily or permanently, those who transferred elsewhere, those who were called to the armed services, those who took courses but were not working for credit toward a degree, etc.—as well as the students still in school.

Whichever group or groups are selected, the surveyor should be aware that he would probably obtain entirely different results if other groups had been included in the sample. Furthermore, generalizations can be made only for the universe which the sample represents. In his article "Sampling in Psychological Research" (630) McNemar questions whether the vast array of information that has been accumulated on college sophomores is of any great value in describing and predicting the generality of human behavior.

5. CLIENTS OF SOCIAL AND OTHER PUBLIC AGENCIES:

Strange as it may seem, few social agencies know how many individuals or families are listed in their files. At any given time they may be able to tell which people are receiving aid or attention, but the figures over a period of time are not so readily available. If their cases are inactive at the time, the clients who return several times are usually listed separately each time. This means that in drawing a sample of clients during a given year, the "repeaters" have a greater chance of being selected because they are listed more than once. Hence, before using a list from one of these agencies, the surveyor should find out whether it is an active list, and how long a client's name remains on this list if he does not ask for or receive assistance. At one time the U. S. Employment Service required each individual to register once a month if he wished to keep his name on the active list. In view of this definition of an "active" case, it is not possible to draw a random sample of the unemployed over a period of a year without making provision for correcting the multiple listings of those who have been unemployed for the longest time.

The definition of "case" differs from agency to agency. The sampler should realize that a "case" is not necessarily an "individual," a "household," or a "family." Thus, before drawing his sample from a list of active "cases," he may have to correct the list so that it will be in terms of the units—individuals, households, etc.—that are to be used in the tabulation procedures.

6. AUTOMOBILE REGISTRATIONS:

Contrary to the popular belief that everyone owns a car, automobile owners do not constitute a cross-section of the total population. Car registrations, like lists of telephone subscribers, are more heavily concentrated in the middle- and upper-income groups. Furthermore, they are more likely to be listed in men's than in women's names, thus making this source a poor one for surveys that include both sexes. Before automobile registrations are used in a survey, the question of multiple listings must be considered. Does the owner of two or more cars have a greater chance of being included in the sample than the owner of one car? Does the two-car family have a greater chance of being included in a household sample? If the cars used for business purposes are listed with private passenger cars, the number of registrations will probably be disproportionately large for self-employed businessmen and individual proprietors.

State laws regarding car registrations are not uniform, so no rule-of-thumb suggestions can be made as to what to look for when examining them as a source for sampling. Are people who are delinquent in paying for their licenses listed with those who are not, or are they in a different file? When the act imposing a tax of $5 on every car in the United States was enacted in 1941 and the procedure for locating every car owner was being discussed, it was pointed out that compiling such a list in one state would cost several thousand dollars. Therefore, before designing a sampling plan based on car registrations, the surveyor should make certain what type of list is available in the state to be surveyed.

7. LISTS OF VOTERS:

A list of the eligible voters in each district is sometimes used for polls of the electorate. These lists can be obtained from the registrar of voters at either local or county headquarters. Such lists usually include the full name of the voter, his age, his party affiliation, and his address at the time of registration or at the last election. The extent to which they represent those who will be eligible to vote on an approaching election day depends on the date of the list. The surveyor should ascertain whether or not the list includes (a) persons who have moved into the district since the last election, (b) those who have reached voting age since the last election, (c) those who have not paid their poll tax (in states that require this), (d) those who voted in the last election but have since moved out of the district, (e) the voters who have died, (f) people who have not voted in one of the preceding two general elections or who have in any other way become disqualified to vote, and (g) absentee voters.

If a sample drawn from a list of voters is to be polled for the purpose of forecasting election results, the surveyor will have to make adjustments for the fact that only a certain proportion of the registered voters actually cast a ballot in any given election. The number who vote varies with such factors as the weather, rural-urban areas, type of election—local, state, national, presidential—the strength and work of the party machine, the coercion of pressure groups, the issues involved, etc. When a large percentage of the young men are in the armed forces, a disproportionate number in this group may not bother to vote even though listed as registered voters.

8. LISTS OF CUSTOMERS AND CONSUMERS, CREDIT LISTS:

Assuming that the highly selected character of lists of consumers or customers is no deterrent to the agency sponsoring the survey, such lists should be carefully examined. The qualifications required for being listed and the situations in which a name is added or dropped should be known. Are the eligibility rules always or only occasionally followed? What checks insure that they are consistently applied?

One of the most discouraging features about drawing a sample from a list compiled for some purpose other than the survey is the frequency with which the rules for adding or dropping a name are violated. Few lists are comprised *only* of those whom the compilers claim are included. Thus one of the surveyor's first duties is to familiarize himself both with the conditions under which the list was compiled and with the definitions employed for including names. For example, does a list of customers include only charge customers? How are cash customers identified? Are all customers included in the list, regardless of whether they live in the city, in the suburbs, or outside the state? Which member or members of a family are most likely to be listed? Is each wage earner in the family likely to be listed?

9. PAYROLL LISTS:

Surveys of occupational differences and of earnings of family members frequently draw their samples from the lists of employees of large business concerns. Usually these samples do not represent the groups for which the surveyor plans to generalize, for occupational groups affiliated with large business concerns are a selected group of the population. Self-employed persons, workers who reside in but work outside the city being surveyed, unemployed people, and numerous other groups are not covered by these payroll lists. Furthermore, if the investigator is interested in studying heads of families, the lists are loaded in favor of families with multiple earners and therefore families in which the earnings may be greater than they are in the general population. The surveyor should examine the census figures on the occupational groups which he plans to include before he decides to concentrate on the employees of a few concerns that have agreed to cooperate with the study.

10. POST OFFICE LISTS:

Populations in rural areas are particularly difficult to sample because few directories of rural inhabitants have been compiled. If the post offices make available the lists of addresses or box numbers prepared for each mail carrier, a fairly comprehensive coverage of the area is possible. But some individuals cannot be reached through a delivery service; they may call for their mail at the nearest country store or at some other designated place. When the plans were being drafted for checking the unemployment census of 1937, the problem of how to sample people in nondelivery areas was raised, but it was decided to omit them entirely from the enumerative check census. Since the sample in the check census was used as a measure of the completeness of the voluntary registration rather than as a representative sample of the entire population, the omission of the 18 per cent these people comprised did not seriously affect the findings. A surveyor who decides to use the postal route source must make some provision for locating and getting in contact with the groups who live in nondelivery areas if he wishes to secure a true cross-section of the population.

11. TAX ASSESSORS' LISTS; OTHER LOCAL GOVERNMENT LISTS:

Although the availability of tax lists in local government administrations varies from community to community, it may be worth while to canvass these sources when planning a survey. A list of every address in the city will be found in the tax assessor's office, and sometimes the number of dwelling units in each building also is indicated; hence this list may prove valuable for a sample survey of households. One of the difficulties likely to be encountered, however, is securing access to books or cards which are constantly in use. Because the records usually may not be taken away from the office, the survey samplers must find space in which to work in what frequently are congested quarters. A tax list of properties is an ideal source if the records are clear-cut and up to date, but it may be unusable if the material is scattered in many files and if there are multiple listings of properties.

12. CITY DIRECTORIES:

Almost every city has a city directory, and most of them are issued annually. Because the author has found these directories so valuable for selecting survey samples, a detailed discussion of them is presented.

A few large concerns publish most of the directories in this country. Some of the data are secured from such sources as employers, public utility companies, and moving and storage concerns, but most of the information is secured by personal interviews. A corps of enumerators usually completes the census in one city in a few months and then moves on to another. As a rule, the name and address listings are quite complete, because payment is based on the number of names the enumerators turn in, so that they have a real incentive to secure as many names as possible. A lazy enumerator might just copy the data from the preceding year's directory, but he would probably be detected because the alphabetical name list kept in the office of the compiler would show more than one address for every person who had moved. Even if he were not detected, the error would occur in the *name* of the occupant rather than in the *address* (except, of course,

that buildings or dwelling units constructed since the preceding enumeration would be omitted). An address omitted one year would probably be included the next year, certainly after two years, unless the
same investigator covered the area each year. Because of this cumulative effect, the address listings of city directories tend to become more
and more complete as the years pass. To be sure, if a city has an
unprecedented building boom, there is greater chance of an under-
enumeration of addresses than if new construction constitutes only a
small fraction of the total. A directory known to be deficient in listing
new dwelling units can be supplemented by addresses taken from the
list of building permits issued during the past year.

The population lists in city directories usually appear in two sections
(aside from the business or classified section). The first section lists
alphabetically all the adults in the city; the second section lists the
householders by address.

In the alphabetical list, the wife's given name appears in parentheses
after her husband's name. Other members of the family are listed separately. In some communities every child is also listed, but most directories include only individuals over 18 years of age. Each person's
occupation and place of work as well as his home address are also
supposed to be listed. Although the occupational data are often incomplete, they are useful for checking purposes in the collection stage
of a survey.

This alphabetical name list is not satisfactory for a sample of households because families that contain several adults have a better chance
of being sampled than do those with one or two members. For sampling individuals also, this list has certain limitations. The names listed
are those of persons who resided at the addresses specified when the
directory was compiled. Changes of address within the city or the
suburbs, movement to and away from the city, changes in name because of marriage or divorce, and deaths will have occurred since the
directory data were collected. If their work is not carefully controlled,
the directory agents may be careless about securing the correct names
of the inhabitants; hence the task of locating or tracing a sample drawn
from the name list is often extremely difficult.

The second section, often printed on pink paper, lists the householders classified by address. The streets are usually arranged alphabetically or numerically, and street numbers are listed in sequence from

the beginning to the end of each street. This list is a very good source for drawing a sample of dwelling units in a city since households or families reside in dwelling units. It is important to bear in mind, however, that the occupant residing in the dwelling unit at the time of the survey agent's visit is the one to be included in the sample. Thus the name of the occupant listed in the directory need not be correct so long as the dwelling unit or address is correct.

In order to formulate a logical plan for using the address list as the source of a sample, it is necessary to know what the list contains. The following items are usually found in the address section of directories compiled by national directory concerns:

1. *Addresses.* A list of addresses giving the house number, the dwelling unit within the house if it contains more than one unit, and the name of the householder. For example, in a two-family house two householders are listed; in a ten-family apartment house ten household units are listed. If a caretaker or janitor lives on the premises, his dwelling quarters are also listed.

2. *Vacant dwelling units.* If any dwelling unit in a structure is vacant, the word "vacant" usually appears instead of a householder's name. Often it is not possible to determine from the directory whether the vacant unit is a business or a dwelling unit. Of course, if the vacancy is listed in a large office building that contains no living quarters, it may be assumed to be a business vacancy. In many cases, however, the distinction between a vacant business address and a vacant dwelling unit cannot be made from the directory.

3. *Miscellaneous information.* Directories include street names and intersections, railroad crossings, notations like "Blank Street ends" or "Don Street begins," etc.

4. *Names of buildings.* The names of buildings, such as Corona Apartment House or The Times Building, usually are given in addition to the addresses or apartment units within them.

5. *Places of business, government buildings, offices, etc.* The names of concerns are given. From the directory listing it is not possible to ascertain whether or not someone lives on the premises, for what appears to be a business unit often includes a resident. For example, in some cities the gas station attendant lives in one of the buildings on the lot. It is usually necessary to find out whether he has another place of residence as well as the one on the business premises.

6. *Combination business and dwelling units.* It is not unusual to find family living quarters in the rear of beauty shops, tailor shops,

grocery stores, etc. Sometimes it is possible to determine whether the business establishment is the home by checking the name of the occupant against the name and address information in the first section of the directory. If the home and business address are the same, "ditto" or "do" appears after the address.

7. *Hotels.* The listing of rooms or suites for transients is usually omitted from most directories. However, if the hotel contains suites or apartments for more or less permanent residents, the directory may list them. In order to be sure, however, a personal investigation of apartment entries is required. The question of what constitutes a "permanent" rather than a "temporary" resident, what is a household dwelling unit and what is a "room" rather than an "apartment," what is a "lodger" and what is a "household" is usually not settled by directory compilers to the satisfaction of surveyors and samplers.

8. *Rooming houses.* The directory usually lists the landlady or operator of a rooming house. Occasionally roomers are also listed, but as a rule this list is incomplete. For a sample of householders this incomplete list of lodgers is not important because only the householder's name belongs in the sample. If roomers happen to be listed and are drawn in the household sample they should be dropped (after a visit to the address has shown that the person is a lodger).

In a city like Washington, D. C., with so many borderline lodgers and light housekeepers, the definition of what constitutes a lodger and what is a one-person household may noticeably affect the type of sample drawn from the address list of the city directory.

If a sample of individuals rather than families is wanted, it is advisable to compile a directory of lodging houses and lodgers to supplement the address sample. This was done in the St. Paul survey mentioned earlier, where tabulations for both the family and the individual populations were to be made from the relatively small sample covered in the field investigation. If only one large rooming house were drawn in the sample, the lodgers in that one dwelling unit would distort the findings for the individual population, unless lodgers were sampled separately from a complete list of the lodging-house population.

9. *Social agencies and institutions.* Usually the directory lists only the name of the agency or institution, not the resident personnel, the transient residents, the inmates, or other residents. It is usually necessary to investigate such places if drawn in samples to determine whether or not they contain sample cases. If members of various quasi-families are to be included in samples of individuals, institutions should probably be treated like rooming houses.

10. *Clubs, schools, dormitories.* Usually only the names of clubs,

schools, and dormitories are entered. As in the case of other agencies, they may or may not house family units. For samples of residents for the quasi-family sample, the number and type of occupants should be specially investigated.

11. *Homeownership.* In addition to the specially investigated name of the householder, the address list in many directories indicates whether the home is owned or rented by the occupant.

12. *Telephone.* Some directories indicate whether or not the occupant has a telephone.

13. *Suburban address.* It is not uncommon for city directories to list addresses outside the corporate boundaries of the city. Because the task of going through the directory and eliminating these addresses before the sample is drawn is too time-consuming, it is recommended that the sample be drawn as if all the addresses were in the city. Then when the district code is applied to each case drawn in the sample, those outside the area included in it can be eliminated.

14. *Errors.* A few errors in address are usually found. Sometimes owners changed the street numbers, or the names of the streets themselves are changed, and the directory may not have caught the changes. Occasionally buildings which have been demolished are listed. Such errors usually are detected during the field work. The method of handling them should be determined with a logical sampling plan in mind.

The completeness of the address list can be checked by numerous devices. If it is suspected that new buildings are omitted, building permits can be compared with the address entries, and the omissions added to the directory list. Certain types of dwellings, such as alley dwellings, river flats, and trailer and tourist camps within the city limits may be omitted by the directory compilers, but a day of field work by a reliable investigator can reveal the extent of these omissions. In one city containing 80,000 dwelling units, this effort did not reveal enough cases to necessitate adding one address to the sample. If the under listing in the directory is known to be significant, its cause can usually be determined and the missing addresses located.

That the address list is an excellent source for a sample of households was shown by two studies made in 1934. The author supervised the selection of a sample from this source in New Haven, Connecticut. The sample was used in a study to determine the extent to which families were listed with social agencies, and to measure the characteristics of the relief group as compared with those of the general population.

In 1935 this sampling procedure was employed in Meriden, Connecticut, under the supervision of T. A. Dreis, in a study of the employment situation of the general population. So successful was it in these two studies that when the sample was selected for the Urban Study of Consumer Purchases in 1936, city directories were used in more than thirty cities where a random sample of households was desired. The sample survey of the Employment Stabilization Institute of the University of Minnesota used a directory sample in 1940 for its study of the characteristics of the labor force in St. Paul. The data from the sample were compared with the federal census data for the same year; the figures were remarkably close. In number of dwelling units, for example, the 10 per cent sample and the census figures are as follows:

	U. S. Census	10% Sample from Directory
Total number of dwelling units	83,324	8358
Occupied dwelling units	80,575	8042

As a matter of fact, even small subsamples of .5 of 1 per cent proved to agree exceedingly well with the census figures and other total enumerations on all of the characteristics examined.

Advantages of the City Directory Method. Using a city directory as a basis for sampling has the following advantages:

1. The sample is selected in the office by a few persons who can be trained in the procedure. This means that too much responsibility need not be placed on the field workers.
2. The spacing between each sample case can be done systematically without ringing doorbells to find out how many families live at each address. (Although it is possible to guess the number of household units in a one-family dwelling, this procedure is quite unreliable in multiple-family houses. Therefore careful sampling in the field would involve a complete canvass of every dwelling to select each sample case.) Such items as the following can be easily checked and eliminated:
   a. Mistakes in the numbering of cases.
   b. Confusion in sampling families in apartment houses, rear dwellings, etc.
   c. Errors in the number of families excluded or that fall in the interval between each family selected.

d. Omissions of sections of the city resulting from the investigator's failure to cover the area assigned.
3. The sample is known in advance; hence any deviations from expected results can be checked up immediately.
4. If the sample is drawn from the street address section of the directory, the assignment of cases can be facilitated by putting the enumeration district number or the ward number on each card sampled.
5. The reliability of the sample can be assessed because the sampling has been methodically carried out in accordance with the demands of the theory of probability.

Preliminary Steps in Sampling

STUDY THE SOURCE LIST:

After the surveyor has tentatively selected the source, he should examine it carefully to see whether it actually covers the population he wishes to sample. The following questions are particularly important:

1. Are all the economic, age, sex, or other groups to be surveyed included in the source? If the list is one of individuals, are the more mobile groups represented? The surveyor should keep in mind the fact that transients and others who move frequently are seldom listed; if they are listed, they cannot be located for survey purposes.
2. What period does the list cover? Does it cover many years? What was exceptional about that period? Are present conditions the same as they were then? If not, does the list still describe the population the surveyor is interested in sampling? Is there a more up-to-date list? The older the list is, the fewer people can be located. Are the addresses up to date? If not, how much work would it involve to make the list up to date?
3. Over what geographic areas are the addresses distributed? Do the limits coincide with areas for which statistical background data are available? Lists of social or service organizations frequently are not restricted to areas for which population statistics are available. Thus when the sample is tested, the areas it covers are not comparable with census or statistical divisions. Does the list include residents of the suburbs? If so, is the entire suburban area covered?
4. If the list is one of individuals, what proportion of them will the

surveyor be able to locate if they are drawn? How do those that cannot be located differ from those who can be found? Are they older, more mobile, in different types of occupations, married, deceased, no longer on the list because of lack of interest, etc.?

5. How can the main list be supplemented in order to make the enumeration complete for the population about which generalizations are to be made?

6. Is the arrangement of the list convenient for sampling purposes? Are all the files or lists required for the sample in one room? Is there sufficient space for the survey staff to work in while drawing the sample? Are the files constantly in use? If so, will the sampler be in the way or be unable to use them when he needs to? Are the active cases filed with the inactive? If not, will the active file be accessible to the sampler long enough to draw a sample? Will the list change while the sample is being drawn? If the sample is to represent only active cases, and if the active and inactive cases are filed together, how is the sampler to pull out the active cases? Are the lists filed in folders with so much other material that the task of pulling them out becomes prohibitive from the point of view of the time required? Are the lists legible, or will considerable time have to be spent trying to decipher names?

7. Are any names or addresses listed more than once? If so, how much work will be required to correct this situation?

8. What determines the arrangement of cases as they appear on the list? On the page? In the drawer? Is the list arranged according to:

   a. Geographic location: Blocks, townships, counties, postal routes, segments of larger areas, wards, enumeration districts, census tracts, city streets, etc.

   b. Time: Date of being listed.

   c. Alphabetical sequence: Name of person, or name of street.

   d. Numerical sequence: The amount or extent of a given characteristic.

   e. Combinations of the above arrangements.

The effect of the order upon the resulting sample is discussed on page 267.

PREPARE THE SOURCE FOR SAMPLING:

Before the selection of the cases is begun, a final check should be made to make sure that the entire population to be sampled is included on the list. In a sample to be drawn from a card file, the sampler should find out whether some cards are in use or will be used by others than himself while the sample is being drawn, whether there are any cards waiting to be filed, whether there is a separate file of "problem cases" which should be either filed or sampled separately, whether all the active cases are in the file.

If the list to be sampled is a list of addresses, it should be checked to see that practically every address in the community is listed. If necessary, one or two interviewers who are familiar with the city should check the list and the community for such places as alley dwellings, shacks along river bottoms, converted railroad cars, houses in the rear of lots, trailer camps within the city limits, vacant dwelling units, all dwelling units in various-sized apartment houses, stores with a dwelling unit on the second floor or in the rear, and other places which are likely to have been overlooked by the compilers of the source list. If residential developments have sprung up in the city, they should be included. It is also important to find out how the source list disposes of people in hotels, flophouses, rooming houses, institutions, social agencies, school dormitories, residential clubs, etc. To be sure, it is not possible to pick up all the omissions from the list by this procedure, but it should give the surveyor some idea of the confidence he may have in the list as a sample of the various types of addresses in the city. If certain types of places that are omitted are essential for a true cross-section of the city, a supplementary list should be compiled and a sample drawn from it and added to the main sample. In one study of the incidence of employment and unemployment among residents of a certain city, the directory used as the source of addresses did not list separately the number of occupied and vacant rooms in each rooming house. It was necessary therefore to compile a directory of rooms in lodging houses from a direct field study. To obtain a true picture of the lodging house population, this second list was then sampled to yield a cross-section of the adults who were not householders but who nevertheless constituted a sizable proportion of the labor market.

The source list should be studied to find out what types of cases are listed that are not included in the universe to be sampled. For example, in an address sample of a city, the suburbs might be listed. If it is relatively easy to eliminate entire streets which are not in the city proper this should be done before the sample is drawn. However, the not infrequent practice of running through the original list and crossing out scattered ineligible items and then taking the trouble to avoid these items when counting for the sample is unnecessarily laborious. Generally speaking, it is easier to leave the unwanted cases on the list and to eliminate the ones that happen to be drawn in the sample. Thus the sampler proceeds just as if all the cases on the list are eligible. When he is through counting and drawing he will find that in a 10 per cent sample, for instance, he has drawn 10 per cent of all eligible cases and 10 per cent of the ineligible. These latter cases can then be discarded.

A list of names should be brought up to date if possible. If it is complete but out of date, it is probably easier to correct only the cases drawn in the sample. Thus data on changes in address or in names because of marriage or divorce, deaths, etc., would be corrected only in the actual sample. If there are many such changes, the surveyor should make certain that the final sample will include the group in which he is interested.

Multiple listings should be eliminated. If every case is to have an equal chance of being selected, every name or address or any other sampling unit that is used should appear only once on the list. Hence it is necessary to go through the list and cross out the extra listings or remove the duplicate cards from the card file. However, this must not be construed to mean that in a dwelling unit sample several dwelling units that have one house number should be discarded, because here the sampling unit is the dwelling unit, not the house number.

If the sample is to be drawn from card files on the basis of a definite interval measured in inches between each case, the files should be packed tightly before the sample is drawn. Similarly, if it is to be selected from long lists of names and the intervals between each case selected or measured in inches, the lists should be pasted together so that no blank spaces will erroneously be included in the measuring. In drawing samples at measured intervals the space taken by the names at the end of a page or filing case must be carried over to the succeeding page or filing case; this task is simplified by having the pages or filing cases as full as possible.

Before the sampling is actually begun, the number of cases in the list should be determined or estimated. This figure should be compared with figures obtained from other sources as a check on the completeness of the list. In a city directory address listing, for example, counting the number of dwelling units listed per column in about twenty columns selected at random from the entire address section makes it possible to estimate fairly closely the number of dwelling units listed. If there is a serious discrepancy between this figure and the number of families shown by the latest census of the city, the reason for it should be sought before the directory address list is used.

Methods of Selecting Sample Cases

Regardless of the type of sampling employed—stratified, random, or purposive—the final choice of cases should be based on random selection, whether within small groups, larger strata, or the total population. The following techniques have been used to obtain random samples: selection by lot; selection at regular intervals; selection at fixed positions from line numbers; selection from a grid placed on a map; and selection by trained interviewers.

SELECTION BY LOT:

Since it is impossible to put the human population that is to be sampled into a hat and have the sampler close his eyes and pull out a sample, many substitute procedures have been devised. In one such procedure, all individuals in the universe to be sampled are assigned numbers that are recorded on small equal-sized slips of paper. These slips are put in a hat or a box and thoroughly mixed, either mechanically or otherwise; the sampler then draws them out without looking into the container. In selecting draftees in 1940, the numbered slips were placed in small capsules which were put in a large goldfish bowl and mixed before the drawing took place. It is interesting to note that on the basis of the published list of the order in which the numbers were drawn, statisticians have discovered that the mixing was not as thorough as it might have been. Apparently an up-and-down motion was used to too great an extent; there was not enough circular motion which would reach the middle and edges of the bowl more thoroughly.

The above procedure is very time-consuming. It is necessary to prepare equal-sized slips of paper, number every name or case in the universe, record the numbers on the slips, and, after the drawing, locate the names on the original list.

A simpler procedure for drawing random numbers is provided by Tippett's Tables of Random Numbers (966). Although the numbers are supposed to be arranged randomly, some statisticians have found certain limitations to the list (507, 508, 1139). Instructions for using these tables are given in Pearson, *Tables for Statisticians and Biometricians* (727), although the surveyor can set up his own procedure.

A roulette wheel has also been used to obtain a random set of numbers. The various digits that come up when the wheel is spun can be used as sample numbers, but care is necessary to make certain that the wheel is not biased in favor of certain numbers.

Playing cards can be used if the universe is not too large. Each case is recorded on a card, the deck is shuffled, and the cards are counted off, every *n*th card being a sample case.

All these methods necessitate numbering the entire universe from which the sample is drawn, and then identifying the sample number on the list which is being sampled. In most large-scale studies this task is so great that it makes these procedures impracticable.

SELECTION AT REGULAR INTERVALS:

Much the same result can be achieved by sampling at regular intervals. In some cases, depending on the arrangement of the source list, this method gives a better sample than the lottery drawing. Furthermore, this method precludes any chance of drawing a poor random sample such as is possible, but very rare, with the lottery technique. Selecting the sample cases at evenly spaced intervals guarantees that a cross-section of the entire universe will be secured. These intervals can be determined by counting a number of cases passed over between each one selected, or measuring the distance between the cases selected in inches of cards or inches of names on a list.

SAMPLING AT REGULAR INTERVALS FROM A LIST:

Suppose, for example, that one-tenth of all the names on a list will yield the number wanted for the sample study. The first case for the sample is selected by lot, as follows: Ten equal-sized slips of paper are numbered from 1 to 10. They are put face down in a box and mixed, and one slip is drawn. If the one drawn is "7," the seventh name from the top of the list is the first one in the sample. The tenth name following this one is the second case in the sample. In other words, the 7th, 17th, 27th, 37th, etc., names constitute the sample.

If the list of names takes up several pages, the names at the end of each page below the last sample case must be carried over when counting cases for the intervals. In the above example in which a sample of one in ten is wanted, if there are four names after the last sample on the first page, the first name on the second page will be "5," and the sixth name from the top of the page will be the sample case. This carrying-over guarantees that the total number drawn for the sample will comprise one out of every ten names in the list. If the carry-over system is used, it is not necessary to draw by lot the first sample case on any page except the first page.

Effect of the Arrangement or the Order of Names on the List. The arrangement of names on the list should depend on the type of cross-section desired in the sample—alphabetical, chronological, or geographic. If the names on the list are arranged alphabetically, taking one in every *n*th case at regular intervals assures the sampler that he will have a good cross-section of names beginning with the various letters of the alphabet. To be sure, such letters as "Q" or "Z" may not happen to be selected in the sample, but since surnames rarely begin with them and they therefore have a very small representation in the list as a whole, the sampler would not éxpect them to appear very often if he were drawing by lot. Similarly, if he is working with a list of addresses classified alphabetically on the basis of street names (as in the address list of a city directory), he can be certain that selecting every *n*th case at regular intervals will give him a good geographic cross-section of the city as well as a good alphabetical sample of street names.

A chronological list—for example, graduates of a certain college listed by year of graduation—should yield a good cross-section of the graduates in various years if every *n*th case is drawn. Had the sample been drawn by lot instead of at regular intervals, it might, if it were small, happen to be a relatively poor sample of the various years in the total. To be sure, if a great many samples were drawn by lot from the list, they would tend to be a good cross-section, chronologically as well as for other characteristics, but any single sample might not be good. Thus, if the sampler wants to make certain that the various years are proportionately represented in a single sample, drawing at regular intervals from a chronological list will give him this assurance. Similarly, if he wants a good geographical' cross-section, the source list should be arranged geographically.

Aside from this assurance, it makes no difference whether the list is classified alphabetically, numerically, by type of case, or on any other basis, so long as the classification has no relation to the sampling ratio. The spacing between various types of cases should not be regular, so that it more or less coincides with the spacing between the sample cases. For example, if every tenth name on a list was a home owner and all the other names were tenants, a sample covering one in every ten names might either exclude the home owners entirely or be composed solely of them.

SAMPLING AT REGULAR INTERVALS FROM A CARD FILE: If a card file is to be used for sampling, all the cards should be filed before the sampling is begun. If there is one card for each individual in the file, the procedure is essentially the same as that recommended for sampling from a list of names, i.e., the cards should be counted and those at regular intervals, such as every tenth, should be taken out or marked for the sample. If the file is very large and time considerations make it inadvisable to count the cards between the sample cases, a space interval can be used. After being packed closely together, the cards are measured with a ruler and the card at the end of every five inches, or any other interval, is selected for the sample. If the sample is selected on the basis of space intervals, all the cards should be of the same thickness. If the thickness varies, it should vary at random; i.e., a thick card (or a thin one) should not always be used for a particular type of entry.

If the cards are in drawers or boxes, the cards remaining in the drawer after the last sample has been drawn must be carried over to those in the next drawer.

Unless the total number of cards in the files is known, it is advisable to ascertain it. This can be done by counting the number of cards there are in an inch at various places through the file. If the average remains stable, the number in an inch can be used in estimating the total. For most purposes, about 10 one-inch counts are sufficient to give the average number of cards per inch.

A different situation arises when there is an unequal number of cards per individual but a sample of individuals at measured intervals is wanted. The first step is to group together all the cards for each individual. Since those individuals with the greatest number of cards will have a better chance of being chosen for the sample, their chances of selection must be equalized. If the interval chosen for sampling is every 5 inches, the sampler can select the card of the individual following the one that comes at the end of the fifth inch. In other words, if the sampling measure falls on the third card of a person who has ten cards in the file, the sampler will overlook the remaining seven cards and select the next name in the file. This same technique may be used if a person's name appears more than once in a card file from which a sample of individuals is wanted. In order to ascertain the approximate ratio when the total number of individuals in the file is unknown, it would probably be necessary to count several one-inch units to obtain an estimate of the average number of different individuals per inch of cards.

SELECTION AT FIXED POSITIONS ON A PAGE OR FROM
LINE NUMBERS:

If the sample is to be selected from a page listing of names or households it is possible to arrive at a random selection by choosing the cases on every *n*th line on the page. The 1940 Sample Census was of this type. Each side of the schedules contained 40 lines on which the enumerator recorded the names and characteristics of persons enumerated. Two out of the 40 lines were designated as the sample lines and instructions printed in the margins indicated to enumerators that they were to ask the supplementary questions desired for the sample cases. This yielded a 5 per cent sample of the population. Since enumerators were instructed to begin at a corner and proceed around the blocks in their districts, naturally a great many schedules would have a corner address listed on the first line of schedule. In deciding which lines were to be chosen for the sample, the sample designers did not want to get a disproportionate number of families who lived in corner houses. If line *1* had been used on all schedules, too many corner houses would have been drawn. If line *1* had been omitted, too few would have been included. The aim of the designers was to get the same proportion of "heads, wives, heads of corner houses, male children 19 years of age, blanks, notes of explanation, etc." as were found in the entire population of the lines that were turned in on the schedules of the enumerators for a given area (927). To avoid the "line bias" which using the same lines on every schedule would have resulted in, it was decided to vary the lines for different schedules. Since only certain lines seemed to be affected by the line bias, it was possible to design a good sample of lines by using five different schedules (styles V, W, X, Y, Z). Style V, with lines 14, 29, 55, and 68, was employed in 16 out of 20 districts, while each of the other styles was used in 1 out of 20 districts. Each enumerator was given one type of schedule only. The schedules were "distributed to enumeration districts according to the following rotation scheme: V V W V V V V X V V V V Y V V V V Z V V, repeated over and over, county after county, without any break at county or state lines" (927). This procedure yielded the correct proportions of each style for the tabulations.

When line samples are employed in connection with telephone directories or other lists, the sampler would do well to consider the possibilities of line biases. How do people happen to be listed first on a page? Does each new letter of the alphabet begin on a new page? If so, people whose names begin with the letters which have few names will have a greater representation than their frequencies warrant in a proportional sample. If line sampling is adopted, every effort should be made to permit each line to be sampled with equal frequency. Thus some type of rotation system is necessary. From the point of view of simplicity, a regular interval system such as was described on page 266 is preferable to line sampling and is much less subject to bias.

SELECTION FROM A GRID PLACED ON A MAP:

One procedure that has been employed in sampling of areas is the grid system. A screen in which squares have been numbered is placed over a map of the area to be sampled. Those areas falling under certain predesignated squares are regarded as the sample areas. In studies of the number of acres devoted to a given type of farming, for example, it is possible to secure a random selection of acres in this manner. This type of selection yields a good area sample but has serious limitations for population sampling. If, for example, a grid were placed over a map of a city and the population in those blocks falling in squares numbered 1, 10, 20, 30, 40, etc., were regarded as the sample, the population of the city could not be gauged from such a sample. Blocks with little or no population would have the same chance of being selected as would densely populated ones.

SELECTION BY INTERVIEWERS:

Unless exceedingly detailed instructions are issued on how to make a random selection of informants, interviewers will almost certainly introduce biases into their selections when respondents are not predesignated. Instructions such as those issued by the National Opinion Research Center (675, pages 74–84) deserve careful study by survey designers who plan to ask interviewers to make the final selection of the sample. Such topics as the following are covered in these instructions and summarized here: (1) Studiously avoid any conscious selection of respondents. Do not seek out people because of their availability, interest in polls, educational background, because they have definite opinions, or are "typical" people. (2) Do not concentrate your interviews in certain districts or in certain places such as retail stores or factories. (3) Never interview your relatives or close friends. (4) Do not seek respondents just because they might cooperate or have interesting opinions. (5) Do not avoid people because they might be difficult to interview or uninformed. (6) Interview in respondents' homes (when interviews are assigned by rent levels the home interview is a necessity). (7) Conduct some interviews during evenings or on weekends. (8) When a woman answers the door ask for the man of the house (interview her only if he is not there). (9) Get a good cross-section of the area assigned to you by approaching houses in all neighborhoods and at random within each. Choose low economic respondents from at least two neighborhoods and the middle ones from at least three. (10) Select neighborhoods impartially—not just because you are familiar with them, or because they are easily accessible. Study a map of the city and learn the character of the various districts. (11) Approach houses at random—do not avoid those that are difficult to reach, unattractive in appearance, or likely to contain foreign-born residents. Also do not concentrate on single-family houses or on too many next-door neighbors. (12) Do not interview more than one member of a family for a given survey, and do not interview the same person more than once in six months. (13) Do not interview persons in groups.

Despite these cautions to the investigator, the NORC sample seems to include too many people with college education. Other surveys or polls have similar difficulty with interviewer-selected samples. Most of them also have pronounced economic biases.

GEOGRAPHICALLY CONTROLLED SAMPLING—SAMPLING THE NATION:

The geographic units which have been employed in social science samplings have varied with the size of the area to be investigated. In sampling the population of the United States, for example, surveyors have drawn samples by states, counties, cities, postal routes,[3] market areas, industrial and farming areas, and by numerous other characteristics which are distributed geographically.

The areas may be listed in an arrangement showing the area with the greatest amount of the characteristic under consideration to the one with the least. Then the sampler may choose sample areas by going straight down the list and choosing every nth area. He may proceed another way by choosing one area with the highest rate, one with an average rate, and one with the lowest rate.

Perhaps the most usual procedure is to select "typical" or "representative" areas. For example, the country is sometimes divided into industrial, mining, farming, and manufacturing areas, and "typical" areas are selected within each. In view of the wide divergence of opinion as to what constitutes a "typical" area, this type of classification is pretty elusive.

Degree of urbanization or city size is a somewhat more objective classification. Even this system of stratification has been subjected to criticism. It is claimed that it is practically impossible to select cities to represent other cities of approximately the same size because so many other factors influence the character of a city. Its proximity to a large metropolitan center, for example, may have a much greater effect on its characteristics than does size alone.

The National Opinion Research Center has been able to make some accurate national estimates on the basis of a small sample of some 2500 cases distributed in representative areas of the nation. The particular cities, towns, and rural areas chosen for the sample are supposed to be

---

[3] For a discussion of the problems and procedures used in postal route sampling in the Enumerative Check Census of Unemployment and Partial Employment in the United States in 1937 see the Appendix (933), Vol. IV.

representative localities—that is, they are chosen because their characteristics resemble the sectional average and the city-size average within each section. The characteristics tested against the section average are: (1) housing characteristics, such as electricity, cooking fuel, and mechanical refrigeration; (2) median contract and estimated rent; (3) persons with eight years or less of schooling and persons with twelve years or more of schooling; (4) total population, native white population, population over twenty-one, and native white population over twenty-one; and (5) industrial distribution of the population fourteen years and over. The criteria in rural areas are the ratio of rural farm to the rural nonfarm population, housing characteristics, median rent, median years of schooling completed, and the ratio of agricultural workers to employed workers (among farm residents). Rural areas are chosen which are not close to large cities and which are adjacent to small villages and towns. Special efforts are made to select farmers in more remote rural areas and to avoid those with above-average mechanization, electrification, and other urban characteristics.

In the NORC sampling process, all cities with a population of 25,-000 and over are classified into types, such as industrial, market, institutional, or mixed. Their proper weight within city sizes and geographic sections of the country is the first consideration in the choice of interviewing spots. Each city with a population of one million or over is included in the cross section. Other size cities are allocated by their proper weights, but of course not every individual city is included in the sample.

It has been assumed by some that a "high," "medium," and "low" spot (economically, educationally, and in housing characteristics) should be selected to yield proper representation in all geographic regions and city sizes. NORC has substituted an "average" concept, and conducts interviews in representative cities. . . . The technical advantage of using interviewing spots which are representative of the geographical section and size of community is especially important when the unavailability of certain interviewers within the survey interval necessitates substitutions, because there is no need to balance a "high" spot with a "low." In the long run, therefore, there is less danger that the sample will become biased either by mistake or necessity (through practical considerations of operation. (674, p. 4).

In 1946 NORC's social cross-section of the civilian adult population was controlled within the areas by sex, color, and standard-of-living level. The age variable was partially controlled by assignment of age quotas under and over 40 years of age. The proportions used in the quotas were based on the distributions reported by the 1940 census with constant adjustments for major population changes such as migrations to and from various sections of the country and in cities and towns of various sizes, and in rural areas. Changes in the numbers of young males in civilian life during the war years and after discharges from the army were also taken into account in planning the sample proportions. Special efforts were made to improve the economic distribution of the sample by assigning quotas to interviewers by rent levels rather than permitting the interviewer to choose respondents on the basis of his subjective judgment of their socio-economic level. In 1946 about two-thirds of the assignments were by rent levels. The proportions in the various rent groups were constantly being adjusted to take into account changing rental values and home evaluations.

The current labor force surveys of the Bureau of the Census employ 68 areas for their sample of approximately 25,000 people. Regional as well as national estimates are obtained from this sample.

The area sample design used in the Surveys of Consumer Finances has been fully described by Goodman and Maccoby of the Survey Research Center of the University of Michigan (**371**). The sample, consisting of 3000 cases located in sixty-six areas of the nation, is referred to as a "probability sample" because each element in the population has a known chance of being included in the sample, and the sampling error can be computed according to probability theory. The considerations which led to the choice of the particular design used in these Surveys of Consumer Finance is discussed in detail in this article and should be referred to directly by persons contemplating a sample of this type. The following summary of the design is presented to acquaint the reader with the various steps that are involved in planning a nation-wide sample of this nature.

I. Selection of sample points
   A. Some interviews were taken in each of the (12) major metropolitan areas of the county (these areas contained about 30 per cent of the nation's population).
   B. A sample of counties was selected from the remaining 70 per cent of the population.
      1. For each county the following information was placed on punch cards:
         (a) Per cent of population living in urban areas

(b) The amount of U.S. Government bonds sold per capita in 1943

(c) Per cent of the employed persons working in manufacturing industries

(d) Per cent of the population who are native white

(e) Average size of farm

(f) The 1940 adult population of the county

2. The cards, arranged in order of degree of urbanization (highest to lowest proportion of urban areas as shown in item a) were cumulated in a pack until one-third of the population had been included (item f).

3. The cards of these most urbanized counties were then separated and rearranged according to per capita bond sales—highest to lowest.

4. The population was then cumulated as before and when one-third of the population was covered, this group of high-capita bond sales counties was withdrawn from the pack.

5. This pack of high-urban, high-bond sales counties was then rearranged according to the per cent of employees engaged in manufacturing.

6. The one-third with the highest proportion of employees working in manufacturing was rearranged by per cent native white.

7. This last group was then classified into the half with the highest per cent native white and the half with the lowest per cent native white.

8. Procedures 1 through 7 were followed for the middle third of the counties and the lower third, except that some groups of counties with little urbanization were arranged by average size of farm instead of per cent in manufacturing.

9. The above procedures yielded 54 groups of counties of approximately the same size adult population. One county was chosen for the sample from each of these 54 groups.

C. The sample county from each of the 54 groups of counties was selected so that every county was given a chance of selection proportional to its 1940 adult population. This was accomplished as follows:

1. A number was assigned to every 100 adults in the county, numbers being consecutive within counties and states, and drawing at random one number from each stratum—e.g., County 1, in Stratum 1, with a population of 30,100 was assigned numbers 1 to 301 inclusive; County 2, in Stratum 1, with a population of 40,800 people, was assigned numbers 302 to 709. The total numbers in this stratum went to 10,836.

2. A number chosen at random determined which county from the stratum was to be the sample county. The number chosen in first stratum happened to be 2147. Thus county-coded number 3034 happened to be the one chosen from Stratum 1 because it had numbers 1873 to 2255.

D. According to the above method of selection, counties with the largest population had the greatest chance of being chosen (because they were assigned more numbers). To give the residents of thinly populated areas the same chance of being included as people from the densely populated counties, the number of interviews assigned each chosen county was inversely proportional to its 1940 adult population.

II. Selection of dwellings within sample points

A. Each of the sample counties was divided into open-country areas and towns.

1. The open-country parts of the county were divided into segments (small areas bounded by easily-identified boundaries, such as roads, fences, or streams, and usually containing two to five dwellings). Maps, aerial photographs, and materials from the Master Sample of Agriculture (478, 512) were used for this purpose. Segments were chosen by random methods and every dwelling in the selected segments was considered to be in the sample.

2. For the town and city sample, the largest town in the county was usually chosen as a separate stratum. Within the town, blocks were selected at random and from each sample block chosen, a subsample of dwellings was selected. Upper-income groups were sampled at a higher rate than the low because income holdings and savings are more variable in the more prosperous classes.

B. For cities in the sample with populations over 50,000, block statistics showing average rent per block were used.

1. A large sample of blocks was chosen, with probabilities proportional to the number of dwellings per block. (Within blocks, sampling rates were inversely proportional to the number of dwelling units.)

2. These blocks were arranged according to average rent, and a sub-sample was drawn—the high-rent blocks being oversampled as compared with the low. Usually high-rent blocks were sampled at four times the basic sampling rate, medium-rent blocks at twice the rate.

3. Interviewers visited the over-sampled blocks and rated each dwelling there according to whether they thought it was occupied by a high, medium or low income family.

4. Only those dwellings rated as having high or medium income families were sampled at the high rate. Low income families living in high-rent blocks were sampled at the basic rate.

C. In towns with fewer than 50,000 people, interviewer ratings were used for oversampling, because block rent statistics were not available.

D. Selection of the sample dwelling units

1. A dwelling unit listing sheet was prepared for every sample block. Interviewers recorded each address encountered as they proceeded clockwise around a block, beginning at a particular corner. Each unit in an apartment house was listed as a separate dwelling. Three listing sheets were used in blocks where interviewers rated dwellings as high, medium and low. At every *n*th line—depending on the sampling ratio to be applied—a check mark indicated the dwellings belonging in the sample. Interviews on the survey topic were held with every spending unit (or family) in the dwelling thus checked.

CITY SAMPLING UNITS:

The sampling units used to provide a cross-section of a city are, of course, much smaller than the geographic areas required for a picture of the entire country. The divisions which have been used for city sampling include wards or other administrative and service areas, census tracts, census enumeration districts, city blocks, and block segments. Address sampling is discussed on pages 256–260.

Wards or Other Administrative and Service Areas. The city ward is a political subdivision of the modern American city which may change from one administration to another. The size of population varies greatly from one ward to another, and the population within a ward may be extremely heterogeneous. Since there are relatively few wards in most cities, it is practically impossible to select a random sample of wards which will contain a satisfactory cross-section of a city's families. Therefore the ward has not proved popular for random samples; its use has been confined to "typical" area samples.

Social service districts, credit areas, customer service districts of large stores, etc., have all been found unsatisfactory as sampling units. Not only are these districts usually too large, too heterogeneous, and too few in number to yield a reliable sample of households or individuals, but the statistical background data needed for testing and evaluating the samples selected are often not available in terms of these nonstandardized divisions.

Census Tracts. In cities in which the census classifies and furnishes data by statistical tracts, a tract sample is much preferable to a ward sample. Not only are the tracts smaller, but they tend to be more homogeneous and more uniform in size than do the wards. The tract boundaries are clearly defined and remain fixed from one decade to another.

Census Enumeration Districts. The enumeration district (E. D.) is the administrative unit employed by the Bureau of the Census for the collection of data. One enumerator is supposed to canvass the area or population covered in one enumeration district, and therefore this unit is much smaller than the census tract described above. Although tabulations for enumeration districts are published only for large cities, they may be obtained from the Census Bureau by special arrangement. Because the population changes from one census to another, the E. D. boundaries also change; hence, before this unit is used it is wise to secure the latest description of the enumeration districts from the Census Bureau.

City Blocks. The closer the collection unit approaches the unit that is to be used in tabulations, the better for sampling purposes. The city block contains fewer households than does the E. D., and the average city has more blocks than the E. D.'s; therefore, sampling by city blocks gives a better sample of households than does E. D. sampling, with comparable effort. However, the tests of block sampling as used in family surveys have shown that the chances of securing a poor sample of households is very great. City blocks tend to be exceedingly heterogeneous; many have no inhabitants while others may contain well over a hundred families. It is possible, however, to plan a block sample to give satisfactory results. The procedure adopted in the surveys of congested production areas might well be followed if block sampling is employed (see pp. 239–242 for a discussion of the procedure). Using block statistics from the 1940 census, all the blocks in the city were arranged according to the number of dwelling units; then every *n*th block was chosen for the stratified sample. Within these blocks every *n*th dwelling unit was enumerated for the final sample.

Block Segments. Since the city block is too large a sampling unit for households, it has been suggested that portions of blocks be sampled instead. In this procedure a segment of each block is used—a half, a quarter, or some such segment. The segment can be chosen on the basis of a list of addresses. If this list is not up to date, this method makes it possible to insure that all new building structures will be sampled; the enumerator is merely instructed to canvass every building between two specified numbers. This last does not seem to be sufficient justification for employing block segment sampling, however, because an out-of-date address list can be brought up to date from building permits. In block segment sampling, more schedules are required to yield a reliable household sample than in dwelling unit sampling. The block segment is also difficult to select and canvass because interviewers are likely to become confused as to the limits of the areas assigned to them. Many houses display no numbers; in these cases the interviewer has to ask the occupants for their addresses to determine the beginning and the end of each segment. Finally, the main responsibility for locating the households in the segment rests with the interviewer; this makes it much more difficult to keep an accurate check in the sampling.

With the use of the Sanborn maps by the Census Bureau, block segment sampling has found wider use than ever before. These maps are kept up to date and enable the surveyor to specify exactly the addresses the interviewer is to survey.

In view of the necessity of call-backs in any properly conducted survey, the saving of travel time by interviewers to adjacent dwellings is questionable. If the interviewer has to make another visit, he might as well go to another section of the city to a randomly chosen address as go to an address in the same block where he has already completed one or more interiews.

Just why so many attempts have been made to find a sampling unit which could be used instead of the individual or household to give a cross-section of the population is explained by the fact that the sampling of individuals presented too many problems. Larger units seemed to have several advantages, chief of which was the fact that lists of such units were available. Whereas lists of political or geographic areas could be had with relatively little work on the part of the sampler, complete up-to-date lists of individuals were thought to be nonexistent. Actually, the address lists of city directories have been tested and found satisfactory in many cities, particularly when supplemented by lists compiled from building permits and special lodging house and quasi-family enumerations. Another reason larger units have been employed is because of the alleged saving in travel time and the consequent saving in the cost of securing schedules. If interviewers covered entire blocks, enumeration districts, wards, or other large sampling units, they could complete many more schedules in a given time than would be possible if they had to spend a great deal of time going from one preselected address to another. But in view of the greater number of schedules required to give a reliable sample of households when a larger sampling unit is employed, this saving of time is more than offset by the time required to visit a larger number of households and to process the schedules obtained. As mentioned before, in view of the need for call-backs among the not-at-homes, areas cannot be covered completely without numerous revisits and consequent high time and travel costs. The interviewer might just as well cover scattered addresses in the first place.

Still another reason claimed for using a large sampling unit and canvassing it completely is the ease of making assignments and checking the work of the interviewers when they must cover every address in their assignment. This reason is open to question, because it is an enormous task to see that interviewers enumerate only the addresses within their assigned areas and that they include all of them. If a sample of dwelling units is selected in the office and if a sample of each interviewer's work is check interviewed, the assignment and checking process can be systematically organized and simplified. To be sure, it requires sampling in advance of the field work, but in view of the gains in accuracy and time, preselection pays high dividends.

Problems of Time Sampling and of Panels

Difficult as it is to select a sample which will constitute a cross-section of the population to be surveyed at any given time, the problem is far more difficult when data for periodic indexes are to be secured by repeated surveys. How can a sample be selected which will continue to be a cross-section of the community? This is the panel problem discussed in Chapter III. What time period can be chosen which will remain comparable from year to year or month to month? What period should be chosen for an index of employment or unemployment, for example? A certain date in each month? How representative of a month is a day? What if this is a holiday or a Sunday? A given week in the month? Should this week include the 15th of the month? The end? The beginning? Should the week be "typical" of the month or of the "peak load?" The entire month? An average of weeks during the month? Should the sample be spread over each week? Should a total for the month be obtained? What about changes during the month? How is a comparable period from month to month to be determined?

The above are but a few of the problems which must be worked out if the time chosen for the sample is to yield meaningful trend figures. The dwelling unit panel or variations of it described in Chapter III seems to provide the most representative population cross-section for periodic surveys.

Additional Steps in Sampling

After the method of sampling has been decided upon and the source list selected and prepared for the drawing, the sampling supervisor should test the plan before the clerks actually start drawing the sample. If necessary, the tentative sampling instructions should be revised or enlarged so that all the sampling clerks will handle every detail logically and uniformly. The mechanics of selecting a sample involves the following procedures:

1. A colored check mark or dot should be placed beside each case which is to be included in the sample. If regular interval sampling is used, the source list should be kept intact so that the interval count can be checked. If a card file is used, the cards chosen for the sample should be tabbed in some way, not removed from the file.

2. The selection should be checked before the sample is numbered. This check should be made by a different clerk from the one who made the original selection.

3. The sample cases chosen should be numbered consecutively and the numbers recorded on the source list.

4. The numbering should be checked to see that there are no duplications, omissions, or other errors.

5. The total number drawn should be compared with the number ex-

pected in view of the sampling ratio used. If there is any discrepancy, its cause should be discovered and its validity determined. At this stage of sampling, it is often possible to detect and correct limitations in the source list. When the exact sampling ratio is not known, as for example in regular interval sampling, it is advisable to make enough sample counts of the number of cases covered by the interval so that an approximate sampling ratio can be arrived at and used in this check.

6. The sample cards should be prepared. It is advisable to use colored cards for this purpose. These cards should not be taken out of the office but should be available for reference throughout the survey.

7. Certain identifying information about each sample case should be transcribed (preferably typed) from the source list. Such data as the following are important: Sample number, name of individual, address, type of dwelling or place of business.

8. The information on the cards should be checked against the data on the source list.

9. The district (ward, census tract, E. D., or other district classification used) in which each address is located should be recorded on the sample card. A street index guide that classifies addresses by districts is available for many cities. The district entered on the card should be checked.

10. Further information on the sample case should be secured from secondary sources. For example, the first section of city directories often lists the wife of a family head, and gives the head's occupation and place of work. Even though this information is not always up to date or reliable, it frequently provides a clue as to the type of informant the interviewer will see and thus aids in the assignment of cases. The telephone directory also contains useful data. If the information obtained from the various sources is conflicting, the discrepancies should be cleared up by the interviewer.

11. A master list should be typed as soon as the sample has been selected and checked. Sheets of paper which can later be stapled together should be used, rather than cards, for cards are apt to be lost, misplaced, or withdrawn for use, whereas a list can be kept intact. The master list should be kept under lock and key. In large-

scale studies, the original source list which was marked during the drawing of the sample may serve as the master list. In this case, the office or interviewing staff should not have access to the source list lest it be damaged or worn out during the survey.

12. Any supplementary cases which are needed to make the sample representative of the universe should be added to the master list. If the source list does not contain new dwelling units, for example, the sample of new dwelling units should be added to the master list. The selection of the sample should not be considered complete until the sample has been tabulated and compared with outside sources and proved to be unbiased.

The various steps for drawing a predesignated sample may be summarized as follows:

1. Locate a list of the universe to be sampled. If one cannot be located, prepare a list.
2. Study the list for its content and limitations.
3. Choose the sampling method and test it to see if it is practicable. Then prepare written instructions.
4. Prepare the source for drawing the sample.
5. Select the sample cases.
6. Check the sample.
7. Prepare the sample cards.
8. Type the master list of the original sample.
9. Prepare sampling tables to test the sample before field work is begun.

A number of additional suggestions on the technique of drawing samples deserve attention:

1. Whatever procedure is chosen, it should be followed systematically and consistently until the entire sample is drawn. The sampler should make no change in technique or in definitions during the selection. If the instructions have been properly tested before the drawing, there should be no need for changing the plan. If the routine work of counting and choosing the sample cases is done by several persons, the sampling supervisor should see that all of them are following instructions.
2. Sufficient time should be allowed for drawing the sample so that no field work will have to be done before the sample is ready for

assignment. The time required can be estimated if the sampler starts to draw the sample and times the various operations. Generally speaking, the time varies with such factors as:

a. The sampling ratio (if regular numbered interval sampling is employed). The greater the number of names or addresses to be counted between each sample case, the fewer cases can be selected per day.

b. The condition of the list from which the sample is being drawn. If it is difficult to identify a sample case—for example, if the list includes other members of the family but only the head is to be drawn—considerable time is consumed in scrutinizing each name on the list.

c. The amount of data transcribed. The more information to be recorded about each sample case, the longer it will take to draw the sample. More time will be required if the facts about each case are handwritten instead of typed. (As a rule, surveyors tend to underestimate the time required to select the sample and transcribe the necessary data. In one study in which a random sample of one in every ten addresses was selected from a list of addresses from a local census, recorded on large sheets of paper, the rate for these two operations was about 500 cases per day per clerk. In another survey in which regular interval sampling was used to select one in ten addresses from a city directory address list in a city of 80,000 households, selection was made at a rate of 1,000 sample cases per day per clerk, and transcription was done at a rate of 500 per day.)

d. The extent to which each process is verified. Even though it may take as long (or longer if serious errors are found) to verify as to select the sample cases and record the data, sufficient time should always be allowed for verification.

3. Whenever possible, draw a larger sample than will be surveyed by the field workers; the part which is not used in the main investigation can be employed for checking or increasing the sample. The subsamples into which the total sample is divided should, of course, be random cross-sections of the total number drawn. For example, by using every other case for the field work and the alternate cases for comparisons with the field sample (e.g., by districts, telephone homes, or home ownership) the surveyor

can obtain some evidence of the difference to be expected if another sample of the same size were drawn. Adding the two samples together will show the effect of doubling the sample. To be sure, a single sample like this will not indicate the variation to be expected as a result of the laws of chance (see the discussion on the size of sample, Chapter IX), but it is an empirical example of what might have happened if the surveyor had started to count his sample in between the first two numbers he actually chose.

Another advantage of this extra sample is the fact that it can be used if for some reason the sample has to be enlarged. The tabulations which are to be made may be too detailed for the number of cases; if these tabulations are important, it may be necessary to extend the field work to include the second sample. If the refusal rate is high in certain districts or occupational groups, substitute cases may have to be drawn from the extra sample so that data for tabulating will not be lacking for these districts or groups. This substitution procedure, however, is not recommended except as a last resort; it should not be used unless the causes of the refusals are understood and corrected in the analysis.

In sampling human populations the drawing of the sample is not synonymous with obtaining information from the sample selected. Unless detailed plans are prepared and followed out for the control of the sample during field work, the sample originally drawn may be very different from that reaching the final tabulations.

OFFICE CONTROL OF THE SAMPLE:

Unless a well-organized office procedure is set up for keeping close tab on the schedules assigned, returned to the office, in the hands of interviewers, and undergoing various processes in the office, the loss of schedules before final tabulation is inevitable. Interviewers occasionally lose schedules or destroy "refusal" or "difficult" cases. Schedules are mislaid in the office, accidentally thrown away, filed among schedules which have already been tabulated, or left on the top or in a drawer of someone's desk. It is surprising how many schedules get lost even within the four walls of a survey office. Without careful accounting procedure the losses may reach such significant proportions that the sample finally tabulated is meaningless. On the other hand, the final tables may erroneously include a number of duplicate cases which may bias the final sample. Duplications arise when incomplete or faulty schedules are returned to the investigator or to a check interviewer for further field work, and a second code card is prepared as the schedule goes through the coding procedures and the original is not destroyed.

One of the most effective ways of assuring good field work is the maintenance of record system whereby the fate of each case drawn in the sample is known and approved by the sampling supervisor. In order to accomplish this goal it is necessary to have a master list (preferably typed) of the original sample—a list which can be referred to throughout the survey. This list must at all times be kept intact; otherwise there is great likelihood of misplacing or losing the cases which are "borrowed" when some problem arises. If the sample is drawn from a city directory household listing, the directory itself, with each sample case marked and numbered, might serve this purpose. In such a case, another directory for use of the interviewers and office assistants should be available. Each sample case should be typed from the master list and placed on a card for office use only. This card could contain such identifying information as: sample number, address, name of householder, wife's name, occupation of householder, telephone number, type of dwelling or business structure, home tenure. This information can be obtained from most city directories. In addition, the final disposition of the case should be indicated on this sample card. These cards could be arranged so that sample cases which were interviewed and accepted for tabulation could be filed together and a count of their number should equal that actually appearing on the summary tables. Other notations as to disposition might include such facts as: Vacant, business or non-dwelling, outside of city, building demolished, cannot locate person, etc., depending on whether the sample happened to be one of dwelling units, specified individuals, householders, or others.

In addition to the master list and the sample cards, careful control should be kept of every card assigned to interviewers, in the hands of interviewers, and returned to the office. If interviewers must sign when they receive assignments, and if the assignment clerk indicates the return of schedules by the interviewer, the losses due to lack of responsibility as to the whereabouts of cards can be avoided. It is particularly important to see that interviewers return assignments to the office, whether completed or not on the due date. Otherwise the "problem" cases will be retained in the possession of the interviewers until the end of the field work. Then there may not be sufficient time to complete them or to reassign them to other interviewers. Since interviewers' ratings should take into account the number of refusals as well as the number of completed and acceptable schedules turned in, interviewers are often reluctant to report refusals. Thus, they may destroy, lose, or fail to return schedules which represent uncooperative cases. Then again, if the interviewers are quite certain that there will not be sufficient time to reassign problem cases to check interviewers, refusals may be reported as "not at home" when the interviewer called, or as "willing but unable to give the desired information." A "due" date stamped or recorded on each schedule assigned would do much to prevent the losses in the sample resulting from such field work.

When the schedules are returned to the office, all the incomplete ones should contain full notes by the interviewer so that the "recapture" of such cases can be made as efficiently as possible. Frequently, the interviewer who has been refused has much knowledge about the reason for refusal or suggestions as to lines of approach which may be more fruitful. Discussion of the case with the interviewer just after he has attempted the unsuccessful interview often yields information of considerable use to the interviewer who makes the next contact. The intake editor should not accept incomplete schedules until the interviewer has recorded "all he knows" about each case. Especially important is a record of the type of dwelling, the estimated rental value of the dwelling unit, the sex and estimated age of the uncooperative case, and the remarks made by the informant which might give a clue as to the reason for refusal. Other minimum information to be required on all incomplete schedules would depend on the nature of the survey.

In order to insure that the field work will improve as the survey continues, adequate provision should be made for analyzing records which are kept on each interviewer. Daily or weekly summaries of such items as the number of completed interviews, the number "not at home," number refusing all or refusing part of the data called for, and the number who are unable to give the facts asked for on the schedule. The sampling supervisor should inspect these tabulations periodically in order to detect poor field work and, if necessary, to remove interviewers from the field if they seem to be "antagonizing" too many people. Dishonesty may also be detected by an analysis of tabulations of schedules turned in by interviewers. In one public opinion poll the responses of informants are tabulated for each interviewer and compared with the responses found by other interviewers in comparable districts. If one agent seems to be getting "unusual" results, his work is checked by sending another interviewer into his neighborhood to verify the results. If faked returns were not detected until the field work was complete, the schedules of dishonest interviewers might have to be eliminated from the tabulations, thus distorting the sample.

Aside from the distortion to the sample resulting from poor field work, other biases might result from differential refusal rates of various economic groups. Since amount of rent or the rental value of owned homes is correlated with the amount of income received, it is possible to use rent as an economic index. A tabulation of the proportion of schedules in various rent classes which are completed and the proportion which are incomplete should reveal whether or not uncooperative cases constitute a biased economic group. If such a bias is detected early in the survey, special efforts might be made to overcome it. Assignment of schedules representing residents of the high rent areas of the city to the most skilled interviewers is one method of preventing refusals. Another procedure is to contact community leaders in the upper-income groups and to get them to assist. Publicity for the survey directed at upper-income groups might do much to forestall refusals.

An analysis of incomplete returns by geographic areas, political wards, census tracts, or ecological areas might reveal that refusals are concentrated among certain nationality groups, political groups, relief clients, trade union groups, or others who could be appealed to and "converted" to the survey if the differential refusal rate were discovered early in the survey.

A file of all "problem" cases should be kept and a systematic effort made tó classify and reassign these cases until all schedules are completed. Cases which are incomplete because at the time of the first interviewer's call the prospective informant was ill, not at home, on vacation, entertaining guests, or for some other reason could not give the interview, should then be reassigned to the original interviewer at the time decided upon when the schedule was turned in to the office. Other problem cases might require a telephone call to some other member of the family to get information which the informant did not know. Partially completed schedules should not be kept in the file longer than necessary, since the missing information is usually easier to obtain when relevant facts or references are fresh in the mind of the interviewer.

The best way of insuring that the sample collected in the field is as good as or better than that drawn in the office is the appointment of a competent sampling supervisor whose task is to watch the sample from the beginning to the end of the survey. Such a person should not only be responsible for observing what happens to the sample, but should have authority over check interviewers and the recapture program.

Selected References

American Marketing Assn. (9), Assoc. of North American Directory Pub. (17), Borden (92), Bowley (99, 102, 103), Brandt (109), Breyer (111), Brown (114, 116, 119, 120), Brunsman (122, 123), Callander and Sarle (132), Cassady (149), Chapin (166), Churchman et al. (174), Cochran (178, 179), Corby (195), Cornell (198, 199), Crossley (214), Curtis Pub. Co. (224), Deming (235, 236, 239), Deming and Hansen (241), Deming and Simmons (242), Dodge and Romig (251), Dunlap (260), Eckler and Staudt (272), Employment Stabilization Inst. (287), Ferber (297), Gallup (343), Goodman (370), Goodman and Maccoby (371), Hagood (389), Hagood and Bernert (390), Hansen (394), Hansen and Hauser (395), Hansen and Hurwitz (396, 397, 398, 399), Hansen et al. (400), Hauser (422), Hauser and Hansen (424), Hitt (442), Hochstim and Smith (444), Holmes (447, 448), Houseman (455, 456), Jensen (473, 474, 475), Jessen (477, 478, 479), Kameda (486), Katz (493, 496, 497, 498), Kendall and Smith (507, 508), Kiaer (510), King (512), King and McCarty (513), King and Simpson (514), Kiser (522), Larsen (540), Lindquist (570), Madow (609), Mangus (612), Manheimer and Hyman (614), McNemar (630), Meier and Burke (634), Moser (658), NORC (674, 677), Neyman (693, 694, 695), Pearson (727), Peatman (728), Sarle (835), Schoenberg and Parten (847), SSRC (898), Stephan (918, 920, 921, 922, 923, 924), Stephan and Deming (925), Stephan et al. (927), Stock and Hochstim (930), Tippett (966), U.N. (979, 980), U.S. (993, 1003, 1004, 1010), Vickery (1043), Yule (1139), Zeisel (1141).

CHAPTER IX

Size of Sample

Early in the development of plans for the survey a decision must be reached as to the approximate number of cases to include in the sample. The plans for most phases of the investigation will be affected by the size of sample decided upon. In order to make this decision, the survey designer must have a fair idea of how the returns are likely to come out. Such information can be gained from a small pilot study of the type described earlier, from some previous study of a similar nature, or from secondary sources such as the census or public records. Given the probable distribution of the data, the requisite size of sample can be estimated.

The problem of this chapter, then, is to predetermine the size of sample necessary to yield significant results; the problem of evaluating the significance of the results, once they are found, is discussed in Chapter XVI.

A review of the literature in the survey field reveals many misconceptions as well as much contradictory and misleading advice regarding sample size. One erroneous idea is that sheer numbers of cases can serve as a guarantee of correct results. This idea should have been completely exploded by the *Literary Digest* debacle mentioned previously. With more than two million ballots returned, out of ten million distributed, this poll underestimated the popular vote of the winner by 19.8 per cent. On the other hand, the *Fortune* poll, with 4500 interviews, predicted the vote on the winning candidate within 1 per cent. The millions of cases in the *Digest* poll were less predictive than a sample of fewer than 100 cases would have been if chosen by proper sampling procedure from a representative group of the electorate.

Another misconception is that biases in samples can be overcome or corrected merely by increasing the sample size. Only the fluctuations in the data arising from chance factors tend to be evened out with the increase in sample size. Biased errors are noncompensating and cannot be corrected (and usually will not even be revealed) by enlarging the sample.

Another mistaken idea is implicit in such comments as the following: "A mere 3,000 cases certainly is not a large enough sample to portray the opinions of 50,000,000 voters!" or "A sample should be at least 10 per cent of the total population to be surveyed." The misconception here is that the size of the universe from which the sample is drawn determines the number of cases needed to yield an adequate sample of that universe. Formulas for measuring the sampling error, presented later, will show that the emphasis should be placed not upon the number of cases in the *universe*, but rather on the number in the *sample*.

Sample Sizes in Actual Use

Some feeling for the problem of choosing a suitable sample size can be gained by consideration of the numbers of cases actually employed by experienced investigators in important surveys. These sample sizes have been found practicable in the surveys using them.

The National Opinion Research Center has been drifting toward smaller and smaller samples. In 1946 its standard poll covered about 2500 cases; in 1948 about half this number or samples of 1300 were used generally, although larger ones were also employed. Telegraphic surveys conducted by this agency utilize samples of 1100 or even 550 cases to represent the American public. In the prediction of the 1944 presidential election, the NORC used about 2000 voters and came within 2 per cent of predicting the popular vote. No published forecast was made in 1948. The Office of Public Opinion Research at Princeton also based its estimate of the 1944 vote on about 2000 cases, and came within a half of 1 per cent of being correct. Gallup, using the quota sampling technique popular among pollers and market research agencies in 1948, employed about 3000 cases. On certain questions he increases the sample. For example, in the 1948 presidential prediction, he used a cumulative sample of approximately 60,000 cases spread over a two-month period. He underestimated the Truman vote by 5.5 per cent. Roper, who did not make state-by-state predictions in his election forecast, used about 5000 simultaneous interviews in 1944 and again in 1948. He predicted the Democratic vote very closely in 1936, 1940, and 1944 but in 1948 missed it by more than 12 per cent. The poor forecast in 1948 was attributed to factors other than size of sample. For his consumer samples, Roper covers a sample of 3500, and for his sample of management 4000 or more cases are usually employed. In September of the 1944 presidential election year, Crossley interviewed a sample of 20,000 cases distributed over the entire nation. Then in October he surveyed another sample of 20,000, but that time only in the 19 states where the September poll indicated the election was likely to be close. The Brand Barometer studies conducted by the Psychological Corporation, in which detailed figures on family purchases are obtained, cover 10,000 households quarterly. On the other hand, the Index of Public Opinion published by this corporation in 1946 used 2500 cases in each of two samples. Since 1945, the Monthly Report of the Labor Force, prepared by the Bureau of the Census, uses about 25,000 interviews distributed in 68 regions of the United States. This same area sample of the Census was utilized by the Columbia Broadcasting System in a survey of radio ownership, etc., conducted in 1947. Since regional predictions were not made, only 5000 homes were covered in this sample for a national estimate. In a survey of farmers' supplies conducted on a sample of 2678 farmers, the Bureau of Agricultural Economics estimated 1,981,-000 tractors on farms, which compared to an estimate of 1,937,000 based on the 1940 census and sales and other figures (78).

The Consumer Requirements surveys conducted during World War II used samples of 5000 for estimating the number of homes in the nation with such home appliances as electric irons, washing machines, refrigerators, etc. Estimates were also made on purchases of various appliances, equipment and types of clothing. The sample estimates for the 37,500,000 households represented were close to independent estimates obtained from industry reports. For example, according to the estimate based on the sample, 1,800,000 extension cords were purchased in the first quarter of 1944. The estimate based on records supplied from shipments reported by industry was 2,000,000 cords. The estimate of the number of scissors purchased was 1,000,000 for the sample and 1,200,000 for the industry estimate.

Surveys of cities usually employ samples of about the same size as those used in national estimates. Parten, in the random sample of New Haven, Connecticut, in 1931 surveyed about 2000 households. The distribution of cases approximated that of the Census taken a year earlier in every respect for which it was compared. As is shown later in this chapter (p. 322) even subsamples of less than 200 cases proved to be sufficiently close to the Census count to justify their use for certain purposes.

The St. Paul, Minnesota, study of employment in 1941 adopted a panel sample of 400 (287). Here again, comparison with the 1940 Census figures showed the sample to be very representative. In August, 1946, Roper conducted a poll on the mayoralty election in New York City using 515 cases spread over 5 boroughs, and his prediction of the winning candidate was within 3 per cent of the actual election outcome. Cantril cites a poll of a county of 100,000 population in which a sample was taken of 233 cases distributed proportionally by economic status, age, and sex. The prediction based on this small sample came within 0.6 per cent of the actual election figure for the winning candidate (142, p. 151).

While sample sizes in actual use can be seen to vary over an enormous range, four-place figures are very common and so afford some basis for planning. Not infrequently, successful surveys have employed samples of the order of 1000 or 2000 cases.

Definition of an Optimum Sample

An optimum sample in a survey is one which fulfills the requirements of efficiency, representativeness, reliability, and flexibility. The most efficient sample is commonly considered to be the one which provides the most useful information per dollar rather than per case. The sample should be small enough to avoid unnecessary expense and large enough to avoid intolerable sample error. It should be large enough to yield statistically representative and significant results in all the proposed tabulations of importance; but not so large as to waste funds, retard the project, and achieve needlessly high precision. The sample should yield the desired information with the required reliability at the minimum cost. The reader may be reminded that in practice efficient sampling involves making the most of available resources in statistical data, technique, and organization, and adjusting as well as possible to any originally imposed limitations of time, cost, and personnel. In addition, it should be possible in some instances to expand or contract the sample size to meet unforeseen developments during the course of the survey. While it is likely to prove confusing and expensive to change the sample size once the survey is under way, situations occasionally arise in which both reliability and efficiency can be improved by such a change of size. If this can be achieved without introducing bias into the sample, the requirement of flexibility also has been fulfilled.

In practice ideals may be approached but rarely realized, and so one cannot expect to choose exactly the correct sample size. While the cost of the survey can be multiplied many times by drawing a sample which is much too large, it is sound practice to err on the side of too large rather than on the side of too small. A sample which is somewhat too large may be somewhat wasteful, but if properly drawn it should provide adequate prediction. A sample which is too small, on the other hand, is likely to lead nowhere and in that sense prove the most wasteful of all.

Factors Affecting the Sample Size

Several general factors which affect the choice of size of the sample, directly or indirectly, will be considered in some detail. These factors will be seen to be interrelated rather than independent, and to vary greatly in different surveys with respect to their relative importance in determining the sample size.

1. HOMOGENEITY OR HETEROGENEITY OF THE POPULATION:

The size of the sample required in a survey will depend, among other things, upon the degree of homogeneity of the population. The more homogeneous the population, the fewer the cases required to yield a reliable sample of it; conversely, the more heterogeneous the population, the more cases required. To take an extreme example, if a surveyor wanted to know the language usually spoken in the home in a small town of native-born American inhabitants, a very few cases might prove to be adequate. On the other hand, the same survey question might require a sample of hundreds of families in the foreign-born sections of a large city.

Homogeneity is a matter of degree; the term refers to the degree of similarity among the individuals of the population with respect to the particular characteristic being studied, or to some other variable which is correlated with that characteristic. Thus, any given population might be relatively homogeneous or heterogeneous, depending upon the characteristic in question. A small settlement of white, native-born married couples under 45 years, all of whom profess the Protestant faith, could be classed as homogeneous in a study of family size (if the investigator knows that the number of individuals in a family is closely related to religion, age, and nativity). The same settlement could be classed as heterogeneous in a study of foreign languages taken up in school (if the amount of schooling in the settlement varied greatly).

The size of sample required for a satisfactory survey of a heterogeneous population can be cut down by classifying that population into strata or sections. Some of the strata may be relatively homogeneous, while others are relatively heterogeneous; the aim is to get as much homogeneity as practicable. More homogeneous strata can be represented by smaller samples than more heterogeneous strata. This is because the more homogeneous any stratum is, the better can a random sample of given size represent it, *viz.*, the more alike will be the cases in the sample and the less variable their mean. By sampling the heterogeneous strata more heavily, the requisite reliability can be secured for predicting the population as a whole.

To return to the example of the presidential election poll. Those southern states whose voters are predominantly Democratic might be regarded as homogeneous, while the northern states which are more mixed in political affiliation might be looked upon as relatively heterogeneous. A relatively small sample would be required to convince a surveyor that the Democrats in the south were following their traditional voting behavior, and would favor the Democratic candidate. The other states which might swing either way would require a larger sample for an equally reliable prediction. Thus, a saving in sample size could be affected in the south, and the total sample size could be reduced accordingly. For the prediction of the national popular vote, of course, the results from the less heavily sampled states would have to be weighted by a factor to give correct representation for these states in the total estimate for the nation.

The surveyor may not be sure that the characteristic being surveyed is related to the variable by which it seems feasible to stratify the population. In the Presidential election poll, for instance, it would be feasible to stratify by income, but the surveyor might not be sure that income is related to political affiliation. Under such circumstances, a small pilot survey might be made to find out. The saving in size of the survey sample might be quite significant. If the pilot study were not made, the surveyor might guess wrong and his stratification might not bring about homogeneity with respect to the subject of inquiry. The error could be rectified by increasing the size of sample in the strata where the surveyor had mistakenly counted on homogeneity to keep the sample small. The administrative problem of adding the necessary cases with the survey actually under way might prove rather complicated and expensive. Unless one is quite certain of the homogeneity and importance of a stratum, therefore, he will probably do well to sample generously in the first place.

2. THE BREAKDOWN PLANNED IN TABULATION:

The choice of size of sample must also take into account the number of categories and classes into which the findings are to be grouped and analyzed. The greater the number of subgroups or minor universes, the larger the total sample needed to yield reliable statistical measures of them. Let us take an example from the straw poll field. A prepresidential election poll in which the popular vote for the country as a whole is to be forecast does not require a breakdown by states. As few as 2400 cases might be sufficient to predict a popular vote which ranged around 55 per cent for the winner. Since a candidate might receive the majority of the popular vote and still lose the election because he failed to secure a majority of the electoral votes (which are apportioned by states), a presidential forecaster must be able to predict the electoral majority. This means that a breakdown by states is necessary. Thus, instead of 2400 cases, the poller might under certain conditions require 48 times this number. As a matter of practical procedure, however, it is not usually necessary to have the same size sample for every state, since the closeness of the contest varies in the different states. Pollers can devise numerous ways of cutting down the sample required for the prediction, but the necessary number of cases will inevitably run far greater when state-by-state tabulations are required than for a poll in which state tabulations are unnecessary.

Inexperienced surveyors frequently are surprised at the rapidity with which the number of cases in their survey samples dwindle when subgroupings are made. Even though the sample seems quite adequate for the principal tabulation, the number is likely to peter out very quickly when more detailed tabulations are prepared. For example, a sample of 1000 voters might seem like an adequate number for a survey of the percentage of persons favoring the state retail sales tax in a given county. Supposing that 25 per cent favored and 75 per cent opposed the tax; there would be 250 in the former group and 750 in the latter. If the surveyor is interested to learn the type of people who voted in the affirmative, he might wish to classify his respondents further. Are they city or rural residents? What income groups do they represent? How many are farmers? A rural-urban breakdown might yield 150 urban and 100 rural residents. If the rural group were further classified into 5 income classes, the upper-income group might very likely contain only about 5 cases. To determine whether the upper-income rural residents were farmers or in some other occupation, would be out of the question with only 5 cases.

If the frequency in the subclass is treated as a sample of a sub-universe—as in the above case, where the surveyor wishes to describe the characteristics of upper-income rural residents who voted for the sales tax—the 5 cases in the category constitute the sample from this universe, and the reliability of measures of this population is a function of this number, i.e., 5. This subclass is called an "independent" subclass, since the sample taken of it purports to represent the universe described by it and not the universe of the larger sample of voters as a whole. Therefore, in computing percentages or averages or other measures of the rural, high-income voters who favored the tax, the total or n is 5. On the other hand, subclasses which are merely a *portion of a larger group,* and therefore not independent universes for purposes of analysis, are not to be confused with such. If the analyst were concerned only with the 1000-case sample and what it represents, the number 1000 would be regarded as the base, and the 5 cases would be expressed merely as a percentage (or other measure) of the 1000, the latter purporting to be a sample of the entire voting population in the county surveyed. In this latter case, n in the sampling error formula obviously would be 1000 and not 5.

The sample size chosen should be large enough to give reliable measures of the smallest important breakdowns. When data are broken down into smaller and smaller subclasses, the number of cases falling in the various cells soon becomes so small that statistical measures computed from the cell entries are likely to be unreliable. It is common practice in surveys to set some arbitrary lower limit, below which statistical measures will not be computed. For example, the U. S. Census does not publish percentages for which the base is less than 100 cases. Some surveyors suggest that the base or total used in computing averages should contain no less than 25 or 30 cases. In computing percentages, it is the *base* which affects the reliability. A percentage consisting of only two cases might be quite reliable if these two were drawn in a sample of 1000 cases, while if they were drawn in a sample of 5 cases, the resulting percentage would be quite unreliable.

One procedure for determining the minimum number of classes into which to break down a base figure is to divide the base number by the proposed number of categories. The resulting figure should not be lower than 10. In other words, if the data were distributed equally into each class, there would be no fewer than 10 cases in each class. According to this rule, a sample of 100 should not be broken down into more than 10 classes; a sample of 50 into more than 5 classes. Working this rule in reverse, the surveyor should be able to estimate roughly the minimum number of cases needed in the sample to give him all the breakdowns desired. This estimate could be improved, of course, if he had some knowledge of the frequencies in the proposed sub-universes, but at best this is only a rule-of-thumb procedure.

The type of statistical measure to be computed from the figures obtained in the given breakdown plays a part in determining how few cases will be useful in a given cell. A simple average, for example, would ordinarily require fewer cases than a standard deviation, or a three-fold percentage grouping.

3. SAMPLE SIZE AND COLLECTION PROBLEMS:

Usually the size of the sample must be kept within the number of cases which can be secured with given funds and time. The number is affected by the length of the schedule, the number of field workers, the specificity as to the person or persons who must be interviewed, the extent to which the cases are concentrated in one district or spread over a large area, the refusal rate, the losses of cases, the type of sampling employed, and finally, the method of data collection—i.e., whether mail, personal interview, etc.

An important factor to consider when deciding on the size of sample is the transportation cost involved in getting from one address to another in the sample and in call-backs when the first visit is unsuccessful. The wider spread geographically the sample is, the fewer schedules per day may be expected—since bus, car, walking, or streetcar transportation are time-consuming. To be sure, geographic dispersion is not so important a consideration if the mail questionnaire is employed. However, if nonrespondents to the questionnaire are followed up by personal interviews to insure an unbiased sample, the dispersion of addresses must be taken into account.

When planning the sample size, the surveyor must always expect to fall short in the collection of the number assigned for interview. People move within or out of the city, die, are unable to give the information because of illness, go out of town on vacations or business, cannot be located, or refuse to give the information, the addresses may be wrong, or the building may have been torn down; some schedules are lost, and others may not pass the editing examination, etc. In general, it is a good policy to plan to obtain information from *every* case in the sample if humanly possible. This means that considerably more time will be required for collection than would be the case if only the most cooperative and accessible cases were obtained. However, it is far better to have a small sample without bias than a large sample which is unrepresentative of the universe. Still, a biased large sample can be corrected if a subsample of unobtained cases is followed up and the resulting information used as a corrective factor.

If the planned sampling ratio is very large, there comes a point when it is just as economical to study the universe as to survey the sample. For instance, a sample representing 80 per cent of the universe would involve the task of drawing the sample, preparing sampling instructions, checking the sample, etc., which often would not be justified by the difference in number of cases and results obtained from a complete canvass.

When controlled or "quota" sampling is employed, and only cases having a *number* of specified characteristics are eligible for inclusion in the sample, the practical problem of locating cases which have the desired characteristics is so great that the surveyor usually must be satisfied with a small sample.

Market surveyors have suggested that the size should depend on the proportion of people familiar with the product under investigation. If the survey purpose is to discover the features most favored by the consumer of a particular product, and if only 5 per cent of the population in the community use the product, the collection plans might need to provide for skimming over the entire population to locate the consumers. If tabulations were to be prepared on only that portion of the population familiar with the product, the sample would need to be large enough so that 5 per cent of it would be sufficient for the tabulations. When a product or a characteristic is found in only 5 per cent of the general population, it is probable that a more efficient sampling plan can be devised than one in which 95 per cent of the interviews (as in the above example) are unproductive. The survey designer might, for example, locate some source list in which only the product users are included—or in which a high proportion are likely to be acquainted with the product. It would be very wasteful, for instance, to draw a sample of the general population in a large city to locate new Cadillac car owners. Such a sample should be drawn from such sources as motor vehicle registrations or from the middle and upper income groups of the city.

As mentioned earlier, the *mobility* of the group being studied must be taken into account when planning the size of the sample. If, for example, one had to survey specific individuals in apartment house areas of a city where in normal times as many as half the residents move every year, the final sample would inevitably be much smaller than that drawn unless substitutions of incoming residents were permitted.

4. SAMPLE SIZE AND TYPE OF SAMPLING:

The principle was mentioned earlier that the more homogeneous the population the smaller the sample needed for the required reliability. Thus, we may ordinarily expect that a smaller sample will suffice when stratification is employed instead of unrestricted random selection. This is because the effect of stratification is to resolve the relatively heterogeneous total into a number of individually homogeneous subsamples. The more heterogeneous the population, the greater the possible saving of cases through stratification.

The use of double or mixed sampling described in Chapter VII enables the surveyor to combine a large sample for the collection of a few basic items with a very small controlled or stratified sample from which detailed or complicated information is secured. By using the frequencies from the large random sample as multiplying factors (or weights), the detailed data from the small controlled sample can be expanded to represent the universe. Since the collection of detailed schedules from a large sample is usually prohibitive, this double sampling procedure has been developed to give substantially the same results more efficiently. Usually the number of cases in each stratum or cell of the controlled sample is limited to just enough to produce reliable averages or frequencies for the cell. Since each stratum is homogeneous, the cell figures tend to be stable and reliable. The cases in each stratum are selected from the larger random sample in accordance with several controls based on information collected for the entire random sample. The numbers of cases meeting each cell characteristic are thus known from the random sample. They serve as weights for the stratified sample, so it can be built up for the universe. The size of the random sample must be large enough to yield reliable weights for the various strata; otherwise the cell frequencies will be improperly adjusted and the predictions from the sample may be seriously thrown off.

The controlled sample itself requires fewer cases than the random sample which determines the weights, because the sample in each stratum need be representative only of that stratum and not of the whole population. In the Study of Consumer Purchases (1010), for instance, approximately 250,000 (short) random sample schedules were collected in 32 cities in the United States, while only about 26,-000 (detailed) schedules had to be secured from the controlled sample. The latter was weighted by the random sample frequencies to provide the over-all picture. The process of weighting is discussed on pages 230, 483–484.

Another important factor in determining the necessary number of cases is the size of the sampling unit. The use of large sampling units is inefficient when the data are to be tabulated with respect to households or individuals. In fact, the larger the sampling unit the greater the number of cases which will be needed for such individual tabulation. Block sampling, enumeration district sampling, and postal route sampling all require much larger samples for estimating the amount of unemployment, for instance, than would a sample of *individuals*.

Requisite Precision of Predictions

The factors already discussed, including degree of homogeneity, amount of breakdown, and type of sampling, all affect the number of cases which must be taken to achieve the degree of precision which is desired. The basic practical question of this section is that of determining the sample size which will yield this requisite precision in the sampling problem at hand.[1] The sampling problem at hand is of the same type in all surveys, i.e., to estimate or predict something about the universe from something about the sample.

The surveyor must know not merely what this something is but also what kind of statistics on it will suffice, e.g., percentages, percentiles, averages, standard deviations, or other measures for summarizing data or predicting population characteristics. This is important because different kinds of statistics require different sample sizes to yield a given desired precision. Percentages or averages are the most commonly desired statistics.

The surveyor should also consider the method of sampling he plans to use, because, as noted above, different methods of sampling involve different sample sizes. The calculation of the necessary sample size can be most simply described in general by reference to the method of unrestricted random sampling, and that is what will be done in the following pages. The practical problem, however, with which the surveyor is actually faced is what to do about the particular sample which he intends to draw by a particular method. An exact solution to the problem requires an appropriate formula for computing

---

[1] The treatment of statistical concepts in this section is intended for readers who have to face the practical question with little statistical background. This discussion is offered with the risk of oversimplifying a rather complicated matter and of giving the novice unwarranted confidence, but the risk does not seem serious. The author's view is that errors of surveying lie not so much in failures to choose correct sample size or to make proper allowance for chance fluctuations, as in failure to secure unbiased samples of the universe or valid information from individuals contacted.

the precision or sampling error corresponding to any method of sampling which the surveyor might legitimately use. Only recently has anyone assembled different formulas appropriate for calculating the standard errors corresponding to the several methods of survey sampling; and to these formulas the mathematically minded reader is herewith referred (142, 179, 236, 631, 1132).

The nonmathematically minded reader may be content with the fact that there is an essentially random element to be found in any acceptable method of sampling which can be chosen; and for that reason the principles of random sampling can generally be of considerable use in the estimation of a necessary sample size. Let us see then, briefly, to what extent the formulas and tables presented in this chapter may be expected to apply directly to different methods of sampling.

First of all, there is the obvious fact that our formulas apply to the method of pure or unrestricted random sampling, because that is the method for which they were derived. Pure random sampling is not ordinarily used, however, because it is generally recognized to be an unnecessarily expensive method. The common practice is to substitute for it some form of quasi-random sampling such as drawing the cases from a random list at regular intervals. Usually this method seems close enough to random sampling to permit a useful estimate regarding necessary sample size; and the more carefully planned and executed the drawing procedure, the closer the estimate. In the method of stratified sampling, the principle of random sampling applies to each stratum taken separately, provided the cases are properly drawn. The actual drawing of the cases in the given stratum may be either purely random or quasi-random. Thus the surveyor can estimate the necessary sample size for each stratum and then add the several estimates together to approximate the total sample size. In the method of subsampling, the random principle must be applied to each sampling stage separately. In general, and in this latter method especially, it is important to observe that the calculation of sample size always refers to the sampling unit. Thus, if the sampling unit is the city block, the calculated sample size will come out in terms of number of blocks; or if the sampling unit is the dwelling, the calculated sample size will come out in terms of number of dwellings. With these thoughts in mind, we may proceed with the problem of how to calculate the number of cases on the basis of random sampling.

COMPUTATION OF NECESSARY SAMPLE SIZE:

Since percentages are most frequently desired in survey analyses, and since averages are perhaps next most common, this section will deal specifically with sample sizes for requisite precision of percentages and averages. While some of the same general principles apply in the estimation of the precision of other statistics, it may be noted here that appropriate estimates from the mean and the percentage are among the most trustworthy that can be made.

Since the sample drawn is only one of many samples that the surveyor might have happened to choose, he needs to know how much reliance he can place in the sample as a miniature of the universe in which he is interested. If he is about to draw a sample, he needs to know how large it should be to give him a satisfactory reliability. This calculation is possible because in random sampling the precision of the estimate is known to be related to the square root of the number of cases in the sample.

When making a survey the usual practice is to attempt to make predictions with respect to several items of interest. Consequently, if the optimum sample size is computed for any single statistic, e.g., an average, the result cannot be expected to be optimum for other items of interest. The safest procedure, therefore, is to make the calculation on the basis of the largest sample size required.

Before proceeding with the calculation, which is itself very simple, there are two things which must always be done in actual practice. The first of these is to secure some *preliminary information* about the population. If the surveyor plans to use the sample to make a percentage estimate of the universe, he needs some advance idea of the approximate size of this percentage in the universe, i.e., about how his prediction eventually will come out. On the other hand, if his purpose is to predict the average of the universe from the average of the sample, he needs a preliminary estimate of the standard deviation. Since the standard deviation of the (finite) universe may be taken for practical purposes to be around one-sixth of the full range of scatter or variation, the surveyor who happens to know the range of the universe can divide it by 6 to get a preliminary estimate of the standard deviation. As a rule, however, the advance information for either the percentage or the average prediction is based upon sampling of some kind. The various procedures which have been discussed earlier include the small pilot study, results of past surveys, experience of experts in the field, and so on. Fortunately, the information can be approximate or even rough and still prove very useful. Indeed, no matter how rough the preliminary estimate may be, there need be no doubt about the precision of the sample because that can be calculated after the data have been taken.

The second thing to do is to decide on the *requisite precision* of the prediction. This decision will itself depend upon two subsidiary questions: (1) how much of an error in the estimate to be derived from the sample will be permissible, and (2) how much assurance is required that the estimate will fall within the permissible error. These two latter questions will now be considered in some detail for the case of the percentage, and then the calculation of the necessary sample size will be illustrated.

1. **The Permissible Error or Tolerance.** How much can the percentage to be secured from the sample vary from the true (unknown) value for the universe or population and still be acceptable? Suppose a surveyor has to discover whether a large or a small percentage of women in a certain area are on part-time jobs. Will it be sufficient for him to demonstrate that the correct percentage for such women is something under 20 per cent, or does he have to show that it is less than 20 per cent but more than 18 per cent? The general answer to such questions is that whether the tolerance is high, low, or medium depends upon the particular object of the survey or the specification of its sponsor. The sponsor might tolerate a 20 per cent error, or he might require accuracy to within 2 per cent. It all depends upon how exactly he happens to need or wants to know certain facts.

Usually the surveyor is in a position to make very helpful suggestions concerning a feasible tolerance because of his knowledge of the technical requirements of the survey. Indeed there are frequent occasions when the tolerance really depends more on those requirements than on the preferences of the sponsor. His purposes and wishes, however, must obviously be paramount considerations. Consider the case of the sponsor who wishes to know in advance which of two candidates is going to win an election. Here the sponsor does not specify the desired precision of the critical percentage; it is the surveyor who must make the decision. If the vote is going to be close, the surveyor can tolerate only a small error if he is to be practically certain, for example, that the 52 per cent which is shown by a straw vote is significantly above the 50 per cent deadline. Obviously, the permissible error here is less than 2 per cent; otherwise the outcome of the election could not be predicted. On the other hand, the outcome of a one-sided election could be predicted (and so the sponsor satisfied) with a much larger error in the estimate. If the preliminary poll had revealed 60 per cent of the votes in favor of the leading candidate, an error as high as 9 per cent might be tolerated. Then, even though the poll happened to draw the most unfortunate sample, deviating the full 9 per cent above the true value, the latter still would figure at 51 per cent. Thus both the true value of 51 per cent and the estimate of 60 per cent would be above the critical 50 per cent, and the prediction would be valid. In brief then, the permissible error is the largest deviation from the true value which would be acceptable to the sponsor or which would permit the surveyor to solve the essential question or questions of the survey.

2. **Assurance of Not Exceeding the Permissible Error.** There is no such thing as being *absolutely sure* that the sample estimate will not exceed the permissible error. The surveyor has to decide what degree of assurance or probability of staying within the tolerance will be sufficient for the situation at hand. In one situation, for instance, he may want to be *exceedingly sure* that his estimate will be within 2 per cent of the true value, while in another situation, he may be satisfied with only fair assurance of the 2 per cent accuracy. If the project is important and facilities and appropriations are adequate, there is no point in taking unnecessary chances. On the other hand, if time and funds are very limited, the surveyor (and sponsor) may have to be satisfied with less assurance. Two levels of assurance, two degrees of significance or probability, are very well known because most investigators have found the one or the other to be satisfactory for their purposes. One of these, referred to as "significant," is such that there are about 19 chances out of 20 (or a probability of 0.95) of not exceeding the tolerance; the other or "very significant" level is such that there are 99 chances out of 100 (or a probability of 0.99) of not exceeding the tolerance. A still more rigorous standard, which is not so frequently applied and which might be described as "practical certainty," yields 999 chances out of 1000 (or a probability of 0.999). On the other

hand, the other extreme of probability sometimes is approached. Thus, for instance, some of the census publications have employed a 2 out of 3 level of assurance (or a probability of 0.67).

The chances that the particular sample drawn in the survey will yield an estimate of the universe which is within the permissible error depend upon the variation among samples drawn from that universe. If the samples tend to deviate considerably from the true value, then the chances of any given sample staying within the permissible limits are not so good; on the other hand, if the samples tend to deviate only slightly from the true value, the chances of not exceeding the tolerance are better. Since the chances of not exceeding the tolerance depend upon the sampling fluctuation, any suitable measure of it can tell us what those chances are. The so-called *standard error* is such a measure. It is a measure of the variation in estimates which could be expected in random sampling. Unbiased samples drawn at random tend to follow the laws of chance, and the sample estimates tend to cluster around the true value for the universe. Estimates of means or percentages can be represented by a bell-shaped curve which is high in the middle and which tapers toward nothing at each end. When there is no bias, the midpoint of the curve represents the true value, and the maximum variation of a random sample estimate from it is about three times the standard error. The standard error does not equal the whole range of random sampling variation, but only a fraction of it—or about ⅙ of the entire range of variation. The more extreme variations occur so rarely, however, that for some practical purposes the standard error may be said to be equal to about ¼ of the entire range. In other words, if we have a symmetrical distribution and lay off a distance equal to twice the standard error (or "2 standard errors") in both directions from the midpoint of the range, we will include most of the sampling fluctuations. Probability tables indicate that there are 19 chances out of 20 that the given sample will not be off by more than about twice the standard error. This means that about ¹⁹⁄₂₀, or 95 per cent of sample estimates can be expected to fall within the limit of plus or minus 2 standard errors. Whenever in practice, then, we will be satisfied with an assurance of 19 chances out of 20 of staying within our tolerance, our problem is merely to draw a random sample with a standard error which is about one-half as large as our tolerance (because this will make the latter equal to 2 standard errors). If we wish greater assurance of staying within our tolerance, we must arrange for a sample with a standard error which is a still smaller fraction of our tolerance. The smaller this fraction, the greater the assurance or the chances of staying within the tolerance.

Since the degree of assurance depends upon the ratio of the tolerance to the standard error, let us now look at the usual formula for calculating the standard error of a percentage:

$$\sigma_{\text{p.c.}} = \sqrt{\frac{\text{p.c.} \, (100 - \text{p.c.})}{n}}$$

Here, p.c. stands for percentage, n for size of sample, and $\sigma_{\text{p.c.}}$ for standard error of the percentage. Consider the example of the straw vote. If it showed 360 people out of a sample of 600 voting in favor of Candidate A, the percentage in favor would be $360/600(100) = 60\%$ and the standard error of this percentage would be found by substituting in the above formula, thus:

$$\sigma_{\text{p.c.}} = \sqrt{\frac{60 \, (100 - 60)}{600}} = \sqrt{\frac{2400}{600}} = 2\%$$

This calculation can be verified by reference to Table 1 which was, in fact, made up by means of this formula. (At the junction of the column headed 60 per cent and the row labelled 600, will be found this standard error, 2 per cent.) Twice this standard error is, of course, 4 per cent. This means that there are about 19 chances out of 20 that the true value lies somewhere between 56 and 64 per cent (or 39 chances out of 40 that it simply lies above 56 per cent. Reference to probability tables (or Table 2) will show that there are nearly 999 chances out of 1,000 that the true value lies between plus and minus 3 standard errors, that is between 54 and 66 per cent (or 1999 chances in 2,000 that it lies above 54 per cent). What we want to be sure of here is that the correct value and our estimate are both on the same side of 50 per cent. But we know that our estimate, being 60 per cent, is above 50 per cent, and that there is an exceedingly high chance that the true value is above 50 per cent. The chance or probability is called "exceedingly high" because our estimate was 60 per cent and the standard error was 2 per cent; and this means that the estimate is 5 standard errors (5 times 2 per cent) above the 50 per cent deadline.

Reference to Table 2 shows how high a probability is associated with a 5 standard error limit. Therefore, we may state with confidence that if only random sampling errors operated, our prediction that candidate A would get more than 50 per cent of the votes would be correct.

TABLE 1. STANDARD ERRORS OF VARIOUS PERCENTAGES[a]
WITH GIVEN SAMPLE SIZES

Sample Size	Percentages																		
	99.5 / 0.5	99 / 1	98 / 2	97 / 3	96 / 4	95 / 5	94 / 6	93 / 7	92 / 8	91 / 9	90 / 10	85 / 15	80 / 20	75 / 25	70 / 30	65 / 35	60 / 40	55 / 45	50
100	.7	1.0	1.4	1.7	2.0	2.2	2.4	2.5	2.7	2.8	3.0	3.6	4.0	4.3	4.6	4.8	4.9	5.0	5.0
125	.6	.9	1.2	1.5	1.7	1.9	2.1	2.3	2.4	2.6	2.7	3.2	3.6	3.9	4.1	4.3	4.4	4.4	4.5
150	.6	.8	1.1	1.4	1.6	1.8	1.9	2.1	2.2	2.3	2.4	2.9	3.3	3.5	3.7	3.9	4.0	4.1	4.1
175	.5	.7	1.1	1.3	1.5	1.6	1.8	1.9	2.0	2.2	2.3	2.7	3.0	3.3	3.5	3.6	3.7	3.8	3.8
200	.5	.6	1.0	1.2	1.4	1.5	1.7	1.8	1.9	2.0	2.1	2.5	2.8	3.1	3.2	3.4	3.5	3.5	3.5
250	.4	.6	.9	1.1	1.2	1.4	1.5	1.6	1.8	1.8	1.9	2.3	2.5	2.7	2.9	3.0	3.1	3.1	3.2
300	.4	.6	.8	1.0	1.1	1.3	1.4	1.5	1.7	1.6	1.7	2.1	2.3	2.5	2.6	2.7	2.8	2.9	2.9
400	.3	.5	.7	.8	1.0	1.1	1.2	1.3	1.6	1.4	1.5	1.8	2.0	2.2	2.3	2.4	2.4	2.5	2.5
500	.3	.4	.6	.8	.9	1.0	1.1	1.1	1.4	1.3	1.3	1.6	1.8	1.9	2.0	2.1	2.2	2.2	2.2
600	.3	.4	.6	.7	.8	.9	1.0	1.0	1.2	1.2	1.2	1.5	1.6	1.8	1.9	2.0	2.0	2.0	2.0
800	.2	.3	.5	.6	.7	.8	.9	.9	1.0	1.0	1.1	1.3	1.4	1.5	1.6	1.7	1.7	1.8	1.8
1000	.2	.3	.4	.5	.6	.7	.7	.8	.9	.9	.9	1.1	1.3	1.4	1.4	1.5	1.5	1.6	1.6
1250	.2	.3	.4	.5	.5	.6	.7	.7	.8	.8	.8	1.0	1.1	1.2	1.3	1.3	1.4	1.4	1.4
1500	.2	.3	.4	.4	.5	.6	.6	.7	.7	.7	.7	.9	1.0	1.1	1.2	1.3	1.3	1.3	1.3
1750	.2	.2	.3	.4	.4	.5	.6	.6	.6	.7	.7	.8	1.0	1.0	1.1	1.1	1.2	1.2	1.2
2000	.2	.2	.3	.4	.4	.5	.5	.5	.6	.6	.7	.8	.9	1.0	1.0	1.1	1.1	1.1	1.1
2500	.1	.2	.3	.3	.4	.4	.5	.5	.5	.6	.6	.7	.7	.9	.9	.9	1.0	1.0	1.0
3000	.1	.2	.3	.3	.4	.4	.4	.5	.5	.5	.5	.6	.7	.8	.8	.9	.9	.9	.9
4000	.1	.2	.2	.3	.3	.3	.4	.4	.4	.4	.5	.6	.6	.7	.7	.7	.8	.8	.8
5000	.1	.1	.2	.2	.3	.3	.3	.4	.4	.4	.4	.5	.6	.6	.6	.7	.7	.7	.7
6000	.1	.1	.2	.2	.2	.3	.3	.3	.3	.3	.3	.4	.5	.6	.6	.6	.6	.6	.6
8000	.1	.1	.2	.2	.2	.2	.3	.3	.3	.3	.3	.4	.4	.5	.5	.5	.5	.6	.6

[a] Since each percentage and its difference from 100 both have the same standard errors, the two percentages are given at the head of each column.

GENERAL PRECAUTION IN PROBABILITY INTERPRETATIONS: When determining suitable sample sizes, the reader is asked deliberately to assume and maintain an appropriately cautious frame of mind with respect to the meaning of all numerical probabilities and size estimates associated therewith. The general difficulty and rarity of ideal sampling should make one properly skeptical about securing results which are exactly coincident with expectation. Of course, this does not mean that the surveyor should not use the exact sample size computed from the probability formula; in fact, that is exactly what he should do because it is his best bet. He should not insist, however, on this exact size if practical considerations make it inexpedient. On the other hand, practical aspects would have to be increasingly important to cause him to depart increasingly from the calculated sample size. Bearing these precautions in mind, let us proceed to a consideration of the meaning and uses of the tables.

Table 1 which may be used in connection with the choice of sample size (as well as for estimating the precision of the sample estimates, Chapter XVI) shows the standard errors corresponding to various sample sizes and percentages. For instance, if the per cent were 25 (in the row across the top of the table) and the sample size were 1,000 (in the column at the left), the standard error would be 1.4 per cent (at the junction of the column headed 75–25 and the row labelled 1000).

It is important to notice that the standard error is expressed in the same units as the percentage estimate itself. For instance, if the percentage estimate is 60 per cent and the standard error is 2 per cent, it means that the latter represents the range of the estimate from 60 to 62 per cent on the plus side and from 60 to 58 per cent on the minus side. This is what the formula gives and what is regularly found in tables of this type. Infrequently, however, the standard error is expressed as a percentage of the percentage estimate, and this, of course, would be a different figure. For instance, 2 per cent of 60 per cent would be not 2 per cent, but 3.3 per cent.

Notice how the standard error gets smaller (higher precision) as the samples get larger. Looking down the columns, one can partly verify the rule that the sample size must be multiplied by 4 to double the precision, multiplied by 9 to triple the precision, by 16 to quadruple it, etc. This is a way of saying what was mentioned earlier, *viz.*, that the precision increases as the square root of the number of cases in the sample. Notice also that the standard errors become greater as the percentage estimates approach 50 per cent. We shall see later that this relation is worth considering in making the preliminary estimate of the percentage.

Table 2 shows the assurances, chances, or probability of the estimate coming within various standard error limits. These limits are conventionally stated as plus or minus. A little care is necessary to make the correct interpretation of these limits. Take the figure 1.96 in the first column, for instance; this sometimes refers to the full range of plus *and* minus 1.96 standard errors. This is the correct interpretation when reading across the row and finding that 19 out of 20, or 95 per cent, of the estimates in random sampling fall within this range. This is the same as saying that there are 19 chances out of 20, or a probability of 0.95, that the particular random sample we draw in our survey will fall within the range of plus *and* minus 1.96 standard errors. Similarly, the table shows only 2 chances out of 3, or a probability of about 0.68, that the sample estimate will fall within the limits of plus *and* minus 1 standard error. The probability of falling within the limits of plus *and* minus 2.57 standard errors is seen to be 0.99, or 99 chances out of 100.

It is well to note that when the predicted percentage is extremely low or high (say around 5 or 95), and the sample is quite small (say

TABLE 2. THE PROBABILITY (CHANCES) OF FALLING WITHIN OR EXCEEDING
VARIOUS LIMITS IN RANDOM SAMPLING

Limits in Standard Errors (+ or −)	Probability (Chances) of				
	Falling Within			Exceeding	
	p	Chances		p	Chances
0.13	0.10	1 in 10		0.9	9 in 10
.32	.25	1 in 4		.75	3 in 4
(1) .6745	.50	1 in 2		.50	1 in 2
1.00	.68	2 in 3		.32	1 in 3
1.15	.75	3 in 4		.25	1 in 4
1.64	.90	9 in 10		.10	1 in 10
(2) 1.96	.95	19 in 20		.05	1 in 20
2.33	.98	49 in 50		.02	1 in 50
(3) 2.57	.99	99 in 100		.01	1 in 100
(4) 3.29	.999	999 in 1000		.001	1 in 1000
4.89	.999999			.000001	
5.99	.999999999			.000000001	

(1) "Probable error" limit. The probability of not exceeding this limit in random sampling is the same as that of exceeding it, viz., 0.50 or 1 out of 2.
(2) "Significant" limit, that is, there are about 19 out of 20 chances of falling within it.
(3) "Very significant" limit, that is, there are about 99 chances out of 100 of falling within it.
(4) "Huge error" limit, that is, there are about 999 chances out of 1000 of falling within it.
The first column of the above table gives various limits of sampling variation in terms of the standard error as a unit. The next two columns give the probability or chances of the given sample falling within the specified limits, while the last two columns give the probability or chances of exceeding the limits. For instance, with limits of plus or minus 1.64 standard errors, there are 9 chances out of 10 that the random sample will fall within those limits, or only 1 chance in 10 that it will exceed the limits. Notice that as the limits are made greater the chances of falling within them increases; the last few rows of the table show that the chances increase much more rapidly than the limits.

around 100), it is not always possible to secure the desired level of probability. This difficulty may occur occasionally in dealing with sub-samples. Graphs have been prepared showing the limiting sample sizes for various predicted percentages and ranges of error (877).

CALCULATION OF THE SIZE OF SAMPLE:

Having considered (1) the question of the permissible error or tolerance, and (2) the question of the chances or probability of staying within the tolerance, we may now proceed to the calculation of the sample size which may be expected to fulfill these two requirements. This calculation can be demonstrated best by a concrete example. Suppose we are permitted a 5 per cent error in estimating the percentage of home telephone calls that will be answered by men on Saturday afternoons, and suppose that the requirements of our survey or the sponsor will be satisfied with 19-out-of-20 assurance that the estimate will fall within the 5 per cent tolerance. We already know (from Table 2) how to tell that *any* tolerance must be equivalent to nearly twice the standard error to permit a 19-out-of-20 assurance of staying within it. Therefore, the present problem could be reduced to computing the size of sample required to yield a standard error equal to one-half our tolerance, that is, a standard error of 2.5 per cent. In any case, we should have to have some advance idea of the thing we are supposed to estimate when we draw our sample, viz., the percentage of home telephone calls answered by men on Saturday afternoons. Ordinarily we do have some idea, and in this example there is reason to believe that the correct figure is somewhere around 10 per cent. The following transposed variation of the standard error formula will give the necessary size of sample:

$$n_s = \frac{p.c.(100 - p.c.)z^2}{T^2}$$

Here, p.c. is the preliminary estimate of the percentage (10 per cent), z is the number of standard error units (2) which are found from a normal probability table to correspond to the required probability (0.95), and T is the required precision or tolerance (5 per cent). The symbol n_s, of course, represents the sample size desired. Substituting in the formula, we have:

$$n_s = \frac{(10 \cdot 90)2^2}{5^2} = \frac{3600}{25} = 144$$

This means that a random sample of only 144 cases should give us an estimate with an assurance of 19 out of 20 that it is within the 5 per cent tolerance.

Various market research groups have prepared tables by applying this formula for n_s. These tables conveniently provide the size of sample required when the approximate percentage and the degree of accuracy are given. Theodore Brown, for instance, in his publication *The Use of Statistical Techniques in Certain Problems of Market Research* (116), presents a table which gives sample sizes required for 3 sigma accuracy (997 chances out of 1000). Such high assurance with respect to range of sampling variation is not usually needed in general survey work. The two tables prepared by Smith (882) which give the limits corresponding, respectively, to 99 chances out of 100, and to 19 chances out of 20, are sufficient for usual survey purposes. These two tables are reproduced as Tables 3 and 4.

Table 3 applies when a study is being planned in which we must be *quite sure* (99 out of 100 assurance) that the estimate from our sample will fall within whatever limits of tolerance have been specified. Suppose, for example, that the surveyor has to be accurate to within 4 per cent and that he has reason to anticipate getting a percentage around 70. He looks down the column headed 70 in Table 3 until he comes to the horizontal row labelled 4, and at the intersection of column and row he reads the answer, 871 cases. So, if the sampling is random and the preliminary estimate is approximately verified, there are about 99 chances out of 100 that the estimate from 871 cases will be correct to within 4 per cent. If the preliminary percentage estimate should be too far off, 4 per cent accuracy would not necessarily be secured. Suppose that the sample returned a percentage of 50, as compared with the forecast of 70; then the sample of 871 cases would be insufficient to yield 4 per cent accuracy with equal assurance. Though the table shows that 1,037 cases would be needed for 4 per cent accuracy at 50 per cent, it still shows (by interpolation) that 871 cases would yield about 4.5 per cent accuracy. This means that a preliminary guess as much off as 20 per cent may not render useless the drawn sample. In fact, if the guess should prove to be off by *any* amount in the *opposite* direction (the direction of decreasing standard error), the drawn sample will be more than adequate in size. For example, if the sample had returned a percentage of 90, as compared with the original guess of 70, then 373 cases would be enough to yield 4 per cent accuracy, and the 871 cases actually drawn would be providing significantly more than 4 per cent accuracy. When in doubt about the preliminary estimate, one can always resort to the conservative expedient of leaning in the direction of 50 per cent.

Table 4 may be used when it is sufficient to be *fairly or moderately*

TABLE 3. SIZE OF SAMPLE NECESSARY TO BE VERY SURE (99 CHANCES IN 100) OF ACCURACY TO WITHIN SPECIFIED LIMITS

Limits of Error in % + and −	Percentages																
	1 / 99	2 / 98	3 / 97	4 / 96	5 / 95	6 / 94	7 / 93	8 / 92	9 / 91	10 / 90	15 / 85	20 / 80	25 / 75	30 / 70	35 / 65	40 / 60	50 / 50
.25	15,510	20,807	30,892	40,765	50,425	59,873	69,109	78,133	86,944	95,543	135,352	169,853	199,047	222,933	241,510	254,780	265,396
.50	2,627	5,202	7,723	10,191	12,606	14,968	17,277	19,533	21,736	23,886	33,838	42,463	49,762	55,733	60,378	63,695	66,349
.75	1,168	2,312	3,432	4,529	5,603	6,653	7,679	8,681	9,660	10,616	15,039	18,873	22,116	24,770	26,834	28,309	29,488
1	657	1,300	1,931	2,548	3,152	3,742	4,319	4,883	5,434	5,971	8,459	10,616	12,440	13,933	15,094	15,924	16,587
2		325	483	637	788	936	1,080	1,221	1,358	1,493	2,115	2,654	3,110	3,483	3,774	3,981	4,147
3			215	283	350	416	480	543	604	663	940	1,180	1,382	1,548	1,677	1,769	1,843
4				159	197	234	270	305	340	373	529	664	778	871	943	995	1,037
5					126	150	173	195	217	239	338	425	498	557	604	637	663
6						104	120	136	151	166	235	295	346	387	419	442	461
7							88	100	111	122	173	217	254	284	308	325	339
8								76	85	93	139	166	194	218	236	249	259
9									67	74	104	131	154	172	186	197	205
10										60	85	106	124	139	151	159	166
15											38	47	55	62	67	71	74
20												27	31	35	38	40	41
25													20	22	24	25	27
30														13	17	18	18
35															12	13	14
40																10	10

TABLE 4. SIZE OF SAMPLE NECESSARY TO BE FAIRLY SURE (19 CHANCES IN 20) OF ACCURACY TO WITHIN SPECIFIED LIMITS

Limits of Error in % + and −	Percentages																
	1 99	2 98	3 97	4 96	5 95	6 94	7 93	8 92	9 91	10 90	15 85	20 80	25 75	30 70	35 65	40 60	50 50
.25	6,085	12,047	17,886	23,602	29,195	34,665	40,013	45,237	50,338	55,317	78,366	98,341	115,244	129,073	139,829	147,512	153,658
.50	1,521	3,012	4,471	5,900	7,299	8,666	10,003	11,309	12,585	13,829	19,591	24,585	28,811	32,268	34,957	36,878	38,415
.75	676	1,339	1,987	2,622	3,244	3,852	4,446	5,026	5,593	6,146	8,707	10,927	12,805	14,341	15,537	16,390	17,073
1	380	753	1,118	1,475	1,825	2,167	2,501	2,827	3,146	3,457	4,898	6,146	7,203	8,067	8,739	9,220	9,604
2		188	279	369	456	542	625	707	787	864	1,224	1,537	1,801	2,017	2,185	2,305	2,401
3			124	164	203	241	278	314	350	384	544	683	800	896	971	1,024	1,067
4				92	114	135	156	177	197	216	306	384	450	504	546	576	600
5					73	87	100	113	126	138	196	246	288	323	350	369	384
6						60	69	79	87	96	136	171	200	224	243	256	267
7							51	58	64	71	100	125	147	165	178	188	196
8								44	49	54	77	96	113	126	137	144	150
9									39	43	60	76	89	100	108	114	119
10										35	49	61	72	81	87	92	96
15											22	27	32	36	39	41	43
20												15	18	20	22	23	24
25													12	13	14	15	15
30														9	10	10	10
35															7	8	8
40																6	6

sure (19 out of 20 assurance) that the estimate will fall within the prescribed limits. This is a fairly good assurance and often considered enough. It will be observed, too, that with this less rigorous criterion much smaller samples suffice. Consider the example mentioned above in connection with Table 3. In that table the sample size for 4 per cent accuracy was 871 cases, whereas in Table 4 the corresponding figure is only 504 cases.

Calculation of Size of Sample for Averages.   Another important case of calculation of necessary sample size is the case of the average or arithmetic mean estimate, which is analogous to the case of the percentage estimate described above. The problem now is to calculate the size of sample necessary to predict the average of the universe, within a given range of error with a given probability. To take a concrete example, one surveyor was faced with the problem of securing a reliable estimate of average yearly income of families in the $10–$15 monthly rent stratum. Three figures were needed by the surveyor to compute the necessary sample size: (1) the required precision or permissible error, T—let us assume this to be $100 in this illustrative example; (2) the required probability, P, of staying within the range of error, which we will place at 0.99; and (3) a preliminary estimate of the standard deviation of the universe, σ, which we will call $500. The first two requirements are simply matters of technical decision as in the case of the percentage estimates discussed above. The third requirement demands some knowledge or feeling for the data and can be met by reference to past experience, a pilot study, or some other source of information. Of course, this estimate is always subject to empirical check against the standard error of the sample, once it has been drawn. The sample size, n_s, may be easily computed by the following formula:

$$n_s = \left(\frac{\sigma z}{T} \right)^2$$

As noted above, σ is the preliminary estimate of the standard deviation of the universe and T is the permissible error or tolerance. Since z is the number of standard error units corresponding to the required probability, z can be read from a normal probability table. Thus, for present purposes we can enter Table 2 with P = 0.99 and come out with 2.57, which is the desired value of z. Substituting in the above formula:

$$n_s = (500 \times 2.57/100)^2 = 165$$

This means that a random sample of 165 cases should give us an estimate of the mean of the population with an assurance of 99 out of 100 that it is within the permissible error range of plus and minus $100. Incidentally, the average income predicted by the surveyor in the above example from the actual sample of 360 families was $1263 and the standard deviation was $420.

TABLE 5. SAMPLE SIZES PROVIDING THREE DIFFERENT DEGREES OF ASSURANCE THAT ESTIMATES IN THE NEIGHBORHOOD OF 50 PER CENT WILL FALL WITHIN THE SPECIFIED LIMITS OF ERROR

Limits of Error in % (+ or −)	Percentage Estimate								
	50			55 or 45			60 or 40		
	Chances in 1000			Chances in 1000			Chances in 1000		
	950	990	999	950	990	999	950	990	999
0.5	38,400	66,000	108,240	38,016	65,340	107,156	36,864	63,360	103,912
.6	26,667	45,833	75,166	26,400	45,375	74,413	25,600	44,000	72,161
.7	19,592	33,673	55,224	19,306	33,337	54,671	18,808	32,326	53,016
.8	15,000	25,781	42,281	14,850	25,523	41,857	14,400	24,750	40,590
.9	11,852	20,370	33,407	11,733	20,166	33,072	11,378	19,555	32,071
1.0	9,600	16,500	27,060	9,504	16,335	26,789	9,216	15,840	25,978
1.5	4,267	7,333	12,027	4,224	7,260	11,906	4,096	7,040	11,545
2.0	2,400	4,125	6,765	2,376	4,084	6,697	2,304	3,960	6,494
2.5	1,536	2,640	4,329	1,521	2,613	4,286	1,474	2,534	4,163
3.0	1,067	1,833	3,006	1,056	1,185	2,976	1,024	1,760	2,886
3.5	784	1,347	2,209	776	1,333	2,186	752	1,293	2,121
4.0	600	1,031	1,691	594	1,021	1,674	576	990	1,624
4.5	474	815	1,336	469	807	1,323	455	782	1,283
5	384	660	1,082	380	653	1,071	369	634	1,039
6	267	458	752	264	454	744	256	440	722
7	196	337	552	194	333	547	100	323	530
8	150	258	423	148	255	418	144	247	406
9	119	204	334	117	202	331	114	195	321
10	96	165	270	95	163	268	92	158	260

It is of some interest to work the above formula with this actual sigma value of $420 from the actual sample substituted for our preliminary estimate of $500. When this is done, the calculation comes out $n_s = 116$ instead of 165. If the preliminary estimate of the standard deviation of the population proves to have been too large, as in this illustration, the computed sample size also will have been larger than necessary and in that sense conservative; of course, it may come out too small with the opposite result. It is apparent, then, that a preliminary estimate may be quite rough and still be close enough to provide a useful prediction. It is an instructive exercise to try in the formula various values for the estimate of the standard deviation and note what effect each has on the computed value of the sample size. This will help one to gain some feeling for the question of how rough a preliminary estimate may be and still prove useful for setting the sample size.

Let us now leave the problem of computing the sample size which may be expected to yield a satisfactory estimate of the mean, and return to a final table and illustration involving percentage estimates.

Table 5 is designed for use in predicting any result which is likely to come out somewhere around 50 per cent. This table may help not merely in deciding on the size of sample to be drawn but it may also be used in assessing the precision of the percentages actually obtained in the survey (discussed in Chapter XVI). The general arrangement is like Tables 3 or 4, but sample sizes around 50 per cent are shown in greater detail and there are three different levels of assurance included, viz., those corresponding to 1.96 σ, 2.57 σ, and 3.29 σ. These levels may be indicated by the descriptive phrases "fairly sure," "very sure," and "almost certain." If one is concerned with the sampling fluctuations at both ends of the range, the respective chances are: 19 in 20, 99 in 100, and 999 in 1000. When predicting a majority, however, one is concerned only with the fluctuations toward one end of the range. What one wants to be sure of, then, is that a sample estimate above 50 per cent means that the true value is also above 50 per cent, but one may not care how far above 50 per cent; the upper limit may be of no concern. The chances of an estimate falling anywhere above a fixed value are greater than the chances of falling between that fixed value and another fixed value. Thus, there are 19 out of 20 chances of an estimate falling between plus and minus 1.96 standard errors, but 39 out of 40 chances of its falling between minus 1.96 standard errors and the extreme upper end of the distribution. Similarly, for 2.57 σ, the chances increase from 99 out of 100 to 199 out of 200; and for 3.29 σ, from 999 in 1000 to 1999 in 2000. Of course, the surveyor might wish to know only what the chances are that a true value is really below some fixed deadline percentage, and in that case also these somewhat greater assurances apply. They apply, too, in some of the problems investigatable with Tables 3 or 4.

The following example may be useful in illustrating the application of Table 5. A very close state election is expected in which only two candidates are entered. If the poller can be quite sure that one of these candidates will get more than 50 per cent of the votes, he can be quite sure that this candidate will be elected. If the poller believes that the election will be very close, he looks at Table 5 and at tentative budgets or appropriations with the resolve to draw a sample which will provide as much safety margin as could be useful. He decides that there is not much point in trying to predict from the straw vote alone if that vote shows less than 51 per cent for the leading candidate. (This is because last-minute upsets could account for as much as 1 per cent quite readily.) Looking in the table under 51 per cent (50 per cent is close enough), he finds that a sample size of 9600 would provide 39 in 40 assurance of an estimate of 51 per cent being above 50 per cent. The next column shows that size 16,500 would provide 199 in 200 assurance. Since a sufficient time and a large appropriation happen to be available, the surveyor decides to take the larger sample and secure the added safety margin which it provides. Now when the straw vote is completed, let us say that it shows a larger percentage than was expected, e.g., 52.5 per cent. Looking in the table opposite the 2.5 limit, it is clear that a sample of only 2640 would give as much assurance for 52.5 per cent as 16,500 gave for 51 per cent. With the larger sample size already drawn, there is practical certainty that the estimate will be in the correct direction at the time it is made. This unexpectedly high assurance is all to the good, because it means that minor disturbing changes can be discounted. The safety margin decided upon might even mean the difference between success and failure of prediction, if the estimate had come out in the other direction. Suppose, for instance, that the straw vote had shown only 50.75 per cent. The sample employed would still yield an assurance of nearly 39 out of 40; and so the surveyor could still feel fairly confident that he had a correct estimate of the sentiment at the time of his poll.

Empirical Determination of Sample Size

An empirical procedure for deciding upon the size of sample is that of collecting the data for relatively small subsamples, and keeping a running record of the distribution of the returns. When the addition of more subsamples does not change the results significantly, one may assume that the total sample has become adequate.

This procedure can be regarded as wasteful of time because it is in effect a series of separate surveys strung out over a considerable period. It has been claimed also that this procedure is wasteful in that more schedules are collected than are needed, because the tapering off to the point of approximate stability cannot be located with any certainty until the curve has maintained its level for awhile. This does not seem to be a serious limitation when compared with the conservative practice of many reputable studies which collect more than the necessary minimum number, either for the sake of playing safe or for less acceptable reasons.

The chief and rather apparent advantage of this type of stability test is that instead of depending upon calculation based on preliminary information, one simply increases the over-all sample size until it is observed to be sufficient. The empirical check of watching the returns and stopping when they stabilize seems straightforward and convincing.

The chief danger lies in the fact that the successive subsamples collected are not likely to be spread over the universe. Results can stabilize even though they do not represent the parent population. In fact, the less representative the subsample, the more likely is the addition of more cases to yield the same result and give the appearance of stabilization. Unless each subsample is a cross-section of the universe, there will not be a representative sample upon which to observe approaching stabilization. The basic requirement of the procedure is that a growing representative sample be available for observation. The expense and the difficulty of collecting successive subsamples which are spread over the universe are the reasons why that is not likely to be done, and why the total sample is not likely to be representative.

The empirical stability test can be very effective, however, when the subsamples are properly drawn and collected. The method is most appropriate for interview surveys covering relatively small areas, such as a town or a city, because then it is not so difficult or expensive to make each subsample a random sample of the population.

The extent to which the character of the universe can be gauged from relatively small random samples may be demonstrated from a study made by the author. In 1931 a random sample of families living in New Haven, Connecticut, was interviewed in a Sample Family Survey. A comparison of the random sample of 2,097 families with the 40,000 families enumerated in the Federal Census of New Haven conducted more than a year earlier indicated that the sample was a good cross-section of the total (446).

Tables 6 and 7 present the comparison between the sample and the Census.

TABLE 6. SURVEY SAMPLE[a] COMPARED WITH CENSUS: TOTAL POPULATION 15 YEARS AND OVER, OF EACH SEX—BY AGE

| | Males | | Females | |
| | Census | Sample Survey | Census | Sample Survey |
Age	1930	1931	1930	1931
15–19	13.5%	13. %	13. %	12. %
20–24	11.5	11.5	12.5	11.
25–29	10.5	11.	11.	11.5
30–34	10.5	10.	10.5	11.
35–44	21	21.5	19.5	21.
45–54	16	16.5	15.	16.
55–64	10	9.	10.5	10.
65 or over	7	6.	8.	6.5
Unknown	. . .	1.5	. . .	1.
Total	100%	100%	100%	100%

a 1931 New Haven Sample Survey, 2097 family interviews in sample (*446*).

TABLE 7. SURVEY SAMPLE[a] COMPARED WITH CENSUS: TOTAL GAINFUL WORKERS OF EACH SEX—BY INDUSTRY

| | Males | | Females | |
| | Census | Sample Survey | Census | Sample Survey |
Industry	1930	1931	1930	1931
Agriculture, forestry, fishing, mining	1.5%	1.5%	. .	.5%
Manufacturing minus building	36.5	33.	34.5	33.5
Building and construction	10.5	10.	.5	.5
Transportation minus construction	13.5	13.5	6.5	5.5
Trade	20.	21.5	15.	16.
Public service	3.	3.5	1.	1.
Professional	7.	6.	18.5	19.
Domestic and personal	6.	7.5	22.5	21.5
Unknown and unattached	2.	3.5	1.5	2.5
Total	100%	100%	100%	100%

a 1931 New Haven Sample Survey (*446*).

In 1933, another study was conducted of the same families supplemented by a sample of newly established families as well as those which had moved into the city since 1930. The 1933 sample contained 2406 families. The data for each family were placed on cards and the cards were arranged in alphabetical order of surnames. A sample of 1,000 cards was drawn at regular intervals from the 2406. The 1,000 cards were subsampled by drawing cards at regular intervals and setting aside one sample and breaking down the other into smaller and smaller subsamples. In this manner the following series of random samples were secured:

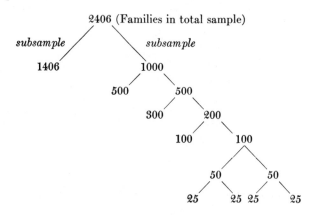

2406 (Families in total sample)

subsample   *subsample*
1406   1000
      500   500
            300   200
                100   100
                      50   50
                  25   25 25   25

The percentage distribution of ten different types of items was tabulated for each of these samples (719). Since the tabulations on all ten characteristics demonstrated the same points, only two of these tables are shown on pages 323 and 325.

The following observations may be made on the data of Table 8:

1. If only 25 cases had been secured, it would have been possible to conclude that the majority of the chief earners in families are over 30 years of age, and conversely, that relatively few are under 30. Also, the surveyor could have learned that a very small percentage of ages were likely to be unreported.

2. With only 25 cases, it would have been impossible to determine whether the 30–44 year age group contained more members than that of 45 years and over. To be sure, in three of the four samples of 25, the 30–44 year percentage was larger, but the one sample of 25 which

TABLE 8. AGE OF HEAD EARNER AS SHOWN BY SAMPLES OF VARIOUS SIZES[a]

Age of Head Earner	Number of Cases in Sample						
	25	25	25	25	50	50	100
Under 30	8.	20.	16.	8.	14.	12.	13.
30–44	56.	32.	44.	52.	44.	48.	46.
45 and over	28.	36.	28.	28.	32.	28.	30.
Inapplicable	8.	8.	12.	8.	8.	10.	9.
Unknown	0.	4.	0.	4.	2.	2.	2.
	100%	100%	100%	100%	100%	100%	100%

Age of Head Earner	Number of Cases in Sample						
	100	200	300	500	500	1000	1406	2406
Under 30	14.	13.5	17.0	15.6	16.0	15.8	15.7	15.7
30–44	44.	45.0	38.7	41.2	42.4	41.8	39.3	40.4
45 and over	34.	32.0	37.0	35.0	34.0	34.5	39.1	37.2
Inapplicable	6.	7.5	6.0	6.6	6.0	6.3	4.3	5.1
Unknown	2.	2.0	1.3	1.6	1.6	1.6	1.6	1.6
	100%	100%	100%	100%	100%	100%	100%	100%

[a] 1933 New Haven Sample Survey.

indicated the opposite situation might have been the one chosen in the survey.

3. Percentages obtained in all sizes of samples, even those of 25 cases, tend to follow a pattern not unlike that obtained in the largest sample. The 15.7 per cent, which is the best measure we have of the true percentage, is never greater than 20 per cent nor less than 8 per cent. The 40.4 per cent appeared in a range from 56 per cent to 32. The 37.2 per cent varies from 39.1 per cent to 28 per cent. The lowest percentage, 1.6 per cent, does not exceed 4 per cent and does not appear at all in two of the smallest samples. Finally 5.1 per cent ranges from 12 per cent to 4 per cent.

4. From samples of 50 and upward, the surveyor would have been correct in deducing that the 30–44 year age group was probably larger than the 45 and over class. The amount of the difference, however, could not have been very closely determined. With the 2406 sample, it is evident that the two percentages are pretty close. According to methods for computing the significance of the difference between two percentages (discussed in Chapter XVI) there is great likelihood that the 40.4 per cent figure is greater than the 37.2 per cent in the universe.

5. Deviations from the percentages found with 2406 cases, are sometimes positive and sometimes negative, in the different samples.

6. As the size of the sample is increased, the fluctuations around the percentages for 2406 cases tend to be smaller and smaller.

The samples in Table 9, on the nativity of the head earner, follow much the same pattern as those on age. With 2406 cases the surveyor can be practically certain that 58.5 per cent is greater than the 38 per cent in the universe from which this sample is drawn, so there is little question but what the native population is more numerous in the total of chief earners than is the foreign white. From 50 cases upward, this modal group of native white would have been ascertained from the sample. With 25 cases, the surveyor could have been quite sure that Negroes, other races, and unknown nativity comprised a relatively small portion of the total head earners in this city.

This empirical study of sample size is here presented (in part) to give the inexperienced surveyor a concrete example of what he is likely to find in samples as small as 25 for the census-type information which is often secured in surveys. The effect of increasing the size of

TABLE 9. NATIVITY OF HEAD EARNER AS SHOWN BY SAMPLES OF VARIOUS SIZES[a]

Nativity of Head Earner	Number of Cases in Sample						
	25	25	25	25	50	50	100
Native White	64.	48.	72.	52.	56.	62.	59.
Foreign-Born White	32.	48.	28.	44.	40.	36.	38.
Native Negro	4.	0.	0.	0.	2.	0.	1.
Others	0.	0.	0.	0.	0.	0.	0.
Unknown	0.	4.	0.	4.	2.	2.	2.
	100%	100%	100%	100%	100%	100%	100%

Nativity of Head Earner	Number of Cases in Sample						
	100	200	300	500	500	1000	1406	2406
Native White	72.	65.0	58.0	60.8	58.4	59.6	57.7	58.5
Foreign-Born White	24.	31.5	38.3	35.6	38.4	37.0	38.7	38.0
Native Negro	2.	1.5	1.3	1.4	1.2	1.3	2.1	1.8
Others	0.	0.	1.0	.6	.4	.5	.1	.2
Unknown	2.	2.0	1.4	1.6	1.6	1.6	1.4	1.5
	100%	100%	100%	100%	100%	100%	100%	100%

[a] 1933 New Haven Sample Survey.

the sample can also be observed. It should be borne in mind, however, that some of these samples are cumulative. The first two samples of 25 comprise the first sample of 50; similarly, the two samples of 50 make up the first sample of 100, etc. This is not quite the same as drawing each sample independently from the 2406 cases.

SEQUENTIAL ANALYSIS:

A more refined form of empirical control than the above stability test is the recent development called sequential analysis (1047). The general procedure is to keep adding cases to the sample and at the same time to keep testing for significance until the minimum sample has been accumulated which will provide the required significance. This technique was developed primarily for the purpose of efficient inspection sampling of industrial production items.

Unfortunately, insofar as usual sociological surveys are concerned, sequential analysis is subject to the same technical limitations as the stability test described above; in other words, the usual survey setup does not lend itself to either continuous random sampling or uniform gradual expansion of sample size. On the other hand, there is some reason for surveyors to keep this technique in mind, because special situations may arise where it would be applicable and because it permits a substantial saving in the number of cases in situations where it is applicable. Samples accumulated sequentially appear to require, on the average, only 30 to 70 per cent as many cases as the usual calculations (illustrated in the preceding section).

General Summary

Samples drawn in carefully conducted surveys vary in size from a few hundred cases to many thousand cases. This is because there is great variation in the size of sample required to furnish a sufficiently representative and precise estimate of the population surveyed. Among the factors which affect the necessary sample size are degree of heterogeneity, amount of breakdown, and type of sampling. Relatively heterogeneous populations require large samples as compared with relatively homogeneous populations; surveys making detailed breakdowns require large samples as compared with surveys using only coarse breakdowns; and unrestricted random sampling demands large samples as compared with stratified sampling. Of course, several such factors may be operating at once to affect sample size in a given survey.

While representativeness or freedom from bias is impossible without a certain minimum sample size, representativeness depends mainly on proper procedure in the drawing and collection of the sample. Precision, on the other hand, depends primarily on the size of the sample. Given a certain heterogeneity, breakdown, and kind of sampling, the precision of the sample should increase about as the square root of the number of cases. Because of this property, it is common practice to control the precision of the estimate by the size of the sample. The three principal steps in determining the necessary number of cases in random sampling are summarized below.

1. Make a preliminary estimate or guess as to the most essential percentage (or other statistic) which the sample will yield. This preliminary estimate is important because it is used in computing the size of the sample to be drawn, but fortunately it does not need to be accurate. Reading across Table 1 will show that considerable differences in percentages are required to make much difference in the standard error. Reading across Table 1 will also show that the standard errors increase progressively toward, and are largest at, 50 per cent. When in doubt, then, one can always be conservative by erring in the direction of 50 per cent; or when in complete doubt, one can simply make the preliminary estimate 50 per cent. If the size of sample calculated on that basis is sufficient, that size of sample should be more than sufficient to control any lesser per cent which may turn up when the sample is drawn.

More important than the preliminary estimate of any particular percentage, however, is adequate planning for all the main tabulations of the survey. Many surveys aim at one or a few main figures, but the tabulations often will include numerous secondary estimates which are also worthy of consideration. The surveyor should plan to draw a large enough sample to take care of important subclasses even though that may result in an unnecessarily large safety margin for his most important percentage.

2. Make decisions regarding permissible error and degree of assurance or certainty. The sponsor may tell the surveyor what the largest permissible error is, or the two can make the decision together. This last-mentioned procedure is often desirable because the surveyor's technical knowledge usually enables him to explain to the sponsor how

he can get the most for his money. In any case, however, the tolerance for error must be small enough to permit the purpose of the survey to be accomplished. If the sponsor is content simply to state the desired objective, the surveyor can set up a tolerance which in his expert judgment will permit the achievement of the objective.

The degree of certainty of the estimate falling within the tolerance should ideally represent a compromise between the importance of not exceeding the tolerance and the difficulty or expense involved. In general, most investigators accept a moderate certainty for small tolerances because otherwise the sample size must be very large. If the tolerance is relatively high, on the other hand, it is good practice not to skimp on sample size; indeed, it is better to gain the added assurance which is achieved without much added expense. Such a feasible conservatism will help the surveyor maintain a good "batting average" even though his predictions occasionally fail under very low tolerance.

3. Determine the necessary sample size. With tables available, no calculation is necessary if it is a percentage which is being predicted. With the preliminary estimate of the percentage in mind, together with the tolerance and the degree of certainty, one merely glances at the appropriate table and reads off the sample size. For instance, if the estimated percentage is 95, the tolerance is 4 per cent, and the degree of certainty is 99 out of 100, the surveyor looks at Table 3 and reads 197 cases. In this particular example, the number of cases required is so small, that it would be easy to secure significantly higher assurance of staying within the tolerance; and therefore, the careful surveyor would probably do so. Reference to Table 1 will show that a sample as small as 400 has a standard error of 1.1 in relation to 95 per cent. But this standard error is considerably less than ⅓ of our 4 per cent tolerance, and reference to Table 2 will show that a tolerance somewhat more than 3 standard errors corresponds to 999 chances in 1,000. In brief, doubling the sample size in this instance, would cause the assurance to rise from 0.99 to 0.999.

A simple though different procedure can be followed when the problem is to determine the sample size for predicting an average rather than a percentage. In this case, the surveyor first makes a preliminary estimate of the standard deviation (rather than the percentage). Suppose we are sampling salaries and we let the estimate of the standard deviation be $700, the required precision or tolerance be $200, and the required probability of staying within the tolerance be, say, 999 out of 1000. First one enters a normal probability table, e.g., Table 2, with the required probability which is 0.999 in this example, and comes out with the corresponding x/σ range which is 3.3. The next step is to divide the estimated standard deviation, which is $700, by the tolerance, which is $200; and the result is 3.5. When this 3.5 is multiplied by the 3.3 obtained above, and the product is squared, we have the required number of cases in the sample. Thus $(3.3 \times 3.5)^2 = 133$. This means that if the σ of the population is $700, a suitably drawn sample of 133 cases should permit prediction of the average salary of the population to within $200, with a probability of 0.999. If the tolerance had been lowered to say $20, *viz.*, one-tenth of what it was, and the probability had been held at 0.999, the sample size would have had to be increased one hundredfold, *viz.*, to 13,340 cases. On the other hand, if the tolerance had been held at $200 but the required probability had been lowered to 0.9, the necessary sample size would drop to about 10.

The repeated use of such terms as permissible error and degree of certainty, together with numerical expressions of exact probabilities and sample sizes, must not lead the reader to feel that a sample size read from a table or computed by a formula will guarantee a desired precision. Indeed, the reader has been reminded already that the relations in the above tables represent normal expectation in ideal or true random sampling. It is essential to be cautioned by that limitation and to keep it ever in mind. To the extent that actual sampling is not ideal, the relations in the tables cannot be expected to hold. One might expect from the tables, for instance, that with a certain sample of 1,000 there would be 99 chances out of 100 of making an estimate within 3 per cent of the correct figure. Unless the sample is carefully planned and drawn, however, it will contain irregularities or biases, and the normally expected relations cannot be expected to hold.

A very different approach to the problem of determining an adequate sample size is the stability test. This consists in continuing to take relatively small subsamples until the accumulated total sample provides sufficient stability for predictive purposes in all breakdowns of interest. The applicability and limitations of this empirical approach were discussed and illustrated in some detail.

Selected References

Statistical Methods

Arkin and Colton (15), Bailey and Cummings (22), Bowley (99, 101, 102), Brown (116), Cantril (142), Chaddock (155), Chapin (166), Cochran (179), Croxton and Cowden (216, 217), Davies and Crowder (229), Deming (236), Desing (246), Dodge and Romig (251), Dunlap and Kurtz (262), Eastwood (266), Employment Stabilization Inst. (287), Fisher (307, 308), Frederick (333), Hagood (388), Hogg (446), Holzinger (449), Kendall (506), Kurtz and Edgerton (539), Lindquist (569), McCormick (623), McNemar (629, 632), Mills (646), Mudgett (660), Neiswanger (681), Parten (716), Pearson (727), Peatman (728), Simon (877), Smith (882), U.S. (1004, 1010), Wald (1047), Walker (1049), White (1084), Yates (1132), Yule (1140).

CHAPTER X

Interview Procedures

While it is possible for surveyors to perform statistical operations and prepare reports on data which have no accuracy, consistency, or validity, it is much less expensive not to bother about making a pretense of surveying unless the returns are reliable, relevant to the problem, and representative of the population sampled. If the survey is to be made at all, the material should be collected in accordance with the best and most effective standards of scientific procedure.

To insure that the data are worth analyzing, it is imperative to control the processes by which the information is obtained. If it is secured by personal interviews, all significant elements in the interview situation—the interviewer, the surroundings of the interview, the informant, and the process of questioning and recording—should be so controlled that the resulting record will be a true account of the situation which the survey is designed to describe. Similarly, surveys conducted by telephone interview, mail questionnaire, or any of the other techniques mentioned in Chapter III should utilize effective controls in order that the data represent what the survey designers think they represent.

Space does not permit a full treatment of all data collection techniques, so discussion in this book is limited to the three most frequently used: mail surveys, telephone surveys, and personal interview surveys. Mail surveys are discussed in Chapter XI, and telephone surveys were treated in Chapter III. In personal interview surveys the interviewer may survey predesignated persons or residents of specified addresses or, as in many public opinion polls, he may select the informants in accordance with specifications set up at headquarters. The work of interviewers may be controlled by personal supervision, or by mail, telephone, or telegraph.

Basic Training of Interviewers

Prerequisite to the training of good investigators is the hiring of promising candidates. Too often surveyors are forced to hire the friends or relatives of survey sponsors, regardless of their qualifications as interviewers. The characteristics of good investigators have already been discussed on page 138. Qualifications of candidates for interviewing positions may be determined before they are hired if they attend a training school of the type described on page 136. When no such selection procedure is used, the director usually tries to choose the most promising candidates from among the applicants. Only those who can grasp instructions and apply them to specific instances should be hired. This ability can best be detected by an objective examination given after applicants have had time to study the instruction manual. This procedure was employed in the selection of enumerators for the 1940 Census of the United States.

Ability to pass a paper and pencil test, however, is no guarantee that the applicant will be an honest, successful interviewer who obtains and records information in accordance with instructions. If he receives thorough instruction in the survey procedures and if, also, regular checks are made upon the quality of his work, failure to meet and maintain high standards will be discovered. Unsatisfactory interviewers should be dropped from the field force before they have much chance to complicate the collection and editing problems.

Instruction of investigators may take several forms. In the most thorough training programs a variety of devices insure that investigators collect correct and complete data. Some of the better-known training devices are:

1. FIRST STAFF CONFERENCE:

Before field work is undertaken, interviewers should be called together and given a general background of information on the survey— the purpose of the survey, who sponsors it, and its scope and methods. If interviewers have a bird's-eye view of the study as a whole, they are better able to meet objections from informants and to convince them of the importance of the inquiry, and thus to decrease the likelihood of refusals.

The statement of the purpose of the survey should include a discussion of the general types of tabulations which may be expected to come out of the study. Such knowledge enables the interviewer to interpret or recognize marginal cases, and makes him aware that he must refer certain questions to his supervisor.

The discussion of sampling should be a popular or nontechnical account of the theory of random sampling, together with the application of the principle to surveys conducted by the agency. If the interviewers, rather than the central office, are to select the respondents, the special precautions required to insure a good spread of sample cases should be given. Such points as the following might be covered: the desirability of interviewing strangers rather than relatives or friends; the importance of seeking interviews in a variety of places— street, home, office; the importance of getting a spread of cases over different neighborhoods; the restriction of interviewing to a single member of a family; and the advisability of not reinterviewing a given person before the passage of a year.

The need for collecting accurate data, for maintaining good relations with the community, and for completing the survey within a specified time should be stressed at this first conference. Upon the interviewer rests the most important responsibility of the study, that of securing and recording information that is reliable and meaningful enough to justify all the effort and expense that goes into the survey.

Staff conferences discussed later should be held frequently during the course of the survey.

2. TESTS AND NARRATIVES:

After interviewers have had time to study their instructions, their ability actually to apply the instructions should be tested. A description of a hypothetical case—one involving a number of different problems—might be presented to the agent, who might then be asked the correct procedure for recording such information. The example below is taken from the 1940 Federal Census Correspondence Training Course:[1]

Mr. Simons, who had worked for three years as a full-time stoker on a steamship, lost his regular job on April 1, 1939. From July 1, 1939 to March 1, 1940 he worked by the hour as a dock laborer

[1] Form FZ-202, Sixteenth Decennial Census of the United States, Department of Commerce, Bureau of the Census, Washington, D. C., January, 1940.

wherever he could find work, and seldom worked at a single job for more than two or three days. He averaged about 10 hours of work per week during the period from July 1 to January 1 and he does not know what constitutes a full-time week for a dock hand. Since March 1, he has had no work, although he has sought work at the docks every day.

a. What is the correct entry for column 27, "duration of unemployment"?

b. What is the correct entry for column 31, "number of weeks worked in 1939"?

Tests of this type may be used to eliminate candidates who cannot apply instructions. It also gives the field supervisor clues as to weaknesses in the written instructions—points which should be remedied before field investigation begins.

When interviewers are stationed in places located long distances from the survey headquarters, it is possible to train them with written instructions. If studied carefully, a book of comprehensive instructions such as the one published by NORC (675) should enable interviewers to pass tests and to conduct practice interviews upon which their knowledge of instruction and ability to carry out an assignment could be judged.

3. DEMONSTRATION AND TRIAL INTERVIEWS:

Demonstration interviews in which a supervisor acts as the informant while another person acts as investigator have been useful for training. Trainees may be asked to fill in the schedule as if they were conducting the interview. Group criticism and discussion of the interview procedures and methods of recording the information serve to bring out problems and to achieve uniformity of interpretation.

In addition to the demonstration interview, the training program should give each agent a chance to conduct trial interviews. Interviewers may serve as informants for one another. The informant may respond to the interview questions as if he were someone else with whose situation he is thoroughly familiar. Some agents have found their own families good practice "subjects." If the survey sample is likely to include many interviewers' families, the above suggestion is not recommended.

4. MOTION PICTURES AND PHONOGRAPH RECORDS OF INTERVIEWS:

During the training of enumerators in the 1940 Population Census, four reels of sound motion pictures were used. Whether this method of instruction is more effective than other procedures involving as much expenditure of time and money can be answered only after further study of the question. Phonograph records of sample interviews could also be used in the training program.

5. SPOT SUPERVISION:

Supervisors who observe the agent conduct the interview and discuss it with him right after it has taken place can give invaluable critical appraisal of his technique and recording of replies. With the details of the conversation fresh in the interviewer's mind, it is relatively easy for the supervisor to point out errors or inefficient procedures.

Some large survey agencies employ squad leaders to train investigators. The new agent accompanies the squad leader on an interview and stands by while it is being conducted. After several such illustrations of the interview technique, the student is permitted to carry on a few trial interviews in the presence of the squad leader. Suggestions and corrections based on mistakes and omissions are offered by the supervisor. The new agent then conducts a few more interviews until he seems to have mastered a satisfactory technique. As a rule, it is more difficult to conduct a satisfactory interview in the presence of a third person who the informant may feel is an unwelcome witness, than it is to carry on an interview without an onlooker. A frank explanation of the situation to the informant or a case in which permission is asked for the "trainee" to listen in on the interview may ease the tension.

6. EXPERIENCE IN EDITING AND CODING:

One of the best ways to train interviewers on definitions and instructions is to give them experience in editing or coding the schedules in the office. A few days of such experience gives the interviewer an idea of the processing of the schedules and impresses him with the need for accuracy and completeness of information. One of the dangers of this technique is that it gives him a knowledge of the sort of information obtained so he can "fake" schedules effectively. But every study should be so organized that checks on the field work are sufficiently frequent to insure the detection of dishonest entries.

7. EARLY EVALUATION OF FIELD WORK:

An early check-up of the interviewers' work is an essential part of the training program. The first schedules turned in should be carefully examined to be sure that the interviewer understands the instructions and is following them. These schedules should be edited in his presence so he can receive any necessary individual instruction immediately and correct his mistakes before they become habitual. Unless this early editing takes place, moreover, a large number of so-called completed schedules will be unacceptable and require revisits.

A member of the schedule review staff should rate the production of each interviewer for both quality and quantity. When the report is turned over to the proper squad leader, he either gives additional training to the interviewer or recommends his removal from the field. Poorly trained investigators make trouble in the field and create additional labor for the office staff.

8. TESTS DURING FIELD WORK:

Even though interviewers memorize the instructions before undertaking the field work, a test or two during the course of the field work often prevents forgetting them. Too often enumerators fall into slipshod or incorrect habits of recording information or do not keep up to date with changed rulings on detailed interpretations of schedule items. This creates unnecessary work for the editors and requires them to return schedules to experienced interviewers who should know better. If interviewers are aware that a test may be given to them at any staff meeting, they may try to keep fully and accurately informed.

Topics to Be Covered in Interviewer's Instructions

In large-scale investigations by personal interview, instructions to interviewers must be prepared well in advance of the date for starting the field work. This provides sufficient time for training interviewers and for getting the instructions themselves into final form. The person who drafts the instructions should be thoroughly familiar with the entire plan of the study, including the sampling and the editing phases. Otherwise data collected may be unreliable, and the sample taken may not coincide with that chosen in the office in accordance with the laws of sampling. No amount of statistical manipulation or analysis can ever produce findings of value if the data are collected with inadequate instructions. The details of these instructions naturally will vary with the data desired, but the topics covered below are common to most survey investigations.

INSTRUCTIONS ON GENERAL POLICIES OF THE SURVEY OR POLLING AGENCY:

1. The need for the interviewer to be *thoroughly* familiar with the instructions has been emphasized already. He should be prepared to take a test on the instructions at any time without notice. Periodic reviews during the course of the survey will combat forgetting and faulty habits of interviewing or reporting. The enumerator should know to whom to appeal when instructions are not clear or do not seem to cover questions arising in the field. Generally, the squad leader assumes this task. If he cannot settle the problem from printed instructions, he should take the problem to a designated supervisor.

2. The interviewer must keep up to date on instructions. Whenever changes in or additions to the printed instructions are issued, he should secure such revisions from his squad leader or supervisor and incorporate them in his own copies.

3. Interviewers should know to whom they are directly responsible. In very large surveys, about ten investigators work under the direction of a squad leader who spends part of his time in the field where he meets the investigators daily to collect their schedules, inspect their completed work, answer questions, make assignments, and check up in general on production. The extent to which the supervisor is responsible for the quality and quantity of each interviewer's work, and for the allocation of time among interviews, travel, and office work, should be specified in the instructions.

4. Copies of the schedules, forms, and instructions must be filed systematically so as to be readily available to the interviewer. Incidentally, enumerators should carry enough forms to last through at least two days and so avoid unnecessary trips to the office.

5. No copies of questionnaires should be distributed by interviewers without the permission of the supervisor. Schedules may get into the newspapers, for instance, and thereby complicate the collection problem.

6. Full-time interviewers should not be permitted to engage in any other work or combine work such as the sale of magazines with their interviewing function. The instructions should contain a specific statement forbidding such practice. It is not a good idea for interviewers such as those employed by public opinion polls to do interviewing for more than one agency at a time. Claims of misrepresentation and other difficulties may arise from divided interviewing interests.

7. The interviewer should not be permitted to delegate authority for collecting schedule information. Cases have been reported in which the person hired as an interviewer turned over the work to another member of his family who was not a qualified investigator.

8. Except when instructed to the contrary, the interviewer should not permit the informant to fill out or check the answers himself. Neither should he be allowed to take the schedule and look it over before responding. If the respondent learns what questions are coming next, his answers may be influenced, particularly those to opinion questions. Of course, "card questions" or those designed for the informant's inspection are another matter.

9. The interviewer may telephone or write for an appointment for an interview, but unless instructed to do otherwise he is never permitted to secure schedule information by such means. A personal interview requires the actual presence at the same place of both people concerned.

10. A letter of identification should be carried to supply proof of the genuineness of the survey in case the informant inquires. One case was reported in which a field worker called the office from the police station stating that a sensitive informant had questioned his intentions and called the police. If male agents are employed, suspicious women and those living in poor economic neighborhoods may refuse to give an interview without acceptable identification.

The identification letter, signed by the survey director or sponsor, should state the name of the agent, the name of the agency conducting the survey, the purpose of the survey, and a request for cooperation. A letter similar to the following may be satisfactory:

LETTERHEAD OF AGENCY

Date

To Whom it may Concern:

This certifies that Miss Jane Doe is an interviewer for the Survey Research Agency of Blank City. We hope that you will cooperate with us by giving her an interview in our survey of . . . .
The information given by you will be treated with strictest confidence and will be seen only by the research staff of this agency which prepares the statistical reports.

With sincere appreciation,

John A. Jones
President of Survey Research Agency

11. Appropriate appearance and behavior of the interviewer help him to secure the schedule information and to create an impression favorable to future cooperation. Interviewers should be clean and reasonably neat in appearance, and careful to avoid body odors. They should keep their hands and nails clean, and not wear badly spotted clothes. It is well to avoid appearing so neat that the housewife refuses admission to her dusty or disorderly home for fear of being censored.

Similarly, it is best not to appear too prosperous. There is evidence for the view that plainly attired interviewers are likely to be more successful than others (115). Occasionally during an interview it may be necessary to appeal to the housewife to give information merely as a kindness to one who appears to have to make his living by interviewing. It is not unusual to encounter an interviewee with the type of attitude suggested in the following: "Well, I think those are silly questions, but it won't hurt me to give the information and it helps you to make a living." An interviewer who appears to be sincere, sober, and healthy is more likely to inspire a positive response than one who looks shifty, intoxicated, or diseased.

A favorable appearance is, to a considerable extent, a matter of the interviewer's manner, which should be confident and businesslike but still frank and pleasant. A well-timed smile will do much to "break the ice." Experienced interviewers are aware of the readiness with which the average person responds to an appropriate approach by a total stranger. This willingness to cooperate obligates the investigator to evince a real interest in the opinions, information, problems, and

personality of the respondent. Not only is the interviewer consuming
the respondent's time and diverting him from other closer interests, but
he is offering nothing tangible in return for this imposition (18). It is
not necessary to have an apologetic manner, however, because most
people are flattered by being asked for their views and enjoy telling
them to a stranger.

While evincing interest in the informant's remarks, the investigator
must tactfully avoid time-consuming tangents leading away from the
schedule questions. The respondent should be allowed some latitude,
however, because his comments may reveal the reasons for his reactions. Usually his meandering can be cut off when he pauses by some
such remark as, "That's very interesting; now I'd like to get your opinion on another question. . . ."

It is advisable for the interviewer to remind himself occasionally
not to talk too much. Not only is it a waste of interviewing time, but
there is a danger of revealing the interviewer's personal opinion and
thus of coloring the respondent's reactions.

The interviewer should always be calm and composed and avoid
showing anger or surprise. He should strive to be absolutely neutral,
never indicating disbelief, disapproval, or approval. For opinion polls
particularly, it is important that the informant give his honest views
and not an opinion which has been distorted by the interviewer. Even
voice inflection or facial expression may provide clues of the interviewer's attitude, and thus give moral support to respondents whose
views might otherwise be uncertain. Should the respondent ask "Is
that right?" or "Don't you think so?" or "What do you think?" the interviewer should either say frankly that he is not allowed to express his
views and that the respondent's view is the important thing at the moment, or he should be noncommittal with a remark such as "Well I've
heard so many different answers that I'll have to make up my mind all
over again."

12. While it is inadvisable to specify the number of interviews expected per hour, some idea of what is "par" for an average day may
be given (see page 143). When respondents live in widely separated
areas, more time will have to be spent in traveling than when several
are concentrated in one small area. Also, interviewing to clear up problem cases or call-backs on the not-at-homes is more time-consuming
than skimming over the original assignment. If the interviewer is supposed to select his respondents in accordance with a "quota system,"

he may be expected to get relatively few cases toward the end of his assignment because of the difficulty of locating eligible respondents. A long, complicated questionnaire also will require more time.

13. The relative amount of time the interviewer should spend studying instructions, interviewing, and checking schedules should be suggested. The NORC instructions state that from half an hour to one or two hours may be needed for study, depending on the complexity of the questionnaire.

14. The manner of payment of interviewers should be made clear from the start. If they are expected to turn in a time and expense report periodically or after completing an assignment, the items for which they are to be paid should be listed in detail. When interviewers are paid by the hour, their bill may include the time spent in (a) studying the assignment, (b) practice interviewing, (c) actual interviewing, (d) checking over each completed schedule after each interview, (e) going from one interview to the next (usually the trip to the first interview and from the last one for the day are not remunerated), (f) filling out various forms (except in rare instances interviewers should not be paid for copying over completed schedules, since the originals should be satisfactory), (g) office consultations or conferences, (h) meetings with squad leader.

When interviews are in rural areas or away from the home town of the interviewer, it is customary to pay for the transportation and time costs to and from the interview area and car mileage from one farm to another (if a car is used). The NORC instructions specify that automobile mileage costs in cities are not paid unless such costs are lower than time costs accumulated in waiting for riding in public conveyances. Other expenses for which the interviewer is remunerated include telephone, postage, and streetcar or bus fares. Receipts for larger expenditures, such as for hotel bills on an overnight assignment, should be presented with the bill. It is important for interviewers to keep accurate time and expense records as they go along so that the itemized bill can be quickly and easily prepared. Interviewers should not depend on memory over a period of several days because they may cheat themselves as well as the survey agency.

15. The necessity of keeping confidential the information obtained in interviews cannot be stressed too strongly. The information or opinions secured should not be disclosed or discussed with anyone outside of authorized members of the survey staff. The envelope containing

questionnaires should never be left carelessly about, and the address of the survey headquarters should always be on the envelope in case it is lost.

In addition to *general* instructions, each assignment should be accompanied by *specific* instructions. These should include detailed information concerning with whom, how, when, and where interviews are to be conducted; detailed specifications as to the meaning of each question, and the manner of asking it and recording the response; also, detailed instructions on the mechanics of filling out the questionnaire and the various reports required of interviewers. Information on many of these specific matters is presented below.

LOCATING THE INFORMANT:

Before starting the day, interviewers should map out their course for the entire day. By spotting addresses on a map which contains the city bus or streetcar routes, the interviewer should be able to work out the most efficient program. Searching for addresses in the wrong vicinity and retracing steps is often unnecessary if proper planning is employed.

The training of field workers should cover general instructions on the sampling procedure of the survey. For example, interviewers should be aware of the fact that in a 1 per cent sample every loss of a case or erroneous inclusion of a case in the sample may be multiplied a hundredfold when the estimates for the total population are made from the sample. Interviewers should receive some instructions on the procedure by which the sample was selected, and the reasons for the choice of the given sampling method as well as detailed warnings on the many ways in which the sample will be distorted if interviewers fail to follow instructions. They must also be told to report unusual situations encountered in the field so that the method of handling such cases may be worked out logically with the sampling director.

Investigators need to be given specific instructions as to whom to interview. The importance of not deviating from the chosen sample should be stressed. Detailed instructions should be provided on how to proceed if the interviewer runs into difficulties in locating, making contact with, or securing cooperation from the assigned cases. The investigator should know just what to do if any one of the following situations is encountered:

1. No one answers the door.
   a. The occupant is not at home.
      (1) He is away for the day—working, visiting, shopping, etc. The interviewer should try to ascertain (probably from neighbors) when the occupant is expected or likely to be home.
      (2) The family is out of the city on vacation or business.
   b. The occupant is at home but does not wish to answer the door. It may be necessary to telephone or write for an appointment, or maybe a call in the evening when the husband returns from work may bring an answer.
   c. There is no occupant—the house is vacant, according to neighbors.
2. The address assigned is or appears to be nonexistent.
   a. The building has been demolished.
   b. The house number has been changed.
   c. The original assignment is in error
      (1) Because of an error in the source list.
      (2) Because of clerical error in the office.
      (3) Because the street name was changed after the source list was compiled.
   d. The interviewer is on the wrong street and so cannot find the correct house number.
3. The dwelling unit assigned is vacant.
   a. Shall the sample case assigned be traced to his new address? If so, what if he has moved out of the city?
4. The original building has been demolished and a new, different type of structure replaces the old.
5. The person or family assigned by the office has moved and a new occupant has moved in.
6. The dwelling unit assigned is not that of the householder but of a roomer.
7. The address assigned contains no dwelling units, only a place of business.
8. The address assigned is both a dwelling unit and a place of business.
9. The building is divided differently from that indicated by the source list; e.g., according to the source this is a one-family house,

but since the source was compiled the house has been altered to accommodate three families. Which one or ones shall be scheduled? What shall be done about the others?

10. The address assigned is a rooming house. Shall some or all the lodgers or only the householder's family be scheduled?

11. The address assigned is a social agency, hotel, hospital, or other institution. What information shall be obtained regarding tran. sients, permanent residents, employees, inmates, etc.?

12. The individual assigned is now deceased, has moved out of the city, has moved within the city.

13. The address assigned is not inside the city boundaries.

14. The family assigned sublets light-housekeeping rooms to another family. Shall the subtenant be scheduled on the same or on a separate form?

15. The address assigned is a business structure, but a janitor lives on the premises.

16. The interviewer discovers that the janitor's quarters were not listed on the original source, and so did not have a chance to be included in the sample.

17. The occupants of the dwelling are living in the country during the summer months.

    a. They have subleased their quarters for a short time during the summer. The original family may or may not come back to the address in the fall.

    b. They have merely closed their homes during the summer, leaving their furniture in the home.

18. The sample case is unable to give the schedule information.

    a. Interviewee is not competent to give information because he is too young, ignorant, sick, or has a language difficulty.

    b. The information called for on the schedules is not applicable to situation of the sample case.

19. Sample case is uncooperative.

    a. Refuses to answer any questions.

    b. Refuses to answer some questions.

Distortion of the original samples may occur if schedules are omitted when sample cases live in an apartment house in which the janitor refuses the interviewer access to the building; are temporarily in hospitals or other institutions; are sick, or entertaining, or are not in a situation to be interviewed when the interviewer first calls; are not accessible because of a recent death, accident, or some unusual circumstance in the household. To be sure, the importance to the sample of any of the various reasons for omission will vary with the nature of information collected. In a health survey, for example, the omission of individuals in hospitals, rest homes, health camps, or even in their own homes, if they are too ill to be interviewed, would give quite an erroneous picture of the health of the population. As pointed out before, however, social characteristics tend to be interrelated, so omissions which would produce a biased sample for one purpose would do so for another.

If no one is at home at the address assigned or the inhabitant refuses to cooperate, the interviewer should estimate the probable rental value of the assigned dwelling. In some cases this figure can be obtained from an informant who refuses all other information; or it may be estimated by the interviewer on the basis of other rents in the neighborhood with which he is familiar. Such rental figures are valuable for estimating the possible economic bias which is introduced into the sample by the unobtained cases.

If the sample cases are not predesignated for the interviewer and he is expected to secure a random sample of informants drawn from various strata of the population, the instructions for filling the "quota" need to be very explicit. The best of such instructions known to the author are those prepared by NORC. The surveyor will do well to go directly to these instructions for details. Such topics as the following are discussed in *Interviewing for NORC* (675): stratified random sampling, how to approach people at random, how to avoid introducing a bias in their selection, selecting the neighborhood, houses to approach, types of people never to interview, avoidance of interviewing persons in groups.

WHEN TO CALL:

The time of day which is most productive for interviewing depends primarily upon the type of person to be reached. Men are seldom found at home during usual working hours but are more likely to be there evenings, Saturday afternoons, or Sundays. In small communities, if most of the workers are employed in one or two large plants which operate on day and night shifts, daytime calls may reach a significant proportion of the men at home. Calls around noon are not resented by most night workers since they usually have had their morning sleep.

The availability of various family members during different hours of the day has been investigated by radio research workers in both urban and rural areas. The accompanying data on urban radio family availability, published by Stanton, is based on 40,000 urban interviews (909, p. 182).

URBAN RADIO FAMILY AVAILABILITY
"AT HOME AND AWAKE"
MONDAY–FRIDAY, COAST-TO-COAST AVERAGES

Eastern Standard Time	% Any Man	% Any Woman	% Adolescents	% Children
10:00–10:30 A.M.	23.1	80.1	4.8	7.6
2:00– 2:30 P.M.	17.9	64.5	3.5	6.9
5:00– 5:30 P.M.	27.3	70.1	17.8	16.9
7:30– 8:00 P.M.	63.2	85.0	24.2	21.1

100%—Total U. S. Urban Radio Families

According to this table, some man was home in the early evening between 7:30 and 8:00 P.M. (Eastern Standard Time) in almost two-thirds of the homes. The proportion would undoubtedly be higher if only the eastern area were considered, since 7:30 P.M. (E.S.T.) is only 3:30 P.M. along the west cost. It is interesting to note, however, the relatively small percentage of homes in which a man is home in the early afternoon as compared with the evening.

Chappell and Hooper have prepared charts showing the available radio audience, i.e., homes in which someone is at home and awake during the daytime and evening and over the various months of the year (170). The figures refer only to homes in which there is a telephone, and to war years, but the information should be of help in planning a schedule. According to the charts the fewest daytime not-at-homes in 1940 occurred during January and the greatest number during August. The figure ranged roughly from 18 per cent in the summer to 27 per cent in the winter. Evenings are slightly more variable. During that same year, approximately 17 per cent of the homes had no available audience in January as compared with 29 per cent in August. During the war years, various influences such as gas rationing, wartime measures, and increased employment tended to make the figures more erratic.

In a study of consumer requirements in November, 1944, a war year, a national sample of 3265 urban households was surveyed in cities of 2500 or more. In over one-third (36 per cent) of the homes, no one was at home at the time of the first visit by a survey interviewer. A second call to such addresses yielded 22 per cent additional schedules, and a third or later call resulted in the remaining 14 per cent being contacted. The effect on the survey results which the omission of the not-at-homes would have made is so significant that callbacks are essential in any well run survey. (See bias resulting from not-at-homes, p. 409.)

Sayre reported that the refusal rate was significantly different for women in high and low income groups in the morning and afternoon (838, p. 25). For the high income groups, 36 per cent of the refusals occurred in the morning and 64 per cent in the afternoon, while in the lower groups 61 per cent of the refusals were in the morning and 39 per cent in the afternoon. This she explains by the fact that women at higher income levels are more apt to be busy socially in the afternoon than are women at low income levels, and that the latter are less willing to be distrubed in the morning at their work than the former. Sayre also reports that her interviewers experienced difficulty in finding men at home during the day.

As for the proportion of successful interviews, Sayre says that out of 1032 calls, 29 per cent were interviewed, 23 per cent refused interviews, and 47 per cent were not at home (838, p. 25). The last figure corresponds remarkably with the 48 per cent who did not answer the doorbell in the study reported by Louis Bader (20). He conducted a "Survey of the Effectiveness of House to House Canvassing" in which 581 housewives were interviewed in three typical suburban towns to determine their attitude toward bell ringers. Mature students in a class in marketing research were used as investigators in Rutherford, N. J., Freeport, L. I., and White Plains, N. Y.—towns representing largely the moderately well-to-do and the well-to-do. Of the 1120 doorbells rung 51.8 per cent were answered by the occupants, and 48.2 per cent did not answer. All calls were made between 9:00 A.M. and 4:00 P.M.; the best hours in all homes and in all towns were from 10 to 12 A.M. and 2 to 3 P.M.

Certain days of the week may be preferable for interviewing women because of their shopping habits. "Market Records of the Buying Habits of Consumers in Sixteen Cities" (856) indicated that women prefer to do their shopping downtown on the following days:

% Preferring to Shop on Various Days	
Monday	15.0%
Tuesday	8.6%
Wednesday	15.5%
Thursday	10.9%
Friday	13.0%
Saturday	36.5%

These figures seem to suggest Tuesday and Thursday as days when the housewife is more likely to be at home and Saturday as the least likely day.

FAVORABLE INTERVIEWING CONDITIONS:

As soon as the interviewer is sure that the person to whom he is speaking is the desired informant, the conditions of the interview should be made conducive to eliciting accurate information. One important condition is that the interview be held in private. As a rule, the presence of a "listener" or witness is not conducive to a frank, uninhibited response. Neighbors, friends, or relatives occasionally will be encountered in the home of a prospective informant, and though a housewife may not be willing to admit that their presence disturbs her, the interviewer should either try to secure privacy or set another date for the interview. This is especially important if the questions relate to personal family situations.

A second essential condition of the interview is that there be no effective distractions or disturbing interruptions. Constant ringing of a telephone, people coming and going, the crying of a baby, loud-voiced conversations, and numerous other situations occasionally encountered may necessitate the postponement of the visit. An informant who cannot give her undivided attention to the questions of the agent may unintentionally give incorrect information. On the other hand, it is often true that a housewife may give an excellent interview while carrying on routine household tasks such as ironing, washing dishes, or stringing beans. The mere fact that the interviewer has offered to conduct the interview while such tasks are being performed may cause the housewife to agree to being interviewed. If the questions are interesting to her, she may stop working of her own accord and give full attention to the interview. The interviewer must try to sense situations and decide whether to go ahead or to make a return visit.

Informants who are in a hurry may give satisfactory responses to a short factual questionnaire, but they should not be asked to furnish information for opinion schedules which require concentrated thought.

If the interviewer discovers that he has selected a smart-aleck or "freshie," the interview should be dropped, providing the case was not preselected as the sample case. If such a person is definitely in the sample, the interviewer needs great tact and skill to get at least the minimum information required. Another interviewer at another time may be more successful, so a complete record of the situation should be made to facilitate the follow-up.

TECHNIQUE OF APPROACH:

Skillful interviewers soon develop their own approaches and adapt their opening remarks to the situation in hand, but suggestions on the technique of approach are helpful to beginners.

Knocking on the Door or Ringing the Bell.   The interviewer should ring the bell or knock on the door rather briefly. He should not act impatient but should give the inhabitant sufficient time to answer. While waiting for a response, he should note the address, time of day, or other facts which he may need to record on the schedule or on his report.

After a reasonable time, the interviewer should ring or knock again. Sometimes the front doorbell does not ring, or the radio is on and the potential informant does not hear. Before deciding that no one is at home, therefore, the investigator should try the rear or the side door. The housewife may be out in the backyard or down in the basement. Then again, she may be in the kitchen where she can see the interviewer if he comes to the rear door. Sometimes the back door stands open, particularly in warm weather, and when the interviewer knocks, the housewife may feel obliged to respond.

The interviewer can often tell from drawn shades, locked doors, washing on the line, a child crying, or other signs whether or not someone is home. If no one comes to the door, the neighbors may know the whereabouts of the person to be located; they may even know when he or she is expected to return. In one study a neighbor reported that the housewife who did not answer the door was at home, but that she never answered the door. In such a case, a repeat call was planned at a time when the woman's husband was at home and would answer the door. Possibly a telephone call to make an appointment might also have been successful.

In one survey, it was suggested that after the knock on the door, the interviewer should step back three or four feet to avoid the appearance of "pressing" the door. In this position he could be seen from windows beside the door, or from above if there were no porch. Thus, housewives who do not answer the door unless they first satisfy themselves regarding the appearance of the caller could see the interviewer.

To avoid being mistaken for sales persons, interviewers should not carry brief cases. Most schedules and supplies can be carried in manila envelopes or folders.

Opening Remarks. The interviewer should first greet the informant with a smile and a pleasant "Good morning" or some other remark appropriate to the time of day. He should then proceed to tell whom he represents and how long an interview he desires (providing it is short). These introductory remarks should be brief, but should satisfy most informants that a harmless "study" is being made. Words such as "Survey," "Statistics," "Population," "Opinion Poll," "Research,"[2] and phrases such as "not interested in names," "there's nothing personal in this study, we only want statistics," "University research," and "families in cities all over the country are giving this information" (if such is the case), may convey the desired impression of a statistical survey which will not harm the interests of the informant. In explaining the purpose of the survey, the interviewer should not use the term "investigation," which may have an invidious meaning to the informant, but use a more neutral word such as "study." The interviewer must, in a few words, convince the informant that he has nothing to sell or to advertise. One interviewer employed in a study of the effectiveness of various types of advertising appearing in certain maga-

---

[2] The use of the phrase "census-type questions" is very effective, since practically all people are familiar with the census and have confidence in its impersonal purpose. It is not permissible or advisable for the interviewer to masquerade as a census taker, however, since the good will established by the Census Bureau should not be impaired through indiscriminate use of its name by numerous surveys.

zines had to carry several magazines containing the advertising about which she was to question the informant. In order to dispel any ideas that she was "selling magazines," she raised her right hand and in a half-humorous tone remarked, "I swear I'm not selling magazines or anything else. I'm just making a survey." This approach was effective since it did not give the respondent time to say that he was not interested. Few people question the right of the particular agency to conduct the survey, and few care who is making the survey or for what the information will be used. All that needs to be conveyed in the opening remarks is the general impression of an impersonal or a statistical research project.

The NORC instructions advise making a casual and brief introduction such as "Good morning. I'm working on a national survey and I'd like to get a few of *your* ideas. For instance, . . ." By getting to the first question as quickly as possible, the interviewer often finds that he can complete the entire interview without having to give further explanations. The interviewer should assume that the informant will be interested in the questions, because he usually is both interested and flattered to be interviewed. He should not be given an opportunity to turn down the interviewer in response to poor questioning, such as: "Are you busy?" or "Would you mind answering some questions?" or "Could you spare a couple of minutes?" (675, p. 14).

Immediately after the greeting, the interviewer must make sure that he is talking to the proper party. If a servant or a child, or an aged person, or anyone else who is obviously not the desired informant, comes to the door, the interviewer should ask for the person from whom he is supposed to get the interview. If the name of the informant has been predesignated and the person at the door may be he, the interviewer should ask if he (or she) is Mr. (or Mrs.) Blank. Should the person answering the door prove to be a lodger or someone other than the desired informant, the interviewer should find out when the desired person is expected to return. When the proper person is contacted, the interviewer should repeat his opening remarks and proceed with the interview.

Answering Objections. While over 90 per cent of the housewives are exceedingly cooperative when they learn that a statistical survey is being conducted, a few object to giving information and have to be "won" over to the idea by the investigator. Occasionally the housewife happens to be busy with something which cannot easily be interrupted; others may have guests or may not be in the "mood" to answer questions. If enumerators are aware of and anticipate the types of remarks which informants may make, they can have ready answers to forestall definite refusals. The interviewer must be able to "size up" the informant and to decide quickly whether to postpone the interview or try to get it before the informant feels even more strongly that she does not wish to cooperate. Some of the objections most frequently met are classified as follows:

1. Those indicating the housewife does not wish to be disturbed at that moment:
   "I haven't time."
   "I'm too busy."
   "I can't spare that much time."
   "I'm going out."
   "Someone is sick in the house."

If the investigator has indicated how long the questions will take and the housewife still is too busy, the interviewer should try to set another time—a definite time, if possible, e.g., "Will you be in at 3 o'clock this afternoon? I'll be in this neighborhood then and would certainly appreciate it if you would let me drop in," or "If you have no objections, I'll come over in a day or two," and then set a specific time.

2. Remarks indicating informant is not sympathetic to surveys:
   "I'm not interested."
   "I don't care to give any information."
   "It's my own business what I do or think."

Try to find out why informant has this attitude. (a) Does she object to the agency sponsoring the study? (b) Is she afraid her confidence will be violated? If so, try to convince her of the anonymity of the survey data and of the fact that no names are taken (if such is the case). "We are not interested in you as a person—this is a nationwide study" (if true) and "We send the results into the Central Office in Blank City—so no one will see them here." (c) Does she think she has something to lose? Assure her that it will not hurt her to give the information and it will be a favor to you, since you are making a living at surveying.

3. Remarks which suggest that informant will answer only if required by law to do so:

"Is it compulsory to tell you?"

"Do I *have* to answer those questions?"

"Is this necessary?"

The agent should assure the informant that cooperation will be appreciated, but that the giving of information is not mandatory. If the reason for refusal cannot be anticipated, use a number of appeals such as: "The results will be in statistical form." "Other families are cooperating." "The study is being made in cities all over the country." "We are not interested in names." "It will take only ten minutes," etc.

4. Questions indicating suspicion of the survey:

"Are you selling something?"

"What is the information going to be used for?"

"Who did you say this is for?"

"Why didn't you go next door?"

In this last case, a frank statement of the sampling process often satisfies the informant. For example, "We just draw every twentieth address from the city directory, and yours happened to be the one we drew."

Occasionally the respondent becomes suspicious only after he has begun giving answers and realizes that he hasn't found out what it's all about. He may ask "What's this for?" or "Who's doing this?" The NORC instructions suggest an explanation such as: "(My name is Mary Jones). I'm working for the National Opinion Research Center (at the University of Denver). They do these surveys all over the country to find out people's ideas. And you know the only way to find out what people think is to ask them. It's interesting, don't you think?"—then get on with the interview.

5. Attempts to put off the enumerator:

"I never give out information until I've talked with my husband."

"Leave the blank and I'll look it over and let my husband see it."

"Leave the form and I'll mail it in."

In most such cases, the enumerator had better call again in the evening and explain the survey to the husband. The interviewer should have a better background with which to explain the study and to answer objections than does the housewife. Furthermore, it is more difficult for the husband to turn down the investigator than it is to tell his wife that she should give the blank back to the agent and tell him that he (the husband) does not want to be bothered with such stuff.

As for mailing in the form, many will not do so, and of those who do, the entries are likely to be incorrect because informants do not have copies of the instructions to investigators. Thus, it is better for the enumerator to offer to help fill out the form, and then seal and mail it if the informant wishes.

6. In opinion surveys, informants may lack confidence in their ability to "pass a test" on a subject. They will ask questions such as: "What kind of questions?" or "What's it all about?" The interviewer might reply, "Well, the first question is . . . What do you think about that one?"

The NORC instructions advise the interviewers not to mention the specific subject of the survey or the respondent may say he knows nothing about it (675, p. 15). If he were asked the questions, however, he might answer them all without realizing they were on the subject about which he had just professed ignorance. Sometimes the respondent says, "My opinions aren't worth anything," or "I don't read up on things much," or "Better ask someone else." The interviewer should explain that this is not a poll of experts, that these are not "right" or "wrong" answers, and that the surveyors just want to find out what average people think (675, p. 16).

To be sure, many objections are unvoiced, but a keen interviewer will soon learn to recognize the symptoms and to answer objections which are on the informant's mind. If the more detailed explanation does not seem to satisfy the respondent, the investigator should be able to sense this fact and should proceed with the interview without giving any impression other than complete confidence that cooperation will be gladly given when the matter is fully understood. Very often, when informants see the type of questions asked and the manner in which the replies are recorded, their resistance breaks down.

The process of "selling the interview" will depend to a large extent upon the interviewer's approach as well as upon the informant. Some informants can be appealed to by humor—"give the information to get rid of the 'pest' interviewer." By appearing amazed that anyone would refuse, the interviewer may make the informant feel silly for holding out. Many devices for making friends and influencing people may be applied in securing the cooperation for the interview.

A last resort is to put away the schedule and say, "If you don't want to answer the questions, would you mind telling me two things— First: . . . . , and second: . . . ." These two questions should be carefully chosen and should provide a measure of the sample bias resulting from nonrespondents. In addition to these two questions, the interviewer should, of course, always estimate monthly rent or rental value, and thus secure an economic measure of the refusal.

THE INTERVIEW PROPER:[3]

1. Asking the Questions

A. SEQUENCE OF QUESTIONING. When the schedule is drawn up, particular attention should be paid to the sequence of questions (see Chapter VI). Good arrangement calls for the placing of questions about which informants are likely to be sensitive near the end—but not *at* the end—of a series. The arrangement also takes into account the fact that the interpretation given to certain questions depends upon the type of question immediately preceding the one under consideration. For this reason, it is advisable in most surveys for the interviewer to follow the schedule order of interrogation and not to alter it without permission. Deviations from this rule may be permissible if the questionnaire deals primarily with questions of fact rather than opinion. Should the intervewer happen to volunteer informaton to a question out of sequence, the interviewer can follow it through until the section dealing with that topic is completed. To cite another situation, the reply given to a question placed near the beginning of the interview may be unsatisfactory, but since the informant seems embarrassed by the question, the investigator may pass over it quickly at the time. Then after the completed schedule is secured, he may return to the answer which was "not clear" and get more accurate or complete information. All other conditions being equal, however, the

---

[3] For discussion of the general problem of interviewing in social research, such books as Neely's *A Study in Error in the Interview* (679), Young's *Interviewing in Social Work* (1136), and Bingham and Moore's *How to Interview* (64), *Interviewing for NORC* (675), as well as the other references cited at the end of this chapter contain many useful suggestions.

sequence in which the questions appear on the schedule is preferable
to any other order, since considerable thought and pretesting have
determined the arrangement of the questions.

If it appears that a refusal is likely, the investigator should be instructed to ascertain answers to a few of the most important items. In
such cases he may skip to these essential questions rather than risk a
refusal on less important detailed questions. A partially filled out
schedule is preferable to a refusal of all information, since partial information enables the analysts for the survey to estimate the biases
introduced by refusals.

The flexibility of the question order may vary also in different types
of opinion surveys. Surveys which contain a few well-chosen and
carefully placed questions usually requiring a choice of one of several
predesignated answers generally allow no leeway to the interviewer.
A question asked out of order may seriously influence responses to
later questions. On the other hand, question order is not important in
surveys in which the interviewer rates the intensity of the respondent's
attitude after spending a long time getting acquainted with the informant and his ideas. If certain types of attitude scales are used the
sequence of questions should not affect the results.

B. ASKING EVERY QUESTION UNLESS OTHERWISE SPECIFIED. People
who have one set of characteristics or opinions in common are likely
to have others, so interviewers may sometimes assume that they know
what the answer will be to certain questions and therefore fail to ask
them. Since a true cross-section includes the exceptions, the interviewer should not assume that the case he is dealing with is going
to run true to form. By asking every question, the "surprise answers"
will be given a chance to come up.

Informants occasionally assume they know what questions are
coming next, so they may say "I'm in favor of all those things. Just put
me down 'Yes' for every one." If the respondent were asked and had
a chance to think over each question, he might find one or two that he
was doubtful of—or even definitely opposed to. Sometimes a casual
remark by the respondent may appear to be a satisfactory answer to a
subsequent question, so the interviewer jots it down out of turn, and
then fails to ask the question when he is supposed to. This procedure
not only does not give the respondent the same stimulus question
in the same context as that received by other respondents, but may

even fail to elicit the respondent's true reaction. By a slight change
in wording, such as the printed question contains, an entirely different answer might have been obtained.

In most surveys the interviewer is expected to record certain items
from observation rather than direct questioning. Sex of informant,
race, and socio-economic rating of neighborhood or home usually are
ascertained without asking questions.

C. PHRASING QUESTIONS TO THE INFORMANT. The amount of leeway in phraseology permitted to interviewers should be specified in
the instructions.

Questions on Facts. Informal questioning can be used to obtain replies to census-type or factual questions. Sometimes such questions can
be linked conveniently to remarks made by the informant in the course
of the interview. If the respondent asks why this factual information is
being obtained, the interviewer should have a ready answer. He may
reply, for example, that it is needed to prove that the interviews actually took place so that confidence may be placed in the statistics from
the survey. Neely reports that errors in factual data are frequently
caused by the failure of the interviewer to ask questions in enough
detail (679, p. 90). Rarely should the interviewer be satisfied with the
first response of the informant on questions of fact. By following up
replies, the interviewer may discover that the question was misunderstood, or that the respondent needed some further questioning to
freshen his memory. Questions dependent on the informant's memory
of certain detailed figures may be followed by a request to see any
records or accounts the respondent may have kept. Even a prompt and
confident reply may represent but a fraction of the truth; the interviewer needs to keep ever on the alert.

Questions on Opinions. In opinion surveys, it is important to use
words which are as free from bias as possible, and which express the
exact meaning wanted by the surveyors. Since persons who frame
questionnaires usually know more about the influence of words than
the interviewer, the phraseology used on the schedule is the best. In
fact, some opinion polls require that the questions be asked exactly as
they appear on the questionnaire. Neither conscious nor careless
changes are permissible. The interviewer is cautioned never to explain
or elaborate questions. If informants ask what is meant, the interviewer
is told to repeat the printed wording, slowly and distinctly, emphasiz-

ing the important words. If the respondent still fails to grasp the meaning, his answer is recorded as "Don't know."

If changes are permitted, however, the interviewers should know the "gist" of each question so they can ask them as intended by the question designer. It may be desirable to supply the interviewer with various explanatory phrases or substitute wordings suitable for different educational levels. Particular words or phrases used in a question may need special clarification. Expressions which are likely to prove difficult should be pointed out to the interviewer. Words which may be interpreted by the interviewer and words which the informant should interpret for himself should be specified. Although the interviewer usually may not be called upon to define unusual expressions, he should always be prepared to do so. A statement of just how a question differs from a similar preceding one may be essential to avoid confusion. Then again, a statement of what is *not* meant by a question sometimes is helpful. Getting the respondent to understand the meaning of the question is all-important.

After making sure that the respondent is giving his full attention to the question, the interviewer should make sure that the respondent understands in what terms his answer is to be given, e.g., the respondent should know whether he is to answer "Yes" or "No," or "Approve" or "Disapprove," or some other, possibly longer expression. Some questions tend to bring out a response which is not an answer to the question. People hear a familiar phrase and they assume they know what is being asked. The interviewer should be on guard for such cases, and try to bring out a direct reply to the issue presented. It is helpful if interviewers are supplied with examples of answers which are not acceptable, and the reasons why. It may be necessary for the interviewer to make certain that the respondent understands the conditions of the question, such as the time, place, or issues. Failure of the interviewer to make the conditions clear may result in an answer which seems to dodge the question. By asking the question again, emphasizing the points missed, and giving the respondent enough time to grasp it, the idea may be put across. On *opinion* questions, the interviewer should make sure that he is finding out what the *respondent thinks,* not what he hopes.

If one of several alternatives is to be chosen by the informant, the interviewer may either read out loud the "possible" answers and let the respondent choose the one with which he agrees, or ask only the question and *not* suggest replies. The answer given by the respondent is then interpreted, recorded, or coded by the interviewer. The interviewer should be told which procedure to use.

What introductory phrases may be used preceding a given question or series of questions? In order to change the "set" of the respondent when a shift of subject occurs on the schedule, it may be necessary to prepare him by an introductory phrase such as, "Now I'd like to ask your opinion about . . ." "Now let's see what you think about another question."

Instructions on manner of speaking when asking questions should specify:

(1) Which word or words to emphasize so the respondent will know what is wanted of him.

(2) Points at which to pause, when reading a long or complicated question.

(3) Words or phrases which should be repeated for the sake of emphasis or clarity.

(4) Words which should be "spelled out" if necessary so that the informant will understand.

(5) Unusual words such as names of foreign places which should be correctly pronounced by interviewers. It may be desirable to include a statement of pronunciation of such words for interviewers.

(6) That all questions should be presented in a slow, distinct speech.

When the interviewer reads a list of several alternatives from which the respondent is to choose the one coming closest to his opinion, the propositions should be numbered as they are read off so that the informant can tell where one ends and the next begins. If the list of proposals which is read off to the informant is long, it may be necessary to remind him once or twice before the question is finished as to the terms in which he is supposed to give his answer and what the question is all about.

For administering long or complicated questions involving several alternative propositions, "card questions" may be used. After an introductory statement, the interviewer reads the question proper and hands the informant some cards on which various propositions are recorded. After examining them, the respondent is asked to tell which statement comes closest to expressing his opinion. Cards containing items to be arranged by the informant in order of importance or in some other sequence may also be employed. The technique for giving card questions should be specifically described in the interviewer's instructions. Such points as the following might be mentioned:

(1) If the respondent is unable to read or cannot read easily, the interviewer should read the items on the cards. He must read slowly, repeating the list several times, if necessary, to make sure that the respondent knows the list.

(2) The interviewer should read only the question proper—not the answers—and he should make it clear to the respondent that he wants to know which statement comes closest to his opinion.

(3) If the respondent reads the cards, he must be given ample time to read *all* the alternatives before giving his reply or making his choice. Otherwise, he is likely to react to only part of the question. Interviewers should watch to see that all alternatives are read. It may be necessary to say "Would you mind reading *all* the statements? I want to make sure that I get your opinion right, and there's a chance that one of the later choices might suit you better" (675, p. 41).

(4) When the respondent indicates his choice, the interviewer should read back the answer to make sure it was the one intended.

(5) The order in which the cards are to be arranged as they are handed to the respondent may be specified. To avoid giving any proposition a favored position, it is advisable to rotate the order every time the question is administered.

D. ENCOURAGING THE RESPONDENT TO REPLY. The interviewer's manner may greatly facilitate the response. If he has memorized the questions, they can be asked in a conversational manner, thus creating an informal atmosphere rather than a test situation. The interviewer should avoid a too serious mien, since this may discourage free expression.

The informant should not be required to waste any of his time waiting between questions. While the interviewer is recording the answer to one question, he should ask the next one so that the informant can be thinking it over. A smooth flow of questions is possible if the interviewer is thoroughly familiar with the schedule.

Encouragement to the informant can come through the use of appropriate phrases by the interviewer. Phrases like the following tend to reduce hesitation: "Nobody really knows, we just want your best guess," "Taking everything into account," "On the whole," "In general," "We'd just like your personal opinion," "Judging by what you've heard or read," "Your guess is as good as the next fellow's."

Sometimes a question will be designed to discover how much information on a given subject the respondent possesses. Such questions frequently make the respondent feel ignorant or even inferior. To offset such feelings or the thought that he is "not passing the test," he may be encouraged to reply by such expressions from the interviewer as, "I couldn't tell you all the answers myself," "Nobody has guessed them all so far," "We just want your guess." Occasionally the interviewer will find inconsistencies among various replies, but the respondent should not be accused of anything. In straightening out the inconsistencies, they can be more agreeably referred to as "misunderstandings."

The establishment of good rapport between the interviewer and the interviewee is a more general source of encouragement. The latter must have no fear that his statements will be used in any way which will be harmful to him or to his interests. Interviewers are frequently surprised at the suspicions which informants entertain. In a survey of population fertility, for example, one informant confessed to the interviewer that she thought the government was trying to find out how much room she had in her house so they might force her to house people working in a nearby munitions factory. Another informant said she thought that the survey was for the purpose of finding childless couples who could be compelled to adopt European refugee children. The more skillful the interviewer, the more likely he is to bring these suspicions into the open and to allay the fears which the informant may be harboring. Since few people understand the technical language or procedure of research, the explanations given by the interviewer are usually not comprehended. Thus, it is often more important that the interviewer "sell himself" and obtain the confidence of the informant than that he present a good statement of the purpose of the survey.

E. "DON'T KNOW" ANSWERS. When the respondent says that he does not know or does not have an opinion on the question, the interviewer should know when to "force" an opinion on the question and when to accept the "no opinion" reaction. Following are some of the reasons why persons say they do not know:

(1) They may be thinking aloud—they may not have thought about the question before, but will reach a decision if given time. Such persons say, for example, "Well, I don't exactly know. . . ."

(2) Lack of information on the subject.

(3) Lack of understanding of words or phrasing of the question. Sometimes if the question is repeated, an answer will be forthcoming.

(4) No conception of what the issue is, or what type of answer is expected. If repetition of the question fails to bring a response, this is usually the reason.

(5) Inability to decide between alternatives. Such cases may merely require time.

(6) Fear of possible consequences should the respondent's opinions come to the attention of persons in power over him. A guarantee of confidential treatment of responses may help in such cases.

(7) Belief that his facts are inadequate for him to make a decision.

(8) Belief that it is not his province to hold an opinion on the subject—that it is up to those "in the know" or "in authority" to handle the issue. Such people should be encouraged to express their own views.

(9) Hesitance at expressing an unpopular or minority view. The "Everybody has a right to his own opinion" line may be useful for such cases.

(10) Fear of being wrong. The interviewer may obtain an explicit answer by remarks such as "There aren't any right or wrong answers; we just want to give people a chance to say what they think." When all other efforts have failed, the interviewer may solicit an explanation by a comment such as, "Would you mind telling me why you feel you can't answer?" It is important to ascertain why the respondent has replied "don't know."

2. Recording the Information.   The information given by the informant may be complete and correct, but it will not be usable unless properly recorded.

A. GENERAL INSTRUCTIONS FOR RECORDING ENTRIES ON THE SCHEDULE.   Interviewers should be instructed to write legibly and to keep the schedule as neat as possible. Entries should be made with black ink, indelible pencil, or hard pencil, depending on the preference of the editorial supervisor of the study. Avoid too many erasures or crossed out entries, but make all necessary corrections. Although interviewers are expected to turn in reasonably neat-looking schedules, they are not to take the time from the survey for copying schedules before handing them in.

There should be an entry for every item on the schedule. If the investigator has neglected to ask the informant about any item, he should write "not asked" in the blank space provided for this question. The editors can decide whether the missing item warrants a return call on the informant, or whether the item can be obtained during a check interview.

Appropriate symbols should be recorded if the informant does not know an answer (D.K.), or if the item does not apply (not applic.). If the information is refused (refused), this should be indicated.

Interviewers should be told where to make notes to explain entries which may appear to be inconsistent or unreliable. Notes on the reverse side of the schedule or on special note paper stapled to the schedule may be used. As a rule, the margins of the schedule are needed for code symbols or for editors' comments.

Instructions to interviewers should inform them that check interviewing will take place and that dishonest reporting will be regarded as cause for dismissal.

If more than one schedule form is to be filled out, definite instructions should be issued stating when the different forms are to be used.

B. SPECIFIC ITEMS ON THE SCHEDULE. The instructions should cover definitions of the terms and items on the schedule, the units in which the entries are to be made, e.g., dollars, cents, weeks, days, etc.

If the schedule is properly drawn up, every item requiring an entry will be numbered. Thus, reference to each item and the manner in which it is to be interpreted, as well as the form in which the reply is to be entered, can be made easily. Only by careful pretesting of the schedule questions, however, is it possible to write adequate instructions on each item. The instructions should contain precautions as to what is not meant, how marginal cases are to be entered, what constitutes an adequate reply, and how replies are to be classified (if coded in the field). Sometimes these instructions are so voluminous that it is necessary to prepare a condensed set of instructions which the enumerator can carry with him, as well as detailed instructions for office reference when "problem" cases arise. In the Sixteenth Federal Census, the "abridged instructions" to enumerators of the Population Schedule (997) covered 18 printed pages, and the more detailed one covered 79 pages on population questions. The following instructions on three items—sex, age, and marital status—should give some idea of the detail required to insure accurate returns and uniform interpretations:

Personal Description

452. Column 9. Sex.—Write "M" for male, and "F" for female.

453. Column 10. Color or Race.—Write "W" for white; "Neg" for Negro; "In" for Indian; "Chi" for Chinese; "Jp" for Japanese; "Fil" for Filipino; "Hin" for Hindu; "Kor" for Korean. For a person of any other race, write the race in full.

454. Mexicans.—Mexicans are to be regarded as white unless definitely of Indian or other non-white race.

455. Negroes.—A person of mixed white and Negro blood should be returned as Negro, no matter how small the percentage of Negro blood. Both black and mulatto persons are to be returned as Negroes, without distinction. A person of mixed Indian and Negro blood should be returned as a Negro, unless the Indian blood very definitely predominates and he is universally accepted in the community as an Indian.

456. Indians.—A person of mixed white and Indian blood should be returned as an Indian, if enrolled on an Indian Agency or Reservation roll; or if not so enrolled, if the proportion of Indian blood is one-fourth or more, or if the person is regarded as an Indian in the community where he lives. (See part 455 for mixed Indian and Negro.)

457. Mixed Races.—Any mixture of white and non-white should be reported according to the non-white parent. Mixtures of non-white races should be reported according to the race of the father, except that Negro-Indian should be reported as Negro.

458. Column 11. Age at Last Birthday.—Enter the age of the person at his last birthday before 12:01 A.M., April 1, 1940. Thus a person whose 18th birthday occurred on April 8, 1940, should be reported as 17 years of age because that was his age on his last birthday before April 1, 1940. For persons 1 year old and over, this question calls for the age in completed years at last birthday.

459. Ages of Infants.—The entry in col. 11 for children less than a year old should indicate age in completed months, expressed as twelfths of a year. Ask the following question in each household:

"Are there any children in this household who were born on or after April 1, 1939?" For each child born after April 1, 1939, ascertain the actual birth date and determine the proper entry for col. 11 by referring to the table showing ages by birth dates at the foot of the schedule. Thus the age of a child born on May 2, 1939, should be entered as 10/12. Note that a child born after 12:01 A.M., April 1, 1940, is not to be enumerated (see par. 301).

464. Ages in Round Numbers.—The age of the person will sometimes be reported in a round number, like 30 or 45, or "about 50" when that is not the exact age. If an age ending in "0" or "5" is reported, you should inquire whether that is really the exact age. If, however, the exact age is not known, enter the approximate age, rather than "Unknown."

465. Column 12. Marital Status.—Write "S" for a single person (one who has never been married), "M" for a married person (this includes "separated" persons), "Wd" for a widow or widower, and "D" for a "divorced person."

Few questions exist in which there is no reasonable possibility of misinterpretation. Only inexperienced surveyors think that questions and entries are "self-evident." Familiarity with the topic, trial questioning, or careful thought about each question will bring up problems which should be mentioned in the instructions.

C. RECORDING ANSWERS VERBATIM. The technique for recording exact statements of informants and at the same time keeping the respondent talking and interested in the interview deserves comment. One investigator claims to have solved this problem by employing shorthand. Another who has an exceptionally good memory merely notes the key words of the reply, and as soon as the interview is over she fills in the rest of the statement. A third interviewer found that she could record the verbatim reply while the informant was answering questions which were not on the schedule but were used to fill in time. The additional questions which she used were quite general, such as, "Why do you think so?" "Just what do you mean by that?" "Do you know of any examples?" etc. Such "fill-in" questions can be general or specific—and can be placed in the interviewer's instructions to be used following questions requiring exact quotation of the respondent's reply.

The NORC instructions contain an excellent discussion of what is meant by verbatim reporting. The interviewer is told to listen attentively to what the respondent says—the words he uses, the way he phrases his response—and to quote him exactly (675, p. 49). This means that the respondent's grammar or even his profanity should not be polished before recording. Neither should the interviewer summarize the respondent's remarks. While some of his remarks may not be relevant or may be repetitious, his comments on the specific question under consideration should be written down in full. Seldom will his answer be longer than one or two sentences, and usually he does not mind waiting for it to be recorded completely.

The instructions further suggest that the interviewer be prepared to write as soon as he has asked the question, but he may have to wait for a general introductory remark, such as "If I understand what you mean, I think . . ." To facilitate writing quickly and legibly, common abbreviations may be used, and crossing out mistakes rather than erasing them is preferable.

In addition to checking or encircling the appropriate answer box, interviewers are often asked to record any pertinent comments made by the informant to amplify or explain his point of view. If the comment seems to contradict or alter the meaning of the answer which has already been checked, the interviewer must determine which is the respondent's final or predominant point of view.

When verbatim comments are received at headquarters, they may be studied by a staff whose chief business is comment analysis. As a result, various important leads may be secured. Explanations may suggest themselves as to why the statistics are coming out the way they do. Indications may be revealed regarding worthwhile analyses or significant cross tabulations of the data. Occasionally, the colorful comments of respondents can be employed as "human interest" material to render more readable the published report of the statistical findings. A further purpose of recording comments is the detection of "curbstone" reporters, *viz.*, those interviewers who fake replies. Few people are ingenious enough to "invent" comments which are as varied as those encountered in the real interview situation.

D. QUALIFIED ANSWERS. Sometimes the respondent finds it difficult to align himself with any one of the alternatives presented in opinion questions unless he is permitted to specify the condition or circumstances under which he holds a given view. In other words, he qualifies his answer before or after agreeing with a given proposition. It is not always easy for the interviewer to determine whether or not the restrictions placed upon the statement of the issue are so great as to constitute a rejection of the proposition. If such qualified answers are likely to be encountered with references to any question, the interviewer should be instructed to record the qualifications set up by the respondent. This verbal record may be in addition to a checkmark in the answer box or instead of such a check, depending upon the instructions.

Qualified answers should be distinguished from a mere repetition of the qualifications expressed or implied in the question itself. Thus if the respondent agrees with a proposition as stated in the question, providing the conditions specified in the statement are met, his response is to be classified as one of agreement rather than of qualified agreement.

Qualified replies should not be confused with amplifying comments added by the respondent.

E. OMISSIONS AND ERRORS.   Interviewers need to be checking themselves constantly to see that every question which is supposed to be asked is asked, and conversely that questions which apply only to limited groups should not be asked of everyone. While it is better to require a "not applicable" entry in such a case, some instructions merely ask that the space be left blank. Subquestions or those dependent upon the answer to a preceding question are often overlooked unless interviewers are especially warned. One useful practice is to print on the schedule form, in sizable letters, instructions as to whom to question on each subquestion. Such phrases as the following might be employed: "Ask of *all* people," "Ask of persons who answered 'Yes' to question 3a above," or "Ask only of people replying 'No' to question 6b."

Another common error in reporting is checking or circling the wrong answer box or number. Even though the informant may have made his choice clear, the interviewer may carelessly check the wrong code. Such an error is unpardonable—and cannot be detected unless comments seem to contradict the entry. Careful inspection of the schedule after the interview should reveal such a mistake.

NORC instructions list another reporting error—that of circling more than one answer number. This may happen when the informant changes his mind after the original check has been made. In such cases the informant's final decision should determine where the check is to be placed. Sometimes the check mark or circle is so placed that it falls between two answers and it is impossible to tell where it was meant to be.

Never should the interviewer use dashes instead of writing out the complete answer or marking "Don't know," or "Inapplicable."

F. RECORDING ANSWERS. The interviewer should know exactly what record is to be made for each question. The instructions should cover such points as:

(1) When to place a checkmark in the correct answer box.

(2) When to record comments of the respondent.

(3) When, if ever, more than one alternative may be checked.

(4) When *only* the "free answer" is to be recorded.

(5) When to record qualified answers and when to classify the respondent as "Don't know."

SUPPLEMENTARY QUESTIONS AND OBSERVATIONS:

In addition to the respondent's own statement of the situation surveyed, it may be desirable to secure the interviewer's appraisal of the respondent, the situation as described by him, or his living conditions. The usefulness of such supplementary observations will be enhanced if uniform classifying and reporting procedures are followed. The detailed instructions prepared by NORC for classifying families into economic levels specify several criteria such as rent, occupation, family status and size, income, and comforts and luxuries which the interviewer is to consider when making his judgment. Interviewers' observations of home environment may be definitely improved through the employment of rating scales such as the Chapin Scale for Rating Social Status (158), the Leahy (Shea) Scale for Measuring Urban Home Environment (866), or other scales described in Chapter VI.

INTERVIEWING IN RURAL AREAS:

While most of the suggestions on interviewing procedure thus far discussed are applicable to rural interviewing as well, a few additional points deserve mention. Studies of not-at-homes show that a significantly higher percentage of calls to farm homes find someone home than is the case in city homes. During certain months the farmer is likely to be in the fields[4] during the day, while his wife often can be found in the kitchen. Early morning or evening may find them working in the barn. It is well to keep in mind that they go to bed early, so late interviewing should be avoided. Interviewing frequently must be conducted while the farmer or his wife are doing chores, but if a friendly approach is used, they are usually cooperative.

During the winter and some spring months, roads may be impassable with an ordinary car and equipment. If the interviewer must "get his man" he might as well either arrange to meet the farmer on his day in the "town or village" or see that he has the necessary chains, snow tires, shovels, sand, etc., for a difficult trip. A detailed map and familiarity with the conditions of the roads is a great help.

CLOSING THE INTERVIEW:

Deciding when all pertinent information has been secured and the interview should be terminated requires experience and judgment. According to White, "no interview which is still yielding applicable facts should be summarily ended even though information sufficient to fill in the questionnaire has been obtained" (1085). Since no time should be wasted, the interviewer must decide when he has obtained an adequate reply and can leave.

The problem of achieving diplomatically a quick exit is not always an easy one. Once the informant has become thoroughly interested in the survey topic or in recounting her hopes or troubles to a willing listener, breaking off the interview may prove difficult. The plea of "an appointment" at a specified time in the near future is a plausible excuse for a seemingly hurried departure which frequently proves successful. By standing up and going toward the door as he thanks the informant, the interviewer can sometimes bring the interview to a close. The NORC instructions suggest that if the respondent continues to talk, the interviewer may say he has quite a few calls to make but would like to come back sometime (675, p. 16). Whatever device employed, the interviewer should leave the informant with a feeling of pleasure at having cooperated in a worthwhile undertaking, and with a willingness to be revisited in case "some points were overlooked." This will

---

[4] If the interviewer goes through gates, he should leave them as they were, either opened or closed, because they have usually been left that way intentionally (675, p. 126).

pave the way for the check interviewer, or, if need be, for a return visit of the original investigator.

Personal Supervision and Control of Work of Interviewers

The success of surveys by the personal interview method demands careful attention to the work of the interviewers. Adequate instructions are indispensable in themselves, and they must be supplemented by active supervision and control to ensure the faithful application of the prescribed procedures.

THE SQUAD SYSTEM:

In large-scale surveys, the great number of interviewers make close field supervision difficult. The squad system, mentioned earlier, may be the best solution. Eight or ten enumerators working in each section of the city or other area are supervised by a skilled interviewer, known as the squad leader. He devotes part of his time to directing the work of his squad, and part to obtaining schedule information from the more difficult cases.

The instructions to squad leaders should cover:

1. Making assignments to interviewers.
2. Reviewing schedules turned in.
3. Duties and responsibilities regarding quality and quantity of work.
4. Procedures for reporting and correcting unsatisfactory field work.
5. Necessity for keeping up-to-date on changes in or additions to instructions, and for conveying these instructions to the interviewers.

The supervisor of collection for the survey as a whole can do much to stimulate production by posting on the bulletin board the production record of the various squads. Those squads working in less concentrated population areas of the city or other regions under survey should, of course, not be expected to produce as many complete schedules as squads surveying districts where little travel time is needed between calls. If a squad system is not employed, and if interviewers are remunerated on a time basis, it is difficult to estimate the amount of time actually spent in the field because of claims that families are not at home.

STAFF CONFERENCE OF INTERVIEWERS:

After the field work has been in progress for a few days, the interviewers may be called together to discuss problems arising in the course of the work. Exchanges of experience on the ways of meeting resistance from informants may keep down the refusal rate and thus reduce biases in the sample. Suggestions as to quotas which may reasonably be expected from interviewers may also come out of this conference. In very large-scale studies where the squad leaders have most of the direct contact with the interviewers, the staff conference may give investigators a "feeling" for the study as a whole.

ASSIGNMENT AND INTAKE OF SCHEDULES:

The office set-up should provide for careful control and accounting of all schedules assigned for interview, awaiting assignment, turned in as completed, reassigned for interview, or in hands of interviewers. A control system should be devised which enables the assignment clerk to check up on the number of schedules in the hands of interviewers and the length of time such schedules have been out of the office. Those which they have had for one week should automatically be called in for special consideration and reassignment. It is very important that interviewers turn in assigned schedules at stated intervals, whether or not the schedules are filled out. Otherwise schedules which represent refusals, night calls, or difficult cases will be left until the end of the collection period, when there is not sufficient time to rectify the biases these cases have produced in the sample. As mentioned previously, there is serious danger that the sample of completed interviews will fall short of the original sample unless frequent check-ups of schedules are made.

The instructions should include a statement of whether completed schedules should be turned over to the squad leader daily, brought to the office, or dropped in the mail in an addressed envelope at the end of the day.

It is desirable that interviewers make daily reports to their squad leaders, or report to the office at least every second day. The payroll should be based upon time or production records filled in by the interviewer during these office visits. Interviewers should not spend too much time in the office getting assignments, talking with editors, or writing notes to accompany schedules. Unless a time limit is set for office work, some may spend so much time in the office that the number of interviews secured will be negligible. One hour in the office for every five hours in the field is adequate in most surveys. The experienced interviewers of NORC customarily spend less than half this much on noninterviewing.

The supervisor of sampling should periodically check the schedules representing cases of persons who are not at home, have moved, can be reached only at night, or have refused to cooperate. By careful study of these "problem cases," procedures for "recapturing" them or of substituting cases in the sample to replace those losses and thus to reduce the collection biases can be devised and put into operation. Few surveyors grasp the effect of these losses until the collection task has been completed and it is too late to correct the sample in the field.

Since the refusal of an informant to give the interview data is regarded as an evidence of failure on the part of the enumerator, interviewers often are reluctant to admit that they have been turned down. Instead, they may report that no one was at home. It is necessary, therefore, to keep very careful account of all cases which do not yield completed schedules.

These incomplete or unobtained schedules should be classified by such items as: enumerator, district, type of dwelling, monthly rental value, occupation of head listed in the city directory, or by any other available information. If, as is likely, these incomplete schedules will produce a bias in the sample, a program for correcting the deficiency should be instituted (see pages 483–484 for a discussion of procedure).

PRODUCTION QUOTAS:[5]

After the first week or so the number of satisfactory and completed interviews which may reasonably be expected per day can be gauged. Allowance should be made for differences in production rate in the various economic districts of the community. In high-rent areas, houses may be far apart and more time is consumed getting from one address to another. In apartment house areas, families tend to be away from home more than in single-family house districts. Apartment dwellers are often childless, and both husband and wife tend to be earners; it is

---

[5] See also Chapter V, p. 144.

difficult, therefore, to find them at home during the day. Since only one or two hours can be used for evening interviews, interviewers who work in apartment areas probably should have lower production quotas.

CHECK-INTERVIEWING:

In order to confirm the fact that the reported interviews actually took place and to provide assurance that the data are accurate, it is necessary to reinterview a cross-section of the persons scheduled by each interviewer.

The check-interviewing supervisor selects the schedules to be checked from the enumerator's production record. To begin with, about one in five schedules should be checked. As the study progresses and the honesty and ability of the interviewer becomes apparent, the proportion checked may be reduced to one in ten or twenty.[6] It is important that the process of check interviewing be continued during the entire collection period, since some interviewers might produce slipshod work if there were not the likelihood of discovery. At no time should they be told the method of selecting the cases to be checked.

If the checker suspects the honesty of any interviewer or feels he is not following instructions, *all* his schedules should be reviewed. As soon as possible such interviewers should be removed from the field, since they usually do more harm than good there. Katz and Cantril state that sponsors of polls agreed that about 60 per cent of all interviewers employed in early public opinion polls were not completely reliable. College trained field workers proved no more reliable than others (499, p. 160). It has been claimed that an honest staff is built up only after months or even years of careful selection and training. This need not be the case if sufficient controls are used.

Check interviewers usually use a blank schedule which they fill out in the course of a reinterview. It is then given to a check clerk who compares it with the original schedule and makes a note of the differences. The supervisor examines the indicated differences and, if minor, makes changes in red ink on the original schedule. If the differ-

---

[6] According to market surveyors, normally not over 10 per cent of the work of interviewers needs to be checked to establish that the interview took place (8, p. 183).

ences are significant, they are reported to the squad leaders who take the matter up with the interviewer.

Care should be taken to stamp "check interview" upon all schedules which represent check interviews so that they do not become confused with the original schedules.

In some studies the check interviewer takes the original schedule into the field and asks the informant only about certain items which have been predesignated for checking. One disadvantage of this procedure is that the check interviewer may become careless and make changes directly on the schedule. Also, if he knows whose work he is checking, he may be inclined to pass over the work of persons he knows well or likes.

To conduct a check-interview requires great tact. The interviewer may impress the informant with the careful work being done by the surveyors and point out that this involves checking a certain percentage of all cases. He may indicate that the first interviewer did not complete the record so it is necessary to bother the informant again to secure an item or two of additional information. If the schedule is long and the original interviewer spent considerable time with the informant, the informant may have developed a feeling of friendliness toward him so that a check-up may be resented.

The check interviewer should check the items essential to the study, and if these entries are incorrect he should review the entire schedule. Jenkins and Corbin, who tested the validity of answers in surveys of "Psychological Brand Barometers," reported that the interviewers went out 48 hours later to 150 persons who had granted interviews, claiming to have lost the schedule, and were surprised to find over 90 per cent granted an immediate new interview on a questionnaire with 26 items. A less favorable response would be expected for a longer questionnaire (472).

If only certain items are to be checked, it may be possible to secure the desired information by telephone when the telephone number is noted by the original interviewer.

One procedure employed by a large marketing research agency is to send a short question or two in a stamped self-addressed envelope to a certain percentage of informants. The respondent is asked whether an interviewer has talked with the family about the item in question. After checking "yes" or "no" the reply is mailed to the research agency. If a very short questionnaire is to be checked, it can be mailed back to the respondents with a letter asking them to confirm the entire interview.

ASSIGNMENT OF INTERVIEWERS:

The wise choice of interviewers for various sections of the city may have a pronounced effect upon the number of refusals. Before assignments are made, the district number (i.e., enumeration district number, tract number, ward number, etc.) should be placed on each schedule, and the assignment clerk should know the type of neighborhood in which every address is located. For the higher rent areas of the city, send only the most skilled, most presentable looking, and best informed investigators. A poor interviewer multiplies the collection work manyfold because refusals require much more time and skill to "recapture" than do "untried" cases.

ORDER OF SURVEYING DISTRICTS:

The question of the optimum order in which to survey the various districts of a city must be decided with several factors in mind. If no pilot study is made and if the survey is begun with all unskilled investigators, it is better to conduct the survey in the lower economic areas of the city first. After interviewers have developed skill and a knowledge of the questions, the best workers can be assigned to the upper middle class and high rent areas of the city. It does not necessarily follow, however, that workers who are successful in the low rent areas will be good in the high economic districts, so after an interviewer has been transferred to the upper income areas, his work should be completely checked.

If there is a possibility that the field work may be brought to a close before all schedules can be secured, interviewing should be distributed throughout all the districts from the very start. Then whenever the field work terminates, the schedules are likely to represent a cross-section of the community.

If the data being collected are likely to change much with the passage of time, it is essential that the average date of interview of families residing in the low rent districts of the city differ as little as possible from the date of interviews from high rent areas. Otherwise what may appear to be due to economic differences may actually be some function of time.

4. Assignments and Control by Mail

Various research agencies collect data for nationwide polls or surveys by means of part-time interviewers who reside in the different areas of the survey. Aside from an initial contact with a representative of the headquarters staff, who hires the interviewer and gives him brief training, communication between the interviewer and the survey headquarters is confined to mail, telephone, or telegraph. Assignments, instructions, supervision, and payment are all handled by mail as a matter of regular routine. Every point about which survey interviewers may have questions is covered by written instructions, and insofar as possible all problems which are likely to arise should be anticipated.

The basic training and instructions to interviewers described elsewhere in this chapter (p. 322) also apply to field workers stationed at a distance from headquarters. Additional matters are taken up below.

FAMILIARITY WITH INSTRUCTIONS:

Since each day's work cannot be reviewed by an editor or field supervisor, the interviewer must himself undertake the responsibility for correct procedure. Emphasis should be placed upon the need for studying all instructions pertaining to the particular survey assignment as well as the more general basic instructions. The interviewer should study the instructions, even after he feels that he has mastered them. A rereading after the first few interviews and again at the end of the second day may prevent the fixation of wrong habits of questioning or reporting.

CHECKING OF SCHEDULES:

While all interviewers should carefully check every schedule for completeness at the time of the interview, field workers at a distance from headquarters need to be particularly careful. Since they are not in close touch with the central office, errors will not be detected soon. After completing each schedule, the interviewer should examine it again to assure himself that it has been filled out in accordance with instructions. Then, if errors or omissions are discovered, they should be corrected as soon as a reinterview can be arranged. When the sample case is selected by the interviewer rather than the home office, it may be easier and equally acceptable to reject the incomplete schedule and interview another informant instead.

An announced policy of checking on the interviewer's work either by means of post cards mailed to a certain proportion of respondents or by check interviewers should be included in the basic instructions. In order to make these checks, it is necessary, of course, for names and addresses to be obtained by the original interviewer.

THE ADVANCE NOTICE:

When surveys are conducted at irregular intervals by a permanent staff of interviewers, they should always receive advance notice that an assignment is about to reach them so they can arrange their time accordingly. Current practice is to notify the interviewer from three days to one week before the assignment. If the interviewer finds that he is unable to carry out the work at the specified time, he is asked to notify headquarters by telegraph immediately, so that other arrangements may be made. It also saves the time and expense of mailing the material for the assignment. Items generally included in the advance warning notice are: (1) the date the assignment is to be mailed from the office, (2) the number of work days involved or the number of interviews, (3) the date the interviewer must mail back the completed schedules, and (4) a request to wire immediately if the interviewer cannot handle the job. It has also been suggested that it would be helpful to the interviewer if the warning card also mentioned the subject of the survey, the territory to be covered (urban or rural or both), the groups to be interviewed, and the rate of payment if the company has no fixed policy in this regard (892).

THE ASSIGNMENT ENVELOPE:

A few days after the advance notice reaches the interviewer, he usually receives the necessary instructions and forms for collecting the data and returning them to headquarters. Customarily, the material needed for the successful completion of the assignment comes in a large envelope. The contents of the envelope vary, of course, with the survey procedures adopted by the research agency. The following items suggest the sort of material included:

1. A list of the material contained in the envelope and instructions as to which material is to be returned to headquarters.

2. An addressed, stamped return envelope.

3. A sufficient number of schedules or questionnaires to cover the interviews assigned, plus several for trial interviews and wastage. If the interviewer must select eligible informants, some wastage may be expected. If the sample cases are predesignated by the office, only a few extra schedules need to be included.

4. Specific instructions for collecting the information for each item on the schedule. These instructions usually range from one to ten pages in length and cover such items as: (a) A general statement of the purpose of the particular survey, (b) specific instructions on how to question the informant, and to secure and record the information on each item (instructions explain how to cope with problems which may be encountered in obtaining the answers to specific questions or to the questionnaire as a whole), (c) additions to or corrections of the basic general instructions already in the hands of the interviewer.

5. The sample assignment or quota sheet. This should indicate the number of interviews the interviewer is expected to complete, and the date by which the returns are to be mailed to headquarters. The NORC sheet also specifies the date it is mailed from headquarters and the date it is received by the interviewer.

If the sample is preselected by the office staff, the assignment may take the form of names or addresses or both, typed on each blank schedule. A summary list of names or addresses should also be included in the envelope so that the interviewer may check his completed schedules against this list before returning them to headquarters. Space should be provided for indicating why the schedule is not completed or why contact has not been made, if such is the case.

If the interviewer selects the sample cases, the assignment should also specify exactly the types or groups of persons to be included in the sample, and the number of schedules to be obtained from each group.

The classes into which the assigned number of cases should fall should be clearly designated. If, for example, the interviewer is to secure thirty-two completed schedules from specified economic, sex, age, and color groups, the exact manner of dividing the groups should be indicated on the quota sheet. An example of a quota specification used by NORC (675) is shown on p. 379.

In this example it will be observed the colored sample and the farm sample are not to be distributed by rental groups.

NATIONAL OPINION RESEARCH CENTER
University of Denver

| This quota is assigned |
| by Rental Groups |

QUOTA SHEET

Survey No. 250   Date mailed from here February 4, 1946

Interviewer SMITH   Date received by you 2/7/46

Place of Interview Detroit N.D., Mich. Date mailed back by you 2/11/46

METROPOLITAN DISTRICT	QUOTA	TALLY INTERVIEWS HERE	TOTAL
Detroit	30	₦₦ ₦₦ ₦₦ ₦₦ ₦₦ ₦₦	30
Wyandotte	12	₦₦ ₦₦ //	12

Tally each interview as you obtain it--under the proper Sex-Age column
opposite the proper Residence or Economic Level category

If you have a Metropolitan District assignment, tally if interview was
made in central city or suburban section. Remember to record the total
number of interviews you obtain.

Tally here all persons who refuse to be interviewed for any reason whatsoever. none

		MEN			WOMEN		TOTAL
		21-39	40 & Over		21-39	40 & Over	
	QUOTA	9	11	QUOTA	11	11	42
White Farm	-			-			
Colored Farm	-			-			
Cont.or $74.50 Est. Rent & over	1	/		-			/
Cont.or $52.50 to Est. Rent 74.49	2	/	/	2	/	/	4
Cont.or $31.50 to Est. Rent 52.49	8	////	////	11	₦₦	₦₦ /	19
Cont.or $31.49 Est. Rent & less	6	///	///	6	///	///	12
Colored Non-Farm	3		///	3	//	/	6
TOTAL	20	9	11	22	11	11	42

Fill Quota Exactly as Assigned.

The above-designated interviews are all bona fide, which I have obtained acting as
an independent interviewer for NATIONAL OPINION RESEARCH CENTER. According to your
Basic Instructions, I will not reveal the answers of any respondent.

Signature John Smith

FIGURE 2. Quota Sheet. (From National Opinion Research Center, *Interviewing for NORC*, 1945.)

6. Time and expense record. Whether or not payment is to be on a daily, hourly, or interview basis, it is desirable to secure a detailed statement of the time spent and expenses incurred. This record may be used as the "bill" submitted by the interviewer. A sample time and expense sheet is presented below:

INTERVIEWER'S TIME AND EXPENSE RECORD

Survey No. ....

Interviewer .... Address ....
        Name   No.   Street   City   State

Date: From .... To .... Number of schedules completed ....

Hours spent
    Studying instructions and practice interviews   ....
    Interviewing and transportation in own town   ....
    Interviewing outside of *own* town   ....
    Traveling to and from *other* towns or rural areas   ....
    Re-checking schedules before return   ....

Total hours

Cost of interviewer's time @ $0.00 per hr.

Expenses incurred
    Streetcar or bus fares* $........
    Railroad fare, Hotel Room, meals (on overnight assignment)   ....
    Auto
        Mileage in own town   ....@ 0¢ per mile ....
        Mileage outside of own town ....@ 0¢ per mile ....
    Other expenses (specify) ....

* Except to first interview and from last interview

Total Cost $........

Use this space for figures needing explanation

I hereby certify that these expenses are true and correct.

Signed..................... Date ....

7. Sheet for interviewers suggestions. When contact with the interviewer is limited largely to correspondence by mail, it is desirable to provide a form on which the interviewer can give his reactions to the job required of him and of the public's response to the questionnaire.

The interviewer's comments or criticism of the schedule as a whole, of specific questions, or of the instructions enable the survey designer continually to improve his techniques. Misunderstandings or wrong procedures by the interviewers are often brought to light through these comments. Questions which proved very interesting, complicated, or hard to put across should be pointed out by the interviewer. These suggestions and comments may be of great value in the analysis stage of the survey. An account of unusual or humorous experiences may serve to "pep up" what might otherwise be a rather dull statistical report.

8. When the interviewer's own opinion of the topic of the survey is desired, an "Interviewer's Questionnaire" may sometimes be included, or may even be sent out in advance of the main assignment. It is usually important that this questionnaire be filled out and mailed back before the interviewer begins his assignment. It is possible by this means to determine the relationship between the interviewer's own opinion and the returns he gets from others.

9. Acknowledgment and comments upon interviewer's work. Good work on the part of interviewers can be stimulated and maintained if properly detected and acknowledged. Snead (892) points out that constructive praise and encouragement is very important to the field worker who seldom comes in contact with his employer or supervisor. Too many survey agencies write to their field workers only when they have negative criticism to offer; but a merited "pat on the back" should not be neglected because it is even more important.

10. A list of all the forms and material which is to be returned to headquarters at the completion of the assignment.

CHECKS ON THE HONESTY OF INTERVIEWERS:

The headquarters staff should be on guard for faked returns. Sometimes only part and sometimes all of the returns may be faked or made to agree with what the interviewer believes the opinion *should* be. Several devices may be used to detect such returns. The statistics which interviewers are asked to collect on such factual items as telephone or car ownership can be compared with the known figures for the total population in the area covered by the interviewer. His work should be scrutinized if the returns deviate too much from the expected percentages. It is also possible to insert factual questions on

current events. Interviewers have no way of knowing what their percentages are likely to be. A third device is to compare the responses on
certain opinion questions to the average response secured by all interviewers in a given section or in the type of neighborhood in which a
given interviewer is supposed to have been operating.

Selected References
Interview Procedures and Problems

Bader (18, 19), Baker and Stanton (26), Bancroft (29), Bell (40),
Bennett (44, 45), Bevis (60), Bingham and Moore (64), Blankenship (74, 77, 78), Blankenship et al. (82), Bogardus (84), Borg
(94), Crespi (208), Elinsen and Cisin (283), Family Welfare Assn.
(294), Friedman (334), Guest (382, 383), Harriman (407), Harris
and Connelly (409), Hilgard and Payne (436), Huey (460), *In-
ternational Journal of Opinion and Attitude Measurement* (467),
Katz (492, 495), Maccoby (604), McPeak (633), Merton and
Kendall (641), Moore (653), Morgan (656), NORC (675, 676),
Neeley (679), Rademacher (755), Radvanyi (756), Rice (771),
Rose (813), Shapiro and Eberhart (864), Sheatsley (867, 870),
Snead (892), Stanton and Baker (912), Strang (939), Symonds
(950), Udow (978), U.S. (984, 996, 997), Wechsler (1073),
Williams (1096), Williams and Cantril (1098), Woodworth (1122),
Wrenn (1124), Young (1136, 1137).
See also discussion in books on Social Surveys, Market Research, and
Polling Methods.

CHAPTER XI

Mail Questionnaire
Procedures

Since the organization, training, and supervision of a staff of investigators is unnecessary when data are secured through mail questionnaires, the collection work consists primarily of designing the questionnaire, inducing people to respond to it, and analyzing and correcting the sample with a view to presenting representative returns.

DESIGN OF THE MAIL QUESTIONNAIRE:

Most of the principles of framing questions and designing schedules discussed in Chapter VI apply also to mail questionnaires. One important difference between schedules presented by interviewers and those sent by mail should be noted here. In the former case, the printed questions may be orally interpreted or rephrased by the interviewer and so rendered intelligible to any informant, whereas in the latter case such flexibility does not exist. The same phrasing is used for every type of individual from the college president to the person with less than fourth grade education. Opinion surveys in which the interviewer is not permitted to alter or explain the wording used on the questionnaire are similar in this respect to mail surveys. Some leeway, however, such as the change in emphasis of certain words is usually allowed, even though no substitute words can be used. Of course, if the persons covered by the survey belong to a more or less homogeneous group such as school teachers, or students, or social workers, or bank executives, the problem of designing questions is much simplified.

The appearance of the questionnaire is much more important in the mail survey than in the interview, since the impression gained from a hasty glance at the form may determine whether or not an attempt will be made to answer it. The psychological devices for gaining the favorable attention of the recipient, as well as the techniques for sustaining his interest until the task is completed, should be carefully considered.

Sletto's work before the adoption of a mail questionnaire deserves study. He carried on extensive pretesting in order "to select an aesthetically pleasing cover design for the questionnaire, to find a title which would arouse interest, to choose an attractive page format, to determine upon a size and style of type that would make the final printed questionnaire easily readable even under poor illumination and by people with less than normal vision, and to find photographs of high interest value and appropriateness to illustrate the various sections of the questionnaire (878, p. 198). Other aspects, such as length of questionnaire, nature of appeals employed in the letter of solicitation, the use of postal cards instead of letters in sending follow-up notices, were also experimented with before the final procedure was adopted in the Sletto study. These and other mail survey matters deserve further experimentation, especially on different elements of the population.

Since adequate quantitative evidence is lacking on the effectiveness of various features of questionnaires mailed to the general public, the surveyor must be guided by the recommendations most often appearing in the literature on the questionnaire method.

1. Appearance. The questionnaire should be attractive in appearance. This can be accomplished by the appropriate use of colors, pictures or pictorial material, spacing, type, arrangement, etc. (see Toops, 971). It is important to bear in mind, however, that what appeals to the survey designers is usually not the same as what appeals to the public. Market researchers have shown in many studies that the choices of specialists in the advertising offices regarding titles of promotion pieces, colors, or other copy invariably differ from the selections of the public at large.

It is also desirable to have the questionnaire look as if it were easy to fill out. This can be accomplished by requiring very little writing of the informant, and/or so arranging the various items so that the questionnaire does not appear crowded.

2. Content. The variety of the topics about which the informant is to report should be as limited as possible. Franzen (329) suggests that a number of unrelated subjects dealt with is an even more objectionable feature in a questionnaire than is considerable length.

3. Length. Most recommendations for the best length for the questionnaire point to the rule, "as short as possible to get all the information needed by the survey." Still, there is experimental evidence which suggests that certain groups of the population, given the proper incentives and presented with a carefully pretested form, will respond to a very long schedule.

In the process of testing the effect of the length of questionnaire on the proportion of returns, Sletto (878) mailed schedules of 10 pages, 25 pages, and 35 pages to three groups of university alumni of 100 persons each. He found no significant difference in the percentage of returns from the three groups. He suggests, however, that although the factor of length does not seem important between the ranges of 10 and 35 pages, it is quite possible that there might be a pronounced difference in percentage of returns between one and 10 pages.

Norton, in the National Education Association study of 136 questionnaires, came to the conclusion that the shorter the questionnaire, the larger the percentage of replies. He found that the per cent of returns on 20 questionnaires with five items or less was 78.5%, while the median per cent on all 136 questionnaires was 69% (701). Stanton (910) reported that 28.3% of the persons sent a three-page questionnaire responded, as compared with 50.2% who replied to a double government post card containing a single question which could be answered by making a single check.

One difficulty about a long questionnaire is that the schedules returned are likely to be poorly filled out. Curtis (223) sent out 795 copies of a questionnaire to individuals who had requested a radio program. This questionnaire contained 45 items. Within 15 days 53.5 per cent of the forms had been returned. Double post cards were then sent to these prompt respondents, asking for only two items of information. Within three weeks, 73.7 per cent of the post cards had been returned. Curtis points out that one difference between the checking of the original long list and the post cards was in the greater proportion of unchecked items in the former. In 51 of the original returns, a particular item was unchecked, whereas on only four post cards was the item unchecked. This result seems to indicate that the more items on the questionnaire, the greater the chance that the informant will skip over any one item.

4. Letter of Transmittal. A letter of transmittal soliciting cooperation should accompany the questionnaire blank. It should be written on the official stationery of one of the survey sponsors. When possible, indicate by a letterhead that the survey has the backing of some agency with prestige in the community, such as a university or leading civic organization, or even the backing of a committee of leading citizens. The letter of transmittal should contain a statement of the purpose of the survey and the uses to be made of the data, together with instructions on how to fill out the form if such instructions are not printed on it. In market surveys of reactions to a particular product, Eastwood suggests that a "dummy company" be used to avoid bias in the result arising from the tendency of people to say things they think will please others (266). Frank and open criticisms of the product and policies of a company are possible only when steps are taken to prevent the respondent from identifying the investigation with the company.

It has been found that a personal touch in the letter of transmittal is quite effective in bringing in returns. A postscript which looks as if it were written by hand or a personal signature of the sender whose name appears on the stationery have proved effective. One mail advertiser even suggests making a mistake in spelling and correcting it in what appears to be his own handwriting! Many other suggestions of this type are to be found in the literature of advertising research.

It is surprising what seemingly insignificant factors influence the number of returns received. Market surveyors have found, for example, that the color of the stamp or printing permit on the card or envelope effects the results. According to Mayer (620), the relative order of color appeal in stamps is: purple, blue, red, brown, green, and black. New stamps or commemorative stamps affect results if used immediately after their issue, when they are still a novelty.

The kind of appeal which seems likely to bring in the highest proportion of returns should be pretested before adoption. Both quality and quantity of returns should be considered. In an examination of 500 questionnaire studies, Davis and Barrow (231) found that in educational surveys the most frequently used type of approach is "intercession," i.e., the investigator appeals first to someone in a position of either direct or indirect authority over the potential respondent. The authority then exerts pressure to see that the replies are filled out. This common procedure is not recommended because the informant resents the pressure placed upon him and the resulting responses are likely to be inaccurate. Various other types of appeals found by Davis and Barrow, listed in order of frequency, are: teacher-pupil; personal approach; appeal to interest; waiver of signature; committee or organization; letter preceding the questionnaire to learn whether recipient will agree to cooperate; promise of a summary.

Sletto tried three different appeals to comparable groups of former university students. "The first letter called upon the individual to help improve education for the thousands of young people who would be entering the university during the year. The second letter directed attention to the changes occurring in education and requested help to guide these changes 'in the right direction.' The third letter challenged the recipient to help do something that people say 'can't be done.' The letter explained that many people believed a study like this could not succeed because former university students are too much concerned with their personal affairs, or too uninterested in education to respond to a lengthy questionnaire" (878). The altruistic appeal of the first-mentioned letter proved to be the most effective, bringing in 67 per cent returns.

In market surveys, a promise that no salesman will follow up the reply may be needed to convince the respondent that the survey is not part of a sales campaign. A promise to quote neither name nor information without permission, or some other emphasis on the anonymity of the replies, may serve further to allay suspicion.

INDUCEMENTS TO REPLY:

Financial reward is not invariably effective. For instance, enclosing a 25-cent piece with the questionnaire has been tried, but the effectiveness of such an incentive varies, Watson (1064), points out that according to market research experience, letters appealing for information as a personal favor have been more productive than letters offering a trivial reward or stressing some alleged advantage to the respondent who answers. Shuttleworth (872) on the other hand, found in a study of adult attitudes toward the financial support of health work in New York State, that from the area in which a 25-cent coin accompanied the letter there was a return of 52 per cent of the blanks, while in the non-coin area the returns were only 19 per cent. Though the percentage of returns received from mail questionnaires in general was much lower than that obtained through interviews in the Hancock study of reaction to retail stores (392), the mail technique in which the letter to the addressee contained 25 cents brought a greater return (47.2%) than when no coin was enclosed (9.56%). When a promise to forward 25 cents upon receipt of the filled-out questionnaire was used, an intermediate percentage replied (17.6%).

A self-addressed envelope, whether stamped or business-reply-permit, seems to help. Practically all surveyors who have used the mail technique recommend enclosing a self-addressed stamped envelope of some sort with the questionnaire blank. A permit-return envelope or business reply envelope in which the recipient pays only for the envelopes actually returned may prove cheaper in some large-scale mail surveys than would the prestamped envelope. Existing evidence suggests, however, that the percentage of returns is significantly greater (about double) for the regular stamped envelope than for the business reply envelope (1064).

It has been claimed, however, that double return post cards are just as effective as stamped envelopes. Since the card must necessarily be limited to only a few items, the reason it is effective may be due to its brevity.

In view of the savings which could be made if the mail questionnaire brought in as large a proportion of the sample as could be obtained by interview, it might be worthwhile to experiment with really large inducements. For example, if a prize of $1,000 were to be given by the survey agency and the lucky winner was to be drawn by lot from among the respondents, it is quite likely that the response would be pretty good. Possibly a first, second, and third prize might be offered. The specifications for being eligible for the drawing might be that the questionnaire (1) was filled out only by the person to whom it was addressed, (2) that it was completely filled out, (3) that the information given was accurate (or in the case of an opinion poll, the *true* opinion of the informant), and (4) that the response was mailed back by a specified date.

The relatively few people who would not respond to an incentive of this type could be traced through secondary sources to determine what their characteristics were so that a technique for reaching them and securing their cooperation could be worked out. For some, a flat rate of $10 for their replies might be sufficient, while for others, some other appeal made through business associates, neighbors, or telephone, might work better. In other words, for the few nonrespondents, an individualized approach would be necessary.

This "prize" technique would be especially adapted to national surveys in which the sample was distributed at random over the entire country. Since many cities would have only one or even no cases, a personal approach for the entire sample would be financially prohibitive. On the other hand, it might be quite feasible to make contact with the small number of nonrespondents—or as a last resort, of a small random sample of nonrespondents, so their characteristics and reactions could be determined (see discussion on page 401) and the appropriate weights secured.

Before adopting any "prize" technique, the surveyor should acquaint himself with the federal laws on the prohibition of conducting a lottery through the mails. In designing the plan, federal postal authorities should be consulted to make certain that the plan is acceptable. If the questionnaire must be in the form of a contest, it is possible to give a prize for the best reason given for the informant's answers to a certain question on the schedule.

PRETESTING THE QUESTIONNAIRE:

Before the final form and procedure are adopted, preliminary experiments should be tried out on a sample population as is done in pilot interview surveys. When questionnaires are to be distributed on a large scale, it is absolutely essential to test the forms. If time is short, several small random samples may be used simultaneously, each one for a different schedule or technique. Sletto (878) spent more than six months constructing, testing, and revising a questionnaire before it was considered in final form, and the excellent results achieved indicated that pretesting paid.

The preliminary tests can answer questions about which one of several drafts (1) brings in the highest percentage of returns, (2) best fulfills the need for facts on the survey topic, (3) yields data which are suitable for tabulation, (4) indicates the informants have grasped what is wanted of them, (5) seems to yield the most reliable, accurate and complete information, and (6) is the simplest, shortest, and apparently most interesting.

When pretesting mail questionnaires, it is important always to cover a cross-section of the population eventually to be surveyed. When the sample is drawn, it should be broken down into various subsamples by taking, for instance, every tenth or every hundredth case from the entire list. If several such subsamples of, say, 25 or 50 cases each are available, the pretesting of subsamples is facilitated.

It is important for the pretester to bear in mind that he can test only *one* type of item at a time if he is interested in the percentage of returns received. He may vary color, size, method of mailing, appeal, printing, or any one of the other factors which may be likely to influence returns. In order that the results be clear-cut, he should make it a point to send out the questionnaire to comparable samples on the same day (unless he is testing day of mailing).

Testing, revising, and retesting questionnaires yield high dividends. Even persons most allergic to writing can, with proper inducement, be prevailed upon to answer questionnaires. It is the surveyor's job to find out what these appeals are.

MECHANICS OF SENDING THE QUESTIONNAIRE:

The sampling problems arising in connection with the choice of a list of persons who will be representative of the population about which information is desired has already been discussed. The problems of locating specific persons and of securing an up-to-date address list for them are especially troublesome in surveys conducted through the mail. When a significant proportion of the people fails to respond, it is important to learn whether or not the questionnaire was ever received. This may be accomplished with follow-up devices discussed later in this chapter.

Assuming that the mailing list is satisfactory, the most opportune time for sending out the questionnaire must be chosen. If it is desirable that all potential informants receive the letters at the same time, and if the survey is national in scope, those addressed to the distant points should be mailed first. The season of the year, the month, week, or time of the week during which a questionnaire should arrive in order to have the best chance of being filled out, will vary with the type of informants. Toops suggests that questionnaires to school men should be sent early in the school year before the pressure of duties decreases the chances of attention (969). Toops also reports that questionnaires tend to be filled out during weekends. He suggests that the questionnaire should not arrive so early in the week that it is laid aside, forgotten, or thrown in the wastebasket, but rather should arrive about Friday night or Saturday morning, whereupon it may receive immediate attention (967, p. 158). Such a rule would not apply to groups of the population, such as clergymen, who are busiest over weekends. Its effectiveness during summer vacation seasons, when people flock to shore resorts, is also questionable. Questionnaires sent to New York doctors concerning child health care were frequently answered the first part of the week. The general public probably differs from all of these selected groups. Certainly periods such as holidays, extremely hot weather, important national events, should be considered when mailing questionnaires.

NUMBER AND BIAS IN RETURNS TO BE EXPECTED:

Although the number of replies received will depend to a large extent on the amount of experimentation which has gone into the survey design and mailing technique, a certain proportion of nonrespondents cannot be prevented. Surveyors have found that such factors as (1) the characteristics such as sex, economic status, and educational level of the groups solicited; (2) the interest in the subject of the investigation; (3) the prestige of the sponsoring groups among the recipients of the questionnaires; (4) the appeal of the particular questionnaire; and (5) strong agreement or disagreement with the propositions about which they are surveyed, are all related to the proportion of replies obtained.

It has long been known that people who return questionnaires or who write to their congressmen are a highly selected element of the population.[1] Just what the characteristics are that are associated with mailed returns is becoming the object of much recent research. To begin with, in terms of numbers, the returns from mail questionnaires

---

[1] The Gallup Poll release of July 1, 1946, indicated that only one voter in seven had ever written to his Congressman, but more than twice as many business and professional people wrote such letters as white-collar workers or farmers.

are usually quite small, but as we shall see later, it is possible greatly to increase the proportion of returns by various devices—most important of which perhaps are the "follow-up" or "reminder" letters. By an analysis of the returns which are induced by the follow-up letters, it is possible to gauge the type of biases which would have existed in the sample and the data had the surveyor stopped with the single questionnaire. In some studies, the nonrespondents have been called upon by field interviewers who have secured the questionnaire information and thus rounded out the sample. The information gained about these "nonrespondents" thus is piling up rapidly. While it is impossible to cover *all* the literature about them, the mention of a few sources should serve to prove the biased nature of the population and of the data returned from mail questionnaires. Thus, unless the surveyor intends to see that in so far as possible every person to whom a questionnaire is mailed responds either by mail, telephone, or personal interview, or that a small random sample of the nonrespondents is covered by some means, he had better refrain from conducting the survey. The findings obtained almost certainly will be so biased that no statistical tabulation would be meaningful.

While the proportion of returns varies from survey to survey, and within a survey among various classes of the population, the experience of mail surveyors is that the percentage of replies varies by economic classes.

Katz and Cantril (499), in discussing the returns received by public opinion polls conducted by mail, reported that usually less than one-fifth of the mailed ballots are returned. A disproportionately high number came from people with intense opinions (reformers, arch conservatives, radicals) rather than those who were lukewarm or undecided, and from more highly educated and economically secure persons as well as from men. The American Institute of Public Opinion found that the highest returns (about 40 per cent) came from people listed in *Who's Who*, while 18 per cent of the people on telephone lists, 15 per cent of the registered voters in poor areas, and 11 per cent of people on relief returned their ballots.

During the 1944 presidential election campaign, ballots were mailed to names taken from telephone directories in five states and to persons who had passenger cars as well as telephones in eleven states. The returns for these sixteen states averaged 25.6 per cent (51).

The experience of the Literary Digest Poll in 1936 was in line with the above facts; slightly more than one-fifth of the ten million ballots which were sent out were returned. In attempting to check the findings during the course of the election campaign, the Literary Digest conducted a mail survey of *every third registered voter* in Chicago, *every other registered voter* in Scranton, Pennsylvania, and *every registered voter* in Allentown, Pennslyvania (582). In Chicago, one in five of the voters replied, and of these there was a preponderance of supporters of Mr. Landon. From the mail ballots it appeared that Landon would receive 48 per cent of the vote and Roosevelt 47.56. In the actual election, the vote was 65.24 per cent to 32.26 per cent in favor of Roosevelt in this city. In Allentown about one-third of the ballots were returned and these indicated 53.32 per cent for Landon. Actually he received 41.17 per cent and Roosevelt carried the city with 56.93 per cent of the vote. So even with a better sample source, that is, *registered voters* instead of *telephone lists* and *car registrations* such as were used in the countrywide poll, the Literary Digest Poll would have failed because of the unrepresentative character of mail respondents.

About 4 months before the 1936 election, the American Institute of Public Opinion said publicly that the Digest Poll was reaching too many upper income people and would forecast the Landon victory by 56 per cent to 44 per cent for Roosevelt. Digest Editors were indignant over the criticism which, however, proved to be accurate. The American Institute of Public Opinion in August, 1936, showed that 59 per cent of telephone owners were for Landon, that 56 per cent of automobile owners were for Landon and only 18 per cent of people on relief were for him.

The differential rate of mail return by economic classes is pointed out by Starch (914). In one survey in which 200 questionnaires were mailed out to each of four income groups, the returns varied as follows:

Income Class	% Returned
$0–999	2.6
1,000–1,999	2.5
2,000–4,999	14.1
5,000 and over	9.0
All classes	7.0

Studies by Reilly (764) and Stanton (910) show that in marketing surveys persons who are users of products are more apt to respond to mail questionnaires than are nonusers. Stanton reports a study in which a three-page questionnaire was sent to a list of 11,169 school teachers inquiring, among other things, about their possession and use of classroom radio receiving facilities. Approximately 28 per cent responded. Follow-ups to nonrespondents revealed that teachers without classroom radio facilities were more reluctant to reply and required the stimulus of reminders before responding. Reilly, in one mail survey of housewives, found that 92 per cent of the respondents were users of the product in question, while only 8 per cent were nonusers. Among those who did not answer the questionnaire, 40 per cent were users of the product and 60 per cent were nonusers.

Hancock (392) in a study of methods of surveying, employed three mail survey techniques and one personal interview method. The proportion of returns were as follows:

	% of Returns from All Solicited	Store Owners
Method I. Mail letter with appended explanation of purpose and instructions for filling in questionnaire.	9.56	12.5
Method II. Mail questionnaire accompanied by 25 cents to be kept for the trouble of filling out the form.	47.2	12.0
Method III. Mail questionnaire with promise of payment of 25 cents upon receipt of filled-in return.	17.6	10.5
Method IV. Personal interview method.	85.5	6.8

It is interesting to note that the subject matter of the above survey—attitude toward retail chain stores—resulted in a greater proportion of returns from store owners by the mail methods than by the personal interview method, thus confirming the findings of other research studies that intense feeling and familiarity with the subject brings disproportionately greater mail returns from the interested groups. The proportion of responses from store owners by the above methods is shown in the last column.

Suchman and McCandless (943) in a study of radio listening of 600 women whose names were selected from telephone directories, found that the factors of interest and familiarity with the topic under investigation and the education of the respondent influenced the number of returns from mail questionnaires (p. 769). This study pertained to listening to a child training program. Two "waves" of questionnaires were sent out. On the first, 16.8 per cent replied; on the second, 34.1 per cent answered. Then a random sample of the remaining cases were contacted by telephone, and 97.2 per cent cooperated. The authors state, "If we had stopped with the original returns . . . it would have been claimed that almost twice as many women knew about the program as really do" (p. 760). As for the educational bias of the replies from the first questionnaire, the authors report ". . . the percentage of highly educated informed listeners who returned the first wave of questionnaires in this case was more than eight times as great as the percentage of less-educated, uninformed, non-listeners" (p. 760).

The assumption often made by mail surveyors that the early returns come from as good a cross-section of the total as do the replies drifting in after several weeks is not borne out by a study reported by Toops (968). He claims that "there is a decided tendency for those recipients who are best known to the sender to reply earlier than strangers" (p. 96).

Deming and Simmons reported that in a survey of the stocks of retail tire dealers, the tire dealers who responded to the second follow-up letter had on hand an average of 10 tires per dealer as compared with an over-all average of 6 tires per dealer among those who had already responded (242, p. 18). Among the nonrespondents who were later contacted by personal interview, the average number of tires per dealer was 50 per cent higher than the average for all other dealers.

The same authors report that in September, 1944, during tire rationing, a survey by OPA of 140,989 retail tire dealers asking them for information on the number of tires held by them resulted in 83 per cent responses, even though a reply was more or less mandatory. In a later survey of the same group, in which personal interviews were used to follow up a sample of nonrespondents, the returns jumped to 99 per cent.

Biases in mail questionnaire returns are also likely to occur when the universe being sampled is that of business concerns instead of individuals. Lloyd, in commenting upon the sampling problems encountered in current trade statistics, said that there is a positive correlation between the size of individual firms and their willingness and ability to contribute figures (583, p. 374).

SPECIAL REASONS FOR NONRESPONSE:

Although the main task of persons in charge of sampling when mail questionnaires are used is to induce people to return the forms which they received, another set of problems arises when questionnaires are not received or are no longer applicable to the situation of the informant. When the failure to respond is due to lack of interest or unwillingness to cooperate in the survey, there is a chance of inducing replies by the follow-up procedures discussed later. There are many other reasons, however, for unreturned questionnaires, and these are not so easily solved.

Most questionnaires are sent to specific people who have once belonged to a given group, or in some way have become identified with it so as to get on a list. This list is usually out of date. People who once were members or once were interested in a given activity may no longer be interested or eligible to reply at the time the questionnaire is sent to them. For example, if a survey were being made of the number of patients seen by physicians during a specified week, several physicians who received the questionnaire might no longer be practicing, so the questionnaire would not be applicable to them. Those who had retired permanently would probably need to be differentiated from those who (1) had gone on a short vacation, (2) were ill and (a) might never practice again, (b) would probably begin practicing within a week or two. To ascertain the approximate number of patients visiting doctors, the surveyor would have to decide what effect the omission or inclusion of these cases would have on the averages or frequencies resulting in the survey.

Since the address list is usually dated, a number of persons to whom questionnaires were mailed would have moved—some in the city and some to other communities or even farther. Other people will have disappeared or died. Still others will be away temporarily—on vacation, on business, in hospitals, in the armed forces.

An incorrect address on the original list or a mistake made when the questionnaire was addressed may also result in failure to respond. If the address on the list is a business address, the questionnaire may not come to the attention of the informant desired.

If the mailing list happens to be an address list, and the questionnaire is addressed to "the householder" at a given address, failure to respond may mean (1) that it is a business address and has no householder (2) that the building which formerly had that address has been torn down, or (3) that the address is a multiple-family dwelling unit and there is no *one* householder.

Sometimes it takes a long time for mail to return to the original sender when not claimed by the addressee. So, if there is any doubt about the availability of or likelihood of there being a respondent, a special delivery letter may be used with a notice of delivery. The number of cases lost for such reasons, of course, will vary with the recency of the list and with the mobility of the people surveyed. Before deciding to omit all cases which are difficult or impossible to trace, the sampling supervisor should carefully consider the effect these omissions will have upon the generalizations and decide whether it is necessary to add to the sample people who have become eligible for the list by reason of their immigration to the community.

FOLLOW-UP EFFORTS:

Even with careful pretesting of all forms and techniques, complete returns cannot be secured without reminders to those who do not respond. As is shown in Chapter XII, the nonrespondents are from highly selected groups. To omit their replies from most tabulations of mail results is likely to leave the findings open to question. This applies especially to tabulations of subgroups or cross-classifications.

Aside from the reduction or elimination of bias, it is cheaper to use small samples with follow-up letters than larger samples without reminders. Lindsay points out that in his surveys the follow-up card and letter were of much greater value in securing returns than was the original questionnaire (571, p. 305). This finding is corroborated by Suchman and McCandless who found that a higher total response was obtained with a follow-up to nonrespondents than would have been secured if the original sample had been doubled (943, p. 766). Lundberg states that the amount of follow-up required will vary with (1) the mandatory power or prestige of the surveyor, (2) the simplicity of the schedule, (3) the educational level of the recipients of the questionnaire, (4) interest in the survey topic, and (5) the need for precision in the results (597, p. 205).

1. Form of Follow-Up.   The first follow-up usually takes the form of a short note or post card reminding the recipient that he has not yet sent in the form. A tactful suggestion may be included to the effect that the reply may be on the way, in which case to disregard the reminder.

The second reminder may include a copy of the original questionnaire because by this time it may have been misplaced. Another follow-up device is the use of a special delivery letter. In case the name or address is incorrect, a deliver-to-addressee-only, return-receipt requested, registered mail, is likely to reveal such an error. Shuttleworth (873) employed this technique with some success in a survey of former graduates of a university. His last resort was a systematic personal canvass of those who still failed to reply. This procedure yielded a return from every case outstanding for which a sufficient address could be obtained.

The follow-up of those persons on the mailing list who have telephones may take the form of a telephone call. If the budget permits, more drastic measures such as sending a telegram may bring in returns from the last remaining cases. If all efforts to bring in the last replies fail, the following procedure for correcting the bias in the sample might be employed: A random subsample of, say, 300 cases could be drawn from the list originally sent the questionnaire. The nonrespondents in this subsample should constitute a manageable number. If the survey is limited to the inhabitants of one community, a field worker could be employed to conduct a personal interview with the nonrespondents. The oral replies of these informants might be regarded as representative of the other nonrespondents and weighted to take care of the nonrespondents in the sample as a whole.

2. Number of Follow-Ups.   Apparently, the greater the number of follow-up letters, the higher the proportion of returns which may be expected (within certain limits, of course). Toops (968) sent as many as six letters and in the sixth promised not to bother his informants again if they heeded this last appeal. In this way he secured 100 per cent returns on a questionnaire to trade school graduates.

3. When to Send Follow-Up Letters.   Two procedures have been followed in mailing follow-up letters. One, recommended by Lindsay (571), consisted in sending out the first follow-up at the end of 16 days when the curve of replies started to show a definite decline. Then, instead of waiting for a second downward trend, the second follow-up was sent out approximately one week after the first. The third follow-up was sent out two weeks after the second. This close spacing of the first and second follow-up letters was in accord with the theory that the stimuli to strengthen recall should come soon after the original impression and be repeated thereafter at gradually increasing intervals. Lindsay's questionnaire, which required about one-half day to fill out, was sent to public officials who were not accustomed to cooperating on mail surveys. Nevertheless, this follow-up procedure resulted in returns from more than 90 per cent of those solicited.

The more usual timing of follow-up letters consists in waiting until daily returns have dwindled low before sending out a reminder. Suchman and McCandless (943) waited until not more than one return per day (of a total of 600 names drawn from the telephone directory) was received in five successive days before dispatching a second "wave" of questionnaires. After a similar period of waiting, every second person from among those who had not responded was called by telephone. It was assumed that the sample called by telephone was representative of the others who had not returned questionnaires. For each wave, the proportion returned of those sent out was: original questionnaire, 16.8 per cent; second wave, 34.1 per cent; residual sample (telephone) 97.2 per cent. In another survey conducted among persons known to be interested in the subject matter of the survey (a survey on music of subscribers to a booklet listing the music broadcasts of a radio station) the same authors report the percentage of returns received from each wave of questionnaires: (uncumulated percentages) first wave, 44.3 per cent; second, 46.4 per cent; third, 50.3 per cent; and fourth, 66.5 per cent. The cumulated per cent of the total amounted to 95.1 per cent of the 820 persons solicited in the sample.

Stanton reports receiving a 94 per cent return to a nine-page questionnaire by means of three follow-ups. The first was dispatched when 54 per cent of the replies had been received (910, p. 102). Stanton also points out that in commercial studies mail is usually accepted for three weeks before tabulation is begun. It is assumed that 90 per cent of the total possible returns are in by that time (910, p. 99, footnote). In two studies which he conducted, 95 per cent of the questionnaires received were returned within 30 days.

The question of the validity and the reliability of data received from mail questionnaire surveys is discussed in Chapter XVI. The surveyor should be familiar with these concepts before proceeding to set up a survey by mail. Equally important, however, is the need for understanding the effect of selective returns upon the findings of mail surveys. As has been pointed out, there is abundant evidence that the people who reply to the first wave of questionnaires are not representative of the total population solicited. Unless every effort is made to secure a high percentage of returns, the mail technique should not be employed.

CONTROL OF THE SAMPLE:

While the drop between the number of cases drawn in a sample and the number finally tabulated is often rather marked in surveys conducted through field visits and telephone interviews, the loss can in no way compare with the drops usually occurring when mail questionnaires are employed. Most mail questionnaires bring so few returns, and these from such a highly selected population, that the findings of such surveys are almost invariably open to question.

Although most surveys conducted by mail are failures from the scientific viewpoint, it is possible to make a mail survey which will stand the test of scientific scrutiny—a survey in which the returns tabulated will come from or be representative of the population solicited.

After the questionnaire has been devised and tested, and the sample selected, a very strict control system should be set up to try to get returns from individuals belonging in the sample. This means, first of all, keeping very close tab on the identity of every case to whom the form is sent. If the informant is not asked to sign his name, an identifying number should appear on the form so that the surveyor will know whether or not a reply has been received. In one study, the surveyor thought he would get better and more frank returns if he indicated that he was not interested in the identity of the informants, so he devised a code for identifying the returned questionnaires. The code used was a number which he called the "Room Number" at the address to which the informants were to send their replies. Every schedule mailed out had a different room number listed for the designated address, and thus to the office (798). Such deception is probably unnecessary, since few people question the use of a serial number on the form if they are assured that their replies are to be tabulated in statistical tables and that the information given by any individual will be seen only by staff members who are pledged to respect the confidence of the informant.

If follow-up letters and letters of appeal do not bring in replies from all nonrespondents to the first questionnaire, it is necessary to determine their number and characteristics. If the survey is conducted within a given city or within a short distance of the survey headquarters, it is possible to call upon the nonrespondents and explain the situation to them. If a good interviewer is employed for this purpose, it should be possible to "recapture" all outstanding cases. A telephone call to those listed in the directory may save interviewers' time, but there will always be some who cannot be reached this way. If a few still remain after field efforts have failed, an analysis by characteristics listed below, or some other facts gleaned either from the desired informant, from neighbors, or from secondary sources should enable the surveyor to piece out a sample which is a true cross-section of the population surveyed. By analyzing the reasons for the uncooperative attitude and the characteristics of the few who refused to give the schedule information, it may be possible to suggest where such cases would fall in the main tabulation of the survey, had they been included. The best procedure, however, is to sample the nonrespondents and call upon them personally or by telephone interview to get the data. The sample can then be weighted before it is combined with the larger sample of respondents.

ANALYSIS OF UNRETURNED QUESTIONNAIRES:

Following is a list of checks which can be made upon the characteristics of persons returning and those not replying to questionnaires:

1. The geographical distribution of the addresses from which a reply was received can be compared with those from which no return was made. This distribution could be by states, counties, cities, wards, census tracts, or enumeration districts. Data available about the districts, e.g., average rent, per cent of owned homes, and much other census data should throw considerable light on the type of people who are not responding and thus on biases which are developing in the sample.

2. In any city, the proportion of each group who are telephone users should indicate possible economic biases.

3. By checking the sample against the city directory list, one could get a rough indication of the occupational composition, home owner-ship, or marital status of the nonrespondents as compared with the respondents.

4. A comparison of the percentage of car owners (from automobile registrations) of the respondents and nonrespondents should give a clue as to possible sampling biases.

5. Other lists such as those mentioned in discussing Social Background Data should be examined to determine which groups are dispropor-tionately represented among those who did not fill in the question-naire.

Selected References

Bain (25), Benson (51), Bevis (61), Cahalan and Meier (131), Cassady and Haas (150), Corey (196), Dartmouth (227), Davis and Barrow (231), Desing (246), Edgerton et al. (274), Fallon (293), Frank (325), Franken (327), Franzen (329), Franzen and Lazarsfeld (332), Gerberick and Mason (354), Hancock (392), Hankinson (393), Hobson (443), Hubbard (459), Kelley (500, 501), Koos (531, 532), Lawson (541), Lazarsfeld (546), Lazarsfeld and Franzen (553), Lindsay (571), *Literary Digest* (581, 582), Manfield (611), Mayer (620), Meredith Pub. Co. (638), Mitchell (649), Moore (654), Norton (701), Pace (710), Perry (733, 734), Phillips (742), Reid (763), Reuss (768), Rit-tenburg (784), Rollis (798), Ruckmick (822), Rushmore (827), Salisbury (830), Shannon (863), Shuttleworth (872, 873), Sletto (878), Smith (890), Stanton (910), Stapel (913), Stoke and Lehman (932), Suchman and McCandless (943), Toops (967, 968, 969, 970, 971), Wagner (1045), Watson (1064), Weaver (1065, 1066, 1069), Whitney (1087), Wilson (1110), Wyant (1129), Wylie (1130).
See also books on Social Surveys or Market Research.

Sources of Bias

Statisticians have grouped errors into two types—*random, chance, or accidental errors*—those which arise from a multiple number of small factors and which will tend, in the long run, to have a nullifying effect on each other since they are as likely to be in one direction as the other —and *constant, noncompensating or biased errors.* The first type of error is treated fully in most statistical textbooks, but biased error is passed over with more or less general statements that such errors exist and should be avoided. Ways in which to discover biased errors and methods of avoiding them have received very little treatment by social statisticians. It is not unusual to find very refined statistical techniques used to measure random errors in data which are so biased that all the corrective devices known would not enable the surveyor to determine what the correct results should be. As a matter of fact, research in the social sciences is still at a stage where biased errors are likely to be twenty to a hundred times as great as random errors unless the survey and sampling are very carefully designed and executed.

At every stage of survey procedure biases may creep in and vitiate the findings, unless the surveyor is on guard. Even though some of the biases may not significantly influence the findings as a whole, they may affect certain subgroups of the survey. Unless the surveyor is aware of possible biases and is constantly testing their magnitude, his findings may be the reverse of what they would have been had he had unbiased data. But unfortunately, neither he nor anyone else is likely to know the true situation from the survey data.

It is impossible to present a list which will cover the infinite number of points in survey procedure at which biases may enter. The most that can be accomplished is to make the surveyor aware of common procedures which result in biased data, and to familiarize him with some approaches which are used to detect, prevent, and correct biasing elements. Most of the chapters in the present book include discussions of error-producing procedures which should be avoided if biased results are to be prevented.

A BIASED SOURCE LIST:

Beginning with the determination of what constitutes the universe of discourse, the surveyor must recognize that he can generalize with certainty only for the universe which he has sampled. If certain parts of it are not given a chance to be sampled, the definition of the universe must be changed or else the surveyor must admit that he has a biased portion of the universe for which he is generalizing. Often the source or list from which the sample is to be selected is biased because it contains only easily accessible cases. In order to get on a list, the individual usually has to belong to some organization, subscribe to something, have a more or less permanent address, or take part in activities of the community.

A concrete example of how great the temptation is to select an "easy" source for a sample may be cited. In one city it was decided to investigate the economic and social conditions of domestic servants. The suggestion was made that all employment agencies in the city be contacted and a list of their applications and placements in domestic service during the past year (or some other period of time) be sampled. Had this source been used, it is not likely that the sample would have been representative of domestic servants in the city. Without looking at the records it was possible to think of a number of factors which would differ among the servants who had not been to the employment exchange. Are servants who are not listed by the employment exchanges like those who are? In the first place, those who had not changed positions or who had not contemplated changing positions would not have been listed. Are steady workers more satisfied with their lot than are the more mobile groups? If so, is it because their condition of employment is better? In the second place, servants who have secured positions through recommendations of friends or relatives would not be listed. If the payment of minimum wages were required by employment exchanges from prospective employers, the rates of pay might conceivably be lower among employers who hired their servants without the aid of an employment agency. In the third place, those servants who could not afford to pay an agency commission or who thought they might have to pay an agency commission would not be included in the sample. Probably such servants come from lower economic groups than those listed with agencies. Still another selective factor operated to keep certain servants away from employment exchanges. Those whose families were receiving public relief and who did not want to report income from domestic work might not go to an employment agency where a record would be made of their employment. The preceding considerations represent the type of reasoning which should be applied to any source which is used as a basis from which a sample is drawn. If, in the above study, one were interested only in the type of case handled by employment exchanges and not in the type of case which such agencies conceivably might handle through a process of public education with regard to the facilities of the exchange, a sample drawn from the exchange records might be quite satisfactory. But the source must be chosen from the point of view of the population for which the surveyor hopes to generalize.

If the source is known to be biased or deficient in any respect, it is still possible to use it providing it is supplemented by other sources which contain the missing groups.

In line with material presented later in this chapter, the assumption that certain groups can be omitted entirely from the sample and still "not have any effect upon the results" is one of the most dangerous assumptions one can make. For example, if the list from which a sample was to be drawn did not contain cases who had become eligible for inclusion on the list but had not been added, for instances, because of the clerical time required to make such additional entries, the surveyor should admit that his findings did not relate to the current group of eligible cases, but only to those who were listed on a given date. If the surveyor did not make this admission but generalized for current cases as well, it might legitimately be said that he had a biased sample of the cases in his universe. In other words, a population which might be a good sample of one universe might be a biased sample of another. Polls in which the surveyor expects to measure the voting intention of people who are going to vote in the next election cannot draw the sample solely from lists of persons who voted at the preceding election. Persons just reaching voting age, for example, would not be on such a list. And, as Katz and Cantril pointed out, a correlation exists between age and conservatism (499, p. 169).

Surveyors who wish to survey a cross-section of the family population and who draw their samples from the telephone directory are biasing their sample in favor of the middle and upper income groups. Similarly, radio audience research conducted by means of telephone interviews does not tap the lower economic groups in the correct proportion. For many purposes such a universe is satisfactory, but the findings of such surveys should not be regarded as applicable to the entire family population.

One mistaken assumption is that even though one bias is known to exist in the sample, all other "relevant" factors in the survey are unbiased. It would be more correct to assume that if the existence of a single bias has been demonstrated, others are likely to be found. The reason for this assumption is that social and economic factors are all so closely associated. If the surveyor knows, for example, that his sample is biased in that it contains more telephone subscribers than are found in the community as a whole, what other biases are likely to exist? We have already mentioned the economic bias—the income groups will not be proportionate to their distribution in the city as a whole; the lower income groups will be underrepresented. Home tenure also will be misrepresented; a much higher percentage of telephone subscribers are home owners than of non-telephone subscribers. Other characteristics are associated with home ownership—mobility, for instance. The people reached by telephone are much more stable residents of the community than are the nonusers. Their purchases will be of a different type from those of tenant families. Furthermore, the family composition, religion, political affiliation, the number of earners, the age of the family head and countless other factors are correlated either directly or indirectly with the telephone subscription bias. In view of these many known interrelationships, it is much safer to assume that any known bias is a signal that other biases exist in the sample and in the data secured from the sample than to assume that the data are "O.K. except for this one item."

ERRORS DURING DRAWING OF SAMPLES:

In addition to the bias which may result from the definition of the universe and from the selection of a source list which is supposed to constitute the universe, numerous biases may arise when the sample is being selected from the source list. The discussion of the errors which can arise in the drawing of samples is described in Chapter VIII.

NONRANDOM FIELD SELECTION:

When sample cases are to be selected by interviewers in accordance with a "quota" assignment, the sampling tends to be biased unless carefully controlled. Surveyors have found that interviewers tend to choose respondents who belong to the same social and economic groups as themselves. They have also found that interviewers contact too many residents of one-family houses, American-born, and next-door neighbors. Katz pointed out that interviewer selectivity gives the well-educated groups about 15 per cent overrepresentation in quota samples (495). Assignment by rent levels, such as is done by the National Opinion Research Center, partially overcomes this tendency.

POOR QUESTION FRAMING:

This is one of the greatest sources of bias in surveys. Many examples of the effect of question wording and sequence of questions were given in Chapter VI. Leading questions, those which state the issues in a biased manner, questions which are misunderstood by most respondents, and questions which assume knowledge on the part of the informant in fields where his knowledge is very slight or lacking entirely will all lead to biased replies. Suchman and Guttman (942) cite one example of what soldiers thought about the army. Two sets of six questions each were used; one set stressed the undesirable aspects of army life while the other set secured opinions on the desirable features. The surveyor might have concluded from one set that majority opinion was unfavorable to the army, but if he had used the other set of questions he would have come to the opposite conclusion. Biases of this type might be avoided if the techniques outlined by these authors are followed (942).

POOR ASSIGNMENT AND OFFICE PROCEDURES:

Oversights in the office which result in the failure to assign schedules or to process them when they are turned in may produce serious biases in the findings. If schedules for families located in certain sections of the city are misplaced or lost, the omission from tabulation may not come to light until the field work has been completed and the final inventory has been made.

Biases in the sample may occur if the schedules have been assigned by districts and the study terminates before all districts have been assigned or surveyed. Usually the poor sections of the city are scheduled first, because interviewers are less likely to be refused in these areas, and because the experience gained from such interviews enables interviewers to handle the more difficult cases in the upper income districts. In such cases, a sudden termination of field work before the higher economic areas have been covered may leave a decidedly biased sample.

FAULTY INTERVIEWING:

Unless interviewers are adequately trained in the art of asking questions and reporting opinions they are likely to bias returns. Rice (771) analyzed data on homeless men collected by two investigators, one of them a prohibitionist and the other a socialist. The former reported that in a preponderance of cases the difficulties were caused by liquor, while the latter found that the primary cause lay in industrial factors. One suggestion for minimizing interviewer bias is to employ an equal number of interviewers who are biased in different directions. This is not practicable, however, for surveys which cover a wide variety of topics or which employ the same interviewers for periodic surveys. It is far better to frame questions which can be presented and recorded objectively by skilled interviewers.

Interviewers may falsify information and thus make it necessary to discard their schedules. Proper survey procedures should, however, require enough check interviewing of the schedules turned in by each agent to discover unreliable agents before many schedules have been taken. It would be inadvisable to penalize agents for a high percentage of refusals without such a check, since there is some danger that interviewers might begin reporting families as "not at home" rather than as "refusing." Interviewers may keep in their possession schedules for which the information has been refused and report them as "in process." This is more likely to happen in large-scale studies which do not exercise careful control of the assignment and intake of cards. Often these biases in the sample are not discovered until the final inventory of collection is made.

UNTRUTHFUL INFORMANTS:

Unless questions are very carefully framed, there is danger that informants will be tempted to overstate or understate answers to certain questions. It is well known, for example, that educational attainment tends to be exaggerated unless the question is properly framed (see page 170). Other questions involving the prestige of the informant are also subject to misstatement in the reply. In three studies of the redemption of war bonds, display of government posters, and absenteeism, those questions with prestige value resulted in distorted responses amounting to as much as 42% when checked with actual records (462). When respondents are asked to classify themselves into economic groups, the top groups tend to regard themselves as middle class as do the lowest groups.

NOT-AT-HOMES:

Perhaps the greatest cause of biased returns is to be found in the omission of sample cases who are not at home when the interviewer calls. Many of these represent cases in which both the husband and wife work outside the home during the day. Hence there is less chance of finding anyone at home and of obtaining information. Such families are less likely than the general population of families to have small children; they have more earners than the average family, and therefore often represent a somewhat higher income group than the average of the population.

If the collection work of the survey extends over the summer months, it is almost impossible to find well-to-do families in their city homes. During the Urban Study of Consumer Purchases in Chicago, for instance, over half of the families in the better districts moved to resort or vacation places during the summer months.

Among families who may be at home there is less chance of making contact with families in the upper class apartments than in the one or two family units. In some of these apartment buildings the interviewer will not be admitted unless he specifically asks for a family by name. Since apartment dwellers move frequently, it is difficult to obtain the name of the particular family drawn in the sample. Inasmuch as the refusal of a single building superintendent or janitor is often equivalent to the refusal of all families in the building who were chosen in the sample, a significant underrepresentation of those upper income apartment dwellers is inevitable. Generally speaking, no such barriers exist in interviewing families residing in middle and low rent dwellings.

In one study made by the Bureau of Agricultural Economics it was found that people who are at home at the time of the first call by the interviewer are more likely to have home gardens than are those who are away. Also those home on the second call are more likely to have gardens than are those located on the third call. In a study of consumer requirements, the not-at-homes on the first call differed little in their replies about possessions of electric irons, radios, or refrigerators, but they differed significantly in their ownership of homes, washing machines, and sewing machines (436).

Among telephone users surveyed for radio research, from 20 to 30 per cent of the calls indicate that no one is at home and awake. As was pointed out in Chapter III, real differences in family composition are associated with staying or not staying at home.

Kiser (522) describes certain difficulties encountered when trying to secure a representative sample for the study of birth dates. In the original survey no attempt was made to revisit "missed" families, i.e., those not at home on the first call. Neither did the first survey secure fertility data for secondary families, i.e., married persons in the household other than the head and wife. In order to secure such information more field work was conducted and data obtained from persons missed in the original survey. On the basis of this additional sample, Kiser analyzed the selective factors involved in the failure to make recalls and in the failure to enumerate secondary families. He found that the original sample contained too many large families. This he attributed to the fact that the "not at home" group were more likely to be married women who work away from home and who are more often childless. The analysis confirmed this hypothesis: 18.6 per cent of the women in the original sample, 23.4 of those scheduled on the return call to primary families, and 28.5 of the women in secondary families were childless. "The greatest difference between the samples was found among women 30–44. In this age group only 15.3 of the women in the original primary sample were childless, as compared with 22.3 per cent of those in the additional primary, and 34.4 per cent of those in the secondary sample" (522, pp. 255–256).

The omission of the secondary families in the first survey led to an age bias in which the younger married women, the daughters and daughters-in-law, and the older ones, the mothers and mothers-in-law of the family head were omitted.

Another bias in the original sample was noted. "The women included in the secondary families were survivors of broken unions to a greater degree than those in primary families. Many were doubtless living in the households of their parents or children simply because their own homes were broken" (522, p. 256). Only 47.2 per cent of the women of secondary families were living with their husbands at the time of the enumeration, 89.1 per cent of the women in the original sample, and 84.8 per cent in the additional primary sample.

A study of the selective factors involved in trying to reinterview a sample who have once cooperated is reported by Gaudet and Wilson (348). A sample of 2800 individuals in an Ohio county were interviewed in May, 1940, on their radio and reading habits, political opinions, and personal characteristics. From this sample a representative sample of 1800 was selected to be reinterviewed a couple of months later. Of these 3 per cent refused, 6 per cent were unavailable or impossible to locate owing to vacations, illness, death, and migration, and 91 per cent cooperated. Significant differences were found in the economic status, educational level, occupation, and age of the three groups—Refusals, Cooperative Cases, and Unavailable. The political opinion held by each of these groups on the initial interview also indicated important differences. Lack of interest in the coming election, for example, was found to be much higher among the refusals and unavailable cases than in the cooperative group.

The expense of call-backs on the not-at-homes has led surveyors to search for some more economical way of avoiding biases due to failure to interview such persons. One proposal which was first discussed by H. O. Hartley, commenting on a paper by Yates (1132) in 1946, was independently put forth by Politz and Simmons (747). The plan assigns to each individual found at home a weight equal to the reciprocal of the time he spends at home. It is assumed that visits are scheduled at times chosen at random, and therefore whether or not a particular individual is at home is a function of the amount of time he spends at home. According to the plan suggested by the last-mentioned authors, each person in the sample is visited only once. Those who are contacted are asked whether they were at home on specific instances during the week. This permits an estimate of the proportion of time the informant was at home during hours when interviewers call. Schedules are then classified into, e.g., six groups according to the estimated proportion of time people in each group are at home—one-sixth, two-sixths, three-sixths, etc. Estimates for any variable being surveyed are produced by weighting the results for each group by the reciprocal of the estimated per cent that persons are at home.

The following type of questioning is recommended for assisting the informant to recall how often he was at home during the interview period of the past week, e.g., on a Saturday night interview the remarks would be: "We are interested in finding out how often people go out in the evening at various times and on various days of the week. I wonder if you would mind telling me

1. Whether or not you happened to be at home last night at just this time?
2. How about the night before last at this time?
3. How about Wednesday night?
4. How about Tuesday night?
5. Monday night?

According to one study, the proportion of time informants were at home according to a record kept by interviewers was 61.1. Basing the answer on respondents' answers as to the nights they were at home, the percentage was almost identical, 61.5 (747).

REFUSALS AND OMISSIONS:

Uncooperative and inaccessible people, for example, are serious threats to the representativeness of the final sample. Social statisticians frequently assume that families who refuse to give information requested by interviewers represent a cross-section of all families surveyed.[1] On a priori grounds it has been argued that refusals are dependent upon such a variety of causes, the most important of which is the mood of the moment, and that the final inventory should show a random selection of unobtained schedules. Unfortunately, there is considerable evidence to show that this assumption is false. Not only are

---

[1] This section, through page 417, is a revision of a paper by the author on "The Analysis and Treatment of Refusals and Partial Information Schedules in Social Surveys," delivered at the Annual Meeting of the American Sociological Society, December 28, 1937.

refusals highly selected with respect to certain characteristics, but missing items on partially completed schedules are also concentrated in certain questions and in selected groups of the population.

Unlike surveys conducted by mail in which only a small percentage of families usually respond, social surveys conducted by means of trained interviewers often yield 90 per cent or more of the families selected. While such a high return is often regarded by surveyors as entirely adequate, this confidence is often unwarranted. Even though unobtained schedules may not distort the averages for the total community very seriously, subclasses of the population may be thrown out of line by differential refusal rates.

Once the interviewer has access to the family, selective factors operate to produce more refusals on the part of the upper income groups than among the lower groups. To begin with, servants answering doors may have blanket instructions to turn away all solicitors. It may be difficult for the interviewer to convince servants that he does not fall in this category. Upper income groups sometimes regard themselves superior to the interviewer and unless they are convinced of the value of the cause served, they may not hesitate to refuse. Persons of superior economic status are apt to be reticent about personal affairs; this is not characteristic, in general, of the wage earner group. Families receiving relief especially are more or less accustomed to giving out information and may feel that there is something to be gained by divulging their situation to the interviewer.

Middle and upper income families are more often members of pressure groups than are the lower. Thus these higher income groups may have a tutored negative reaction to the agency making the survey. For example, just before the 1936 presidential election, many Republican organizations voiced opposition to any New Deal enterprises. In one of the cities surveyed by a government agency during this period, members of a Republican women's organization decided to refuse to give the information solicited. It was only after special efforts were made to convince the women of this community that the survey was to their advantage that this "organized resistance" was overcome. Cases have also been reported in which one or two women have caused a number of refusals through their influence upon residents of the same block or neighborhood or members of the same bridge club. In such cases if the ringleader is "won over" to the survey, it is usually possible to secure the desired information from the others. Most of such instances have been reported for middle and upper income group families rather than for the lower.

Other potential informants may be temporarily or permanently unable to give the desired information. For example, families in which there is sickness or those in which a death has occurred recently may not be in a position or mood to respond to a questioner. In some cases a return visit to such families may yield the desired information. In a health survey or in studies of expenditures for medical care, the failure to get information from such families may seriously bias the results.

The inability of some of the lower income groups to speak or understand English may result in too few schedules from such families. Usually, however, neighbors or older children in the family may be used as interpreters. Some surveys employ interviewers who can speak the most prevalent foreign language in the survey area, but this is usually not necessary unless the community contains a large recent immigrant group.

Aside from these factors producing refusals on the part of the family, the interviewing technique as well as errors of the interviewer may be responsible for failure to obtain complete schedules. The interviewer may not be competent to "sell the survey" to the person interviewed or he may have an antagonistic personality which produces refusals. In higher economic districts particularly, interviewers who do not make a good appearance or who are relatively uneducated have difficulty. Generally speaking, very little "selling" of the survey is necessary in poor districts of most cities, so refusals attributable to the enumerator or to his technique tend to produce an underrepresentation of higher economic groups.

In any large-scale survey it is inevitable that a number of schedules will be only partially completed and so may have to be discarded. Although the types of questions or the subject matter of the survey may determine the extent to which schedule data are incomplete, the amount of supervision and training given the interviewers also affects the usability of returns.

Consider first the reasons respondents refuse to answer certain questions. Resistance may be due to the wish to conceal certain facts, particularly those relating to financial status if there is any doubt about the uses to be made of such information. Wealthy informants may feel that information on income may be used for taxation purposes or to check on income tax returns. Families receiving relief may think that the relief agency is checking up on their income, so they may not admit earnings from private employment. In one of the national surveys conducted with relief workers as interviewers, relief officials drawn in the sample of one of the cities refused to answer the income items because they did not want their relief employees to know this information. The schedules were completed, however, by sending the filled in questionnaire to headquarters in another city. In a survey in which doctors were asked to cooperate, a number were uncooperative because they feared the findings when published would lead to socialized medicine.

In addition to fear of the uses to be made of the information there is also the feeling among families that certain questions are of a private nature and should not be made public. Women, for example, are less likely than men to tell their ages. The same women may report the ages of their husbands, while failing to give their own. Reluctance to give age may be especially prevalent among unmarried spinsters or any older married women who are trying to compete with younger women in occupations outside their homes. The nature of certain illnesses also may be concealed. Marital status is an item about which divorced or separated persons tend to be sensitive.

Aside from deliberate intention to conceal or give misleading information, respondents may not know the information asked for. For example, persons who own and operate small business enterprises may find it extremely difficult or often impossible to differentiate between business and personal or family income. Farmers also have difficulty estimating their incomes. Wage and salary workers, on the other hand, are likely to be able to supply this information.

Incomplete schedules may be due in a large measure to faulty procedure by the interviewer. He may omit certain questions intentionally or accidentally. If he is rushed, he may skip over items which are time consuming; he may also omit items to avoid a refusal or to prevent antagonizing the informant; he may think certain questions are inapplicable and therefore omit them; he may develop faulty recording habits and consistently fail to fill in an item or enter it incorrectly. In other cases the entries made by the agent may be so illegible that they cannot be interpreted. The interviewer may also misunderstand the questions or the answers and thus record a meaningless or wrong entry. He may not follow the instruction for recording the information and thus make data unusable for tabulation.

If the interviewer leaves the items blank it may mean one of several things. It may mean that the question was not applicable to the particular family situation; it may mean that the question was not asked; it may mean the answer was "no" or "zero"; or it may indicate that the informant was unable to or unwilling to answer the question. When the question is not asked or an answer is refused by the informant, bias is probably indicated.

Despite efforts to obtain complete schedules from all families in a sample, it is practically impossible to secure completed and acceptable information on *every item*, not only because of time limitations which are imposed on every field survey, but also because of the expense of maintaining a special staff for contacting resistant or inaccessible families. There comes a point at which all field work must cease, regardless of the stage of completion. From this point on the analysis of what was not obtained becomes very important to a proper interpretation of the data.

In the New Haven Random Sample Family Survey, in which 2097 families were scheduled during the months of May and June in 1933, 12 families had moved to the country for the summer months. It was possible to obtain some information on every one of the remaining cases. The extent to which the schedules were incomplete for various items gives us a clue as to types of data most difficult to obtain. Since no special effort was made to obtain one type of information instead of another, the frequency with which the various items were omitted may be similar to what other surveyors would find if they did not emphasize the need for certain minimum information.

Of eight types of items analyzed, education of the head of the family seemed to be the greatest stumbling block—slightly over one-tenth of the persons interviewed either refused this information or were unable to give it. Family income ran a close second with 10 per cent lacking this item. Third position among the missing items was shared by the rent item (4 per cent) and religion of the family head (4 per cent). The other four items—country of birth of head, number of persons in the family, occupation, and age of family head—were lacking in fewer than one per cent of the schedules.

Since many surveys attempt to ascertain the economic level of persons surveyed, the characteristics of families in which income data are not obtained is of interest. Since the schedules with income unreported were complete for certain other items, it was possible to glean something about the composition of families who failed to report their incomes. The distribution of families with known income was compared with the distribution of those with unreported income for seven types of items. The analysis showed that schedules which lack the income item are not a true cross-section of all schedules. For the most part, those with the income omission tended to contain a disproportionately large number of persons in the upper economic and educational levels, older family heads, white collar managerial and professional workers, Protestant and Jewish groups, American born, and small families. The median rental of those reporting their incomes was $26, while that of those not reporting income was $35.

A similar analysis of schedules in which the education of the head of the family was unreported showed a different type of selection. Possibly because of the difficulty of translating foreign education into American equivalents, the omission of years of schooling occurred most frequently among foreign-born heads of families. Unskilled occupational groups, Jewish family heads, heads over 50 years of age, and the extremes of low and high income groups also had a disproportionately large representation among cases of unreported education.

ARITHMETICAL ERRORS:

Although most mistakes in arithmetic are of a chance nature and as likely to be in one direction as another, occasional errors may be definitely biased and of sufficient magnitude to distort the results entirely. Failure of one clerical worker, for example, to include a major item when making a certain addition on a set of schedules may, if not corrected, affect the major findings of the survey. By providing checks of every operation in the survey the surveyor will avoid errors of this type.

ERRORS IN ADJUSTING THE RETURNS:

1. The Nonvoter. When the surveyor attempts to predict the outcome of an election he has a threefold task. First, he must know accurately the sentiment revealed by his poll. Second, he must be able to

predict which of the respondents are likely to turn out to vote on election day. Third, he must know how the sentiment of those who vote differs from that of the nonvoter. If the surveyor errs in these estimates he might present a biased picture of the forthcoming election. In the 1944 presidential campaign, one poller estimated that the turnout would be 40 million or less. Such a low turnout would, he thought, be unfavorable to the Democrats. So he subtracted two percentage points from the national and state percentages for Democrats in his published results. He was criticized for this adjustment by a Congressional investigating committee, and suggestions were made that in the future the poller should publish the results based upon the poll separately from his adjustment for anticipated election turnout.

A valuable contribution to the polling field was made by Connelly and Field in their analysis of the characteristics of nonvoters (187). Although the number of registered or qualified voters in 1940 was 60,576,979, only 82 per cent of this number cast their ballots on the election day. In 16 southern states the average turnout was 34%, with only 10% voting in South Carolina. No northern state had less than a 65% turnout. The greatest percentage of voters was found among college educated people, highest economic groups, persons 40 years or over, white collar workers, men, and people in large metropolitan districts. Conversely, nonvoters were relatively more numerous among persons with grade school education, low economic groups, persons under 40, service workers, women, and residents of farms.

The above authors also found that persons who held no opinions on current issues were twice as frequent among nonvoters as among voters. These nonvoters also were more opposed to change and were more isolationist than the voters.

Another surveyor found that nonvoters tend to have confidence in public officials. Minority groups, on the other hand, tend to have a relatively high turnout, except for Negroes, who are largely disqualified.

2. **Incorrect Weights.** When controlled sampling is employed and strata are weighted in accordance with their frequency in the total population, the use of incorrect weights will result in a biased picture of the total. Sometimes weights are used also when a deficiency in the sample is shown by checks of factors not used in the controls. Such

adjustments may not improve the sample and they may make it more biased.

SOURCES OF ERROR IN ELECTION POLL PREDICTIONS:

Some pollers hold the view that the prediction of election outcomes is outside the scope of scientific polling. With the present limited knowledge about voting behavior it is true that a large element of guesswork and personal judgment enters into the election predictions. This need not always be the case because with each passing year knowledge of the factors controlling turnout and voting behavior is being advanced. Even when almost everything is known about voting behavior, pollers may find that several forecasts are necessary to cover the various contingencies which may arise the day of the election or the evening before. The public should be informed about the various elements which could turn an election one way or another. They should know that some of these factors are beyond the ability of the poller to foresee. They should be told where polling ends and guessing begins. The pollers of the future may present their predictions with such limiting phrases as "assuming that 75 per cent of the eligible voters vote," or "If there is no concerted effort to influence the vote near the polling booths," or "If the weather is fair in the following states," or "Providing the popular vote is at least 50 million," or "Assuming that the people who are undecided as of November 1st are going to vote just like those who have already decided on their preferences." Insofar as certain elements are unpredictable the pollers could show how their predictions of the election outcome could vary, depending on the course of these extraneous influences. If, to satisfy the general public or the bettors the poller selects a single figure for his prediction, he should caution the public that the figure is his best guess but that the results may differ from this figure, depending upon which factors loom largest on election day. Below are some of the reasons presidential election pollers may forecast incorrectly even though the polling techniques—such as sampling methods, ascertainment of true opinions, interview procedures, interpretations, and all other polling operations—are unbiased and adequate.

1. The turnout on election day may not be predicted correctly.

If a disproportionate number of one party's members stay at home on election day the prediction of votes may be in error. Much has been done in recent years to discover what factors cause people to stay away from the polls and what kinds of people do so. Evidently not enough was known in 1948 because all the pollers expressed surprise at the small turnout.

The turnout may be affected by such a factor as *overconfidence*—the feeling that the preferred candidate will be elected regardless of whether a given voter votes. In 1948 when all the major polls had assured the public that the election was "in the bag" and that Dewey was going to win, a significant number of normally Republican places had low turnouts.

Apathy may affect the turnout; the voter may not be interested in either candidate so he does not bother to vote. This is especially true if apathy toward the candidate is associated with overconfidence that the preferred party will win.

Fear that the preferred candidate may not be elected unless everyone turns out to vote for him may bring out many voters who otherwise might stay home. Voters may also be afraid that a candidate whom they dislike will get in unless they vote against him. So even if they feel neutral to the candidate they vote for, they may come forth with their protest vote.

Enthusiasm—a desire to show by a vote how much a candidate or his policies are appreciated or how much his opponent is disliked—may affect the number who go to the polls.

By 1948 techniques for determining the intensity of feelings toward candidates and issues had been well developed. According to *Fortune* editors (December, 1948), the Roper poll had revealed that enthusiasm for Dewey was not very great. The data had shown also that the public as a whole favored the New Deal and its program. But the editors has mistakenly assumed that the public wanted Dewey to administer the programs.

At one time pollers thought that a small national turnout on election day was favorable to the Republican party. The 1948 presidential vote was the smallest per capita for twenty-eight years, but still the Democrats won. So merely the *number* of people going to the polls cannot be used for forecasting the probable winner; it is the number of people with given sympathies that is important.

Closely allied to turnout is the *failure to vote* for a given position or issue. Even the number who go to the polls and who profess attachment to a given party cannot be relied upon to produce a vote for a given candidate. In 1948, about 683,000 people who voted did not cast a ballot for President. To be sure, this might have been an oversight on the part of some, but for others it indicated a disapproval of both candidates or enthusiasm for a local candidate or issue.

2. The vote on a given candidate may be affected by the entire ballot. Certain candidates or issues on the ballot may draw a large vote because they are popular with the voters while other candidates or issues about which the voters are more neutral may receive large votes merely because they are sponsored by the same political group as the more popular candidate or issue. In presidential elections, city, county, or state candidates of the same party as the President often "ride in on his coattails." If enthusiasm for the presidential candidate is not high but if strong local candidates are listed on the ballot, the reverse situation might result—the presidential candidates might be swept into office on the coattails of popular Congressmen or other state candidates or issues. One of the functions of forecasters is to determine which candidate or issue has the greatest appeal to voters.

3. If the interviews are conducted too long in advance of election day the forecast may be wrong. Polling results may be correct as of the date the poll was taken, but if shifts in opinion occur between the date of the poll and the actual election, the forecast may easily be wrong. Pollers are aware of these shifts and so they usually continue sampling right up to the day before election. The telegraphic polls described elsewhere are particularly useful for these last-minute polls. According to published reports on the 1948 election forecasts, all three of the well-known national pollers stopped polling too soon. One poller, Mr. Roper, took his last poll in September. Crossley's interviewing took place three weeks before the election, and the field work for the Gallup poll ended more than a week before the election. All these pollers had observed a trend toward Truman during the months preceding the election but, as Crossley pointed out, they did not believe the trend would be sufficiently accelerated to overcome the 5-point lead Dewey had in mid-October.

4. The adjustments made by pollers to allow for trends toward or away from a given candidate between the last interviews and the election may be incorrect. Although the Gallup poll reported a sample

of some 60,000 interviews during the period preceding the 1948 November poll, these interviews were spread over two months. Since Truman seemed to be gaining in popularity with each successive sample, Gallup had to guess whether this swing would continue at the same rate right up to election day, whether it would slow down, or whether it would stop or greatly accelerate toward the end of the campaign.

Even if the poll had been taken the day before the election, the poller had to be prepared for shifts which might result from an election eve broadcast or from events which might swing the vote even on election day. A sudden drop in the price of a farm commodity, a Pearl Harbor, a stock market crash, or extensive efforts on the part of one political group or its supporters to get out the vote might upset the best predictions. Even if sudden upsetting factors do not occur, the vote forecaster must guess how to project his figures to carry him beyond his interviews into the day of the election. In a Congressional investigation conducted after the 1944 presidential election, one poller reported that his published forecast of the election was 2 percentage points higher for Dewey than the figure he had obtained through interviews. He justified this on the ground that the trend was toward Dewey and this was his best guess as to what would happen by election time.

5. Events or speeches on election eve or election day sometimes cannot be foreseen by pollers. In an Australian election reported by Morgan (657) voters were handed printed cards by party officials showing them how to mark the ballots on several rather complicated issues being submitted to a referendum. The discrepancy between how the people voted and what they had told pollers was, in one instance, about 8 percentage points. The results of the election corroborated the findings of the polls on several issues in which public opinion and the printed card agreed, but when the two were in disagreement the card won out at the polls. Efficient forecasters need to know about plans such as cards, or other techniques to influence votes during election day. To the extent that such methods come as a surprise to pollers, to that extent may their prognostications be upset.

6. Pollers may make poor guesses as to what the "undecided" groups will do on election day. Several studies have been made about what happens to the people who have not made up their minds about

voting when questioned by interviewers. Techniques have been used such as having interviewers carry a secret ballot box with them, questioning the undecided about what he did or how he voted in the last election, and studying the characteristics of the undecided so that a reasonable guess may be made as to how he is likely to vote, if at all, on election day. In the 1948 election the pollers said that they had divided the undecided cases in the same proportion as the decided votes were distributed among the candidates. After the election, the pollers were of the opinion that most of the undecided votes had swung to Truman. Use of the techniques available to the pollers at that time should have given greater insight into what the undecided were likely to do. If there was no way of determining, the pollers might have warned the public of the possibilities if the undecided all turned toward one candidate. When one poller stopped polling, 15 per cent of the persons interviewed were still undecided. As many as 7 per cent were undecided when the last polls were taken.

7. The election results might be too close to be detectable or predictable from samples. The polls claim that errors of sampling in their polls are almost certain not to exceed 4 percentage points. If the sample happens to be that extreme deviate of one case in a thousand that may occur by the laws of chance, the poll findings may be incorrect. If one major party candidate were to receive 48 per cent of the popular vote and the other 49 per cent, sampling polls could not be reliable within such close percentages. The problem is multiplied manyfold, however, when the forecasters attempt to predict electoral votes. In all the states in which the popular vote for the leading candidates is very close, samples might fall down. In the 1948 presidential election, Truman won over Dewey in Ohio by only about 6000 votes in a total of about 3 million. In Illinois and California Truman led by slightly more than 30,000 votes in a total of about 4 million in each State. Such close margins would require extremely large samples to detect accurately.

8. Any one or more of the techniques of polls may be faulty and thus tend to produce biased results even as of the date of the poll. Quota sampling in which interviewers tend to select biased samples of the voting population, or in which weights assigned various population groups are incorrect, may produce inaccurate results. The greater the time between the federal census and the election to be forecast, the

more hazardous the choice of weights used by pollers who employ quota sampling or other sampling techniques requiring up-to-date census data.

Other distortions can result from the use of mail ballots with inadequate protection from self-selected samples, from faulty interviewing or recording of results, from failure to reveal honest or true opinions or to gauge intensity of feeling, and from failure of analysts to interpret the meaning of the figures obtained. Thus, in addition to unpredictable factors, preventable errors arising at every stage of polling procedure may permanently distort the findings and the forecasts based upon them.

Some of the more important sources of bias have been discussed in this chapter. Preventative techniques for avoiding most of these biases are to be found in good survey procedures—the subject matter of this book.

Selected References

Baker and Stanton (26), Blankenship et al. (82), Brennan (110), Coutant (200), Crespi (208), Deming (238), Deming, Tepping, and Geoffrey (244), Elinsen and Cisin (283), Friedman (334), Gaudet and Wilson (348), Gimbel (360), Hansen and Hurwitz (399), Hilgard and Payne (436), Hinrichs (441), Hyman and Sheatsley (464), Katz (495, 497, 498), Kiser (522), Kornhauser (534, 535), Lawson (541), Link et al. (579, 580), *Literary Digest* (581, 582), Manheimer and Hyman (614), McCormick (622), Mitchell (649), Moore (654), Morgan (657), *New Statesman and Nation* (686), Parten (720), Peatman (729), Reid (763), Reuss (768), Shuttleworth (873), Stephan (922), Stoke and Lehman (932), Suchman and Guttman (942), Suchman and McCandless (943), Terris (955), Toops (968), Wagner (1045), Ziff (1144).
See also references on Interview Procedures and Problems, Phrasing of Questions, Mail Questionnaire Procedure, Validity, and 1948 Election.

CHAPTER XIII

Editing the Schedule Data[1]

The process of examining the data collected in a survey to detect errors and omissions and to see that they are corrected and the schedules prepared for tabulation is known as editing. It may be differentiated from "coding" discussed in Chapter XIV, which is the assignment of classes or class symbols to data already edited. In actual practice, the two operations of editing and coding are often performed together or by the same staff.

Editing Functions

The schedule editor is responsible for seeing that the data to be tabulated are: (1) as accurate and reliable as possible; (2) consistent with other facts secured; (3) uniformly entered; (4) as complete as possible; (5) acceptable for tabulation; and (6) arranged so as to facilitate coding and tabulation. He also should spot comments that are useful in interpreting results.

While some of the problems of editing mail questionnaires differ from those encountered in schedules obtained by interviews, the underlying principles of editing are applicable regardless of the method of data collection. In fact, it is often possible to make returns acceptable by shifting to collection procedures other than those used in gathering the original returns. For instance, returns from mail questionnaires may be followed up by telephoning to informants or even visiting them if given items are not clear. Similarly, data gathered from interviews may be corrected or interpreted by information received by mail. Surveyors would do well, however, to make it a fundamental rule to conduct the survey in such a way that the first returns or replies are

---

[1] Editing instructions and specific problems of editing are described in a manuscript prepared by Dorothy McCamman, formerly chief check editor of the Urban Study of Consumer Purchases (1010). Much of the material in this chapter is adapted from her manuscript.

satisfactory and require no further contact with the informant, except for checking purposes. Not only is it less time consuming to prevent than to correct errors, but the data secured are more likely to be reliable. The various devices by which errors can be prevented have already been discussed under such topics as: pilot surveys, pretesting of questions and questionnaires, and training of interviewers.

Edits in Interview Survey

EDIT IN THE FIELD:

In large-scale studies each schedule is reviewed by a number of editors before it is finally ready for tabulation. In the collection stage, for example, a first edit by the squad leader in charge of ten or twenty enumerators often precedes the office edit. Since it is the duty of the squad leader to supervise the quantity and quality of each interviewer's work, a brief schedule edit in the field often catches omissions and errors.

Furthermore, if an investigator leaves an interview puzzled about the proper method of recording some unusual data, his squad leader should be prepared to advise him. A brief review of the schedule shortly after the interview may reveal certain incomplete entries which the interviewer may be able to complete since the interview is still fresh. Under such circumstances, the squad leader must be certain that the interviewer has really ascertained the answer to the question and is not merely supplying material in order to avoid a return visit.

Under another procedure, one or more editors is assigned to each squad. The advantage of maintaining editors in the various districts to which squads are assigned is greatest in large cities where travel to and from a central office may be expensive and time consuming. It is not necessary to establish a number of offices throughout the city in order to effect such contacts. An unused garage, a room in the home of a staff member, or an automobile may serve as the headquarters of both editor and squad leader.

If two editors work with each squad, both may review a given schedule before it is returned to the interviewer for correction. This second review does much to eliminate the natural irritation which an enumerator feels when the same schedule is returned to him a number of times because the first editor has failed to catch all the necessary corrections.

When the initial edit is made in the field, the enumerator reports to the editor, perhaps twice a day, to consult about any items with which he is having difficulty, to receive new instructions, and to pick up any edited schedules which need revision or further information. The number of contacts between interviewers and editors is usually reduced as the field workers become more experienced.

After an interviewer has made the necessary revisions on an unacceptable schedule, a complete reedit is necessary, preferably by an editor who has not yet reviewed this particular schedule. The review must be thorough in order to make certain that the new information and the revisions are consistent with other data on the schedule.

When interviewers are instructed by mail, they must edit their own schedules before sending them in. Immediately after each interview, the interviewer should inspect each item on the schedule to see that (1) it is filled in, (2) it is legible or checked in the proper answer box, (3) the entry has been made in accordance with instructions, (4) the information given by the informant is accurately reported, and (5) notes accompany any entries which may appear to be inconsistent or inaccurate.

Another review of the schedule should be made just before it is placed in the envelope for mailing to headquarters. Since this is usually on a different day from the interview, the interviewer may catch errors that he overlooked on his first inspection.

Even when squad leaders inspect schedules, it is advisable for interviewers to review their own questionnaires before submitting them to their leader. It might be well for each interviewer to be supplied with a check list of points which he could use when reviewing his entries, e.g., (1) Is there an entry for every question? (2) Is the entry legible and unmistakably clear? (3) Does each answer truthfully represent what the informant said? (4) If the answer to question 5 is "Yes" is question 5a also entered? (5) Do any of the answers seem to be inconsistent, e.g., items 9 and 13? If so, explain why in notes. (6) Is the address and name of informant correct? (7) Have you signed your own name and date? (8) etc.

THE INTAKE EDIT:

The systematic inspection of each schedule before it is accepted, to insure that enumerators are collecting and recording the information in accordance with instructions, is known as the "intake edit." Without this precautionary measure much of the data gathered may prove to be worthless and many schedules may have to be discarded.

The edit of schedules as soon as they are turned in as completed by enumerators serves a number of purposes. In the first place, unless the schedule is reviewed when turned in, the need for additional information may not be discovered until the collection phase of the survey has ceased and the interview staff disbanded. Then it will be too late to ascertain the correct facts. In the second place, if errors and omissions are caught early in the study, the repetition of similar mistakes on later schedules can be avoided. When the intake editor systematically reviews each schedule in the presence of the interviewer, misunderstanding of instructions, careless interviewing, or careless recording can be pointed out and the interviewer instructed to correct the situation. By catching the errors and omissions while the interview is still fresh in the interviewer's mind, it is often possible for him to correct the schedule entry without reinterviewing the informant. Thus, an embarrassing situation as well as a time consuming task is avoided. When a second interview is needed, the investigator who made the initial visit should repeat the call, unless a check interviewer can obtain the missing information during his check call and thus avoid taking up too much of the informant's time.

The intake edit usually includes an examination for legibility and neatness of schedules, so that the coder will not have to guess at the meaning of the entry.

An evaluation of the interviewers' work is possible from this early edit and those who continue to hand in schedules which require further field work before being acceptable should not be permitted to remain on the staff. Those who do not learn the instructions for interviewing and recording information and those whose schedule entries appear illegible or questionable should be discovered while there is still time, organization, and funds to rectify the errors.

Aside from insuring that the enumerators are collecting and recording the information called for, the field edit often reveals deficiencies in the instructions or interpretation of instructions which need revision before too many schedules have been collected. From discussion with enumerators, editors may discover that definitions of terms employed in the study must be clarified or altered. During the field work, ques-

tions of definition, classification, and interpretation are constantly arising. The editors must see that uniform procedures and interpretations
are adopted for handling unforeseen types of cases or problems. In one
large survey a card file was kept of all questions received from the field
offices, and supplementary instructions were issued when it was
thought that any question arising in the field would not be unique.
Since most questions raised in the field are not unique, surveyors
should not settle each new case as if it would not come up again.
Every ruling should be recorded and referred to when interviewers
seek a clarification or application of instructions to what may seem to
be a special case. These rulings should be incorporated in the editing
instructions.

THE DETAILED EDIT:

In small-scale surveys, the schedules may get only one edit, in which
case it should be exceedingly thorough. It is necessary to establish a
routine procedure for examining the completed schedules, requiring
the investigator to adhere to definite standards when filling in the
items and preparing the recorded information for coding and tabulation. Unless this is done, the final account of schedules acceptable for
tabulation will fall far short of the necessary number. Even when
there is a field and an intake edit, a detailed review is necessary in
which each entry is carefully considered. To insure that the data obtained meet the highest standards of scientific procedure, the editor
must search for any irregularities which may throw light on the accuracy and completeness of reporting, misinformation from respondents, and careless or incorrect questioning. The topics discussed later
under "The Editing Process" indicate the wide range of duties of the
editor. The detailed edit should cover all points mentioned there.

An administrative problem arises concerning whether a general edit
of the schedule as a whole should be made by one person, or whether
it is better to divide the schedule into a number of sections, each of
which is reviewed by one person. The latter technique is preferable
for long and complicated schedules, since it permits an editor to concentrate on a limited amount of material about which he may develop
special knowledge and skill. But too much specialization is dangerous
in that inconsistencies which show up only when sections are interrelated may never be discovered. Many studies use a combination of

these two techniques, in which specialists give detailed attention to certain sections while one editor reviews the entire schedule for internal consistency.

Even when a schedule is so simple or its sections are so interrelated that specialized editing is not desirable, it may be advisable to use an additional editor for all arithmetic checking. An arithmetic checker may be equipped with an adding or calculating machine to achieve greater speed and accuracy than is possible when each editor attempts to check figures.

THE CHECK EDITS:

A portion of all edited schedules which are considered complete and correct should be reviewed by the local supervisor of editing. When the schedules reach the supervisor's desk, all editorial comments should be attached. These comments, on slips dated and signed by the editor, form a valuable record of the quality of work which is being performed by both interviewer and editor and of the length of time which elapses between the intake of the schedules and its acceptance. If each office maintains a rigid control system, schedules should not remain too long on an editor's desk or in the hands of interviewers to whom they have been returned for correction.

In large-scale surveys, an additional check edit of a percentage of all completed schedules from each collection office is made by the regional editors, and a further review of certain schedules is undertaken at headquarters. Schedules which have been revised during conference with the enumerator or revisits to obtain further information must be reedited before they are coded.

The Editing Process

OBTAINING ACCURACY AND TRUTHFULNESS:

When the editor examines an entry for accuracy, he must have sufficient knowledge of the subject to recognize answers which are improbable. In some cases it is quite obvious that the enumerator has made a clerical error, e.g., that he has written "years" instead of "months" when giving the age of an infant. The editor must not, however, change entries without carefully checking and confirming his "hunches" with a superior qualified to authorize changes.

Occasional "jokers" may be entered, especially on questionnaires received by mail. It is the task of the editor to spot schedules which obviously are not accurate. In some cases it may be necessary to reject the entire schedule, whereas in others a telephone call or a revisit may produce the correct information.

A check for arithmetical accuracy is a part of the editing process of every schedule on which figures appear. Whether this arithmetical check is made by the editor who examines the schedule for conformity to instructions, consistency, and completeness, or whether it is made by an editing group who are concerned only with the arithmetical accuracy of the schedule, is an administrative problem. It depends upon such factors as the size of the staff and the amount of arithmetical checking involved.

The editor is in a good position to detect "faked" information by comparing the schedule entries of any given enumerator with the replies recorded by other investigators. Cases have been reported in which investigators have found it less troublesome to sit at home and record the answers of an imaginary informant than to obtain the interview as per instructions. One method for detecting such false information is to request the interviewer to record verbatim the remarks of the informant on "opinion" questions. Very few investigators are clever enough to "imagine" comments which are sufficiently varied and which look plausible to the editor who has the opportunity to compare the work of many investigators. Other cheaters may interview someone—but not the assigned respondent—and thereby get varied answers. These can be detected only through check interviews.

Eastwood points out that in mail questionnaires another technique for testing the accuracy and truthfulness of returns is the insertion of one or two quite plausible questions that cannot be answered. An example of this procedure is provided by a brand familiarity rating scale in which the list of bona fide brands or articles includes two fictitious brands that the respondent is expected to rate as "unknown." Any other answer serves to discredit the truthfulness of his ratings on the bona fide brands (266, p. 292).

By eliminating confusing or illegible entries the editor insures greater accuracy in the tabulated results. If the entry is not legible, or seems to be checked between two possible answers, the editor must try to ascertain the correct answer and write in or check an answer which cannot be mistaken by the coder. In a sense all of the editing which reveals deficiencies in the entries may be regarded as a check on the accuracy and reliability of the information.

Sometimes the inaccuracy cannot be detected for an individual but may be detected by examining groups of replies. Bailey and Cummings cite such a case (22, p. 22).

At the census of 1900 it was found upon tabulating the returns that the number of Negroes returned as "unable to speak English" was so large as to be highly improbable. This return could not be edited out of the schedule, because it was entirely possible that any given Negro might be unable to speak English, but it was exceedingly improbable that the number unable to speak English should be so great as developed upon tabulation of the returns. Upon examination of the schedule used at this census, the probable explanation of the erroneous returns became apparent. In contiguous columns the schedule called for answers to the inquiries as to the person's ability to read and to write and to speak English. In the case of whites, the usual and correct return to these inquiries necessitated writing "Yes, Yes, Yes" and in some cases it was "No, No, No." In the case of many illiterate Negroes the enumerators made the partially incorrect return "No, No, No" instead of the correct return "No, No, Yes." In consequence of this accidental arrangement of columns on the schedule, the tabulation relating to ability to speak English for the Negro element had to be abandoned. At the Thirteenth Census the columns were rearranged and much more accurate returns were secured to this inquiry.

Although each study develops its special problems, the following illustrations have relatively wide application since they relate to data commonly included in social surveys: *Age*, which is frequently reported or entered incorrectly can usually be checked against several items on the schedule. The age of parents should be consistent with that of children unless the interviewer has indicated that these are not blood relationships. An indication of whether or not children's ages are approximately correct may be obtained from comparison with school grades, if the latter information has been obtained. The *occupational title* which an informant assigns to his work may be more impressive than accurate. The example probably closest at hand is that of a statistical clerk, engaged in routine computation, who refers to himself as a statistician. When information is available on education and on salary, it is relatively easy for an editor to detect the presence of such misnomers. *Relief status* is another problem which confuses many enumerators. It is sometimes felt that any person connected with a relief agency is "on relief"; this misconception may extend not only to the nonrelief clerical workers employed by the relief agency but to the case workers as well. Again, the internal evidence of the schedule relating to occupation and to salary may reveal a need for further checking.

INSURING CONSISTENCY:

The editor should always be on guard to detect contradictory or inconsistent entries. Often what may appear to be contradictory information may turn out not to be so when explained by the interviewer. In such cases, his instructions may have been deficient, he may not have grasped the instructions, or the informant may not have been consistent in his statements. In this last case, however, the interviewer should have detected this inconsistency and, if the informant insisted upon maintaining it, notes should have been attached to the schedule explaining the situation.

A complete check for consistency is achieved only by a systematic examination of all related replies in a predetermined order of examination. When two answers are contradictory, it may be possible to determine which, if either of the two, is correct. When this cannot be done, it may be necessary to discard both answers and to classify the response as "unknown."

Checks on the consistency of all figures entered on the schedule are usually a separate editing operation. The arithmetic editor sees that totals are consistent with the constituent items, that given figures are within the range of reason and of probability, and that the figures obtained by any one agent do not differ markedly from those obtained by others. If great differences are found, an attempt should be made to verify the figures or to account for the apparent discrepancy. The editor must also examine each schedule to see if it has internal consistency—or reasonableness. If, for instance, a schedule containing data on family expenditures reports the ownership of a home yet shows no entry for taxes paid or taxes due, the editor is justified in returning the schedule to the agent on the grounds of inconsistency.

OBTAINING UNIFORMITY:

Although replies may be correct, they often cannot be coded until the answers are converted into uniform units of measurement. If the instructions to field workers were properly drawn up and followed, the entries would be uniform, but constant checking is essential to insure that such is the case. Then again, the informant may give greater detail than that needed in coding. For example, the informant may give an exact expenditure in terms of dollars and cents, whereas only the number of dollars may be coded. In such cases the editor may merely cross out the cents figures—or he may round the dollar figures.

The editor must make certain that entries on each schedule are uniform with the entries on other schedules. For example, the use of a dash by one investigator to mean "unknown," when this symbol has been adopted by others to indicate "not applicable," results in a lack of uniformity which precludes accurate analysis. On the whole, uniformity is achieved if each interviewer adheres rigidly to the instructions which govern the making of schedule entries.

INSURING COMPLETENESS:

The editor serves an important function when he decides which schedules are incomplete either in record or in information. When an interviewer attempts to make the interview as brief as possible, he may skip an item which he knows to be inapplicable on the basis of his conversation with the informant. Because the coding and tabulating process takes into account only what is actually recorded, this incomplete schedule is unacceptable. By assuring the completeness of a schedule before it is coded, the editor prevents many schedules from falling into the discard pile. When incomplete schedules are returned to the interviewer, it may be a matter of merely entering a dollar sign. On the other hand, the missing data may necessitate a revisit to the interviewee.

After the survey collection office has closed (or in the case of a mailed questionnaire, once the reply has been received from the informant), it is usually difficult or impossible to return the schedule to the interviewer or to reinterview the family for the missing items. So the editor must make the schedule as complete as possible using the information at hand. This editorial process consists first of all in supplying obvious answers where the omission has been an oversight. For example, the first question may be "Do you own a car? Yes—No," and the next question, "What is the make of your car?" If the make of car is given, it may be assumed that the answer to the first question is

"Yes." Great discretion should be used, however, when supplying missing entries. Preferably, the editor should consult his supervisor before deriving the answer to one question from that given in another.

Another process which generally falls to the editor is that of computing or ascertaining data which can be derived from the field entries. For example, the computation of net income from gross income, and other information secured and recorded on the schedule, may be an involved computation which the field agent does not have the time or training to perform. In very large-scale studies, it may be advisable to employ an editor to make this one computation and enter it on the schedule. The editor should enter "no report," "unknown," "refused," "inapplicable," and similar terms when an omission is obvious, in order to make the schedule complete for coding.

The reduction of the number of "unknown" cases is very important. If certain items are lacking, much other information with which it is cross-tabulated is also lost. In the U. S. Census of 1940 it was found that the tabulation of "unknown age" was costly and the cross-tabulations were of little value. So a system was devised by Dr. W. Edwards Deming whereby the age of any individual could be estimated from the other information given about him, such as his schooling, ages of other family members, his occupation, etc. This method of estimating age was found to be exceedingly accurate and was used to estimate age when this fact was unknown. The editing staff was instructed to write in the estimated age on the schedule whenever it had been omitted.

Not only should editors see that the schedule information is as complete as possible, but they should also make certain that all schedules are accounted for. Loss of information because the schedule does not arrive at the "final edit" stage is not unusual. While this check of schedules should be the function of the office control section, another check by the editors gives added certainty that the information collected is not lost before it is tabulated. On the other hand, it is equally important for the editors to see that duplicates of schedules are eliminated before coding and tabulation begins. When schedules are returned to interviewers for correction and revision, duplicate copies of the schedule may be prepared. If the second is not properly labeled "duplicate" both schedules then get into the editing mill and may even be coded and tabulated, unless editors are on guard for such cases. Similarly, follow-up mail questionnaires sent back for missing information may be duplicates of the originals and check editors should see that duplication does not occur in coding and tabulation.

One of the most important functions of the editor is to determine whether or not a schedule is sufficiently reliable and complete, and whether or not it is obtained from the sample case desired and thus acceptable for tabulation. When a specific person or household has been assigned, the editor makes certain that the correct case has been interviewed. Wrong addresses, wrong member of the family, or type of family not in the assigned quota should have been detected by the sample control staff, but a final check by the editor is still necessary. The sampling procedure usually operates in such a way that only eligible cases are assigned to enumerators, but detailed information secured during the course of the interview may reveal the case to be ineligible for the sample. In such a case the editor should see that the schedule is turned over to the person in charge of sampling.

The standards which the schedule must meet should be carefully set up and adhered to by the editors. The effect of rejection of schedules upon the sample and ultimate findings of the study is so important that constant examination of the "rejected schedules" by the chief editor and sampling expert is advised. Sometimes schedules incomplete in certain respects may be acceptable, particularly if it has been decided that all data collected and recorded on the schedule will not be tabulated and analyzed. For example, on schedules relating to family expenditures, detailed questions on certain subcategories of commodities such as food and clothing may be printed on the schedule. These details may be asked by the enumerator primarily to help the informant remember all of his purchases so that he may build up an estimate of total expenditures for this category. If only the figures for total clothing and for total food expenditures, for instance, are to be tabulated, a schedule which lacks the detailed items but has reliable section totals may be acceptable. Again, a schedule constructed primarily to obtain clothing expenditures may include questions on the number of various items purchased; if the family's accounting process or the informant's memory cannot provide figures on quantity but can produce a reliable figure on total expenditure for a commodity, the missing data may not preclude the schedule's acceptability. Editing instructions which outline the minimum essentials of an acceptable schedule should not be made available to enumerators or they may relax their efforts to obtain schedules which are complete in every detail. Finally, all schedules which the interviewer or the editor feel are unreliable should be rejected.

REARRANGEMENT OF ITEMS:

A convenient arrangement of questions or items for interviewing may not be the best arrangement for coding and tabulating. Sometimes it is necessary for the editor to transcribe the entire schedule on a transcription sheet in order to get the best arrangement. When possible, this extra step should be avoided because it not only is time-consuming, but it permits one more source of error to arise from incorrect copying. The alternative is for editors to renumber the items in some distinctive color for the coders.

MARKING PERTINENT COMMENTS:

As the editor goes over each schedule, he often comes across explanations either by the interviewer or by the informant which throw light on the reasons for particular reactions or facts. If the survey analyst or report writer has these comments available, his interpretations should be more meaningful and interesting. The editor may have a copy made of these comments or he may mark them for later study.

Instructions to Editors

A written manual of instructions to editors should be prepared well in advance of the initiation of the field survey. It is necessary, however, to have some trial schedules on hand when drawing up the instructions because the type of problems arising and items needing clarification cannot be foreseen without some practical attempts to obtain the information. The schedules obtained during the pretesting of the schedule and survey procedure should serve as illustrative material during the preparation of the editing manual. The instructions based on such schedules should not be made final, however, until a number of schedules from the main survey have been edited satisfactorily on the basis of the instructions. Of course, repeated surveys or those conducted with a permanent staff of interviewers should have the instructions completely ready for each survey because such surveys usually are conducted and completed in a short period of time. The instructions from one survey to another can usually be used with slight modifications.

A few general rules to include in editing instructions follow:

1. Editors should be thoroughly familiar with the instructions to enumerators and to coders, as well as with their own instructions. Deficiencies in instructions will be caught more readily if editors know what procedures the enumerators are requested to follow. Similarly, if they know the processes through which the edited schedule passes after it leaves the editing divisions, editors will understand why various procedures are adopted.

2. In no case should the editor destroy, erase, or make illegible the original entry filled in by the enumerator.

3. All available space on the schedule may eventually be used, so it is advisable to avoid all unnecessary marking of the schedule, unnecessarily large letters or symbols, or illegible entries, because these will need to be rewritten.

4. All marks on the schedule by the editor should be made in a distinctive color.

5. No answer should be changed without sufficient justification based on other data in the schedule.

6. Editors are authorized to make certain types of changes, but they should consult the supervisor for others.

7. Schedules to be discarded or rejected should be submitted to the chief editor, who consults with the sampling director before placing them in an inactive file.

8. All answers changed or supplied by the editor should be initialed so that if necessary the check editor can verify the reason for the change.

9. If any of the entries to be coded are illegible, confusing, or difficult to read at first glance, cross out original entry, but do not erase. Rewrite clearly.

10. Detailed instructions should be given on how to make alterations on the schedule. (a) To cancel an entry completely, the census procedure is to draw a horizontal line through the entry, e.g., ~~3500.~~ (b) To cancel only part of an entry, the editor may draw oblique lines about one-sixteenth of an inch apart, e.g., 3500.00. (c) To cor-

rect an entry, the editor should cancel the original entry and write the new entry in a designated place (above or beside the old entry).

11. Each editor should be aware that his work will be check edited, and that he may have to justify his interpretations to others.

12. Editor's initials and date of editing each schedule should be entered on each schedule when it is edited.

The manual for editors should preface the discussion of editing techniques with a complete statement of the purpose of editing. Specific instructions should be prepared for each item on the schedule. Since the editor is familiar with the instructions issued to enumerators, the editing instructions should provide additional information relating to the type of entry expected and acceptable, as well as the type of entry which is not acceptable unless accompanied by a note of explanation. The editors should be informed about sections of the schedule which may be cross-checked for consistency with other sections. Frequently the schedule has been constructed primarily from the point of view of efficiency in interviewing; if some other order is better adapted to editing, the instructions should suggest the desirable sequence of sections for review purposes.

The errors which are apt to be most common and the means of detecting such errors should be pointed out in the manual, but this section can be enlarged upon in subsequent memoranda.

A statement of the criteria by which schedules should be judged for acceptance or rejection constitutes an important part of the instructions to editors. In most surveys these requisites concern (1) the eligibility of the individual or case for inclusion in the sample, and (2) the completeness and reliability of schedule entries.

Editors on large-scale studies should be informed as to the correct procedure for obtaining further instructions or interpretation of terms. The editing manual also should include suggestions as to the quickest and most effective distribution of new instructions or revisions to all members of the local staffs.

It is of the utmost importance to keep the number of changes in instructions and interpretations at a minimum. A change usually necessitates the reedit of all schedules which have previously been accepted and may even involve revisiting certain families. But changes are not merely time-consuming. When revisions are numerous, the editors and interviewers lose their respect for the persons in charge of the survey. One evidence of lowered staff morale resulting from frequent revisions in instructions may be seen in the loss of desire of editors in field offices to keep up with the latest instructions. The editors in field offices may no longer bother to write to headquarters for further interpretations and instructions, with the result that the headquarters staff loses its control over the editing procedures.

It is exceedingly important that there be some check on the interpretation which editors as well as interviewers place on the questions. The editing process does much to reveal interviewers' misinterpretations and to reveal faulty instructions. Misinterpretation of instructions is particularly great in large-scale studies where even the editors may not understand the instructions issued by a distant central office. A review of a given proportion of all schedules from each field office by the central editing staff will provide a check and should insure uniformity of interpretation.

In a nationwide study the central editing staff should maintain a record of all technical questions and provisional interpretations which are submitted by the regional offices, accompanied by the answer or confirmation of the headquarters staff. The use of 3 x 5 cards arranged alphabetically by subject or by section of the schedule has proved satisfactory for this type of index. This record should always be referred to before any new interpretations are issued to make certain that they will be consistent with previous instructions. When the index reveals that the requested interpretation is not merely of local application, or when the same question from several regional offices suggests that the original instructions are not adequate, an interpretation should be issued to all regional offices rather than to just those offices requesting the information. After all the editing has been completed, this index of questions and answers should be turned over to the survey analyst or report writer. Incidentally, the chief editor should be present at all sessions where tabulation and analysis are discussed, so that his knowledge of the manner in which the data are used will guide him in making editing decisions.

Organization of Editing Section

In small-scale studies one or two editors can keep pace with the incoming schedules, and during slack periods they may begin coding the data preparatory to tabulation. It is a mistake, however, for the director of the survey to assume that he will have sufficient time to supervise the collection of data and to edit schedules as well. Problems arising during collection of data usually are so numerous and so pressing that no time remains for the director to edit schedules early in the study as should be done.

The editing supervisor in each local collection office not only trains his editors, but he also instructs enumerators in the meaning of schedule items and in techniques for recording responses. Throughout the period of collection this supervisor keeps interviewers, as well as editors, informed of new instructions. He makes certain that all editors proceed under the same instructions and that any interpretations which they place on the instructions are first cleared through him. The close contact of the supervisor and his editors with the interviewers makes it possible to detect those aspects of the schedule which are proving difficult and therefore need further clarification, and to spot interviewers who need additional training.

In order that the editing division does not impede the smooth flow of schedules through the various processes from collection to analysis, the editing supervisor must maintain his editing force at the proper size for the work on hand. For purposes of making production estimates, the supervisor's record of the number of schedules which have been reviewed and his estimate of the average editing time per schedule should be kept up to date at all times. Records of the work of each editor enables the supervisor to determine which ones are not maintaining quantity and quality of production.

Unfortunately, the local supervisor of editing frequently finds it necessary to serve as a buffer between editors and interviewers. Several factors are at work to produce this friction. Often interviewers are convinced that the editor's demand for strict accuracy in the form of the entry is mere pettiness and the editor's way of showing his authority. The interviewer often feels that his job of ringing doorbells and of persuading the interviewee to divulge the most intimate details of his life is much more difficult than that of an editor who sits at a desk all day—an editor who seemingly cannot appreciate a schedule simply because a perfectly obvious entry has been omitted. The discord and protracted discussions which are thus apt to arise between editors and interviewers must be prevented by the supervisor. Editors should be trained to write their comments in such an objective way that the investigator will recognize it as an impersonal correction. It is important that the editors be so well informed that their editorial comments are always accurate. Otherwise, the interviewer loses faith in the ability of the editing staff and refuses to place any confidence in further corrections. A technique which has been used effectively to obtain objectiveness in phrasing and to keep both editor and interviewer familiar with the instructions is the inclusion in the editor's comment of the reference to page and paragraph in the instruction manual which covers the subject in question. Moreover, the changes which the editor suggests must be directed toward the real improvement of the schedule and must not be corrections merely for correction's sake. Often editors have been trained to request an interviewer to attach a note explaining any dubious entry. From this commendable practice, it is a short step to demanding that the interviewer justify even fairly obvious entries. This exchange of useless notes between editors and field workers not only wastes valuable time but destroys confidence and thus weakens the morale of the investigators.

A better understanding between enumerators and editors may be achieved by giving each interviewer some training in editing techniques. Such training, however brief, provides the interviewer with an appreciation of the need for accuracy and a better understanding of what constitutes an acceptable schedule. From the point of the editing supervisor, this training often reveals which members of the staff may later be used for editing. There is one danger, however, in training interviewers to recognize what schedule information will pass an editing staff. An interviewer's desire to produce a perfect schedule might prompt him to omit complex information which would be difficult to record and to manufacture other entries which he knows will be acceptable to an editor because of their consistency and reasonableness. When rigorous check-interviewing is a part of the survey program, however, enumerators are not so prone to falsify material.

The editing staff maintained in the headquarters office should be large enough to review schedules as soon as they are submitted by the collection offices. Prompt correction of errors and misinterpretations before collection proceeds too far holds to a minimum the number of schedules which will need to be revised or rejected. An additional function of this central editing staff is to answer all technical problems pertaining to the schedule raised by field offices.

When the number of schedules sent to the headquarters office for review represents only a portion of all schedules collected, it is important that those schedules submitted should not be handpicked for excellence. The headquarters staff should have an opportunity to review a random sample of schedules so that the general calibre of work in each field office may be measured. In addition, schedules involving special problems which need the expert attention of the headquarters editors should be sent to the central office.

In studies which are organized by regions with several local field offices under the regional supervisor, each regional office maintains an editing division. Responsibility for uniform interpretation of instructions throughout all collection cities in the region should rest with this staff. To achieve this uniformity, regional editors need to review schedules from each field office. The chief editor in each regional office may be permitted to issue provisional instructions and interpretations to his staff and to the staffs of the collection offices, but they must be subject to the confirmation or revision of the headquarters chief editor. When local offices feel the need for additional instructions, they should apply to their regional editing staff rather than to headquarters. When the regional editors do not feel qualified to answer the questions, they should forward the request to headquarters. By eliminating the duplication which would result if each collection office were to appeal directly to headquarters and by issuing provisional rulings, the regional staff relieves the headquarters office of a good deal of repetitious work.

Selected References

Editing
American Marketing Assn. (8), Bailey and Cummings (22), Chapin (157), Eastwood (266), Fry (336), Schluter (842).

CHAPTER XIV

Coding the Data

Coding consists in assigning a number or symbol to each answer which falls in a predetermined class. In other words, coding may be regarded as the classification process necessary for tabulation. Except for schedule entries which merely indicate the presence or absence of a characteristic, or entries which are limited to relatively few alternatives, almost all answers to questions must be grouped into classes before results can be presented.

Coding may take place during three different points in a survey. The informant may be asked to classify his own reaction or situation, such as when he is asked into which of five different income groups his income would fall. The interviewer classifies the informant's response after the details have been supplied. Details are recorded by the interviewer or respondent to mail questionnaires, and classification into groups is performed by office editors or coders. Classification by informants is relatively rare in surveys; grouping by interviewers is somewhat more common, especially in some large-scale public opinion surveys, while coding in the office is the most usual procedure.

The type of codes required for machine tabulation differ from those needed if the data are to be sorted and counted by hand. However, all codes for machine tabulation can be used for hand tabulation. If data are to be sorted manually, word description of the classes is satisfactory. Also, abbreviations or letters of the alphabet may be used as codes. For machine tabulation, however, the classes must be expressed in numerical symbols. Furthermore, the number of different classes which can be shown on the punch card is limited to 12 or 13 groups. The description of the code procedure for punch cards will be presented later in the present chapter.

Codes are usually entered in one of four places:

1. *On precoded schedules.* The code numbers are printed on the schedule opposite the possible answers to each question. When the interviewer or informant encircles or checks the item which represents his response, the code number is thus marked.

The precoded schedule used in data collection saves both time and money. The cost of a special code card, the clerical work of coding in the office, and the supervision of such work is avoided. Another advantage of the precoded schedule is that transcription of the data to a code or transcription sheet is not necessary—punch card operators can work directly from the schedule used in the field. Thus errors in transcription are avoided.

The precoded schedule has several limitations, however, which tend to offset the above advantages. A previous or preliminary survey similar to that undertaken with the precoded schedule must be made in order to ascertain the relative frequency of various items and the types of replies which may be received. If the classes into which replies are divided on the precoded schedule contain unusually large frequencies in groups designated as "all other" or miscellaneous classes, the data are not very meaningful. A classification set up on the basis of actual replies would break down the miscellaneous group into more significant categories.

Another disadvantage of the precoded schedule is that the replies are classified in such general terms that it is difficult to detect errors in interviewing or reporting. Replies expressed in general terms may not appear to be inconsistent, but if the detailed facts were entered, the inconsistency might be evident. In precoded schedules the field worker is often asked to make a number of computations before classifying and recording the answer. Since the original figures are not available, the spotting of errors is either difficult or impossible. The same problem exists when the informant is asked to classify his own response. No check on his computations is possible when the basic raw data are lacking.

If hand tabulation is to be used, the precoded schedule is not very useful. It is usually necessary to prepare a special code card for office use anyway. The size of card which can be sorted and counted rapidly by hand is usually not the type easiest for the field worker to read and fill out. Furthermore, the average schedule receives so much handling during the process of field work and checking and editing of entries that if the schedule is also used for sorting and counting it soon wears out.

2. *On collection schedule near entries made in the field.* The most common code procedure is that of writing the code symbols on the schedule after the field work and editing of the schedule has been completed. Since the original data do not have to be transcribed to a code card, transcription time is saved and errors occurring in the copying process are avoided. The chief disadvantage of placing the code on the original schedule form is that space for coding is often cramped or lacking, since the schedule already contains interviewers' notes, check interview corrections, and editors' corrections and computations. If the color of ink used for codes stands out sharply from other material on the schedule, this is not an insuperable difficulty.

3. *On a transcription sheet.*[1] If a transcription sheet is used and has been designed with coding procedures in mind, the coder enters the codes in designated positions near the raw data. If all the pertinent information has been transferred to the transcription sheet, the coding procedure may be readily accomplished and verified. However, if only part of the information has been transferred, the coder may have difficulty deciding which codes to give various items, unless he goes back to the explanatory notes on the form used by interviewers.

Transcription or summary sheets. The most efficient and desirable arrangement of schedule items for purposes of the interview or data collection may be quite inefficient from the point of view of coding and tabulation. While it might seem a waste of time to transcribe all the information from the schedule to a sheet just to achieve a more convenient arrangement, the transcription sheet may actually prove to be time-saving as well as error-preventing. This is likely to be the case when the task of transcription is combined with editing, arithmetic computations, and coding.

When designing a transcription sheet, several suggestions may be kept in mind:

1. Avoid, if possible, a large unwieldy sheet with each case listed on a line and entries in column headings stretching across the entire sheet. Some disadvantages of the listing on a large sheet are:

---

[1] In the 1940 U. S. Census the transcription sheets for Household and for Sample Family data contained only the coded entries, and not the raw data. The designation "Code Sheet" better describes these forms.

a. Only one person can conveniently work on such a sheet at one time.
b. The difficulty of following a case across a long line and picking out the column in which an entry is to be made increases the chance of error.
c. The sheet must be sufficiently pliable to be rolled without taking up too much space. A sheet that is not pliable may become frayed if it is handled a great deal during coding and tabulation.
d. It is not possible to give individual cases special attention (such as is required when problems in editing or coding arise), because they cannot be separated and removed from the other cases without cutting up the sheet. If possible, therefore, employ individual transcription cards rather than long listings.
e. If cases are listed according to code numbers, insertion of new cases in which the code classification has been changed is not possible, unless the spacing between each case on the list is very great.

2. If hand tabulation is contemplated, try to design the sheet so that it will be small enough and sturdy enough to withstand sorting and counting.
3. Consider not only suitable arrangement for editing and coding, but also consider arrangement to be used on the punch card, if machine tabulation is to be employed.
4. Provide space for the transcription clerk, coder, and the verifiers to enter their names or initials.

4. *On code card.* The fourth system of coding consists in the preparation of a special code card to be filled out by the coder from the original schedule entries. This code card can be used for hand tabulation. If machine tabulation is used, the code card can be arranged to facilitate or speed up the punching process. The chief disadvantage of a special code card is that it is more difficult to check the accuracy of the codes when they are separated from the data to which they apply. The cost of printing a special code card must also be taken into account.

Selection of Codes

The choice of classes into which to group the raw data should be made with the distribution of cases and tabulations in mind. An inspection and preliminary tally of a small cross-section of schedules may reveal that a breakdown different from that selected on a priori grounds is to be preferred. A few general principles and suggestions should help the surveyor to design codes and coding procedures.

1. Use a more detailed classification than will appear in the final published tables. Not until after the first tables have been prepared can one be sure of the breadth of classes justified by the distribution of the data. It is a relatively simple matter to combine classes for presentation purposes. If the classes chosen for tabulation are too broad, there is danger that the real significance of the data will not be revealed. It is better to err on the side of too great detail than on that of insufficient detail.

2. If hand tabulation is proposed, the codes do not have to be expressed in numerical classes. It might be preferable to use letters or abbreviations rather than numerical symbols to express qualitative categories, since errors of coding are less likely to arise if the classification symbol resembles the word or phrases appearing on the schedule. If letters are used as codes, avoid symbols which may be confused in different styles of handwriting and printing.

3. If codes are to be placed on punch cards (see references on page 468), it is desirable to use 10 or fewer classes for most items. The punch card contains ten numbered spaces and an "X" and "Y" in each column, making a total of 12 codes which could be used. It is a rather complicated procedure to get more than one type of item in a column. Thus, for example, sex and age codes cannot be punched in a single column unless only six age groupings are used for each. It is also possible to get a thirteenth punch in a column, by a process known as the "X" over punch. However, it is not always possible to treat the "X" over punch in the same way as the other punches when tabulating the cards. If 14 code symbols are used, two columns are required. So if there is a doubt as to the desirability of a 12-fold or 14-fold classification, preference should be given the 12-fold grouping.

4. During coding, if some of the entries recorded by the enumerator do not need to be coded, the item or number to be punched should be encircled in a distinguishing color.

5. After codes have been entered, check them for accuracy and completeness before they go through the tabulation process. It is much more work to correct tables than to correct individual codes.

6. If complicated arithmetic computations must be made before an item can be coded, it is advisable to separate the two processes. The computor should first make his calculations and have them verified. Then the computation should be coded.

7. Insofar as possible, coding should be a routine operation. Questions requiring special attention should be settled by someone designated to handle problem cases. If necessary, the more involved sections of the schedule could be coded by persons specializing in those sections. However, if the coding is done by a group of persons who specialize in one or two sections, a final review of the schedule as a whole should be made by an editor-coder.

8. The staff of code clerks, under the direction of a coding supervisor, should be drawn from editors and interviewers, or office workers who are familiar with the definitions and methodology of the survey.

9. Detailed written coding instructions should be prepared so that uniform procedures are followed by all coders. Essential items to be included in the instructions are discussed later (page 458).

10. When setting up the codes for numerical data, decide what rounding procedure to use. Most people agree that .49 is to be dropped and .51 increased to the next unit, but few know what to do with .50. The procedure must be specified in the coding instructions.

11. Select standard or commonly used classifications whenever possible. By using classes which have been adopted by other studies, one takes advantage of the background data which can be used for interpreting the findings and testing the sample. The census groupings should be used for those items which are secured in the U. S. Census, unless other more recent or more detailed data happen to be available for the population being investigated.

Some classifications used in the 1940 Census and in later surveys by the Bureau of the Census are presented because these items are so frequently secured in surveys. Some groupings shown are finer than those usually employed in sampling surveys, but combinations may be readily made. The percentage distributions relate to the entire population of the United States. Surveyors of a particular city or rural area would do well to obtain these types of distribution for their own or a similar community in the same general location. If reliable data more recent than the last census are available, they should be used instead of the census figures. It is usually advisable, however, to employ groupings which can be made comparable with the census because inter-censal sampling surveys are frequently being made which contain current population figures. The percentage distributions are shown in the classifications given below so that the survey planner may get a rough idea of the relative frequencies of various groups in the general population. All classifications should make provision for the "unknown" or "not reported" items, even though this grouping does not appear on some of the classifications shown below. Coding instructions employed in the census and in special surveys often can be obtained upon request.

Urban-Rural. Definitions of urban and rural groups are given on page 166. The population of the United States in 1940 was distributed as follows: urban (56.5%) and rural (43.5%). Only 3 tenths of 1 per cent of the population of the nation lived in places the census classified as urban farm. The rural groups were almost equally divided between the rural nonfarm (20.3%) and the rural farm (22.9%).

Race and Nativity. According to the 1940 Census, the population of the United States was divided as follows: White (89.8%), Negro (9.8%), Other races (0.4%). The nativity of the whites was: Native (81.1%) and Foreign born (8.7%), adding up to the 89.8% total.

Age. The age classification used should depend primarily upon the purpose of the survey and on the range of ages covered. If the study deals with unemployment, for example, the age classification should take into account such facts as the minimum age for workers, the Social Security old age pension law, and other age regulations which might affect the labor market. Since the uses to which census material is put are so varied, ages are not grouped by the census for punch card purposes (except for under 1 year and 100 years or more). The published tabulations, however, contain several types of groupings. The following groups may readily be combined into six or eight significant classes: under 5 years (8.0%), 5–9 years (8.1%), 10–14 years (8.9%), 15–19 years (9.4%), 20–24 years (8.8%), 25–29 years (8.4%), 30–34 years (7.8%), 35–39 years (7.2%), 40–44 years (6.7%), 45–54 years (11.8%), 55–59 years (4.4%), 60–64 years (3.6%), 65–69 years (2.9%), 70–74 years (2.0%), 75 years and over (2.0%). The median age of persons 21 years and over is 63.8 years.

In addition to the above groupings, the census also published statistics on the number of persons in the following classes: under 1 year, 14 years, 15 years, 16 and 17 years, 21 years and over. With these classes it is possible to add to or subtract from the main groupings listed above to develop others. For example, by adding the 14-year-olds to the 15 and over group, the number of persons 14 years and over can be obtained. As a matter of fact, employment statistics of the census are given for persons 14 years and over, so this indirect procedure is not necessary for this particular case. For other population statistics, however, derived age groupings might be necessary.

The following statement on age groupings used in the 1940 Census tables appears in the Population Report, second series: "The age classification is based on the age of the person at his last birthday before the date of the census, that is, the age of the person in completed years. . . . In tables showing the population by age for state, counties, urban places, and the larger metropolitan districts, the classification is by 5-year periods up to 75 years. Tables for minor civil divisions, for incorporated places having 1,000 to 2,500 inhabitants, for wards of cities of 50,000 or more and for the smaller metropolitan districts present data for persons under 5 years of age, and then classify the population by 10-year intervals up to 65 years. Age data are also available in various tables for selected additional class intervals. In connection with the statistics relating to school attendance the following age classes are shown: 5, 6, 7–9, 10–13, 14, 15, 16–17, 18–19, 20, 21–24. Data relating to the labor force include the age classification '14 and over'; the data relating to citizenship include the classification '21 and over'; and data relating to highest grade of school completed include the classification '25 and over.' Finally, the classifications 'under 1' and '21 and over' are included in a number of age tables because of the frequent use made of these data" (p. 4).

In most surveys provision should be made for coding "age unknown." The census utilized a procedure for estimating age on the basis of other available information, such as school attendance, employment status, age of other members of the family, etc., so the census tables do not contain the "not reported" age group.

Highest Grade of School Completed. Census data on educational attainment refer to the last full grade completed in the regular school system—public, private, or parochial school, college or university. The published tables usually group the schooling for persons 25 years old and over into the classes which follow (the percentage of such persons who received each amount of schooling according to the 1940 Census is also shown). No school years completed (3.7%); Grade School: 1 to 4 years (9.8%), 5 and 6 years (11.4%), 7 and 8 years (34.6%); High School: 1 to 3 years (15.0%), 4 years (14.1%); College: 1 to 3 years (5.4%), 4 years or more (4.6%); Not Reported (1.4%). The median years of schooling was 8.4 years for the population 25 years and over. More detailed statistics on education and school enrollment and attendance are also published.

Marital Status.   The 1940 Census used the following codes: Single *1*, married *2*, widowed *3*, divorced *4*, married spouse absent *5*. The marital status of persons 14 years old and over and 20 to 44 years in the United States civilian population not in institutions in June, 1946, was estimated by the Census Bureau from a sample survey (Report P-S No. 16). The distribution of males 14 years old and over follows: Single (28.3%), Married (65.9%), Widowed and Divorced (5.8%). The married males were further classified according to those with wife present (64.4%) and wife absent (1.4%). The distribution of the females was Single (22.9%), Married (62.8%), Widowed and Divorced (14.3%). Married women were further grouped into: Husband present (59.3%), Husband absent and in armed forces (1.3%), and Husband absent other reason (2.1%).

The June, 1946, report mentioned above also showed the marital status of heads of families. The distribution was: Male head (82.6%), Female Head (17.4%). Those families with males heads were further classified into: Married, wife present (75 6%), Married, wife absent (0.6%), Widowed and Divorced (3.8%), Single (2.6%). The same breakdown for female heads gave the figures: Married, husband absent (2.4%), Widowed and Divorced (12.3%), Single (2.7%).

Families; Relationship of Members.   The relationship of each person to the head of the household was indicated in the instructions for general population coding by the following code symbols: Head, either male or female, except head of a hotel, institution, etc. (code 0); Wife of head (code 1); Child—either son or daughter, including stepchild but not including son-in-law or daughter-in-law (code 2); Parent— including father-in-law, mother-in-law, stepmother, and stepfather (code 3); Grandchild (code 4); Other relative of head—including son-in-law, brother-in-law, nephew, niece, brother, sister, uncle, aunt,

grandparent, etc. (code 5); Lodger, roomer, boarder, or partner—
wife, son, or daughter of lodger, boarder, etc. (code 6); Servant—
maid, chauffeur, butler, housekeeper, etc. (code 7); Servant's wife,
son, daughter; any other employee's wife, son, or daughter; or any
other person not covered by other codes (code 8); Hired hand or other
employee who is *not* a domestic servant (code x); Resident in a hotel,
institution, prison, school, household with 11 or more lodgers, etc.
(except an employee and the members of his family who occupy a
detached house or structure and are returned as a separate household
in accordance with Paragraph 427, *Instructions to Enumerators*). For
the above residents, the codes used are: Head (that is, manager, offi-
cer, superintendent, or warden) of hotel, institution, etc.—usually the
first person listed—(code v); Any other person in a hotel, institution,
etc. (code 9).

From the detailed codes it was possible to prepare a great variety of
tables on family composition and size. Comparisons of the 1940 data
with estimates obtained from sample surveys in 1946 reveal similar
distributions. In no case is there a difference as large as 2 per cent in
any of the family size groups given below, so the more recent figures
are presented: One-person families (10.3%), 2 persons (27.1%), 3
persons (22.1%), 4 persons (18.0%), 5 persons (10.5%), 6 persons
(5.7%), 7 or more persons (6.3%).

Families were classified as follows by the number of children under
10 years in the February, 1946, sample survey estimate: Families with
no children under 10 years (63.4%); Families with one or more children under 10 years (36.6%). When the number of children under
18 years of age is considered, the distribution is: No children under 18
(47.5%), 1 child under 18 (21.2%), 2 children under 18 (15.4%),
3 or more children under 18 (14.9%).

Doubling of families is also of interest to surveyors. According to
the 1946 estimate, the presence of more than one family in a home
appears as follows: With no subfamily (5.2%), With one subfamily
(4.2%), With two or more subfamilies (0.2%). Definitions of subfamilies, lodgers, etc. are to be found in the Census reports containing
these figures (P.S. 16). Lodgers are found in 8.1% of the households.
Of the 91.9 per cent of the households with no lodgers, 88.1% have
no subfamilies, 3.7% have one subfamily, and 0.1% have two or more
subfamilies.

Housing and Rentals: a. *Type of Structure of Dwelling Units.* The distribution of dwelling units in 1940 in the United States was as follows: 1 family detached (81%), 1 family attached (4.0%), 2 family side by side (2.8%), 2 family other (5.9%), 3 family (1.6%), 4 family (0.7%), 1 to 4 family with business (2.3%), 5 to 9 family (0.8%), 10 to 19 family (0.2%), 20 family or more (0.2%), other dwelling place (0.5%). The definitions of these types of structures appear in the reports on *Population and Housing, Introduction.* Each dwelling unit in a group of three or more row houses is a "1 family attached" structure, but two attached dwelling units by themselves constitute a "2 family side-by-side" structure. Dwelling units in one to four family structures with business are shown in a separate group, but dwelling units in five family or larger structures with business are not separated in the tabulations from those without businesses. "Other dwelling places" such as trailers, tourist cabins, boats, etc., were enumerated only when occupied by persons having no other place of residence.

b. *Monthly Rent or Rental Value.* The contract rents of rented homes and the estimated monthly rents of owner-occupied homes in 1940 were quite different from those found several years after World War II when the housing shortages and restrictions in building had had an effect. The 1940 distribution, however, may be useful if the survey planner keeps in mind that it contains too high a percentage of low rentals and not enough of the high as compared with the late 1940's.

Contract rents and estimated monthly rents of urban and rural nonfarm homes in the United States in 1940 were as follows: Less than $3 (2.2%), $3–4 (3.2%), $5–6 (5.4%), $7–9 (5.1%), $10–14 (12.3%), $15–19 (12.0%), $20–24 (11.6%), $25–29 (11.1%), $30–39 (16.1%), $40–49 (9.2%), $50–59 (4.8%), $60–74 (3.2%), $75–99 (1.9%), $100 or more (1.9%). The estimated value of owner-occupied units over the entire United States in 1940 appears as follows: Less than $300 (6.7%), $300–499 (4.9%), $500–699 (6.1%), $700–799 (5.9%), $1,000–1,499 (10.7%), $1,500–1,999 (8.9%), $2,000–2,499 (0.0%), $2,500–2,999 (7.3%), $3,000–3,999 (13.3%), $4,000–4,999 (8.6%), $5,000–5,999 (6.4%), $6,000–7,499 (5.4%), $7,500–9,999 (3.3%), $10,000–14,999 (2.2%), $15,000–19,999 (0.7%), $20.000 or more (0.7%).

According to the 1940 Census figures, 43.6 per cent of all homes in the United States were owner-occupied dwelling units.

Employment, Occupations, and Earnings: a. *Employment Status*. Facts about employment in 1940 during the week of March 24 to 30 were secured for all persons 14 years of age and over. The most up-to-date material, however, is available from current sample surveys of the labor force conducted by the Bureau of the Census (see page 17). Prior to June, 1947, these reports were known as the *Monthly Report of the Labor Force* or the MRLF series. Since that date the information is published as *Current Population Reports—Labor Force Series P-57*. The release of June 10, 1947, gave the following estimates of employment status of the noninstitutional population of the United States for the week May 4–10, 1947 (P-57 No. 60).

Total noninstitutional population 14 years and over	107,330,000
Total labor force including armed forces	61,760,000
Civilian labor force	60,290,000
Employed	58,330,000
At work	56,470,000
35 hours or more during week	48,270,000
15–34 hours during week	6,440,000
1–14 hours during week	1,760,000
With a job but not at work	1,860,000
Unemployed	1,960,000
Not in labor force	45,570,000

The definitions used in the above classification follow:

Employed—employed persons comprise those who, during the survey week, were either (a) "at work," i.e., those who did any work for pay or profit, or worked without pay for 15 hours or more on a farm or business; or (b) "With a job but not at work," i.e., those who did not work and were not looking for work but had a job or business from which they were temporarily absent because of vacation, illness, industrial dispute, bad weather, or layoff with definite instructions to return to work within 30 days of layoff. Also included are persons who had new jobs but had not yet started to work.

Unemployed—unemployed persons include those who did not work at all during the survey week, and who were looking for work. Also included as unemployed are persons who would have been looking for work except that (a) they were temporarily ill, (b) they expected to return to a job from which they had been laid off for an indefinite period, or (c) they believed no work was available in their line of work in the community.

Labor force—the civilian labor force comprises the total of all civilians classified as employed or unemployed in accordance with the criteria described above. Figures on the net strength of the armed forces at the first of the month are added to the civilian labor force to obtain the total labor force.

Not in labor force—all persons 14 years of age and over who are not classified as employed or unemployed are defined as "Not in the labor force." These persons are further classified as "engaged in own home housework, in school, and other," the latter group including for the most part retired persons, those permanently unable or too old to work, seasonal workers for whom the survey week fell in an "off" season, and the voluntarily idle. Persons doing only incidental unpaid family work (less than 15 hours) are also classified as "not in the labor force."

b. *Class of Worker.* The class of worker is shown in the June 3, 1947, release covering the week of April 6–12, 1947.

Total employed	56,700,000
Employed in nonagricultural industries	48,840,000
Private wage or salary workers	37,230,000
In domestic service	1,740,000
Other wage or salary workers	35,490,000
Government workers	5,270,000
Self-employed workers	5,940,000
Unpaid family workers	400,000
Employed in agriculture	7,860,000
Wage or salary workers	1,370,000
Self-employed workers	5,090,000
Unpaid family workers	1,400,000

"Wage or salary workers" are persons working for wages, salary, commission, tips, pay in kind, or at piece-rates for a private employer or for any governmental unit. "Self-employed workers" are persons working in their own businesses, professions, or trade, or operating a farm, for profit or fees. "Unpaid family workers" are persons working without pay on a farm or in a business operated by a member of the household to whom they are related by blood or marriage.

c. *Occupational Groups.* Occupations of employed persons were distributed in the following classes in the labor force report covering the week April 6–12, 1947: Professional and semi-professional workers

(6.8%), Farmers and farm managers (9.0%), Proprietors, managers, and officials (except farm) (10.2%), Clerical and kindred workers (12.4%), Salesmen and saleswomen (5.8%), Operatives and kindred workers (21.5%), Craftsmen, foremen, and kindred workers (13.3%), Domestic service workers (3.2%), Service workers, except domestic (7.2%), Farm laborers (wage workers) and foremen (4.6%), Laborers, except farm and mine (6.0%). The detailed list of occupations included in the above classes should be consulted for coding purposes (see 991, 994, 995).

d. *Relationship of Earners.* The *Instructions for sample family transcription* (Form P. 426) of the 1940 Census contained the following classifications for earners in a family: No earners; 1 or more earners. The latter group was further classified into: head earner, wife not earner, or no wife; wife earner, head not earner; head and wife both earners; neither head nor wife earners.

e. *Earnings.* Yearly earnings or wage and salary income of individuals for the year 1939 preceding the 1940 census were classified and distributed as follows: None (7.0%), $1–99 (3.7%), $100–199 (6.3%), $200–399 (12.7%), $400–599 (11.2%), $600–799 (12.2%), $800–999 (10.0%), $1,000–1,199 (8.9%), $1,200–1,399 (8.6%), $1,400–1,599 (6.7%), $1,600–1,799 (3.7%), $1,800–1,999 (4.6%), $2,000–2,499 (5.9%), $2,500–2,999 (2.2%), $3,000–3,999 (2.1%), $4,000–4,999 (0.6%), $5,000 and over (1.0%), Not reporting income (2.3%). Median wage or salary income was $877 for the year.

f. *Industry.* The major industry groups used in the 1940 census included: Agriculture, forestry and fishing; construction; mining; manufacturing; transportation, communication, and other public utilities; wholesale and retail trade; finance, insurance and real estate; business and repair services; personal services; amusement, recreation, and related services; government; not reported.

g. *Family Income.* The annual income of families from all sources such as wages, dividends, interest, etc., is frequently included as a survey question. The 1940 Census did not ascertain the amount of income from sources other than wages and salaries, so the total family income is not available from this source. However, the census did ascertain whether or not income which amounted to $50 or more was received from sources other than wages or salaries, so it was possible to obtain the total income from those families who did not receive such supplemental income. The amount of income received by families in the United States from wages or salaries in 1939 and the per cent of families receiving such income was as follows: $1–199 (6.4%), $200–399 (9.2%), $400–599 (8.8%), $600–799 (8.9%), $800–999 (7.8%), $1,000–1,199 (7.7%), $1,200–1,399 (8.3%), $1,400–1,599 (7.4%), $1,600–1,999 (10.8%), $2,000–2,499 (9.8%), $2,500–2,999 (5.2%), $3,000–4,999 (7.3%), $5,000 and over (2.3%). The median family income from wages and salaries was $1,226.

Coding Instructions

The following items should be included in the written instructions to coders:

1. A statement that coders are to familiarize themselves with instructions to enumerators, to editors, and the card punchers or sorters.
2. A description of the purposes of coding and of the various steps involved.
3. Criteria by which the coder can decide whether or not a schedule is acceptable for coding, e.g., certain items must be filled in or the schedule should be rejected. Usually the editors have weeded out the unacceptable ones but the coders may catch oversights.
4. Criteria by which the coder can decide whether any given item is acceptable or ready for tabulation.
5. A statement of the order in which items are to be coded, e.g., whether to take one item at a time or to cover all items on a given schedule before proceeding to the next one. It is usually better for the coder to limit his work to one or two codes at a time so that he can keep the instructions in mind easily.
6. Specifications as to how the code should be entered: (a) Place— in margin of card? Above each item being coded? Below each item? To the right of it? To the left? (b) Which items are to be encircled to indicate that the interviewer's entry is already in code form? (c) What color pencil should be used for codes? (d) Write legibly. (e) Do not erase or write over an item, but draw a line through errors and write another entry clearly.
7. Code only *final* corrected entries. Code the final figure rather than one which has been changed by the interviewer or editor or check editor.

8. If a marginal case arises, or if the case does not seem to fit into the classification prepared, consult with the supervisor of coding.

9. A detailed definition of every item to be coded as well as detailed examples of every type of answer to be assigned each code.

10. Warning to coders about the mistakes or types of errors they may find and which should be corrected before the coding proceeds.

11. Warning to coders about types of errors they are likely to make unless they are very careful.

12. Examples of when it is permissible to code "no report" or "unknown."

13. An example of a correctly coded schedule.

14. Instructions for coder and code verifier to sign his name or initials to coded schedule.

15. Detailed instructions to "code verifiers" or "checkers."

The coding of open-end questions or "free story" answers requires more skill as well as knowledge of the survey topic than does coding of more objective and systematically collected data. Woodward and Franzen found that it is possible to get fairly high agreement among coders for this less-standardized material (**1121**).

Selected References

Coding and Classification of Data
Alderson (**3**), Berkson (**53**), Edwards (**275, 276, 281**), Erdos (**292**), Kolesnikoff (**529**), Lundberg (**596, 597**), Newcomb (**689**), Palmer (**713**), Roper (**805**), U.S. (**991, 994, 995, 1000, 1002, 1012**), Woodward and Franzen (**1121**).
See also discussion in books on Statistical Methods, Research Methods, Market Research, and Social Research.

Census Data
U. S. (**1000, 1002**).

CHAPTER XV

Tabulation of the Data

The essential element of tabulation is the summarization of results in the form of statistical tables. Only when the raw data have been classified into groups and counts made of the number of cases falling in the various groups is it possible for the surveyor to determine what his results mean and to convey his findings to the reader in a form which can be readily understood. To transform the information from the schedules to finished tables requires the various steps of editing, preparation of table forms, classification, coding, punching, and running cards through machines (for mechanical tabulation), sorting or listing and tallying (for hand tabulation), counting, recording of counts, analysis and regrouping of data and computation of summary measures which may appear on the finished tables, and lastly the presentation of the tables in the report. Since all of these topics except the procedures of sorting, counting, and recording counts in tables and the mechanics of table construction have been discussed elsewhere in this book, the present chapter will be devoted to these remaining topics and most basic elements of tabulation.

Inexperienced surveyors seldom concern themselves with tabulation plans until the data have been collected, but experienced workers develop tabulation plans at the same time as they draft the schedule and sampling plans. Although it is impossible for the table designer to foresee all the tabulations which will be desired, he should be familiar enough with the subject of the investigation to draw up tables which will provide answers to the questions which gave rise to the survey. He should know how questions may be interpreted and answered by respondents, and the relative frequency with which various answers may occur. The preliminary knowledge need not be so exact nor in so much detail for subgroups as will be shown in the final tabulations. The surveyor should be able to prepare adequate tabulation plans if he uses the findings from earlier surveys which are similar or have elements in common with the one for which the plans are being drafted. When new fields of human activity are being explored, the safest procedure is to pretest the questionnaire on the same type of population as that to be used for the final survey. In this way the incidence of various responses and population groups can be ascertained and plans made for meaningful tabulations.[1]

If no data are available from a pilot study or a previous survey, sources such as the United States Census, National Surveys, State Censuses, and other local surveys will usually provide enough basic information about the distribution of the population for the surveyor to estimate the number of cases which the survey will yield in the various subgroups of the proposed tables. For example, if less than 1% of the population of a small community belong to the Negro race, a survey which covers 10% of the families in the community is not likely to yield enough Negroes to justify detailed tabulations by race.

The process of tabulation may be accomplished entirely by manual methods, or by machine methods which also require certain hand operations but which utilize fast electrical machines for the bulk of the process. Before detailed tabulation plans can be drafted, the surveyor must decide which method to use. The tabulation cost, forms, cards, instructions sheets, time and personnel required for carrying out the proposed tabulations will depend upon whether the data are to be sorted and tabulated by hand or are to be punched on cards and sorted and tabulated by mechanical means. Whichever method is employed, careful planning of the details will save much time and expense in the long run. Some surveyors assume that plans are necessary only when machine tabulation is contemplated, and that little or no planning is required for hand tabulation. As a result, surveyors using hand tabulation are faced with many problems which arise only because of lack of planning. The relative merits of each will be discussed after the two tabulation procedures have been described below, and the surveyor will be better able to decide which method is better suited to his problems.

---

[1] The importance of examining every question included on the schedule to see how it will fit into the tabulation plans has been discussed in Chapter VI.

Hand Tabulation

Tabulation by manual methods usually is accomplished by one of the following techniques: (1) listing and tallying, or (2) card sorting and counting. One common procedure is to use a counting or listing sheet on which the data from each schedule are posted on a line or two devoted to each case. The sheets are usually large enough to accommodate fifty or a hundred schedules. Tallies are made from this sheet and no sorting takes place. Sometimes schedules are sorted as they come from the editors and separate listing sheets are used for various groups. For example, there may be a sheet for the cases in each income group, or a sheet for each age group, or for some other characteristics for which major tabulations are to be prepared. The most usual procedure is to list the cases by schedule number. The schedule may be copied pretty much as it stands after editing, or just the code numbers may be posted for each item. Counts made from the code numbers are much more likely to be accurate since problems of classification do not come up every time a count is to be made. The technique of cross-fives is often used to count the number of cases on each sheet. Four vertical short strokes represent four cases and an oblique line crossing them is the fifth, e.g., ||||. These tallies can be recorded on a tally sheet set up in the form of a table or they may be placed on numbered sheets attached to the blank table forms. The advantage of the first method is that adequate titles describe each count and it is easy to make the final count and cross-checks from the tallies before entering the figures in the final table, which takes the same form as the tally tables. This counting procedure is time-consuming as well as difficult to check. The eye does not easily follow long columns and rows and select the correct items. It is hard to remember if one has counted a case, since the tallies are being written with one hand while the other follows along the columns, and in glancing from the data sheet to the tally sheet one is likely to lose the place. If large transcription sheets are used, each sheet should be numbered and each column fully described by its title. A subtotal with which each column is to check should be entered on each sheet in order to facilitate the checking of the columns.

Some surveyors work directly from the schedules to the tally sheet without listing the cases first. There are instances when it is not worthwhile to transcribe codes to a hand count card. If, for example, only a few cross-tabulations are planned, or if only a few simple tables are desired, and the schedule entries are clear, it may be quite efficient to tally the returns without sorting them first. Unless the schedules are easy to sort and handle and the coded entries are clear, however, the tallies are likely to be difficult to check. If a great many detailed tables are to be prepared, or if there are numerous items or cases, the listing and tallying methods are usually too cumbersome and inefficient to justify their use. The chief advantage of the listing procedure is that it can run concurrently with the field work and as soon as the schedules have been edited and coded. Card sorting and counting, on the other hand, is efficient only if done as a complete operation according to a prepared plan.

A TALLY CARD:

Instead of using sheets or code cards for each schedule, the tabulator may use an answer card such as that described by Phelps (740). This is designed for exploratory or pilot surveys employing open-ended questions in which the replies cannot be anticipated. The card, prepared in advance of the tabulations, contains a space or cell for each of the population classes or subgroups by which the answers are to be classified. Each card when filled in gives the tabulated characteristics of all persons who gave a particular answer to the question listed on that card. The schedule question is noted at the top of the card and a space is provided for writing in the reply received. If there are twenty questions with an average of ten different replies each, two hundred answer cards will be required.

CARD SORTING AND COUNTING:

Contrary to general belief, hand tabulation may be very rapid and accurate, if the proper techniques are employed. One of the most efficient techniques utilizes a small code card which may be easily sorted and counted. A 3 x 5 index card with a fairly smooth surface is satisfactory. As many or even more codes may be placed on a card this size than on an 80 column punch card. By the use of such devices as colors, heavy lines, encircled figures, and various space positions on the card, the codes may be easily differentiated, and the cards may be efficiently sorted. It is possible, for example, for a relatively unskilled clerical worker to sort 1000 cards into six stacks in less than five minutes. Since few surveys have more than 5000 cases, the actual sorting process is not very time-consuming if the code card is carefully designed. To be sure, subsorts will be wanted, but at the above production rate, the time required for further sorting may be calculated.

Counting the number of cards in each stack is also quite rapid if small cards are used. If the counter holds the two upper corners of a pack of cards and bends the deck with short jerks, the corners of individual cards can be exposed somewhat like a fan. If the fingernail is caught in these corners, the number of cards in the pack can be counted very rapidly. In a series of tests the writer counted 1,000 cards in an average of 4 minutes per 1000.[2]

When a large stack of cards is being counted, it is easy to check errors if the cards are piled in groups of 25 or 50. These may be laid crosswise over each other and the total number of cards may be readily computed when the number of piles of 25 cards is known. If the sum of the separate stacks does not equal the known total (shown on the table or from some previous count) it may not be necessary to count every stack of 25 cards, because the error may be found in the first pile picked up.

In large-scale surveys the instructions for card sorting and counting should cover such items as:

1. The importance of having all coded cards available before the sorting begins.
2. The necessity of keeping cards in files or special boxes properly labeled when the cards are not in use.
3. The desirability of placing rubber bands around each stack as soon as the sorting operation is completed so that cards will not be lost or misplaced.
4. Seeing that every bundle is correctly labeled so that other operators will know what it contains and which sorts it has passed through.
5. Where to obtain cards for a given sort, i.e., from which file, control clerk, or tabulation supervisor.

---

[2] The reader may test his own ability in this field by sorting 200 playing cards into 8 groups—the four suits and face cards and numbered cards in each suit. The time taken to count each of the eight stacks may also be tested. If data on code cards were properly coded and arranged, the time required for counting and sorting would probably not be much greater than that required when playing cards are used.

6. The importance of signing a receipt for cards received and of getting a receipt for cards given to other operators. It should indicate the date received, number of cards in the bundle, and the bundle number.

7. Each bundle received should have a bundle face card containing pertinent information about its contents.

8. Write legibly, do not erase or write over, but draw a line through errors and write another entry.

9. Detailed instructions for filling out each table including the order in which sorts are to be made to get the counts for tables. For example, instructions for sorting and tabulating cards to obtain Table 10—Color of head, might read somewhat as follows:

Step 1. Obtain card bundle number XX21 from clerk R. B., giving receipt.

Step 2. Remove bundle face card and give it to your supervisor.

Step 3. Sort cards into two groups for Question 10—Color of head, according to code X (white) and code Y (Negro). Note there will be no cards in this bundle having code Z (other). If you find such a card report it to your supervisor. It should have been removed for tabulating Table 9.

Step 4. Verify this sort by examining each of the two stacks of cards.

Step 5. Now count the cards in X stack and enter the number in Table 10, Column 4, Row 3.

Step 6. Verify the count. Count the number in stack X again, being careful that cards do not stick together. If your second count differs from the first, count the cards again and keep doing so until the count agrees twice in succession.

Step 7. Verify the position or entry of the number in Table 10, Column 4, Row 3. Is it the same as the corrected count?

Step 8. The total of row 1 minus column 3 (row 1) should equal the figure you have just checked in step 7. If these figures are not identical, consult your supervisor.

Step 9. Count the cards in stack Y and enter the number in Table 10, Column 4, Row 4.

Step 10. Verify the count as in step 6.

Step 11. Verify the entry in Column 4, Row 4.

Step 12. The total of Row 2 minus Column 3 (Row 2) should equal the figure you have just checked in step 11.

Step 13. If the table entries check, place a bundle face card X on stack X, and Y on stack Y, place rubber bands around each and file in file 11-XY.

Step 14. Sign the tabulation control sheet and hand it to control clerk M. B.

Step 15. Give Table 10 to M. B.

Adequate tabulation plans require that:

1. Tentative table forms be drafted when the schedule questions are being planned, and that the basic tables be decided upon before coding is begun.

2. All major tables which are to come out of the various counts should be decided in advance of the sorting and counting operations.

3. The coding operation which precedes sorting should have been done in accordance with the best principles of classification and coding laid down in Chapter XIV. Thus the codes should be correct, easily legible, not easily confused with other codes, and should not require too much attention on the part of the sorter for grouping of codes.

4. In large-scale studies a supervisor of tabulation should organize and direct the work and be responsible for the quality and quantity of work performed.

5. An efficient control system should be set up so that the whereabouts of all cards are known at any given time and no cards are lost or misplaced. Operating files fully labeled may be used for holding cards before and after the various sorts and counts. As the tabulation progresses, files with new labels are set up and old ones discontinued. Full instructions for the preparation of the files, labeling of their contents, and responsibility for their maintenance should be made available before the sorting operation is begun.

6. If a counting sheet is used instead of cards, the instructions for entering and checking the schedule data and the filing system for the schedules should be available to the tabulators.

7. Serial numbers should appear on all schedules, code cards, counting sheets, bundle face cards or sheets, files, and tables. Whenever any of these items are referred to in tabulation instructions, the serial number as well as the title should be used.

8. All table forms should carry clear and complete titles to prevent entries being made on the wrong tables. Serial numbers are also of help in this connection.

9. The principles of correct table construction, to be discussed later, should be followed.

10. The order in which the various tables are to be prepared is carefully worked out in advance of tabulation. The most efficient order would be one that utilizes each major sort for all the counts that are to be made from it before a resorting is made. For example, in a study where the income factor is regarded as very important, once the cards have been sorted by income classes, all subsorts by income groups should be made before the cards are sorted by some other factor such as age. Otherwise it will be necessary to throw the cards back into the income groups again for other tabulations, thus requiring unnecessary duplication of sorting. It is usually desirable to sort first by a factor which appears on a series of tables or even on every table. The stacks of cards from these major sorts then are filed separately and used for all subsequent sorts involving this factor. The total of each stack should be the base total with which all the sums of the detailed tabulations should check. Sometimes surveyors have found it convenient to make a few master sorts for two or three groups such as income groups, age groups, or educational groups. After totals are obtained for these groups the cards are thrown together and the various tables prepared. Totals for checking the figures on each table or series of tables are then made available from the master count. If such main counts are to be valuable they must be accurate, otherwise the detailed tables will not check with them, and the source of error will be hard to find.

11. A routine for checking every sort, every count, and every entry of the count to the tables should be established.

12. Detailed instructions are prepared for sorting, counting, entering the counts in tables, filing and verifying each of these operations.

Machine Tabulation

In the few pages which can be devoted to a description of machine tabulation, only the most basic processes can be mentioned. For a more detailed treatment the reader may consult the bibliography at the end of this chapter, or publications of the commercial agencies which rent the tabulating machines.[3] Representatives of such agencies will acquaint the potential customer with the latest devices for performing various operations.

Readers who are not familiar with the steps in machine tabulation may be interested in a brief description of the process of the punch card, machine sorting, counting, and tabulating, and the machine runs.

The first step in machine tabulation (after data have been coded) is to transfer the codes to the punch card, of which two sizes are in general use—the 80 column card and the 45 column card.[4] The codes are transferred to the cards in the form of punched holes. Each column contains 12 punching positions. Numbers 0–9 are printed on the card while the 11th and 12th punched positions at the top of the card are unnumbered. The 80 column card with its 12 positions gives 960 potential punch positions. As a matter of fact, however, only one position is usually punched in each column. It is possible to utilize a second punch (X over punch) for certain purposes.[5]

The punch card is usually divided into groups of columns known as "fields" where particular types of information appears. The number of columns used for each field depends on the number of digits it may have to accommodate. For example, if the exact age of the informant were to be punched, two columns would be required in the age field, but if seven age groups were coded, one column would suffice. As a rule, the name of the field is printed on the card to facilitate punching and verifying as well as for general usefulness to the survey staff.

Ordinarily the tabulation problems are less complicated if all the data are placed on a single card. If the data for each case require several cards, cross-tabulations of items appearing on different cards are not so easily obtainable. Furthermore, it is necessary to repeat the identifying information on major controls on each card, since most tabulations require such data. It is possible, however, by means of a dupli-

---

[3] The International Business Machine Corporation makes the Hollerith Machine and Remington Rand, Inc.—Powers Accounting Machine Division makes the Powers (8, p. 248).

[4] Since the cost of the 45 column card is about the same as that of the 80 column card, it is rapidly falling into disuse.

[5] Single punching means one hole is punched in each column. Double punching means that two holes may be punched in each column. This is accomplished by using the X and R keys which are on the punch and verifying machines. These letters do not appear on the face of the card (638).

cator to punch the columns of identifying information upon several sets of cards rather than to punch each card individually. A type of tabulator has been placed on the market which enables cross-tabulations to be made of data appearing on different cards, but a special machine device is required for this purpose.

The codes are punched on the tabulating cards by trained punch operators. If the survey is a large-scale undertaking extending over a long period, it may be possible to train punch operators selected from the clerical force. The punches are verified by a second operator who actually punches the data a second time; if an error is found, a bell rings to indicate the error. "The punch designed for the numerical system has a keyboard consisting of twelve keys, one for each punching position of a column. As a key is depressed, a hole is cut and the card advanced automatically to the next column to be punched" (21, p. 7).

The time required to punch codes and to verify the punches is difficult to estimate because it depends upon such factors as: (1) The skill of the punch operator—whether a professional or one trained by the survey for this purpose; (2) the condition of the data to be punched. (If several calculations must be made before the operator punches each key, it will take much longer than if the codes are in form suitable for punching. Furthermore, if the data on the code sheets are arranged in the same order as the fields on the card, the punch operator does not waste time skipping from one section of the code sheet to another. In some cases it may be necessary to take an intermediate step between coding and punching to prepare a code card arranged conveniently for punching purposes. Another factor which is important is the legibility of the data to be punched. If the codes are generally not clearly legible, the punch operator will consume a great deal of time trying to decipher the symbols.) (3) The physical conditions under which the punch operators must work, such as space, lighting, condition of punching machine, etc. (555).

Authorities differ in their estimates of punching speed. Differences are probably due to factors such as those mentioned above. Eckert (269) reports that 125 eighty-column cards can be punched per hour from good typed manuscript. Leahy analyzed card punching from raw data sheets to 80 column Hollerith Cards for 15,000 cases with a code of 563 possible items. Punchers averaged 219 cards a day or 33 an hour, while verifiers averaged 256 cards a day or 39 an hour. The greatest output was in the morning, and the lowest was late in the afternoon, when also the greatest number of errors, 6 to 10 per cent, occurred. Fewest errors were made in the early afternoon and late morning. Those which were made were omissions, misreadings, and misplacements. Leahy found that errors may be reduced by giving attention to the lighting of the laboratory, analysis of errors and omissions, and attention to the vividness of ink used in the data sheets. Deming and others (244) examined errors of punch operators in the Bureau of the Census. From .5 to 5 per cent of the cards of the various operators had to be replaced because of errors. Errors arose when the operator skipped a column, punched a hole in the wrong position, or put a second hole in a column where there should be only one. The net effect of the errors proved to be negligible because errors were compensating and because many of the errors were made in the righthand columns of a field. These columns are the units for numerical data rather than the tens or hundreds so the errors were of small magnitude. Of course, errors in the right columns would be just as serious as those in the left for nonnumerical data.

SORTING AND TABULATING MACHINES:

After the data are on punch cards, many different types of machines may be employed in the production of the tabulations desired.[6] The most essential machines are the card sorters and tabulators.

------

[6] For a description of the following machines, see Baehne (21):

Alphabetic printing punch	Automatic summary punch	Manual code punch
Automatic reproducing punch	Gang punch	Automatic interpreter multiplying punch
Elec. card-operated sorting machine	Elec. card-operated counting sorter	

See also a description of the following special devices:

Card matching device	Class selection device	Collating device
Consecutive number control device	Counter carry over device	Decimal accumulating device
Split column device	Groups sorting device	Pre-set selector
Multiple column selection device	Total transfer device	Universal automatic device
	Test scoring device	

Eckert (269), in addition to discussing the sorting and tabulating machines, gives a full description of the summary punch, the multiplier, the interpreter and the calculation control switch.

Card-Operated Sorting Machine. Cards are sorted by electricity at the rate of 400 cards per minute (21). When the perforated cards pass under brush contacts, an electrical impulse is made through the card at the punched hole. Thus an electrical circuit is closed at a definite time and from a fixed position on the card. This momentary circuit sends the card to a receiving pocket which corresponds to the punched position. Only one column is sorted at a time. Thus a four column field would be run through the sorter four times. For example, if sorting is being done for column 3, a card punched "8" is directed to the 8 pocket, a card punched "5" is directed to the 5 pocket, etc.

The process does not always operate without a slip, however. Cases have been reported in which the brushes have been worn and the machine has made errors. Mechanical defects are unavoidable, and since they do exist, the surveyor should be on guard for errors made by the machine just as he is on guard for clerical errors. One surveyor who has done a great deal of sorting by machine remarked that the sorting machine is apparently a rather delicate mechanism and it may give completely wrong results if the cards are worn. If the box is too full the works may jam and cards in the process of going through may get caught and torn when extricated.

Electric Tabulating Machine. This is a combination adding, subtracting, and printing machine, which operates at a speed of 150 cards per minute (21). With it summary cards can be punched simultaneously with the printing of reports. A trained operator must wire the tabulating machines for each desired tabulation. When the sorting machine causes the cards to drop into pigeonholes the counting sorter counts the number having holes in the various rows in each column and gives a grand total as well. The tabulator can be equipped to provide products as well as counts. The counts are printed by the tabulating machine on large sheets known as "machine runs."

Processes Following Machine Tabulation

EDITING THE MACHINE RUNS:

After the "machine runs" are obtained from the tabulating machine, it is necessary to write in the heading for each column of figures which appears on the long sheet. If this is not done immediately and in detail, the figures on the machine runs may be meaningless. The titles should of course be verified.

One of the next steps is that of "editing" the machine runs. Errors may arise from such causes as: incorrect wiring of the machine; insufficient or indistinct ink on the tabulator; incorrect punching of the cards; worn cards slipping through without being counted, worn "brushes" not making the contact for the count, etc. In addition, errors may have arisen during the sorting process if the sorter is set for the wrong column. The editing of machine runs is essential to pick up errors before they are carried over to the tables prepared from the runs. The clerical force should check questionable figures. It may be necessary to secure a listing of individual cases before the errors can be located.

LISTING:

A listing, indicating the code which has been punched for each case in each column, can be made by machine. The listing is useful because it gives, in compact form, all the data about each case. When the tabulated results do not seem to make sense, a listing of individual cases may reveal errors in punching or coding the original data. Inconsistencies can thus be picked up from the listings. If the machine listing is wrong because the card is punched or coded wrong, it is not sufficient just to correct machine listing or tables.The card must also be repunched so that future runs will not be in error.

TABLE FORMS:

Table forms should be prepared upon which the figures taken from the machine runs are to be entered. The table forms should indicate which machine runs the data are taken from, and should contain the headings and titles necessary to understand the figures. Although some typists can type the figures directly from the machine runs, it is usually preferable for a clerk to fill the tables, and for the typist to work from the handwritten figures. The "uncoding" of data from the machine runs should also be carefully checked.

TYPING AND VERIFYING:

Typing the tables and verifying the typing is the final stage in the machine tabulation process.

Relative Merits of Hand and Machine Tabulation[7]

The following considerations should influence the decision whether to tabulate the data by hand or by machine:

[7] Also see Coutant and Doubman (202), Brown (115), White (1085), American Marketing Association (8), Croxton and Cowdon (216), Paton (723).

1. The amount of clerical work involved. The comparison of manual and machine tabulation should take into account not only the speed with which punched cards pass through the sorting and tabulating machines, but also the steps required for preparing the data for these machines as well as for checking the runs and converting the results into tables from the machine runs. A list of the main steps involving labor in the two processes follows:

Operations in Tabulation

	Operations Needed in	
	Hand Tabulation	*Machine Tabulation*
1. Code data	Preferable	Required
2. Check codes	Required if using codes	Required
3. Punch codes on cards or transcribe codes to hand count cards	Preferable	Required
4. Verify punching or verify transcription	Required	Required
5. Wire tabulating machines	Not needed	Required
6. Verify wiring of machines	Not needed	Required
7. Sort and count cards	Required	Required; but operation is much faster
8. Print or record the count	Required	May be included in operation 8
9. Verify the count	Required	Included in operation 8
10. Write in headings on machine runs	Not needed	Required if not printed
11. Edit machine runs	Not needed	Required
12. Check edit the machine runs	Not needed	Required
13. Prepare blank table forms or posting sheets	Required	Required
14. Uncode figures on machine runs and enter figures on table forms	Not needed	Required
15. Verify the uncoding and figures entered on table form	Not needed	Required
16. Type the table	Preferable	Preferable
17. Check the typing	Preferable	Preferable

From the above, it may be seen that several more clerical operations and jobs requiring specialists are needed for machine tabulation than for hand. The greater speed with which the machine sorts, counts, and records the count on machine runs may or may not compensate for the extra clerical work or the work of other specialists required for machine runs. The computations which the machine can provide also deserve consideration.

2. If the number and types of tables desired are not decided upon

before tabulation is begun, machine tabulation may be more expedient. If hand tabulation is to be efficient, the order in which the various sorts and counts are made must be determined in advance of tabulation. While this is true also for machine tabulation, the actual sorting and counting operations are performed so rapidly by machine that lack of planning does not result in as great inefficiency as in hand tabulation. There is usually little justification for not planning tabulations so that the added cost of manual operations can be avoided.

3. One of the major advantages of machine tabulation is that it lends itself readily to performing cross-classifications. In large-scale studies if every item on the schedule is to be classified by every other item, machine tabulation is to be preferred. It is possible also to secure correlations by machine, so tabulations requiring many intercorrelations may be more quickly obtained by machine. But here again the number of cards to be sorted and counted should be a consideration. The mere process of wiring the machine, putting in cards, and taking them out may be as time-consuming as counting them by hand if the total number of cards is small.

4. When there is a great deal of coded information and several punch cards would be required for each case, hand tabulations may be preferable. However, it is possible to duplicate the identifying data of each card by a mechanical punch and thus save punching time. If several cards are required the tabulation problem becomes more complex. There is no limit to the number of different categories or answers which can be placed on cards for manual sorts, but the limit is soon reached on punched cards.

5. If it is desired to keep the data in a form ready for new tabulations on relatively short notice, the punch cards meet this requirement. They take up relatively little space and can be retabulated quite easily if a machine and funds are available. Government bureaus have found machine tabulation useful for periodic surveys in which the same type of information is collected at frequent intervals. The coding can be standardized and the machines are usually available for runs whenever trends or summaries are wanted.

6. The relative accuracy of hand versus machine tabulation depends on many factors. Since the number of clerical operations is at least as great in machine as in hand tabulation, the chance for clerical errors is just as great by either method. The process of sorting and

counting may, however, be less likely to produce errors if done by machine than if done by hand. While it is possible to train clerks and organize a manual tabulation job so that errors will be discovered during every process, few tabulation supervisors have the ability to set up such an organization or the time to give to supervising the work of the clerks unless it is a very large-scale undertaking. Errors can and do arise in machine tabulation, and when they do they are not easily detected. Machine errors may result in more serious biases than would scattered or compensating errors of hand-tabulation clerks.

One disadvantage of machine tabulation is that errors are often more difficult to check. The more steps between an original set of figures and those appearing in final tables, the more places for errors to occur. If the machine tabulation of the cards has been turned over to an agency which is equipped to perform machine tabulations, any errors discovered in the coding, editing, or field work stages of the survey may hold up machine tabulators while the punch cards are returned to the survey agency for checking. Market research groups have pointed out that often it is desirable to proceed with hand tabulation concurrently with the field work so that errors in field work may be run down without delay and interruption to the rest of the work. With machine tabulation the need for further checking may not come to light until the tabulating is finished (8, p. 235).

7. Cost considerations are usually the paramount concern of surveyors. In estimating the cost of machine tabulation, the surveyor should decide whether the tabulation is to be turned over or "farmed out" to an outside agency equipped to do the work from punching through the typing of completed tables. Such concerns can provide estimates to guide the surveyor in making his choice.

If the surveyor has access to machine tabulation facilities which may be obtained at cost he might make use of such services. Universities and similar agencies often have some cooperative arrangement whereby various departments may use the machines for research purposes. The decision might depend upon whether the survey funds are to bear the entire cost or only part of it. The cost of the punch cards, the rental charge for punching and verifying machines, rent of sorting and tabulating machines, and the extra expense of hiring special operators for the various machine operations often greatly exceeds the clerical cost required for hand tabulation.

8. Time considerations usually are second in importance only to cost. The amount of clerical help needed for hand tabulation will depend primarily on the number of tables to be made and the number of cards to be sorted. The faster the work is to be done, the more clerical employees will be required. To be sure, too large a clerical staff may become unwieldy, and the supervisory and administrative costs will be prohibitive. By the time most surveys reach the tabulation stage, a well-trained staff of clerical workers can be drawn from among interviewers, editors, and coders. If machine tabulation by the survey staff is contemplated, it may be possible to train punch operators and other machine operators. This is time-consuming, however, and must be considered in the calculations. Another point to be kept in mind is that it is not always possible to rent the type of machine desired, especially on short notice. Tabulation work may be held up for a month or more because of inability to secure the type of machine needed.

Those surveyors who plan to tabulate data concurrently with the field work may find that hand tabulation is better suited to their situation, especially if the number of schedules being turned in daily is rather limited. In order to justify machine tabulation, enough schedules must be sent through the machine at any given time to take advantage of the sorting, counting, and tabulating speeds which are the time powers of the machine.

9. If convenience is an item, the manual method sometimes offers an advantage. If the surveyor has to pack and send the questionnaires or code cards to some office far removed from the survey headquarters, packing inconvenience, transportation costs, and other problems will arise. Boxes may be lost, they may be delayed in the mails, or damaged in moving. Most serious of all, however, is the inconvenience of having to check errors by correspondence when field schedules are separated from code cards, punch cards, and machine runs.

10. The amount of commentary material to be recorded and analyzed may also affect the choice of tabulation methods. In some market and opinion surveys, for example, verbatim comments of informants are almost as important as the numerical tables. The hand code card could provide space for such remarks but the space and design of the usual punch cards are unsuitable for such purposes. A combination written data and punch card has been devised which may be the solution to such cases.

The Construction of Tables

GENERAL PURPOSE, REPOSITORY, OR APPENDIX TABLES:

The statistical tables made up from figures secured by the machine runs or by the counts of the code cards usually are quite different from the tables which will eventually appear in the text of the published report. The first tables, often called the general purpose tables, tend to be detailed; typically they present full summations of items from the schedules, classified according to the original categories. Usually they contain the original, unconverted, unrounded figures. The analyst uses these tabulations as study tables to facilitate the analysis and interpretation of the original data. After significant relationships have been discovered by scrutiny or experimentation with such general tables, special tables may be designed to feature those relationships in the body of the report. In addition to serving thus as a source for text tables, the original tables often prove valuable for reference for persons interested in the data from the points of view of their own projects. If tables are to serve this purpose, they must be carefully edited and labeled so that anyone can work with them directly. The arrangement of the table should facilitate ready reference for the location of any given item. Nearly always the most generally convenient order of items is a conventional one, e.g., numerical, geographical, or chronological. Masks, cutouts, movable line headings on cardboard strips, and other simple devices often are a great help in finding or keeping one's place when using a large general purpose table.

SPECIAL PURPOSE, ANALYSIS, OR TEXT TABLES:

The special purpose table, which is often developed from a general purpose table and is published in the body or text of most reports, usually presents selected or summary data in order to emphasize some significant relationships. The data in this table may be grouped, averaged, rounded, derived, or handled in any legitimate manner which will best serve the special functions of clarification and emphasis. The order of items is likely to be determined by the logic of the problem; otherwise, the most convenient conventional order should be used.

The efficient design of special purpose tables is a relatively frequent and exacting problem of the survey analyst. The detailed recommendations discussed below relate primarily to tables of the special purpose

variety, since general purpose tables present a comparatively straightforward problem with little flexibility or choice in arrangement. Some
readers may wish to go directly to Walker and Durost, *Statistical Tables, Their Structure and Use* (**1050**) for an excellent and comprehensive treatment of the many practical problems involved in the
preparation of statistical tables. The common practices and recommendations below constitute an adapted condensation of many suggestions contained in that book.

PARTS OF A TABLE:

A table is an exhibit of numerical data systematically arranged in
labeled columns (vertical) and rows (horizontal). The small space defined by the intersection of a column and row is known as a *cell*. The
line headings of the rows comprise the *stub* which is at the left margin
of the table. The *column headings,* at the top of the table, refer to the
columns of data in the body of the table. There is also, of course, a
column heading over the stub. A heading which extends over more
than one column is a *box heading;* the headings under a box are *subheadings*. The line headings (in the stub) and the column headings
(over the body) provide the two systems of classification by which the
data are identified. The plan of a table following shows the general arrangement of parts:

Number of Table :	Title of Table
Headnote :	
Column heading referring to the stub below	Column headings referring to the vertical arrays below
Total of all classes in stub	Total column
(Stub) Line headings referring to the horizontal arrays to the right	Body of table containing the numerical data in columns and rows[a]

[a] footnote.

TITLE AND NUMBERING:

The table number and the title are always placed above the table. If
the table title is long, instead of centering the title it may be set a few
spaces to the right of the table number. The text tables should be num-

bered consecutively in one number series and the appendix tables in a second series. The trend in table numbering is toward the use of arabic numerals for all tables. Some statisticians, however, still recommend roman numerals if fewer than 20 tables appear in the report. The table number should be followed by a dash. It is not necessary to use the word "number," e.g., "Table 12" not "Table Number 12."

The title should summarize both the captions and the stubs. It should supply sufficient information to make the table fairly comprehensible without the text. This can be done usually by telling the who, what, when, and where of the data in the table, usually in the form of a series of phrases properly separated by commas, semicolons, dashes or parentheses.

The title should be as concise as feasible without being ambiguous or misleading. Subtitles and headnotes sometimes help to shorten the main title. If the title does not give the dates and area covered, a table footnote should contain this information. The reader must also know whether it is a complete canvass or a sampling survey. Related tables should use identical format and bear similarly phrased titles but the essential differences should be readily apparent.

HEADINGS OF COLUMNS AND ROWS:

Each (vertical) column, including the stub column, should have its own heading; the same is true of each row. Long headings can be arranged to fit into the table. Preferably use the stub for long titles, since it can provide the most space for phrases. However, the use of a box heading over a number of columns or the use of a deeper space to accommodate several words in a natural arrangement are also useful devices. Usually column headings are worded in the singular because the given heading refers to the single entry in each cell of the column. If numerous columns are used, they should be numbered to facilitate reference.

TABLE FOOTNOTES:

The purpose of the table footnote is to provide any needed explanation or clarification of part or all of the tabulated data. When an explanation of how to read a table is necessary, it is not run as a footnote but as a separate paragraph in print of the table size. Since the footnote belongs specifically to the table, it is set up as an indented paragraph just below the table. Ordinarily, type smaller than that in the table itself is employed. Reference symbols usually are small alphabetic letters of which several may be used on a table. The symbols should be easily distinguishable from the column or row numbers or letters. It is not necessary to repeat the same footnote on each page of a table containing several pages. Usually the even-numbered pages carry this.

BOXING AND RULING OF TABLES:

Horizontal rules or lines above and below the table are desirable as they make the table stand out from the text, but complete boxing, in the sense of vertical lines at the sides as well as between columns, is never essential for clarity. Column headings are often separated off by rules and the same is true of the columns of data, but too many intersecting rules should be avoided because they are expensive in printed reports. In very complex tables, heavy lines or even logical spacing and grouping of columns and other parts often eliminates the need of many rules. If it is difficult for the eye to follow across a wide table, a series of horizontal dots extending from the stub across the table or just up to the first column is often used.

TABLE DATA:

The figures appearing in tables should conform to acceptable standards of classification, rounding, and labeling. Only a few of the numerous suggestions appearing in Walker and Durost (1050) are given here. For a more detailed discussion of these points the reader should refer to the original treatment as well as to statistical textbooks such as those listed on page 484.

CLASSES AND CLASS INTERVALS:

1. There must be no overlapping of classes, in either the columns or the rows. The classes must be mutually exclusive.

2. When new classifications are set up, class intervals should, if possible, be uniform in width and in convenient multiples like 5, 10, or 20. However, the analyst should take into account how the cases are distributed. For most social data it is better to use groupings such as those described in the chapter on Coding than to stick to the uniform width or convenient multiple principles.

3. The particular width to be chosen will depend upon the range of the data and the number of classes desired. Where feasible this number should provide a readily perceptible picture; it is usually around 6 to 10 and rarely as great as 30. For data tabulated by machine methods, the 12 fold classification is often adopted because the punch card lends itself to this number of positions. For text tables, this number of classes can often be cut in half to give a clearer picture of results.

4. There must be sufficient classes or groups to include every case. Special categories may be required to fulfill this requirement, e.g., the category "not reported" or "not specified." When a category like "all others" or "miscellaneous" is included, it should include a relatively small number of the cases and be a relatively unimportant grouping. The "don't know" group often encountered in public opinion polls should also be kept relatively low. If it is high, it usually means that the question was poorly phrased or that the public is not ready or willing to express an opinion. Sometimes inefficient interviewing techniques are responsible. Further experimentation with the question and topic and better training of interviewers should reduce the "don't know" group.

ROUNDING NUMBERS:

1. The number of places to include in a column of tabulated figures is a matter of judgment depending upon the precision of the individual items and the purpose of the table. In a text table it seems misleading and unnecessarily complicating to retain more places than the original measurements justify. For instance, if most of the entries are known to be in error in the first decimal place, retention of the second or third would be unjustified.

2. A number is rounded off by increasing the last retained digit by one if the following digits amount to more than half a unit, or by decreasing the last retained digit by one if the following digits amount to less than half. For instance, 17.51 will be rounded to 18, while 17.49 will be rounded to 17.

3. When a number falls on the dividing line, as in the above example at 17.50, a convention is applied to assure about equal proportions of increases and decreases. This convention is to round off to the nearest even number. Thus 17.50 would be rounded off to 18, but 18.50 would also be rounded to 18.

4. Successive roundings should be avoided because they are likely to lead to error. For instance, if 17.49 is rounded to the first decimal place the result is 17.5; but if 17.5 is now rounded to no decimal places the result is 18, by the convention above. If both decimal places had been rounded off in the same operation the correct result of 17 would have been secured instead of 18.

5. Examples of correct rounding:

Original Value	Number of Decimal Places to Which Rounded		
	2	1	0
1.377	1.38	1.4	1
6.4955	6.50	6.5	6
35.500	35.50	35.5	36
36.50	36.50	36.5	36
48.639	48.64	48.6	49

LABELING AND ALIGNMENT OF FIGURES:

1. The name of the particular unit of measurement employed must be invariably included and unequivocally expressed. Examples of commonly used units are: time in minutes, age in years, income in dollars, and the relative units of per cent. The unit may be stated in the title or in the column headings.

2. The dollar sign is an exception to the rule in the sense that it never stands alone as a column heading; instead it precedes the first entry in the column and also the last if that is a total.

3. The "per cent" symbol or word may be used to head columns of percentages, but when it is not so used the per cent sign is placed after the first entry and also the last if that is a total.

4. In case of similar items the decimal points should be in alignment and each number carried to the same number of decimal places, if any.

5. In whole numbers of more than three places, a comma may be used to facilitate perception, e.g., 1,129 or 13,619.

INDICATING OMISSIONS, NUMBERS OF CASES, AND PER CENTS:

1. A dash in the empty cell accompanied by a footnote or other explanation is used to indicate actual lack or loss of the datum.

2. A zero is regularly used to represent a real datum of zero magnitude.

3. When entries are percentages or averages the reader needs to know how many cases are involved in order to be able to evaluate the results. Always show the number of cases in the base used for the computation of per cents shown in the table. Since it is difficult for the reader to know whether per cents are figured to add up to 100 vertically or horizontally, it is a good idea to list a row or column of 100%'s so that the reader knows how to interpret the per cent. If the meaning of the per cent figures shown in each cell is not obvious, e.g., when the per cents in a column or row are not to be added together to make 100%, or if the bases used in computing the per cents do not appear in the table, an explanatory note should be appended to the table showing how to interpret the per cent figures. The reader should not be left in doubt as to what the per cent is a percentage of.

4. In percentage tables, the entries rarely sum to exactly 100, though of course they should do so if carried out to enough places. The individual items should be left unchanged, but the total may be stated as 100 per cent, provided an explanatory note is added.

5. The number of cases may be given in the title, subtitle, or footnote of the table. When the cases vary, they may be indicated in parenthesis under line headings or column headings.

WEIGHTED TABULATIONS:

When disproportionate sampling has been employed or when the percentage of returns differs among the various groups in the sampled population, it is necessary to adjust the tabulations in which the groups are combined to get a balanced sample. This adjustment usually is made by multiplying the raw figures for each of the various groups by figures which will take care of their under- or over-representation in the total. Suppose, for example, that a population consists of 600 men and 600 women, and that the women subdivide into 200 homemakers and 400 employed. If the sample yielded only half as many women as men, but there were the same relative numbers of homemakers and employed as in the population, then the returns for women should simply be multiplied by two before being presented in the same table with those for men. If, again, the sample yielded only half as many women as men, but there were now twice as many homemakers as employed represented, then to weight the women correctly it would be necessary to multiply the returns for the employed by four.

Instead of multiplying the under-sampled groups, it is possible to produce a balanced sample by dividing the figures for adequately sampled groups to reduce them to the same level as the deficient groups. Another weighting procedure in the above example would be to quadruple the schedules of the under-sampled group before making tabulations. Still another technique would be to remove from the sample three out of four schedules of men and homemakers for all tabulations in which the sexes were combined. This last procedure wastes available data.

Quota sampling and other forms of disproportionate sampling employ weighting as a necessary step in the sample procedure. Aside from the problem of determining the incidence of the various groups in the population so that correct weights can be set, the problem of avoiding confusion in the handling of weighted and unweighted tabulations should not be underestimated. Only by exceedingly careful labeling of all tabulations and by the use of explanatory footnotes for weighted figures can the surveyor hope to avoid confusion.

Selected References

Tabulation

Arkin and Colton (14), Berkson (53), Blankenship (77), Chaddock (155), Coutant and Doubman (202), Day (234), DuBois (257), Edwards (281), Erdos (292), Hall (391), Holzinger (449), Mills (646), Mudgett (660), New York Department of Social Welfare (688), Paton (723), Phelps (740), Ramsey (758), Reilly (764), Riggleman and Frisbee (780), Saunders and Anderson (836), Truesdell (973), U. S. (982, 987, 988, 1029), Walker and Durost (1050), Zeisel (1141).

Machine Tabulation

American Marketing Assn. (8), Baehne (21), Benjamin (42), Berkson (53), Blankenship (77), Brown (115), Croxton and Cowden (216, 217), Deming et al. (244), DuBois (257), Eckert (269), *Engineer* (289), Hartkemeier (415), Leahy (555), Meredith Pub. Co. (638), Paton (723), Truesdell (973), U. S. (982, 987, 988), White (1085).

Evaluation of the Data
and Sample

Before the surveyor turns to the tabulated results of the survey, he should have some idea of the validity of the data yielded by his procedures. Just what do the results of the survey measure? Do they accomplish what the surveyor has claimed, what he has intended to measure, or what he has attempted to put in quantitative form? This is the problem of validity. The extent to which the survey results agree with some criterion which is regarded as an acceptable measure of the phenomena being studied may be taken as an indication of the validity of the results.

Obviously the criteria by which validity is determined are not to be expected to give results identical with those of the survey. If a criterion were completely satisfactory as a measure of the situation to be surveyed, many surveys would not be undertaken because the desired information would be available in the form of the criterion. For example, data on school grades reached by students have been used as criteria for determining the validity of tests of intelligence. It is assumed that intelligence is required to progress in school and therefore that there should be some relationship between these two factors if the intelligence tests were really measuring intelligence. School grades, however, are not in themselves completely acceptable as a measure of intelligence or educational experts would not bother to develop special tests of this factor. In a like manner, the surveyor should not expect perfect agreement of survey results with the criteria he sets up. If the correlation is reasonably good or if several different criteria all point to a given meaning in the results, the surveyor must be satisfied. If from his findings he is able to predict satisfactorily how people will reply or react in similar situations at another time or place, he will have achieved his goal as a surveyor. How satisfactory the prediction is will depend upon who has to be satisfied and what practical use is to be made of the prediction.

Evidence drawn from validation tests conducted by surveyors and pollers suggests that data collected by survey methods tend, on the whole, to correlate fairly closely with test criteria. Verbal statements of informants agree reasonably well with overt behavior, official records, or data secured through carefully controlled experimental situations. Although the surveyor may place some confidence in data secured by procedures similar to those surveys which have been validated by other surveyors, he should, whenever possible, try to determine the validity of his own data.

Types of Validation Criteria

The choice of criteria by which to validate survey returns varies with the subject matter of the survey, but may be classed into the following groups:

1. COMPARISON OF THE SURVEY RESULTS WITH SUBSEQUENT EVENTS:

One of the most effective checks on polls of candidate preference or of issues which are to be brought before the electorate is the outcome of the election itself. To be sure, the closer the poll is taken to election day, the better measure the election is of the poll because shifts in opinion have less chance to take place in the intervening period. The turnout of voters on election day, i.e., the per cent and type of eligible voters who actually vote on election day, must be estimated closely if the vote is to be taken as a valid indication of the opinion of voters. This and other problems accounting for a possible discrepancy between preelection results and votes have been extensively analyzed and reported by Katz (**493, 496**) and earlier by Katz and Cantril (**499**). Despite expected discrepancies between preelection polls and the elections themselves, most of the modern polls have come sufficiently close to the actual outcome in their preelection estimates to create widespread belief in them as a device for measuring voters' preferences. In 1948, however, this faith on the part of the general public was shattered when a discrepancy of from 5 to 12 percentage points occurred between the predictions and the vote on the candidate. In view of the fact that the polls were taken from ten days to two months or more before the election, and that from 7 to 15 per cent of the persons interviewed had not yet made up their minds how they were going to vote, it is not surprising that the returns deviated this much from the polls.

One very interesting experiment is reported by Field and Connelly of the National Opinion Research Center (304). By arrangement with various state and local officials, the surveyors were permitted to set up a special secret ballot box in each of the official polling precinct stations in Boulder, Colorado, at the time the state elections were being held. As each voter completed his official voting, a survey representative handed him a ballot to be marked secretly and placed in the sealed box. The survey ballot contained three questions—one on each of the following topics: a national sales tax, old age pensions, and a union of nations after the war. The identical questions had been asked previously in a sample poll conducted by home interviews in this community and in accordance with regular interview procedures. The similarity between the returns obtained at the polling station and those secured by personal interview lends support to the belief that opinions expressed to interviewers tend to agree reasonably well with voting behavior. The discrepancy between the prediction based on interviews and the actual vote was 7.2 per cent on the sales tax, 1.1 per cent on old age pensions, and 3.2 per cent on a union of nations. The vote on two candidates was predicted even closer, with only 0.3 per cent and 0.2 per cent error. The error on the sales tax was greater than would have been expected from chance error alone. The authors believe that it may have been due to any or a combination of three things: the hesitance of voters to express their true opinions to the interviewer because of a prestige factor; the position of the question on the form (this was the first question on the form, and the respondent might not have been "warmed up" to thought and expression); and some inherent element of the question for which the sample was not properly representative.

In order to provide a perfect test of the validity of survey questioning as a measure of voting behavior, the two instruments should be applied to strictly comparable populations. This was not feasible in the above experiment because of the fact that all who voted had not been interviewed, and of all interviewed, only some went to the polls. Of those at the polls, 86 per cent who were handed ballots marked them.

Another example may be drawn from the field of marketing research. Questions about purchases people plan to make can be tested at a later date against the purchases they did make. The agreement need not be 100 per cent to be an adequate test of validity, since considerations such as having money to buy or to make down payments may enter into the final purchase of a commodity regardless of the customer's desire in the matter.

Copy testers have asked the public to rank advertisements according to their sales pulling power. The advertiser then may place these ads in a given issue of some magazine which has the "split-run" advertisement facilities, i.e., equal numbers of a given issue will carry one of each of the ads which are to be tested. By use of the keyed coupon method, the advertisers may then determine which ad resulted in the most sales. The few studies of this nature which have been reported reveal close correspondence between consumer preference and keyed coupon returns (77, p. 206).

2. COMPARISON OF SURVEY RESULTS WITH RESULTS OBTAINED USING SOME OTHER SURVEY TECHNIQUE:

For example, data secured through mail questionnaires might be compared with those obtained through interviews; then again, information obtained through interviews may be compared with data from observations without questioning. In radio audience research, a comparison of program ratings obtained through the use of the aided recall technique (see page 75) and the coincidental (see page 85) may be employed to validate one another. Certain differences are to be expected because of the differences in the sample as well as the technique of collecting the information. The recall method, for example, is likely to be affected by factors influencing memory.[1]

3. ANALYSIS OF RESULTS OF PRETESTING OF QUESTIONS:

When the questions were being drafted the effect of different wordings upon the response should have been tested. Emotionally tinged words, suggestive words or phrases, personalized questions, dichotomous versus alternative choices, and confusion in the respondent's

---

[1] For a discussion of these factors see Chappell (169).

mind between means and ends all may lead the surveyor to misinterpret the informants' responses. Payne (725) noticed that two national surveys were reporting apparently widely different results on opinions toward socialized medicine. One showed 16 per cent of the people in favor of a 6 per cent payroll deduction from wages for the federal government to provide medical care and hospitalization, while the other organization reported that 68 per cent thought it would be a good idea for social security to cover doctor and hospital care. The first organization also found that 32 per cent of its respondents approved of increasing social security taxes for federal government use in a medical and hospital insurance program. The difference between 16 and 68 per cent seemed to call for further probing of opinions on this subject, so a repeat survey was set up in which several other questions were added. Among the additional questions the interviewer asked, "When you said a minute ago that the social security plan would be a good idea, were you thinking that the best way to obtain doctor and hospital care would be under the social security law, or were you just saying that some sort of plan is needed?" Thirty-one per cent said that they were thinking that the best way would be under the social security law, 34 per cent remarked that they just meant that some plan was needed, and 3 per cent said that they did not know what they meant. According to these results, when means were separated from ends, only 31 per cent endorsed socialized medicine through the social security law. This figure corresponded closely to the 32 per cent which the first agency found approved the plan to increase social security taxes and have the government use the money for medical care. Further probing was necessary for the surveyor to discover that the responses to a certain question did not mean what the surveyor assumed they meant.

In tests of the wording of opinion questions alternative presentations of issues may give completely different distributions of responses. The surveyor may have difficulty deciding which phrasing is the better index of the informant's actual opinion, i.e., which is more valid. In such cases, more experimentation is needed or more probing is necessary to bring out a meaningful response. By asking several questions instead of only one, it may be possible to determine just which elements in the phrasing or in the questioning procedure respondents are reacting to. Whenever widely divergent replies are secured through alternative phrasing, the surveyor is not justified in saying that one question is a more valid indicator of opinion about the issue in question than is the other, unless he has expanded his questioning and can account for the discrepancy.

If the purpose of the survey is the ascertainment of "general opinion" on such issues as "liberalism," "intervention," "racial tolerance," etc., rather than a definite opinion on a specific candidate or issue, it is especially important to tap all the different sides of the topic in question. The surveyor needs to use a battery of questions which get at opinion in a number of different contests and are surrounded by the sort of contingencies found in life situations. The surveyor would be wise to become familiar with the extensive work in the field of attitude testing before he places too much confidence in his own meager attempts to get at any generalized behavior.

4. CHECKING RETURNS AGAINST OBJECTIVE RECORDS:

When objective facts rather than opinions are called for by the survey, it is often possible to check the individual returns against some data such as public records on marriages, births, deaths, school records, employers' records of wages, etc.

Stoke and Lehman (932) conducted an interesting experiment in this connection. They asked students in psychology to report the number of times they had taken books from the library reserve desk for assigned work. By checking the replies against the library records, it was found that seven out of eight students overestimated the number of checkouts. The best students exaggerated least and the poorer students most.

Track records of 1,000 high school students were used to check statements the students made about their records in a questionnaire. Smith (885) came to the conclusion that questions involving judgment and personal data obtain responses colored by a constant error of overstatement.

Walker (1052) checked returns received from over 2,000 junior college students on questions of age, sex, year of high school graduation, and father's occupation against valid sources. The greatest discrepancy noted was in regard to school progress. Students tended to avoid giving themselves the stigma of retardation.

5. COMPARISON OF RESPONSES TO AN EXISTING SITUATION
WITH THOSE TO A NONEXISTING ONE:

The inclusion of false items in a schedule may give an indication of the validity of the returns. Smith (885) asked students and teachers to tell him which books they had read in a list containing a number of false titles. Over one-fourth of the students made false statements.

Lucas (589, 590) describes a clever technique in which advertisements which had not yet appeared in magazines were shown to informants along with some which actually had appeared. Informants were asked which ads they recalled having seen. *After* the publication of the ads another survey ascertained the number who recalled having seen them. The difference between the recall *before* the publication of the copy and the recall *after* its publication was regarded as the true measure of its attention-getting influence.

6. CHECKING EXPRESSED ATTITUDES OR STATEMENTS
AGAINST SPECIFIC BEHAVIOR:

Jenkins and Corbin have conducted a number of tests on the validity of answers to questions about the purchase of common household articles (470, 472). The respondent's statement about the brand last purchased is compared with what is found through pantry inventories. In one study Jenkins secured the cooperation of grocers who kept records on the brands sold to certain customers. The comparison between the grocer's records and the customer's statement of the name of the brands he last purchased served as a measure of validity.

Link and Freiberg remark that the validity of opinion polls should be established in terms of objective behavior. "For several years the Psychological Barometers have included a scale of attitude toward certain large companies. The favorable, unfavorable, and indifferent attitudes of people to these companies have been correlated with such actions as (1) attendance at World's Fair Exhibits; (2) listening to a company's radio program; (3) knowledge of the company's advertising and products; (4) presence or absence at a company's traveling exhibits" (579, p. 93).

The same authors cite other examples of validating questions in terms of objective behavior. One other may be cited here. In a "test of two products, X was described by the subjects as superior to product Y in respect to eight points and inferior in respect to one, namely, taste. However, when asked which, given the same price, they would probably buy, they chose product Y. Therefore, in terms of behavior, in this case hypothetical behavior, the one factor, taste, outweighed all others" (579, p. 95).

7. VALIDATING RETURNS AGAINST THE JUDGMENT OF EXPERTS OR PERSONS QUALIFIED TO KNOW THE TRUE SITUATION:

If the respondent may be expected to know his true financial state, one test of the validity of the interviewer's ratings may make use of this knowledge. Cantril reports a study in which the respondent was asked to specify the weekly income group to which his immediate family belonged. The answers were correlated with the interviewer's classification of the family's economic status and a correlation of .73 was obtained (142, p. 104). Among residents of large cities the correlation between the interviewer's estimates and those of the respondents was .81.

A subjective classification by the respondent of his own income status, i.e., whether he was a member of the upper, upper middle, middle, lower middle, or lower class, did not correspond so closely as the weekly income group classification with the interviewer's estimate. The correlation was .60. Cantril attributes this lower agreement to the tendency of upper income groups to classify themselves lower than they are and for the poor to claim higher levels than their income warrants.

8. TESTS OF GROUPS KNOWN TO BE BIASED TO SEE WHETHER SURVEY REVEALS SUCH BIASES:

Lundberg lists several devices for estimating the validity of attitude tests which may be applied to opinion surveys also. According to one technique, "Certain groups may in the judgment of competent persons be expected to have certain biases. The ability of the tests to reveal these attitudes is some indication of the validity of the tests" (597, p. 243). Another "method of estimating the validity of a test is to secure a consensus of judgment from a group as to what individuals among their close personal friends hold pronounced attitudes on certain questions. The application of the test to these individuals then gives a measure of the degree to which the test agrees in its findings with the judgment of close associates. Individuals known for their objectivity of mind may also be confronted with their own scores on the tests and the degree of their acceptance of the results may be some indication of the validity of the test" (597, p. 243).[2]

9. TESTS OF KNOWLEDGE USED TO VALIDATE RESULTS:

Increasing use has been made of the "knowledge" test to determine whether or not people understand enough about the topic being surveyed to hold an intelligent opinion.

Link and Freiberg (579) reported an opinion survey in which automobile owners had expressed a decided preference for Pennsylvania oils as compared with non-Pennsylvania oils. A follow-up survey, in which factual and information questions were asked, indicated that many informants did not know which oils were Pennsylvanian and which were not, and many motorists knew very little about the relative merits of oils, even where preference for Pennsylvania oil was expressed. Since the knowledge of motorists about the oils was so limited, their stated opinions were not to be regarded as a valid indication of what they would do in a purchase situation.

10. SIZE OF NO-OPINION VOTE:

In opinion polling, a very high "no opinion" vote should lead the surveyor to suspect the validity of the question. Is the informant really giving his true opinion or is he reacting to some other element in the interview situation? For example, questions which are phrased in too technical language for the average man may elicit a high proportion of "I don't know" responses. Actually, the respondents may be indicating that they do not know what the interviewer is trying to find out. If the same question were reworded in simple language, the informants might express very definite opinions. The original question might be a more valid measure of the educational background of the informants rather than of their views toward the issue in question.

---

[2] In the construction of scales to measure attitudes, an analysis of each item included in the scale is usually made to determine its discriminatory value. If people who hold opposite views, for example, give the same response to certain questions, the item is not sufficiently differentiating and should be dropped (597, p. 295).

11. USE OF COMMON SENSE FOR VALIDATING DATA:

It is frequently assumed that if the findings of a survey seem reasonable or appear to correspond with "common sense," this provides the test of validity. As Lundberg has so aptly put it, "In the absence of other criteria, and always in addition to them, common sense is entitled to consideration. But in view of the fact that systematic questionnaire studies are undertaken because we do not trust the common sense estimates, we can hardly use the latter as sole criteria of the validity of the former" (597, p. 201).

Reliability of the Results

Not only should the survey analyst ascertain whether or not the data assembled constitute valid evidence on the survey problem, but he must also determine the reliability of the information obtained. Would a repetition of the survey on the same topic, using the same collection procedures and covering a comparable sample of individuals, give the same or approximately the same results? To answer this question, the reliability of the survey instrument as a whole—the schedule, the interviewer's techniques, the informants' responses, as well as the reliability of the sample—needs to be examined. Sampling reliability is primarily a function of sample size; techniques for measuring it will be discussed later under the reliability of various statistical measures. Other sources of unreliability have been discussed throughout this book; suggestions have been given for controlling and objectifying procedures so as to avoid getting unreliable returns. When the questionnaire is being designed, its reliability should be determined. The effect of changes in wording, the effect of the position of questions on the schedule, the objectivity and inclusiveness of definitions of items should be tested. Interviewer's instructions and checks upon his work—his honesty as well as his techniques of interviewing, interpreting, and recording of information—should guarantee that the information is objectively obtained and recorded. Various controls should also be set up to discourage dishonesty on the part of the informants and to give them an opportunity to understand the questions and to reply truthfully to them.

Assuming that all possible steps have been taken to insure reliable data, differences in reliability may be expected from survey to survey.

These differences will depend upon such factors as the subject matter of the survey, the method of collecting information, the types of inform-ants, the interval between surveys, and the strength of the influences operating between the initial survey and its reapplication.

Several methods commonly used to test the reliability of schedules and survey procedures are summarized below.

1. ODD-EVEN COMPARISON OF QUESTION RESULTS:

If a series of questions on a schedule can be summarized to form a single score such as an attitude score toward some current issue, the items entering into the score can be numbered consecutively as they appear on the schedule. The scores obtained if only the even-numbered items are employed can then be correlated with those resulting from using the odd-numbered items. If the correlation is high, it may be assumed that the scores obtained are reliable.

A variation of this technique is the comparison of the first half versus the second half of the questionnaire. If the placing of questions in the first or second half of a long series of items is a chance arrange-ment, reliability may be tested by correlating the scores obtained from the first half with those from the second half, correcting for the length of the list.

2. SPLIT-BALLOT TECHNIQUE:

This device has been widely used in market surveys. If a question is worded in two different ways, or placed in a different context on each of two schedule forms, it is possible to determine the effect of the differences in wording (or placing on the schedule) by varying the question form given to every other person interviewed. In a sense, the informants as well as the questions are varied by this technique. On the other hand, the interviewer and his techniques, as well as the time factor, are held constant. The sampling differences, if the sample is large enough, should not have much of an effect upon the result obtained from the different forms. In opinion polls in which the split ballot is used, it is assumed that if the percentages of persons respond-ing in a given way are approximately the same, regardless of the form of question (or its placement on the form), the question is reliable.

In order to keep the informants' errors due to sampling down even more, it is possible to place the two forms of the question on the

same schedule. In order that neither question be given an advantageous (or disadvantageous) position, an equal number of two different
schedule forms might be printed—one with question "A" first, and
the other with question "B" first. When distributing the schedules,
every other informant might receive identical forms.

The above split-ballot technique for two forms of a question might
also be applied to three or more forms of a question, with say every
third informant being given the same form.

3. SUBSAMPLE OR COMPARABLE SAMPLE COMPARISON:

The identical questions and survey techniques might be employed
simultaneously or very close together to similar samples of the population. If given simultaneously, the interviewers as well as the informants would differ for the two surveys. Subsamples such as those described in Chapter IX might be used to advantage in such tests of
reliability. The greater the correspondence between the results from
the different samples, the more confidence the analyst may place in his
findings.

4. REPETITION OF THE SURVEY AFTER A SHORT INTERVAL:

If the identical schedule, interviewers, and procedures were used
to survey the identical informants after a short period, would the same
results be obtained? To be sure, the original situation could never be
reproduced *exactly*—the mere fact that the informant had responded
a certain way the first time might affect his response the next time.
For example, he might have been thinking over his response on the
original interview, and in the process of mulling over the subject
he might have recalled additional material or have come to a different
conclusion. An interviewer in a southern rural community had been
interviewing Negro householders on their income, family size, etc.
One afternoon as she happened to pass a house where she had interviewed the husband in the family the previous morning, a Negro
woman rushed out to the sidewalk to talk with her. It seems her husband had reported to the interviewer that they had twelve
children, and the wife wished to correct this error, since her husband
had forgotten little Amos, who was their thirteenth child.

Cantril found that when the same interviewers reinterviewed their
respondents after three weeks, the classification of income level cor-

related .79 with that in the original interview. The correlation of age information was .90. Car ownership replies were identical in 96 per cent of the sample while responses to an opinion question were identical in 79 per cent of the cases (**142**, pp. 99–100).

Different interviewers also obtained relatively reliable information from a panel of respondents. Age figures obtained by the two sets of interviewers correlated .91. Data on car ownership was identical in 86 per cent of the interviews and that of telephones in the home agreed in 87 per cent of the cases. Answers to the question about whom the informant voted for in the last presidential election yielded identical replies in 87 per cent of the sample (**142**, pp. 102–103).

As a rule, personal factual material tends to be quite consistently reported in repeated surveys. Cavan (**152**) resubmitted a questionnaire to 123 eighth grade pupils after a week's interval. Eighty-seven per cent of the questions yielded replies which were in agreement with those given on the first questionnaire. Factual questions about themselves showed 97 per cent agreement; attitude toward self yielded 78 per cent agreement. Eighty-five per cent of the replies relating to a "neurotic inventory" were in agreement on the two schedules.

Bain (**25**) submitted a questionnaire to a group of college students relating to family data, factual personal data, and subjective personal material. When he repeated the study two and one-half months later, he found that nearly 25 per cent of the 3,050 responses differed from those secured the first time. The greatest shift occurred with subjective personal items, while the least difference was noted in factual personal data. The findings of Smith (**890**) are in agreement with those of Bain and Cavan.

Cuber and Gerberich, who submitted a questionnaire three times, found that 71.9 per cent of the responses were consistent. Contrary to the usual experience of surveyors, they found that the consistency proved to be greatest for questions dealing with ideologies rather than with factual information (**221**).

Questionnaires on regularity of listening to certain radio programs, if repeated within 15 days, give results varying not over 8 per cent (Curtis, **223**). Seventy per cent in one study gave the identical answers on the second questionnaire, while 2 per cent reversed their original answers. Some 10,000 people in rural areas were reinterviewed, and it was found that the "reported average daily listening for the whole group differed by only five minutes for the two studies" (223, p. 129).

Jenkins reports a study of brand preferences (brand last purchased) in which the investigators made a second call on the same families 48 hours after the first visit. Ninety per cent of the replies agreed with those given in the original report (469).

Superstitious beliefs of fifth and sixth grade school children were tested twice after an interval of one month. Peatman and Greenspan, who conducted the study, reported that the retest reliability of the questionnaire was .958.

The longer the interval between the surveys, the greater the chance that the responses of given individuals will differ, especially about subjective or opinion items. The averages or group measures obtained from the survey might, however, remain fairly constant if no significant worldshaking events were taking place to affect the responses of most people. In the absence of a major social, political, or economic happening, it may be assumed that as many individuals will shift their original response in one direction as in the other. Thus, although reversals of position do take place on the resurvey, these shifts tend to balance each other and leave a relatively stable average or other measure of the total.

If the resurvey yields results which do not agree with those secured in the initial investigations, the analyst must look for the explanation in unreliable techniques or interviewers employed, noncomparability of informants in the two surveys, in a change in the phenomenon or situation studied, or in an insufficient number of cases in the sample.

If time has elapsed between the first and second surveys, the situation being measured might have changed so that the answers should be different. A poll on American participation in World War II conducted the week before Pearl Harbor might not have corresponded very closely to one taken the week after. A change in opinion arising from external events, wide publicity of the facts, etc., might produce a decided change in people's reactions. In such a case the reliability of the first survey could not be tested by a single repetition.

Statistical Interpretations

1. SUMMARIZING MEASURES:

Regardless of what particular characteristic is being investigated, some measure is generally required conveniently to express and clarify the various figures shown in tables of results. The most common measures are: frequencies or counts, relative frequencies or percentages, rates, ratios, frequency distributions, averages, measures of dispersion or variability, correlation coefficients, trend lines or time series. In general, the counts and percentages are more frequently employed in surveys than averages and other measures of magnitudes.

The particular summarizing measure or measures which the surveyor uses will depend upon what he intends to find out about the characteristic being investigated. For example, if the problem were simply to discover the number of Negroes in a certain area, a 10 per cent sample might be drawn and a simple count made of the number of Negroes in the sample. Then this count or frequency could be multiplied by 10 to give an estimate of the number of Negroes in the whole area. On the other hand, if the information called for was the average income of a certain group, then obviously that average would have to be computed on the basis of the sample. If the surveyor were commissioned to discover the relative preference of housewives for different kinds of eggbeaters, he could count the frequency in favor of each type in his sample and compute the corresponding percentages. If the problem were to estimate the range of variation in the rentals being paid in a certain residential section, a suitable measure of dispersion or variability (like the standard deviation) might be computed from the sample as an estimate for the population. If the task were to see whether there was a relation between size of a city and the per cent of voters who voted for Republican candidates in a given election, the degree of relation could be estimated by sampling different sized cities, getting the Republican vote in each, and correlating the two variables.[3]

2. RELIABILITY OF SUMMARIZING MEASURES:

Once the characteristic under investigation (e.g., opinion, preference, income) has been sampled and the needed summarizing measure (e.g., frequency, percentage, average) has been calculated, the question immediately arises as to the reliability of that summarizing measure. How much chance is there that another sample would give the same or similar results? How close is the estimate likely to be to

---

[3] The reader is referred to standard statistical handbooks for descriptions and derivations of the various summarizing measures and treatment of tests of statistical significance.

the figure which would have been obtained if every case in the universe had been studied? Suppose we are able to estimate that there are 8,000 Negroes in a certain area; or that the average income of a certain group is $1450; or that 60 per cent of the housewives prefer eggbeater A. None of these estimates is of much value unless its reliability is known. We need some idea of the range of error in our estimate. Is the estimate of 8,000 Negroes probably within 200 of the true number or can we only say that it is probably within 2,000 of the correct value? Is the estimate of $1450 average income within $50 of the correct figure for the universe or may it be off as much as $500? Is the 60 per cent who prefer eggbeater A correct to within 3 per cent or may it be off 15 per cent? In general, the reliability (precision) of an estimate in unbiased random sampling is the closeness with which that estimate approaches the true value for the universe. The statistical measure of the reliability (precision) of the estimate is its standard error. It is clear from earlier discussion in Chapter IX that the smaller the standard error the greater the reliability (precision) of the estimate. The calculation of the standard errors of some of the most generally useful summarizing measures will now be described.

Standard Error of a Percentage. This calculation was referred to in Chapter IX in connection with the predetermination of the size of sample necessary to yield any required reliability. Now we use the standard error formula for evaluating the reliability of the result which has been obtained by actually drawing the survey sample. A sample of 500 "head earners" drawn in the 1933 New Haven Survey showed that 42 per cent were 30–44 years of age. Let us compute the precision of this obtained result. The procedure is the same as that described in Chapter IX.

$$\sigma_{p.c.} = \sqrt{\frac{p.c. (100 - p.c.)}{n}}$$

$$= \sqrt{\frac{42(100 - 42)}{500}} = \sqrt{\frac{2436}{500}} = 2.2\%$$

(1)

Reference to Table 2 (p. 311) will indicate that there are 2 out of 3 chances that the estimate from an unbiased random sample will fall within 1 standard error of the population percentage. Thus we may expect that there are about 2 chances out of 3 that the estimate of 42 per cent from our sample of 500 is within 2.2 per cent of the correct value. In other words, there are 2 out of 3 chances that the population value is somewhere between 39.8 per cent and 44.2 per cent. Similarly, there would be 19 out of 20 chances that the population value lies within about 2 standard errors, that is, between 37.6 per cent and 46.4 per cent. All of this is on the assumption that the sample estimate represents the population percentage, which is the most probable assumption in random sampling; but the sample estimate can be considerably off without greatly affecting the standard error (see Chapter IX).

While the above formula is in general use and is generally close enough, it seems well to note in passing that it applies exactly only in the special case of an infinite population, and is conservative in the sense of yielding a standard error figure which is a little too large for samples of the finite populations with which surveys are so generally concerned. If desired, in a borderline or otherwise crucial case, the exact figure for the finite population can be calculated from the full formula (631). This also applies to the standard error formulas for the statistics given below.

Standard Error of a Frequency. It is unnecessary to convert a simple frequency (absolute frequency) to a percentage (relative frequency) before computing the standard error. The 42 per cent of "head earners" in the above sample of 500 was figured from a frequency of 210 (42 per cent of 500 = 210). The formula for the standard error of a frequency is:

$$\sigma_f = \sqrt{\frac{f(n - f)}{n}} \tag{2}$$

Here f is the frequency returned by the sample, n is the number of cases in the sample, and σ_f is the standard error of the frequency. Substituting in this formula the values for f and n in our example, we have:

$$\sigma_f = \sqrt{\frac{210(500 - 210)}{500}} = 11.0$$

Thus the standard error for the estimate of 210 individuals is 11 individuals, as compared with the corresponding percentage values of

42 per cent and 2.2 per cent. (The results with the two formulas can be shown to agree: $11/210 = 0.05$, and $2.2/42 = 0.05$. By both formulas, the standard error is 0.05 of the estimate.)

Standard Error of a Mean.   This formula assumes that the standard deviation of the sample represents the standard deviation of the population, which is legitimate except for very small samples. The formula for the standard error of the mean is:

$$\sigma_m = \frac{\sigma}{\sqrt{n-1}} \tag{3}$$

Here, σ is the standard deviation of the sample, σ_m is the standard error of the mean, and n is the number of cases in the sample. The -1 may be omitted from the denominator for sample sizes greater than 30. (This formula assumes that the standard deviation of the sample, σ, has already been computed. If not, it can be computed from the re-

lation, $\sigma = \sqrt{\dfrac{\Sigma(x-m)^2}{n}}$, where $(x-m)^2$ is the square of the dif-

ference between any measure x in the sample and the mean m, and Σ is the sign of summation which means to add up all such squared differences before dividing by n. The detailed procedure for calculating the standard deviation from this basic formula is to: (1) find the difference between each individual return and the average return, (2) square all these differences, (3) sum all the squared differences, (4) divide this sum by the number of cases in the sample, and finally (5) take the square root of the result. The analyst should consult a statistical text to find that version of this basic formula which best suits his computational facilities.)

Now let us illustrate the calculation of the standard error of the mean .by reference to income data from the *Study of Consumer Purchases* (1010). In a sample of 360 families paying monthly rents of $10–15, the average income was $1263 with a standard deviation of $420. Substituting in formula (3) we have:

$$\sigma_m = \frac{420}{\sqrt{360-1}} = \$22$$

The standard error of the mean is interpreted much as any other standard error. In unbiased sampling there are about 2 out of 3 chances that the population mean lies somewhere within one standard error of the sample mean, thus in the present example, somewhere between $1241 and $1285. If the limits are made wider, the chances of the population value lying within them become greater, as indicated in Table 2. If the sample had been larger, the standard error would have been smaller (and so the precision greater), as indicated in Table 1.

3. SIGNIFICANCE OF DIFFERENCES:

The statistical significance of a result depends upon the reliability (precision) of that result relative to some critical difference. Sometimes only one observed result (summarizing measure) is involved, the critical difference being the difference between that result and some fixed limit. This type of problem has been considered already in connection with the prediction of the outcome of a majority vote from the outcome of a poll (p. 319). Suppose the estimate from a poll of 800 came out 58 per cent in favor of the proposition. Here we hypothesize that the vote should come out a 50 per cent tie if there is no real majority. Therefore we compute the standard error for 50 per cent, using formula (1), and ask ourselves the chances in random sampling of departing from 50 per cent by as far as the observed 58 per cent. The standard error comes out 1.8 per cent and the observed difference $(58 - 50)$ is, of course, 8 per cent. Dividing this difference by the standard error, we have: $8/1.8 = 4.5$. In other words, the estimated 58 per cent exceeds the fixed limit of 50 per cent by about 4.5 times the standard error. Since there is theoretically less than 1 chance in 20,000 that this would occur by chance, we conclude that the result of 58 per cent is significantly above 50 per cent.

The above procedure applies in principle whenever the problem is to determine whether or not the obtained result is significantly above (or significantly below) some fixed limit. In the particular illustration of the poll the fixed limit was 50 per cent, but that is not always the case. The fixed limit may have any value which happens to be crucial for the particular problem at hand. Suppose, for instance, that a harried school committee discovers that it will be allowed to employ certain funds for the construction of a much needed new building if it can show that at least 75 per cent of the alumni of the school approve of such action. In this example 75 per cent is the fixed limit. When a random sampling of the opinions of 250 of the alumni is secured, 77 per cent are found to favor the project. The question is now whether this 77 per cent in the sample is really indicative of at least 75 per cent in the population. The 77 per cent is not really indicative if it can easily be accounted for as a sampling fluctuation around 75 per cent; because then the true value could easily be less than 75 per cent. Substituting in the standard error formula, we have:

$$\sigma_{p.c.} = \sqrt{\frac{75 \times 25}{250}} = 2.7\%$$

Since the observed difference $(77 - 75 = 2$ per cent) is even smaller than the standard error (2.7 per cent), it can easily be accounted for as a sampling fluctuation; and so the school committee would not be justified in proceeding with the project on the basis of the data collected.

Significance of the Difference Between Two Percentages. The Common problem of calculating the significance of the difference between two percentage estimates may be illustrated with data from a study by R. J. Kennedy of the social adjustment of morons in a Connecticut city. The specific illustrative problem is to demonstrate whether or not there is a significantly greater percentage of morons working as laborers than there is of nonmorons. The survey showed that 84 per cent of a sample of 244 morons were employed in laboring occupations while 56 per cent of a control sample of 120 nonmorons were similarly employed. Thus the difference between the two percentages was $84 - 56 = 28$. The common formula for the standard error of the difference between two percentages is:

$$\sigma_{dif.\ p.c.} = \sqrt{\sigma^2_{p.c.1} + \sigma^2_{p.c.2}} \tag{4}$$

where $\sigma^2_{p.c.1}$ is the square of the standard error of the one percentage, and $\sigma^2_{p.c.2}$ is the square of the standard error of the other percentage. These squared standard errors are easily computed by using formula (1) without the square root sign, viz., p.c.$(100 - $p.c.$)/n$, and come out 5.5 and 20.5, respectively. Substituting these two figures in the formula for the standard error of the difference, we have:

$$\sigma_{dif.\ p.c.} = \sqrt{5.5 + 20.5} = 5.1$$

To estimate the significance of the difference, the latter is divided by its standard error, thus: $28/5.1 = 5.5$. In other words, the difference between 85 per cent and 56 per cent corresponds to over 5 standard errors in extent. This means, according to Table 2, that there is less than 1 chance in a million that this result is a mere fluctuation of sampling. In other words, the percentage of morons employed as laborers in this city is very significantly greater than the percentage of non-morons so employed.

The above formula assumes that the two estimates compared are essentially independent or uncorrelated. This was probably true in the illustration, where the estimates were based on two independent samples, separately drawn. Not infrequently, however, the procedure of sampling or the form of the question in the schedule may serve to limit the response in such a way as to cause some correlation of the results.

In general, correlation is a matter of degree and it is present to the extent that different measures or percentages vary together. Consider, for instance, a survey on the attitude toward the movies, in which the panel technique was employed to reveal the effect of certain experiences on attitude. The same people were interviewed before and after the experiences. Since attitudes tend to persist, the before and after percentages are likely to exhibit some positive correlation; that is, the individuals who were most in favor of the movies on the first occasion tend to remain the ones who are most in favor on the second occasion, the individuals who were less in favor at first tend to remain less in favor, and so on down the line. Some degree of (positive) correlation is to be expected whenever the same sample or panel of individuals is subjected twice to the same test or interview, even though some change which we wish to investigate has been interpolated between the two interviews. Positive correlation is to be expected simply because each individual, being an individual, tends to respond persistently in a more or less characteristic manner. Another useful procedure which gives rise to positive correlation is to interview two individually matched groups once, instead of (as above) interviewing the one group twice. Here the positive correlation is introduced by the matching of the individuals of the one group with individuals of the other group. Since the members of each matched pair are somewhat similar, they tend to react in a somewhat similar manner, and so the results from the two groups tend to exhibit some positive correlation.

Negative correlation, as distinguished from positive correlation, is relatively rare, but it is present if the one variable tends to increase as the other variable tends to decrease, or vice versa. About the only type of extreme or perfect negative correlation to be found in the survey field is the correlation between the frequencies or percentages resulting when every person in a group expresses a preferential judgment for the one or the other of two different things. Here, the more judgments there are in favor of the one thing, the less judgments there are bound to be in favor of the other thing.

The traditional formula for the standard error of the difference between correlated percentages or proportions is:

$$\sigma_{\text{dif. p.c.}} = \sqrt{\sigma^2_{\text{p.c.1}} + \sigma^2_{\text{p.c.2}} - 2r_{12}\sigma_{\text{p.c.1}}\,\sigma_{\text{p.c.2}}} \tag{5}$$

where r is the coefficient of correlation between the percentages in the samples, and the other terms are as above. If the correlation is negative, the sign of the last term becomes plus and this makes the size of the standard error greater than would appear from the previous formula (4). If the correlation is positive, the negative sign remains and the standard error will be less than would appear from the previous formula.

Sometimes we can dispense with a formula for correlated results even though correlation is known to be present. This is because we can usually tell from conditions what kind of correlation to expect, if any, and because in general some degree of positive correlation is far more usual than negative correlation. If positive correlation is present and the standard error calculated by the formula (4) for uncorrelated data yields a seemingly significant difference, then we know that the formula (5) for correlated results would have pointed to a still smaller standard error and so to a still more significant difference. In this instance, then, it would be conservative not to bother with the more complicated formula. On the other hand, if the computation with the formula for uncorrelated data happened to indicate a difference somewhat below the critical level of significance required, that computation would be indeterminate and it would be desirable to take account of the correlation in determining whether or not the required level of significance actually had been reached. Furthermore, in any borderline instances of negatively correlated data the correlation had best be taken account of in the formula, because in such instances the formula for uncorrelated data might have pointed to a difference as significant when actually it was not.

An important aid in deciding whether correlation is worth bothering about is a knowledge of the maximum possible effect of correlation upon the size of the standard error of the difference. The maximum effect of a perfect negative correlation is to make the standard error of the difference about 1.4 times as large as that of zero correlation. The maximum effect of perfect positive correlation is to reduce the standard error of the difference to zero, and so increase infinitely the statistical significance of any finite difference. While the extremes of either positive or negative correlation are rarely approached in practice, it is clear that correlation not only occurs frequently but can have a great influence upon the interpretation of results.

How fortunate, then, that a formula much simpler than formula (5) recently has been derived which does not require the calculation of the separate variances, the standard errors, or even the correlation coefficient (632). The data need be only in the simple and usual dichotomous form of the percentages of responses in the two situations in question. Suppose, for instance, that certain returns from a survey schedule are analyzed for the purpose of deciding whether or not there is a significant difference in household use of two competing brands of bread, X and Y. Suppose, further, that out of $N = 1000$ housewives interviewed, a total of 700 or 70 per cent reported use of brand X, and a total of 350 or 35 per cent reported use of brand Y. Moreover, the number who used brand X but not brand Y was $A = 600$, or $a = 60$ per cent; and the number who used brand Y but not X was $B = 250$, or $b = 25$ per cent. Then the standard error of the difference between the two original percentages, 70 and 35, taking into account the correlation which is present in the data, is given by McNemar's formula:

$$\sigma_{\text{dif. p.c.}} = 10\sqrt{\frac{a+b}{N}} = 10\sqrt{\frac{60+25}{1000}} = 2.9\% \qquad (6)$$

The difference between the two percentages being 35 per cent, and the standard error of the difference being only 2.9 per cent, the critical ratio is $35/2.9 = 12$ and the difference is very significantly in favor of brand X.

When, as in the above example, what one really wants to know is the significance of the difference rather than its standard error, there is a still shorter cut to the solution (632). The observed frequencies, A and B, to which the percentages a and b correspond, are used in a formula which yields the critical ratio directly, thus:

$$cr = \frac{A - B}{\sqrt{A + B}} = \frac{600 - 250}{\sqrt{600 + 250}} = \frac{350}{29.15} = 12 \qquad (7)$$

This is the same result as that obtained above.

Significance of the Difference Between Two Means. The traditional formulas for the significance of the difference between means are the same as those for percentages except that the standard errors of the means are substituted for the standard errors of the percentages. Thus the formula (corresponding to formula 4) for uncorrelated data is:

$$\sigma_{\text{dif. m}} = \sqrt{\sigma^2_{m1} + \sigma^2_{m2}} \qquad (8)$$

As an example, let us calculate the standard error of the difference between two mean incomes. The problem is to see whether there is a significant difference between the average income of families paying a monthly rent of $10 to $15, and the average income of those paying $15 to $20. The preliminary figures are tabulated as follows:

	Monthly Rent $10–$15	Monthly Rent $15–$20
Sample, n	360	716
Mean income, m	1263	1572
Stand. dev., σ	420	460
Stand. error, σ_m	22	17
σ^2_m	484	289

Substituting the squares of the two standard errors in the formula we have:

$$\sigma_{\text{dif. m}} = \sqrt{484 + 289} = 28$$

The difference between the two mean incomes is $1572 − $1263 = 309. Dividing this observed difference by the standard error of the difference, we have 309/28 = 11 as the critical ratio. There is no question about the significance of this difference, because no amount of negative correlation could seriously reduce it.

The best formula for computing the standard error of the difference between two means when the data are correlated is the formula for the standard error of the mean difference between the first and second responses of each individual in the group or panel, or between the performances of the first and second members of matched pairs of individuals. Furthermore, as in the case of the new formula (6) for correlated percentages, it is not necessary actually to calculate either the correlation coefficient or the two standard errors. All that is necessary is to calculate the standard deviation of the differences of the paired measures, $\sigma_{dif.}$, and divide this by the square root of the number of pairs minus one (277, pp. 174, 179–180; 384, p. 141). Thus:

$$\sigma_{dif.\ m} = \frac{\sigma_{dif}}{\sqrt{N-1}} \qquad (9)$$

The standard deviation of the differences is calculated in just the same way as the standard deviation of an original sample, except that one deals with the differences between the paired measures rather than with original measures. The procedure for calculating the standard deviation was outlined in connection with formula (3).

4. SIGNIFICANCE OF MULTIPLE DIFFERENCES:

Sometimes survey results contain a number of percentages or frequencies which were secured under comparable conditions. Then the problem confronting the analyst is likely to be that of testing whether one or a few of the differences of special interest are statistically significant. When there are not many differences to be considered, a simple indicative procedure is to apply repeatedly the most appropriate formula for the standard error of a difference.

The multiple choice survey question yields several frequencies or percentages which ordinarily must be compared. The limited or restricted choice inherent in this type of situation results, of course, in negative correlation of the data being used. Therefore, the formula employed should be one which takes account of correlation. As a final computational example, the returns of a certain survey of 2000 interviews showed the following frequencies of preferences for five competing brands of a certain commodity: V = 800, W = 700, X = 200, Y = 200, Z = 100. The statistical problem here was to discover which brands could be regarded as really in the lead over which others. Since the 99-out-of-100 level of assurance was accepted, and since the corresponding critical ratio is 2.6, the problem reduces to finding out which differences are at least 2.6 times their standard error. Applying formula (7) to the votes for the leading and runner-up brands V and W, we have: 800 − 700 divided by the square root of 800 + 700 gives the critical ratio 2.6. Since this first difference is barely significant, the greater differences, V − X, V − Y, and V − Z also will be significant. Next, applying the formula to brands W and X, we have 700 − 200 divided by the square root of 700 + 200 giving about 17. This is far above the criterion ratio of 2.6; and so differences W − X, W − Y, and W − Z all are significant. Since there is no difference between the frequencies of votes for brands X and Y, there is no problem there, and it only remains to deal with the difference between brands Y and Z. Applying the same formula as before, the critical ratio comes out about 5.7, indicating that this difference also is statistically significant. In brief, then, it so happened in this example that all the observed differences were also significant differences, at least to the chosen criterial level of assurance. The above type of analysis may well be made contingent upon the result of a preliminary overall test to see whether the data as a whole depart significantly from chance expectation, because, if they do not, there is no need to go further. The more differences there are to consider and the smaller they run, the more the preliminary test is indicated. A simple chi-square test is suitable for this purpose (266, pp. 194–195; 629).

While an effort has been made throughout to select for illustration types of problems and methods of solution which are of practical interest and value in survey work, there are of course various valuable techniques and tests which are beyond the scope of this chapter. For further guidance and derivations of formulas, the interested reader is referred to recent articles and texts dealing with statistical analysis.

Selected References

Reliability and Validity of Data
Bancroft (29), Bancroft and Welch (30), Beers (38), Benson (50), Bingham (63), Blanar (67), Blankenship and Manheimer (81), Bonney (90), Cahalan and Meier (131), Cantril (140, 143), Chapin (166), Connelly (186), Corey (197), Crespi (209), Crutchfield and Gordon (220), Cuber and Gerberich (221), Curtis

(223), Deming (238), Dodd (248), Droba (254), Farnsworth (295), Ferraby (302), Field and Connelly (304), Field et al. (305), Fischer (306), Frank (325), Gallup and Rae (345), Gehlke (351), Gosnell (373), Gosnell and deGrazia (374), Hogg (445), Hyman (462), Jenkins (469, 470, 471), Jenkins and Corbin (472), Katz (491, 493, 495, 496, 497), Katz and Cantril (499), King (515), Lawson (541), Lee (557), Lentz (559), Link and Freiberg (579), Link et al. (580), McGeogh (625, 626), Merton (639), Nepprash (683), Newhall (690), Newhall and Rodnick (691), Pace (711, 712), Palmer (714), Peatman (728, 729), Pierce (743), Robeson (785), Rogers (795, 796, 797), Roper (806), Roskelley (814), Seham and Schey (858), Smith (884, 885), Spingarn (904), Stagner (907), Stanton (910), Stephan (918), Stoke and Lehman (932), Symonds (947), Toops (967), Tryon (976), Walker (1052), Warner (1057), Washington Public Opinion Laboratory (1059), Wilks (1091), Williams and Cantril (1098), Wylie (1130), Yates (1131), Young (1138).

Determinants of Opinion

Benson and Perry (48), Beville (58), Campbell (133), Cantril (141, 142), Crespi and Rugg (210), Ferguson (300), *Fortune* (319), Kornhauser (533), Lazarsfeld (543), Lee (556, 557), Lovell (588), Lurie (600), Martin (617), Max (619), Meyrowitz and Fiske (642), Ogburn and Coombs (704), Osgood and Stagner (708), Riesman and Glazer (778), Saenger (829), Smith (886).

Significance of Differences

Chapin (166), Daniel (225), Edgerton and Paterson (273), Edwards (277), Fiske and Dunlap (309), Flanagan (314), Guilford (384), Hart (413, 414), Lindquist (568), McNemar (632), Peek (731), Smith (889), Wilks (1092), Wood (1117), Zubin (1145).

See also books on statistical methods.

CHAPTER XVII

Preparation and Publication
of the Report

No survey, however carefully planned and conducted, should terminate until the published findings have been circulated among the groups for whom the study was intended. To insure that a report will be forthcoming, it is wise to set aside adequate funds and plan to reserve sufficient time for preparing the report. Unless ample time, funds, and personnel are provided in the plans for writing and publishing the findings, there is grave danger that toward the end of the survey adequate resources may not be found to complete it. The persons who organized the study and secured the funds may have left, the source of funds may have run dry, the enthusiasm of the financial sponsors may have died down, or the forces opposing the survey at the start may have gained sufficient strength to prevent further aid being given the study. The countless unpublished and unanalyzed surveys in files of public and private agencies provide ample testimony of the fate of investigations in which the funds were used up in the collection or tabulation stages and the expectation of securing further funds was not realized.

PLANNING THE REPORT:

If the various steps in the preparation and publication of a report are kept in mind, careful budgeting of time, funds, and personnel is facilitated. Since the value of many survey facts lies in their timeliness, the findings should be available within a relatively short period after the collection of the data. Very early in the survey planning, the publication date of the report should be set. Each proposal to expand the investigation, once it is under way, should be considered in terms of its effect upon publication plans.

The time required for the preparation and publication of a report will depend upon numerous factors. The many steps required for preparing reports should convince one that however much time is allotted, it will seem insufficient when the "deadline" date approaches.

WHO WILL PUBLISH THE REPORT?

Before actual writing of the report begins, much time and effort will be saved if certain questions are answered. For example, what individual, agency or organization is sufficiently interested in the results to see that the findings are published and circulated? Do the plans and funds provide for publication of the findings in a special report or monograph, or will the results merely be filed away after they have been seen by the sponsoring agency? If a published report is contemplated, will the sponsoring agency distribute it once it has been printed and after the survey staff has disbanded? Do the survey funds cover the cost of circulating the report after it has been printed or does the work of the survey staff terminate with the publication of the report? Questions on the price of the report, use of funds received from sale of the monograph, possibility of securing advertising to offset printing expenses, etc., may affect the plan of the report.

WHO WILL READ THE REPORT?

The purpose of the survey and the potential readers of the report must be considered by the report writer. If the report is to be prepared for popular consumption by readers not familiar with survey procedure or terminology or not versed in the technical subject matter of the investigation, the plan, emphasis, and style will be different from that employed for specialists. The specialist and scientist are usually interested in detailed results as well as in definitions, sampling, and survey methods. The lay reader is more likely to be interested in the highlights interpreted for him and presented in an interesting style. As a matter of fact, specialists are also interested in the popular presentation, but few of them will be satisfied with reading only the popular report. They will want supporting tables for any generalizations. Reports intended for all types of readers usually combine a popular presentation in the main body of the text with a technical appendix for the specialist. If the report must reach both types of readers, it is well to prepare what Baker and Howell (27) call a "double purpose" report, with one section written from the standpoint of the lay reader and another from that of the scientist. This combined popular and technical report is being employed more and more, especially in government reports. The United States Census of Partial Employment and Unemployment, for example, included an appendix giving the sampling errors in the estimates (993, Vol. IV). Not very long ago, however, one government bureau which published probable errors was criticized by a reader for being so inaccurate as to have errors in its figures!

Another widely adopted procedure for reaching a mixed reader public is the preparation of several separate reports—a press release to the newspapers giving the high spots and general interest material, a semipopular report with the necessary details for understanding the significance of the findings, and articles or tabular material prepared for scientific or technical periodicals.

METHOD OF REPRODUCTION:

In addition to considering the reader, the report writer should bear in mind the process by which the report will be reproduced. That is, he should know whether the report is to be typed, mimeographed, multigraphed, photolithographed, planographed, placed on microfilm, printed, or duplicated by some other method. Each process has certain do's and don't's with respect to such items as arrangement, spacing, use of colors, cost of reproducing tabular material and charts and graphs, and time required for duplication. If the writer knows which process is to be used, he can adapt his plans to take the greatest advantage of whichever process is employed; also, he will know in advance how many chances at "revision" he will have. For example, if some photo offset process is employed, there are no last-minute opportunities to revise or make minor corrections, as is so often done on the galley and page proofs of printed reports.

The method of duplication used should be decided after consideration of the relative costs and merits of the various processes. Invention of new and improved systems of duplicating copies makes it imperative that the surveyor consult publishers and printers before coming to a decision. A voluminous account of techniques of reproduction, equipment, costs and suggestions for organizing the manuscript to facilitate publication may be found in Binkley's *Manual of Methods of Repro-*

ducing Research Material (65). The choice of the method of publication will depend upon such factors as (1) the size of edition; (2) the likelihood that reruns will be wanted; (3) the number and types of tables, illustrations, charts, and photographs to be included; (4) the format desired, number of pages, and number of words to the page; (5) the price at which the report is to be sold; (6) the type of reader to whom the report is addressed; (7) the importance of a "finished-product-look" to accomplish the purpose of the report.

OUTLINING THE REPORT:

Once the writer knows the type of report wanted, who his readers will be, and what process of publishing will be used, he should examine the tabulations and select material for the text, for detailed presentation as well as for omission from the report. It is seldom possible or even desirable to publish all the tables prepared during the analysis of the findings. Assuming that tabulation and preliminary analysis has taken place, the writer next prepares an outline of the chapters and decides on the table order. The mechanics of writing vary from writer to writer, but most report writers find that a logical presentation of results is facilitated by the preparation of an outline. Generally speaking, the report secures greater clarity and unity if the entire report is first outlined under large headings and then filled in by more and more detailed outlines. Suggested outlines are found in many books on the preparation, writing, and planning of reports (see references on page 535). The following outline incorporates the most usual divisions for a report:

Suggested Outline

I. Prefatory material
    a. Title page
    b. Table of contents
    c. List of illustrations, tables, and charts
    d. Preface, foreword, or letter of transmittal
    e. Summary of findings, abstract, or recommendations
II. Text or body of report
    a. Introduction
        1. Aim—statement and definition of the problem
        2. Scope—time, place and materials of the survey
        3. Organization and procedure (general statement here but detailed statement in appendices)
           (a) Methods or techniques employed

        (b) Copy of schedules, or questionnaires, or forms used (Sometimes placed in appendices)
        (c) Pertinent historical or comparable material
    b. Analysis and presentation of results
        1. Report of facts—presentation of the data, tables, graphs, etc.
        2. Analysis and interpretation of data
        3. Conclusions based on the data presented, and possible recommendations
        4. Condensed summary of the important content (if not already presented under Ie. above)
III. Supplementary material
    a. Appendices (often contain detailed report on sampling and other methods used in the survey)
    b. Bibliography
    c. Index
    d. Glossary of terms (if scientific terms needing definition are used)

If the writer keeps in mind the report as a whole, he may often find it advantageous to shift material from one section to another or to present a brief statement in one part of the report and give details in another. The material commonly included in the above-mentioned sections is described below:

The title page includes the title of the report, the name of the person or organization to whom addressed, the author's name, and the place and date of the publication or release. The title should be brief—a few words well selected to indicate the content are most effective.

The table of contents consists of an outline of the topics covered by headings and subheadings, with page references detailed enough to make it possible for the reader to ascertain quickly if the report contains material in which he is interested and where to turn to locate such data. The main headings are usually double spaced, while the subdivisions are single spaced. Numeration is used for the chief headings, and indentation and alignment for the subheadings. The table of contents condenses longer statements by using words for phrases, and phrases for sentences.

The list of illustrations, tables and charts. All illustrations and charts should be numbered consecutively as Fig. 1, 2, 3, 4, etc., with the page reference following. Generally speaking, it is advisable to separate the list of statistical tables from that of charts and illustrations. If there are more than twenty tables, it may be desirable to use arabic numerals; if fewer than twenty, roman numerals may be used.

The preface, foreword, or *letter of transmittal,* with acknowledgments to those who have contributed to the completed form, may contain a statement of the basic purpose, chief phases, and salient aspects of the study, and should fix responsibility for the facts presented. A foreword or preface is used in place of the letter of transmittal or submittal when the report is directed to the public in general. It is a statement regarding the investigator's credentials for undertaking such a study.

A *summary* is sometimes included in the prefatory material and provides a convenient method for the reader to determine whether he is interested in the report as a whole. It should be written as a concise abstract in such a form that abstracting journals or reviewers can use it without rewriting it.

The text or body of the report includes the introduction, presentation and interpretation of the facts, conclusions, recommendations, if any, and a summary of the important content if not already presented in the prefatory material.

The introduction should contain a statement of the problem giving rise to the survey and the methods used to solve it. Both Harrison (410), in his review of 2000 published survey reports, and McNemar (630), in his examination of scientific studies using sampling methods, state that the most elementary information on the "how, why, and what" of the report was either not clear or entirely missing in the majority of published studies reviewed by them. The writer should, therefore, take particular precautions clearly and definitely to cover these details. The description of method and definitions in the text of the report does not need to be so detailed as that appearing in the appendix—if a technical appendix is presented. A specific description of sampling methods and techniques as well as collection procedures employed to secure the data, whether questionnaire, interview, telephone interview, panel, poll, etc., is absolutely necessary, along with a statement of the reason for the choice of the particular technique. Copies of the schedules, questionnaires, or other forms used could appear either in the body of the text or in the appendix. It is not enough, for example, to state that "questionnaires were sent and replies indicated such and such percentages." The writer should state exactly

how many were sent, to whom they were sent, how many were returned, of these how many were eliminated, for what reasons, what
attempts were made to secure more complete returns, and how many
cases constitute the basis for the percentages presented. It is always
desirable, if possible, to include this material in footnotes or in an
appendix if the report is primarily for popular consumption. Pertinent
historical and comparable material, showing familiarity with what has
been done in the past, its relation to the present material, and a statement indicating wherein this report is unique and contributes something additional to the field, may also be included.

Presentation of the facts includes exposition supported by tables,
graphs, and pictorial material. The discussion should not be a mere
repetition of the figures in the tables. It should bring out the most
striking facts or relationships appearing in the table. Of course, the
chief point or over-all picture revealed by the figures should not be
overlooked. The writer can, by taking an example, show the reader
how the figures in the table are to be interpreted. A knowledge of the
fundamentals of statistics is a prerequisite for the social surveyor, but
in itself it is not sufficient. It has been said so often that "figures do
not lie," but inexpertly presented or incorrectly interpreted, they can
give a completely false impression. The structure of the tables has
been dealt with in Chapter XV. It is safe to assume that most readers
will skip over the tables and look at any charts or pictorial material.
Tables should be prepared, however, for those who have a genuine
interest in the study. Graphs, charts, maps, and illustrations all add
considerably to the readability and clearness of a report. A well-
constructed graph or chart can convey compactly, vividly, and logically data which might otherwise require pages of exposition.

Usually the report writer does not have the time, training, or skill to
prepare a finished drawing of graphs or charts which he wishes to
include. He may, however, prepare a rough sketch on cross-section
paper and submit it to a statistical draftsman, who in turn probably
will prepare several working charts before the final form is drawn. It is
advisable to follow standard practices such as those recommended by
the Committee on Standards for Graphic Presentation (10, 11) when
planning the charts.

Many of the principles suggested for tables apply also to charts and other visual aids. It is especially important that the title, placed at the top of the chart, be clear and brief. It should answer the questions of who, what, when, and where. The chart as well as its title should be centered on the page. Boxing of the chart is frequently used to give a pleasing appearance. The chart should not only be easy to read and understand, but it should truthfully present the facts. The draftsman should be aware of common optical illusions which may convey a false impression of the relative size of various elements in the chart. Even though the graph is numerically correct, the impression gained from it may be completely erroneous if techniques such as shading, spacing, or lettering give undeserved emphasis to certain parts of it.

Some of the more commonly used forms of graphic presentation are: bar or column charts, line charts or curves, ratio or logarithmic charts, circle or pie charts, map diagrams, and pictorial charts.

Bar charts are graphs in which numerical values are represented by the length of columns or bars which may be arranged either vertically or horizontally. Bars are particularly adapted for comparisons of size. It is much easier, for example, to compare heights of bars than areas of squares or volumes of circles. The choice of direction for the bars will depend on such factors as the convenience in reading the lettering, captions, or designations, or the natural association which the reader may have with the subject matter of the graph, e.g., heights of persons call for vertical bars while distances at which ratio stations can be heard would best be shown horizontally.

Component parts may be shown for each bar by shading, cross-hatching, or coloring the various subdivisions. This proportional presentation is usually limited to relatively few bars and subdivisions for ease of interpretation. Bar charts are also used for presenting amounts in a single time series. They are not recommended for comparisons of several time series or for series covering a long period and requiring many plottings. For single series, bars should be of equal width and the spaces between them should represent equal periods. Usually the earliest years are shown at the top for horizontal bars and at the left for vertical ones. The same positions are used for emphasis of any facts in charts. Explanations of what the vertical bars represent usually are placed underneath them. If figures are placed above vertical bars the reader gets the impression of added length. Sometimes the designations are placed within the bars. If the space required for such designations varies noticeably from bar to bar, it is better not to insert them in the bar because of the misleading optical illusions.

As a rule, a scale beginning with zero and laid out in round numbers at convenient equal intervals is included with the bars to facilitate correct reading of the figures. Guide lines also are helpful, provided, of course, there are not so many as to be confusing.

Designations of the units represented by the scale are most conveniently read if placed horizontally across the top of the column of scale figures. For horizontal bar charts, the scale is usually placed along the top of the graph just above the bars. A systematic order such as one determined by size or geographic location is desirable but not essential to the presentation. Comparisons of pairs or groups are easier if the bars are spaced so that the pairs or groups stand out.

Line charts or *curves* are constructed by plotting the points representing the observed values of the two variable magnitudes, e.g., number of cases and period of time, and then connecting these points either by straight or smoothed lines. The line graph is particularly useful for plotting time series. Two or three curves may be shown on the same chart if the lines are of different colors or composition, such as a series of dots, dashes, combinations of dots and dashes, etc. In plotting data where time is one of the variables it is customary to lay out the time period horizontally and the other variable vertically. Equal time periods should be equal distances apart so that all sections of the graph are comparable.

The scale intervals should not be too broad or too narrow if the true trends are to be depicted. The wrong choice of intervals may give the impression of violent fluctuations in the data or it may cause the plottings to run beyond the limits of the chart. Trends should be gradual but still should show any significant changes.

Scale designations are best placed outside the coordinate lines—below the chart and to the left. The vertical scale, reading from bottom to top, usually begins with zero, but if it does not the zero line may be shown by a horizontal break in the diagram. When the chart covers a long period a vertical scale is sometimes placed at the right as well as at the left, and at the top as well as at the bottom. Curved lines of the figure should always be sharply distinguished from the rulings.

Semilogarithmic or *ratio charts* are used when the *rate* of change

rather than the *absolute amount* is to be shown graphically. They are
also recommended for series with widely different magnitudes, or for
series expressed in different units. The spacing on the vertical line
(Y axis) is logarithmic, while that on the horizontal line (X axis) is
arithmetic. Equal distances on the vertical axis represent equal percentage changes, so that a series increasing an equal per cent each
period will plot as a straight line on the semilogarithmic paper.

The *circle* or *pie chart,* constructed with the aid of a protractor, is
used for comparing component parts of a total. When the item represented is in terms of dollars, such as family income or expenditures, the
circle presentation is very effective. The reader should not be expected
to compare different sized circles with any accuracy. Subdivision of
the circle should proceed by lines radiating from the center and not
by arcs drawn across sectors. Descriptive matter is usually placed inside sectors and when possible it is readable horizontally. Shading or
coloring is used to differentiate the various sectors, but care must be
taken not to overemphasize by contrasts such as very black and completely white on the same chart.

Map charts are sometimes used to show the geographic distribution
or concentration of variables. Cross-hatching, dots, partially shaded
dots, pictorial symbols, bars, and color are used to show frequencies in
areas. The dot maps, in which each dot represents a given number of
cases and the number of dots indicates the frequency of the item, are
particularly suitable for showing the distribution of population over a
city, state, or nation. It is difficult to compare various sized dots so
numbers of dots rather than *size* are preferred for density distributions.

Pictorial charts or *pictograms* usually have a wide popular appeal.
They consist of pictures which are considered to be descriptive of the
variable plotted. For example, small figures of men are used to represent voters, miniature dollars for money, or raised hands for "yes."
Modley (**650**, p. 12) predicted that a pictorial dictionary of self-
explanatory symbols for general use soon will be compiled. He recommends that only comparisons be charted, since figures are meaningful
only in relation to something already understood.

Because of the difficulty of accurately comparing two-dimensional
volumes, only rough comparisons are to be expected from picture
graphs. The *number* of figures rather than their *size* should indicate
differences. The symbols used should be as simple as possible and still

be eye-catching. Adequate verbal descriptions of the chart should be closely associated with it.

Analysis of tabulations. During the processes of planning the survey, drawing up the questions, and preparing the tabulations, the surveyor has been thinking in terms of analysis. What sort of questions are to be answered by the survey? What hypotheses are the figures supposed to prove or disprove? Which facts will seem most significant from the sponsor's point of view? Which are socially significant? By the time the analyst looks for answers, he usually knows which tabulations are most important, which ones bring out significant but not essential facts, and which are of secondary importance only. He also knows why what originally seemed to be a very simple problem with a clear-cut answer is usually complicated and requires pages of discussion to bring out the facts in their proper perspective.

The procedure usually followed by survey writers is to examine the tables in the order regarded as most important at the time of tabulation. For each table, the analyst asks such questions as:

1. What is the most important point revealed by this table?
2. What other points are brought out?
3. What is significant about the totals shown?
4. Are the averages higher or lower than one would have expected or than were known to have been the case at an earlier period or in another place?
5. Are the averages pretty stable or is there great variability among them and in the components from which the average is computed?
6. Why do the smallest figures shown fall in that particular grouping? How can the infrequent or low numbers be explained?
7. What is the largest figure shown? Does it make sense? How does it compare with numbers or percentages found in comparable items, places, populations, on the same table or on other tables?
8. What general trend seems to exist? If there is none, why not?
9. What conspicuous exceptions to the general situation are observable? Can these exceptions be accounted for?
10. Are any causal relationships apparent? If so, does the cause seem to operate throughout the table or just here and there? What checks from other tables can be made where these causes should also show up?
11. Do certain sequences seem to occur with any amount of regularity?
12. Is there something about the way the sample was drawn, or the questions asked, that could explain why the table shows these particular results?

13. How do these facts compare with those already known or shown by other tables? Are they consistent? Are they more or less pronounced?
14. Which groups could be combined and which could be shown in greater detail to reveal significant facts?
15. Would it be desirable to go back to the original schedules from which the tabulations were made to see what kind of people and what responses account for certain portions of this table?
16. What summary figures should be computed from those appearing on the table? What measures of central tendency, variability, or correlation are desirable?

Questions of the above nature enable the analyst to discover the important similarities, differences, sequences, causal relationships, and limitations of the data. As the various questions are being answered by inspection of the tables, the analyst should jot down his observations so that when he begins writing the report he will need only to select and integrate the most significant findings into a meaningful presentation. The points finally made should be expressed clearly and in a straightforward style. The writer should let the facts speak for themselves and should avoid any special pleas or arguments which look as if he has an ax to grind. It is important to maintain perspective and not to emphasize unduly the data toward which the analyst has a bias—whether conscious or unconscious. Important points should be played up, while minor points should be given a subordinate position. This requires that the analyst distinguish between small fluctuations and general tendencies or between the exceptional case and the general rule. He must also be aware of the difference between chance association and causal relationships. Comparisons should be made only of groups, things, situations or places that have common qualities. When the analyst makes comparisons, he should consider whether differences noted are statistically significant. Use of formulas presented in Chapter XVI should enable the analyst to evaluate observed differences.

Summary and conclusions. The summary may be distinguished from the conclusions in that the former is merely a listing of the main points brought out in the tabulations and discussion. The latter is an attempt to bring these points together into one or more generalized statements. If the summary comes after the body of the report, it usually lists the points in the same order as in the more detailed treatment. If the summary is first, however, there is something to be said for using a newspaper style and arranging the findings in order of importance.

The conclusions should answer the questions which gave rise to the survey. If the survey has been properly designed, the plans will contain the list of questions which the survey is expected to answer. If these have been altered during the course of the survey, a written record to this effect should have been filed with the plans. The writer should make certain that he gives a definite and full answer to all the questions which he agreed to investigate. He may, in addition, supply facts which are as important or even more significant than those originally planned for. He must keep in mind, however, what the reader and his sponsors expect to get out of the report. Only after he has fulfilled his promises to them should he present additional findings.

If the writer examines the various points brought out in the text, he can find general tendencies and significant relationships. He also will find exceptions to the general rules. As long as these exceptions are of minor importance, it is safe to generalize, but if they provide contradictory evidence, they should not be disregarded. It is a common fault for novices in research to expect too much from their data. It is better to err on the side of understatement than of overstatement in order to retain the reader's confidence. Generalizations should always take into account the universe from which the sample has been drawn. If the study has been limited to a given income group, or to homes with telephones, it is not safe to assume that people in general will behave or react the same as did those in such restricted groups. On the other hand, if the writer can bring in outside evidence to support his claims for wider applicability of his findings, he should do so, providing he supplies the reader with enough information to make an independent judgment.

After tentative conclusions are drawn they should be scrutinized to see whether (1) it is possible to come to opposite conclusions with the same material, (2) other persons on the staff would reach the same conclusions with the evidence shown, (3) the conclusions are consistent with one another and with other known facts, (4) they seem to make sense—and if not, why not, (5) they are colored by the writers' personal biases, (6) their meaning is unmistakable and (7) they could be accounted for by the survey techniques used. Suggestions arising during the course of answering these questions should be utilized in preparing the final draft of the conclusions.

Recommendations. Fortified by the facts disclosed in the investigation, the surveyor is in an excellent position to make recommendations or to advise the survey sponsors in courses of action which will take advantage of the added knowledge. Some market surveyors regard the recommendations as the goal of the survey and an essential part of the report. Suggestions may be drawn up in conferences with representatives of the sponsoring organization or without them. Consultation with persons who will carry out the recommendations once they are received is advisable when the surveyor is not familiar with how the recommendations will fit into the program and policies of the organization or with the personalities upon whom the successful working out of the recommendations will depend. Unless suggestions are accepted as administratively practical, they are likely to be ignored. They should also be based upon clear-cut evidence. If the findings do not point unmistakably to some positive course of action, it is better to withhold recommendations.

If the purpose of the survey is to provide facts for the guidance of social or political reformers, the surveyor may accomplish more if he lets the facts and conclusions speak for themselves than if he makes recommendations to which exception might be taken. Ideally, the surveyor should be called in when legislation is being drafted so he can make oral recommendations based on his intimate knowledge of community conditions.

Appendices are placed after the finished report and contain material such as a bibliography, index, unsummarized tabular material or tables that are too detailed for the text discussion, letters of authorization, approval or endorsement, descriptions of methods employed in collecting and analyzing material, and a glossary of terms, if necessary. The discussion of methods should be complete enough to enable the reader to evaluate the survey in terms of standards such as those suggested by Dodd (248). Detailed sampling procedures, pretests of questions, copies of schedules and other forms used, methods of selecting interviewers, instructions to enumerators, test of validity and reliability, and limitations of the findings should appear either in the text or in the appendices. Every survey report writer should make certain that in so far as possible he has adhered to the highest standards of reporting. The pamphlet on the Preparation of Sampling Survey Reports (980), prepared by a United Nations Statistical Commission, contains recommendations as to the various points to be included. If the writer has brought out all the points listed in this publication, he may feel assured that the report is going to be of value not only to the limited group for which the survey was conducted but to the more general as well as to specialized audiences of surveyors the world over.

A *bibliography* accompanying a report makes available additional sources of information and also acknowledges those from whom one has drawn material or techniques. It may be arranged topically according to material in each chapter or it may be classified alphabetically and cover references to material throughout the report. The citations may or may not carry annotations regarding their content. Whatever form of listing is used, the work cited should be described completely enough for the reader to locate it. A suggested form for books is: last name of author, first name in full, initial for second name, title of book, city of publication, publishing house, and year. Omission of the city is permissible for well-known publishers. Periodical articles may be referred to by: name of the author (as for books), title of article, name of periodical, month, year, volume number, and pages. It is not necessary to give the month if the other information is included. Also, either the year or the volume number may be omitted. The bibliography is usually arranged alphabetically by author, and when no author is named, by the name of the organization or periodical responsible for the publication. When there is more than one author for a publication, only the first author is listed by last name first. Government publications appear under the department or bureau responsible for the publication rather than under the author. Several publications by the same author are often arranged by date of publication, the earliest coming first.

The subject index is a list of words or phrases of the important concepts, ideas, terms or significant facts appearing in the report, with a citation of the pages where they appear. The subject matter is arranged alphabetically and cross-referenced to other topics within the index. Most survey reports are not long enough to justify an index, but if the report is voluminous the index is important for making the information easily accessible to the reader. The index is usually begun during the editing of the manuscript but it obviously cannot be completed until the final page proof is ready so the pagination will be correct.

Each reference word or phrase, together with its page reference to the typed manuscript, is placed on a small card (one word or phrase to a card). After the final page numbers have been added, the alphabetical file is prepared. One indexer has found it convenient to type his list of reference words on gummed paper such as that used for sealing cardboard cartons. After the pagination is completed, he cuts the list up and pastes the words in alphabetical order. It may be advisable to check the final index against indexes used by other investigators of the same subject to make certain that all usual references are included. Sometimes a separate index of authors is prepared, but as a rule surveys do not draw upon enough outside sources to justify an author index. A combination of author and subject index also may be used.

A glossary of terms for the lay reader in which all technical terms are defined may be necessary if many such terms are used. A definition of terms rarely employed may be given in the text or in a footnote.

WRITING STYLE:

After the tabulations have been carefully analyzed and detailed notes taken, the outline should be prepared by sorting and resorting the facts to be brought out. Before the writing begins, the writer should know what his results reveal and the relative importance of the various findings. His aim should be to present this material so that the reader will be interested and understand correctly what he has to say. The worth of the entire survey is usually judged by the report that comes out of it. It is up to the writer to see that the survey gets the attention it merits. To be widely read, the report must be interesting looking, easy to read, clear and accurate in statement, meaningful and attractively illustrated.

To develop a clear style, the writer must think logically and know in advance what he wants to say. The purpose of the report is not to present a mass of undigested figures, but to convey interpretations and conclusions after careful analysis of the material. Fortified with facts and an outline of points to be discussed, the report writer might do well to forget about literary style until he has written his first draft. It has been suggested that the author write as rapidly as possible, making sure to cover the necessary points. An uninterrupted period for writing is conducive to an integrated presentation. After the rough draft is completed the style should be examined more closely. Sometimes reports based on tabulations are dull reading because there is no variation in phrasing. "This table shows . . . ." may get to be a very monotonous phrase if repeated in paragraph after paragraph. The writer should make sure that the reader knows which figures are being discussed. The column or row number as well as the table number may need to be cited. If there is likely to be any question regarding the meaning of a word or figure, it should be clearly defined in the text, in a footnote, or in a glossary. If there is any chance of misinterpretation, the writer should try out the sentence or paragraph on someone else, preferably a person of the type who will eventually read it. Lack of clarity seriously limits the usefulness of the report.

All statistical material and figures in a report must be accurate. This can be assured if all text figures, tables and references are systematically checked. If the writer discovers material which needs checking or does not seem to make sense, he should check the figures personally, if possible, and thus familiarize himself with their limitations. He should make sure that all changes in tables are also made in figures cited in the text.

If the manuscript is handwritten, the writer will save himself much grief if his writing can be easily deciphered by the typist. Many errors arise in this process and are carried along from one typing to the next without being discovered. If precautions for preventing and correcting errors in all stages of the survey have been observed, and errors are not permitted to crop up at the writing stage, the facts and figures should be accurate.

Uniformity in presentation is essential to a good report. Reference should be made to standard books on style, composition, and English usage, such as those listed at the end of this chapter. If one manual is followed consistently, uniformity will be assured on such matters as punctuation, capitalization, abbreviations, footnotes, quotations, acknowledgments, bibliography, etc. On many of these points any one of several forms is acceptable, but whichever is used should be followed consistently.

An interesting report may appear dull if set up on a solid page, while a dull report may attract interest if broken up into readable sections.

Readability is facilitated by the use of such devices as: frequent paragraphing; topical or summary sentences at the beginning or end of a paragraph; underlining or capitalization of key phrases or sentences; use of specific illustrations and examples; and use of pictorial and graphic illustrations. When editing the manuscript, each sentence should be examined objectively as if it were a telegram to see which words can be deleted or which expressions simplified. Too many modifications and qualifications of incidental points often merely confuse the reader. Logical relationships of various points may be revealed by the use of correct typography, central headings, subtitles, subheadings and footnotes and by such devices as spacing, capitalization, underlining and boldface type. These devices for emphasis can be overdone, however, and the total effect may still be confusing.

NUMBERING AND LABELING DRAFTS:

Before most survey reports are ready for the printer, every page, and parts of each page, will have been typed a great many times, in what was believed to be the final form at the time. Usually several people must pass on the final report. As each one reads over the report he is likely to revise sections or phrases to conform to his own style or point of view at the moment. Sometimes these suggestions bring about real improvement in the manuscript, while in other cases the revised form may be inferior to that originally prepared by the report writer. In any case, one person should be responsible for seeing that the various changes are completely integrated into the report as a whole.

The various drafts of the manuscript will become hopelessly confused unless each typed page bears a page number, chapter number, draft number, and date. This point cannot be emphasized too strongly. Even if no one other than the report writer makes each revision, he will waste much time and effort searching for drafts and pages unless each one is labeled carefully.

It is also essential to label and place a date upon all tables as they are prepared. It is not an uncommon experience for material to be lost because no title and date appear on the page of figures which once were perfectly clear to someone, but which later could not be identified.

This brings up the question as to what to do with early drafts of the manuscript and with discarded tables. It is unwise to throw material in the wastebasket until one is absolutely certain that there will be no call for it before the report is received from the publishers. In one study a file of discarded copies of manuscript and tables labeled "The Morgue" was useful on a number of occasions, although during most of the time this canceled or discarded material did not lie around on tops of desks to confuse the writers or staff members.

FINAL REEDIT OF MANUSCRIPT:

Prior to the final typing, it is advisable to lay the manuscript aside for a period, so that it "gets cold." Too often one fails to catch the gaps or weaknesses, as one's memory erroneously recalls seeing references in the text that actually are not there. After a lapse of time the material should be reedited for clarity and organization, sentence structure, paragraphing, and wording. It is then well to recheck all figures. Even small errors may seriously detract from the value of the report, because they convey the impression of careless work. Reexamination of the report may reveal further opportunities for deleting material. By eliminating extra words or irrelevant ideas, the finished report may be made about one-half as long as the original. It is generally advisable to ask some other person, or preferably several other persons, to read the material critically before it is sent to the printers. Corrections in the galley or page proofs are costly, as is also loss of reputation and peace of mind when one's errors are perpetuated in a printed document.

TYPING THE REPORT:

It is wise to make an early decision regarding the desired final form, style and size of the report, and whether it is to be mimeographed, processed, or printed, so that the typist can set up the manuscript correctly. If she develops wrong habits of manuscript preparation, such habits may be hard to break and inconsistencies will arise. By the time of the final typing, attention can be given to checking details other than general form and arrangement. In deciding on the typed form, advice should come from the publishers or printers. Many organizations, publishing houses, universities and government bureaus distribute manuals indicating the preferred form and styles. In addition to having a style manual at her disposal, the typist should also be instructed how to set up tables. Chapter XV contains advice on the preparation of tabular material. The following additional suggestions to the typist for final copy may be useful:

1. See that typing is clear.
2. Type on one side of the paper only.
3. Keep copy flat, never roll or fold.
4. Use a good grade of regular sized 8½ by 11 inch white paper.
5. Typing must be double spaced, except for quotations and footnotes which are single spaced and indented. Quotes are entirely indented, while the footnote is indented only in the first line.
6. Fasten pages together by clips or pins which can be removed easily.
7. Number pages in the left upper corner, and leave the upper right corner clear. Numbering permits insertion or elimination of pages, and also enables several typists to work on different sections simultaneously. Collate and renumber consecutively the entire report in the upper right hand corner just before the report is given to the printer. Interpolated pages should be numbered for the preceding page, and lettered, e.g., 10a, 10b, 10c, if the page preceding the insert is numbered 10. Where pages have been eliminated, the page preceding the elimination should carry the numbers of the missing pages. For example, if pages 11, 12, 13 and 14 are taken out, then page 10 will become page 10–14.
8. Make margins at least 1 inch all around—preferably 1½ inches from the top, two inches from the left, and one inch from the right. This permits binding at the left and corrections in the margin.
9. Use center headings to indicate main divisions. They should be written in capitals, but not underlined.
10. Side headings in lower case letters are used to indicate subdivisions. Only the main words are capitalized.
11. Place approximately the same number of words on each page to facilitate estimates on printing or processing.
12. If paragraphs are completed on each page several compositors can work on the manuscript simultaneously.
13. The desired form for footnotes and references must be uniformly adhered to. Footnotes may be typed on separate sheets of paper or they may be placed on the line directly following the text refer-

ence, set off by two horizontal lines entirely across the page, one above and one below the footnote.

14. Each table is typed on a separate sheet. Tables usually require different type from that used in the text so different compositors can be working on them while others set up text.

15. Indicate where cuts or illustrations are to be inserted.

16. When numbers are to be inserted and the exact figure ·is not known at the time of typing, use one or more zeros to indicate number of digits, if possible.

17. Place the author's name near the top of the first page of the manuscript, indicating it is not to be typed or printed.

Additional suggestions for printers' copy are:

1. The original ribbon copy, not a carbon, should be given to the printer.

2. Directions to the printer in the original typed manuscript, or proofs, are made in a differentiating color pencil or ink. Use printer's symbols, which are to be found in most dictionaries or manuals on writing.

3. Written instructions as to size of type, size of page, type of paper, and general set-up should accompany the manuscript.

4. Send illustrations, charts, or other cuts to the printer with the typed manuscript.

5. A dummy may be used to indicate most clearly where cuts, illustrations, or tables are to be placed.

6. Specifications as to the makeup of the pages should be noted on the margins, or on sheets fastened to the manuscript or galley proofs.

7. Indicate to whom proofs are to be sent.

GALLEY PROOF:

The printer sets up galley proofs from the typed copy. These are sent to the writer for correction, and returned to the printer who then sets up page proofs. If a great many corrections are needed, a second galley may be prepared before the material is placed on pages. When galley proofs are received, the writer is responsible for seeing that the proofs agree with the manuscript, and that all genuine errors are corrected. Instructions are given in printer's symbols placed in the margins of the galleys. When the galley is received:

1. It should be read to see that the printer has set up the manuscript as submitted to him. This involves proofreading the typed manuscript against the galley, and watching for errors in names, citations and spelling, as well as for omissions in the text of words, phrases or even pages. Correction of sentences should preferably be typed and the corrected material pasted over the error. If minor corrections are made in the space above, the printer will see them before he reaches the words.
2. Printed tables should be read against the typed tables submitted. In addition, all figures should be checked to see that the totals and subtotals are correct, that the percentages add up to 100 per cent, that the text figures agree with those shown in the tables, and that the latest revised figures were those sent to the printer.
3. It should be read to see that all statements make sense and that they are clear and accurate. Sometimes errors in typing may not have been caught, so that the typed manuscript submitted may not be in the form desired. Then again, when the author sees his material in printed form he may discover points which he overlooked in the typed form.

PAGE PROOF:

When page proof is received:
1. The correct page numbers should be inserted wherever they appear in the report.
2. The page numbers should be placed in the index.
3. The author should check to see that the footnotes appear on the correct page and that the numbering agrees with that of the text.
4. The author should see that illustrations and cuts are placed in the best possible position with respect to the text.
5. The report should be reread to see that all statements make sense, and that the style is clear. This process should be separate from the other steps mentioned at this stage.

PRESS RELEASES:

The preparation of press releases might best be done with the aid of a local news reporter. The writer also might study textbooks in the field of journalism. Sections dealing with feature writing as well as with straight news stories ought to be particularly helpful. Survey releases currently being published in newspapers might also be examined.

Wilbur Lewis, city editor of a Rochester, New York, newspaper, was asked to give some advice on how to get survey material published in newspapers. At the risk of oversimplifying the task of newswriting, a few basic suggestions are offered by him:

Determine whether the story is to be written on a local level or is to be a broadside of general information to a lot of newspapers. If local, put the "local angle" foremost. Make certain that the statistical material is written up in such a fashion that the whole story hangs on its local application. Point out that the community is above or below average, that the total is such and such. Enliven the report with a specific incident if possible.

If the material lacks a specific local approach, select some factor that will "hook in" with the news for that day or week—either domestic or international news. If your organization is keyed to a program of major news coverage, make contacts with the wire services. The editor in another city who tosses your mailed material into the wastebasket is likely to pay attention to the same material if it comes over the wire. So keep the wire service reporters interested in what you are doing and keep them interested by the same methods used in interesting city editors on the local level. If your office is set up to individualize coverage, you can include "local angles" for various editors throughout the country. That generally is an expensive procedure. If, however, you have lists of cities included with your statistical material, be sure to point out to each editor that his "local angle" can be found therein.

All releases should be interesting in both lead and content. Editors, like members of the general public, will succumb to a well-written lead and to an interesting story. Therefore the writer should employ the usual methods of newspaper writing, such as attempting to intrigue the reader at the outset into following his story through to the end, giving complete and accurate information and leaving no "loose ends" unexplained. The usual methods of good expression, such as the use of moving verbs, descriptive adjectives, similes and metaphors that appear in all well-written manuscripts should, of course, be followed. But use care that you do not overdo your writing. An editor is particularly on the alert against being sold on a story that has no meat. So be sure your facts are plentiful. And be sure you do not attempt to sell the editor on tricky phrases such as are employed in display advertising slogans.

DISSEMINATING THE FINDINGS:

It is not possible, in the confines of this book, to discuss extensively methods of disseminating and giving publicity to the results of a survey.

Surveys conducted for profit-making purposes will not, of course, wish to have the results publicized through any but predetermined channels. The surveyor's job usually ends with the writing of recommendations. Social surveys, however, assume importance only when the facts are known and used. The following methods of disseminating information have been used with success, and may prove suggestive:

1. Obtain the endorsement of group leaders in the community, and get them to give publicity to your findings.
2. Arrange for radio resumes or dramatizations.
3. Prepare exhibits and demonstrations to be placed in prominent places and presented at important conferences and meetings.
4. Call special conferences of influential representatives of the community and present the findings to them.
5. Write popular articles for magazines and newspapers, especially local newspapers.
6. Arrange for book reviews if possible.
7. Send complimentary copies of the report to newspapers, reviewers, local business leaders, social agencies and fraternal organizations, or to public officials and the libraries.
8. Circularize lists of persons who might buy the report, using abstracts of or quotations from the report.
9. As material is tabulated, send regular releases to the newspapers on the tentative results.

Selected References

Report Writing

Chapters or discussion of report writing appear in most textbooks on research procedures and methodology, but the following contain extensive treatment of this topic.

Almack (7), American Marketing Assn. (8), Baker and Howell (27), Blankenship (77), Borden and Grover (93), Brown (115),

Cole and Bigelow (182), Coutant and Doubman (202), Dartmouth College (227), Fitting (313), Fowler (323), Good (366), Guam et al. (381), Hendrichs et al. (430), Jones (485), Meredith Pub. Co. (638), Nelson (682), Newson and Walk (692), Norton (700), Ogburn (703), Oliver (707), Reeder (762), Reilly (764), Rhodes (769), Rickard (777), Saunders and Anderson (836), Schluter (842), Seyfried (862), Stevenson et al. (928), Thompson (958), Trelease and Yule (972), Williams and Stevenson (1095).

Bibliographic Citation
Appel (13).

Indexing
Johnston (480), New York State Library (687).

Style Manuals
U. S. Dept. of State (1011), U. S. Government Printing Office (1018), University of Chicago (1035).

Graphic Presentation
Most books on statistical methods contain discussions of graphic presentation. The following references contain detailed or specialized treatments of this topic.

Arkin and Colton (15), Brinton (113), Croxton and Cowden (216), *Engineers* (10, 11), Graeter and Wood (375), Haskell (420), Modley (650), Mudgett (660), Riggleman (779), Wright (1125).

Inference and Interpretation
Blankenship (79), Brown (117), Cohen (180), Crespi (210), Deming (237), Deming and Stephan (243), Max (619), Riesman and Glazer (778), Ross (817), Scates (839), Scates and Hoban (840), Stouffer (936), Studenski (941), Truesdell (974), Wilson (1103, 1104, 1107, 1108).
See also discussions of reliability, validity, and evaluation of data.

Reproducing Material
Binkley (65).

BIBLIOGRAPHY

1) Advertising Research Foundation, *Copy Testing*, Ronald, 1939.
2) Albig, William, *Public Opinion*, McGraw-Hill, 1939.
3) Alderson, Wroe, "Marketing classification of families," *Journal of Marketing*, 1941, 6:143–147.
4) Alexander, Carter, "Research and survey techniques," *Review of Educational Research*, 1932, 2:169–170.
5) Allport, Floyd H., "Toward a science of public opinion," *Public Opinion Quarterly*, 1937, 1:7–24.
6) Allport, Floyd H., "Polls and the science of public opinion," *Public Opinion Quarterly*, 1940, 4:249–257.
7) Almack, John C., *Research and Thesis Writing*, Houghton Mifflin, 1930.
8) American Marketing Association: Committee on Marketing Research Technique, *The Technique of Marketing Research*, McGraw-Hill, 1937.
9) American Marketing Association: Committee on Marketing Research Technique, "Design, size, and validation of sample for market research," *Journal of Marketing*, 1946, 10:221–234.
10) American Society of Mechanical Engineers, *Engineering and Scientific Graphs for Publications*, New York, 1943 (ASA 215.3).
11) American Standards Association and American Society of Mechanical Engineers, Committee on Standards for Graphic Presentation, *Time-Series Charts, A Manual of Design and Construction*, American Society of Mechanical Engineers, New York, 1938.
12) Anderson, Oskar N., "Statistical method," *Encyclopaedia of the Social Sciences*, 1934, 14:366–371.
13) Appel, Livia, *Bibliographical Citation in the Social Sciences*, University of Wisconsin, 1940.
14) Arkin, Herbert, and Raymond R. Colton, *An Outline of Statistical Methods* (4th ed.), Barnes and Noble, 1939.
15) Arkin, Herbert, and Raymond R. Colton, *Graphs, How to Make and Use Them* (revised ed.), Harper, 1940.
16) Arrington, Ruth E., "Some technical aspects of observer reliabil-

ity as indicated in studies of the talkies," *American Journal of Sociology*, 1933, 38:409–417.

17) Association of North American Directory Publishers, *Catalogue and Price List of City, County and State Directories*, 354–60 4th Ave., New York, 1940.

18) Bader, Carolyn F., *The Interviewer's Guide*, Institute of Market Research, Webster Groves, Missouri, 1947.

19) Bader, Carolyn F., "Standardized field practice," *International Journal of Opinion and Attitude Research*, 1948, 2:243–244.

20) Bader, Louis, "Survey of the effectiveness of house to house canvassing," *Journal of Retailing*, 1935, 111–118.

21) Baehne, G. W., *Practical Applications of the Punched Card Method in Colleges and Universities*, Columbia University Press, 1935.

22) Bailey, W. B., and John Cummings, *Statistics*, McClurg, 1917.

23) Bain, Read, "An attitude on attitude research," *American Journal of Sociology*, 1928, 33:940–957.

24) Bain, Read, "Theory and measurement of attitudes and opinions," *Psychological Bulletin*, 1930, 27:357–379.

25) Bain, Read, "Stability in questionnaire response," *American Journal of Sociology*, 1931, 37:445–453.

26) Baker, K. H., and Frank Stanton, "Interviewer-bias and the recall of incompletely learned material," *Sociometry*, 1942, 8:123–124.

27) Baker, Ray Palmer, and Almonte C. Howell, *The Preparation of Reports*, Ronald Press, 1938.

28) Ballin, M. R., and P. R. Farnsworth, "A graphic method for determining the scale values of statements in measuring social attitudes," *Journal of Social Psychology*, 1941, 13:323–327.

29) Bancroft, Gertrude, "Consistency of information from records and interviews," *Journal of American Statistical Association*, 1940, 35:377–381.

30) Bancroft, Gertrude, and Emmett H. Welch, "Recent experience with problems of labor force measurement," *Journal of the American Statistical Association*, 1946, 41:303–312.

31) Barr, Arvil Sylvester, "Research," *Journal of Educational Research*, 1929, 19:56–57.

32) Barr, Arvil Sylvester, and Mabel Rudisill, *An Annotated Bibliography on the Methodology of Scientific Research, as Applied to Education*, Bulletin No. 13 of the Bureau of Educational Research, University of Wisconsin, 1931.

33) Barth, Alan, "The bureau of intelligence," *Public Opinion Quarterly*, 1943, 7:66–76.

34) Bartlett, M. S., "Sub-sampling for attributes," *Journal of the Royal Statistical Society*, Suppl. 1937, 4:131–35.

35) Baur, E. Jackson, "Response bias in a mail survey," *Public Opinion Quarterly*, winter, 1947–1948, 11:594–600.

36) Bean, Louis H., *Ballot Behavior—A Study of Presidential Elections*, American Council on Public Affairs, 1940.

37) Bean, Louis H., *How to Predict Elections*, Knopf, 1948.

38) Beers, Howard W., "The validity of schedule entries," *Sociology and Social Research*, 1936, 21:40–44.

39) Belden, Joe, "Measuring college thought," *Public Opinion Quarterly*, 1939, 3:458–462.

40) Bell, E. P., "Interviewing: its principles and functions," *Proceedings of the American Society of Newspaper Editors*, Washington, D.C., 1927:169–175.

41) Bell, Howard M., *Youth Tell Their Story*, American Council on Education, 1938.

42) Benjamin, Kurt, "Problems of multiple-punching with Hollerith machines," *American Statistical Association Journal*, 1947, 42:46–71.

43) Bennett, Archibald S., "Some aspects of preparing questionnaires," *Journal of Marketing*, 1945, 10:175–179.

44) Bennett, Archibald S., "Observations on the so-called cheater problem among field interviewers," *International Journal of Opinion and Attitude Research*, 1948, 2:89–96.

45) Bennett, Archibald S., *Report on Researching Researchers*, A. S. Bennett Associates Serial Study, 1944–1947, of Part-Time Local Field Interviewers, New York, 1948.

46) Benson, Edward G., "Three words," *Public Opinion Quarterly*, 1940, 4:130–134.

47) Benson, Edward G., and S. H. Northcross, "Customers opinion surveys for public utilities," *Public Utilities Fortnightly*, 1940, 26:847–854.

48) Benson, Edward G., and Paul Perry, "Analysis of democratic-republican strength by population groups," *Public Opinion Quarterly*, 1940, 4:464–473.

49) Benson, Edward G., Cyrus Young, and Claude Syze, "Polling lessons from the 1944 election," *Public Opinion Quarterly*, 1945–1946, 9:467–484.

50) Benson, Lawrence E., "Studies in secret-ballot technique," *Public Opinion Quarterly*, 1941, 5:79–82.

51) Benson, Lawrence E. "Mail surveys can be valuable," *Public Opinion Quarterly*, 1946, 10:234–241.

52) Berelson, Bernard, Clyde Hart, and Philip Hauser, *Do Public Opinion Polls Serve Democracy?* University of Chicago Round Table Discussion, 747 Broadcast No. 536, June 27, 1948.

53) Berkson, Joseph, "A punch card designed to contain written

data and coding," *Journal of the American Statistical Association*, 1941, 36:535–538.

54) Bernard, Jessie, "An experimental comparison of ranking and paired comparisons as methods of evaluating questionnaire items," Papers of American Sociological Society, 1933, 28:81–84.

55) Bernard, Luther Lee, "Sociological research and the exceptional man," Publications of the American Sociological Society, 1933, 27:3–19.

56) Bernard, Luther Lee (ed.), *The Fields and Methods of Sociology*, Farrar and Rinehart, 1934.

57) Bernays, E. L., "Attitude polls—servants or masters?" *Public Opinion Quarterly*, 1945, 9:264–268b, and 1945–1946, 9:407–410.

58) Beville, H. M., Jr., "Social stratification of the radio audience," Princeton University Office of Radio Research, November, 1939.

59) Beville, H. M., Jr., "The A.B.C.D.'s of radio audiences," *Public Opinion Quarterly*, 1940, 4:195–206.

60) Bevis, J. C., "Management of field staffs in the opinion research field," *Journal of the American Statistical Association*, 1945, 40:245–246.

61) Bevis, J. C., "Economical incentive used for mail questionnaires," *Public Opinion Quarterly*, 1948, 12:492–493.

62) Beyle, H. C., "A scale for the measurement of attitudes toward candidates for elective governmental office," *American Political Science Review*, 1932, 26:527–544.

63) Bingham, Walter V. D., "Reliability, validity and dependability," *Journal of Applied Psychology*, 1932, 16:116–123.

64) Bingham, Walter V. D., and Bruce V. Moore, *How to Interview* (3rd ed.), Harper, 1941.

65) Binkley, Robert C., *Manual of Methods of Reproducing Research Materials*, Edward Brothers, 1936.

66) Bird, Charles, *Social Psychology*, Appleton-Century, 1940.

67) Blanar, Abe, "How accurate are public-opinion polls?" *Congressional Record*, May 17, 1940, Appendix, 86 (Pt. 15):3012–3013.

68) Blankenship, Albert, "What happened to the polls?" *International Journal of Opinion and Attitude Research*, 1948, 2:321–328.

69) Blankenship, Albert, "Does the question form influence public opinion poll results?" *Journal of Applied Psychology*, 1940, 24:27–30.

70) Blankenship, Albert, "The influence of the question form upon the response in a public opinion poll," *Psychological Record*, 1940, 3:349–422.

71) Blankenship, Albert, "Pretesting a questionnaire for a public opinion poll," *Sociometry*, 1940, 3:263–269.

72) Blankenship, Albert, "The 'sample' study in opinion research," *Sociometry*, 1940, 3:271–276.

73) Blankenship, Albert, "The choice of words in poll questions," *Sociology and Social Research*, 1940, 25:12–18.

74) Blankenship, Albert, "The effect of interviewer bias upon the response in a public opinion poll," *Journal of Consulting Psychology*, 1940, 4:134–136.

75) Blankenship, Albert, "These opinion polls again!" *Sociometry*, 1942, 5:89–101.

76) Blankenship, Albert, "Psychological difficulties in measuring consumer preference," *Journal of Marketing*, 1942, 6:66–75.

77) Blankenship, Albert, *Consumer and Opinion Research*, Harper, 1943.

78) Blankenship, Albert (ed.), *How to Conduct Consumer and Opinion Research*, Harper, 1946.

79) Blankenship, Albert, "What is public opinion?" *International Journal of Opinion and Attitude Research*, 1948, 2:201–206.

80) Blankenship, Albert, Lawrence Lockley, and Edwin Ghiselli, "Public opinion polls: A symposium," *Journal of Marketing*, 1940, 5:110–119.

81) Blankenship, Albert, and Dean I. Manheimer, "Whither public opinion polls?" *Journal of Psychology*, 1941, 12:7–13.

82) Blankenship, Albert, and six others, "Survey on Problems of Interviewer Cheating," *International Journal of Opinion and Attitude Research*, 1947, 1:93–107.

83) Blumer, Herbert, "Public opinion and public opinion polling," *American Sociological Review*, 1948, 13:542–549; Discussion, 549–554.

84) Bogardus, Emory S., "Methods of interviewing," *Journal of Applied Sociology*, 1925, 9:457–467.

85) Bogardus, Emory S., *The New Social Research*, Los Angeles, California, J. R. Miller, 1926.

86) Bogardus, Emory S., "Measuring public opinion," *Sociology and Social Research*, 1932–1933, 17:465–469.

87) Bogardus, Emory S., "A social distance scale," *Sociology and Social Research*, 1932–1933, 17:265–271.

88) Bogardus, Emory S., *Introduction to Social Research*, Suttonhoose, 1936.

89) Bogardus, Emory S., "Scales in social research," *Sociology and Social Research*, 1939, 24:69–75.

90) Bonney, M. E., "The validity of certain techniques of gathering psychological data, with special reference to personality

questionnaires," *Journal of Social Psychology*, 1941, 13:103–122.

91) Booth, Charles, *Life and Labour of the People in London* (17 volumes), Macmillan, 1892–1897.

92) Borden, Neil H., "Some problems in sampling for consumer surveys," *American Marketing Journal*, 1936, 3:19–24.

93) Borden, Neil H., and Charles H. Grover, *Suggestions on Report Writing*, Baker Foundation, Harvard University, Graduate School of Business Administration, 1925.

94) Borg, Lloyd E., "Interviewing school," *International Journal of Opinion and Attitude Research*, 1948, 2:393–400.

95) Bosse, Paul C., "Polling civilian Japanese on Saipan," *Public Opinion Quarterly*, 1945, 9:176–182.

96) Bower, Robert T., "Opinion research and historical interpretation of elections," *Public Opinion Quarterly*, 1948, 12:455–465.

97) Bower, Robert T., "Public opinion polls and the politician," *Annals of the American Academy of Political and Social Science*, 1948, 259:104–112.

98) Bowers, Curtis A., "Issues in research method," *Journal of Personnel Research*, 1925, 4:155–161.

99) Bowley, Arthur L., "Address to the economic section of British Statistical Association," *Journal of the Royal Statistical Society*, 1906, 69:550–554.

100) Bowley, Arthur L., "Working class households in Reading," *Journal of the Royal Statistical Society*, 1913, 76:672–701.

101) Bowley, Arthur L., *An Elementary Manual of Statistics*, MacDonald and Evans, 1915.

102) Bowley, Arthur L., "Measurement of the precision attained in sampling," *Bulletin de l'Institut Internationale de Statistique*, No. 1, Pt. 3, Rome, 1926, 17:1–62.

103) Bowley, Arthur L., 'The application of sampling to economic and sociological problems," *Journal of American Statistical Association*, September, 1936, 31:474–480.

104) Bowley, Arthur L., *Elements of Statistics* (6th ed.), Scribners, 1937.

105) Bowley, Arthur L., and Alexander Bennett-Hurst, *Livelihood and Poverty*, London, G. Bell, 1925.

106) Bowley, Arthur L., and Margaret Hogg, *Has Poverty Diminished?* London, P. S. King, 1925.

107) Box, Kathleen, and Thomas Geoffrey, "Wartime Social Survey," *Journal of the Royal Statistical Society*, 1944, 107:151–177.

108) Bradford, Ernest S., *Survey and Directory of Market Research Agencies in the United States*, New York City College, Bureau of Business Research, 1945.

109) Brandt, A. E., "Practical difficulties met in the use of experi-

mental designs," *Journal of the American Statistical Association,* 1940, 35:101–106.

110) Brennan, Ellen E., "Last minute swing in New York City presidential vote," *Public Opinion Quarterly,* 1949, 13:285–299.

111) Breyer, R. F., "Some preliminary problems of sample design for a survey of retail trade flow," *Journal of Marketing,* 1946, 10:343–353.

112) Breyer, R. F. (ed.), "Research in marketing," *Journal of Marketing;* see current volumes.

113) Brinton, Willard C., *Graphic Presentation,* Brinton Associates, 1939.

114) Brown, George H., "A comparison of sampling methods," *Journal of Marketing,* 1947, 11:331–337.

115) Brown, Lyndon, *Market Research and Analysis,* Ronald Press, 1937.

116) Brown, Theodore, *The Use of Statistical Techniques in Certain Problems of Market Research,* Harvard University, Graduate School of Business Administration, Business Research Studies No. 12, 1935.

117) Brown, Theodore, "Interpretation of market data," *American Marketing Journal,* 1935, 2:217–223.

118) Brown, Theodore, "Size of a sample in market surveys," *National Marketing Review,* 1935–1936, 1:258–263.

119) Brown, Theodore H., "Scientific sampling in business," *Harvard Business Review,* 1942, 20:358–369.

120) Brown, Theodore H., "Bench marks for marketing research," *Dun's Review,* 1945, 53:9–11.

121) Bruner, Jerome S., and Sheldon J. Korchin, "The boss and the vote: case study of city politics," *Public Opinion Quarterly,* 1946, 10:1–23.

122) Brunsman, Howard G., "The housing census of 1940," *Journal of the American Statistical Association,* 1941, 36:393–401.

123) Brunsman, Howard G., "The sample census of congested production areas," *Journal of the American Statistical Association,* 1944, 39:303–310.

124) Brunsman, Howard G., "Current sources of sociological data in housing," *American Sociological Review,* 1947, 12:150–155.

125) Brunsman, Howard G., "Observations on the provision and use of data from the 1940 Housing Census," *American Economic Review,* 1947, 37:498–507.

126) Buros, Oscar K. (ed.), *Research and Statistical Methodology: Books and Reviews of 1933–38,* Rutgers University, 1938.

127) Buros, Oscar K. (ed.), *The Second Yearbook of Research and Statistical Methodology, Books and Reviews,* The Gryphon Press, 1941.

128) Burtt, Harold E., "Current trends in marketing research," *Journal of Consulting Psychology*, 1941, 5:145–148.

129) Burtt, Harold E., and Harold V. Gaskill, "Suggestibility and the form of the question," *Journal of Applied Psychology*, 1932, 16:358–373.

130) Cahalan, Don, "On the concepts of 'public' and 'public opinion,'" *International Journal of Opinion and Attitude Research*, 1947, 1:99–102.

131) Cahalan, Don, and Norman C. Meier, "The validity of mail-ballot polls," *Psychological Record*, 1939, 3:3–11.

132) Callandar, W. F., and Charles F. Sarle, "The Bureau of Agricultural Economics' program in enumerative sampling," *Journal of Farm Economics*, 1947, 29:233–236.

133) Campbell, A., "Polling, open interviewing, and the problem of interpretation," *Journal of Social Issues*, 1946, 2:67–71.

134) Campbell, A., "Two problems in the use of the open question," *Journal of Abnormal and Social Psychology*, 1945, 40:340–343.

135) Campbell, Angus, "The uses of interview surveys in federal administration," *Journal of Social Issues*, 1946, 2:14–22.

136) Campbell, Angus (ed.), "Measuring public attitudes," *Journal of Social Issues*, 1946, 2:36–45.

137) Campbell, Angus, and George Katona, "A national survey of wartime savings," *Public Opinion Quarterly*, 1946, 10:373–382.

138) Campbell, Angus, Sylvia Eberhart, and Patricia Woodward, "Public reaction to the atomic bomb and world affairs. Part II: Findings of the intensive surveys," Cornell University, 1947, 80–310 (see also Crutchfield **219**).

139) Cantril, Hadley, "Experiments in the wording of questions," *Public Opinion Quarterly*, 1940, 4:330–332.

140) Cantril, Hadley, "The public opinion polls: Dr. Jekyll or Mr. Hyde?" *Public Opinion Quarterly*, 1940, 4:212–217.

141) Cantril, Hadley, "Identification with social and economic class," *Journal of Abnormal and Social Psychology*, 1943, 38:74–80.

142) Cantril, Hadley (ed.), *Gauging Public Opinion*, Princeton University Press, 1944.

143) Cantril, Hadley, "Do different polls get the same results?" *Public Opinion Quarterly*, 1945, 9:61–69.

144) Cantril, Hadley, "The intensity of an attitude," *Journal of Abnormal and Social Psychology*, 1946, 41:129–135.

145) Cantril, Hadley, "Opinion trends in World War II: Some guides to interpretation," *Public Opinion Quarterly*, 1948, 12:30–45.

146) Cantril, Hadley, "Polls and the 1948 U. S. presidential election," *International Journal of Opinion and Attitude Research*, 1948, 2:309–321.

147) Caples, John, *Tested Advertising Methods*, Harper, 1932.

148) Carpenter, Niles, "Social surveys," *Encyclopaedia of the Social Sciences,* Macmillan, 1934, 14:162–165.

149) Cassady, Ralph, Jr., "Statistical sampling techniques and marketing research," *Journal of Marketing,* 1945, 9:317–341.

150) Cassady, Ralph, Jr., and Harold V. Haas, "Analyzing the market of mail order retail stores," *Harvard Business Review,* 1935, 13: 493–502.

151) Caswell, Hollis L., "Survey techniques," *Educational Administration and Supervision,* 1933, 19:431–441.

152) Cavan, Ruth S., "The questionnaire in a sociological research project," *American Journal of Sociology,* 1933, 38:721–727.

153) Cavan, Ruth S., J. David Hauser, and Samuel Stouffer, "Note on the statistical treatment of life-history material," *Social Forces,* 1930, 9:200–203.

154) Cawl, F. R., "The continuing panel technique," *Journal of Marketing,* 1943, 8:45–49.

155) Chaddock, Robert E., *Principles and Methods of Statistics,* Houghton Mifflin, 1925.

156) Chambers, M. M., and H. M. Bell, *How to Make a Community Youth Survey,* American Council on Education, 1938 (pamphlet).

157) Chapin, F. Stuart, *Field Work and Social Research,* Appleton-Century, 1920.

158) Chapin, F. Stuart, *The Social Status Scale* (rev. ed.), University of Minnesota Press, 1936.

159) Chapin, F. Stuart, *The Social Participation Scale,* University of Minnesota Press, 1937.

160) Chapin, F. Stuart, "Design for social experiments," *American Sociological Review,* 1938, 3:786–800.

161) Chapin, F. Stuart, "New trends in social research: some hypotheses and some sociometric scales," *Journal of Educational Sociology,* 1938, 11:561.

162) Chapin, F. Stuart, "The role of experimental design in public opinion research," *International Journal of Opinion and Attitude Research,* 1948, 2:333–340.

163) Chapin, F. Stuart, "Factors related to errors of prediction by public opinion polls in the presidential election of 1948," *International Journal of Opinion and Attitude Research,* 1948–1949, 2:528–530.

164) Chapin, F. Stuart, "Trends in sociometrics and critique," *Sociometry,* 1940, 3:245–262.

165) Chapin, F. Stuart, "New methods of sociological research on housing problems," *American Sociological Review,* 1947, 12: 143–149.

166) Chapin, F. Stuart, *Experimental Designs in Sociological Research*, Harper, 1947.

167) Chapman, J. C., and V. M. Sims, "A revision of the Chapman-Sims socio-economic scale," *Journal of Educational Research*, 1928, 18:117–126.

168) Chappell, Matthew N., *How Adequate is the Telephone Sample for Obtaining Radio Program Ratings?* C. E. Hooper, 1941.

169) Chappell, Matthew N., "Factors influencing recall of radio programs," *Public Opinion Quarterly*, 1942, 6:107–114.

170) Chappell, Matthew N., and C. E. Hooper, *Radio Audience Measurement*, Stephen Daye, 1944.

171) Cherington, Paul T., "Current progress in market research," *Journal of Marketing*, 1941, 5:213–227.

172) Childs, Harwood Lawrence, *Reference Guide to the Study of Public Opinion*, Princeton University, 1934.

173) Childs, Harwood Lawrence, *An Introduction to Public Opinion*, Wiley, 1940.

174) Churchman, C. West, Russell L. Ackoff, and Murray Wax (eds.), *Measurement of Consumer Interest*, University of Pennsylvania, 1947.

175) Clark, Willis W., "Scale for grading social conditions," *Journal of Applied Sociology*, 1922, 7:13–18.

176) Clausen, John A., and Robert N. Ford, "Controlling Bias in Mail Questionnaires," *Journal of the American Statistical Association*, 1947, 42:497–511.

177) Cleveland Foundation, *Cleveland Survey* (7 vols.), 1916 to 1922.

178) Cochran, W. G., "Use of the analysis of variance in enumeration by sampling," *Journal of the American Statistical Association*, 1939, 34:492–511.

179) Cochran, W. G., "Relative accuracy of systematic and stratified random samples for a certain class of populations," *Annals of Mathematical Statistics*, 1946, 17:164–177.

180) Cohen, Jerome B., "The misuse of statistics," *Journal of the American Statistical Association*, 1938, 33:657–675.

181) Colcord, Joanna C., *Your Community*, Russell Sage Foundation (3rd ed.), 1947.

182) Cole, A. H., and K. W. Bigelow, *A Manual of Thesis Writing for Graduates and Undergraduates*, Wiley, 1934.

183) Colley, Russell H., "How to determine the size of a survey sample," *Printers' Ink*, September 6, 1946, 216:35–37.

184) Columbia Broadcasting System, *How Radio Measures Its Audiences: Four Discussions by Research Authorities*, Radio Sales Division of C.B.S., 1941.

185) Columbia Broadcasting System, and National Broadcasting

Company, *The Joint Study of Rural Radio Ownership and Use in the U. S., Markets in Radio Homes by Income Levels and Price Levels*, 1939.

186) Connelly, Gordon M., "Now let's look at the real problem: Validity," *Public Opinion Quarterly*, 1945, 9:51–60.

187) Connelly, Gordon M., and Harry Field, "The non-voter—who he is and what he thinks," *Public Opinion Quarterly*, 1944, 8:175–187.

188) Conover, H. F., *A Selected List of Books on Statistical Methods and Their Applications*, Library of Congress, 1938 (mimeographed).

189) Conover, H. F. (comp.), *List of Recent References on Statistical Methods*, U. S. Library of Congress, Division of Bibliography, 1941.

190) Conrad, H. S., "Some principles of attitude measurement: a reply to opinion-attitude methodology," *Psychological Bulletin*, 1946, 43:570–589.

191) Converse, P. D., *Essentials of Distribution*, Prentice-Hall, 1936.

192) Cook, Stuart W., and Alfred C. Welch, "Methods of measuring the practical effect of polls of public opinion," *Journal of Applied Psychology*, 1940, 24:441–454

193) Cooper, Alfred M., *How to Supervise People*, McGraw-Hill, 1941.

194) Copeland, Herman A., "Validating two tests for census enumerators," *Journal of Applied Psychology*, 1937, 21:230–232.

195) Corby, P. G., "Current sampling problems in public opinion and market research," *American Psychologist*, 1946, 1:243 (abstract).

196) Corey, Stephen M., "Signed versus unsigned attitude questionnaires," *Journal of Educational Psychology*, 1937, 28:144–148.

197) Corey, Stephen M., "Professed attitudes and actual behavior," *Journal of Educational Psychology*, 1937, 28:271–280.

198) Cornell, Francis G., "A stratified-random sample of a small finite population," *Journal of the American Statistical Association*, 1947, 42:523–533.

199) Cornell, Francis G., "Sample plan for a survey of higher education enrollment," *Journal of Experimental Education*, 1947, 15:213–218.

200) Coutant, Frank R., "The difference between market research and election forecasting," *International Journal of Opinion and Attitude Research*, 1948–1949, 2:569–575.

201) Coutant, Frank R., "Supervising the field investigation," *Market Research*, 1938, 8:19–21.

202) Coutant, Frank R., and J. Russell Doubman, *Simplified Market Research*, Walther, 1935.

203) Cover, John H., "Some investigations in the sampling and distribution of retail prices," *Econometrica*, 1937, 5:263–279.

204) Cowell, F. R., "Public opinion polls," *Public Administration*, 1940, 18:250–258.

205) Cowley, W. H., "Two questionnaire devices," *Educational Research Bulletin*, 1931, 10:374–376.

206) Crespi, Leo P., "Elections and poll validity," *International Journal of Opinion and Attitude Research*, 1948–1949, 2:481–488.

207) Crespi, Leo, "The cheater problem in polling," *Public Opinion Quarterly*, 1945–1946, 9:431–445.

208) Crespi, Leo, "The interviewer effect in polling," *Public Opinion Quarterly*, 1948, 12:99–112.

209) Crespi, Leo, "Opinion-attitude methodology and the polls—a rejoinder," *Psychological Bulletin*, 1946, 43:562–569.

210) Crespi, Leo, and Donald Rugg, "Poll data and the study of opinion determinants," *Public Opinion Quarterly*, 1940, 4:273–276.

211) Crossley, Archibald M., "Straw polls in 1936," *Public Opinion Quarterly*, 1937, 1:24–35.

212) Crossley, Archibald M., "Size and distribution of the research sample," *Advertising and Selling*, May 6, 1937, 29:77–78.

213) Crossley, Archibald M., "Methods tested during the 1940 campaign," *Public Opinion Quarterly*, 1941, 5:83–86.

214) Crossley, Archibald M., "Theory and application of representative sampling as applied to marketing," *Journal of Marketing*, 1941, 5:456–461.

215) Crossley, Archibald M., "Why we should bring radio research up to date," *Advertising and Selling*, 1946, 34:41–42.

216) Croxton, Frederick E., and Dudley J. Cowden, *Practical Business Statistics*, Prentice-Hall, 1937.

217) Croxton, Frederick E., and Dudley J. Cowden, *Applied General Statistics*, Prentice-Hall, 1940.

218) Crum, W. L., *Straw Polls*, Harvard University, 1938.

219) Crutchfield, Richard S., "Public reaction to the atomic bomb and world affairs. Part I: Findings of the extensive surveys," Cornell University, 1947, 1–79 (see also Campbell et al. 138).

220) Crutchfield, Richard S., and Donald H. Gordon, "Variations in respondents' interpretations of an opinion-poll question," *International Journal of Opinion and Attitude Research*, 1947, 1:22–31.

221) Cuber, John, and John Gerberich, "A note on consistency in questionnaire responses," *American Sociological Review*, 1946, 11:13–15.

222) Culver, Dorothy C., *Methodology of Social Science Research: A Bibliography*, Bureau of Public Administration, University of California, 1936.

223) Curtis, Alberta, "Reliability of a report on listening habits," *Journal of Applied Psychology*, 1939, 23:127–130.

224) Curtis Publishing Company, *Respondent Pre-Selection*, August, 1946 (pamphlet).

225) Daniel, Cuthbert, "Statistically significant differences in observed percents," *Journal of Applied Psychology*, 1940, 24:826–830.

226) Daniels, John, *Social Surveys, Reasons, Methods, and Results*, National Conference of Charities and Corrections, 1910.

227) Dartmouth College, Amos Tuck School of Administration and Finance, Committee on Research, *Manual of Research and Reports*, McGraw-Hill, 1937.

228) Davie, Maurice R., *Urban Ecology*, Yale University, 1936.

229) Davies, George R., and Walter F. Crowder, *Methods of Statistical analysis in the Social Sciences*, Wiley, 1933.

230) Davis, Ralph Currier, *The Principles of Business Organization and Operation* (4th ed.), Columbus, Ohio, H. L. Hedrick, 254 Oakland Ave., 1937 (processed).

231) Davis, Robert Alexander, and Edwin L. Barrow, "Critical study of the questionnaire in education," *Educational Administration and Supervision*, 1935, 21:137–144.

232) Day, Daniel D., "Methods in attitude research," *American Sociological Review*, 1940, 5:395–410.

233) Day, Daniel D., and O. F. Quackenbush, "Relation between war attitudes and opinions," *Sociology and Social Research*, 1940, 25:19–27.

234) Day, Edmund E., "Standardization of the construction of statistical tables," *American Statistical Association Publications*, 1920–1921, 17:59–66.

235) Deming, W. Edwards, *On the Sampling Problems of the 1940 Census*, Speech delivered at Cowles Conference on Economics and Statistics at Colorado Springs, July 11, 1940.

236) Deming, W. Edwards, *Theory of Sampling*, Wiley, 1949.

237) Deming, W. Edwards, "On a classification of the problems of statistical inference," *Journal of the American Statistical Association*, 1942, 37:173–185.

238) Deming, W. Edwards, "On errors in surveys," *American Sociological Review*, 1944, 9:359–369.

239) Deming, W. Edwards, "On training in sampling," *Journal of the American Statistical Association*, 1945, 40:307–316.

240) Deming, W. Edwards, and Leon Geoffrey, "On sample inspec-

tion in the processing of census returns," *Journal of the American Statistical Association*, 1941, 36:351–360.

241) Deming, W. Edwards, and Morris H. Hansen, "On some census aids to sampling," *Journal of the American Statistical Association*, 1943, 38:353–357.

242) Deming, W. Edwards, and Willard Simmons, "On the design of a sample for dealers' inventories," *Journal of the American Statistical Association*, 1946, 41:16–33.

243) Deming, W. Edwards, and Frederick F. Stephan, "On the interpretation of the censuses as samples," *Journal of the American Statistical Association*, 1941, 36:45–49.

244) Deming, W. Edwards, B. J. Tepping, and L. Geoffrey, "Errors in card punching," *Journal of the American Statistical Association*, 1942, 37:525–536.

245) Deri, Susan, D. Dinnerstein, J. Harding, and A. D. Pepitone, et al., "Techniques for diagnosing and measurement of inter group attitudes and behavior," *Psychological Bulletin*, 1948, 45: 248–272.

246) Desing, Minerva F., "Suggestions to the novice in the mechanics of research," *School Review*, 1941, 49:206–212.

247) Dodd, Stuart C., "Toward world surveying," *Public Opinion Quarterly*, 1946–1947, 10:470–484.

248) Dodd, Stuart C., "Standards for surveying agencies," *Public Opinion Quarterly*, 1947, 11:115–130.

249) Dodd, Stuart C., "The Washington public opinion laboratory," *Public Opinion Quarterly*, 1948, 12:118–125.

250) Dodd, Stuart C., "On predicting elections or other behavior," *International Journal of Opinion and Attitude Research*, 1948–1949, 2:494–502.

251) Dodge, Harold F., and Harry G. Romig, *Sampling Inspection Tables; Single and Double Sampling*, Wiley, 1944.

252) Dreis, Thelma A., *Social Statistics of New Haven, Connecticut*, Yale University, 1936.

253) Droba, D. D., "Methods for measuring attitudes," *Psychological Bulletin*, 1932, 29:309–323.

254) Droba, D. D., "Statements as opinion indicators," *Sociology and Social Research*, 1931, 15:550–557.

255) Droba, D. D., "Methods used for measuring public opinion," *American Journal of Sociology*, 1931–1932, 37:410–423.

256) Droba, D. D., "Social attitudes—topical summaries of current literature," *American Journal of Sociology*, 1934, 39:513–524.

257) DuBois, P. H., "Some statistical operations on the counting sorter," *Psychometrika*, 1941, 6:383–390.

258) Duffy, Ben, *Advertising Media and Markets*, Prentice-Hall, 1939.

259) Dunham, H. Warren, "Social attitudes, topical summaries of current literature," *American Journal of Sociology,* 1940, 46: 344–375.

260) Dunlap, J. W., "Recent advances in statistical theory and applications," *American Journal of Psychology,* 1941, 54:583–601.

261) Dunlap, J. W., and Abraham Knoll, "Observations on the methodology in attitude scales," *Journal of Social Psychology,* 1939, 10:475–487.

262) Dunlap, J. W., and A. K. Kurtz, *Handbook of Statistical Nomographs: Tables and Formulas,* World Book Co., 1932.

263) Dunn, Halbert L., "Census—past and future," *Journal of the American Statistical Association,* 1940, 35:242–252.

264) Dunn, Halbert L., "Plans for vital statistics in 1940," *Journal of the American Statistical Association,* 1940, 35:86–92.

265) Eastman, R. O., "How to spot quack research," *Advertising and Selling,* November, 1939, pp. 40 f.

266) Eastwood, R. Parker, *Sales Control by Quantitative Methods,* Columbia University, 1940.

267) Eaton, Allen, and Shelby M. Harrison, *A Bibliography of Social Surveys,* Russell Sage Foundation, 1930.

268) Eberle, George F., "Population estimates of local communities and economic planning," *Journal of the American Statistical Association,* 1938, 33:694–704.

269) Eckert, W. J., *Punched Card Methods in Scientific Computation,* The Thomas J. Watson Astronomical Computing Bureau, Columbia University, 1940.

270) Eckler, A. Ross, "Employment and income statistics," *Journal of the American Statistical Association,* 1941, 36:381–387.

271) Eckler, A. Ross, "Management of field work and collection of statistics of the labor force," *Journal of the American Statistical Association,* 1945, 40:249–250.

272) Eckler, A. Ross, and E. P. Staudt, "Marketing and sampling uses of population and housing data," *Journal of the American Statistical Association,* 1943, 38:87–92.

273) Edgerton, Harold A., and Donald G. Paterson, "Table of standard errors and probable errors of percentages for varying numbers of cases," *Journal of Applied Psychology,* 1926, 10:378–391.

274) Edgerton, Harold A., Steuart H. Britt, and Ralph D. Norman, "Objective differences among various types of respondents to a mailed questionnaire," *American Sociological Review,* 1947, 12: 435–444.

275) Edwards, Alba M., "A social-economic grouping of the gainful workers in the U. S.," *Journal of the American Statistical Association,* 1933, 28:377–387.

276) Edwards, Alba M., "Occupation and industry statistics," *Journal of the American Statistical Association,* 1941, 36:387–393.

277) Edwards, Allen L., *Statistical Analysis for Students in Psychology and Education,* Rinehart, 1946.

278) Edwards, Allen L., and Kathryn Kenney, "A comparison of the Thurstone and Likert techniques of attitude scale construction," *Journal of Applied Psychology,* 1946, 30:72–83.

279) Edwards, Allen L., and F. P. Kilpatrick, "Scale analysis and the measurement of social attitudes," *Psychometrika,* 1948, 13:99–114.

280) Edwards, Allen L., and F. P. Kilpatrick, "A technique for the construction of attitude scales," *Journal of Applied Psychology,* 1948, 32:374–384.

281) Edwards, T. I., "The coding and tabulation of medical and research data for statistical analysis," *Public Health Reports,* 1942, 57:7–20.

282) Egerton, J. B., *Market Research in the United States,* Market Research Corporation of America, 1939.

283) Elinsen, J., and I. H. Cisin, "Detection of interviewer cheating through scale technique," *Public Opinion Quarterly,* 1948, 12:325.

284) Elmer, Manuel C., "The random sample," *Journal of Applied Sociology,* 1925, 9:422–424.

285) Elmer, Manuel C., *Technique of Social Surveys,* J. I. Miller, 1927.

286) Elmer, Manuel C., *Social Research,* Prentice-Hall, 1939.

287) Employment Stabilization Research Institute, *The Saint Paul Labor Market, Oct. 1941–June 1942, Part I. Summary,* Study II, Minneapolis, University of Minnesota, August, 1942 (processed).

288) *Encyclopaedia of the Social Sciences,* Macmillan, 1930–1934.

289) *Engineer,* "The Hollerith Tabulator," 1934, 157:101–105.

290) England, L. R., "Capital punishment and open-end questions," *Public Opinion Quarterly,* 1948, 12:412–417.

291) Engle, N. H., "Gaps in marketing research," *Journal of Marketing,* 1940, 4:345–353.

292) Erdos, Paul L., "Planning the questionnaire for tabulation," *International Journal of Opinion and Attitude Research,* 1948, 2:401–408.

293) Fallon, John F., "The questionnaire in educational research," *Catholic Educational Review,* 1926, 23:539–545.

294) Family Welfare Association of America, *Interviews, Interviewers and Interviewing in Social Case Work* (reprint of articles published in *The Family*), Family Welfare Association of America, 1931.

295) Farnsworth, Paul, "Shifts in the values of opinion items," *Journal of Psychology*, 1943, 16:125–128.

296) Farnsworth, Paul, "Attitude scale construction and the method of equal appearing intervals," *Journal of Psychology*, 1945, 18: 245–248.

297) Ferber, R., "Disproportionate method of market sampling," *Journal of Business*, 1946, 19:67–75.

298) Ferguson, Leonard W., "The requirements of an adequate attitude scale," *Psychological Bulletin*, 1939, 36:665–673.

299) Ferguson, Leonard W., "A study of the Likert technique in attitude scale construction," *Journal of Social Psychology*, 1941, 13: 51–57.

300) Ferguson, Leonard W., "The relation of the primary social attitude variables to national morale," *American Sociological Review*, 1944, 9:194.

301) Ferguson, Leonard W., "A revision of the primary social attitude scales," *Journal of Psychology*, 1944, 17:229–241.

302) Ferraby, J. G., "Validity of public opinion survey results: methods used by mass-observation," *Sociological Review*, 1944, 36: 43–49.

303) Ferraby, J. G., "Planning a mass-observation investigation," *American Journal of Sociology*, 1945, 51:1–6.

304) Field, Harry H., and Gordon M. Connelly, "Testing polls in public election booths," *Public Opinion Quarterly*, 1942.

305) Fink, Kenneth, and Robert G. Lutz, "Business forecasting through public opinion research," *Public Opinion Quarterly*, 1949, 13:325–328.

306) Fischer, Robert P., "Signed versus unsigned personal questionnaires," *Journal of Applied Psychology*, 1946, 30:220–225.

307) Fisher, Ronald A., *The Design of Experiments*, Oliver and Boyd, 1935.

308) Fisher, Ronald A., *Statistical Methods for Research Workers* (7th ed.), Oliver and Boyd, 1938.

309) Fiske, D. W., and J. W. Dunlap, "A graphical test for the significance of differences between frequencies from different samples," *Psychometrika*, 1945, 10:225–229.

310) Fiske, Marjorie, and Leo Handel, "Motion picture research: content and audience analysis," *Journal of Marketing*, 1946, 11: 129–134.

311) Fiske, Marjorie, and Leo Handel, "Motion picture research: response analysis," *Journal of Marketing*, 1947, 11:273–280.

312) Fiske, Marjorie, and Paul F. Lazarsfeld, "The office of radio research: a division of the bureau of applied social research, Columbia University," *Educational Psychological Measurement*, 1945, 5:351–369.

313) Fitting, R. U., *Report Writing*, Ronald, 1924.
314) Flanagan, John C., "Note on calculating the standard error of measurement and reliability coefficients with test scoring machine," *Journal of Applied Psychology*, 1939, 23:529.
315) Fleiss, Marjorie, "The panel as an aid in measuring effects of advertising," *Journal of Applied Psychology*, 1940, 24:685–695.
316) Flesch, Rudolph, *The Art of Readable Writing*, Harper, 1949.
317) Florence, P. S., "Social survey," *Nature*, 1946, 158:169.
318) *Fortune*, "Fortune survey: wording of questions," June, 1941, 23:70.
319) *Fortune*, "Fortune survey: analysis of survey findings over four-year period reveals political importance of education," October, 1945, 32:282.
320) *Fortune*, "Fortune survey: self portrait of the American people, 1947," 1947, 35:5, 6, 73–79.
321) *Fortune*, "Hindsight," December, 1948, pp. 39–40.
322) Fortune Magazine Editors, "The Fortune survey: its history and development," *Journal of Educational Sociology*, 1940, 14:250–253.
323) Fowler, Henry W., *Dictionary of Modern English Usage*, Clarendon, 1926.
324) Fox, Kirk, "The farmer speaks," *Successful Farming*, 1938, 36:14–15.
325) Frank, B., "Stability of questionnaire response," *Journal of Abnormal Psychology*, 1935, 30:320–324.
326) Frankel, Lester R., and J. Stevens Stock, "On the sample survey of unemployment," *Journal of the American Statistical Association*, 1942, 37:77–80.
327) Franken, R. B., "Formulating questionnaires," *Advertising Fortnightly*, 1924, Jan. 30:22 f., Feb. 13:26 f.
328) Franz, J. G., "Survey of sociometric techniques," *Sociometry*, 1939, 2:76–92.
329) Franzen, R. B., "The construction of a questionnaire," *Market Research*, 1936, 7:17–19.
330) Franzen, R. B., "Use of leading questions in consumer interviews," *Market Research*, 1937, 6:19–21.
331) Franzen, R. B., "An examination of the effect of number of advertisements in a magazine upon the 'visibility' of these advertisements," *Journal of Applied Psychology*, 1940, 24:791–801.
332) Franzen, R. B., and Paul F. Lazarsfeld, "Mail questionnaires as a research problem," *Journal of Psychology*, 1945, 20:239–320.
333) Frederick, J. George, *Business Research and Statistics*, D. Appleton-Century, 1920.

334) Friedman, P., "A second experiment on interviewer bias," *Sociometry*, 1942, 5:378–381.

335) Fromme, Allan, "On the use of certain qualitative methods of attitude research," *Journal of Social Psychology*, 1941, 13:429–459.

336) Fry, C. Luther, *The Technique of Social Investigation*, Harper, 1934.

337) Gage, N. L., and H. R. Remmers, "Opinion polling with mark-sensed punch cards," *Journal of Applied Psychology*, 1948, 32:89–91.

338) Gallup, George H., "Government and the sampling referendum," *Journal of the American Statistical Association*, 1938, 33:131–142.

339) Gallup, George H., "Testing public opinion," *Public Opinion Quarterly Supplement*, January, 1938:8–14.

340) Gallup, George H., "Question wording in public opinion polls: comments on points raised by Mr. Stagner," *Sociometry*, 1941, 4:259–268.

341) Gallup, George H., "Reporting opinion in five nations," *Public Opinion Quarterly*, 1942, 6:429–436.

342) Gallup, George, "The quintamensional plan of question design," *Public Opinion Quarterly*, 1947, 11:385–393.

343) Gallup, George H., *A Guide to Public Opinion Polls*, Princeton University Press, rev. ed., 1948.

344) Gallup, George H., and Saul Forbes Rae, "Is there a bandwagon vote?" *Public Opinion Quarterly*, 1940, 4:244–249.

345) Gallup, George H., and Saul Forbes Rae, *Pulse of Democracy*, Simon & Schuster, 1940.

346) Gallup, George H., and Claude Robinson, "American Institute of Public Opinion—Surveys, 1935–1938," *Public Opinion Quarterly*, 1938, 2:373–398.

347) Gaudet, H., and C. Daniel, "Radio Listener Panels," The Federal Radio Education Committee, Washington, D. C., 1941.

348) Gaudet, H., and E. Wilson, "Who escapes the personal investigators," *Journal of Applied Psychology*, 1940, 24:773–777.

349) Gault, R. H., "History of questionnaire in method of research," *Pedagogical Seminary*, 1907, 14:266–283.

350) Gee, Wilson (ed.), *Research in the Social Sciences*, Macmillan, 1929.

351) Gehlke, C. E., "The use and limitations of statistics in sociological research," *Proceedings of the American Sociological Society*, 1926, 21:141–148.

352) George, R. F., "Sample investigation of the 1931 population census with reference to earners and non-earners," *Journal of the Royal Statistical Society*, 1936, 99:147–161.

353) George, William, *The Scientist in Action,* Williams and Norgate, 1936.

354) Gerberich, G. B., and J. M. Mason, "Signed versus unsigned questionnaires," *Journal of Educational Research,* 1948, 42: 122–127.

355) Ghiselli, Edwin E., "All or none versus graded response questionnaires," *Journal of Applied Psychology,* 1939, 23:405–413.

356) Ghiselli, Edwin E., "Some further points on public opinion polls," *Journal of Marketing,* 1940, 5:115–119.

357) Ghiselli, Edwin E., "The problem of question form in the measure of sales by consumer interviews," *Journal of Marketing,* 1941, 6:170–171.

358) Gill, S. E., "Telephone and listening habits," *Printers' Ink,* December, 1939:32.

359) Gilliland, Adam Raymond, and E. Taylor Katzoff, "A scale for measurement of attitudes toward American participation in the present European conflict," *Journal of Psychology,* 1941, 11: 173–176.

360) Gimbel, E. S., "No opinion group dwindles," *New York Times Magazine,* May 6, 1945, p. 18.

361) Glueck, Sheldon, and Eleanor T., *500 Criminal Careers,* Knopf, 1930.

362) Glueck, Sheldon, and Eleanor T., *Later Criminal Careers,* The Commonwealth Fund, 1937.

363) Goldman, E. F., "Poll on the polls," *Public Opinion Quarterly,* 1944–1945, 8:461–467.

364) Gonner, E. C. K., "The population of England in the eighteenth century," *Journal of the Royal Statistical Society,* 1912, 76:261–296.

365) Good, Carter V. (comp.), "Selected bibliography on the methodology of educational research and related problems, 1939–1940," *Journal of Educational Research,* 1940, 34:57–80.

366) Good, Carter V., "Effective reporting of research," *Phi Delta Kappan,* 1941, 24:178–184.

367) Good, Carter V. (comp.), "Selected bibliography on the methodology of educational research and related problems, 1940–1941," *Journal of Educational Research,* 1941, 35:57–80.

368) Good, Carter V., A. S. Barr, and Douglas E. Scates, *The Methodology of Educational Research,* Appleton-Century, 1938.

369) Goode, Kenneth M., *What About Radio?* Harper, 1937.

370) Goodman, Roe, "Sampling for the 1947 Survey of Consumer Finances," *Journal of the American Statistical Association,* 1947, 42:439–448.

371) Goodman, Roe, and Eleanor E. Maccoby, "Sampling methods

and sampling errors in surveys of consumer finances," *International Journal of Opinion and Attitude Research*, 1948, 2:349–360.

372) Gosnell, Harold F., "How accurate were the polls?" *Public Opinion Quarterly*, 1937, 1:97–104.

373) Gosnell, Harold F., "The polls and other mechanisms of democracy," *Public Opinion Quarterly*, 1940, 4:224–228.

374) Gosnell, Harold F., and Sebastian deGrazia, "A critique of polling methods," *Public Opinion Quarterly*, 1942, 6:378–390.

375) Graeter, Ralph, and Richardson Wood, "Photo charts of survey findings," *Public Opinion Quarterly*, Winter, 1945–46, 9:430.

376) Great Britain, Royal Commission on Unemployment Insurance, *Report, Appendices to the minutes of evidence . . .* Part V: 239–304, London, H. M. Stationery Off., 1932.

377) "Great fiasco," *Time*, November 15, 1948, 52:66.

378) Green, Howard W., "The use of census tracts in analyzing the population of a metropolitan community," *Proceedings of the American Statistical Association*, 1932, 94:147–153.

379) Greenshields, Bruce D., "The photographic method of investigating traffic delays," *American City*, 1934, 49:83.

380) Gruenberg, Sidonie M., *The Use of the Radio in Parent Education*, Report of study conducted by the Child Study Association, the National Council of Parent Education, and the National Advisory Council on Radio in Education, University of Chicago, 1939.

381) Guam, C. G., H. F. Graves, and L. S. Hoffman, *Report Writing* (rev. ed.), Prentice-Hall, 1942.

382) Guest, Lester, "A study of interviewer competence," *International Journal of Opinion and Attitude Research*, 1947, 1:17–30.

383) Guest, Lester, "Have these sources of polling error been fully explored?" *International Journal of Opinion and Attitude Research*, 1948–49, 2:507–509.

384) Guilford, J. P., *Fundamental Statistics in Psychology and Education*, McGraw-Hill, 1942.

385) Guttman, L., "A basis for scaling qualitative data," *American Sociological Review*, 1944, 9:139–150.

386) Guttman, L., "The Cornell technique for scale and intensity analysis," *Educational and Psychological Measurement*, 1947, 7:247–279.

387) Hader, J. J., and Eduard C. Lindeman, *Dynamic Social Research*, Harcourt, Brace, 1933.

388) Hagood, Margaret J., *Statistics for Sociologists*, Reynal and Hitchcock, 1941.

389) Hagood, Margaret J., "Recent contributions of statistics to re-

search methodology in sociology," *Social Forces*, 1947, 26: 36–40.

390) Hagood, Margaret J., and E. H. Bernert, "Component indexes as a basis for stratification in sampling," *Journal of the American Statistical Association*, 1945, 40:330–341.

391) Hall, Ray Ovid, *Handbook of Tabular Presentation*, Ronald, 1943.

392) Hancock, John, "An experimental study of four methods of measuring unit costs of obtaining attitudes toward retail stores," *Journal of Applied Psychology*, 1940, 213–230.

393) Hankinson, Frank, "The blight of the questionnaire," *Educational Review*, 1927, 73:102–103.

394) Hansen, Morris H., "Sampling human populations," Abstract, *Econometrica*, 1948, 16:74–75.

395) Hansen, Morris H., and Philip M. Hauser, "Area sampling— some principles of sample design," *Public Opinion Quarterly*, 1945, 9:183–193.

396) Hansen, Morris H., and William N. Hurwitz, "Relative efficiencies of various sampling units in population inquiries," *Journal of the American Statistical Association*, 1942, 37:89–94.

397) Hansen, Morris H., and William N. Hurwitz, "On the theory of sampling from finite populations," *Annals of Mathematical Statistics*, 1943.

398) Hansen, Morris H., and William N. Hurwitz, *A New Sample of the Population*, U. S. Department of Commerce, Bureau of the Census, October, 1944.

399) Hansen, Morris H., and William N. Hurwitz, "Problem of non-response in sample surveys," *Journal of the American Statistical Association*, 1946, 41:517–529.

400) Hansen, Morris H., William N. Hurwitz, and Margaret Gurney, "Problems and methods of the sample survey of business," *Journal of the American Statistical Association*, 1946, 41:173–189.

401) Haring, Albert, "The evolution of marketing research technique," *The National Marketing Review*, 1935–1936, 1:268–272.

402) Haring, Chester, "How many should we interview?" *Advertising and Selling*, August 7, 1929.

403) Haring, Chester, "What is an adequate audience sample?" *Advertising and Selling*, September, 1939, 32:40, 42, 72.

404) Harley, Dudley, *Surveys of Youth*, American Council of Education, 1937.

405) Harper, Ernest B., "Training in research techniques: discussion," *Sociology and Social Research*, 1934, 18:219–222.

406) Harper, Robert A., "The present status of questionnaire-derived opinion data," *Journal of Social Forces*, 1947, 25:294–298.

407) Harriman, Phillip L., "An objective technique for beginning the interview with certain types of adults," *Journal of Applied Psychology*, 1935, 19:717–724.

408) Harris, Marilyn, D. G. Horvitz, and A. M. Wood, "On the determination of sample sizes in designing experiments," *Journal of the American Statistical Association*, 1948, 43:391–403.

409) Harris, Natalie, and Gordon M. Connelly, "A symposium on interviewing problems," *International Journal of Opinion and Attitude Research*, 1948, 2:69–84.

410) Harrison, Shelby M., *The Social Survey*, Russell Sage Foundation, 1931.

411) Harshe, William R., "The Reed poll," *Public Opinion Quarterly*, 1942, 6:291–294.

412) Hart, C. W., "Bias in interviewing studies of opinions, attitudes, and consumer wants," *American Philosophical Society Proceedings*, 1948, 92:399–404.

413) Hart, Hornell, "What contrasts in percentage distributions are significant," *Journal of the American Statistical Association*, 1924, 19:65–70.

414) Hart, Hornell, "The reliability of a percentage," *Journal of the American Statistical Association*, 1926, 21:40–46.

415) Hartkemeier, Harry Pelle, *Principles of Punch-Card Machine Operation*, Crowell, 1942.

416) Hartshorne, Hugh, and Mark May, *Character Education Inquiries*, Macmillan, 1928–30.

417) Hartwell, Dickson, "Business asks the public how it may serve best," *Nation's Business*, 1940, 28:26–28, 106–108.

418) Hartwell, Dickson, "What the public thinks of food manufacturers: Survey of consumer opinion reveals where public relations are weak," *Food Industries*, May, 1940, 39–41.

419) Harvey, O. L., "The questionnaire as used in recent studies of human sexual behavior," *Journal of Abnormal and Social Psychology*, 1932, 26:379–389.

420) Haskell, A. C., *Graphic Charts in Business*, Codex Book, 1928.

421) Hauser, Philip M., "Research possibilities in the 1940 census," *American Sociological Review*, 1941, 6:463–471.

422) Hauser, Philip M., "The use of sampling in the census," *Journal of the American Statistical Association*, 1941, 36:369–376.

423) Hauser, Philip M., "Proposed annual sample census of population," *Journal of the American Statistical Association*, 1942, 37:81–88.

424) Hauser, Philip M., and Morris H. Hansen, "On sampling in market surveys," *Journal of Marketing*, 1944, 8:21–32.

425) Hauser, Philip M., and William R. Leonard, *Government Statistics for Business Use*, Wiley, 1946.

426) Hayes, Samuel P., Jr., "Occupational and sex differences in political attitudes," *Journal of Social Psychology*, 1937, 8:87–113.

427) Hearings before the Committee to Investigate Campaign Expenditures, House of Representatives, 78th Congress, Part 12 (Anderson Committee, *Report of Technical Sub-Committee*), Washington, D. C., U. S. Government Printing Office (1945).

428) Heidingsfield, Myron, and Albert Blankenship, *Market and Marketing Analysis*, Holt, 1947.

429) Henderson, Harry W., "An early poll," *Public Opinion Quarterly*, 1942, 6:450–451.

430) Hendrichs, King, L. A. Stoddard, and others, *Utah State Manual for Research Writing*, Utah State Agricultural College, 1938.

431) Herzog, Herta, "Radio—the first post-war year," *Public Opinion Quarterly*, 1946, 10:297–314.

432) Hettinger, Herman S., *A Decade of Radio Advertising*, University of Chicago, 1933.

433) Hettinger, Herman S., and Walter J. Neff, *Practical Radio Advertising*, Prentice-Hall, 1938.

434) Hettinger, Herman S., Robert N. King, and Paul A. Peter, "Roster, coincidental, unaided recall: how they compare in counting listeners," *Advertising and Selling*, August, 1940, 33: 20–21.

435) Hildreth, Gertrude, *A Bibliography of Mental Tests and Rating Scales*, Psychological Corporation, 1933.

436) Hilgard, Ernest R., and Stanley L. Payne, "Those not at home —riddle for pollsters," *Public Opinion Quarterly*, 1944, 8:254–261.

437) Hill, Frank Ernest, "Listening groups in the United States," in Institute for education by radio, *Education on the air*: Eleventh Yearbook, 1940:174–178.

438) Hill, Joseph A., "The essentials of a good census," *Journal of the American Statistical Association*, 1930, 17:1–13.

439) Hilton, John, "Enquiry by sample: An experiment and its results," *Journal of the Royal Statistical Society*, 1924, 87:544–570.

440) Hinckley, E. D., and M. B. Hinckley, "Attitude scales for measuring the influence of the work relief program," *Journal of Psychology*, 1939, 8:115–124.

441) Hinrichs, A. F., "Statistical bias in primary data and public policy," *Journal of the American Statistical Association*, 1938, 33:143–152.

442) Hitt, H. L., "Sampling technique for studying population changes in rural areas," *Social Forces*, 1940, 19:208–213.

443) Hobson, Asher, "The use of the correspondence method in origi-

nal research," *Journal of the American Statistical Association*, 1916, 15:210–218.

444) Hochstim, J. R., and M. K. D. Smith, "Area sampling or quota control? Three sampling experiments," *Public Opinion Quarterly*, 1948, 12:73–80. Comments by S. Banks, 316–320. Rejoinder, 320–324.

445) Hogg, Margaret, "Sources of incomparability and error in employment-unemployment surveys," *Journal of the American Statistical Association*, 1930, 195:284–294.

446) Hogg, Margaret, *Incidence of Work Shortage*, Russell Sage Foundation, 1934.

447) Holmes, Irvin, "Results of four methods of sampling individual farms," *Journal of Farm Economics*, 1939, 21:365–374.

448) Holmes, Irvin, *Research in sample farm census methodology, Part I. Comparative statistical efficiency of sampling units smaller than the minor civil division for estimating year-to-year change*, U. S. Dept. of Agriculture, Agricultural Marketing Service, 1939.

449) Holzinger, Karl J., *Statistical Methods for Students in Education*, Ginn, 1928.

450) Hooper, C. E., "Lifting the veil from the radio audience," *Printers' Ink*, June, 1941, 42:37.

451) Hopkins, Florence M., *Reference Guides that Should be Known and How to Use Them*, Willard, 1923.

452) Horst, P., "Measuring complex attitudes," *Journal of Social Psychology*, 1935, 6:369–374.

453) Horwood, Murray P., *Public Health Surveys: What They Are: How to Make Them: How to Use Them*, Wiley, 1921.

454) Hotchkiss, George B., and Richard B. Franken, *The Measurement of Advertising Effects*, Harper, 1927.

455) Houseman, Earl E., "The sample design for a national farm survey by the Bureau of Agricultural Economics," *Journal of Farm Economics*, 1947, 29:241–245.

456) Houseman, Earl E., "Designs of samples for surveys," *Agricultural Economics Research*, 1949, 1:1–11.

457) Houser, J. David, "Measurement of the vital products of business," *Journal of Marketing*, 1938, 2:181–189.

458) "How the election polls went wrong," *Business Week*, November 13, 1948.

459) Hubbard, Frank W., "Questionnaires," *Review of Educational Research*, 1939, 9:502–507, 608–609.

460) Huey, George H. H., "Some principles of field administration in large-scale surveys," *Public Opinion Quarterly*, 1947, 11:244–263.

461) Huff, Henry H., "How to avoid the pitfalls in research," *Advertising and Selling*, 1945, 38:5, 74–79.

462) Hyman, Herbert, "Do they tell the truth?" *Public Opinion Quarterly*, 1944–1945, 8:557–559.

463) Hyman, Herbert, "Community background in public opinion research," *Journal of Abnormal and Social Psychology*, 1945, 40:411–413.

464) Hyman, Herbert, and Paul B. Sheatsley, "The Kinsey Report and survey methodology," *International Journal of Opinion and Attitude Research*, 1948, 2:182–195.

465) *Index to the Journal of the American Statistical Association, Vols. 1–34, 1905–1939*, Prepared by Myron S. Heidingsfield with Harold R. Hosea, Consultant, American Statistical Association, 1941.

466) Institute for Government Research, *The Bureau of the Census*, Brookings Institute, 1929.

467) *International Journal of Opinion and Attitude Research* (entire issues beginning Volume 1, 1947).

468) Jaffee, A. J., "The application of attitude research methodology toward the problem of measuring the size of the labor force," *International Journal of Opinion and Attitude Research*, 1947, 1:45–54.

469) Jenkins, John G., "Dependability of psychological brand barometers, I. The problem of reliability," *Journal of Applied Psychology*, 1938, 22:1–7.

470) Jenkins, John G., "Characteristics of the question as determinants of dependability," *Journal of Consulting Psychology*, 1941, 5:164–169.

471) Jenkins, John G., "Validity for what?" *Journal of Consulting Psychology*, 1946, 10:93–98.

472) Jenkins, John G., and Horace N. Corbin, Jr., "Dependability of psychological brand barometers, II. The problem of validity," *Journal of Applied Psychology*, 1938, 22:252–260.

473) Jensen, Adolph, "Report on the representative method in statistics," *Rome, Bulletin, Institut Internationale de Statistique*, Pt. I, 1928, 22:359–378.

474) Jensen, Adolph, "The representative method in practice," *Rome, Bulletin, Institut Internationale de Statistique*, Pt. I, 1928, 22:381–439.

475) Jensen, Adolph, "Purposive selection," *Journal of the Royal Statistical Society*, 1928, 91:541–547.

476) Jessen, Carl A., "Surveys of youth," *School Life*, 1936, 21:273–275.

477) Jessen, R. J., "An experiment in the design of agricultural surveys," *Journal of Farm Economics*, 1939, 21:856–863.

478) Jessen, R. J., "The master sample of agriculture: design," *Journal of the American Statistical Association*, 1945, 40:46–56.

479) Jessen, Raymond, "On a population sample for Greece," *Journal of the American Statistical Association*, 1947, 42:357–384.

480) Johnston, Mary, "Indexing of social data," *Journal of the American Statistical Association*, 1929.

481) Jones, David C., 'The cost of living of a sample of middle class families," *Journal of the Royal Statistical Society*, 1928, 91:463–502.

482) Jones, David C., *The Social Survey of Merseyside* (3 volumes), University of London, Hodder and Stoughton, 1934.

483) Jones, David C., "Evolution of the social survey in England since Booth," *American Journal of Sociology*, 1941, 46:818–825.

484) Jones, David C., and Colin Clark, "Housing in Liverpool: a survey by sample of present conditions," *Journal of the Royal Statistical Society*, 1930, 93:489–521.

485) Jones, W. Paul, *Writing Scientific Papers and Reports*, Dubuque, Iowa, W. C. Brown, 1946.

486) Kameda, T., "Application of the method of sampling to the 1st Japanese population census," *Rome, Bulletin, Institut Internationale de Statistique*, 1931, 25:121–132.

487) Kaplan, Louis, *Research Materials for the Social Sciences*, University of Wisconsin, 1939.

488) Karol, John J., "Measuring radio audiences," *Public Opinion Quarterly*, 1937, 1:92–96.

489) Karol, John J., "Analyzing the radio market," *Journal of Marketing*, 1938, 2:309–313.

490) Karslake, Ruth H., "A technique for measuring consumer attitude toward any advertisement," *Proceedings Indiana Academy of Science*, 1939, 48:193–195.

491) Katz, Daniel, "Three criteria: knowledge, conviction, and significance," *Public Opinion Quarterly*, 1940, 4:277–284.

492) Katz, Daniel, "The effect of social status or membership character of the interviewer upon his findings," *Psychological Bulletin*, 1941, 38:540.

493) Katz, Daniel, "The public opinion polls and the 1940 election," *Public Opinion Quarterly*, 1941, 5:52–78.

494) Katz, Daniel, "Psychological tasks in the measurement of public opinion," *Journal of Consulting Psychology*, 1942, 6:59–64.

495) Katz, Daniel, "Do interviewers bias poll results?" *Public Opinion Quarterly*, 1942, 6:248–268.

496) Katz, Daniel, "The polls and the 1944 election," *Public Opinion Quarterly*, 1945, 8:468–482.

497) Katz, Daniel, "Polling methods and the 1948 polling failure," *In-*

ternational Journal of Opinion and Attitude Research, 1948–1949, 2:469–481.

498) Katz, Daniel, "An analysis of the 1948 polling predictions," *Journal of Applied Psychology,* 1949, 33:15–29.

499) Katz, Daniel, and Hadley Cantril, "Public opinion polls," *Sociometry,* 1937, I:155–179.

500) Kelley, R. L., "Questionable questionnaires," *Association of American Colleges Bulletin,* 1931, 17:291–293.

501) Kelley, R. L., "Revolt against questionable questionnaires," *Association of American Colleges Bulletin,* 1931, 17:377–390.

502) Kelley, Truman L., *Scientific Method: Its Function in Research in Education,* Macmillan, 1932.

503) Kelley, Truman L., *Fundamentals of Statistics,* Harvard University Press, 1947.

504) Kellogg, Paul U. (ed.), *The Pittsburgh Survey* (6 volumes), Russell Sage Foundation, 1909–1914.

505) Kelsey, George W., and Mary L. Alexander, *A Selection of Books and Articles on the Purpose, Scope and Techniques of Marketing Research,* American Society of Mechanical Engineers, 1935.

506) Kendall, M. G., *The Advanced Theory of Statistics,* Vols. 1 and 2, Charles Griffin, 1946.

507) Kendall, M. G., and B. Babington-Smith, "Randomness and random sampling numbers," *Journal of the Royal Statistical Society,* 1938, 101:147–166.

508) Kendall, M. G., and B. Babington-Smith, "Second paper on random sampling numbers," *Journal of the Royal Statistical Society, Supplement,* 1939, 6:51–61.

509) Key, V. O., Jr., *Politics, Parties and Pressure Groups,* Thomas Crowell, 1942.

510) Kiaer, A. N., "Observations et experiences concernant des denombrements representatifs," *Bulletin IX de l'institute internationale de Statistique,* 1896.

511) Killough, Hugh B., and Barrington Associates, Inc., *The Economics of Marketing,* Harper, 1933.

512) King, Arnold J. "The master sample of agriculture: development and use," *Journal of the American Statistical Association,* 1945, 40:38–46.

513) King, Arnold J., and Dale E. McCarty, "Application of sampling to agricultural statistics with emphasis on stratified samples," *Journal of Marketing,* 1941, 5:462–475.

514) King, Arnold J., and Glenn D. Simpson, "New developments in agricultural sampling," *Journal of Farm Economics,* 1940, 22:341–349.

515) King, Morton B., "Reliability of the idea centered question in

interview schedules," *American Sociological Review*, 1944, 9: 57–64.

516) King, Robert N., "Fallacy of large numbers in survey field work," *Advertising and Selling*, February, 1935:66.

517) Kinsey, A. C., W. B. Pomeroy, and C. E. Martin, *Sexual Behavior in the Human Male*, Saunders, 1948.

518) Kirkpatrick, Clifford, *Report of a Research into the Attitudes and Habits of Radio Listeners*, Webb Book Publishing Company, 1933.

519) Kirkpatrick, Clifford, "Intelligence and the radio," *Sociology and Social Research*, 1935, 19:203–209.

520) Kirkpatrick, Clifford, "Assumptions and methods in attitude measurements," *American Sociological Review*, 1936, I:75–88.

521) Kirsch, Mary M., "Bibliography: an indispensable aid to sociological research," *Library Journal*, 1930, 5:773–774.

522) Kiser, Clyde V., "Pitfalls in sampling for population study," *Journal of the American Statistical Association*, 1934, 29:250–256.

523) Kiser, Clyde V., and P. K. Whelpton, "Progress report on the study of social and psychological factors affecting fertility," *American Sociological Review*, 1947, 12:175–186.

524) Kluckhohn, F. R., "The participant observer technique in small communities," *American Journal of Sociology*, 1940, 46:331–343.

525) Knower, F. H., "Effect of oral argument on changes of attitude," *Journal of Social Psychology*, 1935, 6:315–347.

526) Knower, F. H., "A study of the effect of printed argument on changes in attitude," *Journal of Abnormal and Social Psychology*, 1935–1936, 30:522.

527) Knower, F. H., "Some incidences of attitude changes," *Journal of Applied Psychology*, 1936, 20:114–127.

528) Knutson, Andie L., "Japanese Opinion Surveys: The special need and the special difficulties," *Public Opinion Quarterly*, 1945, 9:313–319.

529) Kolesnikoff, Vladimir, "Standard classification of industries in the United States," *Journal of the American Statistical Association*, 1940, 35:65–73.

530) Komarovsky, Mirra, *The Unemployed Man*, Institute of Social Research, 1940.

531) Koos, L. V., *The Questionnaire in Education*, Macmillan, 1928.

532) Koos, L. V., "Specific techniques of investigation, observation, questionnaire, and rating," *National Society for the Study of Education, 37th Yearbook*, 375–390.

533) Kornhauser, Arthur, "Attitudes of economic groups," *Public Opinion Quarterly*, 1938, 260–269.

534) Kornhauser, Arthur, "Are public opinion polls fair to organized labor?" *Public Opinion Quarterly,* 1946–1947, 10:484–500.

535) Kornhauser, Arthur, "The problem of bias in opinion research," *International Journal of Opinion and Attitude Research,* 1947, 1:1–16.

536) Kriedt, P. H., and K. E. Clark, "Item analysis versus scale analysis," *Journal of Applied Psychology,* 1949, 33:114–121.

537) Kulp, Daniel H., "The forms of statements in attitude tests," *Sociology and Social Research,* 1933, 18:18–25.

538) Kulp, Daniel H., "Concepts in attitude tests," *Sociology and Social Research,* 1939, 19:218–223.

539) Kurtz, Albert K., and Harold Edgerton, *Statistical Dictionary of Terms and Symbols,* Wiley, 1939.

540) Larson, Nellie G. (comp.), *The Sampling Method in Social and Economic Research,* U. S. Dept. of Agriculture, Bureau of Agricultural Economics, 1941 (Bibliography No. 90).

541) Lawson, Faith, "Varying group responses to postal questionnaires," *Public Opinion Quarterly,* 1949, 13:114–117.

542) Lazarsfeld, Paul F., "The art of asking why," *National Marketing Review,* 1935, I:26–38.

543) Lazarsfeld, Paul F., "Interchangeability of indices in the measurement of economic influences," *Journal of Applied Psychology,* 1939, 23:33–45.

544) Lazarsfeld, Paul F., "Radio research and applied psychology, Princeton radio research project and other surveys: Symposium," *Journal of Applied Psychology,* 1939, 23:1–206.

545) Lazarsfeld, Paul F., "Panel studies," *Public Opinion Quarterly,* 1940, 4:122–128.

546) Lazarsfeld, Paul F., "The use of the mail questionnaire to ascertain the relative popularity of network stations in family listening surveys," *Journal of Applied Psychology,* 1940, 24:802–812.

547) Lazarsfeld, Paul F., "Repeated interviews as a tool for studying changes in opinion and their causes," *American Statistical Association Bulletin,* 1941, 2:3–7.

548) Lazarsfeld, Paul F., "Evaluating the effectiveness of advertising by direct interviews," *Journal of Consulting Psychology,* 1941, 5:170–178.

549) Lazarsfeld, Paul F., "Use of panels in social research," *American Philosophical Society Proceedings,* 1948, 92:405–410.

550) Lazarsfeld, Paul F., Bernard Berelson, and Hazel Gaudet, *The People's Choice: How the Voter Makes Up His Mind in a Presidential Campaign,* Duell, Sloan & Pearce, 1944.

551) Lazarsfeld, Paul F., and H. Field, *The People Look at Radio,* Bureau of Applied Social Research, University of North Carolina, 1946.

552) Lazarsfeld, Paul F., and Marjorie Fiske, "The panel as a new tool for measuring opinion," *Public Opinion Quarterly*, 1938, 2:596–612.

553) Lazarsfeld, Paul F., and Raymond Franzen, "Validity of mail order questionnaires in upper income groups," Time, Research Report No. 940, October, 1945.

554) Lazarsfeld, Paul F., and Frank N. Stanton (eds.), *Radio Research*, 1941, Duell, Sloan & Pearce, 1941.

555) Leahy, Alice, "Punching psychological and sociological data on Hollerith cards," *Journal of Applied Psychology*, 1931, 15:199–207.

556) Lee, Alfred McClung, "Social determinants of public opinions," *International Journal of Opinion and Attitude Research*, 1947, 1:12–29.

557) Lee, Alfred McClung, "Sociological theory in public opinion and attitude studies," *American Sociological Review*, 1947, 12:312–323.

558) Lee, Alfred McClung, "A definition of public opinion," *International Journal of Opinion and Attitude Research*, 1947, 1:102–106.

559) Lentz, T. F., "Reliability of opinionaire technique studied intensively by the retest method," *Journal of Social Psychology*, 1934, 5:338–364.

560) LePlay, Frederick, *Les Ouvriers Européens* (six volumes), Paris, France, Imprimeries Impériales, 1855.

561) LePlay Institute, *Social Surveys and Community Organization* (pamphlet), London LePlay House, 65 Belgrave Road, Westminster, S. W., 1933.

562) Levinson, N. C., *Your Chance to Win*, Farrar and Rinehart, 1939.

563) Likert, Rensis, *A Technique for the Measurement of Attitudes*, Archives of Psychology, Columbia University Press, No. 140, 1932.

564) Likert, Rensis, "Survey research center at Michigan," *Higher Education*, May 1, 1947, p. 6.

565) Likert, Rensis, "The sample interview survey," in Dennis, W., *Current Trends in Psychology*, University of Pittsburgh Press, 1947, 196–225.

566) Likert, Rensis, "Why opinion polls were so wrong," *U. S. News*, November 12, 1948, 25:24–25.

567) Lindeman, Eduard C., *Social Discovery*, Republic Publishing, 1924.

568) Lindquist, Everett Franklin, "The significance of a difference between 'matched' groups," *Journal of Educational Psychology*, 1931, 22:197–204.

569) Lindquist, Everett Franklin, *Statistical Analysis in Educational Research,* Houghton Mifflin, 1940.
570) Lindquist, Everett Franklin, "Sampling in educational research," *Journal of Educational Psychology,* 1940, 31:561–574.
571) Lindsay, E. E., "Questionnaires and follow-up letters," *Pedagogical Seminary,* 1921, 28:303–307.
572) Link, Henry C., *The New Psychology of Selling and Advertising,* Macmillan, 1932.
573) Link, Henry C., "How many interviews are necessary for results of a certain accuracy," *Journal of Applied Psychology,* 1937, 21:1–17.
574) Link, Henry C., "The tenth nation-wide social experimental survey," *Journal of Applied Psychology,* 1944, 28:363–375.
575) Link, Henry C., "The Psychological Corporation's index of public opinion," *Journal of Applied Psychology,* 1946, 30:1–9 and 297–309.
576) Link, Henry C., "The psychological barometer of public attitudes," *Journal of Applied Psychology,* 1947, 31:111–128.
577) Link, Henry C., "Some milestones in public opinion research," *Journal of Applied Psychology,* 1947, 31:225–234.
578) Link, Henry C., and Philip Corby, "Studies in radio effectiveness by the Psychological Corporation," *Journal of Applied Psychology,* 1940, 24:749–757.
579) Link, Henry C., and A. D. Freiberg, "The problem of validity vs. reliability in public opinion polls," *Public Opinion Quarterly,* 1942, 6:87–98.
580) Link, Henry C., Albert Freiberg, John Platten, Jr., and Kenneth Clark, "Is Dr. Kornhauser fair to organized pollers?" *Public Opinion Quarterly,* 1947, 11:198–212.
581) *Literary Digest,* "Topics of the day, Landon 1,293,669; Roosevelt, 972,897. Final returns in the Digest's poll of ten million voters," October 31, 1936, 122:5–6.
582) *Literary Digest,* "What went wrong with the polls?" November 14, 1936, 122:7–8.
583) Lloyd, Edward L., "Sampling problems in current trade statistics," *Journal of Marketing,* 1939, 3:373–379.
584) Lockley, Lawrence C., and Alfred N. Watson, "Some fundamental considerations in the conduct of polls," *Journal of Marketing,* 1940, 5:113–115.
585) London School of Economics and Political Science, *The New Survey of London Life and Labour* (9 volumes), P. S. King and Son, 1930–1935.
586) Lorge, Irving, "The Thurstone attitude scales I: The reliability and consistency of attitudes of rejection and acceptance," *Journal of Social Psychology,* 1939, 10:187–198.

587) Lorge, Irving, "The Thurstone attitude scales II: Reliability and consistency of attitudes of younger and older intellectual peers," *Journal of Social Psychology*, 1939, 10:199–208.

588) Lovell, George D., "A sex difference in opinion," *Journal of Social Psychology*, 1945, 22:17–22.

589) Lucas, D. B., "A rigid technique for measuring the impression values of specific magazine advertisements," *Journal of Applied Psychology*, 1940, 24:778–790.

590) Lucas, D. B., "A controlled recognition technique for measuring magazine advertising audiences," *Journal of Marketing*, 1942, 6:133–136.

591) Ludeke, Herbert C., "A test of two methods commonly used in reader interest surveys," *Journal of Marketing*, 1945, 10:171–173.

592) Lumley, Frederick H., *Measurement in Radio*, Columbus, Ohio State University, 1934.

593) Lundberg, George A., "Thoughtways of contemporary sociology," *American Sociological Review*, 1936, I:703–723.

594) Lundberg, George A., *Foundations of Sociology*, Macmillan, 1939.

595) Lundberg, George A., "The measurement of socio-economic status," *American Sociological Review*, 1940, 5:29–39.

596) Lundberg, George A., "Some problems of group classification and measurement," *American Sociological Review*, 1940, 5:351–360.

597) Lundberg, George A., *Social Research* (rev. ed.), Longmans, Green, 1941.

598) Lundberg, George A., Mirra Komarovsky, and Mary Alice McInery, *Leisure: A Suburban Study*, Columbia University, 1934.

599) Lurie, Walter H., "Statistics and public opinion," *Public Opinion Quarterly*, 1937, 1:78–82.

600) Lurie, Walter H., "Measurement of prestige and prestige suggestibility," *Journal of Social Psychology*, 1938, 9:219–226.

601) Lydgate, William A., *What America Thinks*, Thomas Crowell, 1944.

602) Lynd, Robert S., and Helen M., *Middletown*, Harcourt Brace, 1929.

603) Lynd, Robert S., and Helen M., *Middletown in Transition*, Harcourt Brace, 1938.

604) Maccoby, E. E., "Interviewing problems in financial surveys," *International Journal of Opinion and Attitude Research*, 1947, 1:31–39.

605) Maccoby, E. E., and R. E. Holt., "How surveys are made," *Journal of Social Issues*, 1946, 2:45–47.

606) Maclatchy, Josephine H. (ed.), *Education on the Air 1943*, Ohio State University, 1944.

607) Madge, Charles, and Tom Harrison (eds.) *First Year's Work by Mass Observation*, Lindsay-Drummond, 1938.

608) Madge, Charles, and Tom Harrison, *Britain by Mass Observation*, Penguin Books, 1939.

609) Madow, Lillian H., "Systematic sampling and its relation to other sampling designs," *Journal of the American Statistical Association*, 1946, 41:204–217.

610) Malcolm, Theodore, "A new research tool," *Journal of Marketing*, 1940, 1:38–39.

611) Manfield, Manuel N., "A pattern of response to mail surveys," *Public Opinion Quarterly*, 1948, 12:492–495.

612) Mangus, A. R., "Sampling in the field of rural relief," *Journal of the American Statistical Association*, 1934, 29:410–415.

613) Mangus, A. R., *Rural regions of the United States*, U. S. Federal Works Agency, Works Projects Administration, Division of Research, 1940.

614) Manheimer, Dean, and Herbert Hyman, "Interviewer performance in area sampling," *Public Opinion Quarterly*, 1949, 13:83–93.

615) Mann, H. B., "On a problem of estimation occurring in public opinion polls," *Annals of Mathematical Statistics*, 1945, 16:85–90. Correction 1946, 17:87–88.

616) Marsh, Charles J., "The influence of supplementary verbal directions upon results obtained with questionnaires," *Journal of Social Psychology*, 1945, 21:275–280.

617) Martin, Boyd A., "The service vote in the elections of 1944," *American Political Science Review*, 1945, 39:721–732.

618) Mathews, C. O., "The effect of the order of printed response words on an interest questionnaire," *Journal of Educational Psychology*, 1929, 20:128–134.

619) Max, Alfred, *Basic Factors in the Interpretation of Public Opinion Polls*, Ph.D. thesis, The American University, 1941.

620) Mayer, Edward N. "Postage stamps do affect results of your mailing," *Printers Ink*, October 4, 1946, p. 91.

621) McCormick, Thomas C., "Sampling theory in sociological research," *Social Forces*, 1937, 16:67–74.

622) McCormick, Thomas C., "On the amount of error in sociological data," *American Sociological Review*, 1938, 3:328–332.

623) McCormick, Thomas C., *Elementary Social Statistics*, McGraw-Hill, 1941.

624) McCormick, Thomas C., "Note on the validity of mathematical probability in sociological research," *American Sociological Review*, 1945, 10:626–631.

625) McGeogh, J. A., "Influence of sex and age on ability to report," *American Journal of Psychology*, 1928, 40:458.

626) McGeogh, J. A., "The relation between different measures of ability to report," *American Journal of Psychology*, 1928, 40:596–599.

627) McGuire, G. R., "Republican form of government and the straw ballot: an examination," *Vital Speeches*, 1939, 6:73–78.

628) McKenzie, R. D., *The Metropolitan Community*, McGraw-Hill, 1933.

629) McNemar, Quinn, *Psychological Statistics*, Wiley, 1949.

630) McNemar, Quinn, "Sampling in psychological research," *Psychological Bulletin*, 1940, 37:331–365.

631) McNemar, Quinn, "Opinion-attitude methodology," *Psychological Bulletin*, 1946, 43:289–374.

632) McNemar, Quinn, "Note on the sampling error of the difference between correlated proportions or percentages," *Psychometrika*, 1947, 12:153–157.

633) McPeak, W., "Problems of field management in army opinion research," *Journal of the American Statistical Association*, 1945, 40:247–248.

634) Meier, Norman C., and Cletus J. Burke, "Laboratory tests of sampling techniques," *Public Opinion Quarterly*, Winter 1947–1948, 11:586–593.

635) Menefee, Selden C., "The effect of stereotyped words on political judgments," *American Sociological Review*, 1936, 1:614–621.

636) Menefee, Selden C., "Stereotyped phrases and public opinion," *American Journal of Sociology*, 1938, 43:614–622.

637) Menefee, Selden C., *Assignment: U. S. A.*, Reynal and Hitchcock, 1943.

638) Meredith Publishing Co., *Standards of Research*, Meredith Publishing, 1929.

639) Merton, Robert K., "Facts and factitiousness in ethic opinionnaires," *American Sociological Review*, 1940, 5:13–28.

640) Merton, Robert K., Marjorie Fiske, and Alberta Curtis, *Mass Persuasion: The Social Psychology of a War Bond Drive*, Harper, 1946.

641) Merton, Robert K., and P. L. Kendall, "The focused interview," *American Journal of Sociology*, 1946, 51:541–557.

642) Meyrowitz, Alvin, and Marjorie Fiske, "Relative preferences of low income groups for small stations," *Journal of Applied Psychology*, 1939, 23:158–162.

643) Miller, C. R., "Public opinion polls and public schools," *Teachers College Record*, 1942, 43:245–254.

644) Miller, J. Erroll, "Atypical voting behavior in Philadelphia," *Public Opinion Quarterly,* 1948, 12:489–490.

645) Miller, J. T., "The farmer speaks—A survey of farm thinking," *Journal of Marketing,* 1938, 3:44–46.

646) Mills, Frederick C., *Statistical Methods Applied to Economics and Business,* Holt, 1938.

647) Millson, W. A. D., "A review of research in audience reaction," *Quarterly Journal of Speech,* 1938, 24:464–483.

648) Mitchell, Claude, "Do scales for measuring attitudes have any significance?" *Journal of Educational Research,* 1941, 34:444–452.

649) Mitchell, Walter, "Factors affecting the rate of return on mailed questionnaires," *Journal of the American Statistical Association,* 1939, 34:683–692.

650) Modley, Rudolph, *How to Use Pictorial Statistics,* Harper, 1937.

651) Monroe, Walter S. (ed.), *Encyclopedia of Educational Research,* Macmillan, 1941.

652) Monroe, Walter S., and Max Engelhart, *The Techniques of Educational Research,* Bureau of Educational Research, Bulletin No. 138, University of Chicago, 1928.

653) Moore, Bruce V., "Objective methods in the personal interview," *Psychological Clinic,* 1930, 19:105–115.

654) Moore, Clarence Carl, "Increasing the returns from questionnaires,"*Journal of Educational Research,* 1941, 35:138–140.

655) Moreno, J. S., "A frame of reference for testing the social investigator," *Sociometry,* 1940, 3:317–327.

656) Morgan, Roy, "Interviewer introspection on 'bias,'" *Public Opinion Quarterly,* 1947–1948, 11:615–616.

657) Morgan, Roy, "Last-minute changes in voting intention," *Public Opinion Quarterly,* 1948, 12:470–480.

658) Moser, C. A., "The use of sampling in Great Britain," *Journal of the American Statistical Association,* 1949, 44:231–260.

659) Mudge, Isadore Gilbert, *Guide to Reference Books,* American Library Association, 1936.

660) Mudgett, Bruce D., *Statistical Tables and Graphs,* Houghton Mifflin, 1930.

661) Murphy, Gardner, and Rensis Likert, *Public Opinion and the Individual,* Harper, 1938.

662) Murphy, Gardner, L. B. Murphy, and T. N. Newcomb, *Experimental Social Psychology* (rev. ed.), Harper, 1937.

663) Murphy, J. A., "Sleuthing for basic market facts," *Advertising and Selling,* February, 1941:24.

664) Muscio, B., "The influence of the form of the question," *British Journal of Psychology,* 1916, 8:351–389.

665) Myer, W. E., "Studies in public opinion," *National Education Association Journal,* 1937, 26:48.

666) Myers, Howard B., "The general development and present status of the F.E.R.A. Research Program," *Social Forces,* 1934–1936, 13:477.

667) Myers, Howard B., and John N. Webb, "Another census of unemployment," *American Journal of Sociology,* 1937, 42:521–533.

668) Myers, Robert C., "Whose business is polling?" *International Journal of Opinion and Attitude Research,* 1948–1949, 2:543–549.

669) Nafziger, Ralph O., "Problems in reader interest surveys," *Journal of Marketing,* 1945, 9:359–363.

670) *Nation,* "Once more Dr. Gallup hits the news; his analysis of political trends," October 26, 1946, 163.

671) National Association of Broadcasters, *Radio Audience Measurement,* Washington, D. C., 1946.

672) National Education Association, Research Division, "The questionnaire," *Research Bulletin,* 1930, 8:1–51.

673) National Opinion Research Center, *Announcement of Purposes,* University of Denver, 1942.

674) National Opinion Research Center, *How NORC Builds Its Cross-section* (pamphlet), University of Denver, July, 1946.

675) National Opinion Research Center, *Interviewing for NORC,* University of Denver, 1946.

676) National Opinion Research Center, *Proceedings of the Central City Conference on Public Opinion Research: Opera House, Central City, Colorado, July 29, 30, 31, 1946,* University of Denver, 1946.

677) National Opinion Research Center, *The How and Why of Public Opinion Research,* University of Chicago, 1948.

678) National Youth Poll, "Student attitude survey," *Scholastic,* May 5, 1941, 38:1.

679) Neely, Twila E., *A Study of Error in the Interview,* Ph.D. thesis, Columbia University, privately published, 1937.

680) Nielson, Arthur C., "Two years of commercial operation of the audimeter and the Nielson Radio Index," *Journal of Marketing,* 1945, 9:239–255.

681) Neiswanger, William A. *Elementary Statistical Methods,* Macmillan, 1943.

682) Nelson, J. Raleigh, *Writing the Technical Report,* McGraw-Hill, 1947. 2nd ed.

683) Nepprash, J. A., "The reliability of responses to questions on so-

cial attitudes," *Publication of American Sociological Society*, 1934, 28:69–73.

684) Neumeyer, M. H., "Radio and social research," *Sociology and Social Research*, 1940, 25:114–124.

685) Neuner, John J. W., and Benjamin R. Haynes, *Office Management and Practice*, South-Western Publishing, 1941.

686) *New Statesman and Nation*, "The don't knows," January 20, 1940, 19:69–70.

687) New York (State) Library Bulletin, No. 50, *Indexing*, 1923.

688) New York (State) Department of Social Welfare, Division of Research, *Handbook for the Collection and Tabulation of Statistical Information*, J. B. Loyon, 1935.

689) Newcomb, Charles Shelton, *Street Addresses Coding Guide, by Census Areas of Chicago, 1930*, University of Chicago, 1934.

690) Newhall, S. M., "The reliability of order of merit evaluations of advertisements," *Journal of Applied Psychology*, 1930, 14:532–548.

691) Newhall, S. M., and E. H. Rodnick, "The influence of the reporting response upon the report," *American Journal of Psychology*, 1936, 48:316–325.

692) Newson, N. William, and George E. Walk, *Standards of Thesis Writing*, International Textbook Co., 1936.

693) Neyman, J., "On the two different aspects of the representative method," *Journal of the Royal Statistical Society*, 1934, 97:558–625.

694) Neyman, J., *Lectures and Conferences on Mathematical Statistics*, U. S. Department of Agriculture, Graduate School, 1938.

695) Neyman, J., "Contribution to the theory of sampling human populations," *Journal of the American Statistical Association*, 1938, 33:101–116.

696) Nielsen, Arthur C., "Trends toward mechanization of radio advertising," *Journal of Marketing*, 1942, 6:217–228.

697) Niles, Henry, and Mary C. H. Niles, *The Office Supervisor*, Wiley, 1935.

698) Niles, Mary C. H., *Middle Management*, Harper, 1941.

699) Noll, H. V., "Measuring the scientific attitude," *Journal of Abnormal and Social Psychology*, 1935, 30:145–154.

700) Norton, F. H., "Art of writing scientific reports," *Scientific Monthly*, 1920, 11:548–554.

701) Norton, J. K., *The Questionnaire*, National Education Association, Research Bulletin 8, No. 1, 1930.

702) Odum, Howard W., and Katherine Jocher, *An Introduction to Social Research*, Holt, 1929.

703) Ogburn, William F., "On scientific writing," *American Journal of Sociology*, 1947, 52:383–389.

704) Ogburn, William F., and L. C. Coombs, "The economic factor in the Roosevelt elections," *American Political Science Review,* 1940, 34:719–727.

705) Ogg, Frederick Austin, *Research in the Humanistic and Social Sciences,* Appleton-Century, 1928.

706) "Ohio State conducts presidential poll," *Higher Education,* September 1, 1948, 5:6.

707) Oliver, L. M., *Technical Exposition,* McGraw-Hill, 1941.

708) Osgood, C. E., and Ross Stagner, "Analysis of a prestige frame of reference by a gradient technique," *Journal of Applied Psychology,* 1941, 25:275–291.

709) Osgood, C. E., and others, "Separation of appeal and brand name in testing spot advertising," *Journal of Applied Psychology,* 1939, 23:60–75.

710) Pace, C. Robert, "Factors influencing questionnaire returns from former university students," *Journal of Applied Psychology,* 1939, 23:388–397.

711) Pace, C. Robert, "A situations test to measure social-political-economic attitudes," *Journal of Social Psychology,* 1939, 10:331–334.

712) Pace, C. Robert, "Stated behavior versus stated opinion as indicators of social-political-economic attitudes," *Journal of Social Psychology,* 1940, 11:369–383.

713) Palmer, Gladys L., "The convertibility list of occupations," *Journal of the American Statistical Association,* 1939, 34:693–708.

714) Palmer, Gladys L., "Factors in the variability of response in enumerative studies," *Journal of the American Statistical Association,* 1943, 38:143–152.

715) Palmer, Vivian M., *Field Studies in Sociology,* University of Chicago, 1928.

716) Parten, Mildred, "Social background studies," *Journal of Educational Sociology,* 1931, 4:569–580.

717) Parten, Mildred, "A statistical analysis of the modern American family," *Annals of the American Academy of Political and Social Science,* 1932, 160:29–37.

718) Parten, Mildred, "Social participation among pre-school children," *Journal of Abnormal and Social Psychology,* 1932, 27:243–269.

719) Parten, Mildred, "Some methodological problems to be considered in planning family research," paper presented at the Annual Meeting of the American Sociological Society, December, 1934, abstract in *Manual of Abstracts,* 25–26.

720) Parten, Mildred, "The analysis and treatment of refusals and partial information schedules in social surveys," unpublished pa-

per read at the Annual Meeting of the American Sociological Society, December 28, 1937.

721) Parten, Mildred, and R. J. Reeves, "Size and composition of American families," *American Sociological Review*, 1937, 2:638–649.

722) Paterson, Donald G., and M. A. Tinker, *How to Make Type Readable: A Manual for Typographers, Printers and Advertisers*, Harper, 1940.

723) Paton, Mary R., "Selection of tabulation method, machine or manual," *Journal of Marketing*, 1942, 6:229–235.

724) Patte, W. E., "Nomograph for analyzing percentage tolerances," *Chemical and Metallurgical Engineering*, 1944, 51:117.

725) Payne, Stanley L., "Some opinion research principles developed through studies of social medicine," *Public Opinion Quarterly*, 1946, 10:93–98.

726) Pearson, George W., "Prediction in a non-partisan election," *Public Opinion Quarterly*, 1948, 12:112–118.

727) Pearson, Karl, *Tables for Statisticians and Biometricians* (3rd ed.), Cambridge University Press, 1930.

728) Peatman, John Gray, *Descriptive and Sampling Statistics*, Harper, 1947.

729) Peatman, John Gray, "DK's for Truman," *International Journal of Opinion and Attitude Research*, 1948–1949, 2:537–542.

730) Pechanec, J. F., and G. Stewart, "Sagebrush-grass range sampling studies; Size and structure of sampling unit," *Journal of American Society of Agronomy*, 1940, 32:669–682.

731) Peek, R. L., Jr., "Test of an observed difference in the frequency of two results," *Journal of the American Statistical Association*, 1937, 32:532–536.

732) Pemberton, H. Earl, "A technique for determining the optimum rating scale for opinion measures," *Sociology and Social Research*, 1932–1933, 17:470–473.

733) Perry, Harold, "The questionnaire method," *Journal of Applied Sociology*, 1925, 10:155–158.

734) Perry, R., "Putting persuasive power into the questionnaire," *Printers Ink*, 1923, 123:125–164.

735) Peter, P. F., "American listener in 1940," *Annals of American Academy of Political and Social Science*, 1941, 213:1–8.

736) Peters, Charles C., "The individual and his environment," *Review of Educational Research*, 1940, 10:23–29.

737) Pettet, Z. R., "Developments arising out of the trial census in 1938," *Journal of Farm Economics*, 1939, 21:354–355.

738) Phelps, Dudley Maynard, *Marketing Research*, University of Michigan, School of Business Administration, Bureau of Business Research, 1937.

739) Phelps, Harold A., "The case record and scientific method," *The Family*, 1927, 7:103–109.

740) Phelps, Katherine, "A flexible method of hand tabulation," *Journal of Marketing*, 1939, 3:265–269.

741) Phillips, J. B., "Even our best friends tell us; mass observation poll," *Newsweek*, May 19, 1947, 29–50.

742) Phillips, Marjorie, "Problems of questionnaire investigation," *Research Quarterly American Association for Health, Physical Education, and Recreation*, 1941, 12:528–537.

743) Pierce, Walter M., "Climbing on the bandwagon," *Public Opinion Quarterly*, 1940, 4:241–243.

744) Pietra, G., "A particular case of non-representative sampling," *Journal of the American Statistical Association*, 1926, 21:330–332.

745) Poffenberger, Albert T., *Psychology in Advertising*, McGraw-Hill, 1932.

746) Politz, A., "Measuring the size of spot commercial audiences; St. Louis research using double-survey method," *Printers Ink*, April 11, 1947, 219:54.

747) Politz, A., and Willard Simmons, "An attempt to get the not-at-homes into the sample without callbacks," *Journal of the American Statistical Association*, 1949, 44:9–32.

748) Prevette, Earl, *How to Sell by Telephone*, Wilfred Funk, 1941.

749) Psychological Corporation, "Further contributions, 20th anniversary of the Psychological Corporation and to honor its founder," *Journal of Applied Psychology*, 1942, 26:15–17.

750) Psychological Corporation, *Advertising that people remember versus the brands they prefer* (pamphlet), April, 1945.

751) Psychological Corporation, *Psychological Corporation General Clerical Test*, 1945.

752) Quinn, James A., "Community studies in Cincinnati," *Publication of the American Sociological Society*, 1931, 25:143–145.

753) Quinn, James A., "Census population data in community research," *Ohio Social Science Journal*, November, 1932, 4:5–12.

754) Quinn, James A., "Topical summary of current literature on human ecology," *American Journal of Sociology*, 1940, 46:191–226.

755) Rademacher, E. S., "The single interview," *Mental Hygiene*, 1929, 13:81–92.

756) Radvanyi, Laszlo, "Problems of international opinion surveys," *International Journal of Opinion and Attitude Research*, 1947, 1:30–51.

757) Radvanyi, Laszlo (ed.), *International Directory of Opinion and Attitude Research*, Donato Guerra 1 Desp. 207, Mexico, 1948.

758) Ramsey, E. W., "Use of the marginal punch card in tabulating

vital statistics data," *American Journal of Public Health,* 1939, 29:907–909.

759) Ranney, John C., "Do the polls serve democracy?" *Public Opinion Quarterly,* 1946, 10:349–360.

760) Redmayne, Paul, and Hugh Weeks, *Market Research,* Sutterworth, 1931.

761) Reed, Vergil D., *Planned Marketing,* Ronald, 1929.

762) Reeder, Ware G., *How to Write a Thesis,* Public School Publishing Co., 1925.

763) Reid, Seerly, "Respondents and non-respondents to mail questionnaires," *Educational Research Bulletin,* 1942, 21:87–96.

764) Reilly, William J., *Marketing Investigation,* Ronald, 1929.

765) Remmers, H. H., *Studies in Attitudes: A Contribution to Social Psychology Research Methods,* Purdue University, 1934.

766) Remmers, H. H., and E. E. Silance, "Generalized attitude scales," *Journal of Social Psychology,* 1934, 5:298–312.

767) Remmers, H. H., "Purdue opinion poll for young people," *Scientific Monthly,* 1945, 60:292–300.

768) Reuss, C. F., "Differences between persons responding and not responding to a mailed questionnaire," *American Sociological Review,* 1943, 8:433–438.

769) Rhodes, Fred H., *Technical Report Writing,* McGraw-Hill, 1941.

770) Rice, Stuart A., *Quantitative Methods in Politics,* Knopf, 1928.

771) Rice, Stuart A., "Contagious bias in the interview: A methodological note," *American Journal of Sociology,* 1929, 35:420–423.

772) Rice, Stuart A. (ed.), *Statistics in Social Studies,* University of Pennsylvania, 1930.

773) Rice, Stuart A., "Units and their definition in social science," *Social Forces,* 1931, 9:475–478.

774) Rice, Stuart A., *Methods in Social Science,* University of Chicago, 1937.

775) Rice, Stuart A., "Quantitative methods in politics," *Journal of the American Statistical Association,* 1938, 33:126–130.

776) Richards, Edward A., and Edward B. Rubin, *How to Select and Direct the Office Staff,* Harper, 1941.

777) Rickard, T. A., *Technical Writing,* Wiley, 1931.

778) Riesman, David, and Nathan Glazer, "Social structure, character structure, and opinion," *International Journal of Opinion and Attitude Research,* 1948–1949, 2:512–527.

779) Riggleman, John R., *Graphic Methods for Presenting Business Statistics* (2nd ed.), McGraw-Hill, 1936.

780) Riggleman, John R., and I. N. Frisbee, *Business Statistics,* McGraw-Hill, 1938.

781) Riker, B. L., "A comparison of methods used in attitude re-

search," *Journal of Abnormal and Social Psychology*, 1945, 40: 102–103.

782) Riley, John W., Jr., "Opinion Research in Liberated Normandy," *American Sociological Review*, 1947, 12:698–702.

783) Ritchie, Frank, *How to Study your Association and Community*, Association Press, 1926.

784) Rittenburg, Max, *Practical Points in Postal Publicity*, Isaac Pitman, 1927.

785) Robeson, Sophia, *Can Delinquency Be Measured?* Columbia University, 1938.

786) Robinson, Claude E., *Straw-votes: A Study in Political Prediction,* Columbia University, 1932.

787) Robinson, Claude E., "The straw vote," in *Encyclopedia of the Social Sciences,* Macmillan, 1934, 14:417–419.

788) Robinson, Claude E., "Recent developments in the straw-poll field," *Public Opinion Quarterly,* 1937, 1:45–56, 1:42–52.

789) Robinson, Claude E., "Current research of the American Institute of Public Opinion," *Public Opinion Quarterly,* 1938, 2:274–275.

790) Robinson, Claude E., "Pre-election polls in the 1942 elections," *Public Opinion Quarterly,* 1943, 139–144.

791) Robinson, C. S., "The new science of public opinion measurement and its implications for business," *Harvard Business School Alumni Bulletin,* 1939, 3–8.

792) Robinson, D., and S. Rhode, "Two experiments with an antisemitism poll," *Journal of Abnormal Psychology,* 1946, 41:136–144.

793) Robinson, Edgar Eugene, *The Presidential Vote, 1936,* Stanford University, 1940 (supplement to *The Presidential Vote, 1896–1932, 1934*).

794) Robinson, Ray, "Progress in mass-observation," *International Journal of Opinion and Attitude Research,* 1948, 2:369–378.

795) Rogers, Lindsay, *The Pollsters,* Knopf, 1949.

796) Rogers, Lindsay, "Dr. Gallup's statistics," *New Republic,* November 1, 1939, 100:358–359.

797) Rogers, Lindsay, "Do the Gallup polls measure opinion?" *Harpers Magazine,* November, 1941, 623–632.

798) Rollis, Malcolm G., "A practical use of repeated questionnaire waves," *Journal of Applied Psychology,* 1940, 24:770–772.

799) Romine, Stephen, "Criteria for a better questionnaire," *Journal of Educational Research,* 1948, 42:69–72.

800) Root, Alfred R., and Alfred C. Welch, "The continuing consumer study," *Journal of Marketing,* 1942, 7:3–21.

801) Roper, Elmo, "Forecasting election returns," *Review of Reviews,* 1936, 94:58–59.

802) Roper, Elmo, "Three weaknesses of market research," *Market Research,* 1938, 8:16–19.

803) Roper, Elmo, "Wording questions for the polls," *Public Opinion Quarterly,* 1940, 4:129.

804) Roper, Elmo, "Sampling public opinion," *Journal of the American Statistical Association,* 1940, 35:325–334.

805) Roper, Elmo, "Classifying respondents by economic status," *Public Opinion Quarterly,* 1940, 4:270–272.

806) Roper, Elmo, "Checks to increase polling accuracy," *Public Opinion Quarterly,* 1941, 5:87–90.

807) Roper, Elmo, "Sampling technique in surveying occupations," *Occupations,* 1941, 19:504–506.

808) Roper, Elmo, "The Fortune Survey is now aged ten," *Fortune,* 1945, 32:1–263.

809) Roper, Elmo, "New York Elects O'Dwyer," *Public Opinion Quarterly,* 1946, 10:53–56.

810) Roper, Elmo, "Fortune survey; survey pitfalls," *Fortune,* 1947, 35:6.

811) Rorty, James, *Order on the Air,* John Day, 1934.

812) Rosander, A. C., "An attitude scale based upon behavior situations," *Journal of Social Psychology,* 1937, 8:3–16.

813) Rose, A. M., "A research note on experimentation in interviewing," *American Journal of Sociology,* 1945, 51:143–144.

814) Roskelley, R. W., *Attitudes and Overt Behavior; Their Relationship to Each Other and to Selected Factors,* Doctor's Thesis, University of Wisconsin, 1938.

815) Roslow, Sydney, and Albert B. Blankenship, "Phrasing the question in consumer research," *Journal of Applied Psychology,* 1939, 23:612–622.

816) Roslow, Sydney, Wallace H. Wulfeck, and Phillip G. Corbey, "Consumer and opinion research: experimental studies on the form of the question," *Journal of Applied Psychology,* 1940, 24:334–346.

817) Ross, Frank A., "On generalization from limited social data," *Social Forces,* 1931, 10:32–37.

818) Rowntree, B. S., *Poverty, A Study of Town Life,* Macmillan, 1908.

819) Ruch, Floyd L., "Effects of repeated interviewing on the respondent's answers," *Journal of Consulting Psychology,* 1941, 5:179–182.

820) Ruch, Floyd L., *A Research Memorandum on Methods of Studying Public Opinion Reactions to the War,* Social Science Research Council, 1942.

821) Ruch, Floyd L., "Predicting the box office returns of motion pictures," *American Psychologist,* 1946, 1:454 (abstract).

822) Ruckmick, Christian A., "The uses and abuses of the question-naire procedure," *Journal of Applied Psychology*, 1930, 14:32–41.

823) Rudolph, Harold J., *Four Million Inquiries from Magazine Advertising*, Columbia University, 1936.

824) Rugg, Donald, "Experiments in wording questions: II," *Public Opinion Quarterly*, 1941, 5:91–92.

825) Rugg, Donald, and Hadley Cantril, "The wording of questions in public opinion polls," *Journal of Abnormal and Social Psychology*, 1942, 4:469–495.

826) Rundquist, E. A., and R. F. Sletto, *Personality in the Depression*, University of Minnesota, 1936.

827) Rushmore, Elsie M., "How to get results in mail questionnaires," *Printers Ink*, March 22, 1934, 17–21.

828) Sackett, E. S., "Middle towning Peripheryville: Summarization of life in the Canal Zone paralleling the organization of Middletown," *Survey Graphic*, 1936, 25:470–473.

829) Saenger, G. H., "Social status and political behavior," *American Journal of Sociology*, 1945, 51:103–113.

830) Salisbury, Philip, "Eighteen elements of danger in making mail surveys," *Sales Management*, 1938, 42:28, 30, 84, 85.

831) Sarle, Charles Faye, *The theory of sampling as applied to crop estimating; issued for the use of the staff of the Division of crop and livestock estimates*, U. S. Department of Agriculture, Bureau of Agricultural Economics, Division of Crop and Livestock Estimates, 1929.

832) Sarle, Charles Faye, *Adequacy and reliability of crop yield estimates*, U. S. Department of Agriculture Technical Bulletin 311, 1932, 1–39.

833) Sarle, Charles Faye, "Development of partial and sample census methods," *Journal of Farm Economics*, 1939, 21:356–364.

834) Sarle, Charles Faye, "Future improvement in agricultural statistics," *Journal of Farm Economics*, 1939, 21:838–845.

835) Sarle, Charles Faye, *The possibilities and limitations of objective sampling in strengthening agricultural statistics*, U. S. Department of Agriculture, Agricultural Marketing Service, 1939, also in *Econometrica*, 1940, 8:45–61.

836) Saunders, Alta G., and Chester R. Anderson, *Business Reports*, McGraw-Hill, 1929.

837) Sayre, Jeanette, "Progress in radio fan mail analysis," *Public Opinion Quarterly*, 1939, 3:272–278.

838) Sayre, Jeanette, "Comparison of three indices of attitude toward radio advertising," *Journal of Applied Psychology*, 1939, 23:23–33.

839) Scates, Douglas E., "Assumptions underlying research data," *Journal of Educational Research*, 1940, 34:241–254.

840) Scates, Douglas E., and Charles F. Hoban, Jr., "Critical questions for the evaluation of research," *Journal of Educational Research*, 1937, 31:241–254.

841) Schettler, Clarence, "Topical summaries of current literature: Personality traits," *American Journal of Sociology*, 1939, 45:234–258.

842) Schluter, William C., *How To Do Research Work*, Prentice-Hall, 1929.

843) Schmeckebier, Laurence F., *Government Publications and Their Use*, Brookings Institution, 1939.

844) Schmid, Calvin F., *Social Saga of Two Cities*, Minneapolis Council of Social Agencies, Bureau of Social Research, 1937.

845) Schmid, Calvin F., "Theory and practice of planning census tracts," *Sociology and Social Research*, 1938, 22:228–238.

846) Schmid, Calvin F., *Guide to Studies of Social Conditions in the Twin Cities*, Minneapolis Council of Social Agencies, Bureau of Social Research, in cooperation with Works Progress Administration, 1938.

847) Schoenberg, Erika, and Mildred Parten, "Methods and problems of sampling presented by the Urban Study of Consumer Purchases," *Journal of the American Statistical Association*, 1937, 32:311–322.

848) Scholastic, "Public opinion poll, step by step view," *Scholastic*, 1939:35.

849) Scholastic, "Sales are customer's votes: Field of public opinion sampling called consumer research," *Scholastic*, 1939, 35:34.

850) Schreiner, Sam, Jr., "China's first public opinion poll," *Public Opinion Quarterly*, 1943, 7:145–148.

851) Schuler, Edgar A., *Social Status 'and Farm Tenure—Attitudes and Social Conditions of Corn Belt and Cotton Belt Farmers*, U. S. Department of Agriculture, Farm Security Administration, Social Research report 4, 1938.

852) Schuler, Edgar A., and Wayne C. Eubank, "Sampling listener reactions to short-wave broadcasts," *Public Opinion Quarterly*, 1941, 5:260–266.

853) Schultz, T. W., "Scope and method in agricultural economics research: review of bulletins edited by J. D. Black, with reply by J. D. Black," *Journal of Political Economy*, 1939, 47:705–721.

854) Schutz, H. H., "Selection of areas for sample agricultural enumerations, II. Tests of various sampling methods," *Journal of Farm Economics*, 1942, 24:81–95.

855) *Science News Service*, "Study of Radio Audiences," December 18, 1936, 84:31–32.

856) Scripps-Howard Newspapers, "Market records from a home inventory study of buying habits of consumers in 16 cities," Automotive Section, Scripps-Howard Newspapers, 1938.

857) Seashore, R. H., and K. Hevner, "A time-saving device for the construction of attitude scales," *Journal of Social Psychology,* 1933, 4:366–372.

858) Seham, Max, and Ole Schey, "Reliability and validity of the questionnarie method," *Research Quarterly, American Association for Health and Physical Education,* 1934, 5:31–43.

859) Sellers, Marie, "Pre-testing of products by consumer juries," *Journal of Marketing,* 1942, 6:76–80.

860) Sewell, W. H., *The Construction and Standardization of a Scale for the Measurement of the Socio-Economic Status of Oklahoma Farm Families,* Oklahoma Agricultural and Mechanical College, April, 1940, 88 p. (Technical Bulletin No. 9).

861) Sewell, W. H., "A scale for the measurement of farm family socio-economic status," *Southwestern Social Science Quarterly,* 1940, 21:125–137.

862) Seyfried, John E., *Principles and Mechanics of Research: With Emphasis on Term Reports and Theses,* University of New Mexico Bulletin, Education Series, Vol. 9, No. 1, July 1, 1935.

863) Shannon, J. R., "Percentage of returns of questionnaires in reputable educational research," *Journal of Educational Research,* 1948, 42:138–142.

864) Shapiro, S., and J. C. Eberhart, "Interviewer difference in an intensive interview survey," *International Journal of Opinion and Attitude Research,* 1947, 1:1–17.

865) Shaw, Richard, "Public selects cover and title for promotion piece," *Printers Ink,* November 8, 1946, p. 44–45.

866) Shea, Alice Leahy, *The Measurement of Urban Home Environment,* University of Minnesota, 1937.

867) Sheatsley, Paul B., "Some Uses of Interviewing—Report Forms," *Public Opinion Quarterly,* Winter, 1947–1948, 11:601–611.

868) Sheatsley, Paul B., "How Cross-Tabs Can Question Validity," *Public Opinion Quarterly,* Winter, 1947–1948, 11:612–613.

869) Sheatsley, Paul B., "Closed questions sometimes more valid than open," *Public Opinion Quarterly,* 1948, 12:127.

870) Sheatsley, Paul B., "The public relations of the polls," *International Journal of Opinion and Attitude Research,* 1948–1949, 2:453–468.

871) Shryock, Henry S., and Norman Lawrence, "The current status of state and local population estimates in the census bureau," *Journal of the American Statistical Association,* 1949, 44:157–173.

872) Shuttleworth, Frank K., "A study of questionnaire technique," *Journal of Educational Psychology,* 1931, 22:652–658.

873) Shuttleworth, Frank K., "Sampling errors involved in incomplete returns to mail questionnaires," *Journal of Applied Psychology,* 1941, 25:588–591.

874) Sibley, Elbridge, "The size of families, a discussion of sampling," *Journal of the American Statistical Association,* 1926, 21:333–334.

875) Siepmann, Charles, *Radio's Second Chance,* Little, Brown, 1946.

876) Sikes, Allen B., "The continuing study of newspaper audience," *Journal of Marketing,* April, 1942, 6:125–127.

877) Simon, Leslie E., *An Engineer's Manual of Statistical Methods,* Wiley, 1941.

878) Sletto, Raymond F., "Pretesting of questionnaires," *American Sociological Review,* 1940, 5:193–200.

879) Smith, B. O., *Measurement in Education,* Teachers College, Columbia University, 1937.

880) Smith, Bruce L., Harold D. Lasswell, and Ralph D. Casey, *Propaganda, Communication, and Public Opinion: A Comprehensive Reference Guide,* Princeton University, 1946.

881) Smith, Charles W., *Public Opinion in a Democracy,* Prentice-Hall, 1939.

882) Smith, E. Dillon, "Market sampling," *Journal of Marketing,* 1939, 4:45–51.

883) Smith, Elias, and E. A. Suchman, "Do people know why they buy?" *Journal of Applied Psychology,* 1940, 24:673–784.

884) Smith, Francis Ferdinand, "Objectivity as a criterion for estimating the validity of questionnaire data," *Journal of Educational Psychology,* 1935, 26:481–496.

885) Smith, Francis Ferdinand, "Direct validations of questionnaire data," *Educational Administration and Supervision,* 1935, 21:561–575.

886) Smith, G. H., "Note on attitudes and information," *Journal of General Psychology,* 1947, 37:193–197.

887) Smith, G. H., "Liberalism and level of information," *Journal of Educational Psychology,* 1948, 39:65–81.

888) Smith, J. G., and A. J. Duncan, *Sampling Statistics and Applications,* McGraw-Hill, 1945.

889) Smith, John H., Tests of Significance, *What They Mean and How to Use Them,* University of Chicago, 1939.

890) Smith, Mapheus, "A note on stability in questionnaire response," *American Journal of Sociology,* 1933, 38:713–720.

891) Smith, T. V., and Leonard D. White (ed.), *An Experiment in Social Science Research,* University of Chicago, 1929.

892) Snead, Roswell P., "Problems of Field Interviewers," *Journal of Marketing*, 1942, 7:139–145.

893) Snedecor, George W., "Design of sampling experiments in the social sciences," *Journal of Farm Economics*, 1939, 21:846–855.

894) Snedecor, George W., *Statistical Methods, Applied to Experiments in Agriculture and Biology* (3rd ed.), Iowa State College, 1940.

895) Snedecor, George W., and Arnold J. King, "Recent developments in sampling agricultural statistics," *Journal of the American Statistical Association*, 1942, 37:95–102.

896) Social Science Research Council, *Research Method and Procedure in Agricultural Economics* (Advisory Committee on Economics and Social Research in Agriculture, J. D. Black, Chairman), Volumes I, II, 1928.

897) Social Science Research Council, *Government Statistics and Information Services up to 1935,* 1937.

898) Social Science Research Council, *Committee Report on Analysis of Pre-election Polls and Forecasts*, 1948.

899) Social Science Research Council Bulletins, *Research Memoranda on Social Aspects of the Depression* (13 monographs), 1937.

900) Solenberger, Alice Willard, *One Thousand Homeless Men: A Study of Original Records,* Charities Publication Committee, 1911.

901) Spahr, Walter E., and R. J. Swenson, *Methods and Status of Scientific Research*, Harper, 1930.

902) Spencer, Philip, "Pardon me, Madam, how often do you take a bath: a survey of surveys," *Canadian Forum*, 1940, 22:274–276.

903) Spencer, Philip, "We went right to the people: some results of an investigation that probed directly into the minds of the men in the street," *Canadian Forum*, 1941, 20:315–319.

904) Spingarn, J. H., "These public opinion polls, How they work and what they signify," *Harpers Magazine*, 1938, 178:97–104.

905) Stagner, Ross, "The cross out technique as a method in public opinion analysis," *Journal of Social Psychology*, 1940, 11:79–90.

906) Stagner, Ross, "Public opinion polls," *Congressional Record,* May 9, 1941, Vol. 87, p. 3925.

907) Stagner, Ross, "A comparison of the Gallup and Fortune polls regarding American intervention policy," *Sociometry*, 1941, 4:239–258.

908) Stanton, Frank, "Checking the checkers," *Advertising and Selling*, December 19, 1935:24–44.

909) Stanton, Frank, "Factors involved in going on the air," *Journal of Applied Psychology*, 1939, 23:170–187.

910) Stanton, Frank, "Notes on the validity of mail questionnaire returns," *Journal of Applied Psychology*, 1939, 23:95–104.

911) Stanton, Frank, "Problems of sampling in market research," *Journal of Consulting Psychology*, 1941, 5:154–163.

912) Stanton, Frank, and Kenneth Baker, "Interviewer-bias and the recall of incompletely learned materials," *Sociometry*, 1942, 5:123–134.

913) Stapel, J., "Convivial respondent," *Public Opinion Quarterly*, 1947, 11:524–529.

914) Starch, David, "Factors in the reliability of samples," *Journal of the American Statistical Association, Proceedings Supplement*, 1932, 27:190–201.

915) Steiner, Jesse Frederick, *The Social Survey in Community Organization*, Appleton-Century, 1925.

916) Steiner, Jesse Frederick, *The American Community in Action: Case Studies of American Communities*, Holt,\ 1928.

917) Stephan, A., "State and local statistical studies conducted as work relief projects," *Social Forces*, 1934–1935, 13:485–490.

918) Stephan, Frederick F., "Sampling in studies of opinions, attitudes, and consumer wants," *American Philosophical Society Proceedings*, 1948, 92:387–398.

919) Stephan, Frederick F., "Sampling errors and interpretations of social data ordered in time and space," *Journal of the American Statistical Association*, 1934, 29:165–166.

920) Stephan, Frederick F., "Practical problems of sampling procedure," *American Sociological Review*, 1936, 1:569–580.

921) Stephan, Frederick F., "Representative sampling in large scale surveys," *Journal of the American Statistical Association*, 1939, 34:343–352.

922) Stephan, Frederick F., "Weighted proportions and poll reliability," *Public Opinion Quarterly*, 1940, 4:135–136.

923) Stephan, Frederick F., "Stratification in representative sampling," *Journal of Marketing*, 1941, 6:38–47.

924) Stephan, Frederick F., "History of the uses of modern sampling procedures," *Journal of the American Statistical Association*, 1948, 43:12–40.

925) Stephan, Frederick F., and W. Edwards Deming, *Sampling Methods of the 1940 Census*, Technical Bulletin, U. S. Government Printing Office, 1941.

926) Stephan, Frederick F., and Philip J. McCarthy, *Studies in Sampling Under the Committee on Measurement of Opinion, Attitudes, and Consumer Wants*, Social Science Research Council, *Items*, 1947, 1:1–3.

927) Stephan, Frederick F., W. Edwards Deming, and Morris H. Hansen, "The sampling procedure of the 1940 population census," *Journal of the American Statistical Association*, 1940, 35:615–630.

928) Stevenson, B. W., J. R. Spicer, and E. C. Ames, *English in Business and Engineering,* Prentice-Hall, 1938.

929) Stock, J. Stevens, and Lester R. Frankel, "The allocation of samplings among several strata," *Annals of Mathematical Statistics,* 1939, 10:288–293.

930) Stock, J. Stevens, and Joseph R. Hochstim, "Commercial uses of sampling," *Journal of the American Statistical Association,* 1948, 43:509–523.

931) Stoddard, George D., "Observational method," *Review of Educational Research,* 1934, 4:65–66.

932) Stoke, Stuart M., and Harvey C. Lehman, "The influence of self interest on questionnaire replies," *School and Society,* 1930, 32:435–438.

933) Stonborough, Thomas H. W., "Fixed panels in consumer research," *Journal of Marketing,* 1942, 7:129–138.

934) Stone, Abigal, "Efficiency of national samples having the county as a sampling unit," Master's Thesis, Iowa State College, 1946.

935) Stouffer, Samuel A., "Sociology and Sampling," Chapter XVI in *The Fields and Methods of Sociology,* L. L. Bernard, ed., Farrar and Rinehart, 1934.

936) Stouffer, Samuel A., "Statistical induction in rural social research," *Social Forces,* 1935, 13:505–515.

937) Stouffer, Samuel A., "Government and the measurement of opinion," *Scientific Monthly,* 1946, 63:435–440.

938) Stouffer, Samuel A., and Paul Lazarsfeld, *Research Memorandum on the Family in the Depression,* Social Science Research Council, Bulletin 29, 1937.

939) Strang, Ruth M., "The interview," *Review of Educational Research,* 1939, 9:498–501, 607–608.

940) Strang, Ruth M., "Methodology in the study of propaganda and attitudes relating to war," *School and Society,* 1941, 54:334–339.

941) Studenski, P., "How polls can mislead," *Harpers Magazine,* 1939, 180:80–83.

942) Suchman, Edward A., and Louis Guttman, "A solution to the problem of question bias," *Public Opinion Quarterly,* 1947, 11:445–455.

943) Suchman, Edward A., and Boyd McCandless, "Who answers questionnaires?" *Journal of Applied Psychology,* 1940, 24:758–769.

944) "Survey of Consumer Finances," *Monthly Labor Review,* 1948, 67:515–517.

945) Swineford, Frances, "Graphical and tabular aids for determining sample size when planning experiments which involve comparisons of percentages," *Psychometrika,* 1946, 11:43–49.

946) Swineford, Frances, "A table for estimating the significance of the difference between correlated percentages," *Psychometrika*, 1948, 13:23–25.

947) Symonds, Percival M., "On the loss of reliability in rating due to coarseness of the scale," *Journal of Experimental Psychology*, 1924, 7:456–460.

948) Symonds, Percival M., *Diagnosing Personality and Conduct*, Appleton-Century, 1931.

949) Symonds, Percival M., *Psychological Diagnosis and Social Adjustment*, American Book, 1934,

950) Symonds, Percival M., "Securing rapport in interviewing," *Teachers College Record*, 1938, 39:707–722.

951) Symonds, Percival M., "Research on the interviewing process," *Journal of Educational Psychology*, 1939, 30:346–353.

952) Taylor, Carl C., *The Social Survey, Its History and Methods*, Bulletin Vol. 20, No. 28, Social Science Series No. 30, University of Missouri, 1919.

953) Taylor, Carl C., "The social survey and the science of sociology," *American Journal of Sociology*, 1920, 25:731–756.

954) Tepping, B. J., W. N. Hurwitz, and W. E. Deming, "Efficiency of deep stratification in block sampling," *Journal of the American Statistical Association*, 1943, 38:93–100.

955) Terris, Fay, "Are poll questions too difficult?" *Public Opinion Quarterly*, 1949, 13:314–320.

956) Thomas, Dorothy Swaine, et al., *Observational Studies of Social Behavior*, Yale University, 1933.

957) Thomas-Baines, D. M., "The construction and evaluation of a scale to measure attitudes toward any proposed social action," Purdue University, *Studies in Higher Education*, 1936, 37:252–258.

958) Thompson, Karl Owen, *Technical Exposition*, Harper, 1922.

959) Thomson, Charles A. H., "Public relations of the 1940 census," *Public Opinion Quarterly*, 1940, 4:311–318.

960) Thorndike, Edward, *Teachers Word Book of 20,000 Words Found Most Frequently and Widely in General Reading for Children and Young People*, Teachers College, Columbia University, 1932.

961) Thorndike, Edward L., "How we spend our time and what we spend it for," *Scientific Monthly*, 1937, 44:464–469.

962) Thurstone, L. L., "The measurement of social attitudes," *Journal of Abnormal and Social Psychology*, 1931, 26:249–269.

963) Thurstone, L. L., and E. J. Chave, *The Measurement of Attitudes*, University of Chicago, 1929.

964) *Tide*, "Gallup Abroad," August 15, 1945, 19:112–114.

965) *Tide*, "Leadership Survey," January 7, 1949.

966) Tippett, Leonard Henry Caleb, *Random Sampling Numbers, Tracts for Computers,* No. XV, ed. by Karl Pearson.

967) Toops, Herbert A., "Validating the questionnaire method," *Journal of Personnel Research,* 1923, 2:153–169.

968) Toops, Herbert A., "The returns from follow-up letters to questionnaires," *Journal of Applied Psychology,* 1926, 10:92–101.

969) Toops, Herbert A., "Predicting the returns from questionnaires, a study in the utilization of qualitative data," *Journal of Experimental Education,* 1935, 3:204–215.

970) Toops, Herbert A., "Questionnaire construction and analysis," Chapter I, Part V in *Practical Applications of the Punched Card Method in Colleges and Universities,* G. W. Baehne (ed.), Columbia University, 1935, 177–204.

971) Toops, Herbert A., "The factor of mechanical arrangement and typography in questionnaires," *Journal of Applied Psychology,* 1937, 21:225–229.

972) Trelease, S. F., and E. S. Yule, *Preparation of Scientific and Technical Papers,* Williams & Wilkins, 1925.

973) Truesdell, Leon E., "The mechanics of the tabulation of the population census," *Journal of American Statistical Association,* 1935, 30:89–94.

974) Truesdell, Leon E., "Residual relationships and velocity of changes as pitfalls in the field of statistical forecasting," *Journal of the American Statistical Association,* 1938, 33:373–379.

975) Truesdell, Leon E., "New features of the 1940 population census," *Journal of the American Statistical Association,* 1941, 36:361–369.

976) Tryon, Robert C., "Psychological basis of errors in the Gallup election polls," *Psychological Bulletin,* 1941, 38:371, abstract.

977) Turbeville, G., and R. E. Hyde, "Selected sample of attitudes of Louisiana State University students toward the negro: a study in public opinion," *Social Forces,* 1946, 24:447–450.

978) Udow, Alfred B., *The Interviewer-Effect in Public Opinion and Market Research Surveys,* Archives of Psychology, No. 277, 1942.

979) United Nations, Sub-Commission on statistical sampling, *A Brief Statement on the Uses of Sampling in Censuses of Population, Agriculture, Public Health, and Commerce.* By W. Edwards Deming, United Nations Publication Sales number 1948, XVII, No. 1, Lake Success, February, 1948.

980) United Nations Statistical Office, *The Preparation of Sampling Survey Reports,* Statistical papers, Series C. No. 1, Lake Success, January 1949.

981) U. S. Department of Agriculture, Bureau of Agricultural Eco-

nomics, *Conferences on Statistical Methods of Sampling Agricultural Data,* Proceedings of Conference, 1936.

982) U. S. Department of Agriculture, Bureau of Agricultural Economics, *The Preparation of Statistical Tables, A Handbook,* 1937.

983) U. S. Department of Agriculture, Bureau of Agricultural Economics, *Research in Sample Farm Census Methodology: Part I Comparative Statistical Efficiency of Sampling Units Smaller Than the Minor Civil Divisions for Estimating Year to Year Change,* Agricultural Marketing Service, 1939.

984) U. S. Department of Agriculture, Bureau of Agricultural Economics, Division of Program Surveys, Morale Division, *Interviewing Manual,* Washington, D. C., 1945.

985) U. S. Department of Agriculture, Bureau of Home Economics, *Comparison of Schedule and Account Methods of Collecting Data on Family Living,* Technical Bulletin, 386, Government Printing Office, 1933.

986) U. S. Department of Agriculture, Bureau of Home Economics, *Consumer Purchases Reports for Farms, Villages and Small Cities,* Government Printing Office, 1939–1941.

987) U. S. Department of Agriculture, Census of 1935, *Technique of Tabulation,* Descriptive Supplement, Government Printing Office, 1937.

988) U. S. Department of Agriculture, Surplus Marketing Administration, Fruit and Vegetable Division, *Style Manual for the Preparation of Statistical Tables,* August, 1941 (processed).

989) U. S. Department of Commerce, Bureau of the Census, *The Story of the Census,* Government Printing Office, 1915.

990) U. S. Department of Commerce, Bureau of the Census, *Topical Index of Population Census Reports, 1900–1930,* 1934.

991) U. S. Department of Commerce, Bureau of the Census, *Alphabetical Index of Occupations by Industries and Social-Economic Groups,* Government Printing Office, 1937.

992) U. S. Department of Commerce, Bureau of the Census, *Census Tracts in American Cities,* by Howard W. Green and Leon E. Truesdell, 1937.

993) U. S. Department of Commerce, Bureau of the Census, *Unemployment Statistics, Census of partial employment, unemployment and occupations* (4 vols.), 1937.

994) U. S. Department of Commerce, Bureau of the Census, *Alphabetical Index of Occupations and Industries, Sixteenth Census of the United States, 1940,* Government Printing Office, 1940.

995) U. S. Department of Commerce, Bureau of the Census, *Classified Index of Occupations, Sixteenth Census of the United*

States 1940 (prepared by Alba M. Edwards), Government Printing Office, 1940.

996) U. S. Department of Commerce, Bureau of the Census, *Instructions to Enumerators: Population, and Agriculture* (Form Pa-1), *Instructions to Enumerators: Housing* (Form Hc-1) Government Printing Office, 1940.

997) U. S. Department of Commerce, Bureau of the Census, *Population: Abridged Instructions to Enumerators, 16th Decennial Census of United States*, 1940.

998) U. S. Department of Commerce, Bureau of the Census, *Population: Index of Data Tabulated from 1930 Census of Population including Unemployment*, 1940.

999) U. S. Department of Commerce, Bureau of the Census, *Key to the Published and Tabulated Data for Small Areas, Populaulation-Housing-Business-Manufactures-Agriculture, Sixteenth Census of the United States: 1940* (Prepared under supervision of Calvert L. Dedrick).

1000) U. S. Department of Commerce, Bureau of the Census, *Coding Instructions for the Population Schedule*, Government Printing Office, 1940.

1001) U. S. Department of Commerce, "Bureau of the Census," pp. 37–60 in *Annual Report of the Secretary of Commerce, 1940*, Government Printing Office, 1941.

1002) U. S. Department of Commerce, Bureau of the Census, *Sixteenth Census of the United States, 1940*, Government Printing Office. See *Catalog of the Sixteenth Decennial Census Publications*.

POPULATION PUBLICATIONS (1940 census).

VOLUME I. *Number of Inhabitants*: Total population for states, counties, and minor civil divisions; for urban and rural areas; for incorporated places; for metropolitan districts; and for census tracts.

VOLUME II. *Characteristics of the Population*: Sex, age, race, nativity, country of birth of foreign-born white; school attendance, education, employment status; class of worker, major occupational group and industry group.

VOLUME III. *The Labor Force*: Occupation, industry, employment and income. Other subjects included are class of worker, hours worked during census week, and duration of employment.

SPECIAL REPORTS Those below are selected from a long list:

Internal Migration, 1935–1940.

Nativity and Parentage of the White Population
General Characteristics, age, marital status, and education for states and large cities.

Country of Origin of the Foreign stock—by nativity, citizenship, age, and value or rent of home, for states and large cities (112 pages).

Mother Tongue—by nativity, country of origin and age, for states and large cities.

Educational Attainment of Children—by Rental Value of Homes.

The Labor Force (Sample Statistics)

Employment and personal characteristics

Employment and family characteristics of women

Wage or salary income 1939

Industrial characteristics

Occupational characteristics

Characteristics of persons not in the labor force, 14 years old and over by age, sex, household relationship, months worked in 1939, usual major occupation group.

Characteristics by Age; marital status, relationship, education, and citizenship. Also includes limited data on employment status classified by age.

Series P-10—*Summary Statistics* of the United States based on second series of population data.

Series P-14—*Labor Force,* income, occupation releases based on a five per cent sample tabulation.

Series P-15—*General Population*—Releases based on a five per cent sample tabulation.

Bureau of the Census—Sixteenth Decennial Census

HOUSING PUBLICATIONS—1940 Census.

VOLUME I. *Data for small areas.*—Selected housing statistics for states, counties, and minor civil divisions; for urban and rural areas; for incorporated places; and for metropolitan districts.

VOLUME II. *General Characteristics.*—Occupancy and tenure status, value of home or monthly rental; size of household; and race of head; type of structure; exterior material; year built; conversion; state of repair; number of rooms; housing facilities and equipment; and mortgage status.

VOLUME III. *Characteristics by Monthly Rent or Value.*—Type and age of structure, state of repair, number of rooms, size of household, race of head, persons per room, facilities and mortgage status.

VOLUME IV. *Mortgages on Owner-Occupied Non farm Homes*—First mortgages by amount outstanding, type of payment, frequency and amount of payment, interest rate, and holder of mortgage; value of property, estimated rental value, year built, color of occupants.

First Series Housing Supplements:

A series of bulletins one for each of the 191 cities which in 1930 had a population of 50,000 or more, showing selected housing statistics for the city by blocks. Each bulletin includes a map of the given city by blocks.

Analytical Maps Block Statistics A series of bulletins for each city of 100,000 inhabitants or more, comprising sets of analytical maps presenting in graphic form various housing characteristics, in different areas of the city. Includes map for average rent, major repairs, bathing equipment, year built, non-white households, persons per room, owner occupancy, and mortgage status. (Prepared by the New York City W.P.A. War Services and the Bureau of the Census.)

Special Reports on housing:

Series H-5 Summary Statistics for the United States based on first and second series housing data.

Series H-13 Summary Statistics for the United States based on second series housing data: radios, heating, refrigeration, fuels, persons per room.

Population and Housing

Series PH-3 General Population and Housing Statistics.

Series PH-4 Families—General Characteristics

Statistics for Census Tracts: 58 bulletins covering 60 tracted cities and adjacent tracted areas if any. Population data: sex, age, race, nativity, citizenship, country of birth, education, employment status, class of worker and occupation; Housing; occupancy, tenure, value or rent, type of structure, race of household head, persons per room, size of household, state of repair and plumbing equipment, radio, refrigerator, and heating fuel by type of heating.

1003) U. S. Department of Commerce, Bureau of the Census

Population—Special Reports

Series P-44 No. 4 Map showing changes in civilian population of the U. S. by counties, April 1, 1940 to November 1, 1943.

Series P-140b. Supplement

How to List, Current Population Survey, September 1948.

Series P-46 No. 3 Estimated Population of the United States, by States, 1940, 1945.

Series P-46 No. 8 Composition of Families in the United States at the end of the war in Europe, May 1945.

Series P-S *Report No. 5* Reliability of Sampling Estimates.

Report No. 13   Characteristics of Families in the United
   States, February, 1946.
Report No. 14   Migration of Families in the United
   States, April 1940 to February 1946.
Report No. 15   Characteristics of Secondary Families in
   the U. S., February 1946, 9 pages.
Report No. 16   Marital Status of the Civilian population
   and Heads of Families, June 1946, 7 pages.
Report No. 19   Urban and Rural Population of the
   United States, by Age and Sex, 1946, 1945, and 1940,
   3 pages.
Series P-H   Vet. Report numbers 95–113 November and De-
   cember 1946 on housing of veterans.
List of Schedules used by the Bureau of the Census for Col-
   lecting Data, 1946.
Series P-47   *Report No. 3*   Estimated Population of the
   United States by Age, Color and Sex, 1940–1946, 8
   pages.
Report No. 4   Suggested Procedures for Estimating the
   Current Population of Counties, 6 pages.
Series P-MRLF   Monthly report on the Labor Force (to June
   1947 then changed to
Series P-LF   Current Population Statistics—Labor Force).
   Series P-MRLF No. 57-S   Sampling Variability of Estimates
   of the MLRF, a supplement, February 2–8, 1947, 4 pages.
Series P-SC   Special Census of specified areas 1947. Final Figures for certain large cities and metropolitan districts, current information on population characteristics, employment,
   unemployment, and related subjects.
1004) U. S. Department of Commerce, Bureau of the Census, The
   Sampling Staff, *A Chapter in Population Sampling,* Government Printing Office, 1947.
1005) U. S. Department of Commerce, Bureau of the Census—for
   current publications see:
   1. *Catalog* published annually and lists current census pub-
      lications.
   2. *List of Publications*   Issued monthly. It lists special pub-
      lications, reports issued in a series at irregular intervals
      and regular publications issued less frequently than quar-
      terly.
   3. *Subject Guide*   Issued quarterly. It is a classified guide
      to contents of all publications issued to date during the
      year.
1006) U. S. Department of Commerce, Bureau of Foreign and Domestic Commerce, *The Real Property Inventory, 1934,* Gov-

ernment Printing Office, 1935 (reports for 64 cities and general summary).

1007) U. S. Department of Commerce, Bureau of Foreign and Domestic Commerce, *Suggestions for Use in Making a City Survey,* 1938.

1008) U. S. Department of Commerce, Bureau of Foreign and Domestic Commerce, *Results of Test Operations of Audimeters in radio homes,* December, 1940, Business Information Service (processed).

1009) U. S. Department of the Interior, Office of Education, *Youth Community Surveys,* by Charles Arthur Jessen and H. C. Hutchins, Bulletin 18, pt. 6, Government Printing Office, 1936, 1–97.

1010) U. S. Department of Labor, Bureau of Labor Statistics, *Study of Consumer Purchases: Bulletins 642–649,* Government Printing Office, 1938–1940.

1011) U. S. Department of State, *Style Manual of the U. S. Department of State,* by Margaret Hanna and Alice M. Ball, Government Printing Office, 1937.

1012) U. S. Executive Office of the President, Bureau of the Budget, *Convertibility List of Occupations for Reports from Individuals,* 1940, 55 pp.

1013) U. S. Federal Housing Administration, *A Technique for a Real Property Survey* (Federal Housing Administration, prepared jointly with Central Statistical Board and Works Progress Administration), 1935.

1014) U. S. Federal Housing Administration, *Technique for Real Estate Activity Surveys* (prepared jointly by the Federal Housing Administration, the Central Statistical Board, and the Works Progress Administration), 1937.

1015) U. S. Government Printing Office, *Weekly List of Selected U. S. Government Publications* (issued weekly and contains more important government publications for sale).

1016) U. S. Government Printing Office, United States Government Publications, *Monthly Catalog* (issued monthly since 1895).

1017) U. S. Government Printing Office, *1940 Census: Hearings Before the Sub-Committee of the Committee on Commerce, U. S. Senate, 76th Congress, 3rd Session,* Government Printing Office, 1940.

1018) U. S. Government Printing Office, *Style Manual,* Division of Publications.

1019) U. S. Housing Authority, *Plan for the Study of Housing of Low Income Families,* 1937.

1020) U. S. Library of Congress, *List of American Doctoral Dissertations,* U. S. Government Printing Office (issued annually, giving author and title of all doctoral dissertations in all universities and colleges in the United States).

1021) U. S. National Resources Committee, *Consumer Incomes in the United States: Their Distribution in 1935–36*, U. S. Government Printing Office, 1938.

1022) U. S. National Resources Committee, *Consumer Expenditure in the United States: Estimates for 1935–36*, U. S. Government Printing Office, 1939.

1023) U. S. National Resources Committee, *Research: A National Resource*, Government Printing Office, 1939, (pamphlet).

1024) U. S. Public Health Service, Division of Public Health Methods, National Institute of Health, *The National Health Survey, 1935–36*, 1938.

1025) U. S. Social Security Board, Social Security *Bulletins*, Government Printing Office (bulletins issued monthly by Bureau of Research and Statistics, carry current statistical material).

1026) U. S. Social Security Board, Bureau of Research and Statistics, *Plan for a Case Census of Recipients of Public Assistance*, Bureau Report No. 2, 1938.

1027) U. S. Social Security Board, Bureau of Research and Statistics, *Family Composition in the United States*, Social Security Bulletin, April, 1939, 2, No. 4:9–13.

1028) U. S. Works Progress Administration, *Migrant Families*, by John N. Webb and Malcolm Brown, Research Monograph 18, Government Printing Office, 1938.

1029) U. S. Works Progress Administration, *Technique for a Real Property Survey*, 1938 (*Tabulation instructions for dwelling survey*, Reissue of Volume II of *Technique for a Real Property Survey* issued by Federal Housing Administration).

1030) U. S. Works Progress Administration, Division of Social Research, *Urban Housing: A Summary of Real Property Inventories Conducted as Work Projects, 1934–36*, Government Printing Office, 1938.

1031) U. S. Work Projects Administration, *Rural Families*, by Carle C. Zimmerman and Nathan L. Whetten, Research Monograph 17, Government Printing Office, 1938.

1032) U. S. Works Progress Administration, *Index of Research Projects, 1938–1939*, by Harold Hosea.

1033) U. S. Works Progress Administration, Division of Social Research, *Low Income Housing Area Survey*, 1939.

1034) U. S. Work Projects Administration, *Catalog of Research and Statistical Publications*, January, 1940.

1035) University of Chicago, *A Manual of Style* (10th ed.), 1937.

1036) Updegraff, Harlan, *Inventory of Youth in Pennsylvania*, American Youth Commission of the American Council on Education, 1936.

1037) Updegraff, R. R., "Democracy's new mirror: How public opinion polls afford a new check on Congressional action," *Forum*, 1940, 103:11–14.

1038) Van Kleek, M., "The interview as a method of research," *Taylor Society Bulletin*, 1926, 11:268–274.

1039) Vernon, Raymond, "Predetermining the necessary size, of sample in marketing studies," *Journal of Marketing*, 1937, 2:9–12.

1040) Vetter, G. B., "The study of social and political opinions," *Journal of Abnormal and Social Psychology*, 1930, 25:26–29.

1041) Vicary, James M., "Word association and opinion research," *Public Opinion Quarterly*, 1948, 12:81–99.

1042) Vickery, C. W., "Punched card technique for the correction of bias in sampling," *Journal of the American Statistical Association*, 1938, 33:552–556.

1043) Vickery, C. W., "On drawing a random sample from a set of punched cards," *Supplement to the Journal of the Royal Statistical Society*, 1939, 6:62–66.

1044) Waggoner, Frank H., *Premium Advertising as a Selling Force*, Harper, 1939.

1045) Wagner, Isabella F., "Articulate and inarticulate replies to questionnaires," *Journal of Applied Psychology*, 1939, 23:104–115.

1046) Wagner, Isabella F., and M. Erb, "Program preferences of different groups," *Journal of Applied Psychology*, 1939, 23:187–192.

1047) Wald, Abraham, *Sequential Analysis*, Wiley, 1947.

1048) Walker, Helen M., "Testing a statistical hypothesis," *Harvard Educational Review*, 1939, 9:229–240.

1049) Walker, Helen M., *Elementary Statistics*, Holt, 1944.

1050) Walker, Helen M., and Walter M. Durost, *Statistical Tables, Their Structure and Use*, Columbia University, 1936.

1051) Walker, Helen M., et al., "The sampling problem in educational research," *Teachers' College Record*, 1929, 30:760–774.

1052) Walker, Kirby P., "Examining personal information items of a questionnaire study," *Journal of Educational Research*, 1937, 31:281–282.

1053) Walker, R. F., "When the housewife meets you at the door with fire in her eyes," *Sales Management*, February 1, 1938, 42:29–30, 61.

1054) *Wall Street Journal*, "Audience Research Techniques," October 25, 1945.

1055) Wallace, Henry A., and James L. McCamy, "Straw polls and public administration," *Public Opinion Quarterly*, 1940, 4:221–223.

1056) Wallace, J. M., Jr., F. W. Williams, and H. Cantril, "Identification of occupational groups with economic and social class," *Journal of Abnormal and Social Psychology*, 1944, 39:482–485.

1057) Warner, Lucien, "The reliability of public opinion surveys," Yale University Press, *Public Opinion Quarterly*, 1939, 3:376–390.

1058) Warner, W. L., and P. S. Lunt, *Yankee City Series*, Volume I–IV, Yale University Press, 1941–1947.

1059) Washington Public Opinion Laboratory, *Validation*, University of Washington, Seattle, Bul. 1, Section C, April 1948.

1060) Watson, Alfred N., "Use of small area census data in marketing analysis," *The Journal of Marketing*, 1942, 6:42–47.

1061) Watson, Alfred N., *Respondent Pre-Selection. A Statistical Method of Reducing Interviewer Bias in Market Surveys*, Curtis Publishing Co., 1946.

1062) Watson, Alfred N., *Respondent Pre-Selection Within Sample Area. A Statistical Method of Selecting Individuals at Random*, Curtis Publishing Co., 1947.

1063) Watson, J. "Study in urban conversation, sample of 1,001 remarks overhead in Manhattan," *Journal of Social Psychology*, 1948, 28:121–133.

1064) Watson, Richmond, "Investigations by mail," *Market Research*, 1937, 5:11–16.

1065) Weaver, Henry G., "Consumer questionnaire technique," *American Marketing Journal*, 1934, 1:115.

1066) Weaver, Henry G., "Proving ground on public opinion," *Journal of Consulting Psychology*, 1941, 5:149–153.

1067) Weaver, Leon, "How valid is public opinion?" *Social Forces*, 1942, 20:341–344.

1068) Weaver, Otis T., *Estimating the Reliability of a Small Sample (Less than 30) Taken from a Large Universe*, U. S. Department of Agriculture, Bureau of Agricultural Economics, Division of Cotton Marketing, 1932 (processed).

1069) Weaver, S. M., "Public opinion by post card," *Public Management*, 1939, 21:138–140.

1070) Webb, J. N., M. S. Northrup, and S. L. Payne, "Practical applications of theoretical sampling methods," *Journal of the American Statistical Association*, 1943, 38:69–77.

1071) Webb, Sidney, and Beatrice, *Methods of Social Study*, Longmans, Green, 1932.

1072) Wechsler, James, "Polling America," *The Nation*, January 20, 1940, 150:64–67.

1073) Wechsler, James, "Interviews and interviewers," *Public Opinion Quarterly*, 1940, 4:258–260.
1074) Welch, E. H., "Measuring our manpower," *Domestic Commerce*, 1946, 34:13–16.
1075) Weld, L. D. H., "Those election straw votes," *Printers Ink*, November 12, 1936, 177:6–8, 121–183.
1076) Weld, L. D. H., "The problem of measuring radio coverage," *Journal of the American Statistical Association*, 1938, 33:117–125.
1077) Wells, A. F., *The Local Social Survey in Great Britain*, Allen and Unwin, 1935.
1078) Wells, A. F., "Social surveys and sociology," *Sociological Review*, 1936, 28:274–294.
1079) Wheeler, Ferdinand C., "New methods and results in market research," *American Marketing Journal*, 1935, 35–39.
1080) Whelpton, P. K., and Clyde V. Kiser, "The completeness and accuracy of the household survey of Indianapolis," *Milbank Memorial Fund Quarterly*, 1945, 23:254–296.
1081) Whelpton, P. K., and Clyde V. Kiser, "Social and Psychological Factors Affecting Fertility," *Milbank Memorial Fund Quarterly*, 1946, 24:49–93.
1082) Whelpton, P. K., and Clyde V. Kiser, *Social and Psychological Factors Affecting Fertility, Vol. 1, The Household Survey*, Milbank Memorial Fund, 1946.
1083) Whisler, L. D., "Reliability of scores on attitude scales as related to scoring method," *Purdue University Studies in Higher Education*, 1938, 38:126–129.
1084) White, Clyde, *Social Statistics*, Harper, 1933.
1085) White, Percival, *Marketing Research Technique*, Harper, 1931.
1086) Whiteley, R. L., "Interviewing the problem boy," *Journal of Educational Sociology*, 1930, 3:326–340; 1931, 5:89–100; 1931, 5:140–151.
1087) Whitney, F. P., "Questionnaire craze," *Educational Review*, 1924, 68:139–140.
1088) Whitney, Frederick L., *The Organization, Scope, and Cost of a Department of Research, Ninth Yearbook*, The American Association of Teachers Colleges, National Education Association, 1930.
1089) Whitney, Frederick L., *The Elements of Research*, Prentice-Hall, 1937.
1090) Wilder, Frances F., *Radio's Daytime Serial*, Columbia Broadcasting System, 1945.
1091) Wilks, Samuel Stanley, "Representative sampling and poll reliability, *Public Opinion Quarterly*, 1940, 4:261–269.

1092) Wilks, Samuel Stanley, "Confidence limits and critical differences between percentages," *Public Opinion Quarterly*, 1940, 4:332–338.

1093) Willcock, H. D., "Mass observation," *American Journal of Sociology*, 1943, 48:445–446.

1094) Willcox, Walter F., "Census," in the *Encyclopaedia of the Social Sciences*, 3:295–300.

1095) Williams, Cecil B., and A. H. Stevenson, *A Research Manual*, Harper, 1940.

1096) Williams, Douglas, "Basic instructions for interviewers," *Public Opinion Quarterly*, 1942, 6:635 f.

1097) Williams, Frederic, "Polling postwar issues," *Journal of Consulting Psychology*, 1946, 10:35–44.

1098) Williams, Frederic, and Hadley Cantril, "The use of interviewing rapport as a method of detecting differences between 'public' and 'private' opinion," *Journal of Social Psychology*, 1945, 22:171–175.

1099) Williams, J. H., *A Scale for Grading Neighborhood Conditions*, Bulletin No. 5, 1917, Whittier State School, Whittier, California.

1100) Williams, J. N., *A Guide to the Grading of Homes*, Bulletin No. 7, 1918, Whittier State School, Whittier, California.

1101) Willoughby, William F., "A program for research in political science," *American Political Science Review*, 1933, 27:1–23.

1102) Wilson, Charles Morrow, *Money at the Crossroads*, Columbia Broadcasting Company, 1937.

1103) Wilson, Edwin B., "Statistical inference," *Science*, 1926, 63:1–8, 289–296.

1104) Wilson, Edwin B., "What is statistics?" *Science*, 1927, 65:581–587.

1105) Wilson, Edwin B., "Mathematics and statistics," *Journal of the American Statistical Association*, 1930, 25:1–8.

1106) Wilson, Edwin B., "How to study the social aspects of the depression," *Journal of the American Statistical Association*, 1938, 33:505–512.

1107) Wilson, Edwin B., "Methodology in the natural and the social sciences," *American Journal of Sociology*, 1940, 655.

1108) Wilson, Edwin B., "Controlled experiment and the four-fold table," *Science*, 1941, 93:557–560.

1109) Wilson, E. C., "Measurement of public opinion," *Annals of the American Academy of Political and Social Science*, 1947, 250:121–129.

1110) Wilson, P. W., "Question of questionnaires," *North American Review*, 1934, 237:325–330.

1111) Wingate, John W., "A consumer survey of the New York market," *Journal of Retailing*, April, 1934, 5:5–12.

1112) Winslow, H. J., "Sampling technique for obtaining number of covered workers under state unemployment compensation laws," *Social Security Bulletin*, August, 1940, 3–9.

1113) Wirth, Louis (ed.), *Eleven Twenty-Six: A Decade of Social Science Research*, University of Chicago, 1940.

1114) Wolfe, C. H., "Radio Audience Measurement: coincidental, mechanical recorder, recall, diary-methods," *Advertising and Selling*, 1948, 41:37–38.

1115) Wolfe, Harry Deane, "Techniques of appraising brand preference and brand consciousness by consumer interviewing," *Journal of Marketing*, 1942, 6:81–87.

1116) Womer, S. S., "What 'they' think of the two leading methods of measuring radio," *Printers' Ink*, February, 1940, 73–74.

1117) Wood, Ben D., "The reliability of prediction of proportions on the basis of random sampling," *Journal of Educational Research*, 1921, 4:390–395.

1118) Wood, Richardson, "How the Fortune survey is conducted," *Fortune*, October, 1935:58.

1119) Wood, Richardson, "Public Opinion Surveys," *Encyclopaedia Britannica*, 1946.

1120) Woodward, J. L., "Public opinion polls as an aid to democracy," *Political Science Quarterly*, 1946, 61:238–246.

1121) Woodward, J. L., and Raymond Franzen, "A study of coding reliability," *Public Opinion Quarterly*, 1948, 12:253–257.

1122) Woodworth, R. S., "Psychological experience with the interview," *Journal of Personnel Research*, 1925, 4:162–165.

1123) Woofter, T. J., Jr., "Common errors in sampling," *Social Forces*, 1933, 11:521–525.

1124) Wrenn, C. Gilbert, "The interview," *Review of Educational Research*, 1939, 9:201–204.

1125) Wright, John Kirtland (ed.), *Notes on Statistical Mapping with Special Reference to the Mapping of Population Phenomena*, American Geographical Society, 1938.

1126) Wrightstone, J. W., *Wrightstone's Scale of Civic Beliefs*, World Book, 1938.

1127) Wulfeck, Wallace H., "A new application of survey technique to the study of public attitudes toward contribution and social agencies," *Journal of Applied Psychology*, 939:25.

1128) Wulfeck, Wallace H., "The role of the psychologist in market and advertising research," *Journal of Applied Psychology*, 1945, 29:2, 95–102.

1129) Wyant, Rowena, "Voting via the Senate mailbag," *Public Opinion Quarterly*, 1941, 5:359–382.

1130) Wylie, A. T., "To what extent may we rely upon the answers to a school questionnaire?" *Journal of Educational Method*, 1927, 6:252–257.

1131) Yates, F., "Some examples of biased sampling," *Annals of Eugenics*, 1935, 36:202–213.

1132) Yates, F., "Review of recent statistical developments in sampling and sampling surveys; methods of estimating sampling error with discussion," *Journal of the Royal Statistical Society*, 1946, 109:12–43.

1133) Yoder, Dale, D. G. Paterson, H. G. Heneman, C. H. Stone, et al. *Local Labor Market Research*, University of Minnesota Press, 1949.

1134) Young, Donald, "A note on procedure in the planning of research," *American Journal of Sociology*, 1936, 42:95–99.

1135) Young, Kimball, John Lewis Gillen, and Calvert L. Dedrick, *The Madison Community*, University of Wisconsin Studies in the Social Sciences and History, No. 21, 1934.

1136) Young, Pauline V., *Interviewing in Social Work*, McGraw-Hill, 1936.

1137) Young, Pauline V., *Scientific Social Surveys and Research*, Prentice-Hall, 1939.

1138) Young, Pauline V., "The validity of schedules and questionnaires," *Journal of Educational Sociology*, 1940, 14:22–26.

1139) Yule, George U., "A test of Tippett's random sampling numbers," *Journal of the Royal Statistical Society*, 1938, 101:167–172.

1140) Yule, George U., *Introduction to the Theory of Statistics* (12th ed., revised), Lippincott, 1940.

1141) Zeisel, Hans, *Say It with Figures*, Harper, 1947.

1142) Zeisel, Hans, "Coordinating the measurements of radio listening," *Journal of the American Statistical Association*, 1947, 42:512–523.

1143) Zeligs, Rose, and Gordon Henrickson, "Checking the social distance technique through personal interviews," *Sociology and Social Research*, 1934, 18:420–430.

1144) Ziff, R., "Voters' bias in interpreting election poll predictions," *Public Opinion Quarterly*, 1948, 12:326–328.

1145) Zubin, J., "Note on a graphic method for determining the significance of difference between group frequencies," *Journal of Educational Psychology*, 1936, 27:431–444.

Index